D0148366

"E. J. W. GIBB MEMORIAL"
SERIES

NEW SERIES, IV. 6

# THE MATHNAWÍ

OF

# JALÁLU'DDÍN RÚMÍ

EDITED FROM THE OLDEST MANUSCRIPTS
AVAILABLE: WITH CRITICAL NOTES,
TRANSLATION, & COMMENTARY

BY

## REYNOLD A. NICHOLSON

LITT.D., LL.D., F.B.A.

*Emeritus Sir Thomas Adams's Professor of Arabic, Fellow of*
*Trinity College, and sometime Lecturer in Persian*
*in the University of Cambridge*

VOLUME VI
CONTAINING THE TRANSLATION
OF THE FIFTH & SIXTH BOOKS

PRINTED FOR THE TRUSTEES OF
THE "E. J. W. GIBB MEMORIAL"
AND PUBLISHED BY MESSRS LUZAC & CO. LTD
46 GREAT RUSSELL STREET, LONDON W.C.
1968

UNITY SCHOOL LIBRARY
UNITY VILLAGE, MISSOURI 64065

*First published* 1934
*Reprinted* 1968

2/01

PRINTED IN GREAT BRITAIN

gift

PK
6481
.M8
E52
1968
V. VI
C. 1

THIS VOLUME
IS ONE OF A SERIES
PUBLISHED BY THE TRUSTEES OF
THE "E. J. W. GIBB MEMORIAL"

*The funds of this Memorial are derived from the Interest accruing
from a Sum of money given by the late* MRS GIBB *of Glasgow, to
perpetuate the Memory of her beloved Son*

ELIAS JOHN WILKINSON GIBB

*and to promote those researches into the History, Literature, Philo-
sophy and Religion of the Turks, Persians and Arabs, to which, from
his Youth upwards, until his premature and deeply lamented Death
in his forty-fifth year, on December 5, 1901, his life was devoted.*

تِلْكَ آثَارُنَا تَدُلُّ عَلَيْنَا ∗ فَانْظُرُوا بَعْدَنَا إِلَى ٱلْآثَارِ

*" These are our works, these works our souls display;
Behold our works when we have passed away."*

## "E. J. W. GIBB MEMORIAL"

*CLERK OF THE TRUST*

W. L. RAYNES,
90, REGENT STREET, CAMBRIDGE.

*PUBLISHER FOR THE TRUSTEES*

MESSRS LUZAC & CO.,
46, GREAT RUSSELL STREET, LONDON, W.C.

# INTRODUCTION

WITH the publication of the sixth volume this work has reached a turning-point, and I should have liked to call a halt for refreshment, especially as the next stages, though perhaps less tedious, are more difficult and hazardous than those already traversed. It would be pleasant to employ a sabbatical year in studies unconnected with the *Mathnawí*; for example, in making a catalogue of a small but interesting collection of Oriental manuscripts which I hope will go to the University Library after I have done with them. But such diversions, while they might help to relieve the ἀπραγμοσύνη statutorily prescribed for persons of my age, cannot be allowed to interrupt the progress of the work in hand. Now that text and translation are complete, a commentary is needed to give substance to the translation, which by itself is often little more than a shadow; and the commentary must be reasonably full. At present I can only guess how far it may spread: in any case it will not exceed three volumes, and if two suffice, so much the better. Economy of space is comparatively unimportant, but one has to save time.

The Fifth and Sixth Books of the *Mathnawí*, composed when the author was approaching his seventieth year, show signs, I think, of failing power. An abnormally large number of anecdotes belong to the class which booksellers term "facetiae"; certain *motifs*, such as that of "the hidden treasure," are overworked; sometimes the poet lets his habitual bias towards prolixity carry him beyond all bounds; and we seldom meet with passages that lay hold of our imagination like the memorable verses (Book IV, 3637 foll.), where the *Mathnawí* seems to attain its climax[1]. If so, the descent is very gradual, though the latter half of the Sixth Book "drags its slow length along" till it breaks off in the course of an allegory depicting the quest for union with God, which probably was intended to conclude both the Book and the Poem. In the Búláq edition the unfinished Sixth Book is followed not only by two short epilogues ascribed to the poet's son Sultán Walad, but also by a Seventh Book containing 1751 verses. This is a patent forgery and has been generally recognised as such. It was first brought to light in A.H. 1035/A.D. 1626 in Constantinople by Ismá'íl Dedeh of Angora, whose Turkish commentary on the *Mathnawí* is a work of great merit. He professed to have found it in a manuscript of the poem, dated A.H. 814; but even if that were true, it would merely prove that he himself was not the fabricator. The so-called "Seventh

---

[1] There are some striking exceptions to this rule, *e.g.*, Book v, *vv.* 1796–1851, 3260–3274.

Book" is wanting in all MSS. of the *Mathnawi* known to me[1]. Style and matter alike stamp it as the production either of Ismáʿíl Dedeh—and in my opinion the circumstantial evidence is quite enough to convict him—or some learned man who was no poet, however good he may have been at rhyming.

This volume of the translation, like those which have preceded it, gives a literal rendering of the text in English or, where necessary, in Latin. While revising it, I have noted a few errors and misprints that should be added to the List of Errata, Vol. v, pp. xxi–xxiv.

Book v, *v.* ٥٨٨. Delete the *iḍáfat* of معشوق.

  ,,  ١١٧١, Heading, l. 4. Read یَنْهَی.

  ,,  ٢٢١٣. Read تا مُنِی.

  ,,  ٢٩٧٦. Read آنگَه.

  ,,  ٣١٢٣. Read روی‌زرد.

  ,,  ٣٣٩٧. Read یك ستاره.

  ,,  ٣٥١٨. Read وقتِ, with *iḍáfat.*

  ,,  ٣٩١٨. Read قِرْنِ حملهٔ.

Book vi, *v.* ٥٢١. Read كاغذها رقمِ.

  ,,  ١١١٥. Read عاشقان.

  ,,  ٣٣١٣٦. Read پگاه.

  ,,  ٣١٣٩٦. Read خشمِ شـحنه.

  ,,  ١٣٣٣٥. Read همچو دلوت.

No version of a work so idiomatic and ambiguous can be free from faults, but those which I may have committed[2] are at any rate not due to the method of loose paraphrase adopted by some of my predecessors—a method full of pitfalls for the student. Doubts and difficulties will be considered in their proper place; also questions of wider interest. Any one who reads the poem attentively will observe that its structure is far from being so casual as it looks. To say that "the stories follow each other in no order" is entirely wrong: they are bound together by subtle links and transitions arising from the poet's development of his theme; and each Book forms an artistic

[1] Copies are described by Rieu, British Museum Persian Catalogue, Vol. II, p. 587, col. 2, and Fluegel, Vienna Catalogue, Vol. I, p. 518. The latter, dated A.H. 1035, is said to be the first transcript made from the original copy. According to Ḥájjí Khalífa, ed. Fluegel, Vol. v, p. 377, Ismáʿíl Dedeh wrote a commentary on the suspected Book and tried to establish its authenticity.

[2] Some points of detail in the translation of the First and Second Books are corrected in Vol. IV, pp. xiii–xiv.

whole. The subject cannot be discussed here, but I may refer to an excellent analysis and illustration of these technicalities by Dr Gustav Richter which has been published recently[1].

Familiarity does not always breed disillusion. To-day the words I applied to the author of the *Mathnawí* thirty-five years ago, "the greatest mystical poet of any age[2]," seem to me no more than just. Where else shall we find such a panorama of universal existence unrolling itself through Time into Eternity? And, apart from the supreme mystical quality of the poem, what a wealth of satire, humour and pathos! What masterly pictures drawn by a hand that touches nothing without revealing its essential character! In the *Díwán* Jalálu'ddín soars higher; yet we must read the *Mathnawí* in order to appreciate all the range and variety of his genius.

در دائرهٔ سـماع مـا مـی‌نآیـی

تا چرخ زنی چون فلك مینائی ؟

در جذبهٔ رقـص بـشنـوی از نایی

[3] اسـرار ازل از دم مـولانـایـی

---

[1] *Persiens Mystiker Dschelál-eddin Rumi: eine Stildeutung in drei Vorträgen* (Breslau, 1933).

[2] Preface to *Selected Poems from the Díwáni Shamsi Tabríz* (Cambridge, 1898).

[3] This quatrain was composed and sent to me from Constantinople by my friend Ḥusayn Dánish Bey.

REYNOLD A. NICHOLSON

CAMBRIDGE,
*August* 19, 1933

ERRATUM

Book V, *vv.* 2680 and 2756. *For* 'Abbás of the honeyed tongue *read* 'Abbás (the seller) of date-syrup.

# TABLE OF CONTENTS

## BOOK V

# BOOK V

IN THE NAME OF GOD, THE MERCIFUL, THE COMPASSIONATE

Whose help we implore and in whom we trust, and with whom are the keys to our hearts. And God bless the best of His creatures, Mohammed, and all his Family and Companions!

This is the Fifth Book of the Poem in rhymed couplets and the spiritual Exposition, setting forth that the Religious Law is like a candle showing the way. Unless you gain possession of the candle, there is no wayfaring; and when you have come on to the way, your wayfaring is the Path; and when you have reached the journey's end, that is the Truth. Hence it has been said, "If the truths (realities) were manifest, the religious laws would be naught." As (for example), when copper becomes gold or was gold originally, it does not need the alchemy which is the Law, nor need it rub itself upon the philosophers' stone, which (operation) is the Path; (for), as has been said, it is unseemly to demand a guide after arrival at the goal, and blame-worthy to discard the guide before arrival at the goal. In short, the Law is like learning the theory of alchemy from a teacher or a book, and the Path is (like) making use of chemicals and rubbing the copper upon the philosophers' stone, and the Truth is (like) the transmutation of the copper into gold. Those who know alchemy rejoice in their knowledge of it, saying, "We know the theory of this (science)"; and those who practise it rejoice in their practice of it, saying, "We perform such works"; and those who have experienced the reality rejoice in the reality, saying, "We have become gold and are delivered from the theory and practice of alchemy: we are God's freedmen." *Each party is rejoicing in what they have.*

Or the Law may be compared to learning the science of medicine, and the Path to regulating one's diet in accordance with (the science of) medicine and taking remedies, and the Truth to gaining health everlasting and becoming independent of them both. When a man dies to this (present) life, the Law and the Path are cut off (fall away) from him, and there remains (only) the Truth. If he possess the Truth, he will be crying, *"Oh, would that my people knew how my Lord hath forgiven me"*; and if he possess it not, he will be crying, *"Oh, would that I had not been given my scroll and had not known my reckoning! Oh, would that it (death) had been the (final) decision! My riches have not availed me, my authority hath perished from me."*

The Law is knowledge, the Path action, the Truth attainment unto God. *Then whoso hopeth to meet his Lord, let him do good works and associate none other in the service of his Lord.* And God bless the best of His creatures, Mohammed, and his Family and his Companions and the people of his House, and grant them peace!

IN THE NAME OF GOD, THE MERCIFUL, THE COMPASSIONATE.

The (spiritual) King, Ḥusámu'ddín, who is the light of the stars, demands the beginning of the Fifth Book.

O Ziyá'u 'l-Ḥaqq (Radiance of God), noble Ḥusámu'ddín, master to the masters of purity,

If the people were not veiled (from the Truth) and gross, and if their throats (capacities) were not narrow and feeble,

In (my) praise of thee I should have done justice to the reality and expressed myself in language other than this[1];

5 But the falcon's mouthful is not that of the wagtail: now (therefore) recourse must be had to water and oil[2].

'Tis wrong to praise thee to the prisoners (of sensuality): I will tell (thy praise) in the assembly of the spiritual.

'Tis fraud to discourse of thee to the worldly: I will keep it hidden like the secret of love.

Praise consists in describing (excellent qualities) and in rending the veil (of ignorance): the Sun is independent of exposition and description.

The praiser of the Sun is (really) pronouncing an encomium on himself, for (he says implicitly), "My eyes are clear and not inflamed."

10 To blame the Sun of the world is to blame one's self, for (it implies), "My eyes are blind and dark and bad."

Do thou pity any one in the world who has become envious of the fortunate Sun.

Can he ever mask it (the Sun) from (men's) eyes and (prevent it) from giving freshness to things rotten?

Or can they diminish its infinite light or rise in resistance to its power?

Whosoever is envious of (him who is) the World—verily, that envy is everlasting death.

15 Thy dignity hath transcended intellectual apprehension: in describing thee the intellect has become an idle fool.

(Yet), although this intellect is too weak to declare (what thou art), one must weakly make a movement (attempt) in that (direction).

Know that when the whole of a thing is unattainable the whole of it is not (therefore to be) relinquished.

If you cannot drink (all) the flood-rain of the clouds, (yet) how can you give up water-drinking?

If thou wilt not communicate the mystery, (at least) refresh (our) apprehensions with the husk thereof[3].

---

[1] Literally, "I should have opened a lip other than this (ordinary) language."

[2] *I.e.* varnish and veneer, which is merely superficial.

[3] Here the poet identifies himself with Ḥusámu'ddín whom he regards as the source of his inspiration.

(My) spoken words are (only) a husk in relation to thee, but [20] they are a good kernel for other understandings.

The sky is low in relation to the empyrean; else, in respect of the earth-mound, it is exceedingly high.

I will tell thy description in order that they (my hearers) may take their way (towards thee) ere they grieve at the loss of that (opportunity).

Thou art the Light of God and a mighty drawer of the soul to God. His creatures are in the darkness of vain imagination and opinion.

Reverence is the necessary condition for this goodly Light to bestow a salve on these sightless ones.

The ready sharp-eared man gains the Light—he who is not [25] in love with darkness like a mouse.

The weak-eyed (bat-like) ones that go about at night, how shall they make a circuit round the Cresset of the Faith?

Difficult subtle points of disputation are the chains of (hold in bondage) the nature that has become dark (blind) to the (true) Religion.

So long as he (such an one) decks out the warp and woof of (his own) cleverness, he cannot open his eyes to the Sun.

He does not lift up branches (to the sky) like a date-palm: he has bored holes in the earth after the fashion of mice.

This humankind have four heart-oppressing qualities: these [30] four have become the gibbet of Reason.

*Commenting on* "Take four birds and turn them towards thee[1]."

O thou whose intelligence is (resplendent) as the Sun, thou art the Khalíl (Abraham) of the time: kill these four birds that infest the Way,

Because each of them, crow-like, is plucking the eye from the intellect of the intelligent.

The four bodily qualities resemble the birds of Khalíl: their slaughter[2] makes way for the soul (to ascend).

O Khalíl, in (accomplishing) the deliverance of good and bad (alike), cut off their heads that the feet (of the people) may escape from the barrier (which confines them).

Thou art all, and they all are parts of thee: open (the prison), [35] for their feet are thy feet.

By thee the (whole) world is made a place abounding in spirit: a single cavalier becomes the support of a hundred armies.

Inasmuch as this body is the abode (nest) of (these) four dispositions, they are named the four mischief-seeking birds.

[1] *Qur'án*, ii, 262.
[2] Literally, "(saying) *bismilláh* (in God's name) before slaughtering them."

If thou wish the people to have everlasting life, cut off the heads of these four foul and evil birds,

(And then) revive them again in another sort, so that afterwards no harm will be done by them.

40 The four immaterial birds which infest the Way have made their home in the hearts of the people.

Since in this epoch thou, O Vicegerent of God, art the commander of all righteous hearts,

Cut off the heads of these four live birds and make everlasting the creatures that are not enduring for ever.

There is the duck and the peacock and the crow and the cock: these are a parable of the four (evil) dispositions in (human) souls.

The duck is greed, and the cock is lust; eminence is like the peacock, and the crow is (worldly) desire.

45 His (the crow's) object of desire is this, that he forms hopes and wishes for immortality or long life.

The duck is greed, for her bill is always in the ground, seeking what is buried in the wet and dry.

That gullet (of hers) is never idle for a moment: it hearkens unto naught of the (Divine) ordinance save the command " *Eat ye!* "

'Tis like the looter who digs up (ravages) the house and very quickly fills his bag,

Cramming into the bag good and bad (indifferently), single pearls and chick-peas,

50 Cramming dry and wet[1] into the sack, for fear lest another enemy should arrive.

Time presses, the opportunity is small, he is terrified: without delay he heaves it under his arm as speedily as possible.

He hath not (such) confidence in his Sovereign (as to believe) that no enemy will be able to come forward (against him).

But the true believer, from his confidence in that (Divine) Life[2], conducts his raid[3] in a leisurely manner and with deliberation.

He hath no fear of missing his chance or of the enemy, for he recognises the King's dominion over the enemy.

55 He hath no fear of the other fellow-servants[4] coming to jostle him and gain the advantage,

(For) he perceived the King's justice in restraining his followers so that none durst do violence to any one.

Consequently he does not hurry and is calm: he hath no fear of missing his (appointed) portion.

---

[1] *I.e.* articles of every sort.
[2] *I.e.* the living God.
[3] *I.e.* takes his allotted portion of worldly goods.
[4] *I.e.* fellow-worshippers, co-religionists.

He hath much deliberation and patience and long-suffering;
he is contented and unselfish and pure of heart,

For this deliberation is the ray of the Merciful (God), while
that haste is from the impulse of the Devil,

Because the Devil frightens him (the greedy man) away from 60
poverty and kills the beast of burden, patience, by stabbing.

Hear from the *Qur'án* that the Devil in menace is threatening
thee with hard poverty,

That in haste thou mayst eat foul things and take foul things,
(having in thee) no generosity, no deliberation, no merit acquired
by good works.

Necessarily (therefore) the infidel takes his food in seven
bowels: his religion and spirit are thin and lean, his belly fat.

*Concerning the occasion of the coming of the Tradition of
Muṣṭafá (Mohammed), the blessings of God be upon him, that
the infidel takes his food in seven bowels, while the true believer
takes his food in one bowel.*

The infidels became the guests of the Prophet: they came to
the mosque at eventide,

Saying, "We have come here as visitors seeking hospitality, 65
O King, O thou who art the entertainer of (all) the inhabitants
of the world.

We are destitute and have arrived from afar: hark, shed thy
grace and light upon us!"

He said (to his Companions), "O my friends, divide (these
guests amongst you), for ye are filled with me and with my
nature."

The bodies of every army are filled with the King; hence they
would draw the sword against (his) Majesty's enemies.

'Tis because of the King's anger you draw the sword; other-
wise, what (cause of) anger have you against your brethren?

(From) the reflexion of the King's anger you are striking your 70
innocent brother with a mace of ten *manns'* weight.

The King is one soul, and the army is filled with him: the
spirit is like the water, and these bodies are the river-bed.

If the water of the King's spirit be sweet, all the river-beds
are filled with the sweet water;

For only the King's law do his subjects have (as their own):
so hath the sovereign of '*Abas*[1] declared.

Each Companion chose a guest. Amongst them (the infidels)
was one stout and incomparable (in that respect).

He had a huge body: no one took him along, he remained 75
in the mosque like the dregs in a cup.

As he was left behind by all, Muṣṭafá (Mohammed) took him

[1] *I.e.* the Prophet. '*Abas* refers to Súra LXXX of the *Qur'án*, which begins
with the word '*abasa*, he frowned.

away. In the (Prophet's) herd there were seven goats that gave milk,

For the goats used to stay in the house for milking in preparation for meal-time.

That famishing giant[1] son of a Ghuzz Turcoman devoured the bread and (other) food and (drank all) the milk of the seven goats.

The whole household became enraged, for they all desired goat's milk.

80 He made his voracious belly like a drum: he consumed singly the portion of eighteen persons.

At bed-time he went and sat in his room; then the maid angrily shut the door.

She put in (fastened) the door-chain from the outside, for she was angry with him and resentful.

At midnight or dawn, when the infidel felt an urgent need and stomach-ache,

He hastened from his bed towards the door, (but) laying his hand on the door he found it shut.

85 The cunning man employed various devices to open it[2], but the fastening did not give way[3].

The urgency increased, and the room was narrow[4]: he remained in dismay and without remedy and dumbfounded.

He made shift and crept to sleep: in his slumber he dreamed that he was in a desolate place.

Since a desolate place was in his mind, his (inward) sight went thither in sleep.

Cum sese videret in loco vastato et vacuo, tanta necessitate coactus extemplo cacavit.

90 Experrectus vidit stratum lecti in quo dormiverat sordibus plenum: pudore commotus insanire coepit.

E corde ejus ascendunt centum gemitus propter tale opprobrium pulvere non coopertum.

"Somnus meus," inquit, "pejor quam vigilia mea; hic enim edo, illic caco."

He was crying, "Woe and alas! Woe and alas![5]" even as the unbeliever in the depths of the tomb,

Waiting to see when this night would come to an end, that the noise of the door in opening might rise (to his ear),

95 In order to flee like an arrow from the bow, (for fear) lest any one should see him in such a condition.

The story is long: I will shorten it. The door opened: he was delivered from grief and pain.

---

[1] Literally, 'Új, *i.e.* Og the son of Anak.      [2] Delete the *fatḥa* of در.
[3] Literally, "did not become undone."
[4] *I.e.* afforded no means of exit.      [5] Literally, "Alas, destruction!"

*How Muṣṭafá (Mohammed) opened the door of the room for his
guest and concealed himself in order that he (the guest) might not
see the form of the person who opened it and be overcome with
shame, but might go forth boldly.*

At dawn Muṣṭafá came and opened the door: at dawn he gave
the way (means of escape) to him who had lost the way (of
salvation).

Muṣṭafá opened the door and became hidden, in order that
the afflicted man might not be ashamed,

But might come forth and walk boldly away and not see the
back or face of the door-opener.

Either he became hidden behind something, or the skirt 100
(merciful palliation) of God concealed him from him (the infidel).

*The dye of Allah* sometimes makes (a thing to be) covered
and draws a mysterious veil o'er the beholder,

So that he does not see the enemy at his side: the power of
God is more than that, (yea), more.

Muṣṭafá was seeing all that happened to him in the night,
but the command of the Lord restrained him

From opening a way (of escape) before the fault (was com-
mitted), so that he (the infidel) should not be cast into a pit
(of grief) by the disgrace (which he had incurred).

(Otherwise, Muṣṭafá would have let him out in time), but it 105
was the (Divine) wisdom and the command of Heaven that he
should see himself thus (disgraced and confounded).

There be many acts of enmity which are (really) friendship,
many acts of destruction which are (really) restoration[1].

A meddlesome fellow purposely brought the dirty bed-clothes
to the Prophet,

Saying, "Look! Thy guest has done such a thing!" He smiled,
(he who was sent as) *a mercy to all created beings,*

And said, "Bring the pail here, that I may wash all (clean)
with my own hand."

Every one jumped up, saying, "For God's sake (refrain)! Our 110
souls and our bodies are a sacrifice to thee.

We will wash this filth: do thou leave it alone. This kind (of
affair) is hand's work, not heart's work.

O *La-'amruk*[2], God pronounced unto thee (the word) 'life[3]';
then He made thee (His) Vicegerent and seated thee on the
throne.

We live for thy service: as thou (thyself) art performing the
service, what then are we?"

---

[1] Literally, "architecture."

[2] *I.e.* "O thou who art the object of the words *la-'amruka*, 'by thy life'"
(*Qur'án*, xv, 72).

[3] *I.e.* "swore to thee by thy life."

He said, "I know that, but this is an (extraordinary) occasion; I have a deep reason for washing this myself."

115   They waited, saying, "This is the Prophet's word," till it should appear what these mysteries were.

(Meanwhile) he was busily washing those filthy things, by God's command exclusively, not from blind conformity and ostentation;

For his heart was telling him, "Do thou wash them, for herein is wisdom manifold."

*The cause of the guest's return to the house of Muṣṭafá, on whom be peace, at the hour when Muṣṭafá was washing his befouled bed-rug with his own hand; and how he was overcome with shame and rent his garment and made lamentation for himself and for his plight.*

The wretched infidel had an amulet (which he carried) as a keepsake. He observed that it was lost, and became distracted.

He said, "The room in which I lodged during the night—I (must have) left the amulet there unawares."

120   Though he was ashamed, greed took away his shame: greed is a dragon, it is no small thing.

In quest of the amulet he ran hastily into the house of Muṣṭafá and saw him,

That *Hand of God*, cheerfully washing the filth by himself— far from him be the evil eye!

The amulet vanished from his mind, and a great rapture arose in him: he tore his collar,

Smiting his face and head with both hands, beating his pate against wall and door,

125   In such a wise that blood poured from his nose and head, and the Prince (Mohammed) took pity on him.

He uttered shrieks, the people gathered round him: the infidel was crying, "O people, beware!"

He smote his head, saying, "O head without understanding!" He smote his breast, saying, "O bosom without light!"

Prostrating himself, he cried, "O (thou who art) the whole earth, this despicable part[1] is abashed on account of thee.

Thou, who art the whole, art submissive to His command; I, who am (but) a part, am unjust and wicked and misguided.

130   Thou, who art the whole, art humble and trembling in fear of God; I, who am (but) a part, am (engaged) in opposition and in rivalry."

At every moment he was turning his face to heaven, saying, "I have not the face (to look towards thee), O *qibla* of the world!"

[1] *I.e.* "I, who am an insignificant part of the whole."

When he had trembled and quivered beyond (all) bounds, Muṣṭafá clasped him in his arms,

Quieted him and caressed him much and opened his (inward) eye and gave him (spiritual) knowledge.

Till the cloud weeps, how should the garden smile? Till the babe cries, how should the milk begin to flow?

The one-day-old babe knows the way: (its instinct says), 135 "I will cry, that the kind nurse may come."

Do not you know that the Nurse of (all) nurses gives no milk gratis without (your) crying?

He (God) hath said, "*Let them weep much.*" Give ear, that the bounty of the Creator may pour forth the milk.

The cloud's weeping and the sun's burning are the pillar of this world: twist these two strands (together)[1].

If there were not the sun's heat and the cloud's tears, how would body (substance) and accident become big and thick?

How would these four seasons be flourishing unless this glow 140 and weeping were the origin?

Since the burning (heat) of the sun and the weeping of the clouds in the world are keeping the world fresh and sweet[2],

Keep the sun of your intelligence burning, keep your eye glistening with tears like the cloud!

You must needs have a weeping eye, like the little child: do not eat the bread (of worldliness), for that bread takes away your water (spiritual excellence).

When the body is in leaf (well-furnished), on that account by day and night the bough, (which is) the soul, is shedding its leaves and is in autumn.

The leafage (flourishing state) of the body is the leaflessness 145 (unprovidedness) of the soul. Be quick! You must let this (body) dwindle and that (soul) increase.

*Lend unto God*, give a loan of this leafage of the body, that in exchange a garden may grow in your heart.

Give a loan, diminish this food of your body, that there may appear the face (vision) of (that which) eye hath not seen.

When the body empties itself of dung, He (God) fills it with musk and glorious pearls.

He (such a person) gives this filth and gets purity (in return): his body enjoys (what is signified by the words) *He will purify you.*

The Devil frightens you, saying, "Hark and hark again! You 150 will be sorry for this and will be saddened.

If you waste away your body in consequence of these idle whims, you will become very sorry and anxious.

---

[1] *I.e.* combine tearful supplication with spiritual enlightenment.
[2] Literally, "sweet-mouthed."

Eat this, it is hot and good for your health[1]; and drink that for your benefit and as a cure,

With the intention (of acting on the principle) that (since) this body is your riding-beast[2] that to which it is accustomed is best for it.

Beware, do not alter your habit, else mischief will ensue and a hundred maladies will be produced in brain and heart."

155  Such menaces does the vile Devil employ, and he chants a hundred spells over the people.

He makes himself out to be a Galen (for skill) in medicine, that he may deceive your ailing soul.

"This," says he, "is of use to you against any sorrow and pain." He said the same thing to Adam about an ear of wheat[3].

He utters (hypocritical expressions such as) "Ah, ah" and "Alas," while he twists your lips with the farrier's barnacle,

As (the farrier twists) the lips of a horse when shoeing it, in order that he (the Devil) may cause an inferior (worthless) stone to appear as a ruby.

160  He takes hold of your ears as (though they were) the ears of a horse, pulling you towards greed and acquisition (of worldly goods).

He claps on your foot a shoe of perplexity, by the pain of which you are left incapable of (advancing on) the Way.

His shoe is that hesitation between the two works (of this world and of the world hereafter)—"Shall I do these or shall I do those?" Take heed!

Do that which is chosen by the Prophet, don't do that which (only) a madman or (foolish) boy ever did.

"Paradise is encompassed"—by what is it encompassed? By things disliked[4], from which there comes increase of the seed sown (for the future life).

165  He (the Devil) hath a hundred spells of cunning and deceit, which would entrap[5] (any one), even if he is (strong and wily as) a great serpent.

He (the Devil) will bind him, though he be (swift and elusive as) running water; he will make a mock of him, though he be the most learned man of the time.

(Therefore) associate your intelligence with the intelligence of a friend: recite (the text) *their affairs are (carried on by) taking counsel with each other*[6], and practise it.

---

[1] Literally, "a remedy for the temperament."
[2] And therefore (as the Prophet said) to be treated kindly.
[3] *I.e.* the forbidden fruit.
[4] *I.e.* acts of self-mortification.
[5] Literally, "put into the basket"—a metaphor derived from the custom of snake-catchers.
[6] *Qur'án*, XLII, 36.

*How Muṣṭafá, on whom be peace, treated the Arab guest with lovingkindness and calmed his distress and stilled the sobbing and lamentation for himself which he was making in his shame and penitence and fire of despair.*

This topic hath no end. The Arab was astounded by the kindnesses of that (spiritual) King.

He was wellnigh becoming crazed, his reason fled (from him), but the hand (power) of Muṣṭafá's reason drew him back.

He (Muṣṭafá) said, "Come hither." He came in such fashion 170 as one rises up from heavy slumber.

"Come hither," said he, "do not (lose thy wits); hark, come to thyself, for there are (great) things to be done with thee here."

He threw water on his face, and he (the infidel) began to speak, saying, "O witness of God, recite the Testimony (profession of the Faith),

That I may bear witness (to its truth) and go forth (from unbelief): I am weary of this (unreal) existence and will go into the wilderness (of reality)."

In this court[1] of the Judge who pronounces the Decree[2] we are (present) for the purpose of (making good) our claim (to fulfil the covenant signified by the words) "*Am not I (your Lord)?*" and "*Yea*[3]";

For we said, "*Yea*," and (since we are) on trial our acts and 175 words are the (necessary) witnesses and evidence of that (assent).

Wherefore do we keep silence in the court of the Judge? Have not we come (here) to bear testimony?

How long, O witness, wilt thou remain under detention in the court of the Judge? Give thy testimony betimes.

Thou hast been summoned hither that thou mayst give the testimony and show no disobedience;

(But) in thy obstinacy thou hast sat down and closed (both) hand and mouth in this confinement.

Until thou give that testimony, O witness, how wilt thou 180 escape from this court?

'Tis the affair of a moment. Perform (thy duty) and run away: do not make a short matter long (tedious and irksome) to thyself.

As thou wilt, whether during a hundred years or in a moment, discharge this trust and acquit thyself (of it).

[1] Literally, "entrance-hall."
[2] *I.e.* in this world where we are on trial.
[3] *Qur'án*, VII, 171.

*Explaining that (ritual) prayer and fasting and all (such)
external things are witnesses to the inner light.*

This (ritual) prayer and fasting and pilgrimage and holy war
are the attestation of the (inward) belief.

The giving of alms and presents and the abandonment of
envy are the attestation of one's secret thoughts.

185 Dishes of food and hospitality are for the purpose of declaring
that "we, O noble (guests), have become in true accord with
you."

Gifts and presents[1] and offerings bear witness (saying im-
plicitly), "I am pleased with thee."

(If) any one exerts himself in (giving) money or in conjura-
tion[2], what is (the meaning of) it? (He means to say), "I have
a jewel within.

I have a jewel, namely, abstinence or generosity": this
alms-giving and fasting are witnesses in regard to both (these
qualities).

Fasting says (implicitly), "He has abstained from what is
lawful: know (therefore) that he has no connexion with what
is unlawful";

190 And his alms-giving said (implicitly), "He gives of his own
property: how, then, should he steal from the religious?"

If he act as a cutpurse (from self-interest), then the two
witnesses are invalidated in the court of Divine justice.

He is a fowler if he scatter grain not from mercy and muni-
ficence but in order to catch (the birds).

He is a cat keeping the fast and feigning to be asleep at fast-
time for the purpose of (seizing) his ignorant prey.

By this unrighteousness he makes a hundred parties (of people)
suspicious, he causes the generous and abstinent to be in ill
repute.

195 (But) notwithstanding that he weaves crookedly, in the end
the grace of God will purge him of all this (hypocrisy).

His (God's) mercy takes precedence (over His wrath) and
bestows on that treachery (hypocrisy) a light that the full-moon
does not possess.

God cleanses his effort of this contamination: the (Divine)
Mercy washes him clean of this folly.

In order that His great forgivingness may be made manifest,
a helmet (of forgiveness) will cover his (the hypocrite's)
baldness.

The water rained from heaven[3], that it might cleanse the im-
pure of their defilement.

---

[1] *Armaghán*, properly a present given on return from a journey.
[2] *I.e.* in imploring God to preserve him from temptation.
[3] Literally, "from Arcturus."

*How the water cleanses all impurities and then is cleansed of*
*impurity by God most High. Verily, God most High*
*is exceeding holy.*

When the water[1] had done battle (in its task of ablution) and had been made dirty and had become such that the senses rejected it, 200

God brought it back into the sea of Goodness, that the Origin[2] of the water might generously wash it (clean).

Next year it came sweeping proudly along[3]. "Hey, where hast thou been?" "In the sea of the pure.

I went from here dirty; I have come (back) clean. I have received a robe of honour, I have come to the earth (again).

Hark, come unto me, O ye polluted ones, for my nature hath partaken of the nature of God.

I will accept all thy foulness: I will bestow on the demon purity like (that of) the angel. 205

When I become defiled, I will return thither: I will go to the Source of the source of purities.

There I will pull the filthy cloak off my head: He will give me a clean robe once more.

Such is His work, and my work is the same: *the Lord of all created beings* is the beautifier of the world."

Were it not for these impurities of ours, how would the water have this glory?

It stole purses of gold from a certain One[4]: (then) it runs in every direction, crying, "Where is an insolvent?" 210

Either it sheds (the treasure) on a blade of grass that has grown[5], or it washes the face of one whose face is unwashed,

Or, porter-like, it takes on its head (surface) the ship that is without hand or foot (helplessly tossing) in the seas[6].

Hidden in it are myriads of salves, because every salve derives from it its nature and property[7].

The soul of every pearl, the heart of every grain, goes into the river (for healing) as (into) a shop of salves.

From it (comes) nourishment to the orphans of the earth; from it (comes) movement (growth) to them that are tied fast, the parched ones. 215

When its stock (of spiritual grace) is exhausted, it becomes turbid: it becomes abject on the earth, as we are.

---

[1] The water is a type of the saintly spirit which, when it is soiled through contact with human sin, renews its purity by union with God.

[2] Literally, "the Water."      [3] Literally, "trailing its skirt."

[4] *I.e.* it received the treasure of Divine grace.

[5] *I.e.* it endows the vegetable soul with capacity for spiritual progress.

[6] *I.e.* it uplifts those who are struggling with doubt and despair and bears them onward to salvation.

[7] Literally, "because every salve grows from it in such manner (as is its nature to grow)."

*How the water, after becoming turbid, entreats God Almighty
to succour it.*

(Then) from its interior it raises cries of lamentation, saying,
"O God, that which Thou gavest (me) I have given (to others)
and am left a beggar.

I poured the (whole) capital over pure and impure (alike):
O King who givest the capital, *is there any more?*"

He (God) saith to the cloud, "Bear it (the water) to the
delectable place; and thou too, O sun, draw it up aloft."

220    He maketh it to go diverse ways, that He may bring it unto
the boundless sea.

Verily, what is meant by this water is the spirit of the saints,
which washes away your dark stains.

When it is stained dark by (washing) the treason of the in-
habitants of the earth, it returns to Him who endows Heaven
with purity.

From yonder, trailing the skirt (of glory), it brings back to
them lessons concerning the purities of the All-encompassing
(God).

Through mingling with the people (of the world) it falls sick
and desires (to make) that journey, saying, "Revive us, O
Bilál!"[1]

225    O melodious sweet-voiced Bilál, go up into the minaret, beat
the drum of departure."

Whilst the body is standing (in the ritual prayer), the spirit
is gone on its journey: hence at the moment of return it says,
"*Salám!*"

(On its return to the world) it liberates all from performing the
ablution with sand, and seekers of the *qibla* from endeavouring
to ascertain the proper direction.

This parable is like an intermediary in the discourse: an
intermediary is required for the apprehension of the vulgar.

Without an intermediary, how should any one go into the fire,
except (one like) the salamander?—for he is independent of the
connecting link.

230    You need the hot bath as an intermediary, so that you may
refresh your constitution by (the heat of) the fire.

Since you cannot go into the fire, like Khalíl (Abraham), the
hot bath has become your Apostle, and the water your guide.

Satiety is from God, but how should the unclean attain unto
satiety without the mediation of bread?

Beauty is from God, but the corporealist does not feel (the
charm of) beauty without the veil (medium) of the garden.

When the bodily medium is removed, (then) he (who is dis-

---

[1] *I.e.* "chant the *adhán* (call to prayer)." These words were addressed by
the Prophet to Bilál, who was the first muezzin.

embodied) perceives without (any) screen, like Moses, the light
of the Moon (shining) from (his own) bosom.

These virtues possessed by the water bear witness likewise 235
that its interior is filled with the grace of God.

*The testimony of external acts and words to the hidden mind*
*and the inner light.*

Act and word are witnesses to the hidden mind: from these
twain infer the inward state.

When your thought does not penetrate within, inspect the
patient's urine from without.

Act and word are (as) the urine of the sick, which is clear
evidence for the physician of the body.

But the spiritual physician enters into his (patient's) soul and
by the spiritual way penetrates into his (inmost) belief.

He hath no need of fine acts and words: "beware of them 240
(the spiritual physicians), they are spies on (men's) hearts."

Demand this testimony of acts and words from him (only)
who is not united with the Sea like a river.

*Explaining that the light itself from within the illumined person*
*bears witness to his light, without any act or word declaring it.*

But the (inner) light of the traveller (mystic) who has passed
beyond the pale (of selfhood)—the deserts and plains are filled
with his radiance.

(The fact of) his being a witness (to God) is independent of
witnesses and works of supererogation and of self-devotion and
self-sacrifice.

Since the light of that (spiritual) substance has shone forth,
he has gained independence of these hypocrisies.

Therefore do not demand of him the testimony of act and 245
speech, for through him both the worlds have blossomed like
a rose.

What is this testimony? The making manifest of that which
is hidden, whether (by) word or act or something else;

For its object is to make manifest the inward nature of the
spiritual substance: the attributes (of that substance) are per-
manent, though these accidents (such as acts and words) are
fleeting.

The mark of the gold on the touchstone does not remain, (but)
the gold (itself) remains—of good renown and undoubted.

Similarly, (all) this ritual prayer and holy war and fasting
does not remain, but the spirit remains in good renown (for
ever).

The spirit produced certain acts and words of this kind (as 250 proofs): it rubbed its substance on the touchstone of the (Divine) command,

As though to say, "My belief is perfect: here is the witness!" (Yes), but there is doubt as regards the witnesses.

Know that the probity of the witnesses must be established: the means of establishing it is a (great) sincerity: thou art dependent on that.

In the case of the word-witness, 'tis keeping thy word (that is the test); in the case of the act-witness, 'tis keeping thy covenant (to perform these acts).

The word-witness is rejected if it speaks falsely, and the act-witness is rejected if it does not run straight.

255 Thou must have words and acts that are not self-contradictory, in order that thou mayst meet with immediate acceptance.

*Your efforts are diverse*, ye are in contradiction: ye are sewing by day and tearing up (what ye have sewn) by night.

Who, then, will hearken to testimony that contradicts itself, unless indeed He (the Judge) graciously show a (great) forbearance?

Act and word are (for) the manifestation of the inward thought and hidden mind: both are divulging the veiled secret.

When thy witness has been proved honest, it is accepted; otherwise, it is kept in detention as a prisoner.

260 O recalcitrant one, so long as thou contendest (with the holy saints) they will contend (with thee). *Lie in wait for them, then! Verily, they are lying in wait (for thee).*

### How Muṣṭafá, on whom be peace, offered the Testimony (profession of the Faith) to his guest.

This discourse hath no end. Muṣṭafá offered the Faith, and the youth accepted

That Testimony which hath ever been blessed and hath ever loosed the fast-bound chains.

He became a true believer. Muṣṭafá said to him, "Be my guest to-night also."

"By God," said he, "I am thy guest unto everlasting. Wheresoever I be, to whatsoever place I go,

265 I am made living by thee and liberated by thee, and am thy doorkeeper (eating) at thy table in this world and in the next.

Whosoever chooses any but this choice table, in the end his gullet will be torn by the bone (of perdition).

Whosoever goes to the table of any but thee, know that the Devil shares his cup.

Whosoever departs from thy neighbourhood, without any doubt the Devil will become his neighbour;

And if without thee he go on a far journey, the wicked Devil is his fellow-traveller and table-companion;

And if he mount a noble horse, (since) he is envious of the 270
Moon[1], the Devil sits behind him;

And if his Shahnáz[2] be got with child by him, the Devil is
his partner in begetting it."

O thou that glowest (with faith)[3], God hath said in the
Qur'án[4], "*Share with them in their wealth and children.*"

The Prophet, (who drew inspiration) from the Unseen, ex-
plained this (matter) clearly in his marvellous discourses with
'Alí.

"O Prophet of Allah, thou hast displayed (the truth of) thy
prophetic mission completely, like the cloudless sun.

Two hundred mothers never did (to their children) this which 275
thou hast done (to me); Jesus by his (life-giving) spells never
did (so much as this) to 'Ázar (Lazarus).

Lo, through thee, my soul hath been delivered from death:
if 'Ázar was revived by that breath (of Jesus), yet he died
again."

The Arab became the Prophet's guest that night: he drank
half the milk of a single goat and (then) closed his lips.

He (the Prophet) urged him to drink the milk and eat the
scones. "By God," said he, "in all sincerity I have eaten my
fill.

This is not hypocrisy or affectation and artifice: I have become
fuller than I was yesternight."

All the people of the (Prophet's) house were left in astonish- 280
ment (to think that) this lamp had been filled by this one drop
of oil,

And that what is (only) a swift's (portion of) food should
become the (means of) filling the belly of such an elephant.

Whispering arose amongst the men and women—"That man
who has the body of an elephant eats as little as a fly!"

The greed and vanity of unbelief was overthrown: the dragon
was satisfied with the food of an ant.

The beggar-like greediness of unbelief departed from him:
the sweet food of the Faith made him stout and strong.

He who was quivering from ravenous hunger beheld, like 285
Mary, the fruit of Paradise.

The fruit of Paradise sped to his body: his Hell-like belly
gained repose.

The essence of the Faith is a mighty blessing and exceedingly
delicious food, O thou who art content with naught of the Faith
but the profession!

---

[1] *I.e.* the Prophet.          [2] *I.e.* his wife.
[3] Literally, "O (thou who resemblest the) redness of sunset."
[4] xvii, 66.

3

*Explaining that the Light which is the food of the spirit becomes the food of the saint's body, so that it (his body) also becomes friendly with the spirit (according to the saying of the Prophet), "My satan hath accepted Islam at my hands."*

Although that (Light) is the food of the spirit and the (spiritual) sight, the body too partakes of it, O son.

If the devilish body had not become fond of eating it, the Prophet would not have said, "The devil accepted Islam."

290   How should the devil become a Moslem until it drink of the sweet food by which the dead is made living?

The devil is passionately in love with the world, blind and deaf; (but this) love, no doubt, may be cut off by another love.

When it tastes the wine from the cellar of clairvoyance, little by little it will transfer its love thither[1].

O thou whose belly is greedy, turn away thus (from the world): the only method is change of food.

O thou whose heart is sick, turn to the remedy: the entire regimen is change of disposition.

295   O thou who art kept in pawn to food, thou wilt escape if thou suffer thyself to be weaned.

Verily, in hunger there is plenteous food: search after it diligently and cherish the hope (of finding it), O shrinker.

Feed on the Light, be like the eye, be in accord with the angels, O best of mankind.

Like the Angel, make the glorification of God thy food, that like the angels thou mayst be delivered from vexation.

If Gabriel pays no attention to the carcase, (yet) how should he be inferior in strength to the vulture?

300   What a goodly table is spread in the world! But it is quite hidden from the eyes of the vile.

Though the world should become a delightful orchard, still the portion of the mouse and the snake would consist of earth.

*How the corporealists ignore the food of the spirit and tremble with anxiety for the vile food.*

Its (the vile creature's) food is earth, whether in winter or in spring; thou art the lord of creation: how is it thou eatest earth like the snake?

The wood-worm in the midst of wood says, "For whom (else) should be such fine sweetmeat?"

The dung-worm amidst (all) that pollution knows no dessert in the world but filth.

---

[1] Literally, "will take the baggage of love to that place."

*Prayer.*

O God who art without peer, show favour! Since Thou hast 305
bestowed on (our) ear this discourse as an ear-ring,

Take hold of our ear and draw us along to the assembly where
the joyous revellers drink of Thy wine.

Forasmuch as Thou hast caused a waft of its perfume to reach
us, do not stopple the head (mouth) of that wine-skin, O Lord
of the Judgement!

Whether they are male or female, they (all Thy creatures)
drink from Thee: O Thou whose help is besought, Thou art
stintless in giving.

O Thou by whom the unspoken prayer is answered, who
bestowest at every moment a hundred bounties on the heart,

Thou hast limned some letters of writing: rocks have become 310
(soft) as wax for love of them.

Thou hast scribed the *nún* of the eyebrow, the *ṣád* of the eye,
and the *jím* of the ear[1] as a distraction to a hundred minds and
understandings.

By those letters of Thine the intellect is made to weave subtle
coils (of perplexity): write on, O accomplished Calligrapher!

At each moment Thou shapest beauteously pictured forms
of phantasy, suitable to every thought, upon (the page of) non-
existence.

On the tablet of phantasy Thou inscribest wondrous letters—
eye and profile and cheek and mole.

I am drunken with desire for non-existence[2], not for the 315
existent, because the Beloved of (the world of) non-existence is
more faithful.

He (God) made the intellect a reader of those figured characters,
that thereby He might put an end to[3] its contrivances[4].

*Comparison of the Guarded Tablet (the Logos), and the perception*
*therefrom by every individual's mind of his daily fate and portion*
*and lot, to the daily perception (of the Divine decree) by Gabriel,*
*on whom be peace, from the Most Great Tablet.*

Like the Angel, the intellect receives (reads) every morning
its daily lesson from the Guarded Tablet.

Behold the inscriptions made without (use of) fingers upon
non-existence and the amazement of the madmen at the black-
ness of them.

Every one is infatuated with some phantasy and digs in corners
in mad desire for a (buried) treasure.

[1] The letters ن, ص, and ج resemble in shape the eyebrow, eye, and ear
respectively.
[2] *I.e.* the ideal world, which is non-existent *ab extra.*
[3] Literally, "roll up."
[4] *I.e.* render it distraught and bewildered.

320 By a phantasy one person is filled with (desire for) magnificence and turns his face towards the mines (of precious ore) in the mountains;

And, (inspired) by a phantasy, another sets his face with bitter toil towards the sea for the sake of pearls;

And another (goes) into a church to perform religious exercises, while another (betakes himself) to sowing in his greed (for gain).

Through phantasy that one becomes the waylayer (destroyer) of him who has escaped (unhurt); and through phantasy this (other) becomes the salve (deliverer) of him who has been (sorely) wounded.

One loses his soul in the invocation of demons, while another sets his foot upon the stars.

325 He (the observer) sees that these modes of action in the external world are diverse (since they arise) from the various phantasies within.

This man (engaged in some occupation) is amazed at that man (occupied with something else) and says, "What is he about?" Every taster denies the other (whose taste is different).

Unless those phantasies were incongruous, how did the modes of action become diverse externally?

Since the *qibla* (the true object) of the soul has been hidden, every one has turned his face to a (different) quarter.

*Comparison of the different practices and the various aspirations (of mankind) to the disagreement of those who at prayer-time endeavour to find the qibla (direction of Mecca) when it is dark, and to the search of divers (for pearls) at the bottom of the sea.*

(They are) like folk trying to find (the direction of the Ka'ba) and (each) turning in a certain direction which they fancy is the *qibla*:

330 When at dawn the Ka'ba appears, it is discovered who has lost the (right) way;

Or like divers under the depth of the (sea)-water, every one (of whom) picks up something in haste:

In hope of (getting) precious jewels and pearls, they fill their bags with that and this;

When they come up from the floor of the deep sea, the possessor of the great pearls is discovered,

And (also) the other who got the small pearls, and the other who got (only) pebbles and worthless shells.

335 Even thus in the *Sáhira* (place of Judgement) a shameful overwhelming tribulation will afflict them (the followers of phantasy).

Similarly[1], every class of people in the world are fluttering like moths round a candle[2].

---

[1] *I.e.* like the divers and those who seek the *qibla* in the dark.
[2] *I.e.* an object of desire.

They attach themselves to a fire and circle round their own candle

In the hope of (gaining) the blessed fire of Moses[1], by the flame whereof the tree[2] is made more green (flourishing).

Every troop (of them) has heard of the excellence of that fire, and all imagine that any spark is that (same fire).

When the Light of Everlastingness rises at dawn, each (candle) 340 reveals what (manner of) candle it was.

Whosoever's wings were burnt by the candle of victory, that goodly candle bestows on him eighty wings;

(But) beneath the bad candle many a moth, whose eyes were sealed, is left (lying) with burnt wings,

Quivering in sorrow and anguish, lamenting the vain desire that seals the eyes.

Its candle says (to it), "Since I am burnt, how should I deliver thee from burning (grief) and oppression?"

Its candle weeps, saying, "My head is consumed: how should 345 I make another resplendent?"

[*Explanation of* "Alas for the servants (of God)!"][3]

It (the moth) says, "I was deceived by thy (outward) features and (too) late did I regard thy (inward) condition."

The candle is extinguished, the wine is gone, and the Beloved[4] has withdrawn himself[5] from the disgrace of our squintness.

Thy profits have become a loss and penalty: thou complainest bitterly to God of thy blindness.

How excellent are the spirits of brethren trustworthy, self-surrendering, believing, obeying!

Every one (else) has turned his face in some direction, but 350 those holy ones have turned towards that which transcends direction.

Every (other) pigeon flies on some course, but this pigeon (flies) in a region where no region is.

We are neither birds of the air nor domestic (fowls): our grain is the grain of grainlessness.

Our daily bread is so ample because our stitching the coat (of bodily existence) has become the tearing (of it to pieces).

[1] Literally, "the Moses-fire of fortune."
[2] In allusion to the Burning Bush (*Qur'án*, xxviii, 30).
[3] *Qur'án*, xxxvi, 29.
[4] Literally, "he who captivates the heart."
[5] Literally, "has become submerged."

*The reason why the name faraji was first given to the garment known by that name.*

A certain Ṣúfí tore his *jubba* in distress: after (its) tearing, relief (*faraj*) came to him.

355   He bestowed the name *faraji* on that torn (garment): from that man (who was) a confidant (of God) this title became well known.

This title became well known; but (only) the (Ṣúfí) Shaykh apprehended the pure (essence) thereof: in the nature of the (common) people the (mere) letter, (which is) the dregs, remained.

Similarly, (with) every name, he (the Shaykh) has kept the pure (essence) and left the (mere) name behind, like dregs.

Whosoever is a clay-eater (corporealist) took the dregs, (but) the Ṣúfí went impatiently towards the pure (essence).

He said (to himself), "Of necessity the dregs have a pure (essence): by means of this indication the heart advances to purity."

360   The dregs are difficulty and their pure (essence) is their ease: the pure (essence) is like the ripe date, and the dregs (are like) the date in its immature stage.

Ease is accompanied by difficulty; come, do not despair: through this death thou hast the way into Life.

(If) thou desirest (spiritual) peace, rend thy *jubba*, O son, that immediately thou mayst emerge pure[1].

The (true) Ṣúfí is he who has become a seeker of purity: (it is) not from (wearing) the garment of wool and patching (it) and (committing) sodomy.

With these base scoundrels Ṣúfism has become patching and sodomy, and that is all[2].

365   To wear colours (coloured garments) with the fancy of (attaining to) that purity and good name is good (commendable), but

(Only) if, with the fancy thereof, you go on (till you attain) to its (essential) principle; not like those who worship (worldly) fancies manifold.

Your fancy is the baton of (Divine) jealousy (which prevents you from prowling) round about the curtained pavilion of (Divine) Beauty;

It (fancy) bars every seeker, saying, "There is no way (admission)": every fancy confronts him (the seeker) and says "Stop!"—

Except, indeed, that person of sharp hearing and keen in-

---

[1] Literally, "that quickly thou mayst lift up thy head from that (above-mentioned) purity."

[2] Literally, "and farewell," *i.e.* "there is no more to be said."

telligence who possesses enthusiasm (derived) from the host of His (God's) helps (to victory).

He does not recoil from the fancies (which bar the way) nor 370 is he checked: he shows the King's arrow (token); then way is made (for him to enter).

(O God), bestow forethought on this bewildered heart, and bestow the arrow (of resolution) on these bows bent double.

From that hidden goblet (of Thine) Thou hast poured out of the cup of the noble (prophets and saints) a draught over the dusty earth.

From the draught thereof there is a trace on the locks and cheeks (of the fair): hence kings lick the earth (of which the bodies of the fair are made).

'Tis the draught of (Divine) beauty—(mingled) in the lovely earth—that thou art kissing with a hundred hearts day and night.

Since the draught, when mingled with dust, makes thee mad, 375 think how its pure essence would affect thee!

Every one is tattered (torn with emotion) in the presence of a clod that has received a draught of Beauty.

(There is) a draught (poured) on the moon and the sun and Aries; (there is) a draught (poured) on the Throne and the Foot-stool and Saturn.

Oh, I wonder, wilt thou call it a draught or an elixir, since from contact with it so many splendours arise?

Earnestly seek contact with it, O accomplished man: none shall touch it except the purified.

One draught (is poured) on gold and rubies and pearls; one 380 draught (is poured) on wine and dessert and fruits;

One draught on the faces of the charming fair: (consider, then,) how (marvellous) must be that pure wine!

Inasmuch as thou rubbest thy tongue (even) on this (earthly draught), how (enamoured of it) wilt thou be when thou seest (tastest) it without the clay!

When at the hour of death that pure draught is separated from the bodily clod by dying,

Thou quickly buriest that which remains, since it had been made such an ugly thing by that (separation).

When the Spirit displays its beauty without this carcase, I 385 cannot express the loveliness of that union.

When the Moon displays its radiance without this cloud, 'tis impossible to describe that glory and majesty.

How delightful is that Kitchen full of honey and sugar, of which these (worldly) monarchs are (only) the lick-platters!

How delightful is that Stack in the spiritual field, of which every (other) stack is (only) the gleaner!

How delightful is the Sea of painless Life, of which the Seven Seas are (only) a dewdrop!

390    When the Cup-bearer of *Alast*[1] poured a draught upon this nitrous abject earth,

The earth seethed, and we are (the result) of that seething. (O God, pour) another draught, for we are very effortless (unaspiring).

If 'twas permitted, I sang of non-existence[2]; and if 'twas not to be told, lo, I was silent.

This is the account of the bent (grovelling) duck, which is greed[3]: learn of Khalíl (Abraham) that the duck ought to be killed.

In the duck there is much good and evil besides this, (but) I am afraid of missing other (more important) topics of discourse.

*Description of the Peacock and its nature, and the cause of its being killed by Abraham, on whom be peace.*

395    Now we come to the two-coloured (double-faced) peacock, who displays himself for the sake of name and fame.

His desire is to catch people: he is ignorant of good and evil and of the result and use of that (catching).

He catches his prey ignorantly, like a trap: what knowledge has the trap concerning the purpose of its action?

What harm (comes) to the trap, or what benefit, from catching (its prey)? I wonder at its idle catching.

O brother, thou hast uplifted thy friends with two hundred marks of affection, and (then) abandoned (them).

400    This has been thy business from the hour of (thy) birth: to catch people with the trap of love.

From that pursuit (of people) and throng (of friends) and vainglory and self-existence wilt thou get any warp or woof? Try and see![4]

Most (of thy life) is gone and the day is late; (yet) thou art still busy in pursuit of people.

Go on catching one and releasing another from the trap and pursuing another, like mean folk;

Then again release this one and seek the other! Here's a game of heedless children!

405    Night comes, and nothing is caught in thy trap: the trap is naught but a headache (affliction) and shackle to thee.

Therefore (in reality) thou wert catching thyself with the trap, for thou art imprisoned and disappointed of thy desire.

---

[1] The Primal Covenant (*Qur'án*, VII, 171).
[2] *I.e.* the world of esoteric knowledge which has no external existence.
[3] *I.e.* the account of the passion of greed, typified by the duck, is here concluded.
[4] Literally, "apply thy hand (try by touch) whether thou wilt get any warp or woof," *i.e.* experiment will convince thee of the futility of thy occupation.

Is any owner of a trap in the world such a dolt that, like us, he tries to catch himself?

Pursuit of the vulgar is like hunting pig: the fatigue is infinite, and 'tis unlawful to eat a morsel thereof.

That which is worth pursuing is Love alone; but how should He be contained in any one's trap?

(Yet) perchance thou mayst come and be made His prey, thou 410 mayst discard the trap, and go into His trap.

Love is saying very softly into my ear, "To be a prey is better than to be a hunter.

Make thyself My fool and be a dupe: renounce the (high) estate of the sun, become a mote!

Become a dweller at My door and be homeless: do not pretend to be a candle, be a moth,

That thou mayst see (taste) the savour of Life and contemplate the sovereignty hidden in servitude."

In this world you see the shoes upside down[1]: the title of 415 "kings" is conferred on (those who are really) bondsmen.

Many a one who deserves to mount the scaffold[2] with a halter on his throat—a crowd (gathers) round him, crying, "Behold, an emperor![3]"

(They are) like the tombs of infidels, outwardly (resembling) the robes of Paradise, (while) within (them) is the wrath of God Almighty and Glorious.

He (the worldling) has been plastered like the tombs: the veil of self-conceit has been brought before him (drawn over him).

Thy miserable nature is plastered with virtues, like a palm-tree of wax without (real) leaves and fruit.

*Explaining that every one knows the mercy of God, and every one knows the wrath of God; and all are fleeing from the wrath of God and clinging to the mercy of God; but the Most High God has concealed wraths in mercy and mercies in wrath. This is God's mystification and disguise and contrivance to the end that the discerning who see by the Light of God may be separated from those who see (only) the present and the visible; for (He created death and life) that He might try you, which of you is most righteous in his works.*

One dervish said to another, "Tell (me), what was thy vision 420 of the Presence of God?[4]"

He replied, "My vision was ineffable[5]; but for the sake of argument I will briefly declare a parable thereof.

---

[1] *I.e.* everything is topsy-turvy, and its real nature is not apparent.
[2] Literally, "(one who is) the crown of the scaffold."
[3] Literally, "a wearer of the crown."
[4] Literally, "how didst thou behold the Presence of God?"
[5] Literally, "I beheld (Him) nohow."

I beheld Him with a fire on His left, and on the right a stream (like) Kawthar:

On His left an exceedingly world-consuming fire, on His right hand a sweet river.

One party put forth their hands towards the fire, (while) another party were rejoicing and intoxicated (with desire) for that Kawthar.

425 But 'twas a very topsy-turvy (mystifying) game in the path of every one doomed to perdition or blessed with salvation[1].

Whoever went into the fire and sparks was emerging from the midst of the water;

Whoever went from the middle towards the water, he was at once found to be in the fire;

Whoever went towards the right (hand) and the limpid water would put forth his head from the fire on the left;

And he who went towards the fiery left, would emerge on the right.

430 Few were they who hit upon (understood) the mystery of this occult (matter); consequently, seldom would any one go into the fire;

(None would go) except him upon whom felicity was shed, so that he abandoned the water and took refuge in the fire.

The people made the pleasure that was actually present their object of worship; consequently the people were swindled by this game.

Troop by troop and rank by rank, (they were) on their guard against the fire and fleeing greedily and in haste towards the water.

Of necessity, they lifted up their heads (emerged) from (amidst) the fire. Take warning, take warning, O heedless man!

435 The fire was crying, 'O crazy fools, I am not fire, I am a delectable fountain.

A spell has been cast on thine eyes, O sightless one: come into me and never flee from the sparks.

O (thou who art as) Khalíl (Abraham), here are no sparks and smoke: 'tis naught but the sorcery and deceit of Nimrod.

If, like the Friend of God, thou art wise, the fire is thy water, and thou art the moth.'"

The soul of the moth[2] is always crying, "Oh, alas, would that I had a hundred thousand wings,

440 That they might be consumed without mercy by the fire, to the blindness (confusion) of the eyes and hearts of the profane!

The ignorant man pities me from stupidity: I pity him from clairvoyance.

---

[1] Literally, "before the feet of every one (who was) damned or blessed."
[2] The lover of God.

Especially this fire (of Love), which is the soul of (all) waters (delights); (but) the behaviour of the (ignorant) moth[1] is contrary to ours.

It sees the light and goes into a Fire; the heart (of the mystic) sees the fire and goes into a Light."

Such a (deceptive) game is played by[2] the Glorious God in order that you may see who belongs to the kin of Khalíl (Abraham).

A fire has been given the semblance of water, and in the fire 445 a fountain has been opened.

A magician by his art makes a dish of rice (appear to be) a dish full of (tiny) worms in the assembly;

(Or) by the breath (power) of magic he has caused a room to appear full of scorpions, though in truth there were no scorpions.

When sorcery produces a hundred such illusions, how (much greater) must be the cunning of the Creator of sorcery?

Of necessity, through the magic of God generation after generation have fallen down (been vanquished), like a woman (lying) flat beneath (sub marito).

Their magicians were slaves and servants, and fell into the 450 trap (of Divine cunning) like wagtails.

Hark, read the *Qur'án* and behold lawful magic (in) the overthrow of plots (huge) as *the mountains*[3].

"I am not (like) Pharaoh that I should come to the Nile[4]; I am going towards the fire, like Khalíl (Abraham).

'Tis not fire; (in reality) 'tis *flowing water*, (while) the other[5], through (Divine) cunning, is water whereof the (real) nature is fire.

Excellently well said the complaisant[6] Prophet, "A mote of intelligence is better for thee than fasting and performing the ritual prayer,"

Because thy intelligence is the substance, (whereas) these two 455 (things) are accidents: these two are made obligatory in (the case of persons who possess) the full complement of it[7],

In order that the mirror (intelligence) may have (a bright) lustre; for purity comes to the breast (heart) from piety.

But if the mirror is fundamentally depraved, (only) after a long time does the polisher get it back[8] (to purity);

While (in the case of) the fine mirror, which is (like) a goodly planting-ground, a little polishing is enough for it.

---

[1] The lover of the World.
[2] Literally, "came from."          [3] Cf. *Qur'án*, XIV, 47.
[4] The speaker is the "moth" (*v.* 439) which typifies the lover of God.
[5] *I.e.* the water of worldliness in which Pharaoh was drowned.
[6] Literally, "passing easily from one thing to another"; hence "generous in dealing with others."
[7] *I.e.* they are not obligatory in the case of madmen or young boys.
[8] Literally, "bring it to hand again."

*The diversity of intelligences in their nature as originally created;*
*(a doctrine) opposed to (that of) the Muʿtazilites, who assert that*
*particular (individual) intelligences are originally equal, and*
*that this superiority and diversity is the result of learning and*
*training and experience.*

Know well that intelligences differ thus in degree from the
earth to the sky.

460    There is an intelligence like the orb of the sun; there is an
intelligence inferior to (the planet) Venus and the meteor.

There is an intelligence like a tipsy (flickering) lamp; there
is an intelligence like a star of fire,

Because, when the cloud is removed from it, it produces in-
tellects that behold the Light of God.

The particular intelligence has given the (universal) intelli-
gence a bad name: worldly desire has deprived the (worldly)
man of his desire (in the world hereafter).

That (universal intelligence), through being a prey (to God),
beheld the beauty of the (Divine) Hunting, while this (particular
intelligence), through being a hunter (of worldly goods), suffered
the pain of being a prey (to perdition).

465    The former, through service, gained the pride of lordship,
while the latter, through lordship, turned from the path of glory.

The latter, through being a Pharaoh, was taken captive by
the water (of perdition), while the Israelites, through captivity,
became (mighty as) a hundred Suhrábs.

'Tis a topsy-turvy game and a terrible quandary[1]; do not try
(to escape by) cunning: 'tis (all) a matter of (Divine) favour and
fortune.

Do not weave plots[2] in vain imagination and cunning; for
the Self-sufficient One does not give way to the contriver.

Contrive, in the way of (by following the guidance of) one
who serves (God) well, that you may gain the position of a
prophet in a religious community.

470    Contrive that you may be delivered from your own contrivance;
contrive that you may become detached from the body[3].

Contrive that you may become the meanest slave (of God):
if you enter into (the state of) meanness (self-abasement), you
will become lordly.

Never, O old wolf, practise foxiness and perform service with
the purpose of (gaining) lordship;

But rush into the fire like a moth: do not hoard up that
(service)[4], play for love![5]

---

[1] Literally, "a formidable move by the queen (in chess)," when she gives
check to the king and threatens to capture the rook.
[2] Literally, "thread."        [3] Or, reading از حسد, "from envy."
[4] Literally, "do not sew up a purse of that (service)," *i.e.* "do not seek to
profit by it."
[5] Literally, "play cleanly (purged of all self-interest)."

Renounce power and adopt piteous supplication: (the Divine) mercy comes towards piteous supplication, O dervish.

The piteous supplication of one sorely distressed and athirst 475 is real; the piteous (but) cold supplication of falsehood is proper to the miscreant.

The weeping of Joseph's brethren is a trick, for their hearts are full of envy and infirmity.

*Story of the Arab of the desert whose dog was dying of hunger, while his wallet was full of bread; he was lamenting over the dog and reciting poetry and sobbing and beating his head and face; and yet he grudged the dog a morsel from his wallet.*

The dog was dying, and the Arab sobbing, shedding tears, and crying, "Oh, sorrow!"

A beggar passed by and asked, "What is this sobbing? For whom is thy mourning and lamentation?"

He replied, "There was in my possession a dog of excellent disposition. Look, he is dying on the road.

He hunted for me by day and kept watch by night; (he was) 480 keen-eyed and (good at) catching the prey and driving off thieves."

He (the beggar) asked, "What ails him? Has he been wounded?" The Arab replied, "Ravenous hunger[1] has made him (so) lamentable."

"Show some patience," said he, "in (bearing) this pain and anguish: the grace of God bestows a recompense on those who are patient."

Afterwards he said to him, "O noble chief, what is this full wallet in your hand?"

He replied, "My bread and provender and food left over from last night, (which) I am taking along (with me) to nourish my body."

"Why don't you give (some) bread and provender to the 485 dog?" he asked. He replied, "I have not love and liberality to this extent.

Bread cannot be obtained (by a traveller) on the road without money, but water from the eyes costs nothing."

He (the beggar) said, "Earth be on your head, O water-skin full of wind! for in your opinion a crust of bread is better than tears."

Tears are (originally) blood and have been turned by grief into water: idle tears[2] have not the value of earth.

He (the Arab) made the whole of himself despicable, like Iblís: a piece[3] of this whole is naught but vile.

[1] Literally, "canine hunger."    [2] Literally, "blood."
[3] *I.e.* his tears.

490    I am the (devoted) slave of him who will not sell his existence[1]
save to that bounteous and munificent Sovereign,

(So that) when he weeps, heaven begins to weep, and when
he moans (in supplication), the celestial sphere begins to cry,
"O Lord!"

I am the (devoted) slave of that high-aspiring[2] copper which
humbles itself[3] to naught but the Elixir.

Lift up in prayer a broken hand: the lovingkindness of God
flies towards the broken.

If thou hast need of deliverance from this narrow dungeon
(the world), O brother, go without delay (and cast thyself) on
the fire.

495    Regard God's contrivance and abandon thine own con-
trivance: oh, by His contrivance (all) the contrivance of con-
trivers is put to shame.

When thy contrivance is naughted in the contrivance of the
Lord, thou wilt open a most marvellous hiding-place,

Of which hiding-place the least (treasure) is everlasting life
(occupied) in ascending and mounting higher.

*Explaining that no evil eye is so deadly to a man as the eye of
self-approval, unless his eye shall have been transformed by the
Light of God, so that "he hears through Me and sees through
Me," and (unless) his self shall have become selfless.*

Do not regard thy peacock-feathers but regard thy feet, in
order that the mischief of the (evil) eye may not waylay thee[4];

For (even) a mountain slips (from its foundations) at the eye
of the wicked: read and mark in the *Qur'án* (the words) *they
cause thee to stumble.*

500    From (their) looking (at him), Aḥmad (Mohammed), (who
was) like a mountain, slipped in the middle of the road, without
mud and without rain.

He remained in astonishment, saying, "Wherefore is this
slipping? I do not think that this occurrence is empty (of
meaning),"

Until the Verse (of the *Qur'án*)[5] came and made him aware
that this had happened to him[6] in consequence of the evil eye
and enmity (of the unbelievers).

(God said to the Prophet), "Had it been any one except thee,
he would at once have been annihilated: he would have become
the prey of the (evil) eye and in thrall to destruction;

---

[1] *I.e.* himself.
[2] Literally, "cherishing lofty aspiration."
[3] Literally, "offers brokenness (contrition)."
[4] Literally, "may not open an ambuscade."
[5] *Qur'án*, LXVIII, 51.          [6] Literally, "to thee."

But there came (from Me) a protection, sweeping along (majestically)[1], and thy slipping was (only) for a sign."

Take a warning, look on that mountain[2], and do not expose 505 thy (petty) leaf (to destruction), O thou who art less than a straw.

*Commentary on* "And verily those who disbelieve wellnigh cause thee to slip by their (malignant) eyes."

"O Messenger of Allah, some persons in that assembly (of the unbelievers) smite with their (evil) eye the vultures (flying aloft).

By their looks the head of the lion of the jungle is cloven asunder, so that the lion makes moan.

He (such an one) casts on a camel an eye like death, and then sends a slave after it,

Saying, 'Go, buy some of the fat of this camel': he (the slave) sees the camel fallen dead on the road.

(He sees) mortally stricken[3] by disease the camel that used 510 to vie with a horse in speed;

For, without any doubt, from envy and (the effect of) the evil eye the celestial sphere would alter its course and revolution."

The water is hidden and the water-wheel is visible, yet as regards (the wheel's) revolution the water is the source of action.

The remedy of the evil eye is the good eye: it makes the evil eye naught beneath its kick.

(Divine) mercy has the precedence (over Divine wrath): it (the good eye) is (derived) from (Divine) mercy, (while) the evil eye is the product of (Divine) wrath and execration.

His (God's) mercy overcomes His vengeance: hence every 515 prophet prevailed over his adversary;

For he (the prophet) is the result of (Divine) mercy and is the opposite of him (the adversary): that ill-favoured one was the result of (Divine) wrath.

The greed of the duck is single, (but) this (greed of the peacock) is fiftyfold: the greed of lust is (only) a snake, while this (greed for) eminence is a dragon.

The duck's greed arises from the appetite of the gullet and pudendum, (but) twenty times as much (greed) is included in (the ambition to) rule.

He (who is) in power (really) pretends to Divinity: how should one ambitious of co-partnership (with God) be saved?

The sin of Adam arose from the belly and sexual intercourse, 520 and that of Iblís from pride and power.

Consequently, he (Adam) at once besought pardon, while the accursed (Iblís) disdained to repent.

The greed of the gullet and pudendum is in truth (a mark of)

---

[1] Literally, "trailing its skirt."          [2] *I.e.* the Prophet.
[3] Literally, "decapitated."

depravity; but it is not (headstrong like) ambition: it is abasement.

If I should relate the root and branch (the whole story) of dominion, another Book would be needed.

The Arabs called a restive (high-spirited) horse a "devil" (*shayṭán*); (they did) not (give that name to) the beast of burden that stayed (quietly) in the pasture.

525 "Devilry" (*shayṭanat*) in lexicology is (synonymous with) "rebelliousness[1]": this quality is deserving of execration.

There is room for a hundred eaters (guests) round a table, (but) there is not room in the (whole) world for two seekers of dominion.

The one is not willing that the other should be on the surface of the earth; so that a prince kills his father for partaking with him (in sovereignty).

Thou hast heard (the saying) that kingship is childless: the seeker of sovereignty has cut (the ties of) relationship because of (his) fear;

For he is childless and has no son: like fire, he has no kinship with any one.

530 Whatsoever he finds he destroys and tears to pieces: when he finds nothing, he devours himself.

Become naught, escape from his teeth: do not seek mercy from his (hard) anvil-like heart.

After thou hast become naught, do not fear the anvil: take lessons every morning from absolute poverty[2].

Divinity is the mantle of the Lord of glory: it becomes a plague to any one who puts it on.

His (God's) is the crown (of sovereignty), ours the belt (of servitude): woe to him that passes beyond his proper bound!

535 Thy peacock-feathers are a (sore) temptation to thee, for thou must needs have co-partnership (with God) and All-holiness[3].

*Story of the Sage who saw a peacock tearing out his handsome feathers with his beak and dropping them (on the ground) and making himself bald and ugly. In astonishment he asked, "Hast thou no feeling of regret?" "I have," said the peacock, "but life is dearer to me than feathers, and these (feathers) are the enemy of my life."*

A peacock was tearing out his feathers in the open country, where a sage had gone for a walk.

He said, "O peacock, how art thou tearing out such fine feathers remorselessly from the root?

[1] Literally, "raising the neck," "holding the head high."
[2] *I.e.* complete detachment from everything except God.
[3] *I.e.* the pride of power necessarily involves the claim to possess the attributes of Divine majesty.

How indeed is thy heart consenting that thou shouldst tear off these gorgeous robes and let them fall in the mud?

Those who commit the *Qur'án* to memory place every feather of thine, on account of its being prized and acceptable, within the folding of[1] the (Holy) Book.

For the sake of stirring the healthful air thy feathers are used 540 as fans[2].

What ingratitude and what recklessness is this! Dost not thou know who is their decorator?

Or dost thou know (that) and art thou showing disdain and purposely tearing out (such) a (fine) broidery?

Oh, there is many a disdain that becomes a sin and causes the servant to fall from favour with[3] the King (God).

To show disdain is sweeter than sugar; but chew it not, for it hath a hundred perils.

The place of safety is the way of want (lowliness): abandon 545 disdain and make up with (be satisfied with) that way.

Oh, many a disdainfulness flapped its wings and plumes, (but) in the end it became a bane to that (arrogant) person.

If the sweetness of disdain exalts thee for a moment, (yet) its latent fear and dread consumes thee;

(While) this want (lowliness), though it make (thee) lean, will make thy breast (heart) like the brilliant full-moon.

Since He (God) draws forth the living from the dead, he that has become dead (to this world) keeps the right course;

(And) since He brings forth the dead from the living, the 550 living (carnal) soul moves towards a state of death (self-mortification).

Become dead, that the Lord *who brings forth the living* may bring forth a (spiritually) living one from this dead one.

(If) thou become December (Winter), thou wilt experience the bringing forth of Spring; (if) thou become night, thou wilt experience the advent[4] of day.

Do not tear out thy feathers[5], for 'tis irreparable: do not rend thy face in grief, O beauteous one.

Such a face that resembles the morning sun—'tis sinful to rend a countenance like that.

'Tis (an act of) infidelity (to inflict) scratches[6] upon a counte- 555 nance (of) such (beauty) that the moon's countenance wept at parting from it.

Or dost not thou see (the beauty of) thy face? Abandon that contumacious disposition (which prevents thee from seeing it)."

[1] *I.e.* inside of.
[2] Literally, "they make a fan of thy feathers."
[3] Literally, "from the eye of."
[4] Literally, "encroachment (of day upon night)." Cf. *Qur'án*, XXII, 60.
[5] *I.e.* thy spiritual qualities and graces.
[6] Literally, "wounds caused by the nails."

4

*Explaining that the purity and simplicity of the tranquil soul are
disturbed by thoughts, just as (when) you write or depict any-
thing on the surface of a mirror, though you may (afterwards)
obliterate it entirely, (yet) a mark and blemish will remain (on
the mirror).*

The face of the tranquil soul[1] in the body suffers wounds
inflicted by the nails of thought.

Know that evil thought is a poisonous nail: in (the case of)
deep reflection it rends the face of the soul.

In order that he (the thinker) may loose the knot of a difficulty,
he has put a golden spade into ordure[2].

560　Suppose the knot is loosed, O adept (thinker): 'tis (like) a
tight knot on an empty purse[3].

Thou hast grown old in (the occupation of) loosing knots:
suppose a few more knots are loosed (by thee, what then?).

The knot that is (fastened) tight on our throat[4] is that thou
shouldst know whether thou art vile or fortunate[5].

Solve this problem, if thou art a man: spend thy breath (life)
on this, if thou hast the breath (spirit) of Adam (within
thee).

Suppose thou knowest the definitions of (all) substances and
accidents, (how shall it profit thee?): know the (true) definition
of thyself, for this is indispensable[6].

565　When thou knowest the definition of thyself, flee from this
definition, that thou mayst attain to Him who hath no definition,
O sifter of dust[7].

(Thy) life has gone (to waste) in (the consideration of logical)
predicate and subject: (thy) life, devoid of (spiritual) insight,
has gone in (study of) what has been received by hearsay.

Every proof (that is) without (a spiritual) result and effect is
vain: consider the (final) result of thyself!

Thou hast never perceived a Maker except by means of a
thing made: thou art content with a syllogism[8].

The philosopher multiplies links (consisting) of (logical)
proofs; on the other hand, the elect (the mystic) is contrary to
him (in this respect).

570　The latter flees from the proof and from the veil (between
himself and God): he has sunk his head in his bosom for the
sake of (contemplating) the Object of the proof.

[1] The soul at peace with God (*Qur'án*, LXXXIX, 27).
[2] *I.e.* has applied his reason to the futilities of exoteric knowledge.
[3] *I.e.* the solution of the problem is useless.
[4] *I.e.* the vital problem.　　　　[5] *I.e.* damned or saved.
[6] Literally, "there is no escape from this."
[7] *I.e.* "O investigator of worthless matters."
[8] Literally, "an induction based on (the logical) connexion (of proposi-
tions)." Here the syllogism is "The world is made: everything made has a
maker: therefore the world has a Maker."

If to him (the philosopher) the smoke is a proof of the fire, to us (mystics) 'tis sweet (to be) in the fire without the smoke,

Especially this Fire which, through (our) nighness and fealty (to God), is nearer to us than the smoke.

Therefore 'tis black villainy to go (turn away) from the Soul (Reality) towards the smoke for the sake of (indulging) the phantasies (illusions) of the (animal) soul.

*In explanation of the saying of the Prophet, on whom be peace,*
*"There is no monkery in Islam."*

"Do not tear out thy feathers, but detach thy heart from (desire for) them, because (the existence of) the enemy is the necessary condition for (waging) this Holy War.

When there is no enemy, the Holy War is inconceivable; (if) 575 thou hast no lust, there can be no obedience (to the Divine command).

There can be no self-restraint when thou hast no desire; when there is no adversary, what need for thy strength?

Hark, do not castrate thyself, do not become a monk; for chastity is in pawn to (depends on the existence of) lust.

Without (the existence of) sensuality 'tis impossible to forbid sensuality: heroism cannot be displayed against the dead.

He (God) hath said '*Spend*': therefore earn something, since there can be no expenditure without an old (previously acquired) income.

Although He used (the word) *Spend* absolutely, (yet) read (it 580 as meaning) 'Earn, then spend.'

Similarly, since the King (God) has given the command '*Refrain yourselves*,' there must be some desire from which thou shouldst avert thy face.

Hence (the command) '*Eat ye*' is for the sake of the snare (temptation) of appetite; after that (comes) '*Do not exceed*': that is temperance.

When there is no 'predicate' (relative quality) in him (any one), the existence of the 'subject' (the correlative term) is impossible.

When thou hast not the pain of self-restraint, there is no protasis: therefore the apodosis (recompense) does not follow[1].

How admirable is that protasis and how joyful is that apo- 585 dosis (recompense), a recompense that charms the heart and increases the life of the spirit!

[1] Literally, "does not come down (come to pass)."

*Explaining that God (Himself) is the reward bestowed
by Him for the (devotional) work of the lover.*

For (His) lovers He (alone) is (all their) joy and sorrow; He (alone) is their wages and hire for service.

If there be any spectacle (object of regard for them) except the Beloved, 'tis not love: 'tis an idle passion.

Love is that flame which, when it blazes up, consumes everything else but the Beloved[1].

He (the lover) drives home the sword of *Not* in order to kill all other than God: thereupon consider what remains after *Not*.

590    There remains *except God*: all the rest is gone. Hail, O mighty Love, destroyer of polytheism!

Verily, He is the First and the Last: do not regard polytheism as arising from aught except the eye that sees double.

Oh, wonderful! Is there any beauty but from the reflexion of Him? The (human) body hath no movement but from the spirit.

The body that hath defect in its spirit will never become sweet, (even) if you smear it with honey.

This he knows who one day was (spiritually) alive and received a cup from this Soul of the soul;

595    While to him whose eye has not beheld those (beauteous) cheeks this smoky heat[2] is (appears to be) the spirit.

Inasmuch as he never saw 'Umar (ibn) 'Abdu 'l-'Azíz, to him even Ḥajjáj seems just.

Inasmuch as he never saw the firmness (unshakable strength) of the dragon of Moses, he fancies (there is) life in the magic cords[3].

The bird that has never drunk the limpid water keeps its wings and feathers in the briny water.

No opposite can be known except through its opposite: (only) when he (any one) suffers blows will he know (the value of) kindness.

600    Consequently the present life has come in front (first), in order that you may appreciate the realm of *Alast*.

When you are delivered from this place and go to that place, you will give thanks (to God) in the sugar-shop of everlastingness.

You will say, 'There (in the world below) I was sifting dust, I was fleeing from this pure world.

Alas, would that I had died ere now, so that my (time of) being tormented in the mud might have been less!'

---

[1] Delete the *iḍáfat* of معشوق.     [2] *I.e.* the animal soul.
[3] The cords which Pharaoh's magicians caused to move like snakes

*Commentary on the saying of the Prophet, on whom be peace, " None*
*ever died without wishing, if he was a righteous man, that he*
*had died before he (actually) died, in order that he might sooner*
*attain unto felicity; and if he was a wicked man, in order that*
*his wickedness might be less."*

Hence the wise Prophet has said that no one who dies and
dismounts from (the steed of) the body

Feels grief on account of departure and death, but (only) 605
grieves because of having failed (in good works) and missed his
opportunities.

In sooth every one that dies wishes that the departure to his
destination had been earlier:

If he be wicked, in order that his wickedness might have been
less; and if devout, in order that he might have come home
sooner.

The wicked man says, 'I have been heedless, moment by
moment I have been adding to the veil (of sin).

If my passing (from the world) had taken place sooner, this
screen and veil of mine would have been less.'

Do not in covetousness rend the face of contentment, and 610
do not in pride rend the visage of humility.

Likewise do not in avarice rend the face of munificence, and
in devilishness the beauteous countenance of worship.

Do not tear out those feathers which are an ornament to
Paradise: do not tear out those feathers which (enable thee to)
traverse the Way."

When he (the peacock) heard this counsel, he looked at him
(the Sage) and, after that, began to lament and weep.

The long lamentation and weeping of the sorrowful (peacock)
caused every one who was there to fall a-weeping;

And he who was asking the reason of (the peacock's) tearing 615
out his feathers, (he too being left) without an answer repented
(of having asked) and wept,

Saying, "Why did I impertinently ask him (that question)?
He was full of grief: I made him distraught."

From his (the peacock's) moist eyes the water (of tears) was
trickling to the earth: in every drop were contained a hundred
answers.

Sincere weeping touches the souls (of all), so that it makes
(even) the sky and heaven to weep.

Without any doubt, intellects and hearts (spirits) are celestial,
(though) they live debarred from the celestial light.

*Explaining that the intellect and spirit are imprisoned in clay, like*
*Hárút and Márút in the pit of Babylon.*

620    Like Hárút and Márút, those two pure ones (the intellect and
spirit) have been confined here (in this world) in a horrible pit.

They are in the low and sensual world: they have been con-
fined in this pit on account of sin.

The good and the evil (alike) learn magic and the opposite
of magic from these twain involuntarily;

But first they admonish him, saying, "Beware, do not learn
and pick up magic from us:

We teach this magic, O such and such, for the purpose of
trial and probation;

625    (But thou art free to choose), for probation necessarily in-
volves free-will, and thou canst not have any (effective) free-will
without the power (of action)."

Desires are like sleeping dogs: good and evil are hidden in
them.

When there is no power (of action), this troop (of desires) are
asleep and silent like faggots (smouldering in the fire),

Until (when) a carcase comes into view, the blast of the
trumpet of greed strikes on (suddenly rouses) the dogs.

When the carcase of a donkey appears[1] in the parish, a hundred
sleeping dogs are awakened by it.

630    The greedy desires that had gone into the concealment of the
Unseen rush out and display themselves[2].

Every hair[3] on every dog becomes (like) a tooth[4], though they
wag their tails (fawningly) for the sake of gaining their object.

His (the dog's) under-half is cunning, (while) the upper (half)
is anger, like a poor fire that gets faggots (fuel);

Flame on flame reaches (it) from (the realm of) non-spatiality:
the smoke of its blaze goes up to the sky.

In this body (of ours) a hundred such dogs are sleeping: when
they have no prey (in sight), they are hidden.

635    Or they resemble falcons with eyes sealed (covered); (yet) in
the veil (hood) consumed with passion for a prey,

Till he (the Falconer) lifts the hood and it (the falcon) sees
the prey: then it circles the mountains (in pursuit).

The appetite of the sick man is quiescent: his thoughts are
going (are turned) towards health.

When he sees bread and apples and water-melons, his relish
and his fear of injury (to himself) come into conflict.

If he be very self-restrained, the sight (of the food) is a benefit

---

[1] Literally, "when a donkey becomes a carcase."
[2] Literally, "put forth the head from the bosom of the shirt."
[3] Literally, "hair by hair."
[4] *I.e.* stands on end with anger and fury against his rivals.

to him: that stimulation (of appetite) is good for his enfeebled constitution;

But if he have not self-restraint, then it were better he had 640 not seen (the food): 'tis better the arrow should be far from the man who is without a coat of mail.

### The answer of the peacock to his interrogator.

When he (the peacock) had finished weeping, he said, "Begone, for thou art in pawn (bondage) to colour and perfume[1].

Dost not thou perceive that on account of these feathers a hundred afflictions approach me on every side?

Oh, many a pitiless fowler always lays a trap for me everywhere for the sake of these feathers.

How many an archer, for the sake of my plumage, shoots arrows[2] at me (when I am) in the air!

Since I have not strength and self-control (to preserve me) 645 from this destiny and this affliction and these tribulations,

'Tis better I should be ugly and hideous, that I may be safe amidst these mountains and deserts.

These (feathers) are the weapons of my pride, O noble sir: pride brings a hundred afflictions on the proud.

### Explaining that accomplishments and intellectual abilities and worldly wealth are enemies to (spiritual) life, like the peacock's feathers.

Accomplishments, then, are a destruction to the (spiritually) ignorant man, for in his pursuit of the bait he does not see the trap.

Free-will is good for him (alone) who is master of himself in (respect of obeying the command) 'Fear ye (God).'

When there is no safeguarding (of one's self) and piety, 650 beware, put far (from thee) the instrument (that serves as a means to sin): drop free-will.

Those feathers are the object of my display (pride) and free-will: I will tear out the feathers, for they are in quest of my head[3].

The self-restrained man deems his feathers to be naught, in order that his feathers may not cast him into calamity and bale.

Therefore his feathers are no harm to him: let him not tear them out, (for) if an arrow (of temptation) come (against him) he will present the shield (of self-restraint).

But to me my beauteous feathers are an enemy, since I cannot restrain myself from making a display.

[1] *I.e.* outward appearances.
[2] Literally, "draws arrows (from his quiver in order to shoot)."
[3] *I.e.* they endanger my life.

655 If self-restraint and safeguarding had been my guide, my (spiritual) conquest[1] would have been increased by (the exercise of) free-will;

(But) in (the case of) temptations I am like a child or a drunken man: the sword is unsuitable (out of place) in my hand.

Had I possessed an intellect and conscience (to restrain me), the sword in my hand would have been (a means of gaining) victory.

An intellect giving light like the sun is needed to wield the sword that never misses the right direction[2].

Since I do not possess a resplendent intellect and righteousness (in religion), why, then, should not I throw my weapons into the well?

660 I now throw my sword and shield into the well; for (otherwise) they will become the weapons of my adversary.

Since I do not possess strength and aid and support, he (the adversary) will seize my sword and smite me with it.

In despite of this fleshly soul and evil-natured one who does not veil her face, I will rend my face,

That this beauty and perfection (of mine) may be impaired. When my face (beauty) remains no more, I shall not fall into woe.

When I rend (my face) with this intention, 'tis no sin, for this face ought to be covered with wounds.

665 If my heart had a modest disposition, my handsome face would produce naught but purity (goodness).

Since I did not see (in myself) strength and wisdom and righteousness, I saw the adversary and at once broke my weapons,

Lest my sword should become useful[3] to him; lest my dagger should become hurtful to me.

I will continue to flee as long as my veins are running[4], (but) how should it be easy to escape from one's self?

He who is in flight from another obtains rest when he has been separated from him (the pursuer).

670 I, who am the adversary (of myself), 'tis I that am in flight (from myself): rising and departing is my occupation for ever.

He whose adversary is his own shadow is not safe either in India or Khutan.

---

[1] Literally, "attack and retreat."
[2] Literally, "that never is anything but rightly directed."
[3] Literally, "perfection."
[4] Or, "my nerves are vibrating."

*Description of the selfless ones who have become safe from their*
*own vices and virtues; for they are naughted in the everlastingness*
*of God, like stars which are naughted (vanish) in the Sun during*
*the daytime; and he who is naughted hath no fear of bane and*
*(is free from) danger.*

When, through (spiritual) poverty, *faná* (self-naughting) graces
him (such a one), he becomes shadowless like Mohammed.

*Faná* graced (the Prophet who said) 'Poverty is my pride[1]':
he became shadowless like the flame of a candle.

(When) the candle[2] has become entirely flame from head to
foot, the shadow hath no passage (way of approach) around it.

The wax (candle) fled from itself and from the shadow into 675
the radiance[3] for the sake of Him who moulded the candle.

He said, 'I moulded thee for the sake of *faná* (self-naughting).'
It replied, 'I accordingly took refuge in *faná*.'

This is the necessary everlasting radiance, not the radiance
of the perishable accidental candle.

When the candle is wholly naughted in the fire (of Divine
illumination), you will not see any trace of the candle or rays
(of its light).

Manifestly, in dispelling the darkness, the external (material)
flame is maintained by a wax candle;

(But) the candle (which is) the body is contrary to the wax 680
candle, since in proportion as that (the body) dwindles, the light
of the spirit is increased.

This is the everlasting radiance, and that (bodily candle) is
perishable: the candle of the spirit hath a Divine flame.

Since this tongue of fire was (really) light, 'twas far from it
to become a perishable shadow.

The cloud's shadow falls on the earth: the shadow never con-
sorts with the moon.

Selflessness is cloudlessness, O well-disposed one: in (the
state of) selflessness thou wilt be like the orb of the moon.

Again, when a cloud comes, driven along, the light goes: of 685
the moon there remains (only) a phantom.

Its light is made feeble by the cloud-veil: that noble full-moon
becomes less than the new moon.

The moon is made to appear a phantom by clouds and dust:
the cloud, (which is) the body, has caused us to conceive phan-
tasies.

Behold the kindness of the (Divine) Moon; for this too is
His kindness, that He hath said, 'The clouds are enemies to
Us.'

---

[1] Or, *Faná* graced (him who attained to the state denoted by the Prophet's
saying) "Poverty is my pride."
[2] *I.e.* the lover of God.          [3] *I.e.* the Light of God.

The Moon is independent of clouds and dust: the Moon hath His orbit aloft in the (spiritual) sky.

690    The cloud is our mortal enemy and adversary because it hides the Moon from our eyes.

This veil makes the houri (to appear as) a hag: it makes the full-moon less than a new moon.

The Moon hath seated us in the lap of glory: He hath called our foe His enemy.

The splendour and beauty of the cloud is (derived) from the Moon, (but) whoever calls the cloud the Moon is much astray.

Since the light of the Moon has been poured down upon the cloud, its (the cloud's) dark face has been transfigured by the Moon.

695    Although it is of the same colour as the Moon and is associated with (the Moon's) empire, (yet) in the cloud the light of the Moon is (only) borrowed (impermanent).

At the Resurrection the sun and moon are discharged (from their office): the eye is occupied in (contemplating) the Source of (their) radiance,

In order that it may know (distinguish) the (permanent) possession from the (temporary) loan, and this perishable caravanseray from the everlasting abode.

The nurse is borrowed for three or four days: do thou, O Mother, take us into thy bosom!

My feathers are (like) the cloud and are a veil and gross: (only) by the reflexion of God's loveliness are they made lovely.

700    I will pluck my feathers and their beauty from the Way (to God), that I may behold the Moon's beauty (by immediate illumination) from the Moon.

I do not want the nurse; (my) Mother is fairer. I am (like) Moses: (my) Mother (herself) is my nurse.

I do not want (to enjoy) the loveliness of the Moon through an intermediary, for this link is perdition to the people;

Unless (the intermediary be) a cloud[1] (that) becomes naughted in the Way (to God) in order that it may not be a veil to the face of the Moon.

In the aspect of *lá* (self-negation) it (such a cloud) displays His (the Moon's) form, like the bodies of the prophets and saints.

705    Such a cloud is not veil-tying; it is in reality veil-tearing (and) salutary.

'Tis as when, on a bright morning, drops of rain were falling though there was no cloud above (in the sky).

That water-skin was a miracle of the Prophet[2]: from self-effacement the cloud (which replenished it) had become of the same colour as the sky.

---

[1] *I.e.* a perfect saint.    [2] See Book III, *v.* 3130 foll.

The cloud was (there), but the cloud-nature had gone from it: the body of the lover (of God) becomes like this by means of renunciation.

It is body, but corporeality has vanished from it: it has been transfigured, colour and perfume have gone from it.

(My) feathers are for the sake of others, while (my) head is 710 for my own sake: (the head which is) the abode of hearing and sight is the pillar (support) of the body.

Know that to sacrifice the spirit for the sake of catching others is absolute infidelity and despair of good.

Beware! Do not be like sugar before parrots; nay, be a poison, be secure from loss;

Or (otherwise), for the sake of having a 'Bravo' addressed to thee, make thyself (as) a carcase in the presence of dogs![1]

Therefore Khaḍir scuttled the boat for this purpose, (namely), that the boat might be delivered from him who would have seized it by force[2].

(The mystery of) 'Poverty is my pride' is sublime: (it is) for 715 the purpose that I may take refuge from the covetous with Him who is Self-sufficient.

Treasures are deposited in a ruined spot to the end that they may escape the greed of those who dwell in places of cultivation.

(If) thou canst not tear out thy feathers, go, adopt (a life of) solitude, that thou mayst not be entirely squandered (consumed) by that one and this one;

For thou art both the morsel (of food) and the eater of the morsel: thou art the devourer and the devoured. Apprehend (this), O (dear) soul!

*Explaining that everything except God is devouring and devoured, like the bird that was in pursuit of a locust and occupied in chasing it and oblivious of the hungry hawk behind its own back, that was about to seize it. Now, O hunting and devouring man, be not secure against thine own hunter and devourer. Though with the sight of the (physical) eye thou seest him not, (yet) see him with the eye of serious consideration[3] till the opening of the eye of the inmost heart (oculus cordis).*

A little bird was hunting a worm: a cat found its opportunity and seized it.

It (the bird) was a devourer and a thing devoured, and (being 720 engrossed) in its hunting was ignorant of another hunter.

Although the thief is (engaged) in hunting articles of property,

---

[1] *I.e.* "unless thou scorn the world thou wilt become its prey."
[2] *Qur'án*, XVIII, 70 and 78.
[3] Literally, "with the sight that regards the indications given by serious consideration (and takes warning from them)."

(yet) the prefect of police with (the thief's) enemies is behind him (on his track).

His mind is occupied with chattels and lock and door: he is heedless of the prefect and of the outcry (that will arise) at dawn.

He is so absorbed in his passion (for gain) he gives no heed to his seekers and pursuers.

If the herbage is drinking pure water, (yet) afterwards an animal's belly will feed on it.

725   That grass is devouring and devoured: even so (is) everything that exists except God.

Since He is (the subject of the text) *and He feedeth you and is not fed*, God is not devouring and devoured, (like) flesh and skin.

How should that which is devouring and devoured be secure from a devourer who dwells in a (secret) hiding-place?

The security of those who are (liable to be) devoured brings mourning in its train: go to the Portal of Him who *is not fed*.

Every phantasy is devouring another phantasy: (one) thought feeds on another thought.

730   Thou canst not be delivered from any phantasy or fall asleep so as to escape from it (altogether).

(Thy) thoughts are (like) hornets, and thy sleep is (like) the water (in which thou art plunged): when thou awakest, the flies (hornets) come back,

And many hornet-like phantasies fly in and (now) draw thee this way and (now) take thee that way.

This (mental) phantasy is the least of the devourers: the Almighty knows (how great are) the others.

Hark, flee from the troop of huge devourers towards Him who hath said, 'We are thy protector';

735   Or towards one who has gained that (power of) protection, if thou canst not hasten towards the Protector (Himself).

Do not surrender thy hand save to the hand of the Pír (spiritual director); (for) God hath become the aider of his hand.

The Pír (Elder), (which is) thy intellect, has become childish[1] from being a neighbour to the carnal soul which is in the veil (of sensuality).

Associate the perfect intelligence (of the spiritual director) with thy (imperfect) understanding, in order that thy understanding may return (withdraw itself) from that evil disposition.

When thou layest thy hand in his, then thou wilt escape from the hand of the devourers,

740   And thy hand will become one of the Covenanters[2] *above whose hands is the Hand of Allah*[3].

---

[1] Literally, "has made childishness its habitual disposition."
[2] Referring originally to those who took the oath of allegiance to the Prophet at Ḥudaybiya.          [3] *Qur'án*, XLVIII, 10.

When thou hast put thy hand in the hand of the Pír, the Pír of wisdom who is knowing and eminent,

Who is the prophet of his own time, O disciple, so that the Light of the Prophet is manifested by him,

By this means thou hast been present at Ḥudaybiya and hast been associated with the Companions who took the Covenant.

Therefore thou hast become one of the ten Friends to whom the glad tidings were given[1], and hast been made pure like sterling gold.

(This is) to the end that communion may be made perfect; 745 for a man is united with that one whom he has made his friend.

He is with him in this world and in that (other) world; and this is the (meaning of) the Ḥadíth of sweet-natured Aḥmad (Mohammed),

(Who) said, 'A man is with him whom he loves': the heart is not severed from its object of desire.

Do not sit in any place where there is a trap and bait: O thou who regardest (others) as weak[2], go, consider (what becomes of) those who regard (others) as weak.

O thou who regardest the weak as weak (and at thy mercy), know this, (that) there is a hand above thy hand, O youth.

Thou art weak (thyself) and thou regardest (others) as weak. 750 Oh, wonderful! Thou art at once the prey and the hunter in pursuit (of the prey).

Be not (one of those described in the Verse) *before and behind them* (*We will set*) *a barrier*[3], so that thou canst not see the enemy, though the enemy is manifest.

The greed of hunting makes (one) oblivious of being a prey: he (the hunter) tries to win hearts (though) he has lost his own[4].

Be not thou inferior to a bird in (thy) seeking: (even) a sparrow sees (what is) *before and behind*.

When it approaches the grain (bait), at that moment it turns its head and face several times to front and rear,

(As though to say), 'Oh, I wonder whether there is a fowler 755 in front of me or behind, so that for fear of him I should abstain[5] from this food.'

Do thou see behind (thee) the story of (what happened to) the wicked[6]; see before (thee) the death of (many a) friend and neighbour,

Whom He (God) destroyed without (using) any instrument: He is close to thee in every circumstance.

God inflicted torment (on them), and there is no mace or

---

[1] *I.e.* to whom Paradise was promised.    [2] *I.e.* as thy prey.
[3] *Qur'án*, XXXVI, 8.    [4] Literally, "he is without a heart."
[5] Literally, "withdraw my hand."    [6] As related in the *Qur'án*.

hand (employed): know, then, that God is one who deals justice (inflicts chastisement) without hands.

He who was saying, 'If God exists, where is He?' was confessing on the rack (of pain) that 'tis He (God).

760 He who was saying, 'This is far-fetched and marvellous' was shedding tears and crying, 'O Thou who art nigh!'

Since he has deemed it necessary to flee from the trap, ('tis strange that) the trap for thee is in fact stuck fast to thy (gaudy) feathers.

I will tear out the pin of this ill-fated trap: I will not suffer bitter grief[1] for the sake of (indulging) a desire.

I have given thee this answer (which is) suitable to thy understanding: apprehend (its meaning) and do not avert thy face from seeking.

Snap this cord, which is greed and envy: remember (the text) *on her neck a cord of palm-fibres*[2]."

*The reason why Khalíl (Abraham), on whom be peace, killed the crow, indicating (thereby) the subjugation of certain blameworthy and pernicious qualities in the disciple*[3].

765 There is no end and completion to this discourse. O Friend of God, why didst thou kill the crow?

Because of the (Divine) command. What was the wisdom of the (Divine) command? A small part of the mysteries thereof must (now) be shown.

The cawing and noisy cry of the black crow is ever asking for (long) life in this world.

Like Iblís, it (the crow) besought the holy and incomparable God for bodily life till the Resurrection.

He (Iblís) said, "*Grant me a respite till the Day of Retribution.*" Would that he had said, "We repent, O our Lord."

770 Life without repentance is all agony of spirit: to be absent from God is present (instant) death.

Life and death—both these are sweet with (the presence of) God: without God the Water of Life is fire.

Moreover, 'twas from the effect of the (Divine) curse that in such a Presence he was requesting (long) life.

To crave of God aught other than God is (merely) the supposition of gain, and (in reality) it is entire loss;

Especially (to desire) a life sunk in estrangement (from God) is to behave like a fox in the presence of the lion,

---

[1] Literally, "I will not be one whose palate is bitter."

[2] *Qur'án*, CXI, 5.

[3] A more literal translation would be: "and which of the blameworthy and pernicious qualities existing in the disciple are signified and their subjugation indicated (by the killing of the crow)."

(Saying), "Give me longer life that I may go farther back[1]; 775 grant me more time that I may become less[2]."

(The result is) that he (such an one) is a mark for the (Divine) curse: evil is that one who seeks to be accursed.

The goodly life is to nourish the spirit in nearness (to God); the crow's life is for the sake of eating dung.

(The crow says), "Give me more life that I may be ever eating dung: give me this always, for I am very evil-natured."

Were it not that that foul-mouthed one is a dung-eater, he would say, "Deliver me from the nature of the crow!"

### Prayer.

O Thou who hast transmuted one clod of earth into gold, 780 and another clod into the Father of mankind,

Thy work is the transmutation of essences and (the showing of) munificence; my work is mistake and forgetfulness and error.

Transmute mistake and forgetfulness into knowledge: I am all choler, make me patience and forbearance.

O Thou who makest nitrous earth to be bread, and O Thou who makest dead bread to be life,

O Thou who makest the distracted soul to be a Guide, and O Thou who makest the wayless wanderer to be a Prophet,

Thou makest a piece of earth to be heaven, Thou givest in- 785 crease in the earth from the stars.

Whosoever makes the Water of Life to consist of (the pleasures of) this world, death comes to him sooner than to the others.

The eye of the heart (the inward eye) that contemplated the (spiritual) firmament perceived that here (in the sensible world) is a continual alchemy.

The harmonious cohesion of the patched garment, (which is) the body, without being stitched (together), is (owing to) the transmutation of essences and (to) an all-embracing elixir.

From the day when thou camest into existence, thou wert fire or air or earth.

If thou hadst remained in that condition, how should this 790 (present) height have been reached by thee?

The Transmuter did not leave thee in thy first (state of) existence[3]: He established a better (state of) existence in the place of that (former one);

And so on till (He gave thee) a hundred thousand states of existence, one after the other, the second (always) better than the beginning[4].

---

[1] I.e. in disobedience and sin.    [2] I.e. more deficient.

[3] Literally, "From (the action of) the Transmuter thy first state of existence did not endure."

[4] I.e. each one of the series was better than the one which immediately preceded it.

Regard (all change as derived) from the Transmuter, leave (ignore) the intermediaries, for by (regarding) the intermediaries thou wilt become far from their Origin.

Wherever the intermediaries increase, union (with the Origin) is removed: (in proportion as) the intermediaries are less, the delight of (attaining to) union is greater.

795 By knowing the intermediaries thy bewilderment (in God) is diminished: thy bewilderment gives thee admission to the (Divine) Presence.

Thou hast gained these (successive) lives from (successive) deaths: why hast thou averted thy face from dying in Him?

What loss was thine (what loss didst thou suffer) from those deaths, that thou hast clung (so tenaciously) to (this earthly) life, O rat?

Since thy second (life) is better than thy first, therefore seek to die (to the world), and worship the Transmuter.

O contumacious man, thou hast experienced a hundred thousand resurrections at every moment from the beginning of thy existence until now:

800 From inanimateness (thou didst move) unconsciously towards (vegetal) growth, and from (vegetal) growth towards (animal) life and tribulation;

Again, towards reason and goodly discernments; again, towards (what lies) outside of these five (senses) and six (directions).

These footprints are (extend) as far as the shore of the Ocean; then the footprints disappear[1] in the Ocean;

Because, from (Divine) precaution, the resting-places (appointed for the traveller) on the dry land are (like) villages and dwellings and caravanserays,

(While) on the contrary the resting-places of the Ocean, when its billows swell[2], have no floor or roof (to shelter the traveller) during (his) stay and detention.

805 These (Oceanic) stages have no visible beacon[3]: these resting-places have neither sign nor name.

Between every two resting-places Yonder there is (a distance) a hundred times as much as from the vegetal state to the Essential Spirit.

Thou hast seen this life (to be implicit) in (previous) deaths: how, (then), art thou (so) attached to the life of the body?

Come, O crow, give up this (animal) soul! Be a falcon, be self-sacrificing in the presence of the Divine transmutation.

Take the new and surrender the old, for every "this year" of thine is superior to three "last years."

[1] Literally, "are naught."    [2] Literally, "at the time of waves."
[3] Literally, "hump," *i.e.* prominence or elevation which should serve as a mark.

If thou wilt not be lavish (of thyself) like the date-palm, (then) 810
pile old rags on old rags and make a heap,

And offer the stinking and rotten old rags to every blind man.

He that hath seen the new is not thy customer: he is God's
prey, he is not thy captive.

(But) wherever is a flock of blind birds, they will gather
around thee, O brackish flood-water,

That (their) blindness may be increased by (thy) brackish
waters; for brackish water increases blindness.

Hence the worldly are blind of heart: they are drinkers of the 815
brackish water of clay.

Continue to give brackish water and buy (the favour of) the
blind in the world, since thou hast not the Water of Life within
thee[1].

In such a (despicable) state (as has been described) thou
wouldst fain live and be remembered[2]: in blackness of face
(shame and opprobrium), like a negro, thou art rejoicing.

The negro in (his) blackness is pleased (with himself), for he
has (always) been a negro by birth and nature;

(But) he that (even) for a day is beloved and beautiful, if he
become black, will seek to repair (the misfortune).

When the bird that can fly remains (helpless) on the earth, it 820
is in anguish and grief and lamentation;

(But) the domestic fowl walks complacently on the earth: it
runs about picking grain and happy and bold,

Because by nature it was (always) without (the power of)
flight, while the other (bird) was (naturally) a flier and open-
winged.


*The Prophet, on whom be peace, said, " Pity three (classes of men):
the mighty man of a people who is abased, and the rich man of
a people who is impoverished, and a learned man whom the
ignorant make sport of."*

The Prophet said, "Take pity on the soul of him who was
rich and then became poor,

And on him who was mighty and became despised, or on one
(who is) virtuous and learned (dwelling) amongst the (people of)
Muḍar[3]."

The Prophet said, "Show pity to these three classes (of men), 825
(even) if ye are of (the hardness of) rock and mountain:

(Namely), him who was made lowly after having been a chief,
and the rich man, too, who became impecunious,

---

[1] Literally, "in secret."
[2] Literally, "thou desirest life and mention."
[3] *I.e.* the Arab tribes which traced their descent to Muḍar ibn Nizár.
Here the term is equivalent to "the ignorant."

5

And, thirdly, the learned man who in this world becomes
afflicted (by living amongst) the foolish;

For to come (fall) from high to low estate is like the amputa-
tion of a limb from the body."

The limb that is cut off from the body becomes dead: (when)
newly cut off, it moves, but not for long.

830   (Similarly) he who drank of the cup of *Alast* last year, this
year he suffers the pain[1] and headache (in consequence of having
drunk)[2],

While he who, like a dog, is by nature attached to the kennel[3]
—how should he have the desire for (spiritual) sovereignty?

(Only) he that has sinned seeks to repent; (only) he that has
lost the (right) way cries "Alas!"

*Story of the young gazelle being confined in the donkey-stable, and
how the donkey assailed the stranger, now with hostility and
now with mockery, and how it was afflicted by (having to eat)
dry straw which is not its (proper) food. And this is a description
of the chosen servant of God amongst worldlings and those
addicted to passion and sensuality; for "Islam (was) strange
(when it first) appeared, and will become strange again, and
blessed are the strangers." The Messenger of Allah spake the
truth.*

A hunter captured a gazelle: the merciless man put it into
a stable.

(Acting) like oppressors, he made a stable full of cows and
donkeys the prison of the gazelle.

835   The gazelle, wild with terror[4], was fleeing in every direction:
at night he (the hunter) poured (pieces of chopped) straw before
the donkeys.

(Moved) by hunger and (ravenous) appetite, every cow and
donkey was devouring the straw, (as though it were) sweeter
than sugar.

Now the gazelle would run in fright from side to side, now
it would turn its face away from the smoke and dust of the
straw.

Whosoever is left (in company) with his opposite, they (who
are wise) have deemed that punishment (terrible) as death,

So that Solomon said, "Unless the hoopoe make[5] a respectable
excuse for his absence,

840   I will kill him or inflict upon him a torment, a torment severe
beyond (all) calculation[6]."

---

[1] Literally, "to him is the calamity of the pain."
[2] *I.e.* the soul that drank the cup of Divine Love in the state of pre-
existence suffers tribulation in the present life, like a limb recently severed
from the body, on account of being separated from its original home.
[3] *I.e.* the world.      [4] Literally, "from *waḥshat*," *i.e.* fright and distress.
[5] Literally, "speak."              [6] *Qur'án*, XXVII, 20–21

Hark, what is that torment, O trusted (friend)? To be in a cage without thy congener.

O Man, thou art in torment on account of this body: the bird, thy spirit, is imprisoned with one of another kind.

The spirit is a falcon, and the (bodily) properties are crows: it has (receives) painful brands[1] from the crows and owls.

It remains amongst them in sore misery, like an Abú Bakr in the city of Sabzawár.

*Story of Muḥammad Khwárizmsháh who took by war (force) the city of Sabzawár, where all (the inhabitants) are Ráfiẓís[2] (extreme Shí'ites). (When) they begged him to spare their lives, he said, "I will grant (you) security as soon as ye produce from this city a man named Abú Bakr and present him to me."*

Muḥammad Alp Ulugh Khwárizmsháh marched to battle 845 against Sabzawár, (the city) full of refuge (for the wicked).

His troops reduced them (the inhabitants) to straits; his army fell to killing the foe.

They prostrated themselves before him, crying, "Mercy! Make us thy thralls[3], (but) spare[4] our lives!

Whatever thou requirest (in the way of) tribute or presents will come to thee from us with increase (abundantly) at every fixed time (of payment).

Our lives are thine, O lion-natured (prince): let them be on deposit with us for a (little) while."

He replied, "Ye will not save your lives from me unless ye 850 bring an Abú Bakr into my presence.

Unless ye bring to me as a gift from your city one whose name is Abú Bakr, O people who have fled (from righteousness),

I will mow you down like corn, O vile folk: I will accept neither tribute nor blandishments."

They offered him[5] many sacks of gold, saying, "Do not demand an Abú Bakr from a city like this.

How should there be an Abú Bakr in Sabzawár, or a dry sod in the river?"

He averted his face from the gold and said, "O Magians 855 (infidels), unless ye bring me an Abú Bakr as an offering,

'Tis of no avail. I am not a child that I should stand dumbfounded (fascinated) by gold and silver."

Unless thou prostrate thyself (in humble submission to God),

---

[1] *I.e.* it suffers great anguish.

[2] *I.e.* those who reject the Caliphs Abú Bakr, 'Umar, and 'Uthmán, whom they regard as usurpers.

[3] Literally, "Put the ring (the badge of servitude) in our ears."

[4] Literally, "give back."     [5] Literally, "brought in his way."

thou wilt not escape (from punishment), O wretch, (even) if
thou traverse the (whole) mosque on thy séant[1].

They (the inhabitants of Sabzawár) despatched emissaries[2],
(to inquire) where in this desolate (corrupt) place an Abú Bakr
was (to be found).

After three days and three nights, during which they made
haste (in searching), they found an emaciated Abú Bakr.

860    He was a wayfarer and, on account of sickness, had remained
in the corner of a ruin, in utter exhaustion[3].

He was lying in a ruined nook. When they espied him, they
said to him hurriedly,

"Arise! The Sultan has demanded thee: by thee our city will
be saved from slaughter."

He replied, "If I had the foot (power to walk) or any (means
of) arrival, I myself would have gone by my own road to my
destination.

How should I have remained in this abode of my enemies?
I would have pushed on towards the city of my friends."

865    They raised the corpse-bearers' board[4] and lifted our[5] Abú
Bakr (upon it).

The carriers were taking him along to Khwárizmsháh, that
he (the Sultan) might behold the token (which he desired).

Sabzawár is this world, and in this place the man of God is
wasted and good-for-naught.

Khwárizmsháh is God Almighty: He demands from this
wicked folk the (pure) heart.

He (the Prophet) said, "He (God) doth not regard your (out-
ward) form: therefore in your devising seek ye the owner of
the Heart[6]."

870    (God says), "I regard thee through the owner of the Heart,
not because of the (external) marks of prostration (in prayer)
and the giving away of gold (in charities)."

Since thou hast deemed thy heart to be the Heart, thou hast
abandoned the search after those who possess the Heart—

The Heart into which if seven hundred (heavens) like these
Seven Heavens should enter, they would be lost and hidden
(from view).

Do not call such fragments of heart as these "the Heart": do
not seek an Abú Bakr in Sabzawár!

The owner of the Heart becomes a six-faced mirror: through
him God looks upon (all) the six directions.

875    Whosoever hath his dwelling-place in (the world of) six direc-

---

[1] *I.e.* "even if thou frequent the mosque and sit in different parts of it
day after day."
[2] Literally, "advertisers."
[3] Literally, "full of wasting disease."
[4] *I.e.* the bier.                             [5] Literally, "my."
[6] *I.e.* the Perfect Man, the saint united with God.

tions. God doth not look upon him except through the mediation of him (the owner of the Heart).

If He (God) reject (any one), He does it for his sake; and if He accept (any one), he likewise is the authority.

Without him God does not bestow bounty on any one. I have told (only) one sample of (the sublimity of) the possessor of union (with God).

He (God) lays His gift on the palm of his hand, and from his palm dispenses it to those who are the objects of His mercy.

The unitedness of the Universal Sea (of Bounty) with his palm is unqualified and unconditional and perfect.

A unitedness that is not containable in words—to speak of it 880 were a vain task, so farewell.

O rich man, (if) thou bring a hundred sacks of gold, God will say, "Bring the Heart[1], O thou that art bent (in devotion).

If the Heart be pleased with thee, I am pleased; and if it be averse to thee, I am averse.

I do not regard thee, I regard that Heart: bring it, O soul, as a gift to My door!

According as it is in relation to thee, so am I: Paradise is under the feet of mothers[2]."

It (the Heart) is the mother and father and origin of (all) the 885 creatures: oh, blest is that one who knows the Heart from the skin.

Thou wilt say, "Lo, I have brought unto Thee a heart": He (God) will say to thee, "Qutú[3] is full of these hearts.

Bring the Heart that is the Quṭb (Pole) of the world and the soul of the soul of the soul of the soul of Adam."

The Sultan of (all) hearts is waiting expectantly for that Heart full of light and goodness.

Thou mayst wander (many) days in Sabzawár, (but) thou wilt not find (there) a Heart like that by (the most) careful observation.

Then thou wilt lay upon a bier the corrupt heart, whose soul 890 is rotten, to carry[4] (it) Yonder,

And say, "I bring Thee a heart, O King: there is no better heart than this in Sabzawár."

He (God) will answer thee, saying, "O audacious man, is this a graveyard that thou shouldst bring a dead heart hither?

Go, bring the Heart that is kingly, from which is (derived) the security of the Sabzawár of (mundane) existence."

You may say that that Heart is hidden from this world, because darkness and light are opposites.

From the Day of *Alast* there is an hereditary enmity of that 895 Heart to the Sabzawár of the carnal nature;

---

[1] *I.e.* "win the heart of the saint and approach Me through him."
[2] *I.e.* admission to Paradise depends on piety shown towards one's mother.
[3] See translation of Book III, *v.* 1414, note.    [4] Literally, "carrying."

For it is a falcon, while this world is the city of the crow: the sight of one who is uncongenial inflicts pain[1] upon him who is not his congener;

And if he (the worldling) behave with mildness (complaisance), he is acting hypocritically: he is seeking an advantage for himself by conciliating (the owner of the Heart).

He assents[2], not on account of sincere feeling[3], (but) in order that the admonisher may curtail his long admonition;

For this vile carrion-seeking crow hath a hundred thousand manifold tricks.

900 If they (the saints) accept his hypocrisy, he is saved: his hypocrisy becomes identical with the sincerity of him who benefits by instruction,

Because the august owner of the Heart is a buyer of damaged goods in our bazaar[4].

Seek the owner of the Heart, if thou art not soulless: become a congener of the Heart, if thou art not an adversary of the (spiritual) Sultan.

(But) that one whose hypocrisy pleases thee, he is (only) *thy* saint, (he is) not the elect of God.

Whosoever lives in accordance with thy disposition and nature seems to thy (carnal) nature to be a saint and a prophet.

905 Go, renounce sensuality in order that the (spiritual) scent may be thine and that the sweet ambergris-seeking organ of smell may be thine.

Thy brain (organ of smell) is corrupted by sensual indulgence: to thy (olfactory) sense musk and ambergris are unsalable.

This discourse hath no bound, and (meanwhile) our gazelle is running to and fro in flight in the stable.

### The remainder of the Story of the gazelle in the donkey-stable.

During (many) days the sweet-navelled male[5] gazelle was in torment in the donkey-stable,

Like a fish wriggling in the death-agony from (being kept on) dry ground, (or like) dung and musk tortured (by being kept) in the same box.

910 One donkey would say to his neighbour[6], "Ha! this wild fellow[7] has the nature of kings and princes. Hush!"

And the other would mock, saying, "By (constant) ebb and flow[8] he has gained a pearl: how should he sell cheaply?"

---

[1] Literally, "is a (painful) brand."
[2] Literally, "makes 'Yes'"; the German "bejaht."
[3] Literally, "want," "ardent longing."
[4] *I.e.* it is the business of the saints in this world to deal mercifully with the vicious and convert them to righteousness.
[5] *I.e.* vigorous and high-spirited.
[6] Literally, "to him."    [7] Literally, "father of the wild animals."
[8] *I.e.* by running to and fro and searching repeatedly.

And another donkey would say, "With this fastidiousness (of his), let him recline on the imperial throne!"

A certain donkey became ill with indigestion and was unable to eat; therefore he gave the gazelle a formal invitation (to dine)[1].

He (the gazelle) shook his head[2], (as though to say), "Nay, begone, O such-and-such: I have no appetite, I am unwell."

He (the donkey) replied, "I know that you are showing disdain, or holding aloof in regard for your reputation." 915

He (the gazelle) said to himself, "That (which you offer me) is *your* food, whereby your limbs are revived and renewed.

I have been familiar with a (beauteous) pasture, I have reposed amongst (rivulets of) clear water and meadows.

If Destiny has cast me into torment, (yet) how should that goodly disposition and nature depart (from me)?

If I have become a beggar, (yet) how should I have the face (impudence and greed) of a beggar? And if my (bodily) raiment become old, (yet) I am (spiritually) new.

I have eaten hyacinth and anemone and sweet basil too with a thousand disdains and disgusts." 920

He (the donkey) said, "Yes; boast and boast and boast away! In a strange country one can utter many an idle brag."

He (the gazelle) replied, "Truly my navel (musk-gland) bears (me) witness: it confers a (great) favour (even) on aloes-wood and ambergris.

But who will hearken to (perceive) that? (Only) he that hath the (spiritual) sense of smell. 'Tis taboo for the donkey addicted to dung.

The donkey smells donkey's urine on the road: how should I offer musk to (creatures of) this class?"

Hence the Prophet, (who was always) responsive (to the Divine command), spake the parable, "Islam is a stranger in this world," 925

Because even his (the true Moslem's) kinsfolk are fleeing from him, though the angels are in harmony with his essence.

The people deem his (outward) form homogeneous (with theirs), but they do not perceive in him that (spiritual) fragrance.

(He is) like a lion in the shape of a cow: behold him from afar but do not investigate[3] him!

And if you investigate, take leave of the cow, (which is) the body; for that lion-natured one will tear the cow to pieces.

He will expel the bovine nature from your head, he will uproot animality from the animal (soul). 930

(If) you are a cow, you will become a lion (when) near him; (but) if you are glad to be a cow, do not seek to be a lion.

---

[1] Literally, "he called the gazelle with the (ceremonious) form of invitation."    [2] Literally, "put his head so." Cf. Book III, *v.* 2071.
[3] Literally, "excavate, explore."

*Commentary on* "Verily I saw seven fat kine which seven lean
kine devoured." *God had created those lean kine with the
qualities of hungry lions, to the end that they might devour the
seven fat ones with avidity. Although (only) the forms of those
kine were shown as phantoms in the mirror of dream, do thou
regard the reality!*

The Lord of Egypt[1] saw in dream, when the door of his
inward eye was opened,
Seven fat kine, exceedingly well-nourished: the seven lean
kine devoured them.
The lean ones were lions within; else they would not have
been devouring the (fat) kine.

935    The man of (holy) works, then, is human in appearance, but
in him is concealed a man-eating lion.
He (the lion) heartily devours the (carnal) man and makes
him single[2]: his dregs become pure if he (the lion) inflict pain
upon him.
By that one pain he is delivered from all dregs: he sets his
foot upon Suhá[3].
How long wilt thou speak (caw) like the ill-ómened crow?[4]
(Let me return to the parable and ask), "O Khalíl[5], wherefore
didst thou kill the cock?"
He replied, "(Because of) the (Divine) command." "Tell
(me) the wisdom of the (Divine) command, that I may glorify
that (wisdom) punctiliously[6]."

*Explaining that the killing of the cock by Abraham, on whom be
peace, signifies the subdual and subjugation of certain blame-
worthy and pernicious qualities in the heart of the disciple.*

940    He (the cock) is lustful and much addicted to lust, intoxicated
by that poisonous insipid wine.
Had not it (lust) been (necessary) for the sake of procreation,
O executor[7], Adam for shame of it would have made himself
a eunuch.
The accursed Iblís said to (God) the Dispenser of justice,
"I want a powerful snare for this prey."
He (God) showed to him gold and silver and herds of horses,
saying, "By means of this thou canst seduce mankind."

---

[1] Potiphar.
[2] *I.e.* causes him to become entirely detached from his carnal self.
[3] Name of a star.
[4] This question seems to be addressed by the author to himself.
[5] *I.e.* Husámu'ddín. Cf. *v.* 31 *supra*.
[6] Literally, "hair by hair."
[7] *I.e.* "O thou who art charged with the duty of carrying out my in-
junctions."

He (Iblís) cried "Bravo!" but let his lip drop sourly: he became wrinkled and sour like a lemon.

Then God offered to that fallen one gold and jewels from His 945 goodly mines,

Saying, "Take this other snare, O accursed one." He replied, "Give more than this, O most excellent Helper."

(Then) He gave him oily and sweet (viands) and costly sherbets and many silken robes.

He (Iblís) said, "O Lord, I want more assistance than this, to bind them with *a cord of palm-fibre*.

In order that Thy intoxicated (devotees), who are fierce and courageous, may manfully burst those bonds,

And that by means of this snare and (these) cords of sensuality 950 Thy (holy) man may be separated from the unmanly,

I want another snare, O Sovereign of the throne—a mighty cunning[1] snare that will lay men low."

He (God) brought and placed before him wine and harp: thereat he smiled faintly[2] and was moderately[2] pleased.

He (Iblís) sent a message to the eternal Foreordainment of perdition[3], saying, "Raise dust from the bottom of the sea of temptation[4].

Is not Moses one of Thy servants? He tied veils of dust on the sea[5].

The water retreated[6] on every side: from the bottom of the 955 sea a (cloud of) dust shot up."

When He (God) showed unto him (Iblís) the beauty of women that was prevailing over the reason and self-restraint of men,

Then he snapped his fingers (in glee) and began to dance, crying, "Give me (these) as quickly as possible: I have attained to my desire."

When he saw those languorous eyes which make the reason and understanding unquiet,

And the loveliness of that fascinating cheek[7] on which this heart (of man) burns like rue-seed (on the fire),

Face and mole and eyebrow and lip like cornelian, 'twas as 960 though God shone forth through a subtile veil.

He (Iblís) deemed that coquetry and light springing gait to be like the revelation of Divine glory through a thin veil.

---

[1] Literally, "inventive in deceit."   [2] Literally, "half."

[3] *I.e.* to the Divine Name *Muḍill* in virtue of which God "leads those whom He will into perdition."

[4] *I.e.* "make a dry path through the sea, so that the wicked may be tempted and destroyed like Pharaoh and his people."

[5] As explained in the next verse.

[6] Literally, "pulled back the reins."

[7] Literally, "the cheek of those heart-captivating ones."

*Commentary on* "We created Man in the best (physical and
mental) proportion, then We reduced him to the lowest of
the low"; *and on* "And to whomsoever We grant long life,
We cause him to relapse in constitution."

The beauty personified in Adam[1], to which the angels bow
down, is afterwards deposed (from its former perfection), like
Adam (when he fell from Paradise).

It cries, "Alas, after existence non-existence!" He (God) says,
"Thy crime is this, that thou hast lived too long."

Gabriel, dragging it by the hair, leads it away, saying, "Begone
from this Paradise and from the company of the fair ones."

965 It says, "What is (the meaning of) this abasement after
exaltation?" He (Gabriel) replies, "That (exaltation) is a gift
(of God), and this (abasement) is (His) judgement on thee."

(It cries), "O Gabriel, thou didst (formerly) bow down (to
me) with (all) thy soul: why art thou now driving me from
Paradise?

My robes are flying from me in (this hour of) tribulation, like
leaves from the date-palm in the season of autumn."

The countenance whose splendour was moon-like becomes
with old age like the back of the Libyan lizard;

And the fair head and crown (of the head) that once were
radiant become ugly and bald at the time of eld;

970 And the tall proud figure, piercing the ranks like a spear-
point, in old age is bent double like a bow.

The colour of red anemone becomes the colour of saffron;
his lion-like strength becomes as the courage[2] of women.

He that used to grip a man in his arms by skill (in wrestling),
(now) they take hold of his arms (to support him) at the time
of departure.

Truly these are marks of pain and decay: every one of them
is a messenger of death.

*Commentary on* "The lowest of the low, except those who have
believed and wrought good works; for they shall have a
reward that is not cut off."

But if his physician be the Light of God, there is no loss or
crushing blow (that he will suffer) from old age and fever.

975 His weakness is like the weakness of the intoxicated, for in
his weakness he is the envy of a Rustam.

If he die, his bones are drowned in (spiritual) savour; every
mote of him is (floating) in the beams of the light of love-desire.

And he who hath not that (Light) is an orchard without fruit,
which the autumn brings to ruin[3].

[1] Literally, "the Adam of beauty."     [2] Literally, "gall-bladder."
[3] Literally, "turns up and down."

The roses remain not; (only) the black thorns remain: it becomes pale and pithless like a heap of straw.

O God, I wonder what fault did that orchard commit, that these (beautiful) robes should be stripped from it.

"It paid regard to itself, and self-regard is a deadly poison. 980 Beware, O thou who art put to the trial!"

The minion for love of whom the world wept—the world (now) is repulsing him from itself: what is (his) crime?

"The crime is that he put on a borrowed adornment and pretended that these robes were his own property.

We take them back, in order that he may know for sure that the stack is Ours and the fair ones are (only) gleaners;

That he may know that those robes were a loan: 'twas a ray from the Sun of Being."

(All) that beauty and power and virtue and knowledge have 985 journeyed hither from the Sun of Excellence.

They, the light of that Sun, turn back again, like the stars, from these (bodily) walls.

(When) the Sunbeam has gone home, every wall is left dark and black.

That which made thee amazed at the faces of the fair is the Light of the Sun (reflected) from the three-coloured glass.

The glasses of diverse hue cause that Light to seem coloured like this to us.

When the many-coloured glasses are no more, then the colour- 990 less Light makes thee amazed.

Make it thy habit to behold the Light without the glass, in order that when the glass is shattered there may not be blindness (in thee).

Thou art content with knowledge learned (from others): thou hast lit thine eye at another's lamp.

He takes away his lamp, that thou mayst know thou art a borrower, not a giver[1].

If thou hast rendered thanks (to God for what thou hast received) and made the utmost exertion (in doing so), be not grieved (at its loss), for He will give (thee) a hundred such (gifts) in return;

But if thou hast not rendered thanks, weep (tears of) blood 995 now, for that (spiritual) excellence has become quit of (has abandoned) the ungrateful.

*He (God) causeth the works* of the unbelieving people *to be lost; He maketh the state* of the believing people *to prosper.*

From the ungrateful man (his) excellence and knowledge disappear, so that never again does he see a trace of them.

(His feelings of) affinity and non-affinity and gratitude and affection vanish in such wise that he cannot remember them;

[1] Literally, "a generous youth."

For, O ingrates, (the words) *He causeth their works to be lost* are (signify) the flight[1] of (every) object of desire from every one who has obtained his desire (in this world),

1000    Excepting the thankful and faithful who are attended by fortune[2].

How should the past fortune bestow strength (on its possessors)? 'Tis the future fortune that bestows a special virtue.

In (obedience to the Divine command) "*Lend*," make a loan (to God) from this (worldly) fortune, that thou mayst see a hundred fortunes before thy face.

Diminish a little for thine own sake this (eating and) drinking, that thou mayst find in front (of thee) the basin of Kawthar[3].

He who poured a draught on the earth of faithfulness, how should the prey, fortune, be able to flee from him?

1005    He (God) gladdens their hearts, for *He maketh their state to prosper*: He restoreth their (worldly) entertainment after they have perished.

(He says), "O Death, O Turcoman who plunderest the village[4], give back whatsoever thou hast taken from these thankful ones."

He (Death) gives it back; (but) they will not receive it, for they have been endowed with the goods of spiritual life.

(They say), "We are Ṣúfís and have cast off our (bodily) mantles: we will not take (them) back after we have gambled (them) away.

We have seen the recompense (from God)—(and) how (can there be) a (worldly) recompense then (after that)? Want and desire and object are gone from us.

1010    We have emerged from a briny and destroying water, we have attained to the pure wine (of Paradise) and the fountain of Kawthar.

O World, that which thou hast shown unto others—faithlessness and deceit and grievous pride—

We pour (it all) on thy head in repayment, for we are martyrs come to war (against thee)."

(This is) in order that you may know that the Holy God hath servants impetuous and combative,

(Who) tear out the moustache of worldly hypocrisy and pitch their tents on the rampart of (Divine) aid.

1015    These martyrs have become warriors anew, and these captives have gained the victory once more;

They have lifted up their heads again from non-existence, saying, "Behold us if thou art not blind from birth,"

---

[1] Literally, "the springing away."
[2] Literally, "behind whom is fortune."
[3] In Paradise.          [4] The present world.

That you may know that in non-existence there are suns, and
that what is a sun here is (only) a small star yonder.

How, O brother, is existence (contained) in non-existence?
How is opposite concealed in opposite?

*He brings forth the living from the dead:* know that the hope
of (His) worshippers is non-existence[1].

The sower whose barn is empty, is not he joyful and happy 1020
in hope of non-existence—

(Namely, in the hope) that that (crop) will grow from the
quarter of non-existence? Apprehend (this) if thou art aware
of (spiritual) reality.

Moment by moment thou art expecting from non-existence
to gain understanding and (spiritual) perception and peace and
good.

'Tis not permitted to divulge this mystery; else I should make
Abkház[2] a Baghdád.

Non-existence, then, is God's factory from which He con-
tinually produces gifts.

God is the Originator, and an originator is he who produces 1025
a branch (derivative) without root (fundamental principle) or
support (model).

*Parable of the world (really) existent that appears non-existent
and the world (really) non-existent that appears existent.*

He (God) hath caused the non-existent to appear existent
and magnificent; He hath caused the existent to appear in the
form of non-existence.

He hath concealed the Sea and made the foam visible; He
hath concealed the Wind and displayed to thee the dust.

The dust is whirling in the air, (high) as a minaret: how should
the dust rise aloft of itself?

Thou seest the dust on high, O infirm (of sight): the Wind
(thou seest) not, except through knowledge given by induction.

Thou seest the foam moving in every direction: without the 1030
Sea the foam hath no turning-place[3].

Thou seest the foam by sense-perception and the Sea by
induction: thought is hidden, speech manifest.

We deemed negation to be affirmation: we had an eye that
saw (only) the non-existent.

The eye that appeared (came into being) in a state of slumber[4],
how should it be able to see aught but phantasy and non-
existence?

---

[1] *I.e.* they hope to receive a recompense that is not actually existent in
this world.
[2] A mountainous district in Georgia.
[3] *I.e.* no power of turning one way or another.
[4] *I.e.* in the present life.

Necessarily we were bewildered by error, since Reality was hidden and Phantasy visible,

1035 (Wondering) why He (God) set up this non-existence in (full) view and why He caused that Reality to be hidden from sight.

Praise (to Thee), O Master-weaver of magic who hast made the dregs to seem pure (wine) to them that turn away (from the Truth).

Magicians quickly measure moonbeams in the presence of the merchant and receive gold as profit.

(When) by artful tricks of this sort they take money, the money is gone from his (the purchaser's) hand, (but) there is no linen (to be seen).

This world is a sorcerer, and we are the merchants who buy from it the measured moonbeams.

1040 Magician-like, it hastily measures out by the ell five hundred ells of linen from the light of the moonbeams,

(Yet), when it takes the money, (which is) thy life, O slave, the money is gone, there is no linen, and thy purse is empty.

Thou must recite *Say, I take refuge*[1], crying, "O (Thou who art) One, come, save me from *the witches*[2] and from (their) knots.

These sorceresses are blowing on the knots: help, O Thou whose help is besought against (the world's) victory and check-mate."

But invoke (Him) with the tongue of deeds also, for the tongue of words is weak, O honourable man.

1045 In the world thou hast three fellow-travellers: one is faithful and these two (others) are treacherous.

One (of the latter) is friends and the other is goods and chattels; and the third (fellow-traveller) is faithful, and that one is excellence in deeds.

(Thy) wealth will not come with thee out of thy palaces; (thy) friend will come, but he will come (only) as far as thy grave.

When thy day of doom comes to meet thee, thy friend will say (to himself) in the language appropriate to his sentiments[3],

"(I have come) as far as here: I accompany thee no farther, I will stand a (little) while at thy grave."

1050 Thy deeds (alone) are faithful: make of them thy refuge, for they will come with thee into the depths of the tomb.

---

[1] *Qur'án*, CXIII, I.

[2] Literally, "the women who blow (on knots)."

[3] *I.e.* he will express his true feelings towards thee by saying in his heart.

*Commentary on the saying of Muṣṭafá (Mohammed), on whom be peace, "Thou must needs have a familiar who is buried with thee, he being alive, and with whom thou art buried when thou art dead; if he be generous, he will treat thee generously, and if he be base, he will forsake thee. That familiar is thy works, so make them right as far as thou art able." The Messenger of Allah spake the truth.*

Therefore the Prophet said, "For the purpose of (traversing) this Way there is no comrade more faithful than works.

If they be good they will be thy friends for ever, and if they be evil they will be (as) a snake in thy tomb."

How, O father, can one do this work and earning in the Way of righteousness without a master?

The meanest earning that goes on in the world, is it ever (practised) without the guidance of a master?

Its beginning is knowledge; then (follows) action, that it may 1055 yield fruit after a time or after death.

Seek help in (acquiring) crafts, O possessor of intelligence, from a generous and righteous craftsman[1].

Seek the pearl in the oyster-shell, my brother, and seek technical skill from the craftsmen.

If ye see sincere (spiritual) advisers, deal fairly (with them) and be eager to learn[2]: do not show disdain.

If the man (engaged) in tanning wore a threadbare garment, that did not diminish the master's mastery (of his trade);

If the ironsmith wore a patched frock when blowing the bel- 1060 lows, his reputation was not impaired in the eyes of the people.

Therefore strip the raiment of pride from thy body: in learning, put on the garment of humility.

If thou wouldst learn (theoretical) knowledge, the way of (acquiring) it is oral; if thou wouldst learn a craft, the way of (acquiring) it is practical (by practice).

If thou desire (spiritual) poverty, that depends on companionship (with a Shaykh): neither thy tongue nor thy hand avails.

Soul receives from soul the knowledge thereof, not by way of book nor from tongue.

If those mysteries (of spiritual poverty) are in the traveller's 1065 heart, knowledge of the mystery is not yet possessed by the traveller.

(Let him wait) until the expansion (illumination) of his heart shall make it (full of) the Light: then God saith, "*Did not We expand...?*[3]

[1] Literally, "a generous and righteous man belonging to those versed in them."

[2] Literally, "be eager for (their) teaching."

[3] *Qur'án*, XCIV, I.

For We have given thee the expansion (illumination) within thy breast, We have put the expansion into thy breast."

Thou art still seeking it from outside; thou art a source of milk: how art thou a milker of others?

There is an illimitable fountain of milk within thee: why art thou seeking milk from the pail?

1070    O lake, thou hast a channel to the Sea: be ashamed to seek water from the pool;

For *did not We expand...?* Again, hast not thou the expansion? How art thou become a seeker of the expansion and a mendicant?

Contemplate the expansion of the heart within (thee), lest there come the reproach, *Do not ye see?*[1]

### Commentary on "And He is with you[2]."

There is a basket full of loaves on the crown of thy head, and thou art begging a crust of bread from door to door.

Attend to thine own head, abandon giddy-headedness; go, knock at the door of thy heart: why art thou (knocking) at every door?

1075    Whilst thou art up to the knee in the river-water, thou art heedless of thyself and art seeking water from this one and that one.

Water in front; and behind, too, an unfailing supply of water; (but) before thine eyes is *a barrier* and *behind them a barrier*[3].

The horse is under the (rider's) thigh, and the rider is seeking the horse. (When asked), "What is this?" he says, "A horse, but where is the horse?"

"Eh, is not this a horse under thee, plain to see?" "Yes," says he, "but who ever saw a horse?"

He (such a one) is mad with thirst for the water, and it (the water) is before his face: he is in the water and unconscious of the running water.

1080    Like the pearl in the sea, he says, "Where is the sea?" and that shell-like phantasy is his wall[4].

His saying "Where?" becomes for him a screen: it becomes for him a cloud over the radiance of the sun.

His bad (sensual) eye is a bandage on his (inward) eye: his very (awareness of) removing the barrier has become a barrier for him.

His (self-)consciousness has become the plug of his (inward) ear: keep thy consciousness (directed) towards God (alone), O thou who art bewildered in Him.

---

[1] *Qur'án*, LI, 21.        [2] *Qur'án*, LVII, 4.
[3] *Qur'án*, XXXVI, 8.        [4] *I.e.* it obstructs his vision.

*Commentary on the saying of Muṣṭafá (Mohammed), on whom be peace, "Whosoever shall make his cares one care, God will relieve him of all his cares; and whosoever is distracted by his cares, God will not care in what valley He destroys him."*

Thou hast distributed thy consciousness in (all) directions: those vanities are not worth a cress[1].

Every thorn-root draws the water of thy consciousness (to-wards itself): how should the water of thy consciousness reach the fruit? 1085

Hark, smite that evil bough, lop it off: water this goodly bough, refresh it.

Both are green at this (present) time, (but) look to the end (and see) that this one will come to naught, (while) fruit will grow from that one.

To this one the water in the orchard is lawful, to that one (it is) unlawful. In the end thou wilt see the difference, and (so) farewell.

What is justice? Giving water to trees. What is injustice? To give water to thorns.

Justice is (consists in) bestowing a bounty in its proper place, not on every root that will absorb water. 1090

What is injustice? To bestow (it) in an improper place that can only be a source of calamity.

Bestow the bounty of God on the spirit and reason, not on the (carnal) nature full of disease and complications[2].

Load the conflict of (worldly) cares upon thy body: do not lay thy anxiety upon the heart and spirit.

The pack is laid upon the head of Jesus[3], (while) the ass[4] is frisking in the meadow.

'Tis not right to put collyrium in the ear: 'tis not right to demand from the body the work of the heart (spirit). 1095

If thou art a (devotee of the) heart, go, scorn (the world), do not suffer contumely (from it); and if thou art a (devotee of the) body, do not eat sugar but taste poison.

Poison is beneficial to the body, and sugar noxious: 'tis better that the body should be deprived of supplies.

The body is fuel for Hell, do thou weaken it; and if it pro-duce a (new) growth of fuel, go, destroy it.

Else, O (thou who art) firewood, thou wilt be *a carrier of firewood*[5] in both worlds, like the wife of Bú Lahab.

Know (discriminate) the bough of the *Sidra*[6] from the fire-wood, though both are green, O youth. 1100

[1] Literally, "a green herb."
[2] Literally, "dysentery and knots (tumours)."
[3] The spirit. [4] The body.
[5] *Qur'án*, CXI, 4. [6] The celestial lote-tree (*Qur'án*, LIII, 14).

6

The origin of that bough is the Seventh Heaven, the origin of this bough is from fire and smoke.

To sense-perception they are similar in appearance, for the eye and habit of sense-perception is seeing falsely;

(But) that (difference) is manifest to the eye of the heart (spirit): exert thyself, advance towards the heart (spirit) with the exertion of one whose means are small.

And if thou hast no foot (means), (yet) bestir thyself that thou mayst behold every less and more.

*On the meaning of this verse:*

"*If thou fare on the Way, the Way will be revealed to thee; and if thou become non-existent, (real) existence will be conferred on thee*[1]."

1105 Though Zalíkhá shut the doors on every side, still Joseph gained return (to safety) by bestirring himself.

Lock and door opened, and the way (out) appeared: when Joseph put trust in God, he escaped.

Though the world hath no visible crevice (means of exit), (yet) one must run (to and fro) recklessly, like Joseph,

In order that the lock may open and the doorway become clear, and the region of non-spatiality become your dwelling-place.

Thou camest into the world, O afflicted one: dost thou ever see the way of thy coming?

1110 Thou camest from a certain place and abode: dost thou know the way of thy coming? Nay.

If thou knowest (it) not, (yet) beware of saying that there is no way: by this wayless way we (all) shall depart[2].

In dreams thou wanderest happily to left and right: hast thou any knowledge where the way is that leads to that arena?

Shut that (sensual) eye and give thyself up: thou wilt find thyself in the ancient City[3].

How shouldst thou shut thy (sensual) eye when in this direction[4] a hundred inebriated (languishing) eyes are (as) a bandage on thine eye because of (thy) infatuation (with them)?

1115 From love of (having) a purchaser (admirer) thou art (looking) with four eyes (intently) in the hope of (gaining) eminence and chieftainship.

And if thou fall asleep thou seest the purchaser in thy dreams: how should the ill-omened owl dream of aught but a wilderness?

At every moment thou wantest a purchaser cringing (before thee): what hast thou to sell? Nothing, nothing.

If thy heart had any (spiritual) bread or breakfast, it would have been empty of (desire for worldly) purchasers.

---

[1] Literally, "they will turn to thee with (real) existence."
[2] Literally, "there is a going for us."   [3] *I.e.* the world of Reality.
[4] *I.e.* the material world.

*Story of the person who claimed to be a prophet. They said to him,*
*"What hast thou eaten that thou hast become crazy and art*
*talking in vain?" He replied, "If I had found anything to eat,*
*I should not have become crazy and talked in vain"; for whenever*
*they (the prophets and saints) speak goodly words to people*
*unworthy to hear them, they will have talked in vain, although*
*they are (divinely) commanded to talk thus in vain*[1].

A certain man was saying, "I am a prophet: I am superior
to all the prophets."

They bound his neck and took him to the king, saying, "This 1120
man says he is a prophet sent by God."

The people (were) gathered round him (thick) as ants and
locusts, crying, "What deceit and imposture and trap is (this)?

If he that comes from (the realm of) non-existence is a prophet,
we all are prophets and grand (in spiritual eminence).

We (too) came hither as strangers from that place (realm):
why shouldst thou be specially endowed (with prophecy), O ac-
complished one?"

(He replied), "Did not ye come like a sleeping child? Ye
were ignorant of the way and the destination.

Ye passed through the (different) stages asleep and intoxicated, 1125
unconscious of the way and (its) ups and downs;

(But) we (prophets) set out in wakefulness and well (aware)
from beyond the five (senses) and the six (directions) to (this
world of) the five and six,

Having perceived (all) the stages from the source and founda-
tion, possessed of experience and knowing the way like (skilled)
guides."

They said to the king, "Put him to the rack, that a person
of his sort may never (again) speak such words."

The king saw that he was very thin and infirm, so that such
an emaciated man would die at a single blow.

(He thought to himself), "How is it possible to torture[2] or 1130
beat him, since his body has become as (fragile as) a glass?

But I will speak to him kindly and say, 'Why dost thou boast
of (this) high estate?'

For here harshness is of no use: 'tis by gentleness that the
snake puts forth its head (is induced to come forth) from the
hole."

He caused the people to withdraw from around him (the
claimant): the king was a gracious man, and gentleness was
his way.

Then he bade him be seated, and asked him concerning his

[1] *I.e.* to deliver their message notwithstanding that the unbelievers will
accuse them of talking nonsense.
[2] Literally, "squeeze."

dwelling-place, saying, "Where hast thou thy means of liveli-hood and refuge?"

1135    He replied, "O king, I belong to the *Abode of Peace*: I have come from the road (after having journeyed) to this Abode of Blame.

I have neither home nor any companion: when has a fish made its home on the earth?"

Again the king answered him, saying by way of jest, "What (food) hast thou eaten and what provision hast thou (made) for the morning meal?

Hast thou appetite? What didst thou eat at daybreak that thou art so intoxicated and boastful and blustering?[1]"

He replied, "If I had bread, (whether) dry or moist, how should I lay claim to prophecy?

1140    To claim to be a prophet amongst these people is like seeking a heart from a mountain.

No one (ever) sought intellect and heart from mountains and rocks: none sought (from them) understanding and apprehen-sion of a difficult point of discourse.

Whatever you say, the mountain replies the same[2]: it makes a mock (of you) like the scoffers.

What relation exists between this folk and the (Divine) mes-sage?[3] Who can hope for (spiritual) life from a soulless thing?

If you bring (them) a message concerning a woman or gold, they will all lay before you their money and lives[4] (in entire devotion)—

1145    (The message), 'A sweetheart in such and such a place invites thee (to come to her): she is in love with thee, she knows thee.'

But if you bring (them) the honey-like message of God, 'Come to God, O thou who hast a good covenant (with Him);

Go from the world of death towards the (eternal) provision: since everlastingness is possible, do not be perishing'—

They will seek (to shed) thy blood and (take) thy life[4], not in zeal for religion and (spiritual and moral) excellence.

*The reason why the vulgar are at enmity with, and live in estrange-ment from, the saints of God who call them unto God and the Water of Life everlasting.*

Nay, but on account of their sticking to house and goods[5] 'tis bitter (hateful) to them to hear this exposition (given by the prophets).

1150    (Suppose) a rag is stuck fast upon the donkey's sore: when you wish to tear it off, bit by bit,

---

Literally, "full of wind."                   [2] *I.e.* it echoes what you say.
[3] Literally, "Whence this folk and whence the message?"
[4] Literally, "head."               [5] *I.e.* the world and worldly possessions.

The donkey, because of the pain (inflicted on him), will certainly kick: happy the man who abstained from (touching) him!—

Especially (when there are) fifty sores, and a soaked rag[1] stuck on the top of them in every case.

House and goods are like the rag, and this greed (of thine) is the sore: the greater the greed, the greater the sore.

The wilderness alone is the house and goods of the owl: he (the owl) will not listen to descriptions of Baghdád and Tabas.

If a royal falcon come from the road and bring to these owls 1155 a hundred reports of the King,

(With) a full account of the imperial city and the orchards and the rivers—then a hundred enemies will jeer at him,

Saying, 'What has the falcon brought? An old story. He is weaving words of vanity and idle brag.'

('Tis) they (that) are old and rotten unto everlasting; otherwise (they would know that) that breath (of prophetic inspiration) makes the old new.

It gives life to the old dead (spirits): it gives the crown of reason and the light of faith.

Do not steal thy heart away from the spirit-bestowing heart- 1160 ravisher, for he will mount thee on the back of Rakhsh[2].

Do not steal thy head away from the crown-giving one whose head is exalted, for he will untie a hundred knots from the foot of thy heart.

Whom shall I tell? Where in the village[3] is any (spiritually) living one? Where is any one that runs towards the Water of Life?

Thou art fleeing from Love because of a single humiliation: what dost thou know of Love except the name?

Love hath a hundred disdains and prides: Love is gained[4] by means of a hundred blandishments.

Since Love is loyal, it purchases (desires) him that is loyal: 1165 it does not look at a disloyal comrade.

Man resembles a tree, and the root is the covenant (with God): the root must be cherished with all one's might.

A corrupt (infirm) covenant is a rotten root and is cut off (deprived) of fruit and grace.

Although the boughs and leaves of the date-palm are green, greenness is no benefit (when conjoined) with corruption of the root;

And if it (the bough) have no green leaves, while it hath a (good) root, at the last a hundred leaves will put forth their hands.

---

[1] Literally, "a rag immersed in moisture."
[2] The name of Rustam's horse.    [3] *I.e.* in the world.
[4] Literally, "comes to hand."

1170    Be not duped by his (the learned man's) knowledge; seek (to
know whether he keeps) the covenant: knowledge is like a husk,
and his covenant is its kernel.

*Explaining that when the evil-doer becomes settled in evil-doing
and sees the effect of the (spiritual) fortune of the doers of
righteousness, he from envy becomes a devil and preventer of
good, like Satan; for he whose stack is burnt desires that all
(others) should have their stacks burnt: 'hast thou seen[1] him
who forbids[2] a servant (of God) when he performs the (ritual)
prayer?[3]'*

When you see that the loyal have profited, thereat you become
envious, like a devil.

Whenever a man's temperament and constitution is feeble,
he does not wish any one to be sound in body.

If you dislike (to have) the jealousy of Iblís, come (away)
from the door of pretension (and advance) to the portal of loyalty.

When thou hast not loyalty, at least do not talk (presump-
tuously), for words are for the most part self-assertion—'we'
and 'I.'

1175    These words, (whilst they stay) in the breast, are an income
consisting of (spiritual) kernels: in silence the spiritual kernel
grows a hundredfold[4].

When it (the word) comes on to the tongue, the kernel is
expended: refrain from expending, in order that the goodly
kernel may remain (with you).

The man who speaks little hath strong thoughts: when the
husk, namely speech, becomes excessive, the kernel goes.

(When) the rind is excessive, the kernel is thin: the rind
becomes thin when it (the kernel) becomes perfect and goodly.

Look at these three (fruits) when they have passed beyond[5]
immaturity: the walnut and the almond and the pistachio.

1180    Whoever disobeys (God) becomes a devil, for he becomes
envious of the fortune of the righteous.

When you have acted loyally in (keeping) your covenant with
God, God will graciously keep His covenant with you.

You have shut your eyes to keeping faith with God, you have
not hearkened to (the words) *remember Me, I will remember you.*

Give ear, listen to (the words) *keep My covenant*, in order
that (the words) *I will keep your covenant* may come from the
Friend.

What is our covenant and loan[6], O sorrowful one? (It is) like
sowing a dry seed in the earth.

---

[1] *I.e.* "tell me, what thinkest thou of...?"        [2] Read ينهى.
[3] *Qur'án*, XCVI, 9–10.        [4] Literally, "has a hundred growths."
[5] Literally, "when they have escaped from."
[6] Cf. *Qur'án*, LXXIII, 20.

From that (sowing) neither do glory and grandeur accrue to 1185
the earth, nor riches to the owner of the earth.

('Tis nothing) except an indication, as though to say, 'I need
this kind (of produce), the origin whereof Thou didst create
from non-existence.

I ate, and (now) I bring the seed as a token, begging Thee
to send to us such bounty (as before).'

Abandon, then, the dry (verbal) prayer, O fortunate one; for
the tree demands (presupposes) the scattering of seed.

(But) if you have no seed, on account of that prayer God will
bestow on you a palm-tree, saying, 'How well did he labour!'

Like Mary: she had (heartfelt) pain, but no seed: an artful 1190
One made green that (withered) palm-tree (for her sake).

Because that noble Lady was loyal (to God), God gave unto
her a hundred desires without desire on her part.

The company who have been loyal are given superiority over
all (other) sorts (of men).

Seas and mountains are made subject to them; the four ele-
ments also are the slaves of that class.

This (miraculous power) is only a favour (conferred on them)
for a sign, to the end that the disbelievers may see it plainly.

Those hidden graces of theirs, which come not into (the per- 1195
ception of) the senses or into description—

Those are the (real) matter: those are enduring for ever, they
are neither cut off nor reclaimed.

### Prayer.

O Giver of (spiritual) nutriment and steadfastness and stability,
give Thy creatures deliverance from this instability.

Grant unto the soul—for it is bent (crooked)—to stand up-
right (to persevere with rectitude) in the work wherein it ought
to be stable.

Bestow patience upon them and heavy balance-scales[1]: deliver
them from the guile of impostors[2];

And redeem them from envy, O Gracious One, lest from 1200
envy they be devils accursed.

How do the vulgar burn with envy for the fleeting happiness
of riches and (pleasures of) the body!

Behold the kings, how they lead armies (to battle) and slay
their own kinsmen because of envy.

The lovers of filthy dolls (darlings) have sought each other's
blood and life.

Read *Wís and Rámín* and *Khusraw and Shírín*: (you will see)
what those fools did because of envy.

[1] *I.e.* scales laden with good works. Cf. *Qur'án,* CI, 5.
[2] Literally, "picture-makers."

1205 (You will see) that the lover perished and the beloved too: they are naught and their passion also is naught.

Holy is the God who brings non-existence into collision with itself and makes non-existence to be in love with non-existence.

Envies arise[1] in the heart that is no (real) heart: thus doth Being subject not-being to compulsion.

These women, who are kinder than all (other creatures)—(even amongst them) two fellow-wives devour each other from envy,

So that (you may judge) in what degree of envy are the men who indeed are stony-hearted.

1210 If the Law had not exercised a gracious spell (over them), every one would have torn the body of his rival to pieces.

The Law makes a plan for repelling evil: it puts the demon into the bottle of (legal) proof—

Witness and oath and shrinking (from the oath)—till (at last) the insolent demon goes into the bottle (prison).

(The Law is) like the balance whereby the two adversaries are surely united in contentment[2], (whether) in jest or earnest[3].

Know for sure that the Law is like the measure and scales by means of which the litigants are saved from wrangling and enmity.

1215 If there be no pair of scales, how shall the litigant escape from disputing when he suspects[4] fraud and deceit?

(If), then, there is all this jealousy and litigation and injustice in respect of this foul faithless carcase[5],

How, then, must it be when genies and men become envious in respect of that fortune and felicity (hereafter)?

Truly those devils are envious of old: never for a moment do they cease from[6] waylaying;

And the sons of Adam who have sown (the seed of) disobedience—they too have become devils from enviousness.

1220 Read in the *Qur'án* how by Divine transformation the devils of mankind have become homogeneous with the Devil.

When the Devil fails to tempt (any one), he seeks aid from these human (devils),

Saying, 'Ye are my friends: (perform) an act of friendship towards me; ye are on my side: (perform) an act of partiality.'

If they waylay any one in the world, both kinds of devils come off rejoicing;

And if any one has saved his soul and become eminent in religion, those two jealous (parties) keep up lamentation.

1225 Both gnash their teeth in envy at any one upon whom the (spiritual) Teacher has bestowed wisdom."

[1] Literally, "make head."
[2] Literally, "whereby the contentment of two adversaries is surely united."
[3] *I.e.* whether the matter in dispute be trivial or serious.
[4] Literally, "on account of suspicion of."
[5] *I.e.* the world.　　　　　　[6] Literally, "are they devoid of."

*How the king asked the man who claimed to be a prophet, saying,*
*"The person who is a true Messenger (of God) and becomes*
*established (as such)—what has he to give to any one, or what*
*gifts will people obtain by consorting with him and serving him,*
*except the counsel which he utters with his tongue?"*

The king questioned him, saying, "After all, what is inspira-
tion, or what has he got who is a prophet?"

He replied, "What is there indeed that he has not got, or
what fortune is left whereunto he has not attained?

I will suppose (for argument's sake) that this prophetic in-
spiration is not a treasurer (of Divine Revelations); still, it is
not inferior to the inspiration in the heart of the bee.

Since (the words) *God hath inspired the bee* have come (in the
Qur'án), the dwelling-place of its (the bee's) inspiration has
been filled with sweets.

Through the light of the inspiration of God the Almighty 1230
and Glorious, it filled the world with wax and honey.

This one[1] who is (the object of) *We have honoured (the sons*
*of Adam)* and is ever going upward—how should his inspiration
be inferior to (that of) the bee?"

Have not you read (the words) *We have given thee Kawthar?*
Why, then, are you dry and why have you remained thirsty?

Or perchance you are (like) Pharaoh, and for you Kawthar,
like the Nile, has turned to blood and (become) impure, O sick
man.

Repent, renounce every enemy (of God) who hath not the
water of Kawthar in his cup.

Whomsoever you see flushed[2] (with joy) by Kawthar, he 1235
hath the nature of Mohammed: consort with him,

That at the Reckoning you may become (one of those who)
love for God's sake[3]; for with him are apples from the tree
of Aḥmad (Mohammed).

Whomsoever you see with lips unmoistened by Kawthar,
always deem him an enemy like death and fever,

Though 'tis your father or your mother; for in truth he is
a drinker of your blood.

Learn these ways of acting from the Friend of God (Abraham),
who first renounced his father,

That in the presence of God you may become (one of those 1240
who) hate for God's sake, lest the jealousy of (Divine) Love
take offence at you.

Until you recite "*(There is) not (any god)*" and "*except*
*Allah,*" you will not find the plain track of this Way.

---

[1] *I.e.* Man.                    [2] Literally, "red-faced."
[3] These words are taken from the Tradition, "When the true believer
loves, he loves for God's sake."

*Story of the lover who was recounting to his beloved his acts of service and loyalty and the long nights (during which) their sides heave up from their beds¹ and the long days of want and parching thirst²; and he was saying, "I know not any service besides these: if there is any other service (to be done), direct me, for I submit to whatever thou mayst command, whether to enter the fire, like Khalíl (Abraham), on whom be peace, or fall into the mouth of the leviathan of the sea, like Jonah, on whom be peace, or be killed seventy times, like Jirjís (St George), on whom be peace, or be made blind by weeping, like Shu'ayb, on whom be peace; and the loyalty and self-sacrifice of the prophets cannot be reckoned"; and how the beloved answered him.*

A certain lover in the presence of his beloved was recounting his services and works,

Saying, "For thy sake I did such and such, in this war I suffered (wounds from) arrows and spears.

Wealth is gone and strength is gone and fame is gone: on account of my love for thee many a misfortune has befallen me.

1245 No dawn found me asleep or laughing; no eve found me with capital and means."

What he had tasted of bitters and dregs he was recounting to her in detail, point by point,

Not for the sake of reproach; nay, he was displaying a hundred testimonies of the trueness of his love.

For men of reason a single indication is enough, (but) how should the thirst (longing) of lovers be removed thereby?

He (the lover) repeats his tale unweariedly: how should a fish be satisfied with (mere) indication (so as to refrain) from the limpid water?

1250 He (the lover), from that ancient grief, was speaking a hundred words in complaint, saying, "I have not spoken a word."

There was a fire in him: he did not know what it was, but on account of its heat he was weeping like a candle.

The beloved said, "Thou hast done all this, yet open thine ear wide and apprehend well;

For thou hast not done what is the root of the root of love and fealty: this that thou hast done is (only) the branches."

The lover said to her, "Tell me, what is that root?" She said, "The root thereof is to die and be naught.

1255 Thou hast done all (else), (but) thou hast not died, thou art living. Hark, die, if thou art a self-sacrificing friend!"

Instantly he laid himself at full length (on the ground) and gave up the ghost: like the rose, he played away his head (life), laughing and rejoicing.

¹ *Qur'án*, XXXII, 16.          ² Literally, "liver-thirst."

That laughter remained with him as an endowment unto everlasting, like the untroubled spirit and reason of the gnostic.

How should the light of the moon ever become defiled, though its light strike on everything good and evil?

Pure of all (defilements) it returns to the moon, even as the light of the spirit and reason (returns) unto God.

The quality of purity is an endowment (settled) on the light 1260 of the moon, though its radiance is (falling) on the defilements of the way.

Malignity does not accrue to the light of the moon from those defilements of the way or from pollution.

The light of the sun heard (the call) *Return!* and came back in haste to its source.

No disgrace remained with it from the ashpits, no colour remained with it from the rose-gardens.

The light of the eye and the seer of the light returned (to their source): the desert and plain were left in passionate desire thereof.

*A certain man asked a mystic theologian, " If any one weep loudly during the ritual prayer and moan and lament, is his prayer rendered void?" He replied, "The name of those (tears) is 'water of the eye': consider what that weeper has seen: if he has seen (felt) longing for God or repentance for a sin and weeps, his prayer is not spoilt; nay, it attains perfection, for 'there is no prayer without presence of the heart'; but if he has (inwardly) seen bodily sickness or the loss of a son, his prayer is spoilt, for the foundation of prayer is the abandonment of the body and the abandonment of sons, like Abraham, who was offering his son as a sacrifice in order to perfect his prayer and giving up his body to Nimrod's fire; and Muṣṭafá (Mohammed), on whom be peace, was commanded (by God) to act after these manners:* "follow the religion of Abraham[1]." "Verily ye have had a good example in Abraham[2]."

A certain man asked a mufti in private, "If any one weep 1265 lamentably during the ritual prayer,

I wonder, will his prayer be rendered void, or will his prayer be licit and perfect?"

He replied, "Wherefore is it named 'the water of the eye'? You should consider what it (the eye) saw and (then) wept.

Consider what the water of the eye saw in secret, so that on that account it began to flow from its spring.

If the supplicant has seen yonder world, that prayer (of his) gains a lustre from (his) lamentation;

But if that weeping was caused by bodily pain or by mourning 1270 (for the dead), the thread is snapped and the spindle too is broken[3]."

---

[1] *Qur'án*, XVI, 124.    [2] *Qur'án*, LX, 4.    [3] *I.e.* the prayer is void.

*A disciple came in to pay his respects to the Shaykh—and by this
(word) "Shaykh" I do not mean one old in years, but one old
in understanding and knowledge (of God), even if he is Jesus, on
whom be peace, in the cradle, or Yaḥyá (John the Baptist), on
whom be peace, in the children's school. The disciple saw the
Shaykh weeping; he too acted in conformity (with the Shaykh)
and wept. When he had finished and gone forth (from the Shaykh's
presence), another disciple, who was more cognisant of the
Shaykh's spiritual state, impelled by (noble) jealousy, went out
quickly after him and said to him, "O brother, (whatever may
happen) I shall have told you: for God's sake, for God's sake,
beware of thinking or saying that the Shaykh wept and you wept
likewise; you must practise self-discipline without hypocrisy for
thirty years, and you must traverse ravines and seas full of
leviathans, and lofty mountains full of lions and leopards, that
you may attain to that weeping of the Shaykh or not attain.
If you attain, you will often utter thanksgiving (as immense as
is the extent of the earth, described in the words of the Tradition),
'The earth was gathered together for me.'"*

A disciple came into the presence of the Pír: the Pír was
(engaged) in weeping and lamentation.

When the disciple saw the Shaykh weeping, he began to
weep: the tears ran from his eyes.

The man possessed of an ear (sense of hearing) laughs once,
when a friend repeats a joke to a friend; the deaf man (laughs)
twice:

The first time by way of conformity and affectation, because
he sees the company laughing.

1275　　The deaf man laughs then like them, without knowing the
(inward) state of the laughers.

Afterwards he inquires what the laughter was about, and
then, having heard, he laughs a second time.

Hence the mere imitator (of a Shaykh), too, resembles the
deaf man in respect of the (feeling of) joy that is in his head.

It is the Shaykh's reflexion, and its source is in the Shaykh:
the overflow of joy is not (derived) from the disciples; nay, it
is from the Shaykh.

Like a basket in water or a (ray of) light on glass: if they
think it (comes) from themselves, 'tis (owing to) defect (of
intelligence).

1280　　When it (the basket) is separated from the river, that perverse
one will recognise that the sweet water within it was from the
river;

The glass also will recognise, at the setting (of the moon),
that those beams (of light) were from the beauteous shining
moon.

When the (Divine) command "Arise!" opens his (the imitator's) eye, then he will laugh, like the (true) dawn[1], a second time.

He will even laugh at his own (former) laughter which was produced in him in that (period of) imitation,

And will say (to himself), "(Travelling) by all these far and long ways, and thinking that this was the Reality and that this was the Mystery and Secret,

How forsooth, in that valley (of imitation), did I rejoice from 1285 afar through blindness and confusion?

What was I fancying, and what was it (in truth)? My weak perception was showing (only) a weak image (of the reality)."

Where is the thought of the (holy) men in relation to the child of the (mystic) Way?[2] Where is his fancy in comparison with[3] true realisation?

The thought of children is (of) the nurse or milk or raisins and walnuts or weeping and crying.

The imitator is like a sick child, although he may have (at his disposal) subtle argumentation and (logical) proofs.

That profundity in (dealing with) proofs and difficult problems 1290 is severing him from (spiritual) insight.

It took away (from him) the stock (of insight), which is the collyrium of his inmost consciousness, and applied itself to the discussion of (formal) problems.

O imitator, turn back from Bukhárá[4]: go to self-abasement (ba-khwárí) that thou mayst become a (spiritual) hero,

And that thou mayst behold within (thee) another Bukhárá, in the assembly-place whereof the champions *are unlearned.*

Although the courier is a swift runner on land, when he goes to sea his sinews are broken[5].

He is only (like those of whom God says in the *Qur'án*) *We* 1295 *have borne them on the land;* (but) that one who is borne on the sea—he is somebody[6].

The King (God) hath great bounty: run (to receive it), O thou who hast become in pawn to an imagination and fancy.

From conformity that simple disciple, too, was weeping in concert with the venerable (Shaykh);

(For), like the deaf man, he regarded the (Shaykh's) weeping in the manner of a conformist and was unaware of the cause.

When he had wept a long while, he paid his respects and departed: the (Shaykh's) favourite disciple came quickly after him,

[1] The second laughter is compared to the true dawn, which follows the false dawn.
[2] *I.e.* their thought is beyond his apprehension.
[3] Literally, "and where is."          [4] *I.e.* exoteric learning.
[5] Literally, "he is one whose sinews are broken."
[6] *I.e.* all the rest are nobodies.

1300    And said, "O thou who art weeping like a witless cloud in concert with the weeping of the Shaykh (possessed) of insight,

For God's sake, for God's sake, for God's sake, O loyal disciple, although in (thy) conformity thou art seeking (spiritual) profit,

Take heed not to say, 'I saw that (spiritual) king weeping, and I wept like him'; for that is denial (of his exalted state)."

A weeping full of ignorance and conformity and (mere) opinion is not like the weeping of that trusted one.

Do not judge (one) weeping by the analogy of (another) weeping: 'tis a long way from this weeping to that (weeping).

1305    That (weeping) is after a thirty years' (spiritual) warfare: the intellect can never get there[1].

Beyond reason there are a hundred stages: deem not the intellect to be acquainted with that caravan.

His weeping is neither from sorrow nor from joy: (only) the spirit knows the weeping of (him who is) the fountain of beauties.

His weeping, his laughter—(both) are of Yonder (World)[2] and transcend all that the intellect may conceive[3].

His tears are like his eye: how should the sightless eye become a (seeing) eye?[4]

1310    That which he sees cannot be touched (apprehended) either by the analogical judgement of the intellect or by way of the senses.

Night flees when Light comes from afar: what, then, should the darkness of Night know concerning Light?

The gnat flees from the keen wind: what, then, should the gnat know of the (delicious) savour of the winds?

When the Eternal comes, the temporal is made vain: what, then, should the temporal know of Eternity?

When Eternity comes in contact with the temporal, it strikes it dumb; when it has naughted it, it makes it homogeneous[5] (with itself).

1315    You can find a hundred parallels (of this sort) if you wish, but I do not care (to supply them), O dervish.

This *Alif-Lám-Mím* and *Há-Mím*[6]—these Letters become, on (real) comprehension (of their meaning), like the rod of Moses.

The (other) letters resemble these Letters outwardly but are subject (to them) in respect of the (sublime) attributes of the latter.

---

[1] *I.e.* can never comprehend it.      [2] Literally, "of that side."
[3] Literally, "are exempt from that which is the conception of the intellect."
[4] *I.e.* "how should the spiritually blind man become a mystic seer?"
[5] Literally, "of the same colour."
[6] Mysterious combinations of letters which stand at the beginning of certain Súras of the *Qur'án.*

A staff that any one takes on trial—how should it be described as being like that staff (Moses' rod)?[1]

This Breath[2] is (like the breath) of Jesus (in its effects); it is not (like) any wind and breath that arises from joy or sorrow.

This *Alif-Lám-Mím* and *Há-Mím*, O father, have come from 1320 the presence of the Lord of Mankind.

What resemblance has any (other) *alif-lám* to these? Do not regard them with this (external) eye, if you have a (rational) soul.

Although they are composed of letters, O sire, and resemble the composition of (words used by) the common folk, (yet they are not the same).

Mohammed is composed of flesh and skin; (but he is unique) although every body is homogeneous with him in its composition.

It hath flesh, it hath skin and bone; (yet) has this (ordinary) constitution the same (qualities as his)?

(No); for in that constitution (of Mohammed) there appeared 1325 miracles by which all (other) constitutions were vanquished.

Likewise, the composition of the (Letters) *Há-Mím* in the (Holy) Book is exceedingly lofty, while the others are low (in comparison),

Because from this composition comes life, like the blast of the trumpet (of Resurrection), (to those) in helplessness.

By the dispensation of God *Há-Mím* becomes a dragon and cleaves the sea like the rod (of Moses).

Its external appearance resembles (other) appearances, but the disc (round cake) of bread is very far from (being) the disc of the moon.

His (the Shaykh's) weeping, his laughter, and his speech 1330 are not from him: they are the pure nature of *Hú* (God).

Since the foolish took (only) the external appearances (into consideration), and (since) the subtleties (inward aspects) were very much hidden from them,

Necessarily they were debarred from (attaining to) the (real) object; for the subtlety escaped (them) on the occasion when it (the object) presented itself.

---

[1] Literally, "how should it be like that staff at the moment of explanation?"
[2] *I.e.* the above-mentioned Letters.

*Story of the maidservant who cum asino herae suae libidinem exercebat et eum tanquam caprum et ursam docuerat libidinem more humano exercere et veretro asini cucurbitam affigebat ne modum excederet. Her mistress discovered it but did not perceive the device of the gourd; making a pretext, she sent the maid away to a distant place and cum asino concubuit sine cucurbita and perished shamefully. The maid came back late and lamented, crying, "O my soul and O light of my eyes, veretrum vidisti, cucurbitam non vidisti; penem vidisti, illud alterum non vidisti." (According to the Tradition) every deficient one is accursed, i.e. every deficient insight and understanding is accursed; for those deficient in respect of the outward eye are objects of (Divine) mercy and are not accursed. Recite (the Verse), It is no crime in the blind. (In their case) He (God) has removed the crime, He has removed the curse, and He has removed the reproach and the wrath.*

Ancilla quaedam ob multam libidinem immodicamque nequitiam asinum super se injecit.

Asinum ad coitum assuefecerat: asinus ad concubitum hominis viam invenerat.

1335    Technarum fabricatrici cucurbita erat, quam veretro ejus affigebat ut servaret modum.

Cucurbitam peni indiderat illa anus ut trudendi tempore dimidium penis iniret;

Si totum asini veretrum eam iniret, uterus ejus et viscera diruerentur.

The ass was becoming lean, and his mistress remained helpless, saying, "Why has this ass become as (thin as) a hair?"

She showed the ass to the shoeing-smiths and asked, "What is his ailment of which the result is leanness?"

1340    No ailment was discerned in him, no one gave information concerning the secret (cause) thereof.

(Then) she began to investigate in earnest: she became prepared to investigate at every moment.

The soul must needs be devoted to earnest endeavour, for the earnest seeker will be a finder.

Postquam rem asini perscrutata est, ancillulam narcisso similem vidit sub asino cubantem.

Through a crack in the door she saw what was going on: the old woman marvelled greatly thereat.

1345    (Vidit) asinum futuentem ancillam sicut viri ratione et more (concumbunt) cum feminis.

She became envious and said, "Since this is possible, then I have the best right, for the ass is my property.

The ass has been perfectly trained and instructed: the table is laid and the lamp is lighted."

Feigning to have seen nothing, she knocked at the door of the room (stable), saying, "How long will you be sweeping the room, O maid?"

She spoke these words as a blind (and added), "I have come, O maid: open the door."

(Then) she became silent and said no more to the maid: she [1350] concealed the secret for the sake of her own desire.

Thereupon the maid hid all the apparatus of iniquity and came forward and opened the door.

She made her face sour and her eyes full of moisture (tears) and rubbed her lips (against each other), meaning to say, "I am fasting."

In her hand was a soft broom, as though to say, "I was sweeping the room in order to clean it[1]."

When, with the broom (in her hand), she opened the door, the mistress said under her breath, "O crafty one,

You have made your face sour and (taken) a broom in your [1355] hand; what is (the meaning of) the ass having turned away from[2] his fodder?

Re semiconfecta, iratus, agitans veretrum: quia te exspectat ideo (sunt) duo oculi ejus ad januam (conversi)."

This she said under her breath and concealed (her thought) from the maid: at that moment she treated her, like innocent persons, honourably.

Afterwards she said to her, "Put the *chádar* on your head, go and take a message from me to such and such a house.

Say so-and-so and do so-and-so." I abridge the talk of the women.

Take the gist of what is to the purpose. When the discreet [1360] old woman had sent her (the maid) away,

Propter ebrietatem libidinis gaudebat: she shut the door, saying meanwhile,

"I have secured privacy, I will shout in thanksgiving: I am delivered from the four *dángs* and the two *dángs*[3]."

Gaudio hircus (prurigo) feminae quae in igne libidinis asini inquieta erat mille factus est.

Qualis hircus est ille quem tanta libido ludibrium fecit? Stultum deludi non est mirabile.

Lustful desire makes the heart deaf and blind, so that an ass [1365] seems like Joseph, fire (like) light.

Oh, many a one intoxicated with fire and seeking fire deems himself absolute light.

---

[1] Literally, "on account of the unpleasant smell." The term 'aṭan properly denotes the state of a hide which is being tanned or prepared for tanning.

[2] Literally, "having broken off from."

[3] The *dáng* is the sixth part of a dirhem. According to the Turkish Commentator the meaning is "virorum, sive plus valent sive minus, concubitu jam libera evasi."

(He is lost) unless a (chosen) servant of God, or the pull of God (Himself), lead him into the (right) way and turn over his leaf[1],

So that he may know that the fiery phantom (which he mistook for light) in the Path is but a loan (unreal).

(Sensual) cupidity causes foul things to appear fair: among the banes of the Way there is none like lust, none worse.

1370    It has disgraced a hundred thousand good names, it has stupefied (besotted) a hundred thousand clever men.

Since it caused an ass to appear (like) Joseph of Egypt, how (in what aspect) will that (miscreant) Jew cause a Joseph to appear?

Its spell made dung seem honey to you: what, forsooth, will it make honey seem at the time of contest?[2]

Lust arises from eating and drinking: diminish your food, or marry and (so) flee from wickedness.

When you have eaten and drunk (too much), it leads to things forbidden: there must necessarily be some outgoing of income.

1375    Marriage, then, is like (the exorcism), "There is neither power nor (strength except in God)," lest the Devil cast you into temptation.

Since you are fond of eating and drinking, ask a woman (in marriage) at once; else the cat comes and carries off the fat sheep's tail[3].

Quickly put a heavy load on the shying ass before he puts (you) down[4].

(If) you do not know the effect of fire, hold aloof (from it): do not approach the fire with such (little) knowledge (as you have).

If you have no knowledge of the cooking-pot and the fire, neither the pot nor the soup will be spared by the flames.

1380    Water must be there and skill too, in order that the (contents of the) pot may be safely cooked in boiling.

If you are ignorant of the science of the ironsmith, your beard and hair will be burned when you pass by that place (the forge).

Femina januam clausit asinumque animo gaudente attraxit: necessario poenam gustavit.

In medium stabulum eum trahendo duxit: sub asino decubuit supina

In eadem sella quam viderat ab ancilla (adhibitam), ut ista meretrix quoque voto potiretur.

1385 . Pedem sustulit, asinus (veretrum) in eam trusit: asini veretro ignis in ea accensus est.

---

[1] *I.e.* convert and regenerate him.
[2] *I.e.* the contest of passion with reason.
[3] *I.e.* the Devil takes away your righteousness.
[4] *I.e.* before he throws his rider.

Cum asinus eruditus esset, in hera infixit (veretrum) usque ad testiculos: simul hera periit.

Jecur ejus veretri verbere discissum, viscera inter se dirupta.

Extemplo femina, nulla voce facta, animam reddidit: hinc cecidit sella, illinc femina.

Area stabuli sanguine plena, femina inverso capite prostrata: periit, animamque ejus abripuit Fati calamitas.

Ecce mors nefanda cum centum opprobriis, O pater: num 1390 vidisti (quemquam) de veretro asini martyrem?

Hear from the *Qur'án* (what is) *the torment of disgrace*: do not sacrifice your life in such a shameful cause.

Know that the male ass is this bestial soul: to be under it is more shameful than that (woman's behaviour).

If you die in egoism in the way of (for the sake of) the fleshly soul, know for certain that you are like that woman.

He (God) will give our fleshly soul the form of an ass, because He makes the (outward) forms to be in accordance with the (inward) nature.

This is the manifestation of the secret at the Resurrection[1]: 1395 by God, by God, flee from the ass-like body!

God terrified (threatened) the unbelievers with the Fire: the unbelievers said, "Better the Fire than shame."

He said, "Nay, that Fire is the source of (all) shames"—like the fire (of lust) that destroyed this woman.

In her greed she ate immoderately[2]: the mouthful of an infamous death stuck in her throat (and choked her).

Eat (and drink) in moderation, O greedy man, though it be a mouthful of *halwá* or *khabís*.

The high God hath given the balance a tongue (which you 1400 must regulate): hark, recite the *Súratu' l-Rahmán* (the Chapter of the Merciful) in the *Qur'án*[3].

Beware, do not in your greed let the balance go: cupidity and greed are enemies that lead you to perdition.

Greed craves all and loses all: do not serve greed, O ignoble son of the ignoble[4].

The maid, whilst she went (on her errand), was saying (to herself), "Ah, mistress, thou hast sent away the expert.

Thou wilt set to work without the expert and wilt foolishly hazard thy life.

O thou who hast stolen from me an imperfect knowledge, 1405 thou wert ashamed to ask about the trap."

(If) the bird had picked the grain from its stack, the (trap-) cord would not have fallen on its neck (and made it captive).

---

[1] When every one will be raised to life in a shape corresponding to his or her predominating quality.
[2] Literally, "she did not take mouthfuls of food in moderation."
[3] *Qur'án*, LV, 6–8.
[4] Literally, "O radish, son of a radish."

Eat less of the grain, do not patch (the body) so much (with food): after having recited *eat ye*, recite (also) *do not exceed*,

So that you may eat the grain and (yet) not fall into the trap. Knowledge and contentment effect this. And (now) farewell.

The wise man gets happiness from the present life, not sorrow, (while) the ignorant are left in disappointment and regret.

1410 When the trap-cord (of sensuality) falls on their throats, it becomes unlawful (forbidden) to them all to eat the grain.

How should the bird in the trap eat (enjoy) the grain? The grain in the trap is like poison (to him), if he feed (on it).

(Only) the heedless bird will eat grain from the trap, as these common folk do in the trap of the present world.

Again, the knowing and prudent birds have debarred themselves[1] from the grain;

For the grain in the trap is poisonous food: blind is the bird that desires the grain in the trap.

1415 The Owner of the trap cut off the heads of the foolish ones, and conducted the clever ones to the (exalted) assembly-places;

For in the former (only) the flesh is serviceable, but in the clever ones (their) song and warble soft and low.

Deinde venit ancilla perque rimam januae heram vidit sub asino mortuam.

"O hera stulta," inquit, "hoc (facinus ineptum) quid fuit, etsi ea quae perita est technam tibi ostenderat?

Technae quod patebat vidisti, tibi ignotum quod latebat: imperita tabernam aperuisti.

1420 Veretrum tanquam mel vel cibum ex dactylis et butyro comparatum vidisti: cur illam cucurbitam non vidisti, O avida?

Vel cur, cum asini amore obruta esses, cucurbita visu tuo sejuncta manebat?

Docta ab ea quae perita est vidisti technae speciem externam: peritiam ipsa valde gaudens assumpsisti."

Oh, there is many a stupid ignorant hypocrite who has seen nothing of the Way of the (holy) men except the woollen mantle (*súf*).

Oh, there are many impudent fellows who, with little practice (in the religious life), have learned from the (spiritual) kings nothing but talk and brag.

1425 Every one (of them), staff (rod) in hand, says, "I am Moses," and breathes upon the foolish folk, saying, "I am Jesus."

Alas the Day when the touchstone will demand from thee the sincerity of the sincere!

Come, inquire of the Master (what is) the remainder (of the Way)[2]; or are the greedy ones all blind and deaf?

---

[1] Literally, "have made for themselves a dry-bandage."
[2] *I.e.* what lies behind its external forms.

You craved all and you lost all: this foolish flock are the prey of wolves.

Having heard a form (of words), you have become its expounder, (though) ignorant of (the meaning of) your words—like parrots.

*The instruction given by a Shaykh to disciples, or by a prophet to a people, who are unable to receive the Divine lesson and have no familiar acquaintance with God, may be compared with the case of a parrot which has no such acquaintance with the (inward) form of a man, so that it should be able to receive instruction (directly) from him. God most High holds the Shaykh in front of the disciple, as the mirror (is held) in front of the parrot, while He (Himself) dictates from behind the mirror, saying, "Do not move thy tongue to hasten it (the Revelation)[1]; it is naught but an inspiration that is inspired (by God)[2]." This is the beginning of an endless problem. When the parrot, which ye call the image, moves its beak in the mirror, the movement is not (made) by its own volition and power: it is the reflexion of the (movement made in) articulation by the parrot outside, which is the learner; not the reflexion of (the movement made by) the Teacher behind the mirror; but the external parrot's articulation is controlled by the Teacher. This, then, is (only) a comparison, not a (complete) similitude.*

A parrot sees its reflexion (image) facing it in the mirror.   1430
The teacher is concealed behind the mirror: that sweet-tongued well-instructed man is talking.

The little parrot thinks that these words uttered in low tones are spoken by the parrot in the mirror.

Therefore it learns (human) speech from one of its own kind, being unaware of the cunning of that old wolf.

He is teaching it behind the mirror; otherwise (it would not talk, for) it does not learn except from its congeners.

It (really) learned to talk from that accomplished man, but it is 1435 ignorant of his meaning and mystery.

It received speech, word by word, from Man; (but) what should the little parrot know of Man except this?

Similarly, the disciple full (of egoism) sees himself in the mirror of the Shaykh's body.

How should he see Universal Reason behind the mirror at the time of speech and discourse?

He supposes that a man is speaking; and the other (Universal Reason) is a mystery of which he is ignorant.

He learns the words, but the eternal mystery he cannot know, 1440 for he is a parrot, not a boon-companion.

[1] *Qur'án*, LXXV, 16.          [2] *Qur'án*, LIII, 4.

Likewise, people learn the note of birds, for this speech (of birds) is an affair of the mouth and throat;

But (all are) ignorant of the birds' meaning, except an august Solomon of goodly insight.

Many learned the language of (true) dervishes and gave lustre therewith to the pulpit and assembly-place.

Either nothing was bestowed upon them except those (formal) expressions, or at last (the Divine) mercy came and revealed the (right) way.

*A mystic saw a bitch big with young, in whose womb the young were barking. He remained in amazement, saying, " The reason of a dog's barking is to keep watch (against strangers): to bark in the mother's womb is not (for the purpose of) keeping watch; and, again, barking may be a call for help, or its cause may be a desire for milk, etc.; and there is no such purpose in this case." When he came to himself, he made supplication to God—and none knoweth the interpretation thereof except Allah[1]. Answer came: " It represents the state of a party who pretend to (spiritual) insight and utter (mystical) sayings without having come forth from the veil (of materiality) and before the eyes of their hearts have been opened. Thence neither to themselves do strength and support accrue, nor to their hearers any guidance and right direction."*

1445    During a *chila* (forty days' religious seclusion), a certain man dreamed that he saw a bitch big with young on a road.

Suddenly he heard the cry of puppies: the puppies were in the womb, invisible.

The yelps astonished him exceedingly: (he wondered) how the puppies called out in the womb.

Puppies howling in the womb—"has any one," (he thought), "ever seen this in the world?"

When he sprang up from his dream and came to himself, his perplexity was increasing at every moment.

1450    During the *chila* there was none by whom the knot should be untied except the Presence[2] of God Almighty and Glorious.

He said, " O Lord, on account of this difficulty and debate I am deprived of recollection (*dhikr*) of Thee during the *chila*.

Loose my wings, that I may soar and enter the garden of recollection and the apple-orchard (of gnosis)."

At once (in reply) there came to him a mysterious voice[3], saying, "Know that it is an emblem of the idle talk of the ignorant,

Who, without having come forth from the veil and curtain, (being) blindfold have begun to speak in vain."

---

[1] *Qur'án*, III, 5.
[2] Literally, "Portal."        [3] Literally, "the voice of the *hátif.*"

The yelp of the dog in the womb is (useless) loss: (in such 1455 a case) he is neither a starter of hunted animals nor a keeper of watch by night.

He has not seen the wolf, so as to prevent him; he has not seen the robber, so as to repel him.

He (a man of this sort), because of covetousness and desire for eminence, is dull as regards (spiritual) vision and bold in prating.

From desire for the purchaser and warm admirer, (being) devoid of insight, he begins to talk nonsense[1].

Without having seen the Moon, he gives indications: thereby he perverts (misleads) the (ignorant) countryman.

On account of the purchaser he gives a hundred indications 1460 describing the Moon which he has never seen, for the sake of (gaining) power.

There is in truth one Purchaser who is profitable, but concerning Him they (these impostors) have a (great) suspicion and doubt.

In their desire for the inglorious purchaser, these people have thrown the (real) Purchaser to the winds.

He is our Purchaser—*God hath purchased*[2]: hark, rise above anxiety for any (other) purchaser.

Seek the Purchaser who is seeking thee, One who knows thy beginning and end.

Beware, do not try to win[3] every purchaser: 'tis bad to make 1465 love to two sweethearts.

Thou wilt not get interest or capital from him[4], if he purchase (thee): in sooth he has not the price for (thy) reason and intellect.

He has not even the price of half a horseshoe, and thou art offering him (what is precious as) corundum and rubies.

Cupidity hath blinded thee and will deprive thee (of blessedness): the Devil will make thee accursed like himself.

Just as that wrathful (fiend) made accursed like himself the Fellows of the Elephant[5] and the people of Lot.

The patient (devout and self-denying) have gained the Pur- 1470 chaser, since they did not hasten towards every purchaser.

He that averted his face from that Purchaser—fortune and felicity and everlasting life are quit of him.

Grief remains for ever (as a doom) on the covetous, as happened to the people of Zarwán in their envy.

---

[1] Literally, "steps into nonsense."    [2] *Qur'án*, IX, 112.
[3] Literally, "do not draw into thy hand."
[4] *I.e.* the worldly purchaser or the Devil.    [5] See *Qur'án*, CV.

*Story of the people of Zarwán and their envy of the poor. "Our father," they said, "from (foolish) simplicity used to give to the poor the most part of the produce of his orchard." When it was grapes, he would give a tithe; and when they were turned into raisins or syrup, he would give a tithe; and whenever he made halwá or pálúda, he would give a tithe; and he would give a tithe of the corn-sheaves, and when he threshed (the corn), he would give a tithe of the unthreshed ears mixed (with straw); and when he separated the wheat from the straw, he would give a tithe; and when he made flour, he would give a tithe; and when he leavened the dough, he would give a tithe; and when he made bread, he would give a tithe. Consequently God most High had laid such a blessing on his orchard and crops that all the (other) owners of orchards were in need of him, both for fruit and money, while he needed nothing from any of them. His sons saw the repeated payment of tithes, and did not see the blessing, velut illa femina infelix quae veretrum asini vidit, cucurbitam non vidit.*

There was a righteous godly man: he had perfect intelligence and a (great) foresight as to the end.

In the village of Zarwán, near Yemen, (he was) renowned for (his) almsgiving and good disposition.

1475   His abode was the Ka'ba of the poor: the distressed were (always) coming to him.

He would give, unostentatiously, a tithe both of the ears of corn and of the wheat when it was separated from the chaff.

(If) it was made into flour, he would give a tithe of that too; if it was made into bread, he would give another tithe of the bread.

He would never omit (to give) the tithe of any produce: he would give (the tithe) four times on that which he sowed.

That (generous) young man was continually giving many injunctions to all his sons,

1480   Saying, "For God's sake, for God's sake, after I am gone[1], do not on account of your covetousness withhold the portion of the poor,

So that the crops and fruit may remain (as a) permanent (blessing bestowed) on you under the safeguard[2] of your obedience to God."

Without surmise or doubt, (it is) God (who) hath sent all produce and fruits from the Unseen.

If you expend something in the place where the produce comes, 'tis the gateway to profit: you will obtain[3] a (great) profit (thereby).

[1] Literally, "after me."
[2] Literally, "in the refuge."          [3] Literally, "hit upon."

The Turk sows the major part of the produce again[1] in the field, because it (the sown field) is the source of the fruits (crops).

He sows most of it and consumes (only) a little, for he has 1485 no doubt of its growing.

The Turk shakes (moves to and fro) his hand in sowing, because that (former) crop of his has been produced from the same soil.

Likewise the shoemaker buys hide and leather and morocco (with) the surplus left over from (what he spends on) bread,

Saying, "These have (always) been the sources of my income: from these, accordingly, my means of livelihood are flowing[2]."

His income has come from that place: consequently he bestows (it) in the same place with liberality and generosity.

This soil (that produces crops) and (this) morocco are only 1490 a veil (secondary cause): know that at every moment the (real) source of livelihood is in God.

When you sow, sow in the soil of the Origin, that for every single (seed) a hundred thousand (blessings) may grow.

If just now (recently) you have sown seed, (as) I will suppose, in a soil which you thought (would be) a means (of producing crops)—

When it (the seed) does not grow during two or three years, how can you do aught but put your hand (to your head) in supplication and prayer?

You will beat your hand on your head in the presence of God: (your) hand and head bear witness to His giving sustenance;

So that you may know that He is the Source of the source 1495 of (all) sustenance, and that the seeker of sustenance may seek only Him.

Seek sustenance from Him, do not seek it from Zayd and 'Amr: seek intoxication from Him, do not seek it from beng and wine.

Desire wealth from Him, not from treasure and possessions: desire aid from Him, not from paternal and maternal uncles.

At the last you will be left without (all) these things: hark, unto whom will you call then?

Call unto Him now, and leave (all) the rest, that you may inherit the kingdom of the world.

When comes (the Day on which) *a man shall flee from his* 1500 *brother* and on such a Day the son will flee from his father,

In that hour every friend will become your foe, because (in the world) he was your idol and one who hindered (you) from (following) the (right) Way.

You were averting your face from the Painter of the face, since you were gaining heart's delight from a (mere) picture.

---

[1] *I.e.* sows seed derived from the former crop.
[2] Literally, "are untying the knot."

If at this (present) time your friends become hostile to you and turn aside from you and quarrel (with you),

Take heed and say, "Lo, my fortune is triumphant: that which would have happened to-morrow (at the Last Judgement) has happened to-day.

1505   The people of this caravanseray (the world) have become my enemies, in order that the Resurrection might be made clearly visible to me beforehand,

Ere I should lose my time and associate with them to the end of my life[1].

I had bought defective goods: thanks (to God) that I have become aware of their defectiveness in time,

Ere the stock-in-trade should go out of my hands and finally come forth (be exposed) as defective.

My wealth was (all but) gone, my life was (all but) gone, O man of noble lineage: I had (all but) given away my wealth and life for damaged goods.

1510   I sold my merchandise, I received base gold: I was going home in great jubilation.

Thanks (to God) that this gold was shown to be base now, before too much of my life had passed.

The base coin would have remained (as a shackle) on my neck for ever: to waste my life (thus) would have been an iniquity.

Since its (the coin's) baseness has been revealed earlier (in good time), I will step back from it very quickly."

When your friend displays enmity (and when) the itch of his hatred and jealousy shoots forth (manifests itself),

1515   Do not bewail his aversion, do not make yourself (do not let yourself behave as) a fool and ignoramus;

Nay, thank God and give bread (alms), (in gratitude) that you have not become old (and rotten) in his sack,

(But) have quickly come out of his sack to seek the true Eternal Friend,

The delectable Friend whose friendship's cord becomes three-fold (thrice as strong) after thy death.

That friend, in sooth, may be the (Divine) Sultan and exalted King, or he may be one accepted of the Sulṭan and one who intercedes (with Him).

1520   You are (now) delivered from the false coiner and (his) hypocrisy and fraud: you have seen his tumour (imposture) plainly before death.

If you understood (aright) this injustice shown towards you by the people in the world, it is a hidden treasure of gold.

The people are made to be thus evil-natured towards you, that your face may inevitably be turned Yonder.

---

[1] Literally, "bring my life to its end in company with them."

Know this for sure that in the end all of them will become adversaries and foes and rebels.

You will be left in the tomb, lamenting and beseeching the One (God), (and crying), "*Do not leave me (here) alone!*

O Thou whose harshness is better than the troth of the 1525 faithful, the honey (kindness) of the faithful is also from Thy bounty."

Hearken to your own reason, O possessor of a granary, and commit your wheat to the *earth of Allah*,

That it may be safe from thieves and weevils. Kill the Devil with the wood-fretter (of reason) as quickly as possible;

For he is always frightening you with (the threat of) poverty: make him your prey like a partridge, O valiant hawk.

It would be a shame for the falcon of the mighty and fortunate Sultan to be made a prey by the partridge.

He (the father) gave many injunctions (to his sons)[1] and 1530 sowed the seed of exhortation, (but) as their soil was nitrous (barren), 'twas of no avail.

Although the admonisher have a hundred appeals, counsel demands a retentive ear.

You counsel him (the heedless man) with a hundred courtesies, and he turns aside from[2] your counsel.

A single person who obstinately refuses to listen[3] will baffle a hundred (eloquent) speakers.

Who should be more persuasive in counselling and sweeter-tongued than the prophets, whose words made an impression (even) on stones?

(Yet) the bonds of the ill-fated (infidel) were not being loosed 1535 by that whereby mountain and stone were moved[4].

Such hearts as had egoism[5] were described (in the words of the *Qur'án*) *nay, harder (than stone).*

*Explaining that the bounty of God and of the (Divine) Omnipotence is not dependent on receptivity, as human bounty is; for in the latter case receptivity is necessary. (In the former case it is not) because (the Divine) bounty is eternal, whereas receptivity is temporal. Bounty is an attribute of the Creator, while receptivity is an attribute of the creature; and the eternal cannot depend on the temporal, otherwise temporality (origination in time) would be absurd.*

The remedy for such a heart is the gift bestowed by a Transmuter: receptivity is not a necessary condition for His bounty.

Nay, His bounty is the necessary condition for receptivity: Bounty is the kernel, and receptivity the husk.

[1] Cf. *v.* 1479.     [2] Literally, "makes his side empty of."
[3] Literally, "who from obstinacy and repugnance does not listen."
[4] Literally, "came into action."     [5] Literally, "we and I."

The change of Moses' rod into a serpent and the shining of his hand like a (resplendent) sun,

1540 And a hundred thousand miracles of the prophets which are not comprehended by our mind and understanding—

(These) are not derived from secondary causes but are (under) the (direct) control of God: how can receptivity belong to non-existent things?[1]

If receptivity were a necessary condition for God's action, no non-existent thing would come into existence.

He (God) hath established a (customary) law and causes and means for the sake of those who seek (Him) under this blue veil (of heaven).

Most happenings come to pass according to the (customary) law, (but) sometimes the (Divine) Power breaks the law.

1545 He hath established a goodly law and custom; then He hath made the (evidentiary) miracle a breach of the custom.

If honour does not reach us without a (mediating) cause, (yet) the (Divine) Power is not remote from the removal of the cause[2].

O thou who art caught by the cause, do not fly outside (of causation); but (at the same time) do not suppose the removal of the Causer[3].

The Causer brings (into existence) whatsoever He will: the Absolute Power tears up (destroys) the causes;

But, for the most part, He lets the execution (of His will) follow the course of causation, in order that a seeker may be able to pursue the object of his desire.

1550 When there is no cause, what way should the seeker pursue? Therefore he must have a visible cause in the way (that he is pursuing).

These causes are veils on the eyes, for not every eye is worthy of (contemplating) His work.

An eye that can penetrate the cause is needed to extirpate (these) veils from root and bottom,

So that it may behold the Causer in (the world of) non-spatiality and regard exertion and earnings and shops as (mere) nonsense.

Everything good or evil comes from the Causer: causes and means, O father, are naught

1555 But a phantom that has materialised on the King's highway[4] in order that the period of heedlessness (the reign of ignorance) may endure for some (little) time.

---

[1] Literally, "whence do things (which are really) non-existent possess receptivity?"

[2] I.e. can remove the cause and act without it.

[3] I.e. "do not suppose that where there is no cause there is no exercise of Divine Power."

[4] I.e. on the way to God.

*On the beginning of the creation of the body of Adam, on whom*
*be peace, when He (God) commanded Gabriel, on whom be*
*peace, saying, "Go, take a handful of clay from this Earth,"*
*or according to another relation, "Take a handful from every*
*region."*

When the Maker willed to bring Man into existence for the
purpose of probation with good and evil,

He commanded Gabriel the true, saying, "Go, take a handful
of clay from the Earth as a pledge[1]."

He girt his loins and came to the Earth, that he might execute
the command of *the Lord of created beings*.

That obedient one moved his hand towards the Earth: the
Earth withdrew herself and was afraid.

Then the Earth loosed her tongue and made supplication, 1560
saying, "For the sake of the reverence due to the unique
Creator,

Take leave of me and go! Spare my life! Go, turn aside
from me the reins of thy white steed!

For God's sake, leave me and do not plunge me into the
troubles of (moral) obligation and danger[2].

(I beseech thee) for the sake of the favour by which God
chose thee out and revealed to thee the knowledge (written) in
the Universal Tablet,

So that thou hast become the teacher of the Angels and art
conversing with God continually;

For thou wilt be the messenger sent to the prophets: thou 1565
art the life of the inspired spirit, not (the life) of the body.

Thou (ever) hadst superiority over Seraphiel because he is
the body's life, (while) thou art the spirit's.

The blast of his trumpet is (producing) the growth of bodies;
thy breath is (producing) the growth of the single heart.

The life of the heart is the soul of the soul of the body: there-
fore thy gift is superior to his.

Again, Michael gives the sustenance (proper) for the body,
(but) thy labour gives the sustenance (proper) for the illumined
heart.

He has filled his skirt with gifts (of sustenance dispensed) by 1570
measure, (but) thy gifts of sustenance are immeasurable[3].

Moreover, thou art better than Azrael the tyrannous and
enraged, even as (Divine) Mercy is prior to Wrath.

These four (Angels) are the bearers of the (Divine) Throne,
and thou (art their) king: thou art the best of all of the four
from being (spiritually) awake[4].

[1] *I.e.* as a deposit to be returned.
[2] *I.e.* "do not involve me in the tribulations of Man."
[3] Literally, "are not contained in (any) measure."
[4] *I.e.* "on account of thy (superior) state of consciousness."

On the Day of the (Last) Congregation thou wilt see that its bearers are eight: at that time also thou wilt be the most excellent of its eight (bearers)."

Thus was she (the Earth) enumerating (his qualities) and weeping: she guessed what was the object of this (mission).

1575 Gabriel was a mine of reverence and respect: those adjurations barred the way against him[1].

Inasmuch as she entreated and adjured him, he returned and said, "*O Lord of Thy servants*,

(I protest) that I have not been remiss in Thy affair, but Thou knowest what happened better (than I).

She (the Earth) pronounced the Name from awe of which, O All-seeing One, the Seven Heavens would cease from their course.

(A feeling of) shame came over me, I was abashed by Thy Name; else, 'tis easy to convey a handful of earth,

1580 For Thou hast bestowed such a strength upon the Angels that they can tear these celestial spheres to shreds."

*The sending of Michael, on whom be peace, to take a handful of clay from the Earth for putting together the frame of the blessed body of the Father of Mankind, the Vicegerent of God, Adam, on whom be peace, the Adored of the Angels and their Teacher.*

He (God) said to Michael, "Do thou go down and seize, like a lion, a handful of clay from her."

When Michael reached the Earth, he put forth his hand to seize (the clay) from her.

The Earth trembled and began to flee (recoil): she became suppliant and shed tears.

Her breast burning (with grief), she made supplication and earnest entreaty: with bloody tears she adjured (him),

1585 Saying, "(I beseech thee) by the gracious incomparable God who hath made thee the bearer of the majestic Throne.

Thou art the overseer for measuring (and dispensing) the world's means of sustenance: thou art the ladler[2] to them that thirst for the (Divine) bounty"—

Because (the name) Míká'íl (Michael) is derived from *kayl* (measure), and he has become the measurer (*kayyál*) in dispensation of the means of subsistence.

"Give me quarter, set me free! See how I am uttering words stained with blood."

The Angel is a mine of God's mercy: he (Michael) said, "How should I sprinkle this salt on that wound?"—

1590 Just as the Devil is a mine of (God's) wrath, for he has raised up a roar (of lamentation) from the sons of Adam.

---

[1] *I.e.* prevented him from carrying out his purpose.
[2] Properly, "one who scoops water with his hand."

The precedence of Mercy over Wrath exists (as a fact),
O youth: clemency was (eternally) predominant in the nature
of God.

His (chosen) servants necessarily possess His disposition:
their water-skins are filled from the water of His stream.

The Messenger of God and the Guide on the (mystic) journey
said that men follow the usage of their kings.

Michael went (back) to the Lord of the Judgement, with hand
and sleeve empty of the object of his quest.

He said, "O Knower of the secret, O peerless King, the Earth 1595
bound me (tied my hands) by lamenting and weeping.

Tears were (ever) precious with Thee: I could not feign not
to have heard.

Moaning and wailing (ever) had great value with Thee:
I could not leave their rights unheeded.

With Thee the moist eye is much prized: how should I have
become quarrelsome in resisting (her)?"

There is a summons to the servant (of God) to lamentation
five times a day—"come to (perform) the ritual prayer, and
make lament."

The muezzin's cry is "hasten to welfare," and that welfare 1600
is this lamentation and petitioning.

He whom Thou wishest to make sorrow-stricken—Thou dost
bar against his heart the way to lamentation,

In order that affliction may descend (upon him) without (there
being) anything to repel it, when there is no intercessor (in
the form) of humble entreaty;

And (on the other hand) Thou dost lead to humble entreaty
the spirit of him whom Thou wishest to redeem from affliction.

Thou hast said in the *Qur'án* that (as regards) those peoples
on which that heavy vengeance fell,

'Twas because at that moment they would not[1] make humble 1605
entreaty that the affliction might be averted from them;

But since their hearts had been hardened, their sins appeared
(to them) as obedient service (rendered to God).

Until the sinner deems himself rebellious, how can tears run
from his eye?

---

[1] Or, "Why at that moment did they not...?"

*The Story of the people of Yúnus (Jonah), on whom be peace, is
a demonstration and manifest proof that humble entreaty and
lamentation avert affliction sent from Heaven. And God most
High acts by free choice: therefore humble entreaty and reverence
avail with Him. The philosophers, however, say that He acts
by (the necessity of His) nature and as a cause, not by free
choice: therefore humble entreaty (is useless, for it) cannot alter
nature.*

When the affliction became visible to the people of Yúnus,
a cloud full of fire departed (descended) from heaven.

It was shooting (flashes of) lightning, the rocks were burning;
the cloud was roaring, cheeks were shedding colour.

1610    All (the people) were on the roofs at night, when that woe
came into view from on high.

All came down from the roofs and went bare-headed towards
the open country.

Mothers cast out their children, that all might raise wailing
and distressful cries.

From (the time of) the evening prayer till the hour of dawn,
those folk were throwing dust on their heads.

(Then) all voices were hushed: the (Divine) mercy came upon
that perverse people.

1615    After despair and unrestrained lamentation, little by little
the cloud began to turn back.

The story of Yúnus is long and broad: it is time (to speak)
of the Earth and (resume) the far-spread tale.

Since humble entreaty has (such) value with God—and where
(else) has lamentation the price (reward) that it has there?—

Oh, (take) hope! Now (to-day) gird thy loins tight! Arise,
O weeper, and laugh continually,

For the glorious King is ranking tears as equal in merit to
the blood of the martyr.


*The sending of Isráfíl (Seraphiel), on whom be peace, to the Earth
with orders to take a handful of clay for moulding the body of
Adam, on whom be peace.*

1620    Our God said to Seraphiel, "Go, fill thy hand with that clay
and come (back)."

Seraphiel, likewise, came to the Earth: again the Earth began
to moan,

Saying, "O Angel of the trumpet (of Resurrection) and O Sea
of life, by whose breaths the dead are revived,

Thou blowest one terrible blast from the trumpet, and the
place of Judgement becomes full of people (raised) from rotten
bones.

Thou blowest on the trumpet and criest, 'Hark, spring up, O ye slain of Karbalá![1]

O ye who have perished by the sword of Death, put forth 1625 your heads from the earth (grave), like bough and leaf!'

From thy bringing the dead to life this world is filled with thy mercy and with that potent breath of thine.

Thou art the Angel of mercy: show mercy! Thou art the bearer of the Throne and the *qibla* of (Divine) gifts[2]."

The Throne is the mine (source) of justice and equity: beneath it are four rivers filled with forgiveness:

A river of milk and a river of honey everlasting; a river of wine and a river of running water.

Then from the Throne they flow into Paradise; some little 1630 thing (offshoot) appears in this world too,

Although here those four (rivers) are defiled—by what? By the poison of mortality and indigestion.

From (each of) those four (rivers) a draught has been poured on the dark Earth and a temptation has been offered,

In order that these vile wretches may seek the source thereof; (but) these worthless folk are content with this (draught).

He (God) hath given milk and nourishment for babes: He hath made the breast of every wife a fountain (of milk).

(He hath given) wine to drive away grief and care: He hath 1635 made of the grape a fountain to inspire courage.

(He hath given) honey as a remedy for the sick body[3]: He hath made the inward part of the bee a fountain (of honey).

He gave water universally to high and low[4] for cleanliness and for drinking.

(The object is) that you may follow the track from these (derivatives) towards the origins; but you are content with this (offshoot), O trifler.

Now hear the story of the Earth and what she is saying to enchant the disturber (of her peace).

With frowning (unsmiling) looks in the presence of Seraphiel, 1640 she is practising a hundred sorts of coquetry and blandishment,

Saying, "By the truth of the holy essence of the Almighty, (I beseech thee), do not regard this violence to me as lawful!

I have a presentiment of this change: suspicious thoughts are running in my head.

Thou art the Angel of mercy: show mercy, for the *humá*[5] will not harm any (common) bird.

O (thou who art) healing and mercy to the sorrowful, do thou the same as those two benefactors[6] did."

[1] See translation of Book III, *v.* 72, note 1.
[2] *I.e.* the Mediator to whom the Divine gifts are directed for transmission.
[3] Literally, "as a bodily remedy for the sick."
[4] Literally, "to root and branch."
[5] See translation of Book III, *v.* 1620, note 2.   [6] *I.e.* Gabriel and Michael.

8

1645 At once Seraphiel returned to the King: in God's presence he excused himself and told what had passed,

Saying, "Outwardly (formally) Thou gavest (me) the command to take (the clay), (but) Thou didst inspire my conscience to do the opposite of that.

The command to take Thou didst address to my ear, the prohibition against hardheartedness Thou didst address to my understanding.

Mercy, being prior[1], prevailed over wrath, O Lord whose actions are incomparable and whose dealings are gracious."

*The sending of Azrael, the Angel of firm resolution and strong mind, on whom be peace, to seize a handful of clay in order that the body of Adam, on whom be peace, might be quickened.*

Straightway God said to Azrael, "Behold the Earth full of vain imagination!

1650 Find that feeble unjust old crone: hark, fetch a handful of clay and make haste![2]"

Azrael, the captain of the (Divine) Decree, went off towards the terrestrial globe for the purpose of requisition.

The Earth, according to rule, began lamenting loudly: she adjured him, she swore many an oath,

Crying, "O favourite youth (page-of-honour), O bearer of the Throne, O thou whose command is obeyed in heaven and earth,

Depart, for the sake of the mercy of the Merciful (God)! Depart, for the sake of Him who hath shown kindness unto thee!

1655 (Depart), for the sake of that King who alone is worshipped and with whom no one's lamentation is rejected!"

He replied, "These conjurations cannot move me to[3] avert my face from (disobey) the Giver of (all) commands secret or manifest."

She said, "After all, He hath commanded forbearance: both (severity and forbearance) are commanded: take (choose) the latter on the ground of[4] knowledge."

He replied, "That would be an interpretation or an inference: do not seek to confuse the plain meaning of the command.

If thou interpret (alter) thine own thought (so as to make it agree with the command), 'tis better than that thou shouldst interpret (pervert) this unequivocal (command).

1660 My heart is burning (melting) at thy supplication, my bosom is filled with blood on account of thy salty tears.

---

[1] Literally, "the priority of mercy."    [2] Literally, "with haste."
[3] Literally, "I cannot because of these conjurations."
[4] Literally, "by the way of."

I am not pitiless; nay, I have greater pity than those three holy ones[1] for the sorrow of the sorrowful.

If I am slapping an orphan, while a mild-natured person may put *halwá* (sweetmeat) in his hand,

Those slaps (of mine) are better (for him) than the other's *halwá*; and if he be beguiled by the *halwá*, woe to him!

My heart is burning at thy lamentable cry, but God is teaching me (to know) a (great) kindness—

The kindness concealed amidst cruelties, the priceless cornelian 1665 hidden in filth.

The cruelty done by God is better than a hundred clemencies of mine: to withhold the soul from God[2] is agony to the soul.

His worst cruelty is better than the clemency of both worlds: how excellent is *the Lord of created beings* and how excellent (His) help!

In His cruelty there are secret kindnesses: to surrender the soul for His sake increases (the life of) the soul.

Hark, dismiss suspicion and error: make thy head a foot (to hasten towards Him) since He hath bidden thee come.

His 'Come' will give (thee) exaltations; it will give (thee) 1670 intoxication and (spiritual) brides and couches.

In short, never, never can I weaken (the force of) that sublime command and complicate it (by prevarication)."

The wretched Earth heard all this (counsel), (but) in her ear was a plug arising from that evil suspicion.

Once more in another fashion the lowly Earth made entreaty and prostrated herself, like a drunken man.

He said, "Nay, arise! There is no loss (to thee) from this (thing), I lay my head and life as a pledge and guarantee.

Do not think of entreating (me), do not make further entreaty 1675 except to that merciful and justice-dealing King.

I am a slave to (His) command, I dare not neglect His command which raised dust from the sea.

Save from the Creator of ear and eye and head I will hear (accept) neither good nor evil—not even from my own soul.

My ear is deaf to all words but His: He is dearer to me than my sweet soul.

The soul came from Him, not He from the soul: He bestows a hundred thousand souls free of cost.

Who is the soul that I should prefer her to the Gracious (God)? 1680 What is a flea that I should burn the blanket on account of it?

I know no good but His good: I am *deaf and dumb and blind* to all but Him.

My ear is deaf to those who make lamentation, for I am as the spear in His hand.

[1] Gabriel, Michael, and Seraphiel.
[2] *I.e.* "to resist God's command and not resign thyself to Him.'

[*Explaining that when injury befalls you from a creature of God, he in reality is like an instrument. The gnostic is he that refers (all action) to God, not to the instrument; and if he refer it to the instrument formally, he does so not in ignorance but for a purpose. Thus Abú Yazíd, may God sanctify his spirit, said, "During all these years I have never spoken to any creature or heard any creature speak to me; but people fancy that I am speaking and listening to them, because they do not see the Most Great Speaker, of whom they in relation to me are (only) the echo." The intelligent hearer pays no heed to the echo. There is a well-known proverb to this effect, (namely), "The wall said to the nail, 'Why are you splitting me?' The nail replied, 'Look at him who is hitting me.'"*]

Do not foolishly beg the spear for mercy: beg (mercy) of the King in whose hand it (the spear) is (held).

How shouldst thou supplicate the spear and sword which are captives in the hand of that Exalted One?

1685 He is (like) Ázar in craftsmanship, and I am the idol (made by Him): whatever instrument He may make of me, I become that.

If He make me a cup, I become a cup; and if He make me a dagger, I become a dagger.

If He make me a fountain, I give water; and if He make me fire, I give heat.

If He make rain of me, I give a cornstack; and if He make an arrow of me, I dart into the body.

If He make me a snake (*márí*), I emit venom; and if He make me a friend (*yárí*), I do (kindly) service.

1690 I am as a pen between His two fingers: I am not a waverer[1] in the ranks of obedience (to Him)."

He (Azrael) engaged the Earth in (this) discourse, (and meanwhile) he snatched from the old Earth a handful (of clay).

(Deftly) like a magician he snatched it from the Earth, (whilst) the Earth was absorbed, like those beside themselves, in (listening to) his words.

He brought the inconsiderate clay to God: (he brought) the runaway (back) to school.

God said, "(I swear) by My resplendent knowledge, I will make thee the executioner of these (My) creatures."

1695 He replied, "O Lord, Thy creatures will regard me as their enemy when I strangle them at death.

Dost Thou deem it right, O exalted Lord, to make me hated and like a foe in appearance?"

He (God) said, "I will bring into clear view certain causes, (such as) fever and dysentery and phrenitis and spear(-wounds);

---

[1] Literally, "betwixt and between."

For (so) I will turn their attention from thee to the diseases and threefold[1] causes (of death)."

He (Azrael) replied, "O Lord, there are also servants (of Thine) who rend (shatter the illusion of) causes, O Almighty."

Their eye pierces through the cause: by the grace of the Lord, 1700 it has passed beyond (all) veils.

It has obtained the collyrium of Unity from the oculist of ecstasy and has been delivered from ailment and infirmity.

They do not look at fever and dysentery and consumption: they do not admit these causes into their heart;

For every one of these diseases has its cure: when it becomes incurable, that is the act of the (Divine) Decree.

Know for certain that every disease has its cure, as (for example) a fur is the cure for the pain of cold;

(Yet), when God wills that a man shall be frozen, the cold 1705 penetrates even a hundred furs

And puts into his body a tremor that will not be made better by (wrapping himself in) clothes or by (snuggling in) the house[2].

When the Decree comes, the physician is made foolish, and the medicine too loses its beneficial effect[3].

How should the perception of the (mystic) seer be veiled by these (secondary) causes, which are a veil to catch the dolt?

When the eye is quite perfect, it sees the root (origin); when a man is squint-eyed, it sees the branch (derivative).

*The (Divine) answer, (namely), "One who does not regard causes and diseases and sword-wounds will likewise pay no regard to thy action, O Azrael, for thou too art a (secondary) cause, although thou art more concealed than those (other) causes." And maybe it (the real nature of Azrael) is not concealed from the sick (dying) man, for He (God) is nigher to him than ye are, but ye do not see[4].*

God said, "He who perceives the origin (does not regard the 1710 derivative): how, then, should he be conscious of thy intervention?[5]

Although thou hast concealed thyself (thy real nature) from the vulgar, still to the clear-eyed (mystics) thou art (no more than) a veil (instrument)."

And (indeed) those to whom death is (sweet) as sugar—how should their sight be intoxicated (dazzled) with the fortunes (of this world)?

[1] *I.e.* according to the commentators, "physical, mental, and spiritual"; but the word seems to be used here in the sense of "manifold."
[2] Literally, "nest."
[3] Literally, "loses its way in respect of doing good."
[4] *Qur'án*, LVI, 84, where the text has "We are nigher."
[5] Literally, "how, then, should he see thee in the middle?"

Bodily death is not bitter to them, since they go from a dungeon and prison into a garden.

They have been delivered from the world of torment: none weeps for the loss of (what amounts to) nothing, nothing.

1715  (If) an elemental spirit[1] breaks the bastion of a prison, will the heart of any prisoner be angry with him?

(Will they say?) "Alas, he has broken this marble stone, so that our spirits and souls have escaped from confinement.

The beautiful marble and the noble stone of the prison-bastion were pleasing and agreeable (to us).

Why did he break them, so that the prisoners escaped? His hand must be broken (cut off) as a penalty for this (crime)."

No prisoner will talk such nonsense except that one who is brought from prison to the gallows.

1720  How should it (death) be bitter to one whom they take from amidst snake-poison towards sugar?

The soul, freed from the turmoil of the body, is soaring on the wings of the heart (spirit) without bodily feet (means of movement),

Like the prisoner in a dungeon who falls asleep at night and dreams of a rose-garden,

And says, "O God, do not bring me (back) to my body, (but let me alone) in order that I may walk as a prince[2] in this garden."

God says to him, "Thy prayer is granted: go not back"—and God best knoweth the right course.

1725  Consider how delightful is such a dream! Without having seen death, he (the dreamer) goes into Paradise.

Does he feel any regret for (his former) wakefulness and for the body (which he has left) in chains at the bottom of the dungeon?

(If) thou art a true believer, come now, enter the ranks of battle, for a feast has been (prepared) for thee in Heaven.

In the hope of journeying upwards, (arise and) take thy stand before the *miḥráb*[3], (to pray and weep) like a candle, O youth!

Let thy tears fall like rain, and burn (be ardent) in search (aspiration) all night long, like the candle beheaded (by the flame).

1730  Close thy lips against food and drink: hasten towards the Heavenly table.

Continually keep thy hope (fixed) on Heaven, dancing (quivering) like the willow in desire for Heaven.

Continually from Heaven (spiritual) water and fire will be coming to thee and increasing thy provision.

---

[1] *I.e.* an earthquake or lightning.
[2] Literally, "advance and retreat (on the battlefield)."
[3] *I.e.* the niche (in the wall of a mosque) showing the direction of Mecca.

If it (thy aspiration) bear thee thither, 'tis no wonder: do not regard thy weakness, regard thy search (aspiration);

For this search is God's pledge (deposited) within thee, because every seeker deserves something sought (by him).

Strive that this search may increase, so that thy heart (spirit) 1735 may escape from this bodily dungeon.

People will say, "Poor so-and-so is dead," (but) thou wilt say, "I am living, O ye heedless ones!

Though my body, like (other) bodies, is laid to rest, the Eight Paradises have blossomed in my heart."

When the spirit is lying at rest amidst roses and eglantines, what does it matter if the body is (buried) in that dung?

What should the spirit (thus) laid asleep know of the body, (or care) whether it (the body) is in a rose-garden or an ashpit?

(For) in the bright[1] (celestial) world the spirit is crying, 1740 "*Oh, would that my people knew!*"

If the spirit shall not live without this body, then for whom shall Heaven be the palace (of everlasting abode)?

If thy spirit shall not live without the body, for whom is the blessing (promised in the words) *in Heaven is your provision?*

*Explaining the banefulness of the fat and sweet things of the World and how they hinder one from (receiving) the Food of God, as he (the Prophet) hath said—"Hunger is the Food of God with which He revives the bodies of the true (witnesses to Him)," i.e. in hunger the Food of God is (forthcoming); and he hath said, "I pass the night with my Lord and He gives me food and drink"; and God hath said, "being provided for, rejoicing."*

(If) you are delivered from this provision of gross scraps, you will fall to (eating) dainty viands and noble food.

(Even) if you are eating a hundred pounds' weight of His viands, you will depart pure and light as a peri;

For they will not make you a prisoner of (incapacitated by) 1745 wind and dysentery and crucify you with gripes[2].

(In the case of material food) if you eat (too) little, you will remain hungry like the crow; and if you eat your fill, you will suffer from eructation[3].

If you eat (too) little, (the result will be) ill-temper and anaemia[4] and consumption; if you eat your fill, your body will incur (the penalty of) indigestion.

Through (partaking of) the Food of God and the easily digested (delicious) nutriment, ride like a ship on such a (spiritual) ocean.

---

[1] Literally, "water-coloured."
[2] Literally, "that which wrings the stomach (with pain)."
[3] For the use of دماغ (brain) in this phrase, cf. the Arabic جَشَأَتْ نَفْسُهُ.
[4] Literally, "dryness."

Be patient and persistent in fasting: (be) always expecting the Food of God;

1750    For God, who acts with goodness and is long-suffering, bestows (His) gifts (on them that are) in expectation.

The full-fed man does not wait expectantly for bread, (wondering) whether his allowance will come soon or late;

(But) the foodless man is always asking, "Where (is it)?" and expecting it hungrily and seeking and searching (for it).

Unless you are expectant, that bounty of manifold felicity will not come to you.

(Practise) expectation, O father, expectation, like a (true) man, for the sake of the dishes from above.

1755    Every hungry man obtained some food at last: the sun of (spiritual) fortune shone upon him.

When a magnanimous guest will not eat some (inferior) food, the host brings better food,

Unless he be a poor host and a mean one. Do not think (so) ill of the generous Provider!

Lift up your head like a mountain, O man of authority, in order that the first rays of the Sun may strike upon you;

For the lofty firm-based mountain-peak is expecting the sun of dawn.


*Reply to the simpleton who has said that this world would be delightful if there were no death and that the possessions of the present life would be delightful if they were not fleeting, and (has uttered) other absurdities in the same style.*

1760    A certain man was saying, "The world would be delightful, were it not for the intervention of death."

The other said, "If there were no death, the tangled world would not be worth a straw.

It would be (like) a stack heaped up in the field and neglected and left unthreshed.

You have supposed (what is really) death to be life: you have sown your seed in a barren soil.

The false (discursive) reason, indeed, sees the reverse (of the truth): it sees life as death, O man of weak judgement."

1765    Do Thou, O God, show (unto us) everything as it really is in this house of illusion.

None that has died is filled with grief on account of death; his grief is caused by having too little provision (for the life hereafter);

Otherwise (he would not grieve, for) he has come from a dungeon into the open country amidst fortune and pleasure and delight;

From this place of mourning and (this) narrow vale (of tribulation)[1] he has been transported to the spacious plain.

('Tis) *a seat of truth*, not a palace of falsehood; a choice wine, not an intoxication with buttermilk.

('Tis) *the seat of truth*, and (there) God is beside him: he is delivered from this water and earth of the fire-temple[2]. 1770

And if you have not (yet) led the illuminative life, one or two moments (still) remain: die (to self) like a man!

*Concerning what may be hoped for from the mercy of God most High, who bestows His favours before they have been deserved— and He it is who sends down the rain after they have despaired[3]. And many an estrangement produces intimacy (as its result), and there is many a blessed sin, and many a happiness that comes in a case where penalties are expected, in order that it may be known that God changes their evil deeds to good[4].*

In the Traditions (of the Prophet) it is related that on the Day of Resurrection every single body will be commanded to arise.

The blast of the trumpet is the command from the Holy God, namely, "O children (of Adam)[5], lift up your heads from the grave."

(Then) every one's soul will return to its body, just as consciousness returns to the (awakened) body at dawn.

At daybreak the soul recognises its own body and re-enters its own ruin, like treasures (hidden in waste places). 1775

It recognises its own body and goes into it: how should the soul of the goldsmith go to the tailor?

The soul of the scholar runs to the scholar, the spirit of the tyrant runs to the tyrant;

For the Divine Knowledge has made them (the souls) cognisant (of their bodies), as (happens with) the lamb and the ewe[6], at the hour of dawn.

The foot knows its own shoe in the dark: how should not the soul know its own body, O worshipful one?[7]

Dawn is the little resurrection: O seeker of refuge (with God), judge from it what the greater resurrection will be like. 1780

Even as the soul flies towards the clay (of its body), the scroll (of every one's good and evil actions) will fly into the left hand or the right.

Into his hand will be put the scroll (register) of avarice and

---

[1] Literally, "place where camels are made to kneel."
[2] *I.e.* from the material world where men are consumed with afflictions.
[3] *Qur'án*, XLII, 27.   [4] *Qur'án*, XXV, 70.
[5] ذراير is used here for ذراری as in the *Dīwán-i Shams-i Tabríz* (Tabríz, A. H. 1281), 32 marg., 5 fr. foot.
[6] *I.e.* as the lamb knows its mother.   [7] Literally. O idol."

liberality, impiety and piety, and all the (good or evil) dispositions that he had formed yesterday[1].

At dawn when he wakes from slumber, that good and evil will come back to him.

If he has disciplined his moral nature, the same (purified) nature will present itself to him when he wakes;

1785   And if yesterday he was ignorant and wicked and misguided, he will find his left hand black as a letter of mourning[2];

But if yesterday he was (morally) clean and pious and religious, when he wakes he will gain the precious pearl.

Our sleep and waking are two witnesses which attest to us the significance of death and resurrection.

The lesser resurrection has shown forth the greater resurrection; the lesser death has illumined[3] the greater death.

But (in the present life) this scroll (of our good and evil actions) is a fancy and hidden (from our sight), though at the greater resurrection it will be very clearly seen.

1790   Here this fancy is hidden, (only) the traces are visible; but there He (God) from this fancy will produce (actual) forms.

Behold in the architect the fancy (idea) of a house, (hidden) in his mind like a seed in a piece of earth.

That fancy comes forth from within (him), as the earth bears (plants) from the seed (sown) within.

Every fancy that makes its abode in the mind will become a (visible) form on the Day of Resurrection,

Like the architect's fancy (conceived) in his thought; like the plant (produced) in the earth that takes the seed.

1795   My object in (speaking of) both these resurrections is (to tell) a story; (yet) in its exposition there is a moral for the true believers.

When the sun of the Resurrection rises, foul and fair (alike) will leap up hastily from the grave.

They will be running to the *Díwán* (Chancery) of the (Divine) Decree: the good and bad coin will go into the crucible—

The good coin joyously and with great delight; the false coin in anguish and melting (with terror).

At every moment the (Divine) probations will be arriving (coming into action): the thoughts concealed in the heart will be appearing in the body,

1800   As when the water and oil in a lamp are exposed to view, or like a piece of earth from which grow up the (seeds) deposited within.

From onion, leek, and poppy the hand of Spring reveals the secret of Winter[4]—

---

[1] *I.e.* in this world.
[2] *I.e.* the black list of his actions on earth will be placed in his left hand, since he is one of the damned.
[3] Literally, "burnished."   [4] Literally, "December."

One (party) fresh and green, saying, "We are the devout";
and the other drooping their heads like the violet,

Their eyes starting out (of the sockets) from (dread of) the
danger, and streaming like[1] ten fountains from fear of the ap-
pointed end;

Their eyes remaining in (fearful) expectation, lest the scroll
(of their deeds) come (to them) from the left side;

Their eyes rolling to right and left, because the fortune of the 1805
scroll (that comes) from the right (side) is not easy (to win).

(Then) there comes into the hand of (such) a servant (of
God) a scroll headed with black and cram-full of crime and
wickedness;

Containing not a single good deed or act of saving grace—
nothing but wounds inflicted on the hearts of the saintly;

Filled from top to bottom with foulness and sin, with mockery
and jeering[2] at the followers of the Way,

(With all) his rascalities and thieveries and Pharaoh-like ex-
pressions of self-glorification[3].

When that odious man reads his scroll, he knows that he is 1810
(virtually) on the road to prison.

Then he sets out, like robbers going to the gallows; his
crime manifest, and the way (possibility) of excusing himself
barred.

The thousands of bad pleas and (false) speeches (made during
his life) have become like an evil nail (seal) on his mouth.

The stolen property has been discovered on his person and
in his house: his (plausible) story has vanished.

He sets out, therefore, to the prison of Hell; for thorns have
no means of escape from (being burnt in) the fire.

The angels that (formerly) were hidden, (whilst they walked) 1815
as custodians before and behind (him), have (now) become
visible like policemen.

They take him along, prodding him with the goad and saying,
"Begone, O dog, to thy own kennels!"[4]

He drags his feet (lingers) on every road, that perchance he
may escape from the pit (of Hell).

He stands expectantly, keeping silence and turning his face
backward in a (fervent) hope,

Pouring tears like autumn rain. A mere hope—what has he
except that?

(So) at every moment he is looking back and turning his face 1820
to the Holy Court (on high).

Then from God in the realm of light comes the command—
"Say ye to him, 'O ne'er-do-well destitute (of merit),

[1] Literally, "having become."    [2] Literally, "(derisive) hand-clapping."
[3] Literally, "(saying) 'I' and 'verily, we.'"
[4] Literally, "straw-barns" or "places which contain straw."

What art thou expecting, O mine of mischief? Why art thou looking back, O giddy-headed man?

Thy scroll (record) is that which came into thy hand, O offender against God and worshipper of the Devil.

Since thou hast seen the scroll of thy deeds, why dost thou look back? Behold the reward of thy works!

1825   Why art thou tarrying in vain? Where is hope of light in such a (deep) pit as this?

Neither outwardly hast thou any act of piety (to thy credit), nor inwardly and in thy heart an intention (to perform one);

No nightly orisons and vigils, no abstinence and fasting in the daytime;

No holding thy tongue to avoid hurting any one, no looking earnestly[1] forward and backward.

What is (meant by looking) forward? To think of thy own death and last agony. What is (meant by looking) backward? (To remember) the predecease of thy friends.

1830   Thou hast (in thy record) no wailful penitence for thy injustice, O rogue who showest wheat and sellest barley.

Since thy scales were wrong and false, how shouldst thou require the scales of thy retribution to be right?[2]

Since thou wert a left foot (wert going to the left) in fraud and dishonesty, how should the scroll come into thy right hand?

Since retribution is (like) the shadow, accordingly thy shadow, O man of bent figure, falls crookedly before thee.'"

(To him) from this quarter (Heaven) come (such) harsh words of rebuke that even the back of a mountain would be bowed by them.

1835   The servant (of God) answers: "I am a hundred, hundred, hundred times as much as that which Thou hast declared.

Verily, in Thy forbearance Thou hast thrown a veil over worse things (than those mentioned); otherwise (Thou mightst have declared them, for) Thou knowest with Thy knowledge (all my) shameful deeds;

But, outside of my own exertion and action, beyond good and evil and religion and infidelity,

And beyond my feeble supplication and the fancy and imagination of myself or a hundred like me,

Beyond living righteously or behaving disobediently—I had a (great) hope in Thy pure lovingkindness.

1840   I had hope in the pure bounty (flowing) from Thy spontaneous[3] lovingkindness, O Gracious Disinterested One.

I turn my face back to that pure grace: I am not looking towards my own actions.

---

[1] Literally, "with serious consideration (so as to take warning)."
[2] *I.e.* "how shouldst thou expect to receive full measure from God?"
[3] Literally, "unpaid."

I turn my face towards that hope, for Thou hast given me
existence older than of old.

Thou gavest (me) existence, free of cost, as a robe of honour:
I have always relied upon that (generosity)."

When he recounts his sins and trespasses, the Pure Bounty
begins to show munificence,

Saying, "O angels, bring him back to Us, for his inward 1845
eye has (ever) been (turned) towards hope.

Like one who recks of naught, We will set him free and cancel
all his trespasses.

(To say) 'I reck not' is permitted to that One (alone) who
loses nothing by perfidy and (gains nothing) by probity.

We will kindle up a goodly fire of grace, in order that no sin
and fault, great or small, may endure—

Such a fire that the least spark of the flame thereof is con-
suming (all) sin and necessity and free-will.

We will set fire to the tenement of Man and make the thorns 1850
(in it) a spiritual garden of roses.

We have sent from the Ninth Sphere (the highest Heaven)
the elixir (namely), *He will rectify for you your actions.*"

What in sooth is Adam's[1] (Man's) sovereignty and power of
choice beside the Light of the Everlasting Abode?

His speaking organ is a piece of flesh; the seat of his vision
is a piece of fat;

The seat of his hearing consists of two pieces of bone; the
seat of his (intellectual) perception is two drops of blood, that
is to say, the heart.

Thou art a little worm and art stuffed with filth; (yet) thou 1855
hast made a (great) display of pomp in the world.

Thou wert (originally composed) of seed: relinquish egoism!
O Ayáz, keep in mind that sheepskin jacket!

*The Story of Ayáz and his having a chamber for his rustic shoon
and sheepskin jacket; and how his fellow-servants thought he
had a buried treasure in that room, because the door was so strong
and the lock so heavy.*

Impelled by sagacity, Ayáz hung up his sheepskin jacket and
rustic shoon.

Every day he would go into the private chamber, (saying to
himself), "These are thy shoon: do not regard thy (present)
eminence."

They (his rivals) said to the King (Maḥmúd), "He has a
chamber, and in it there is gold and silver and a jar (of treasure).

He admits no one into it: he always keeps the door locked." 1860

---

[1] Literally, "the Father of mankind's."

The King said, "Oh, I wonder what in sooth that servant (of mine) has that is hidden and concealed from me."

Then he gave orders to a certain Amír, saying, "Go at midnight and open (the door) and enter the room.

Whatever you find is yours: plunder him, expose his secret to the courtiers.

Notwithstanding such innumerable kindnesses and favours (as I have bestowed upon him), does he meanly hide silver and gold (from me)?

1865 He professes loyalty and love and enthusiasm—and then (after all) he is one who shows wheat and sells barley!

To any one who finds life in love, aught but (devoted) service would seem infidelity."

At midnight the Amír with thirty trusted (officers) set out[1] to open his chamber,

And all these valiant men, carrying[2] torches, moved joyfully in that direction,

Saying, "'Tis the Sultan's command: let us raid the room and each of us pocket[3] a purse of gold."

1870 "Hey!" cried one of them, "why trouble about gold?[4]" Talk (rather) of cornelians and rubies and (all sorts of) jewels.

He is the most privileged (keeper) of the Sultan's treasury: nay, he is now (as dear) to the King (as) life itself."

What worth[5] should rubies and corundums and emeralds or cornelians possess in the eyes of this man (so) beloved (of the King)?

The King had no evil thoughts of him: he was (only) making a mock (of the courtiers) by way of trial.

He knew him to be free from all deceitfulness and guile; (yet) again his heart was shaken with misgiving,

1875 Lest this (charge) might be (true) and he (Ayáz) should be wounded (in his feelings). "I do not wish," (he said), "that shame should come over him.

He has not done this thing; and if he has, 'tis right: let him do whatever he will, (for) he is my beloved.

Whatever my beloved may do, 'tis I have done (it). I am he, he is I: what (matter) though I am (hidden from view) in the veil?"

Again he would say, "He is far removed from this disposition and (these bad) qualities: such wild accusations (on their part)[6] are (mere) drivel and fancy.

(That) this (should proceed) from Ayáz is absurd and incredible, for he is an ocean whereof none can see the bottom."

---

[1] Literally, "resolved."    [2] Literally, "having raised."
[3] Literally, "put under his arm."
[4] Literally, "what occasion is there for (mentioning) gold?"
[5] Literally, "place (of honour)."
[6] Cf. v. 1909 infra, where تخليط means "raving." But it is possible to translate: "such malversation (as they attribute to him)."

The Seven Seas are (but) a drop in it[1]: the whole of existence 1880 is (but) a driblet of its waves.

All purities are fetched from that ocean: its drops, every one, are alchemists[2].

He is the King of kings; nay, he is the King-maker, though on account of the evil eye his name is "Ayáz."

Even the good eyes are evil to him in respect of (their) jealousy[3], for his beauty is infinite.

I want a mouth as broad as heaven to describe the qualities of him who is envied by the angels;

And if I should get a mouth like this and a hundred times as 1885 (broad as) this, it would be too narrow for (utterance of) this longing's distressful cry.

(Yet), if I should not utter even this (little) amount, O trusted (friend), the phial, (which is) my heart, would burst from weakness (inability to contain its emotion).

Since I have seen my heart's phial (to be) fragile, I have rent many a mantle in order to allay (my pain).

Beyond doubt, O worshipful one, I must become mad for three days at the beginning of every month[4].

Hark, to-day is the first of the triduum: 'tis the day of triumph (*pírúz*), not (the day of) the turquoise (*pírúza*)[5].

Every heart that is in love with the King, for it (for that heart) 1890 'tis always the beginning of the month.

Since I have become mad, the story of Maḥmúd and the description of Ayáz are now out of order[6].

*Explaining that what is related (here) is (only) the outward form of the Story, and that it is a form befitting these (hearers) who apprehend (no more than) the external form and suitable to the mirror of their imagination, whereas the real essence of the Story is so transcendent that[7] speech is ashamed to reveal it, and from (being overcome with) confusion (the writer) loses head, beard, and pen. And a hint is enough for the wise.*

Forasmuch as my elephant has dreamed of Hindustán[8], abandon hope of (receiving) the tax[9]: the village is ruined.

How should poesy and rhyme come to me after the foundations of sanity are destroyed?

[1] Here the author begins to describe the Perfect Man, of whom Ayáz is a type.
[2] *I.e.* they can work a spiritual regeneration.
[3] *I.e.* they wish that his beauty should be revealed to none but themselves.
[4] Referring to the old belief that madness was influenced by the moon.
[5] *I.e.* spiritual bliss, not worldly fortune.
[6] *I.e.* "I have lost the thread of the story."
[7] Literally, "on account of the transcendence which belongs to the real essence of the Story."
[8] *I.e.* "my spirit has had a vision of its original home."
[9] *I.e.* "of hearing the tale."

'Tis not (merely) one madness I have amidst the sorrows of love; nay, but madness on madness on madness.

1895    My body is wasted away by secret indications of the mysteries[1], ever since I beheld eternal life (*baqá*) in dying to self (*faná*).

O Ayáz[2], from love of thee I have become (thin) as a hair: I am unable to tell (thy) story, do thou tell my story.

Many a tale of thy love have I recited with (all) my soul: (now) that I have become (unsubstantial as) a tale, do thou recite mine[3].

Verily thou art reciting, O model (for all), not I: I am Mount Sinai, thou art Moses, and this (discourse) is the echo.

How should the helpless mountain know what the words are? The mountain is empty of that (meaning) which Moses knows.

1900    The mountain knows (only) according to its own measure: the body hath (only) a little of the grace of the spirit.

The body is like the astrolabe in respect of (the use of the latter in) calculation (of altitudes): it is a sign (for seekers) of the sun-like spirit.

When the astronomer is not keen-sighted, an astrolabe-moulder is required,

To make an astrolabe for him in order that he may gain some knowledge[4] concerning the state of the sun.

The soul that seeks (to learn) the truth from the (bodily) astrolabe—how much should it know of the (spiritual) sky and sun?

1905    You who observe (them) with the astrolabe of the eye are certainly very far short (of perfection) in your view of the (spiritual) world.

You have seen the (spiritual) world according to the measure of your eye, (and) where is the (spiritual) world (in relation to that)? Why, (then), have you twisted your moustache (so boastfully)?

The gnostics (mystics) possess a collyrium: seek it, in order that this eye which (now) resembles a river may become an ocean.

If a single mote of reason and consciousness is (remaining) with me, what is this melancholy madness and distracted speech?

Since my brain is empty of reason and consciousness, how then am I at fault in this raving?

1910    No; the fault is his, for he robbed me of my reason: in his presence the reason of all rational beings is dead.

O thou who causest the reason to wander and the understanding to go astray, intelligences have no object of hope but thee.

[1] Literally, "the metonymies."
[2] Probably Husámu'ddín is addressed here.
[3] Literally, "me."
[4] Literally, "scent."

I have never desired reason since thou mad'st me mad: I have never envied beauty since thou didst adorn me.

Is my madness for love of thee approved? Say "Yes," and God will reward thee.

Whether he speak Arabic or Persian, where is the ear and mind by means of which you should attain to the apprehension of it?

His wine is not suitable to every mind, his ring is not subject 1915 to every ear[1].

Once again I have become mad-like: go, go, my (dear) soul, quickly fetch a chain;

(But if you bring any) except the chain of my beloved's curl— though you bring two hundred chains, I will burst them (all).

*The wise purpose (of Ayáz) in looking at his rustic shoon and sheepskin jacket*—then let Man consider from what he was created[2].

Bring back (to my mind) the story of Ayáz's love; for 'tis a treasure full of mystery.

Every day he is going into the uppermost chamber to see his rustic shoon and sheepskin jacket,

Because (self-)existence[3] produces grievous intoxication: it 1920 removes intelligence from the head and reverence from the heart.

From this ambush this same intoxication of (self-)existence waylaid a hundred thousand generations of old.

By this (self-)existence an 'Azázíl was made to be Iblís, saying, "Why should Adam become lord over me?

I too am noble and nobly-born: I am capable of receiving and ready for (receiving) a hundred excellences.

In excellence I am inferior to none, that I should stand before my enemy to do him service.

I am born of fire, he of mud: what is the position (rank) of 1925 mud compared with fire?

Where was he in the period when I was the Prince of the World and the glory of Time?"

*(On the words of God)* "He created the Jinn from smokeless fire[4]," *and His words concerning Iblís:* "verily[5] he was one of the Jinn, and he transgressed."

The fire (of pride and jealousy) was flaming in the soul of the fool (Iblís), because he was (born) of fire: the son is (endued with) the inward nature of his father.

No; I have spoken in error; 'twas the compelling might of God: why, (then), adduce any cause (for it)?

---

[1] *I.e.* the capacity for hearing his words may be compared to an ear-ring which not every ear is worthy to possess.

[2] *Qur'án*, LXXXVI, 5.    [3] *I.e.* egoism and worldly pride.

[4] *Qur'án*, LV, 14.    [5] *Qur'án*, XVIII, 48, where انّه is omitted.

9

The causeless action (of God) is quit of (all) causes: it is lasting (without change) and firmly stablished from eternity.

1930    In the perfection of the holy work sped on (by Him) what room is there for (any) temporal cause or temporal thing?

What is (the real meaning of) "the inward nature of (his) father"? His (God's) work (creative energy) is our father: (His) work is the kernel, and the formal (physical) father is the skin (shell).

O nut-like body, know that Love is thy friend: thy soul (inspired by Love) will seek thy kernel[1] and batter thy shell (to pieces).

The man doomed to Hell whose skin is his friend—(God who hath said) "*We will give them (other) skins in exchange*"[2] bestows a (new) skin upon him[3].

Thy spiritual principle and kernel is dominant over the Fire, but thy skins (sensual faculties) are fuel for the Fire.

1935    (In the case of) a wooden pot in which river-water is (contained), the power of fire is entirely (directed) against the vessel containing it.

Man's spiritual principle is a ruler over the Fire: when is Málik (the Ruler) of Hell destroyed therein?

Do not, then, increase (pamper) thy body; increase (cherish and cultivate) thy spiritual principle, in order that thou mayst be the Fire's sovereign, like Málik.

Thou hast ever been adding skins to thy skin: necessarily thou art (black) as a skin (enveloped) in (layers of) soot.

Since the Fire hath no fodder (fuel) except the skin, the vengeance of God will tear the skin off that pride (of thine).

1940    This arrogance is a product of the skin; hence power and riches are friends to that pride.

What is this arrogance? (It consists in) being oblivious to the essential principle and frozen (insensible)—like the oblivion of ice to the sun.

When it (the ice) becomes conscious of the sun, the ice does not endure: it becomes soft and warm and moves on rapidly.

From seeing the kernel (essential principle) the whole body becomes (filled with) desire: it becomes miserable and passionately in love, for "Wretched is he who desires."

When it does not see the kernel, it is content with the skin: (then) the bondage of "Glorious is he who is content" is its prison[4].

1945    Here glory is infidelity, and wretchedness is (true) religion:

---

[1] *I.e.* God.              [2] *Qur'án*, IV, 59.
[3] *I.e.* in order that his torment may be renewed.
[4] *I.e.* his contentment, in which he takes pride, prevents him from seeing and seeking Reality.

until the stone became naughted[1], when did it become the gem set in a ring?

(To remain) in the state of stoniness and then (to say) "I" (is absurd): 'tis time for thee to become lowly and naughted (dead to self).

Pride always seeks power and riches because the bath-furnace derives its perfection from dung[2];

For these two nurses increase (foster) the skin: they stuff it with fat and flesh and pride and arrogance.

They have not raised their eyes to the kernel of the kernel: on that account they have deemed the skin to be the kernel.

Iblís was the leader on this way, for he fell a prey to the net 1950 (temptation) of power (eminence).

Riches are like a snake, and power is a dragon: the shadow (protection and guidance) of (holy) men is the emerald (which is fatal) to them both.

At (the sight of) that emerald the snake's eye jumps (out of its head): the snake is blinded and the traveller is delivered (from death).

When that Prince (Iblís) had laid thorns on this road[3], every one that was wounded (by them) cried, "Curse Iblís!"

Meaning to say, "This pain is (fallen) upon me through his treachery": he (Iblís) who is taken as a model (by the wicked) was the first to tread the path of treason[4].

Truly, generation on generation came (into being) after him, 1955 and all set their feet on his way (followed his practice).

Whosoever institutes an evil practice, O youth, in order that people may blindly fall in after him,

All their guilt is collected (and piled) on him, for he has been (as) a head (to them), while they are (like) the root of the tail.

But Adam brought forward (and kept in view) the rustic shoon and sheepskin jacket[5], saying, "I am of clay."

By him, as by Ayáz, those shoon were (often) visited: consequently he was lauded in the end.

The Absolute Being is a worker in non-existence: what but 1960 non-existence is the workshop (working material) of the Maker of existence?

Does one write anything on what is (already) written over, or plant a sapling in a place (already) planted?

(No); he seeks a sheet of paper that has not been written on and sows the seed in a place that has not been sown.

Be thou, O brother, a place unsown; be a white paper untouched by writing,

---

[1] *I.e.* lost the qualities in virtue of which it is a mere stone.
[2] Used as fuel.           [3] *I.e.* the road to salvation.
[4] Literally, "is he whose track as regards treachery is prior (to all others)."
[5] *I.e.* he remembered his humble origin.

That thou mayst be ennobled by *Nún wa 'l-Qalam*[1], and that the Gracious One may sow seed within thee.

1965   Assume, indeed, that thou hast never licked (tasted) this *pálúda* (honey-cake)[2]; assume that thou hast never seen the kitchen which thou hast seen,

Because from this *pálúda* intoxications arise, and the sheepskin jacket and the shoon depart from thy memory.

When the death-agony comes, thou wilt utter a (great) cry of lamentation: in that hour thou wilt remember thy ragged cloak and clumsy shoon;

(But) until thou art drowning in the waves of an evil plight in which there is no help (to be obtained) from any refuge,

Thou wilt never call to mind the right ship (for thy voyage): thou wilt never look at thy shoon and sheepskin jacket.

1970   When thou art left helpless in the overwhelming waters of destruction, then thou wilt incessantly make (the words) *we have done wrong* thy litany;

(But) the Devil will say, "Look ye at this half-baked (fool)! Cut off the head of this untimely bird (this cock that crows too late)!"

Far from the wisdom of Ayáz is this characteristic, (namely), that his prayer should be uttered without (being a real) prayer.

He has been the cock of Heaven from of old: all his crowings are (taking place) at their (proper) time.

> *On the meaning of this (Tradition), "Show unto us the things as they are (in reality)"; and on the meaning of this (saying), "If the covering were lifted, my certainty would not be increased"; and on his (the poet's) verse:*
>
> *"When thou regardest any one with a malign eye, thou art regarding him from the hoop (narrow circle) of thy (self-)existence."*
>
> *(Hemistich): "The crooked ladder casts a crooked shadow."*

O cocks[3], learn crowing from him: he crows for God's sake, not for the sake of pence[4].

1975   The false dawn comes and does not deceive him: the false dawn is the World with its good and evil.

The worldly people had defective understandings, so that they deemed it to be the true dawn.

The false dawn has waylaid (many) caravans which have set out in hope of the daybreak.

May the false dawn not be the people's guide! for it gives many caravans to the wind (of destruction).

---

[1] *I.e.* "N. By the Pen," *Qur'án*, LXVIII, 1. The Pen may denote Universal Reason.

[2] *I.e.* the pleasures of this world.

[3] *I.e.* preachers.          [4] Literally, "the sixth part of a dirhem."

O thou who hast become captive to the false dawn, do not regard the true dawn also as false.

If thou (thyself) hast no protection (art not exempt) from hypocrisy and wickedness, wherefore shouldst thou impute the same (vices) to thy brother? 1980

The evil-doer is always thinking ill (of others): he reads his own book[1] as referring to his neighbour.

The wretches who have remained (sunk) in (their own) un-righteous qualities have called the prophets magicians and unrighteous;

And those base Amírs, (who were) forgers of falsehood, con-ceived this evil thought about the chamber of Ayáz,

(Supposing) that he kept there a buried hoard and treasure. Do not look at others in the mirror of thyself!

The King, indeed, knew his innocence: (only) on their account was he making that investigation, 1985

Saying, "O Amír, open the door of the chamber at midnight, when he (Ayáz) will be unaware of it,

In order that his (secret) thoughts may come to light: after-wards it rests with me to punish him.

I bestow the gold and jewels upon you: of those riches I desire naught but the information (concerning them)."

Thus he spoke, while his heart was throbbing on account of the incomparable Ayáz,

(Thinking), "Is it I who am uttering this (command)?[2] How (grieved) he will be if he hear of this injustice!" 1990

Again he says (to himself), "By the truth of his religion, (I vow) that his constancy is too great

For him to be annoyed by my foul aspersion and heedless of my purpose and meaning.

When an afflicted person has perceived the (true) interpreta-tions (reasons) of his pain, he sees the victory: how should he be vanquished by the pain?

The (true) interpreter (of suffering) is (like) the patient Ayáz, for he is contemplating the ocean of ends (ultimate consequences).

To him, as to Joseph[3], the interpretation of the dream of these prisoners (in the world)[4] is evident. 1995

How should the goodly man who is aware of the meaning of the dreams of others be ignorant of (the meaning of) his own dream?

If I give him a hundred stabs with my sword by way of trial, the union (concord) of that loving one (with me) will not be diminished.

He knows I am wielding that sword against myself: I am he in reality and he is I[5]."

[1] *I.e.* his own character.
[2] Literally, "on whose tongue this (command) is being uttered."
[3] Cf. *Qur'án*, XII, 35 foll.        [4] *I.e.* the accusers of Ayáz.
[5] Literally, "he am I," indicating that real being belongs to God alone.

*Setting forth the real oneness of the lover and the beloved, although they are contrary to each other from the point of view that want is the opposite of wanting nothing. So a mirror is formless and pure, and formlessness is the opposite of form, yet in reality they have a oneness with each other which is tedious to explain: a hint is enough for the wise.*

From grief for a (long) separation (from Laylá) there came suddenly a sickness into the body of Majnún.

2000 (Heated) by the flame of longing his blood boiled up, so that (the symptoms of) quinsy appeared in that mad (lover).

Thereupon the physician came to treat him and said, "There is no resource but to bleed him.

Bleeding is necessary in order to remove the blood." (So) a skilled phlebotomist came thither,

And bandaged his arm and took the lancet (to perform the operation); (but) straightway that passionate lover cried out,

"Take thy fee and leave the bleeding! If I die, let my old body go (to the grave)!"

2005 "Why," said he, "wherefore art thou afraid of this, when thou hast no fear of the lion of the jungle?

Lions and wolves and bears and onagers and (other) wild animals gather around thee by night;

The smell of man does not come to them from thee because of the abundance of love and ecstasy in thy heart[1]."

Wolf and bear and lion know what love is: he that is blind to love is inferior to a dog.

If the dog had not a vein of love, how should the dog of the Cave have sought (to win) the heart (of the Seven Sleepers)?[2]

2010 Moreover, in the world there is (many a one) of its kind, dog-like in appearance, though it is not celebrated (like the dog of the Cave).

You have not smelt (discerned) the heart in your own kind: how should you smell the heart in wolf and sheep?

If there had not been Love, how should there have been existence? How should bread have attached itself to you and become (assimilated to) you?

The bread became you: through what? Through (your) love and appetite; otherwise, how should the bread have had any access to the (vital) spirit?

Love makes the dead bread into spirit: it makes the spirit that was perishable everlasting.

2015 Majnún said, "I do not fear the lancet: my endurance is greater than the mountain formed of rock.

I am a vagabond: my body is not at ease without blows; I am a lover: I am always in close touch with blows.

---

[1] Literally, "liver."          [2] Cf. *Qur'án*, XVIII, 17.

But my (whole) being is full of Laylá: this shell is filled with the qualities of that Pearl.

I am afraid, O cupper, lest if you let my blood you suddenly inflict a wound with your lancet upon Laylá.

The (man of) reason whose heart is enlightened knows that between Laylá and me there is no difference."

*A beloved asked her lover, "Do you love yourself more or me?"*
*He replied, "I am dead to myself and living by thee; I have*
*become non-existent to myself and my own attributes and existent*
*through thee; I have forgotten my own knowledge and have*
*become knowing through thy knowledge; I have lost all thought*
*of my own power and have become powerful through thy power.*
*If I love myself, I must have loved thee, and if I love thee,*
*I must have loved myself."*
*(Verse): "Whoever possesses the mirror of clairvoyance sees God*
*(even) though he see himself."*
*(God said to Báyazíd): "Go forth with My attributes to My*
*creatures. Whoso shall see thee shall see Me and whoso shall*
*betake himself unto thee shall betake himself unto Me"; and*
*so on.*

At the hour of the morning-drink a beloved said to her lover 2020 by way of trial, "O such-and-such son of such-and-such,

I wonder, do you love me or yourself more? Tell the truth, O man of sorrows."

He replied, "I have become so naughted in thee that I am full of thee from head to foot.

Of my existence there is nothing (left) in me but the name: in my being there is naught but thee, O thou whose wishes are gratified.

By that means I have become thus naughted, like vinegar, in thee (who art) an ocean of honey."

As the stone that is entirely turned into pure ruby: it is filled 2025 with the qualities of the sun.

That stony nature does not remain in it: back and front, it is filled with sunniness.

Afterwards, if it love itself, that (self-love) is love of the sun, O youth;

And if it love the sun with (all) its soul, 'tis undoubtedly love of itself.

Whether the pure ruby loves itself or whether it loves the sun,

There is really no difference in these two loves: both sides 2030 (aspects) are naught but the radiance of the sunrise.

Until it (the stone) has become a ruby, it is an enemy to itself, because it is not a single "I": two "I's" are there;

For the stone is dark and blind to the day(-light): the dark is essentially opposed to light.

(If) it love itself, it is an infidel, because it offers intense re-sistance to the supreme Sun.

Therefore 'tis not fitting that the stone should say "I," (for) it is wholly darkness and in (the state of) death.

2035 A Pharaoh said "I am God" and was laid low; a Manṣúr (Halláj) said "I am God" and was saved.

The former "I" is followed by God's curse and the latter "I" by God's mercy, O loving man;

For that one (Pharaoh) was a black stone, this one (Halláj) a cornelian; that one was an enemy to the Light, and this one passionately enamoured (of it).

This "I," O presumptuous meddler, was "He" (God) in the inmost consciousness, through oneness with the Light, not through (belief in) the doctrine of incarnation.

Strive that thy stony nature may be diminished, so that thy stone may become resplendent with the qualities of the ruby.

2040 Show fortitude in (enduring) self-mortification and affliction; continually behold everlasting life in dying to self.

(Then) thy stoniness will become less at every moment, the nature of the ruby will be strengthened in thee.

The qualities of (self-)existence will depart from thy body, the qualities of intoxication (ecstasy) will increase in thy head (thy spiritual centre).

Become entirely hearing, like an ear, in order that thou mayst gain an ear-ring of ruby[1].

If thou art a man[2], dig earth, like a well-digger, from this earthen body, that thou mayst reach some water;

2045 (And) if the pull (inspiration) of God come (to thee), the running water will bubble up from the earth without thy well having been dug.

Be always working, do not pay heed to that (hope of being enabled to dispense with work): keep scraping away the earth of the (bodily) well little by little.

To every one who suffers a tribulation there is revealed a treasure: every one who makes an earnest endeavour comes into a fortune.

The Prophet hath said that acts of genuflexion and prostration (in the ritual prayer) are (equivalent to) knocking the door-ring of (mystical) attainment on the Divine Portal[3].

When any one continues to knock that door-ring, felicity peeps out[4] for his sake.

---

[1] Literally, "an ear-ring (consisting) of a ruby ring."
[2] Literally, "somebody."
[3] *I.e.* prayer is the means of attaining to union with God.
[4] Literally, "puts forth a head."

*How the Amír who was the author of the mischievous intrigue came
at midnight with his officers to open the chamber of Ayáz, and
saw the sheepskin jacket and rustic shoon hanging (there) and
supposed that this was a trick and pretence; and how he dug up.
every suspected corner and brought excavators and made holes in
the walls and discovered nothing and fell into confusion and
despair. So (it is with such) evil-thinking men (as those) who
imagined vain things about the work of the prophets and saints,
saying that they were magicians and self-advertisers and (only)
sought to occupy the chief position (among their people): after
having investigated, they are covered with confusion, but it does
not avail them.*

Those trusted (officers) came to the door of the chamber: they  2050
began to search for the treasure and the gold and the jar.

A number of them, (urged) by vain desire, unlocked the
door with infinite[1] dexterity and skill;

For it was a formidable lock with intricate bolts: he (Ayáz)
had selected it from (many other) locks,

Not that he was avaricious of silver and riches and crude
(uncoined) gold, (but) in order to hide that secret (of his) from
the vulgar,

"Lest" (so he thought) "some people imagine evil[2], (while)
others call me a hypocrite."

With the man of lofty aspiration the soul's secrets are kept  2055
from the base (worldlings) more safely than the ruby in the
mine.

To fools gold seems better than the soul; in the opinion of
(spiritual) kings gold is to be scattered on the soul (as an offering).

In greed of gold they (the officers) were hastening rapidly (to
the chamber), (though) their reason was saying, "No; not so
fast[3]."

Greed runs in vain towards the mirage, (though) reason says,
"Look carefully: it is not water."

Greed was predominant (in them), and gold had become (dear
to them) as their souls: at that moment the cry of reason was
unheard[4].

Greed and its clamours had become hundredfold; wisdom and  2060
its suggestions had vanished[5],

To the end that he (the greedy man) may fall into the pit of
delusion, and then hearken to the reproaches of Wisdom.

When his wind (idle self-conceit) is broken by imprisonment
in the trap, *the rebuking soul* gets the upper hand over him[6].

[1] Literally, "two hundred."
[2] Literally, "attach themselves to an evil fancy."
[3] Literally, "more slowly."    [4] Literally, "hidden."
[5] Literally, "had become concealed."
[6] *I.e.* his conscience upbraids him.

Until his head comes against the wall of affliction, his deaf ear will not listen to the counsel of his heart.

Greed for walnut-cake and sugar makes the ears of children deaf to admonitions;

2065 (Only) when the pain of his abscess begins do his (the child's) ears become open to good advice.

Then the party (of searchers)[1], with cupidity and a hundred kinds of vain desire, opened the chamber.

They swarmed in[2] through the doorway, jostling each other, like vermin[3] (falling) on fetid buttermilk.

They (the insects) fall on it triumphantly[4], like lovers, (but) there is no possibility of drinking, and both wings are stuck.

They (the officers) looked to the left and to the right: there was (only) a torn pair of shoon and a sheepskin jacket.

2070 After (having looked), they said (to one another), "This place is not without balm[5]: the shoon are only (displayed) here as a blind.

Hey, bring sharp picks: try excavation and tunnelling."

The (searching) party dug and searched in every direction: they dug holes and deep cavities.

Thereupon the holes were (virtually) crying out to them, "We are empty holes, O ye stinkers!"

Accordingly they (the officers) were ashamed of that (evil) thought (concerning Ayáz) and filled up the holes again.

2075 In every breast were innumerable (sighs of) lá ḥawl[6]: the bird, their greed, was left without any food to peck.

The holes in the walls and in the door were informers against them (giving intelligence) of their futile aberrations.

The wall could not possibly be plastered (repaired): there was no possibility of denying before Ayáz (what they had done);

(For) if they make a pretence of being innocent, the wall and floor will bear witness (against them).

(With such reflections) they were returning to the King, covered with dust and pale-faced and ashamed.

---

[1] Literally, "those several persons."
[2] Literally, "they fell in."
[3] *I.e.* flies and other noxious insects.
[4] Literally, "with pomp and parade."
[5] *I.e.* gold and treasure.
[6] Equivalent to "God help us!"

*How the plotters returned from the chamber of Ayáz to the King*
   *with empty bags and overcome by shame, as those who thought ill*
   *of the prophets, on whom be peace, (shall be confounded) at the*
   *time when their (the prophets') innocence and holiness shall be*
   *made manifest; for (God hath said), "on the Day when (some)*
   faces shall be white and (some) faces shall be black," *and He*
   *hath said,* "and thou shalt see those who lied against God, their
   faces blackened."

The King, (speaking) with a purpose, said, "What has hap-  2080
pened? for your arms are empty of gold and purses;
   And if ye have concealed the pounds and pence[1], (then) where
is the brightness of joy (that should appear) on cheeks and
countenance?
   Although the roots of every rooty (tree) are hidden, (yet) the
leaves—*their marks (upon) their faces*[2]—are green[3].
   Lo, the lofty bough is proclaiming what the root has imbibed,
whether it be poison or sugar.
   If the root is leafless and without sap, what (then) are (signify)
the green leaves on the bough?
   The earth lays a seal on the root's tongue, (but) the bough, its  2085
hand and foot, is bearing witness."
   All those trusted (officers) began to excuse themselves: they
fell prostrate, like a shadow in the presence of the moon.
   In excuse for that heat (hot-headedness) and boasting and
egoism they went to the King with sword and winding-
sheet[4],
   All of them biting their fingers from shame, and every one
saying, "O King of the world,
   If thou shed (our) blood, 'tis lawful, lawful (for thee to do so);
and if thou forgive, 'tis (an act of) grace and bounty.
   We have done those deeds that were worthy of us: consider  2090
what thou wilt command, O glorious King.
   If thou forgive our crime, O thou who makest the heart
radiant, the night will have shown the qualities of night, and the
day (those of) day[5].
   If thou forgive, despair will be removed; and if not, may a
hundred like us be a sacrifice to the King!"
   The King replied, "Nay, I will not show this clemency or deal
this punishment: that (right) belongs to Ayáz.

---

   [1] Literally, "*dínár* and *tasú* (the twenty-fourth part of a dirhem)."
   [2] *Qur'án*, XLVIII, 29.
   [3] *I.e.* the leaves show the nature of the root, just as the piety of the true
believers is shown in their faces.
   [4] *I.e.* to throw themselves on his mercy.
   [5] *I.e.* "we shall have acted in accordance with our character, and thou in
accordance with thine."

*[How the King referred to Ayáz the question of accepting the re-
pentance of the plotters who had opened his chamber or of punish-
ing them, because he judged that[1] the offence had been committed
against his honour.]*

This is an offence against his person and honour: the blow is
(inflicted) on the veins of that man of goodly ways.

2095   Although we are spiritually one, formally I am far from (I am
unaffected by) this profit and loss."

An accusation against a (guilty) servant is no disgrace to the
King: it is only (a means of) increasing (His) forbearance and
(the servant's) reliance (on His protection).

Inasmuch as the King makes one who is accused (rich as)
Qárún (Korah), consider how He will act towards one who is
innocent.

Deem not the King to be ignorant of any one's actions: 'tis
only His forbearance that prevents it (the evil action) from being
brought to light.

Here who shall recklessly intercede with His knowledge—
(who) except His forbearance?

2100   The sin arises at first from His forbearance; otherwise, how
should His awful majesty give (any) room for it (to arise)?[2]

(Payment of) the blood-price for the crime of the murderous
carnal soul falls on His forbearance: the blood-wit is (an obliga-
tion) on the (murderer's) kin.

Our carnal soul was intoxicated and made beside itself by that
forbearance: during its intoxication the Devil snatched away its
cap[3].

Unless the *Sáqí*[4], Forbearance, had poured (the intoxicating)
wine, how should the Devil have quarrelled with Adam?

At the time of (his being in possession of) knowledge, who was
Adam in relation to the angels? (He was) the teacher of know-
ledge and the assayer of (its) coins.

2105   After he had drunk the wine of (God's) forbearance in
Paradise, he was confounded[5] by a single trick of Satan.

The doses of anacardium[6], (namely), the lessons (given to
him) by the Loving One, had made him sagacious and wise and
clever;

(But) afterwards the potent opium of His forbearance brought
the Thief[7] to (carry away) his (Adam's) property.

Reason comes to seek refuge with His forbearance, (saying),
"Thou hast been my *Sáqí* (Thou hast intoxicated me): take my
hand (succour me)!"

---

[1] Literally, "meaning that."     [2] *I.e.* no one would dare to sin.
[3] *I.e.* triumphed over it by means of a trick.     [4] *I.e.* the cup-bearer.
[5] Literally, "was made pale-faced."
[6] Anacardium was supposed to stimulate the intelligence.
[7] Satan.

*How the King said to Ayáz, "Choose either to pardon or to punish,*
*for in the present case 'tis (equally) right whether you do justice*
*or show mercy; and there are advantages in each." Within justice*
*a thousand mercies are enclosed: (God hath said), "and for you*
in retaliation there is a life." *He who deems retaliation abomin-*
*able is regarding only the single life of the murderer and does not*
*consider the hundreds of thousands of lives that will be protected*
*and kept safe, as in a fortress, by fear of punishment.*

"O Ayáz, pass sentence on the culprits! O incorruptible Ayáz
who takest infinite[1] precautions (to keep thyself pure),

Though I boil (test) thee in practice two hundred times, I do 2110
not find any refuse in the foam of thy boiling.

A countless multitude of people are ashamed of (being put to)
the test, (but) all tests are ashamed of (being tried on) thee.

It (thy knowledge) is a bottomless ocean: it is not (creaturely)
knowledge alone; it (thy forbearance) is a mountain and a
hundred mountains: indeed, it is not (creaturely) forbearance."

He (Ayáz) replied, "I know that this is thy gift; otherwise I
am (nothing except) those rustic shoon and that sheepskin
jacket."

Hence the Prophet expounded this (matter), (when he said),
"Whoso knoweth himself knoweth God."

The seed (from which you were conceived) is your shoon, and 2115
your blood is the sheepskin jacket: (all) the rest, O master, is His
gift.

He hath given it to you in order that you may seek more: do
not say, "He has only this amount (to give)."

The gardener shows a number of apples, to the end that you
may know the trees[2] and produce of the orchard.

He (the wheat-merchant) gives the purchaser a handful of
wheat, in order that he may know (the quality of) the wheat in
the granary.

The teacher explains a nice point in order that you may
recognise that his knowledge exceeds (those limits);

And if you say, "This is all (the knowledge) he has," he will 2120
cast you far (from him) as sticks and straws (are cast) from the
beard.

"Now come, O Ayáz, and deal justice: lay the foundation of a
rare justice in the world.

Those who have sinned against thee deserve to be killed, but
in hope (of escaping death) they are attending (waiting upon) thy
pardon and forbearance,

To see whether mercy will prevail or wrath, whether the water
of Kawthar will prevail or the flames (of Hell)."

[1] Literally, "a hundred."
[2] Literally, "palm-trees."

From the (ancient) Covenant of *Alast*[1] (until now) both (these) boughs, (namely) forbearance and anger, are in existence for the purpose of carrying men (up to God).

2125    Hence the perspicuous word *Alast* is (a case of) negation and affirmation joined in one word,

Because this (*Alast*) is an affirmative question, but (nevertheless) the word *laysa* is buried in it[2].

Leave off[3], and let this exposition remain incomplete[4]: do not lay the bowl for the elect on the table of the vulgar.

('Tis) a wrath and a mercy like the zephyr (*ṣabá*) and the plague (*wabá*): the former is (like) the iron-attracting (magnet) and the latter (like) the straw-attracting (amber).

The truth draws the righteous to righteousness; the false class (of things) draws the false (the wicked).

2130    (If) the belly be sweet, it draws sweets (to itself); (if) the belly be bilious (acid), it draws vinegar (to itself).

A burning (hot) carpet takes away coldness from one who sits (on it); a frozen (cold) carpet consumes (his) heat.

(When) you see a friend, mercy is aroused in you; (when) you see an enemy, violence is aroused in you.

"O Ayáz, finish this affair quickly, for expectation is a sort of vengeance."

*How the King bade Ayáz make haste, saying, "Give judgement and bring the matter to decision immediately, and do not keep them waiting or say, 'We shall meet after some days[5],' for expectation is the red death"; and how Ayáz answered the King.*

He said, "O King, the command belongs entirely to thee: when the sun is there[6], the star is naughted.

2135    Who is Venus or Mercury or a meteor that they should come forth in the presence of the sun?

If I had omitted (to look at) the cloak and sheepskin, how should I have sown such seeds of blame[7]?

What was the (use of) putting a lock on the door of the chamber amidst a hundred envious persons addicted to false imagination?

Every one of them, having put his hand into the river-water, seeks (to find there) a dry sod.

[1] Referring to the words *Alastu bi-rabbikum*, "Am not I your Lord" (*Qur'án*, VII, 171).

[2] Though *Alast*, "Am not I?" is equivalent to the affirmation, "I am," it also contains the negation denoted by the word *laysa*, "is not," from which it is derived.

[3] Here the poet addresses himself.

[4] Literally, "raw."

[5] Literally, "(there are) days between us," *i.e.* "some time must elapse before our affair can be settled."

[6] Literally, "with the existence of the sun."

[7] *I.e.* "I should not have given occasion for calumny."

How, then, should there be a dry sod in the river? How should a fish become disobedient to the sea?

They impute iniquity to poor me, before whom loyalty (itself) 2140 is ashamed."

Were it not for the trouble caused by a person unfamiliar (with my meaning), I would have spoken a few words concerning loyalty;

(But) since a world (multitude of people) is seeking (to raise) doubt and difficulty, we will let the discourse run beyond the skin[1].

If you break your (material) self, you will become a kernel and will hear the tale of a goodly kernel[2].

The voices of walnuts are in their skins (shells): where, indeed, is any voice in the kernel and the oil?

It (the kernel) has a voice, (but one that is) not suited to the 2145 (bodily) ear: its voice is hidden in the ear of ecstasy[3].

Were it not for the sweetness of a kernel's voice, who would listen to the rattling voice of a walnut-shell?

You endure the rattling of it (only) in order that you may silently come into touch with a kernel.

Be without lip and without ear for a while, and then, like the lip, be the companion of honey.

How long have you been uttering poetry and prose and (proclaiming) mysteries! O master, try the experiment and, for one day, be dumb!


*Story in confirmation of the saying, "We have tried speech and talk all this time: (now) for a while let us try self-restraint and silence."*

How long have you been cooking (things) sour and acid and 2150 (like the fruit of) the white tamarisk? For this one time make an experiment and cook sweets.

On waking at the Resurrection, there is put into the hands of a (wicked) man the scroll of his sins: (it will be) black,

Headed with black, as letters of mourning; the body and margin of the scroll completely filled with (his) sins—

The whole (of it) wickedness and sin from end to end, full of infidelity, like the land of war[4].

Such a foul and noxious scroll does not come into the right hand; it comes into the left hand.

Here also (in this world) regard your scroll (the record of your 2155 actions), (and consider) whether it fits the left hand or the right.

[1] *I.e.* "we will not discuss the subject, because words are mere symbols ich cannot be understood by non-mystics except in a superficial sense."
*I.e.* "you will receive spiritual communications."
Literally, "drinking," *i.e.* mystical perception.
*I.e.* all territory not under Moslem rule.

In the (bootmaker's) shop, can you know before trying (them) on that the left boot or shoe belongs to the left (foot)?

When you are not "right," know that you are "left"; the cries of a lion and an ape are distinct (from one another).

He (God) who makes the rose lovely and sweet-scented—His bounty makes every "left" to be "right."

He bestows "rightness" on every one belonging to the "left": He bestows *a* (fresh) *running water* on the (salt) sea.

2160   If you are "left," be "right" (in perfect harmony) with His Lordship, that you may see His mercies prevail (over His wrath).

Do you think it allowable that this vile scroll (of yours) should pass from the left hand and come into the right?

How indeed should a scroll like this, which is full of iniquity and injury, be fit (to place) in the right hand?

*Explaining the case of a person who makes a statement when his be-haviour is not consistent with that statement and profession, like the infidels (of whom God hath said): "and if thou ask them who created the heavens and the earth they will surely say, 'Allah.'" How is the worship of a stone idol and the sacrifice of life and wealth for its sake appropriate to a soul which knows that the creator of heaven and earth and (all) created beings is a God, all-hearing, all-seeing, omnipresent, all-observing, all-dominating, jealous, etc.?*

A certain ascetic had a very jealous wife: he also had a maid-servant (beautiful) as a houri.

The wife used to watch her husband jealously and not let him be alone with the maid.

2165   For a long time the wife watched them both, lest an opportunity should occur for their being alone (together)—

Until the decree and fore-ordainment of God arrived: (then) the watchman, Reason, became giddy-headed and good-for-nothing.

When His decree and fore-ordainment arrives unawares, who is Reason? Eclipse overtakes (even) the moon.

The wife was at the (public) bath: suddenly she remembered the wash-basin and (that) it was (had been left) at home.

She said to the maid, "Hark, go like a bird and fetch the silver basin from our house."

2170   On hearing this, the maid came to life, for (she knew that) now she would obtain (a meeting with) the master,

(Since) the master was then at home and alone. So she ran joyously to the house.

For six years the maid had been longing to find the master alone like this.

She flew off and hastened towards the house: she found the master at home and alone.

Desire took possession of both the lovers so (mightily) that they had no care or thought of bolting the door.

Ambo summa alacritate coierunt: copulatis corporibus anima 2175 cum anima conjuncta est.

Then the wife recollected (and said to herself), "Why did I send her (back) to the house?

I have set the cotton on fire with my own hand, I have put the lusty ram to the ewe."

She washed off the clay (soap) from her head and ran, beside herself (with anxiety): she went in pursuit of her (the maid), drawing the *chádar* (over her head as she ran).

The former (the maid) ran because of the love in her soul, and the latter (the wife) because of fear. What is fear in comparison with love?[1] (There is) a great difference.

The mystic's progress is (an ascension) at every moment to 2180 the throne of the (Divine) King; the ascetic's progress is one day's journey every month.

Although, for the ascetic, one day is of great value, (yet) how should his one day be (equal to) *fifty thousand (years)*?[2]

The length of every day in the life of the adept[3] is fifty thousand of the years of the world.

Intellects are excluded[4] from this mystery: if the heart[5] of Imagination burst, let it burst!

In the sight of Love, fear is not (so much as) a single hair: in the law of Love, all things (else) are (offered) as a sacrifice.

Love is an attribute of God, but fear is an attribute of the ser- 2185 vant (of God) who is afflicted by lust and gluttony[6].

Since you have read in the *Qur'án* (the words) "*they love Him*" joined in a certain place[7] with (the words) "*He loves them*,"

Know, then, that love (*maḥabbat*), and excessive love (*'ishq*) too, is an attribute of God: fear is not an attribute of God, O honoured sir.

What relation exists between the attributes of God and those of a handful of earth? What relation exists between the attributes of him who is originated in time and those of the Holy (Eternal) One?

If I should continue to describe Love, a hundred Resurrec-

---

[1] Literally, "where is love and where is fear?"
[2] *Qur'án*, LXX, 4.
[3] Literally, "the man of (spiritual) efficiency."
[4] Literally, "are outside of the door of."
[5] Literally, "gall-bladder."
[6] Literally, "pene et ventre."
[7] Literally, "in (reference to) a certain question." See *Qur'án*, v, 59.

10

tions would pass, and it (my description would still be) in-
complete;

2190    For there is a limit to the date of the Resurrection, but what
limit can there be where the Divine attributes are (concerned)?

Love hath five hundred wings, and every wing (extends) from
above the empyrean to beneath the earth.

The timorous ascetic runs on foot; the lovers (of God) fly
more quickly than the lightning and the wind.

How should those fearful ones overtake[1] Love?—for Love's
passion makes the (lofty) heaven its carpet—

Unless perchance the favours of the (Divine) Light come and
say, "Become free from the world and from this wayfaring;

2195    Escape from thine own *qush* and *dush*, for (only) the royal
falcon has found the way to the King."

This "*qush* and *dush*" is necessity and free-will: the pull of the
Beloved (who draws you to Himself) transcends these twain.

When the wife arrived home, she opened the door: the sound
of the door fell on their ears.

The maid jumped up in consternation and disorder; the man
jumped up and began to say his prayers.

The wife saw that the maid was dishevelled and confused and
excited and witless and unmanageable.

2200    She saw her husband standing up (and engaged) in the ritual
prayer: the wife was made suspicious by (all) that agitation.

Periculi nulla ratione habita, mariti laciniam sustulit: testi-
culos et penem vidit semine inquinatos.

Seminis quod reliquum erat e pene stillabat: femur genuque
inquinata et spurca evaserant.

Caput ejus colapho percussit et "O vilissime," inquit, "num
hujusmodi sunt testiculi viri preces sollennes rite facientis?

Num iste penis cum Dei commemoratione precibusque sol-
lennibus conveniens est? Num femur tale et inguen sordibus
plenum?"

2205    Deal equitably (answer fairly): is a scroll (a register of actions)
full of injustice and wickedness and unbelief and enmity fit (to
be placed) in the right hand?

If you ask an infidel, "By whom were this heaven and these
creatures and this world created?"

He will reply that they were created by the Lord to whose
Lordship the Creation bears witness.

Do his unbelief and great wickedness and wrong-doing fit
(properly agree with) such a confession by him?

Do those infamous deeds and that vicious conduct go fitly
with such a true confession?

2210    His actions have given the lie to his words, so that he has be-
come fit for (deserving of) the awful torment.

----

[1] Literally, "reach the dust of."

On the Day of Resurrection every hidden thing will be made manifest: every sinner will be ignominiously exposed by himself.

His hands and feet will give evidence and declare his iniquity in the presence of Him whose help is sought.

His hand will say, "I have stolen such and such"; his lip will say, "I have asked such and such questions";

His foot will say, "I have gone to (enjoy) things desired[1]"; his pudendum will say, "I have committed fornication."

His eye will say, "I have cast amorous glances at things for-   2215 bidden"; his ear will say, "I have gathered evil words."

Therefore he is a lie from head to foot, for even his own members give him the lie,

Just as, in (the case of) the specious prayers (performed by the ascetic), their fine appearance was proved to be false testimonio testiculi.

Act, then, in such wise that the action itself, without (your) tongue (uttering a word), will be (equivalent to) saying "I testify" and (to making) the most explicit declaration,

So that your whole body, limb by limb, O son, will have said "I testify" as regards both good and ill[2].

The slave's walking behind his master is a testimony (equi-   2220 valent to saying), "I am subject to authority and this man is my lord."

If you have blackened the scroll (record) of your life, repent of the deeds you did formerly.

Though your life has (almost) passed, this (present) moment is its root: water it with repentance if it lacks moisture.

Give the Living Water to the root of your life, in order that the tree of your life may become verdant.

By this (Water) all past (sins) are made good: by this (Water) last year's poison is made (sweet) as sugar.

God hath changed your evil deeds (to good)[3], in order that   2225 what has preceded[4] may become wholly (acts of) piety.

O master, cleave bravely to a repentance (like that) of Naṣúḥ[5]: strive earnestly both with body and spirit.

Hear from me the description of this repentance of Naṣúḥ: (if) you have believed (in it before), (yet now) believe afresh.

---

[1] Reading تا مَنِی.
[2] Literally, "benefit and injury."
[3] Cf. *Qur'án,* xxv, 70.
[4] *I.e.* the sins committed before repentance.
[5] *I.e.* "a sincere repentance," which is the meaning of the phrase *tawbat[an] naṣúḥ[an]* (*Qur'án,* LXVI, 8).

*Story explaining the repentance of Naṣúḥ. As milk that flows from the teat never returns to the teat, so he who has repented like Naṣúḥ will never think of that sin in the way of desire; nay, his loathing will increase continually, and that loathing is a proof that he has experienced the delight of being accepted (as a sincere penitent), and that the old lust has ceased to give delight, and that the former (delight) has established itself in the place of the latter, as it has been said (in verse):*

*" Nothing breaks off (one) love except another love: why don't you take a friend (who is) fairer than he?"*

*And when his (the penitent's) heart desires to sin again, it is a sign that he has not experienced the delight of acceptance, and that the delight of acceptance has not superseded the delight of sin, and that he has not (yet) become (like the righteous of whom God saith),* "We will surely dispose him to ease[1]," *but that the (sinful) delight (spoken) of (in the text),* "We will surely dispose him to hardship[2]," *is still remaining in him.*

There was aforetime a man named Naṣúḥ: he earned his livelihood by shampooing women.

His face resembled a female countenance: he was disguising his manliness.

2230　He was a shampooer in the women's bath, and very active in (contriving) fraud and deceit.

For (many) years he went on shampooing, and no one suspected the (real) nature and secret of his fondness (for that employment).

('Twas) because, (though) his voice and countenance were woman-like, yet his lust was at full strength and wide-awake.

He wore the *chádar* and snood and veil, (but he was) a man lustful and in the prime of youth.

In this fashion that enamoured man was massaging and washing the daughters of emperors,

2235　(And though) he often resolved on repentance and was turning his back[3] (on sin), the miscreant carnal soul would always tear his repentance to pieces.

That evil-doer (Naṣúḥ) went to a gnostic and said, "Remember me in a prayer[4]."

The holy man[5] knew his secret but, (acting) like the forbearance of God, he did not divulge it;

(For) on his (the gnostic's) lips is a lock, while his heart is full of mysteries: his lips are silent, though his heart is filled with voices.

---

[1] *I.e.* "We will make it easy for him to enter Paradise" (*Qur'án*, XCII, 7).
[2] *I.e.* "We will make it easy for him to enter Hell" (*Qur'án*, XCII, 10).
[3] Literally, "was drawing his foot back."
[4] *I.e.* "invoke God on my behalf."
[5] Literally, "the man who was (spiritually) free."

Gnostics, who have drunk of the cup of God, have known the mysteries and kept them hidden.

Whosoever has been taught the mysteries of the (Divine) 2240 action, his lips are sealed and closed.

He (the holy man) laughed softly and said, "O evil-natured one, may God cause thee to repent of that which thou knowest!"

*Explaining that the prayer of the gnostic who is united with God and his petition to God are like the petition of God to Himself, for "I am to him an ear and an eye and a tongue and a hand." God hath said, "And thou didst not throw when thou threwest, but God threw"; and there are many Verses (of the Qur'án) and Traditions and Narrations on this subject. And (what follows is) an exposition of the way in which God devises means in order that, taking hold of the sinner's ear, they may lead him to the repentance of Naṣúḥ.*

That prayer traversed the Seven Heavens: the fortune of the miserable wretch (Naṣúḥ) at last became good;

For the prayer of a Shaykh (Spiritual Director) is not like every prayer: he is naughted (*fání*) and his words are the words of God.

Since God asks and begs of Himself, how, then, should He refuse to grant His own prayer?

The action of the Almighty produced a means that delivered 2245 him (Naṣúḥ) from execration and woe.

(Whilst) he was filling a basin in the bath, a jewel belonging to the King's daughter was lost.

A jewel was lost from her ear-rings, and every woman (in the bath began to take part) in the search (for it).

Then they bolted the door of the bath (and made it) fast, in order that they might first look for the jewel in the folds of the furniture[1].

They searched (all) these articles, but it was not brought to light (there), nor was any person who had stolen the jewel discovered either.

Then they began to search incontinently with all their might 2250 in the mouths and ears (of the bathers) and in every cleft.

In rima inferiore et superiore and everywhere they searched for the pearl belonging to a beauteous oyster-shell.

Proclamation was made: "Strip, all (of you), whoever ye are, whether ye are old or young!"

The lady-in-waiting[2] began to search them, one by one, (in the hope) that the marvellous pearl might be discovered.

---

[1] *I.e.* rugs, cushions, towels, clothes, etc.
[2] Literally, "the lady chamberlain (*ḥájiba*)," who had accompanied the princess to the bath.

Naṣúḥ, (stricken) with fear, went into a private place: his face (was) yellow (pale) and his lips blue on account of a (great) terror (which possessed him).

2255   He saw death before his eyes: he went (to hide himself), trembling like a leaf.

He cried, "O Lord, many a time have I turned away (from evil courses) and (then) broken my vows of penitence and my promises.

I have done the (foul) things that were fit to be done by me, so that such a black flood (of calamity) has arrived.

If my turn to be searched shall come, oh, what cruel sufferings must my soul endure!

A hundred sparks of fire have fallen on my heart[1]: perceive in my orisons the smell of my (burning) heart.

2260   May anguish like this not be the infidel's (portion)! I clutch the skirt of (Thy) mercy. Help, help![2]

Would that my mother had not borne me, or that a lion had devoured me in the pasture!

O God, do Thou what is worthy to be done by Thee, for from every hole a snake is biting me.

I have a soul of stone, and my heart is of iron, otherwise they would have turned into blood in this sorrow and lamentation.

The time presses and I have (only) one moment (left): act in kingly fashion, come to my aid!

2265   If Thou wilt cover me up (conceal my sin) this time, (hence-forth) I repent of everything that ought not to be done.

Accept my repentance this once more, that I may gird myself with a hundred belts for repentance.

If I commit any fault (in keeping my vow) this time, then do not hearken again to my prayer and words (of entreaty)."

Thus was he moaning while a hundred tears[3] flowed (from his eyes). "I have fallen," he cried, "into the hands of the executioner and policeman.

Let no Frank die such a death: may no *mulḥid* (Ismáʿílí or 'Assassin')[4] have (cause to make) this lamentation!"

2270   He was uttering cries of mourning over his soul, (for) he saw the face of Azrael (coming) nearer and nearer[5].

He cried "O God, O God" so often that door and wall joined with him (echoed his words).

He was deep in[6] "O Lord" and "O Lord" (when suddenly) from amidst the (people engaged in) search came the (following) announcement[7].

---

[1] Literally, "liver."          [2] Literally, "Bounty, bounty!"
[3] Literally, "drops."
[4] Probably this is the meaning of *mulḥid* here; but the term may be applied to any freethinker or materialist.
[5] Or "very close (to him)."
[6] Literally, "he was in the midst of."          [7] Literally, "shout."

[*How the turn came for Naṣúḥ to be searched, and how a voice pro-
claimed—"We have searched them all, (now) search Naṣúḥ";
and how Naṣúḥ became senseless from terror, and how after ex-
treme oppression of spirit the way of deliverance was opened to
him[1], as the Prophet of God—may God bless and save him!—
used to say, whenever sickness or anxiety overtook him, "O dis-
tress, become severe: then thou wilt pass away."*]

"We have searched them all: come forward, O Naṣúḥ."
Thereupon he lost his senses, his spirit took wing.

He fell like a broken wall: his consciousness and understanding
departed, he became like lifeless matter.

When his consciousness went without delay from his body,   2275
at that moment his inmost soul was united with God.

When he was emptied (of self) and his (self-)existence re-
mained not, God called the falcon, his soul, into His presence.

When his ship was wrecked and every hope had failed[2], he
was cast on the seashore of (Divine) Mercy.

His soul became united with God: at the moment when he
lost consciousness the waves of Mercy began to surge.

When his soul was freed from the disgrace of the body, it went
rejoicing towards its Origin.

The soul is like a falcon, and the body is its fetter: ('tis) a foot-   2280
bound broken-winged creature;

(But) when its self-consciousness is gone and its foot untied,
that falcon flies towards the King[3].

When the seas of Mercy begin to surge, even stones drink the
Water of Life.

The frail mote becomes stout and strong; the carpet of earth
becomes (like) satin and cloth of gold.

He that has been dead a hundred years comes forth from the
grave; the accursed devil becomes an object of envy to the houris
on account of his beauty.

The whole face of this earth becomes verdant; the dry wood   2285
buds and becomes flourishing.

The wolf becomes the cup-companion of the lamb; the de-
spairing become courageous and valiant[4].

*The finding of the jewel, and how the ladies-in-waiting and hand-
maids of the princess begged Naṣúḥ to exonerate them.*

After that soul-destroying fear, came the good news—"Here
is the lost (jewel)!"

Suddenly rose a shout—"The danger is past: the single pearl
that was missing has been found.

---

[1] Literally, "how his affair was loosed after having been extremely tied."
[2] Literally, "without (the attainment of) the object of desire."
[3] Literally, "Kay Qubád," a monarch of the legendary Kayání dynasty.
[4] Literally, "of good nerve and of good sinew."

It is found, and we are penetrated with joy[1]: give us the reward[2], for we have found the pearl."

2290 The bath-house was filled with clamour and screams and clapping of hands (because) sorrow had disappeared.

Naṣúḥ who had gone (out of himself) came to himself again: his eye saw in front (of him) the splendour of a hundred (shining) days.

Every one was begging him to exonerate them and giving his hand many a kiss.

(They said), "We had evil thoughts (of thee), and (we pray thee to) exonerate us. We were backbiting thee[3] in our talk";

For the suspicion of all (the women) against him had been increased by the fact that he was in higher favour (with the princess) than all (the rest of them).

2295 Naṣúḥ was her private shampooer and confidant; nay (they were) as two bodies with one soul[4].

(Hence the women had said), "If (any one) has taken the pearl, only he can have taken it: none is more closely attached to the Lady than he.

At first she wished to search him forcibly, (but) from respect for his reputation she delayed,

In the hope that he might drop it (the pearl) somewhere and (thus) save himself during the respite."

They were begging him to grant these absolutions and were rising up to excuse themselves.

2300 He replied, "'Twas the grace of God, who deals justice; else I am worse than what has been said (of me).

Why should absolution be begged of me? for I am the most sinful of (all) the people in the world.

The evil they spoke of me is (but) a hundredth part (of that which I have committed): this is clearly known to me, if any one has a doubt (concerning it).

What does any one know of me but a little—(what but) one of my thousand sins and evil deeds?

I know, and He who draws a veil (of concealment) over me (knows) my sins and the wickedness of my conduct.

2305 At first an Iblís was my teacher; afterwards Iblís was (mere) wind in comparison with me.

God saw all that (iniquity), (but) made as though He saw it not, lest I should be openly dishonoured[5] by its exposure.

Moreover, (the Divine) Mercy exercised the furrier's craft on me[6] and bestowed on me a repentance sweet as life.

---

[1] Literally, "we are woven into (wholly commingled with) joy."
[2] *I.e.* the reward given to those who bring good news.
[3] Literally, "we devoured thy flesh."
[4] Literally, "having become one soul."
[5] Literally, "become pale-faced."
[6] *I.e.* "repaired the tattered coat of my piety."

Whatever (ill deeds) I had done, it took them as not having been done; and my undone (acts of) obedience it took as having been performed.

It made me free (pure and noble) as the cypress and the lily; it made me glad of heart as fortune and felicity.

It inscribed my name in the register of the righteous: I was 2310 one doomed to Hell; it gave me Paradise.

(When) I cried 'Alas,' my 'Alas' became a rope, and the rope was let down into my well.

I clutched that rope and climbed out: I became glad and strong and stout and rosy.

(Formerly) I was lying in misery at the bottom of a well: now I am not contained in the whole world.

Praises be unto Thee, O God! Thou didst suddenly put me afar from sorrow.

If the tip of every hair of me should gain a tongue (power to 2315 speak), (yet) the thanks due to Thee are inexpressible.

Amidst these gardens and fountains I am crying to the people, '*Oh, would that my folk did but know!*'"

*How the princess again invited Naṣúḥ to shampoo her, after his repentance had taken firm hold and was accepted (by God), and how he made an excuse and refused to comply.*

Afterwards some one came (to Naṣúḥ), saying, "The daughter of our sovereign graciously invites thee.

The King's daughter invites thee: come and wash[1] her head now, O devout one.

Her heart desires no shampooer except thee to massage her or wash her with clay."

He answered, "Begone, begone! My hand is not in practice, 2320 and thy (friend) Naṣúḥ is now fallen sick.

Go, look for some one else hastily and speedily, for by God my hand has gone out of business."

(Then) he said to himself[2], "My sin passed beyond (all) bounds: how should that terror and anguish (ever) go from my mind?

I died (to self) once (and for all), and (then) I came back (to spiritual life): I tasted the bitterness of death and non-existence.

I have turned to God with real repentance: I will not break (that vow) till my soul shall be parted from my body.

After such a tribulation, whose foot should move towards 2325 danger a second time, unless it be (the foot of) an ass?"

---

[1] Literally, "that thou mayst wash."
[2] Literally, "to his heart."

*Story demonstrating that (when) a person repents and feels remorse and then forgets his feelings of remorse and tries again what he has tried (before)[1], he falls into everlasting perdition. Unless his repentance be reinforced by a (great) firmness and strength and by a (great) sweetness and acceptance (experienced inwardly), it is like a rootless tree, more faded and withered every day. We take refuge with God (from that).*

(Once) there was a washerman, who had an ass with a sore on its back and empty-bellied and lean.

(He kept it) in ground covered with stones, where no grass grew: from morning till night it went without food and shelter.

Except water, there was nothing for it to eat or drink: the ass was in that miserable state[2] by day and by night.

In the neighbourhood was a reed-bed and a jungle, where a lion lived whose occupation was hunting.

2330   A battle took place between the lion and a fierce elephant: the lion was wounded and disabled from going to hunt.

On account of his weakness he was unable to hunt for some time, and the (smaller) wild animals were deprived of their morning-meal;

For they used to eat the lion's leavings: when the lion became ill they suffered distress.

The lion gave orders to a fox, saying, "Go and hunt an ass for me.

If you find an ass round about the meadow, go, charm him with specious talk[3], beguile him, and bring him (here).

2335   As soon as I gain some strength from (eating) the flesh of the ass, then afterwards I will seize another victim.

I will eat (only) a little, ye (shall have) the rest: I am the means (appointed) for you as regards (your supply of) food.

Procure for me either an ass or an ox: address (to them) some of the charming words that you know (how to use).

Deprive him of his wits[4] by flatteries and fair words and bring him here."

---

[1] *I.e.* the sin of which he already has experience.
[2] See Book I (translation), p. 52, note I.
[3] Literally, ' recite spells over him.''
[4] Literally, "make him (to be) out of his head (mind).''

*Parable of the Qutb (Pole), who is the gnostic united with God, in
respect of his dispensing to the people their rations of forgiveness
and mercy in the order and degree which God inspires him to
observe; and a comparison of him with the lion, for the (smaller)
wild animals partake of the lion's rations and eat his leavings in
proportion to their nearness to him—not nearness in space but
nearness in quality. The details of this (subject) are many[1], and
God is the (best) Guide.*

The Quṭb is (like) the lion, and it is his business to hunt: (all)
the rest, (namely), these people (of the world), eat his leavings.

So far as you can, endeavour to satisfy the Quṭb, so that he 2340
may gain strength and hunt the wild beasts.

When he is ailing, the people remain unfed, for all food pro-
vided for the gullet comes from the hand of reason[2],

Since the ecstasies (spiritual experiences) of the people are
(only) his leavings. Keep this (in mind), if your heart desires the
(spiritual) prey.

He is like the reason, and the people are like the members
of the body: the management of the body depends on the
reason.

The weakness of the Quṭb is bodily, not spiritual: the weak-
ness lies in the Ship (Ark), not in Noah.

The Quṭb is he who turns round himself, (while) round him is 2345
the revolution of the celestial spheres.

Lend some assistance in repairing his (bodily) ship, if you
have become his favourite slave and devoted servant.

Your assistance is (really) advantageous to you, not to him:
God hath said, "*If ye help God, ye will be helped[3].*"

Hunt like the fox and sacrifice your prey to him (the Quṭb),
that you may gain in return a thousand preys and more.

The prey caught by the (obedient) disciple is (presented alive)
after the manner of the fox, (but) the froward hyena[4] catches
prey (that is already) dead.

If you present the dead (prey) to him (the Quṭb), it will be- 2350
come living: filth (when placed) in the orchard will produce
(fruit).

The fox said to the lion, "I will serve thee (obediently): I will
contrive expedients and rob him (the ass) of his wits.

Cunning and enchantment is my business: it is my business to
beguile and lead astray."

Hastening from the mountain-top towards the river, he found
that miserable emaciated ass.

[1] *I.e.* would take much time to explain.
[2] *I.e.* as the discursive reason is the source of material livelihood, so all
spiritual food comes from the Quṭb, who is the organ of Universal Reason.
[3] *Qur'án*, XLVII, 8, slightly altered.
[4] *I.e.* the worldly and sensual man.

Then he saluted him cordially and advanced: he advanced to meet that poor simpleton,

2355 And said (to him), "How are you in this arid desert (where you live) amidst stones and on sterile ground?"

The ass replied, "Whether I am in pain or in Iram[1], God has made it my portion, and I am grateful for it.

I give thanks to the Friend (God) in good and evil estate, because in (the Divine) destiny there is worse than (the present) ill.

Since He is the Dispenser of portions, complaint is (an act of) infidelity. Patience is needful: patience is the key to the gift (bounteous reward).

All except God are enemies: He (alone) is the Friend: how is it good (seemly) to complain of a friend to an enemy?

2360 So long as He gives me buttermilk I will not desire honey, for every pleasure has a pain joined with it."

*Story of an ass belonging to a seller of firewood, which saw some well-fed Arab horses in the royal stable and wished for the same fortune. (This story is intended) to convey the lesson that one ought not to wish for anything but (God's) forgiveness and favour; for though you are in a hundred kinds of pain, they all become sweet (to you) when you feel the delight of being forgiven; and for the rest, every fortune that you wish for before you have experienced it is accompanied by a pain which you do not perceive (at the moment); as (for example) in every trap the bait is visible while the snare is concealed. You (who) have been caught[2] in this one trap are (still) wishing (and saying to yourself), "Would that I had gone after those (other) baits!" You fancy that those baits are without a trap.*

There was a water-carrier[3] who owned an ass that had been bent double like a hoop by affliction.

Its back was galled by the heavy load in a hundred places: it was passionately desiring the day of its death.

What of barley? It never got its fill (even) of dry straw: at its heels a (cruel) blow and an iron goad.

The Master of the (royal) stable saw it and took pity—for the man was acquainted with the owner of the ass—

2365 So he saluted him and asked him what had happened, saying, "What is the cause of this ass being bent double like a *dál*?[4]"

He replied, "On account of my poverty and destitution this dumb animal[5] is not getting even straw."

---

[1] *I.e.* an earthly Paradise.     [2] Literally, "have remained."

[3] Apparently he, or rather his ass, carried firewood too. See the Heading.

[4] The Arabic letter ‫د‬.

[5] Literally, "this one whose mouth is closed."

"Hand him over to me," said the other, "for a few days, that in the King's stable he may grow strong."

He handed the ass over to him, and that merciful man tethered him in the Sultan's stable.

The ass saw on every side (of him) Arab horses, well-fed and fat and handsome and glossy[1];

(He saw the ground) swept (clean) under their feet and 2370 sprinkled with water; the straw coming at the (proper) time, and the barley at the hour (when it was expected).

He saw the horses curry-combed and rubbed down. (Then) he lifted up his muzzle, crying, "O glorious Lord,

Am not I Thy creature? I grant that I am an ass, (but) wherefore am I wretched, with sores on my back, and lean?

At night, because of the pain in my back and the (pangs of) hunger in my belly, I am always wishing to die.

These horses are so happy and prosperous: why am I singled out for torment and tribulation?"

Suddenly came the rumour of war: 'twas the time for the 2375 Arab horses to be saddled and brought into action.

They were wounded with arrows by the foe: the barbs entered them on every side.

(When) those Arab horses returned from the campaign, they all fell down and lay on their backs in the stable.

Their legs were tightly bandaged with (strips of) canvas: the farriers were standing in file,

Piercing their bodies with the scalpel in order to extract the barbs from their wounds.

The ass saw (all) that, and was saying, "O God, I am satisfied 2380 with poverty and health.

I have no taste for that (plentiful) food and those hideous wounds." Every one who desires (spiritual) health abandons the world.

### How the fox disapproved of the saying of the ass, "I am satisfied with my lot."

The fox said, "It is an (indispensable) obligation to seek lawful provision in obedience (to the Divine command).

(This) is the world of means: nothing is obtained without a means: therefore it is important (necessary) to seek (provision).

'And seek ye of the bounty of God' is a (Divine) command, lest they (men) should seize (the property of others) by violence, like the leopard.

The Prophet hath said, 'The door is shut against (the arrival 2385 of) provision, O youth; and on the door there are locks.'

---

[1] Literally, "new."

Our movement (exertion) and our going to and fro (in search)
and our acquisition is a key to that lock and barrier.

Without the key there is no way to open the door: bread with-
out endeavour is not (according to) God's law."

### How the ass answered the fox.

He (the ass) replied, "That is (the result) of weak faith[1]; else
He who gave (us) life (also) gives (us) bread.

Whoever seeks (spiritual) sovereignty and victory, a mouthful
of bread will not fail (him), O son.

2390　All wild animals, both the herbivorous and the predatory, are
devourers of the (Divine) provision: they neither go in quest of
work (to get a livelihood) nor do they support (the burden of)
providing (for themselves).

The Provider gives their daily bread to all: He lays before
each one the portion allotted to him.

The (Divine) provision comes to every one who seeks (to show)
patience: the trouble of making efforts arises from your want of
patience."

### How the fox answered the ass.

The fox replied, "Such trust in God is exceptional: few are
proficient in (the practice of) trust in God.

'Tis (a mark of) ignorance to concern one's self with the ex-
ceptional: how is the King's highway (available) for every one?

2395　Since the Prophet hath said that contentment is a treasure,
how should the hidden treasure be gained by every one?

Recognise your (proper) limit and do not fly aloft, lest you fall
into the abyss of woe and bane."

### How the ass answered the fox.

He (the ass) replied, "Know that you are speaking (just) the
reverse (of the truth), (for) woe and bane come to the soul from
cupidity.

No one was (ever) deprived of (spiritual) life by contentment;
no one was (ever) made a (spiritual) king by covetousness.

(The daily) bread is not withheld (even) from pigs and dogs:
this rain and (these) clouds are not earned by Man[2].

2400　Just as you are pitiably enamoured of the daily bread, so the
daily bread is enamoured of its consumer[3].

---

[1] Literally, "weakness of trust in God."
[2] *I.e.* they are the gift of God.
[3] *I.e.* "it is seeking you: there is no need for you to seek it."

*Exposition of the meaning of trust in God, (which is illustrated by)
the Story of the ascetic who, making trial of his trust in God,
abandoned his property and (native) town and went far away
from the beaten tracks and thoroughfares of men to the foot of a
remote and inaccessible mountain, (where) in extreme hunger he
laid his head upon a stone and fell asleep, saying to himself,
'I put trust in Thy providing the means (of livelihood) and daily
bread; and I cut myself off from (all) means (secondary causes)
in order that I may experience the causation of trust in God.'*

A certain ascetic had heard the saying of Muṣṭafá (Mohammed)
that the daily bread surely comes from God to the spirit,

(And that), whether you will or no, your daily bread comes
running to you because it is (so) fond of you.

By way of trial that man went into the desert and immediately
lay down near a mountain,

Saying, 'I will see whether the daily bread will come to me:
(my object is) that my belief in the daily bread may become
firm.'

A caravan lost its way and marched towards the mountain: 2405
(the travellers) saw lying (there) him who was making the
trial.

(One) said (to another), 'How is this man destitute here in
the wilderness, far from road and town?

Oh, I wonder, is he dead or alive? (Evidently) he has no fear
of wolves or enemies.'

They came on and touched him with their hands: that vener-
able man deliberately said nothing.

He did not stir, he did not even move his head or open his
eyes, because he was making a trial.

Then they said, 'This poor disappointed man has had a stroke 2410
of[1] apoplexy caused by hunger.'

They fetched bread and (also) food in a kettle, that they might
pour it into his mouth and (down) his throat[2].

Thereupon the man purposely clenched his teeth, in order to
see (test) the truth of that promise.

They felt pity for him and said, 'This man is starving and
perishing with hunger and at the point of death';

(So) they brought a knife and hastily made[3] a rift in his closed
teeth.

They poured soup into his mouth and forced into it fragments 2415
of bread.

He said (to himself), 'O (my) heart, even though thou art
keeping silence, thou knowest the secret and art showing a
(great) disdain.'

[1] Literally, "has fallen into."
[2] Literally, "into his throat and palate."
[3] Literally, "hastened and made."

His heart replied, 'I know (the secret) and am purposely be-having (thus): God is the provider for my soul and body.'

How should there be a trial more (perfect) than this? The daily bread comes with joy to those who have patience."

*How the fox answered the ass and urged him to seek a livelihood.*

The fox said, "Leave these stories and apply all your poor efforts to earning a livelihood[1].

2420 God has given you hands: do some work, earn something, help a friend.

Every one takes steps to earn something and (thereby) helps other friends (to earn),

Because all the earning is not done by one (craftsman): (there is) a carpenter and also a water-carrier and a weaver.

By means of this partnership (the order of) the world is main-tained: every one, (being impelled) by want, chooses some work.

'Tis not right to be a lick-platter (idle parasite) in the midst (of them): the way of the Sunna is to work and earn."

*How the ass answered the fox, saying, "Trust in God is the best way of earning a livelihood, for every one needs to trust in God and cry, 'O God, bring this work of mine to success'; and prayer involves trust in God, and trust in God is the (only) means of livelihood that is independent of any other means, etc."*

2425 He (the ass) said, "In the two worlds I do not know any means of livelihood superior to trust in my Lord.

I know nothing to be compared with the acquisition of thanks-giving to Him, in order that thanksgiving to God may bring (in its train) the daily bread and the increase (thereof)."

Their dispute was prolonged in mutual altercation (till) they became incapable of (further) questioning and answering.

Afterwards he (the fox) said to him, "Mark in the (Divine) kingdom the prohibition, *Do not cast yourselves into destruction.*'

In a barren desert covered with stones self-denial is folly: God's world is wide.

2430 Move from this place towards the meadow, and browse there on the verdure round about the river—

A meadow verdant like Paradise, where the verdure grows up to (as high as) the waist.

Happy the animal that goes thither: amidst the verdure a camel would become invisible.

There, on every side, is a running fountain; there the animals are in comfort and security."

[1] Literally, "set your hands to earning with the utmost exertion of one who has little."

From asininity he (the ass) did not say to him, "O accursed one, thou art (come) from there: how art thou so wretched?

Where is thy gaiety and fatness and comeliness? What is (the meaning of) this lean starved[1] body of thine? 2435

If thy description of the meadow is not (mere) falsehood and fiction, then why is thine eye not intoxicated (enraptured) by it?

These greedy looks and this blindness are the result of thy beggarliness, not of (spiritual) sovereignty.

Since thou hast come from the fountain, how art thou dry (thirsty)? And if thou art (fragrant like) the gland of the musk-deer, where is the fragrance of musk?

How is there no trace in thee of that which thou sayest and describest, O exalted one?"

*Parable of the camel, explaining that when some one tells of his good fortune and you do not perceive in him any appearance or sign of welfare, there is reason to suspect that he is an imitator therein (of those who have really attained to spiritual felicity).*

A certain man asked a camel, "Hey, whence comest thou, O thou whom fortune attends?[2] 2440

He replied, "From the hot-bath in thy street." Said the other, "Truly, 'tis manifest in (the state of) thy knees!"

(When) Pharaoh, the obstinate rebel, saw Moses' snake, he begged for a respite and showed meekness.

The men of intelligence said, "This man (Pharaoh) ought to have been fiercer, since he is the Lord of the Judgement.

Whether the miracle was a dragon or a snake, what has become of the pride and wrath proper to his divinity?

If he is the Supreme Lord seated on the throne, what is this blandishment on account of a single worm?" 2445

So long as your fleshly soul is intoxicated with the dessert and date-wine (of sensuality), know that your spirit has not beheld the cluster belonging to the World Unseen,

For the signs of that vision of the Light are (consist in) your withdrawal from the abode of delusion.

Since the bird[3] is frequenting a briny (piece of) water, it has not seen (found) help (for its thirst) in the sweet water;

Nay, its faith is (mere) imitation: its spirit has never seen the face of faith.

Hence, because of the accursed Devil, the imitator is in great danger from the road and the brigand; 2450

(But) when he beholds the Light of God, he becomes safe: he is at rest from the agitations of doubt.

[1] Literally, "reduced to the last extremity."
[2] Literally, "O thou whose track is fortune."
[3] *I.e.* the worldly man.

11

The sea-foam (scum) is (always) in collision[1] till it comes to the earth (land) which is its origin.

The foam (scum) is earthly: it is an exile in the water: in exile agitation is inevitable.

When his (the imitator's) eye is opened and he reads those characters (of Reality), the Devil hath no power over him any more.

2455 Although the ass spoke of (spiritual) mysteries to the fox, he spoke superficially and like an imitator.

He praised the water, but he had no longing (for it); he tore his face and raiment, but he was no lover.

The excuse made by the hypocrite was bad, not good, because it was (only) on their lips, not in their hearts.

He (the hypocrite) has the smell of the apple, but no part of the apple (itself); and in him (even) the smell is only for the purpose of (coming into) contact (with the true believers).

The charge of a woman in battle does not break the (hostile) ranks; nay, her plight becomes pitiable.

2460 Though you see her take the sword (and fight) like a lion amidst the ranks, (yet) her hand trembles.

Alas for him whose reason is female, while his wicked fleshly soul is male and ready (to gratify its lust)!

Of necessity, his reason is vanquished: his movement is towards naught but perdition.

Oh, blest is that one whose reason is male, while his wicked fleshly soul is female and helpless;

Whose particular (individual) reason is male and dominant, (so that) his intellect deprives the female fleshly soul (of power to do mischief).

2465 The attack of the female, too, is bold in appearance; her defect, as (in the case of) that ass, arises from asininity.

The animal nature prevails in woman, because she has an inclination towards colour and scent.

(When) the ass heard of the colour and scent of the meadow, all arguments (in favour of trust in God) disgusted him[2].

The thirsty man wanted rain, and there was no cloud; the fleshly soul was ravenously hungry, and there was no self-restraint.

Self-restraint is an iron shield, O father: upon the shield (of self-restraint) God hath written (the words), "Victory will come."

2470 The imitator brings forward a hundred proofs in his exposition, (but) he speaks (gives) them from ratiocination, not from immediate experience.

He is tinctured with musk, but he is not musk: he has the scent of musk, but he is only dung.

---

[1] *I.e.* some parts of it are continually being dashed against others.
[2] Literally, "fled from his disposition."

In order that a piece of dung may become musk, O disciple, one must browse for years in that (spiritual) garden.

One must not eat straw and barley, like asses: browse on *arghawán*[1], like the musk-deer in Khutan.

Do not browse on aught but clove, jasmine, or roses: go to the plain of Khutan in company with those (saintly) personages.

Accustom your belly to the sweet basil and the rose, that you 2475 may gain the wisdom and (spiritual) food of the prophets.

Break your belly of its habit of (eating) this straw and barley: begin to eat the sweet basil and the rose.

The corporeal belly leads to the straw-barn; the spiritual belly leads to the sweet basil.

Whoever feeds on straw and barley becomes a sacrifice (*qurbán*); whoever feeds on the Light of God becomes the *Qur'án*.

Beware! Half of you is musk and half is dung. Beware! Do not increase the dung, increase the Chinese musk.

The imitator brings on to his tongue a hundred proofs and 2480 explanations, but he has no soul.

When the speaker has no soul and (spiritual) glory, how should his speech have leaves and fruit?

He boldly directs people in the Way (to salvation), (though) he is more tremulous (infirm) in soul than a blade of straw.

Therefore, though his discourse may be splendid, tremor (infirmity) is also latent in his discourse.

*The difference between the call of the perfect Shaykh who is united with God and the words of imperfect men whose (spiritual) virtues are acquired and artificial.*

The illumined Shaykh makes (his disciples) cognisant of the Way; moreover, he causes the light (of faith) to accompany his words;

Strive to become intoxicated and illumined, in order that his 2485 light may be (like) the rhyme-letter to[2] your discourse.

Whatever (fruit or vegetable) is boiled in grape-juice, the flavour of grape-juice will be (tasted) in its syrup.

(Whether it be syrup) of carrots or apples or quinces or walnuts, you will taste in it the delicious flavour of grape-juice.

When your knowledge is steeped in the light (of faith), then *the contumacious folk* derive light from your knowledge.

Whatsoever you say, too, will be luminous, for the sky never rains aught but pure (water).

Become (like) the sky, become (like) the cloud and shed rain: 2490 the spout rains (too), (but) it is not at work (productively)[3].

[1] The flowers of the Judas-tree.
[2] *I.e.* be inseparable from.
[3] *I.e.* the spout has nothing to do but discharge the rain-water which passes through it.

The water in the spout is borrowed; the water in the cloud and in the sea is original.

Your thought and cogitation resemble the spout; inspiration and revelation are (like) the cloud and the sky.

The rain-water produces a many-coloured garden; the spout causes your neighbour to quarrel (with you).

The ass disputed twice or thrice with the fox, (but) since he was (only) an imitator he was beguiled by him.

2495    He had not the glorious power[1] of perception possessed by a (true) seer: the fox's palaver brought upon him (a stroke of) apoplexy[2].

Greedy desire to eat and drink made him so despicable that he submitted to him (the fox) notwithstanding five hundred arguments (to the contrary).

*Fabula cinaedi cui paedicator tempore paedicandi "Quamobrem," inquit, "hic pugio est?" Respondit: "Ut, siquis mihi injuriam facere cogitaverit, ventrem ejus diffindam." Paedicator super eo ultro citroque se movebat et aiebat, "Deo gloria quod ego injuriam tibi facere non cogito."*

"*My tent (verse) is not a tent, it is a continent; my jest is not a jest, it is a lesson.*"

Verily, God is not ashamed to set forth as a parable a gnat or what exceeds it, *i.e.* "*what exceeds it in respect of the corruption of (men's) souls by disbelief[3]*"; (for the infidels ask), "What is it that Allah means by using this as a parable?" *and then He answers (them),* "I mean this: He lets many be led astray thereby and He lets many be guided aright thereby." *Every temptation is like a pair of scales: many come off with honour[4] and many with disgrace[5]; and if you were to meditate on it (this parable) a little, you would feel many of its excellent effects.*

*Juvenem imberbem paedicator quidam domum duxit, capite deorsum verso stravit, et in eum trusit.*

The accursed wretch saw a dagger on his waist, so he said to him, "What is this on your waist?"

He replied, "'Tis in order that, if any evil-minded person should think of committing evil against me, I may rip his belly."

2500    The *lúṭí* said, "God be praised that I have not thought of plotting evil against you."

When there is no manliness, of what use are daggers? When there is no heart (courage), the helmet avails not.

---

[1] Literally, "resounding peal."
[2] *I.e.* destroyed his spiritual life.
[3] *I.e.* something even viler than a gnat and accordingly more calculated to cause incredulity.
[4] Literally, "red-faced."      [5] Literally, "disappointed."

You may have (the sword) Dhu 'l-faqár as a heritage from 'Alí, (but) have you the (stout) arm of the Lion of God?[1] (If so), produce it!

Though you may remember a (life-giving) incantation derived from the Messiah, where (in you) are the lips and teeth of Jesus, O abominable man?

You may build a ship with money collected (from your friends) or freely given[2], (but) where is a captain of the ship like Noah?

I grant you have (formally) broken the idol, like Abraham, 2505 (but) what of devoting the idol, (which is) your body, to the fire (of self-mortification)?

If you have the proof (that you are a true saint), put it into practice: by means of that (practice) make your wooden sword (sharp) as Dhu 'l-faqár.

The proof that hinders you from the practice (of saintly works) is (the cause of your incurring) the vengeance of the (Divine) Maker.

You have emboldened those who are afraid of (travelling on) the Way, (but) underneath (inwardly) you are more tremulous (infirm) than all (the rest).

You lecture to them all on trust in God, (while) you are slitting the vein of the gnat in the air[3].

O pathice, qui exercitum praecessisti, barbae tuae mendaciam 2510 penis tuus testatur[4].

When the heart is filled with unmanliness, the beard and moustache are a cause of laughter.

Make a (vow of) repentance, shed tears like rain, redeem your beard and moustache from laughter.

Restore your manliness (by engaging) in (devotional) works, that you may become (like) the hot sun in (the sign of) Aries[5].

Leave the belly and stride towards the heart (spirit), in order that the salutation may come to you from God without (any) veil[6].

Advance one or two paces, make a good endeavour: Love will 2515 lay hold of your ear and then draw (you onward)[7].

[1] A title of 'Alí.

[2] Literally, "by contribution on demand or by free gift." This verse is said to refer to Şúfís who got convents built for them in this way but were not qualified to act as spiritual guides.

[3] I.e. you employ every device to gain wealth and power. The greedy impostor is compared to one who catches and kills flies.

[4] I.e. testatur te non nisi specie virum esse.

[5] I.e. that your power to foster the spiritual growth of your disciples may be as great as that of the sun to make the plants blossom in spring.

[6] I.e. in order that you may receive a direct revelation from God.

[7] كَش for كِشِد. Cf. v. 2567 infra.

*How the cunning of the fox prevailed over the desire of the ass to
preserve and restrain himself (from yielding to temptation), and
how the fox led the ass to the lion in the jungle.*

The fox embarked[1] on the plot: he seized the ass's beard
and led him away.

Where is the musician of that Ṣúfí monastery, that he may
quickly play the tambourine (and sing), "The ass is gone, the
ass is gone"?[2]

Since a hare brings a lion to the well[3], how should not a fox
lead an ass to the grass?

Shut thine ear and do not swallow (beguiling) spells: (swallow
naught) but the spell of the righteous saint—

2520    That spell of his, (which is) sweeter than *halwá*, that (spell) of
whose feet a hundred *halwá's* are (only) the dust.

The imperial jars full of the wine (of mystical knowledge) have
drawn their stock from the wine of his lips.

(Only) that alien soul which has never seen the wine of his
ruby lips is a lover of the wine (of conventional knowledge).

Since the blind bird does not see the sweet water, how should
not it circle round the brackish water?

The spiritual Moses makes the breast a Sinai: he makes the
blind parrots able to see.

2525    The Khusraw[4] (who is the lover) of the spiritual Shírín has
beaten the drum (of sovereignty); consequently sugar[5] has be-
come cheap in the city.

The Josephs of the unseen world[6] are marching: they are
bringing bales of candy and sugar.

The faces of the camels of Egypt[7] are (turned) towards us:
hearken, O parrots, to the sound of the (camel-)bell.

To-morrow our city will be filled with sugar; sugar is cheap
(to-day): (to-morrow) it will be cheaper.

O confectioners[8], wallow in sugar, like the parrot, in despite
of the bilious ones[9].

2530    Pound the sugar-cane: this is the only work (of importance);
lavish your souls (on him): this is the only Beloved.

Now not a single sour one is left in our city, since Shírín has
seated the Khusraws on the throne (of Love).

'Tis dessert on dessert and wine on wine! Ho, go up on the
minaret and proclaim that all are welcome (to the feast).

---

[1] Literally, "planted his foot."
[2] Referring to a story told in Book II, v. 514 foll.
[3] Referring to the story of the Lion and the Beasts, Book I, v. 900 foll.
[4] *I.e.* the Quṭb or Perfect Saint, who is the king of all the lovers of God.
[5] *I.e.* the delights of mystical experience.
[6] *I.e.* the saints.
[7] *I.e.* the holy men who are carriers of Divine gifts.
[8] *I.e.* mystics.                    [9] *I.e.* sceptics.

The nine years old vinegar is becoming sweet; the stone and marble are becoming ruby(-like) and golden.

The sun in heaven is clapping his hands: the motes are dancing like lovers.

(All) eyes are intoxicated with the orchard abounding in 2535 greenery, (where) the blossoms are budding on the boughs.

The eye of blessedness works absolute magic: the spirit is made victorious (*manṣúr*)[1], crying "I am God."

If the fox is seducing an ass, let him seduce (him)! Do not thou be an ass, and be not troubled.

*Story of the person who rushed into a house in terror, with cheeks yellow (pale) as saffron, lips blue as indigo, and hands trembling like the leaves of a tree. The master of the house asked, "Is all well (with you)? What is the matter?" He replied, "Outside they are taking asses by force." "Bless you!" cried the other; "they are taking asses, (but) you are not an ass: what are you afraid of?" He said, "They are taking (them) in a great hurry: (all) discrimination has ceased. To-day I am afraid they will take me for an ass."*

A certain man took refuge in a house: his face was yellow, his lips blue, and his colour had ebbed away.

The master of the house said to him, "Is it well (with you)? for your hand is trembling like (that of) an old man.

What has happened? Why have you taken refuge (here)? 2540 How have you lost the colour of your face so (entirely)?"

"To-day," said he, "they are seizing asses outside (in the streets) to do forced labour for the tyrannical[2] king."

He (the householder) replied, "O beloved of your uncle, they are taking it because it is an ass: since you are not an ass, go (your way): why are you troubled at this?"

He answered, "They are very urgent and furious in taking (them): 'twill be no wonder if they take me too for an ass.

They have put their hands with all their might to (the job of) taking asses: accordingly discrimination has ceased."

Since undiscriminating persons are our rulers, they carry off 2545 the owner of the ass instead of the ass.

(But) the King of our city is not one who takes at random: He has discrimination, He is *hearing and seeing*.

Be a man and do not be afraid of those who take the asses: thou art not an ass: be not afraid, O Jesus of the (world of) Time[3].

[1] Alluding to Ḥusayn b. Manṣúr al-Ḥalláj.
[2] Literally, "refractory."
[3] In this and the following verses the Perfect Man is addressed.

The Fourth Heaven[1], moreover, is filled with thy light: God forbid (that I should say) that the Stable[2] is thy abode.

Thou art higher even than the sky and the stars, though for a good reason thou art (temporarily) in the Stable.

2550   The Master of the Stable is one thing and the ass another: not every one who has entered the Stable is an ass.

Why have we fallen in behind the ass? Tell of the Rose-garden and the fresh roses,

And of the pomegranate and the citron and the apple-bough, and of the wine and the fair youths innumerable,

Or of the Sea whose waves are pearls and whose pearls are speaking and seeing,

Or of the Birds which pick roses and lay eggs of silver and gold,

2555   Or of the Falcons which foster the partridges and fly both with their bellies turned downward and also on their backs.

In the world there are invisible ladders, (leading) step by step up to the summit of heaven.

There is a different ladder for every class, there is a different heaven for every (traveller's) way.

Every one is ignorant of another's condition (in) the kingdom (which is) wide and without end or beginning.

This one is amazed at that one and asks wherefore he is happy, while that one is astounded at this one and asks why he is amazed.

2560   The area of *God's earth* is *spacious*: every tree springs up from a certain soil.

The leaves and boughs on the trees are giving thanks (to God), crying, "Oh, what a fine kingdom! Oh, what a broad expanse!"

The nightingales are (flying) round the knobby[3] blossom, saying, "Give us some of that which thou drinkest."

This discourse hath no end: return to the fox and the lion and the (lion's) sickness and hunger.

*How the fox brought the ass to the lion, and how the ass jumped away from the lion, and how the fox reproached the lion, saying, "The ass was still far off: you were too hasty"; and how the lion made excuses and entreated the fox to go and trick him a second time.*

When he (the fox) brought him (the ass) up the hill towards the meadow, in order that the lion might pulverise him with a (sudden) charge,

2565   He (the ass) was (still) far from the lion, but the lion would not wait for him to come near before attacking[4].

---

[1] Which, according to Moslem belief, is the abode of Jesus.
[2] *I.e.* the terrestrial world.
[3] The "knob" is the round head of the fruit which appears after the blossom is gone.
[4] Literally, "had not patience (enough) to refrain from battle till his approach."

The terrible lion made a spring from an eminence, (though) indeed he had not the strength and power to move (effectively).

The ass saw him from afar and turned and fled to the bottom of the hill, dropping his shoes as he ran[1].

"O king of us (all)," said the fox to the lion, "why didst not thou restrain thyself in the hour of battle,

In order that that misguided (creature) might come near thee and that thou might'st vanquish him with a small attack?

Precipitation and haste is the Devil's wile; patience and cal- 2570 culation is God's grace.

He (the ass) was far off and saw the attack and fled: thy weakness is made manifest and thy prestige is destroyed[2]."

He (the lion) replied, "I thought my strength was restored[3]: I did not know my feebleness was so great[4].

Moreover, my hunger and need had passed beyond bounds: through starvation my patience and understanding had been lost.

If by (using) your wits you can reclaim him and bring him back once more[5],

I shall be much obliged to you: try hard, maybe you will fetch 2575 him by cunning."

"Yes," said the fox, "if God should give (me) help and set a seal of blindness on his heart

(For) then he will forget the terror which he felt on seeing (thee): this will not be alien to his asininity.

But when I bring him, do not thou rush (at him), lest thou lose[6] him again by overhaste."

"Yes," replied the lion; "I have found by experience that I am very ill and that my body has become shaky.

Until the ass comes quite near to me, I will not move, I will 2580 (apparently) be sound asleep[7]."

(Thereupon) the fox departed, saying, "O king, (offer) a prayer that a (great) heedlessness may muffle his reason.

The ass has made vows of repentance to the Creator (and resolved) that he will not be duped by any ne'er-do-well.

We by cunning will cause his vows to collapse, (for) we are the enemy of reason and of the splendid covenant (with God).

The ass's head is a ball for our children: his thought is a plaything for our guile."

The reason that belongs to (is affected by) the revolution of 2585 Saturn hath no position (of honour) in the sight of Universal Reason.

---

[1] Literally, "running, dropping shoes (in his haste)."
[2] Literally, "thy water is spilt."
[3] Literally, "was in its place."          [4] Literally, "to this extent."
[5] Literally, "bring him back once more, reclaimed."
[6] Literally, "give to the wind."
[7] Literally, "asleep in (a state of) consistency (soundness)."

It is made knowing by Mercury and Saturn; we (organs of) Universal Reason) by the bounty of the gracious Creator.

The twisted script[1] of our sign-manual is *He taught Man*: our aims are (expressed in the words) *the knowledge is with God*.

We are (the object of) the nurture of that resplendent Sun: on that account we are crying, "(Glory to) my Lord the Supreme!"

(The fox said), "If he (the ass) possesses experience, nevertheless a hundred experiences will be shattered by this deceitful palaver (of mine).

2590 Maybe that weak-natured one will break his (vow of) repentance, and the bad luck of his breaking it will overtake him."

*Explaining that the violation of a covenant and (vow of) repentance is the cause of affliction; nay, it is the cause of metamorphosis, as in the case of the "Fellows of the Sabbath[2]" and in the case of the "Fellows (who disbelieved in the miracle) of the Table of Jesus[3]," for (God hath said), "And He turned them into apes and swine[4]." And in this community[5] there is (only) metamorphosis of the spirit, but at the Resurrection the form of the spirit will be given to the body[6].*

To violate a pact and break vows of repentance becomes the cause of accursedness in the end.

The violation of vows of repentance by the "Fellows of the Sabbath" became the cause of their metamorphosis and destruction and abomination.

Therefore God turned those people into apes, since they rebelliously broke their covenant with God.

In this community there has never been metamorphosis of the body, but there is metamorphosis of the spirit, O man endowed with perception.

2595 When his spirit becomes the ape-spirit, his clay (body) is debased by the ape-spirit.

How should the ass be debased by his (bodily) form, if his spirit had possessed the virtue (that is derived) from (rational) experience?

The dog of the Companions (of the Cave)[7] had a goodly character: was he any the worse[8] on account of his (bodily) form?

The "Fellows of the Sabbath" suffered outward metamor-

---

[1] Literally, "the twist."
[2] Certain Jews who broke the Sabbath. See *Qur'án*, ii, 61.
[3] See *Qur'án*, v, 112 foll.
[4] *Qur'án*, v, 65.
[5] *I.e.* all those to whom the Prophet Mohammed was sent, including both Moslems and non-Moslems.
[6] *I.e.* every one will be raised from the dead in the bodily form appropriate to his or her spiritual nature.
[7] *I.e.* the Seven Sleepers.
[8] Literally, "had he any detriment?"

phosis, in order that the people might behold outwardly their ignominious fall.

Through breaking (vows of) repentance a hundred thousand others have become hogs and asses inwardly.

*How the fox approached the runaway ass a second time in order to beguile him once more.*

Then the fox came quickly towards the ass: the ass said, "One 2600 must beware of a friend like you.

Ignoble creature, what did I do to you that you brought me into the presence of a dragon?

What but the malignity of your nature was the cause of your enmity to my life, O perverse one?"—

Like the scorpion, which bites a man's foot though no inconvenience has come to it from him,

Or like the Devil who is the enemy of our souls, though no inconvenience or injury has befallen him from us;

Nay, but he is naturally the adversary of the human soul and 2605 rejoices at the destruction of Man;

He never breaks off his pursuit of any human being: how should he abandon his wicked disposition and nature?

For, without any cause, his essential malignity pulls him on[1] to (commit) injustice and tyranny.

He continually invites thee to a spacious tent in order that he may cast thee into a pit,

Saying, "In such and such a place there is a tank of water and (many) fountains," that he may cast thee headlong into the tank.

That accursed one caused an Adam, notwithstanding all his 2610 inspiration and insight, to fall into woe and bane,

Without any sin (having been committed against him) and without any previous harm having been wrongfully done to him by Adam.

The fox replied, "It was a spell of magic that appeared in your eyes as a lion;

Else I am more puny in body than you, and I always feed there by night and day.

If he (the magician) had not wrought a spell of that kind, every famishing (animal) would have run thither.

(In) a foodless world full of elephants and rhinoceroses how 2615 should the meadow have remained verdant without (the protection of) a spell?

Truly, I meant to tell you, by way of instruction, not to be afraid if you should see a terrible thing like that;

But I forgot to impart (this) knowledge to you, because I was overwhelmed with grief and pity[2] on your account.

----

[1] Literally, "is a puller."      [2] Literally, "heart-burning."

I saw you were ravenously hungry and without food, (therefore) I was making haste so that you might attain to the remedy;

Otherwise I would have explained the spell to you: it (the lion) presents itself as an apparition, it is not a (real) body."

### The reply of the ass to the fox.

2620 "Hark," cried the ass, "begone, begone from my presence, O enemy, that I may not see your face, O ugly one!

That God who made you ill-fated hath made your ugly face detestable and impudent.

With what face do you come[1] to me? The rhinoceros has not such a hard skin (as you have).

You manifestly attempted to shed my life-blood, saying, 'I will guide you to the meadow,'

So that I beheld the face of Azrael; (now) again you have brought cunning and plausible suggestion (to bear on me).

2625 Though I am a disgrace to the asses or an ass (myself), (yet) I am possessed of life, I have a vital spirit: how should I purchase (accept and believe) this (palaver)?

If a child had seen the pitiless horror that I saw, it would instantly have become old.

Deprived of heart and soul by dread of that awful object, I threw myself headlong from the mountain.

My legs were tied (paralysed) by terror as soon as I perceived that (cruel) torment without (any) barrier (between it and me).

I made a promise to God, crying, 'O gracious One, do Thou loose my legs from this bondage,

2630 So that henceforth I may not listen to any one's temptation: I promise, I vow (that I will not listen), O Helper!'

Thereupon God loosed my legs because of my prayer and humble entreaty and indication (of abasement);

Else the fierce lion would have overtaken me: how would an ass have fared in the grip of a lion?

Now the lion of the jungle has sent you to me again for the purpose of deceit, O *evil companion that you are!*"

(I swear) by the truth of the Holy Person of Allah, the Lord, that a malign snake is better than a malign friend.

2635 The malign snake takes a soul (life) from the man it has bitten; the malign friend leads him into the everlasting Fire.

Thy heart secretly steals its disposition from the disposition of thy companion, without speech and talk on his part.

When he casts his shadow over thee, that unprincipled one steals away thy principles from thee.

[1] *I.e.* "how dare you come?"

(Even) if thy reason has become (as strong as) a furious dragon,
know that the evil companion is an emerald to it[1].

Through him the eye of thy reason starts out (of the socket)[2]:
his (vicious) thrusts deliver thee into the hands of pestilence[3].

### The answer of the fox to the ass.

The fox said, "There are no dregs in my pure liquor, but the 2640
illusions of imagination are not small.

All this is your imagination, O simpleton, for I bear no malice
and rancour against you.

Do not regard me from (the standpoint of) your evil fancy:
wherefore do you cherish ill thoughts against your lovers?

Think well of the sincere, even though unkindness come from
them in appearance.

When this evil fancy and imagination is manifested, it severs
a hundred thousand friends from one another.

If an affectionate (friend) has behaved unjustly and made a 2645
trial (of one's loyalty), understanding is needed to prevent one
from thinking ill (of him).

In particular, I, who have a bad name, was not evil-natured
(in regard to you): what you saw was nothing evil, it was (only)
a magic spell;

And if, hypothetically, that purpose (of mine) had been evil,
(still) friends pardon such a fault."

The world of imagination and the phantom of hope and fear
is a great obstacle to the traveller (on the mystic Way).

The pictures (illusions) of this picture-making phantasy were
harmful (even) to one like Khalíl (Abraham), who was (firm as)
a mountain.

The noble Abraham said, "*This is my Lord*[4]," when he fell 2650
into the world (fell under the sway) of imagination.

That person who bored the pearl of interpretation[5], inter-
preted the mention of *the star* thus—

(That) the world of imagination and blinding[6] phantasy up-
rooted such a mountain (of wisdom) from its foundation,

So that the words, "*This is my Lord*," were uttered by him:
what, (then), must be the case with a goose or an ass?

Understandings (strong) as mountains have been submerged
in the seas of imagination and the whirlpools of phantasy.

Mountains are put to shame by this Flood: where is any safety 2655
(to be found) but in the Ship (Ark) of Noah?

---

[1] *I.e.* the evil companion is as destructive to thy reason as the emerald to
the eye of the snake. See translation of Book III, *v.* 2548, note 2.
[2] *I.e.* becomes blind.
[3] *I.e.* his corrupting influence makes thee spiritually dead.
[4] See *Qur'án*, VI, 76.
[5] *I.e.* gave a profound and convincing interpretation.
[6] Literally, "eye-bandaging," "binding as with a spell."

By this phantasy, which infests the road of Faith like a brigand, the followers of the (true) Religion have become (split into) two and seventy sects.

The man of sure faith is delivered from imagination and phantasy: he does not call a hair of the eyebrow the new moon,

While he that has not the (spiritual) light of 'Umar as his support is waylaid (deceived) by a crooked hair of the eyebrow[1].

A hundred thousand awful and terrible ships have been shattered to pieces[2] in the sea of imagination.

2660    The least (of them is) the energetic and ingenious Pharaoh: his moon was eclipsed in the mansion of imagination.

Nobody knows who is the cuckold, and he that knows has no doubt concerning himself[3].

Since thine own imagination keeps thee giddy-headed, wherefore shouldst thou revolve round the imagination of another?[4]

I am helpless against my own egoism: why hast thou, full of egoism, sat down beside me?[5]

I am seeking with (all) my soul one who is free from egoism, that I may become the ball of that goodly bat.

2665    In sooth any one who has become without ego is all egos: when he is not loved by himself he becomes loved by (them) all.

(When) a mirror becomes devoid of images, it gains splendour because (then) it is the reporter (reflector) of all images.

### Story of Shaykh Muḥammad Sar-razí of Ghazna, may God sanctify his spirit!

In Ghazna there was an ascetic, abounding in knowledge (of divinity): his name was Muḥammad and his title Sar-razí.

Every night he would break his fast with vine-tendrils (sar-i raz): during seven years he was continually (engaged) in one quest.

He experienced many marvellous things from the King of existence, but his object was (to behold) the beauty of the King.

2670    That man who was surfeited with himself went to the top of a mountain and said, "Appear, or I will fall (throw myself) to the bottom."

He (God) said, "The time for that favour is not (yet) come, and if thou fall down, thou wilt not die: I will not kill thee."

He, from love (of God), threw himself down: he fell into the depths of a (piece of) water.

When he (found that he) was not dead, on account of the

---

[1] An allusion to a story told in Book II, v. 112 foll.
[2] Literally, "have become plank (torn asunder from) plank."
[3] I.e. no one is conscious of being a slave to illusion, and no one who recognises it in others suspects it in himself.
[4] I.e. "first heal thyself before attending to others."
[5] I.e. "why dost thou expect me to act as thy spiritual teacher and guide?'

shock (of disappointment) that man who was sick of life made lament over himself for having been parted from death;

For this (present) life seemed to him like a (state of) death: in his view the thing had become reversed[1].

He was begging death (as a gift) from the Unseen, he was 2675 crying, "Verily, my life is in my death."

He had embraced[2] death as (other people embrace) life, he had become in full accord[3] with the destruction of his life.

As (with) 'Alí, the sword and dagger were his sweet basil[4], the narcissus and eglantine[5] were his soul's enemies.

A Voice came (to his ear), "Go from the desert to the city"— a wondrous Voice transcending the occult and the manifest.

He cried, "O Thou that knowest my secret, hair by hair, tell me, what service am I to do in the city?"

It (the Voice) said, "The service is this, that for the purpose 2680 of self-abasement thou shouldst make thyself (like) 'Abbás of the honeyed tongue[6].

For a while take money from the rich and then deliver it to the lowly poor.

This is the service thou must do for some time." He replied, "To hear is to obey, O Thou who art my soul's refuge."

Many questions and answers and much conversation passed between the ascetic and the Lord of mankind,

Whereby earth and heaven were filled with (spiritual) light: all that is recorded in the *Maqálát*[7];

But I will cut short that dialogue, in order that every worth- 2685 less person may not hear (such) mysteries.

*How after many years the Shaykh came from the desert to the city of Ghazna and carried round the basket (as a beggar) in obedience to the behest from the Unseen and distributed amongst the poor all (the money and food) that was collected.*

*"When any one possesses the spirit of the glory of Labbayka (devoted service), letter on letter and messenger after messenger are (sent to him),"*

*as (when) the window of a house is open, sunbeams and moonbeams and rain and letters and so forth never cease (from coming in).*

That (Shaykh who was) obedient to the (Divine) command turned his face towards the city; the city of Ghazna became illumined by his face.

A (great) multitude joyfully went out to meet him, (but) he entered (the city) in haste and furtively.

[1] *I.e.* he held the converse of the ordinary view.
[2] Literally, "accepted."   [3] Literally, "one in heart."
[4] *I.e.* delightful to him.   [5] *I.e.* the pleasures of life.
[6] Literally, "'Abbás of the date-syrup (or honey)." Shaykh 'Abbás of Níshápúr was a famous beggar and story-teller.
[7] *I.e.* in the collection of the saint's discourses and sayings.

All the notables and grandees rose up and made their palaces ready to receive him,

(But) he said, "I do not come from (motives of) self-advertisement: I come not save in humility and beggary.

2690 I have no intention of talking and discoursing: I will go about from door to door with a basket in my hand.

I am devoted to the (Divine) edict, for 'tis commanded by God that I should be a beggar, a beggar, a beggar.

I will not use choice expressions in begging: I will tread the way of none but the vile beggars,

That I may be completely overwhelmed with abasement, and that I may hear abusive words from high and low.

God's command is my (very) soul, and I am its follower: He has commanded me to be covetous, (for) 'base is he that covets.'

2695 Since the Sultan of the Judgement desires covetousness from me, dust on the head of contentment henceforth!

He has desired covetousness: how should I be ambitious of glory? He has desired beggary: how should I exercise sovereignty?

Henceforth beggary and abasement are my (very) soul: in my wallet are twenty (consummate beggars like) 'Abbás."

The Shaykh would go about, with a basket in his hand, (saying, "Give) something, Sir, for God's sake, if He prompt you (to be generous)[1]."

His inward experiences were higher than the Footstool and the Throne (of God); his (external) business was (to cry), "Something for God's sake, something for God's sake!"

2700 The prophets, every one, ply this same trade: the people (to whom they are sent) are (really) destitute, (yet) they (the prophets) practise beggary,

Crying, "*Lend to God, lend to God*," and persevering contrariously in (the exhortation) "Help God!"

This Shaykh is going as a suppliant[2] from door to door, (while) in Heaven a hundred doors are opened for the Shaykh,

Because the beggary that he practised (so) diligently was for the sake of God, not for the sake of his gullet;

And even if he had done it for the sake of his gullet, that gullet hath (is endowed with) exorbitance by the Light of God.

2705 As regards him, the eating of bread and honey and the drinking of milk is better than the forty days' seclusion and the three days' fast of a hundred dervishes.

He eats Light, do not say he eats bread: he sows anemones (though) in appearance he feeds (on them).

Like the flame that consumes the oil (wax) in a candle, from his eating and drinking there is an increase of light for the company.

God hath said, "*Be not immoderate*," in reference to the eating

---

[1] Literally, "Have you a Divine prompting, Sir, (to give) something for God's sake?"    [2] Literally, "is offering supplication."

of bread; He hath not said, "Be satisfied," in reference to the eating of Light.

The former was the gullet subject to probation, while this (saintly) gullet was free from immoderation and secure from exorbitance.

(In the case of the Shaykh) 'twas (by) the (Divine) command 2710 and order, not (from) greed and cupidity: a spirit like that is not a follower of greed.

If the elixir say to the copper, "Give thyself up to me," cupidity does not prevail (over it)[1].

God had offered to the Shaykh (all) the treasures of the earth down to the seventh tier;

(But) the Shaykh said, "O Creator, I am a lover: if I seek aught but Thee, I am impious.

If I should bring into view the Eight Paradises, or if I should serve Thee from fear of Hell,

(Then) I am (only) a believer seeking salvation, for both these 2715 (motives) are concerned with the body."

A hundred bodies are not worth a bean[2] in the eyes of the lover who has received nutriment from God's love;

And this body which the Shaykh of insight possesses has become something different: do not call it a body.

(To be) in love with God's love and then (desire) a wage! (To be) a trusted Gabriel and then a thief!

In the eyes of that wretched[3] lover[4] of Laylá the kingdom of the world was (worthless as) a vegetable.

Earth and gold were alike in his eyes. What of gold? (Even) 2720 his life had no value (for him).

Lions and wolves and wild beasts were acquainted with him and gathered round him like kinsfolk,

(Knowing) that this man had become entirely purged of animality and filled with love, and that his flesh and fat were poisonous (to them).

The sweets scattered by Reason are poison to the wild beast, because the good of (that which is) good is antagonistic to (that which is) evil.

The wild beast dare not devour the flesh of the lover: Love is known both to the good and the evil;

And if the wild beast devour him even parabolically[5], the 2725 lover's flesh will become poison and kill him.

Everything except love is devoured by Love: to the beak of Love the two worlds are (but) a single grain.

---

[1] *I.e.* it is not impelled by cupidity.

[2] تّرهتوت, said to be a leguminous plant resembling *cassia fistula*.

[3] Literally, "blind and blue."       [4] Majnún.

[5] In Arabic and Persian the metaphorical expression, "to devour a person's flesh," means "to backbite and calumniate him."

Does a grain ever devour the bird? Does the manger[1] ever feed on the horse?

Do service (to God), that perchance thou mayst become a lover: (devotional) service is a means of gaining (Love): it comes into action (produces an effect).

The servant (of God) desires to be freed from Fortune; the lover (of God) nevermore desires to be free.

2730   The servant is always seeking a robe of honour and a stipend; all the lover's robe of honour is his vision of the Beloved.

Love is not contained in speech and hearing: Love is an ocean whereof the depth is invisible.

The drops of the sea cannot be numbered: the Seven Seas are petty in comparison with that Ocean.

This discourse hath no end. Return, O reader, to the story of the Shaykh of the time.

### On the meaning of " But for thee, I would not have created the heavens."

A Shaykh like this became a beggar (going) from street to street. Love is reckless: beware!

2735   Love makes the sea boil like a kettle; Love crumbles the mountain like sand;

Love cleaves the sky with a hundred clefts; Love unconscionably makes the earth to tremble.

The pure Love was united with Mohammed: for Love's sake God said to him, "But for thee."

Since he alone was the ultimate goal in Love, therefore God singled him out from the (other) prophets,

(Saying), "Had it not been for pure Love's sake, how should I have bestowed an existence on the heavens?

2740   I have raised up the lofty celestial sphere, that thou mayst apprehend the sublimity of Love.

Other benefits come from the celestial sphere: it is like the egg, (while) these (benefits) are consequential, like the chick.

I have made the earth altogether lowly, that thou mayst gain some notion of the lowliness of lovers.

We have given greenness and freshness to the earth, that thou mayst become acquainted with the (spiritual) transmutation of the dervish."

These firm-set mountains describe (represent) to thee the state of lovers in steadfastness,

2745   Although that (state) is a reality, while this (description) is (only) an image, O son, (which is employed) in order that he (who offers it) may bring it nearer to thy understanding.

They liken anguish to thorns; it is not that (in·reality), but they do so as a means of arousing (thy) attention.

---

[1] Literally, "the trough containing (cut) straw."

When they called a hard heart "stony," that was (really) in-appropriate, (but) they made it serve as a similitude.

The archetype of that (object of comparison) is inconceivable: put the blame on thy conceptual faculty, and do not regard it (the archetype) as negated (non-existent).

*How the Shaykh, in obedience to the intimation from the Unseen, went with his basket four times in one day to the house of a certain Amír for the purpose of begging; and how the Amír rebuked him for his impudence, and how he excused himself to the Amír.*

One day the Shaykh went four times to the palace of an Amír, in order to beg like a dervish,

(With) a basket in his hand, crying, "Something for God's 2750 sake! The Creator of the soul is seeking a piece of bread."

'Tis preposterous[1], O son: it makes even Universal Reason giddy-headed (astounded).

When the Amír saw him, he said to him, "O impudent man, I will tell you something, (but) do not fasten on me the name of niggard.

What callousness[2] and effrontery and (insolent) behaviour is this, that you come in (here) four times in one day?

Who here is attached to you, Shaykh? Never have I seen a sturdy beggar like you.

You have brought (all) beggars into contempt and disgrace[3]: 2755 what abominable importunity, worthy of 'Abbás (himself), is this that you have shown!

'Abbás of the honeyed tongue[4] is (merely) your groom[5]: may no freethinker (*mulḥid*) have such an ill-starred soul!"

He replied, "O Amír, I am devoted to the (Divine) command. Be silent! Thou art not acquainted with my (inward) fire: do not boil (rage) so much!

Had I found in myself any greed for bread, I would have ripped my bread-craving belly.

During seven years, (inspired) by the ardour of Love that cooks the body, I have eaten (nothing but) vine-leaves in the wilderness,

So that, from my eating withered and fresh leaves, this bodily 2760 colour of mine had turned green."

So long as thou art in the veil of the Father of mankind (Adam)[6], do not look slightingly on the lovers (of God).

The acute men who have split hairs (in profound investigation)

---

[1] Literally, "'tis (a case of) reversed shoes," *i.e.* it is contrary to reason that the saints, who are spiritually the richest of mankind, should beg their bread from those who, though rich in worldly goods, are spiritually destitute.

[2] Cf. *v.* 2622 *supra.*

[3] Literally, "you have taken away the respect and honour of the beggars."

[4] See p. 161, note 6.

[5] Literally, "one who carries a horse-cloth on his shoulder," "a menial.'

[6] *I.e.* in the bonds of the flesh.

and with (all) their soul have (studied and) apprehended the science of astronomy,

And the sciences of sorcery and magic and (natural) philosophy, and, though they do not know (these sciences) with real knowledge,

Yet have endeavoured (to know them) as far as they possibly can, and have surpassed all their rivals—

2765    Love was jealous and withdrew from them: such a (manifest) Sun became invisible to them.

(I marvel), how did such a Sun withdraw its face from the light of an eye that observed a star in the daytime?

Abandon this (revilement); hark, accept my counsel: regard the lovers (of God) with the eye of love.

(Their) time is precious[1] and their souls are on the watch (for the Beloved): at that moment they cannot excuse themselves to thee.

Apprehend (their real state), do not be dependent on their words, do not wound the breasts (hearts) of the lovers.

2770    Hast not thou formed a bad opinion of this enthusiasm (of theirs)? (Thou hast done so from prudence): do not abandon prudence, always act with caution;

(But) it (prudence) is either necessary or allowable or absurd: take this middle course in prudence, O interferer.

*How the admonition of the Shaykh and the reflexion of (the impression produced by) his sincerity moved the Amír to weep; and how after (having shown) that irreverence he gave up (to him the contents of) his treasury; and how the Shaykh preserved himself (from temptation) and refused to accept (the gift) and said, "I cannot take any action in the absence of an intimation (from God)."*

He (the Shaykh) said this and began to weep with ecstatic cries[2], the tears rolling hither and thither down his cheeks.

His sincerity touched the Amír's heart: Love is ever cooking a wondrous potful[3].

The sincerity of the lover affects (even) an inanimate thing: what wonder if it make an impression on the mind of one possessed of knowledge?

2775    The sincerity of Moses made an impression on the rod and the mountain; nay, on the majestic sea.

The sincerity of Aḥmad (Mohammed) made an impression on the beauty of the moon; nay, it stopped the course of the shining sun.

With face turned to face in lamentation, both the Amír and the Dervish had fallen to weeping.

---

[1] *I.e.* their spiritual moods and feelings are delicate (*názuk*) and all-engrossing.          [2] Literally, "crying, 'háy, háy!'"
[3] *I.e.* producing an infinite variety of miracles.

After they had wept much for a while, the Amír said to him,
"Arise, O worthy man,

And choose from the Treasury whatever thou wilt, albeit thou
deservest a hundred such (treasuries).

The (treasure-) house is thine: choose anything thou desirest, 2780
(though) in truth the two worlds are little (in thy estimation)."

He replied, "I have not been given permission (by God) to
pick out anything with my own hand.

I cannot of my own accord commit such an impertinence as
to intrude in this way like an interloper."

He made this excuse and took his leave[1]: what prevented (him
from complying) was (the fact) that the (Amír's) munificence
was not sincere.

Was it not (the case) that it (the munificence) was sincere and
unmixed with rancour and wrath? (Yes; but) every (kind of)
sincerity did not come into the Shaykh's consideration[2].

He said, "God hath so commanded me, saying, 'Go as a 2785
beggar and ask for a piece of bread.'"

*How the (following) intimation came to the Shaykh from the Un-
seen: "During these two years thou hast taken and given by Our
command; henceforth give but do not take; always put thy hand
under the mat which on thy behalf We have made to be like the
wallet of Abú Hurayra, and thou wilt find (there) whatever thou
mayst desire." (The object of such miracles is) that the people of
the world may gain certainty that beyond this (world) is a world
where, if you take a handful of earth, it will turn to gold; if a
dead man enter it he will become living; if the most ill-starred[3]
enter it he will become the most fortunate[4]; if infidelity enter
therein, it will become faith; if poison enter therein, it will become
an antidote (to poison). It (that world) is neither inside of this
world nor outside; neither beneath it nor above it; neither joined
with it nor separate from it: it is devoid of quality and relation.
At every moment thousands of signs and types are displayed by it
(in this world). As manual skill to the form of the hand, or glances
of the eye to the form of the eye, or eloquence of the tongue to the
form of the tongue, (such is the relation of that world to this): it
is neither inside of it nor outside, neither joined with it nor
separate. And indication is sufficient for a person of intelligence.*

For two years that man of (high spiritual) accomplishment
carried on this business (of begging); after that (time) the com-
mand came to him from the Creator—

---

[1] Literally, "removed the piece (from the board)," as in chess or back-
gammon.

[2] *I.e.* he had no regard for sincerity of the ordinary kind.

[3] Literally, "(one under the influence of) 'the greatest inauspiciousness'
(Saturn)."

[4] Literally, "(one under the influence of) 'the greatest auspiciousness'
(Jupiter)."

"Henceforth continue to give, but do not beg from any one:
We from the Unseen World have bestowed on thee this power.

Whoever begs of thee (any amount), from one (piece of money)
to a thousand, put thy hand beneath a (certain) mat and produce
(what he wants).

Hark, give (it) from the incalculable treasure of (Divine)
mercy: in thy hand earth will become gold: give (it)!

2790    Give whatsoever they ask of thee: have no anxiety as to that:
know that the bounty of God is more than (every) more.

In Our bounty there is no retrenchment or reduction; no
sorrow or regret for (having shown) this generosity.

Put thy hand beneath the mat, O trusted man, in order to
blindfold (deceive) the evil eye[1].

Fill thy fist, therefore, from beneath the mat and give (the
money) into the hand of the beggar whose back is broken (by
poverty).

Henceforth give from the wage that is not grudged[2]: give the
hidden pearl to every one who desires (it).

2795    Go, be thou (what is signified by) *the Hand of God is above
their hands*[3]: do thou, like the Hand of God, scatter the daily
bread recklessly[4].

Release those in debt from their responsibility: like rain, make
the carpet of the world green."

During another year this was his work, that he was always
giving gold from the purse of the Lord of the Judgement.

The black earth turned into gold in his hand: beside him[5]
Ḥátim of (the tribe) Ṭayyi' was a beggar.

*How the Shaykh knew the unspoken thoughts of those who begged
of him and the sums owed by the debtors without their telling him,
which is a sign of (his being endowed with Divine attributes, in
accordance with the command), "Go forth with My attributes
unto My creatures."*

If a dervish said nothing about his need, he (the Shaykh)
would give (what he required) and would know his secret
thought;

2800    He would give that bent-backed one the amount that he had
in mind, neither more nor less.

Then they would ask, "How didst thou know, uncle, that he
was thinking of this amount?"

He would reply: "My heart's house is empty: it is void of
beggary, like Paradise.

---

[1] *I.e.* to disguise the fact that the money comes from the Unseen World.
[2] Cf. *Qur'án*, LXXXIV, 25.
[3] *Qur'án*, XLVIII, 10.
[4] *I.e.* without counting the cost.        [5] Literally, "in his row."

There is no work (being done) in it except love of God: there is no inhabitant except the idea of union with Him.

I have swept the house clean of good and evil: my house is filled with love of the One.

When I see in it anything other than God, (I know that) it 2805 (the thing seen) is not mine but is reflected from the beggar (who is with me at the moment)."

If a date-palm or a raceme of dates has appeared in a piece of water, it is only the reflexion from the tree outside.

If you see a form (of something) at the bottom of the water, that image is reflected from outside, O youth;

But it is necessary to cleanse the canal, (which is) the body, until the water[1] is cleared of scum[2],

In order that no obscurity and rubbish may remain therein and that it may become trustworthy[3] and that the reflexion of the (inward) aspect (of everything) may appear (in it).

Where in your body is aught but muddy water, O you who 2810 are (spiritually) destitute? Make the water pure (and free) from mud, O enemy of the heart.

By (indulgence in) sleeping and eating and drinking you are ever intent on pouring into this canal more (and more) earth.

### The means of knowing people's hidden thoughts.

(Only) when the heart of that water is void of these (defilements), does the reflexion of the (inward) aspects (of all things) dart into the water.

Therefore, unless your interior has been purified, (and while) the (heart's) house is full of demons and monsters[4] and wild beasts,

O ass who have obstinately remained in asininity, how will you get scent of (apprehend) the (life-giving) breaths which resemble those of the Messiah?

If a phantasy appear (in your heart), how will you know from 2815 what hiding-place it springs forth?

Ere (all) phantasies are swept from the inward part, the body will become (insubstantial) as a phantasy in (consequence of) renunciation.

### How the cunning of the fox prevailed over the attempt of the ass to preserve himself from falling into temptation.

The ass strove long and argued (stoutly) against him, but ravenous hunger never quitted[5] the ass.

Greed prevailed, and his self-restraint was (too) weak: many are the gullets that are cut by love of the loaf.

---

[1] *I.e.* the heart.          [2] *I.e.* sensual and material affections.
[3] *I.e.* a faithful reflector.
[4] *Nasnás.* See translation of Book IV, *v.* 761, note.
[5] Literally, "was united with."

From the Messenger (Prophet) to whom the realities revealed themselves[1] has come down (the saying), "A (great) penury is near being infidelity."

2820　The ass had been made prisoner by hunger: he said (to himself), "If it is a plot, (what then?). Suppose I am dead once and for all,

At any rate I shall be delivered from this torment of hunger: if this is life, I am better dead."

If at first the ass repented and swore (to keep his vow), in the end, because of his asininity, he made a (great) lapse.

Greed makes one blind and foolish and ignorant: to fools it makes death (seem) easy;

(But) death is not (really) easy to the souls of asses who do not possess the splendour of the everlasting soul.

2825　Since he (the ass) does not possess the everlasting soul, he is damned: his boldness in (facing) death is the result of folly.

Endeavour that your soul may become immortal, so that on the day of death you will have a (goodly) store.

Again, he (the ass) had no confidence in the Provider (to assure him) that He would scatter over him largesse from the Unseen.

Until now, the (Divine) Bounty had not kept him without the daily provision, though at times He subjected his body to a (severe) hunger[2].

Were hunger absent, in consequence of indigestion a hundred other afflictions would raise their heads in you.

2830　Truly the affliction of hunger is better than those maladies in respect both of its subtilty and its lightness and (its effect on devotional) work.

The affliction of hunger is purer than (all other) afflictions, especially (as) in hunger there are a hundred advantages and excellences.

### Explaining the excellency of abstinence and hunger.

Indeed hunger is the king of medicines: hark, lay hunger to thy heart[3], do not regard it with such contempt.

Everything unsweet is made sweet by hunger: without hunger all sweet things are unacceptable.

### Parable.

A certain person was eating bread made of bran[4]: some one asked him, "How are you so fond of this?"

2835　He replied, "When hunger is doubled by self-denial, barley bread is (as sweet as) ḥalwá in my opinion;

---

[1] Literally, "gave their hand," "made themselves accessible."
[2] Literally, "set a (severe) hunger over his body."
[3] Literally, "put hunger in thy soul."　　[4] Or, "mouldy bread."

Therefore when I deny myself once, I can eat *ḥalwá* entirely, (so) of course I am very self-denying (abstinent)."

Hunger, in truth, is not conquered by every one, for this (world) is a place where fodder is abundant beyond measure.

Hunger is bestowed as a gift on God's elect (alone), that through hunger they may become puissant lions.

How should hunger be bestowed on every beggarly churl? Since the fodder is not scarce they set it before him,

Saying, "Eat! This is all thou art worth: thou art not a water- 2840 fowl, thou art a bread-fowl."

*Story of the disciple of whose greediness and secret thoughts his Shaykh became aware. He admonished him with his tongue and in the course of his admonition bestowed on him, by Divine command, the food of trust in God.*

The Shaykh, accompanied by a disciple, was going without delay towards a certain town where bread was scarce,

And the dread of hunger and famine was continually presenting itself to the disciple's mind on account of his heedlessness[1].

The Shaykh was aware (of this) and acquainted with his secret thoughts: he said to him, "How long wilt thou remain in torment?

Thou art consumed (with grief) because of thy craving for bread: thou hast closed the eye of self-denial and trust in God.

Thou art not (one) of the honoured favourites (of God) that 2845 thou shouldst be kept without (deprived of) walnuts and raisins[2].

Hunger is the daily bread of the souls of God's elect: how is it amenable to (in the power of) a beggarly fool like thee?

Be at ease: thou art not (one) of those, so that thou shouldst tarry without bread in this kitchen."

There are always bowls on bowls and loaves on loaves for these vulgar belly-gods.

When he (such a person) dies, the bread comes forward, saying, "O thou who didst (almost) kill thyself from fear of having no food,

Thou art gone (from the world), (but) the bread is still there: 2850 arise and take it (if thou canst), O thou who didst (almost) kill thyself in agony!"

Hark, put trust in God, do not let thy feet and hands tremble (with fear): thy daily bread is more in love with thee than thou (with it).

It is in love (with thee) and is lingering (only) because it knows of thy lack of self-denial, O trifler.

---

[1] *I.e.* he had forgotten that God is the Provider.
[2] *I.e.* "thou art as an ignorant child, and childish things are suited to thee."

If thou hadst any self-denial, the daily bread would come and throw itself upon thee as lovers do.

What is this feverish trembling for fear of hunger? In (possession of) trust in God one can live full-fed.

*Story of the cow that is alone in a great island. God most High fills the great island with plants and sweet herbs which are cows' fodder, and the cow feeds on all that (vegetation) till nightfall and grows fat (and big) as a mountain-crag. When night comes, she cannot sleep for anxiety and fear, (for she thinks), "I have fed on the whole field: what shall I eat to-morrow?" So in consequence of this anxiety she becomes thin like a toothpick. At daybreak she sees the whole field is greener and richer than it was yesterday, and again she eats and grows fat. Then again at nightfall the same anxiety seizes her. For years she has been experiencing the like of this, and (yet) she puts no confidence (in the Provider).*

2855    There is in the world a green island where a sweet-mouthed cow lives alone.

She feeds on the whole field till nightfall, so that she grows stout and big and choice.

During the night she becomes thin as a hair from anxiety, because she thinks, "What shall I eat to-morrow?"

At rise of dawn the field becomes green: the green blades and grain have grown up to (a man's) middle.

The cow falls to ravenously[1]: till night she feeds on that (vegetation and devours it) entirely.

2860    Again she becomes stout and fat and bulky: her body is filled with fat and strength.

Then again at night she (is stricken) by panic (and) falls into a fever (of anxiety), so that from fear of seeking (vainly) for fodder she becomes lean,

Thinking, "What shall I eat to-morrow at meal-time?" This is what that cow does for (many) years.

She never thinks, "All these years I have been eating from this meadow and this pasture;

My provender has never failed (even) for a day: what, (then), is this fear and anguish and heart-burning of mine?"

2865    (No); when night falls that stout cow becomes lean again, thinking, "Alas, the provender is gone."

The cow is the carnal soul, and the field is this world, where she (the carnal soul) is made lean by fear for her daily bread,

Thinking, "I wonder what I shall eat in the future: whence shall I seek food for to-morrow?"

---

[1] Literally, "with the cow's hunger (βουλιμία)."

Thou hast eaten for years, and food has never failed: leave the future and look at the past.

Bring to mind the food and viands thou hast eaten (already): do not regard what is to come, and do not be miserable.

*How the lion made the ass his prey, and being thirsty after his exertions went to the spring to drink. Before his return the fox had eaten the liver together with the lungs, heart, and kidneys, which are the choicest parts. The lion looked for the heart and liver, and when he did not find them asked the fox where they were. The fox replied, " If he had possessed a heart and liver, how should he have come back to thee after receiving such a stern lesson on that day and (only) saving his life by means of a thousand devices?"* " If we had hearkened or considered with understanding we should not have been among the fellows of Hell-fire[1]."

The little fox brought the ass into the presence of the lion: 2870 the courageous lion tore him to pieces.

The King of the Beasts was made thirsty by his exertions and went to the spring to drink some water.

Meanwhile the little fox, having got an opportunity, ate his (the ass's) liver, lungs, and heart.

When the lion returned from the spring to eat (his prey), he looked in the ass to find the heart, (but) there was neither heart nor liver.

He said to the fox, "Where is the liver? What has become of the heart?—for no animal can do without these two (organs)."

He (the fox) replied, "If he had possessed a heart or liver, 2875 how should he have come here a second time?

He had experienced that tremendous agony and turmoil[2], the scramble down the mountain, the terror, and the flight;

If he had had a liver or heart, how could he have come a second time into thy presence?"

When there is no light in the heart, 'tis no heart; when there is no spirit (in the body), 'tis naught but earth.

The (heart resembling) glass that hath no spiritual light is (like) urine and the urine-phial: do not call it a lamp.

The light in the lamp is the gift of the Almighty; the glass and 2880 earthenware (vessels) are His creatures' handiwork.

Necessarily in respect of the vessels there is number, (but) in respect of the flames (of light) there is naught but unity.

When the light of six lamps is mingled together, there is no number and plurality in their light.

The Jew has become a polytheist from (regarding) the vessels;

[1] *Qur'án*, LXVII, 10.
[2] Literally, "the resurrection and the rising from the dead."

the true believer regarded the light and (consequently) has become endowed with (spiritual) perception.

When the sight falls upon the spirit's vessel, it regards Seth and Noah as being two.

2885    When there is water in it (the canal), (only then) is it (really) a canal: the (real) man is he that hath the spirit (within him).

These (others) are not men, they are (mere) forms: they are dead with (desire for) bread and killed by appetite.

*Story of the Christian ascetic who went about with a lamp in the daytime in the midst of the bazaar because of the ecstasy which he had (in his heart).*

That person was going about in a bazaar in the daytime with a candle, his heart full of love and (spiritual) ardour.

A busybody said to him, "Hey, O such-and-such, what are you seeking beside every shop?

Hey, why are you going about in search (of something) with a lamp in bright daylight? What is the joke?"

2890    He replied, "I am searching everywhere for a man that is alive with the life inspired by that (Divine) Breath.

Is there a man in existence?" "This bazaar," said the other, "is full: surely they are men, O noble sage."

He answered, "I want (one who is) a man on the two-wayed road—in the way of anger and at the time of desire.

Where is (one who is) a man at the moment of anger and at the moment of appetite? In search of (such) a man I am running from street to street.

Where in the world is (one who is) a man on these two occasions, that I may devote my life to him to-day?"

2895    "You are seeking a rare thing," said he; "but you take no heed of the (Divine) ordinance and destiny. Consider well!

You regard (only) the branch, you are unaware of the root: we are the branch, the ordinances of the (Divine) decree are the root."

The (Divine) destiny causes the rolling sphere (of heaven) to lose its way; the (Divine) destiny makes a hundred Mercuries[1] to be ignorant;

It makes the world of (our) contrivance to be straitened[2]; it makes iron and hard rock to be (unresisting as) water.

O thou who hast resolved upon the way (thou wilt go), step by step, thou art the rawest of the raw, the rawest of the raw, the rawest of the raw.

2900    Since thou hast seen the revolution of the millstone, come now, see also the water of the river.

---

[1] Those born under the planet Mercury are supposed to be clever and talented.    [2] *I.e.* it makes human expedients of no avail.

Thou hast seen the dust rise into the air: amidst the dust see the wind.

Thou seest the kettles of thought boiling: look with intelligence on the fire too.

God said to Job, "I have graciously bestowed a (gift of) patience upon every hair of thee.

Hark, do not pay so much regard to thy patience: thou hast seen (thy) patience, (now) look at (My) giving (thee) patience."

How long wilt thou behold the revolution of the water-wheel? 2905 Put forth thy head and behold the rapid water (that turns it).

Thou wilt say, "I am beholding it"; but there are many good signs of (really) beholding it.

When thou hast taken a summary view of the circling movement of the foam[1], look upon the Sea[2] if thou wantest (to feel) bewilderment.

He that regards the foam tells of the mystery, while he that regards the Sea is bewildered[3].

He that regards the foam forms intentions, while he that regards the Sea makes his heart (one with) the Sea.

He that regards the foam-flakes is (engaged) in reckoning (and 2910 calculation), while he that regards the Sea is without (conscious) volition.

He that regards the foam is in (continual) movement[4], while he that regards the Sea is devoid of hypocrisy[5].

### How a Moslem called a Magian (to accept Islam).

A certain man said to a Magian, "O such-and-such, hark, become a Moslem, be one of the true believers!"

He replied, "If God will, I shall become a true believer; and if He increase His grace, I shall become possessed of intuitive faith."

He (the Moslem) said, "God wills thy true belief, in order that thy spirit may be delivered from the hand (power) of Hell;

But thy ill-omened carnal soul and the wicked Devil are 2915 dragging thee towards infidelity and the fire-temple."

He replied, "O reasonable man, since they are predominant I shall (necessarily) be on the side of the stronger[6].

I can side (only) with him who is predominant: I (must) fall in the direction to which the predominant one is pulling (me).

Since (according to thy assertion) God was desiring of me a firm belief (in Islam), what is the use of His desire when He does not succeed (in attaining His object)?

---

[1] *I.e.* phenomena.          [2] Reality.          [3] *I.e.* unable to speak.
[4] *I.e.* he moves in the world of secondary causes and self-activity.
[5] *I.e.* he knows that secondary causes have no real existence.
[6] Literally, "the friend of him who is strong."

The carnal soul and the Devil have carried their will to success, while that act of (Divine) favour has been defeated and pulverised.

2920    ('Tis as if) thou hadst built a palace and pavilion and erected therein a hundred beautiful (ornamental) designs[1],

And desired that that goodly place should be a mosque—and (then) some one else had come and made it a Christian monastery;

Or (as if) thou hadst woven a piece of linen cloth, in order deftly to make it a coat for some one to wear,

And (when) thou wert desiring (it to be) a coat, a rival, from (motives of) hostility, made the linen stuff into a pair of trousers in spite of thee.

What resource has the linen, my dear friend[2], but to submit to the purpose of the one who is predominant?

2925    (Since) he (the owner of the cloth) is reduced to submission, what is the crime of this linen? Who is he that is not dominated by the predominant?

When some one has forced his way in against his (the householder's) will and planted a thornbush in his property and house,

The master of the house is humiliated because such a shabbiness (abasement) is inflicted on him.

I too, though I am fresh and new, would become shabby (abased) through being associated with such a contemptible person.

Since the will of the carnal soul is besought for help, 'tis mockery (to say) that whatever God wills shall come to pass.

2930    (Even) if I am a disgrace to the Magians or am an infidel, I am not such (a miscreant) as to think this of God,

That any one should seek to exercise authority in His kingdom against His will and in spite of Him,

And thus should occupy His kingdom, so that the Creator of the breath dare not breathe a word (in opposition),

(And that though) He wishes to repel him and must needs (do so), (yet) the Devil at every moment is increasing His anxiety.

(On this hypothesis) I must worship the Devil, inasmuch as he is predominant in every assembly,

2935    Lest the Devil take vengeance on me—and then in that case how can the Gracious (God) lend me a (helping) hand?

That which he (the Devil) wills, his desire (therein) is fulfilled: by whom (except him) shall my affairs be restored to prosperity?

[1] Probably friezes formed of Qur'ánic texts.
[2] Literally, "my soul."

*Parable of the Devil at the door of the Merciful God.*

God forfend! Whatsoever God wills shall come to pass. He is the Ruler over the worlds of space and non-spatiality.

Without His command no one in His kingdom shall add (so much as) the tip of a single hair.

The kingdom is His kingdom, the command is His: that Devil of His is the meanest dog at His door.

If a Turcoman's dog is lying at the door (of the tent), with his face and head resting on the threshold[1], 2940

(Though) the children of the house keep pulling his tail, he will be humble (submissive) in the children's hands.

If, however, a stranger pass by, he (the dog) will rush at him like a fierce lion;

For he is *hard on the unbelievers*: to a friend he is (as) the rose, to an enemy as the thorn.

He has become so faithful and vigilant on account of the *tutmáj* broth that the Turcoman has given him.

The dog, then, namely the Devil, whom God causes to exist and in whom He creates[2] a hundred thoughts and cunning plans, 2945

And whom He feeds with (men's) honours, so that he takes away the honour of the virtuous and the wicked—

(For) the honour of the populace is the *tutmáj* broth by which the Devil-dog is fed—

Tell me, how should not his soul be devoted to the (Divine) decree at the door of the tent of Omnipotence?

Troop on troop of obedient and rebellious (devils), like the dog (of the Seven Sleepers) *spreading his fore-paws on the threshold*[3],

Are (stationed) like dogs at the door of the Cave of the God- 2950 head, (eagerly) seeking the (Divine) command with every particle (of their bodies), and with every nerve agog[4] (to hear the command),

(Namely), 'O Devil-dog, inflict tribulation in order that (thou mayst see) how these creatures (of Mine) set foot on this Way.

Continually rush (at them), prevent (them from advancing), and look to see who (among them) is female (weak) in respect of sincerity, and who is male (strong).'

For what purpose, then, is (the cry), 'I take refuge (with God)' when the Dog in his arrogance has run swiftly (to the attack)?

This (cry), 'I take refuge,' is (as though you should say), 'O Turcoman of Khitá, call thy dog off and leave the way clear,

That I may come to the door of thy tent and beg what I need 2955 from thy bounty and high estate.'

---

[1] Literally, "(and) has laid his face and head on the door."
[2] Literally, "weaves."        [3] *Qur'án*, XVIII, 17.
[4] Literally, "with veins (arteries) that have jumped (throbbed in tense expectation)."

When the Turcoman is incapable of (restraining) the dog's fury, this (expression), 'I take refuge,' and this cry of distress are improper (inadmissible),

(Since) the Turcoman too will say, 'I take refuge from the dog; for I too am helpless against the dog in my home.

Thou canst not come to this door, nor can I go forth from the door.'

Now dust be on the head of the Turcoman and the stranger-guest, since one dog binds the necks of (subjugates) them both!

2960   God forfend! (If) the Turcoman[1] utter a shout, what of the dog?[2] (Even) a fierce lion would (be terrified and) vomit blood."

O thou who hast called thyself "the Lion of God," for (many) years[3] thou hast been powerless against a dog[4].

How should this dog hunt on thy behalf when thou hast manifestly become a prey to the dog?

*The reply of the Sunní (orthodox) believer to the Necessitarian infidel, and the proof by which he established the power of choice possessed by (every) servant of God. The Sunna is a road trodden by the feet of the prophets, on whom be peace. On the right hand of that road lies the desert of Necessity ( jabr), where he (the Necessitarian) regards himself as having no power of choice and denies the (Divine) command and prohibition and employs (false) interpretation (ta'wíl); and from the (Divine) command and prohibition being denied there necessarily follows the denial of Paradise, since Paradise is the reward of those who obey the (Divine) command, while Hell is the reward of those who disobey it. I will not state to what else it ultimately leads: an indication is enough for the wise. And on the left hand of that road lies the desert of Free-will (qadar), where he (who holds that doctrine) regards the power of the Creator as overcome by the power of the creatures; and thence arise the corruptions (vicious opinions) which have been enumerated (above) by the Magian who was a Necessitarian.*

The true believer replied, "O Necessitarian, hear the words addressed (to you); you have said your say: lo, I bring the answer.

You have seen your own game, O chess-player: (now) see your adversary's game in all its breadth and length[5].

2965   You have read (to me) your letter of apology: (now) read the Sunní's letter. Why have you remained (an infidel)?

You have discoursed in Necessitarian fashion on the (Divine) destiny: (now) hear from me the mystery thereof in (this) debate.

Beyond doubt we possess a certain power of choice: you cannot deny the plain evidence of the (inward) sense.

[1] *I.e.* God.    [2] *I.e.* the Devil.    [3] Literally, "years have passed."
[4] The carnal soul.    [5] Literally, "broad and long."

One never says ' Come' to a stone : how should any one request
a brickbat to keep faith?

One never says to a human being, 'Hey, fly!' or 'Come, O
blind man, and look at me!'

God hath said, ' *There is nothing intolerable (laid) upon the* 2970
*blind*': how should the Lord who bestows relief lay upon any
one what is intolerable?

Nobody says to a stone, 'Thou hast come late' or (to a stick),
'Why didst thou strike a blow at me, O stick?'

Will any one address demands like these to a person who is
compelled, or strike a person who is excused (from complying
with them)?

Command and prohibition and anger and conferment of
honour and (bestowal of) rebuke concern him (only) who
possesses the power of choice, O pure-bosomed one.

There is (such) a power of choice in regard to injustice and
wrong-doing: this (is what) I meant by this Devil and carnal soul[1].

The power of choice resides in your inward part, (but) it does 2975
not wound its hand till it sees a Joseph[2].

The power of choice and the instinct (to choose) were (latent)
in the soul: (when) it beheld his (Joseph's) face, then[3] it spread
wings and pinions (to fly towards him).

When the dog is asleep its power of choice is lost, (but) when
it sees the tripe it wags its tail.

A horse, too, whinnies when he sees barley, and when the
meat is moved, the cat miauls.

Sight (of the desired object) is the means of moving the power
of choice (to exert itself), just as a blowing (of breath) raises
sparks from the fire.

Therefore your power of choice is moved (to action) when 2980
Iblís becomes a go-between (*dallála*) and brings (to you) a mes-
sage from Wís[4].

When he presents an object of desire to this person (who
possesses the power of choice), the sleeping power unrolls itself[5]
(begins to move towards that object);

And (on the other hand), in despite of the Devil, the Angel
presents (to you) good objects (of desire) and makes an outcry
in your heart,

In order that your power to choose the good may be moved
(to action); for, before presentation[6], these two dispositions (to-
wards good or evil) are asleep.

[1] Cf. *v.* 2915.
[2] *I.e.* it only exerts itself when stimulated by the appearance of an object
of desire. There is an allusion to the Egyptian women who cut their hands
on beholding the beauty of Joseph (*Qur'án*, XII, 30 foll.).
[3] Read اكنف.
[4] *I.e.* your beloved.          [5] Literally, "opens its folds or coils."
[6] *I.e.* so long as nothing is presented.

13

So the Angel and the Devil have become presenters (of good or evil objects of desire) for the purpose of setting the power of choice in motion[1].

2985   Your power to choose good or evil is increased tenfold[2] by inspirations (of the Angel) and suggestions (of the Devil).

Hence, when thy ritual prayer is finished[3], O excellent man, it behoves thee to offer a salutation to the Angels,

Saying, 'Through your goodly inspiration and incitement, my power to choose this ritual prayer was set going.'

Again, after (having committed) sin thou wilt curse Iblís, because through him thou art inclined (towards sin).

These two adversaries are making offers to thee in secret and presenting (objects of desire) in the (state of phenomenal existence which is a) curtain over the Unseen.

2990   When the curtain over the Unseen is raised from before thee, thou wilt behold the faces of thy (two) brokers,

And from their words wilt recognise without trouble that these were they who spoke (to thee) invisibly.

The Devil will say, 'O thou who art a captive to thy (sensual) nature and body, I was (only) presenting to thee (objects of desire): I did not force (them upon thee).'

And the Angel will say, 'I told thee that thy sorrow would be increased in consequence of this (sensual) joy.

Did not I tell thee on such and such a day that the way to Paradise is in that (spiritual) direction?

2995   (That) we are lovers of thy soul and fosterers of thy spirit and sincere worshippers of thy Father?

(That) at this time also we are serving thee and inviting thee (to advance) towards sovereignty?

(And that) that party (the Devils) were thy Father's enemies who refused to obey the (Divine) command, *Worship (Adam)*?

Thou didst accept that (offer made by them), thou didst reject ours: thou didst not acknowledge the debt (of gratitude) due for our services.

Now look on us and them in clear view, and recognise (each party) by voice and speech.'

3000   If you hear a secret from a friend at midnight, you will know that it was he when he speaks (to you again) at dawn;

And if two persons bring news to you in the night, you will recognise both of them in the daytime by their (manner of) speaking.

(If) during the night the sound of a lion and the sound of a dog

[1] Literally, "for the purpose of stirring the veins (*or* stimulating the nerves) of the power of choice."
[2] Literally, "becomes as much as that of ten persons."
[3] Literally, "at the moment of annulling the obligations of the ritual prayer," (so as to allow the worshipper to resume his worldly avocations).

have come (into some one's ear) and he has not seen their forms on account of the darkness,

When day breaks and they begin to make (the same) sound again, the intelligent (hearer) will know them by the sound (which they make).

The upshot is this, that both the Devil and the (angelic) Spirit who present (objects of desire to us) exist for the purpose of completing (actualising) the power of choice.

There is an invisible power of choice within us; when it sees 3005 two (alternative) objects of desire it waxes strong.

Teachers beat (school-)children: how should they inflict that correction upon a black stone?

Do you ever say to a stone, 'Come to-morrow; and if you don't come, I will give your bad behaviour the punishment it deserves'?

Does any reasonable man strike a brickbat? Does any one reprove a stone?

In (the eyes of) reason, Necessitarianism (*jabr*) is more shameful than the doctrine of (absolute) Free-will (*qadar*), because the Necessitarian is denying his own (inward) sense.

The man who holds the doctrine of (absolute) Free-will does 3010 not deny his (inward) sense: (he says), 'The action of God is not mediated by the senses, O son[1].'

He who denies the action of the Almighty Lord is (virtually) denying Him who is indicated by the indication[2].

That one (the believer in absolute Free-will) says, 'There is smoke, but no fire; there is candle-light without any resplendent candle';

And this one (the Necessitarian) sees the fire plainly, (but) for the sake of denial he says it does not exist.

It burns his raiment, (yet) he says, 'There is no fire'; it (the thread) stitches his raiment, (yet) he says, 'There is no thread.'

Hence this doctrine of Necessity is Sophisticism (Scepticism): 3015 consequently he (the Necessitarian), from this point of view, is worse than the infidel (believer in absolute Free-will).

The infidel says, 'The world exists, (but) there is no Lord': he says that (the invocation) 'O my Lord!' is not to be approved.

This one (the Necessitarian) says, 'The world is really naught': the Sophist (Sceptic) is in a tangle (of error).

The whole world acknowledges (the reality of) the power of choice: (the proof is) their commanding and forbidding (each other)—'Bring this and do not bring that!'

He (the Necessitarian) says that commanding and forbidding

---

[1] *I.e.* he holds that human actions, which involve sense-perception, cannot be attributed to God.

[2] *I.e.* the (Divine) Agent indicated by the (Divine) action.

are naught and that there is no power of choice. All this (doctrine) is erroneous.

3020    Animals (too) acknowledge (the reality of) the (inward) sense, O comrade, but it is a subtle (difficult) matter to apprehend the proof (of this).

Inasmuch as (the reality of) our power of choice is perceived by the (inward) sense, responsibility for actions may well be laid upon it.

*The inward consciousness of having the power to choose or of acting under compulsion, of anger or self-restraint, of repletion or hunger, corresponds to the senses that know and distinguish yellow from red and small from great and bitter from sweet and musk from dung and hard from soft—by the sense of touch—and hot from cold and burning (hot) from lukewarm and wet from dry and contact with a wall from contact with a tree. Therefore he who denies inward consciousness denies the senses, and (he does) more (than that), (for) inward consciousness is more evident than the senses, inasmuch as one can bind the senses and prevent them from functioning, while it is impossible to bar the way to the experiences of inward consciousness and stop their entrance. And an indication is enough for the wise.*

Inward consciousness corresponds to (external) sensation: both run in the same channel, O uncle.

'Do' or 'don't,' command and prohibition, discussions and talk¹ are suitable to it (the inward consciousness).

(The thought), 'To-morrow I will do this or I will do that,' is a proof of the power to choose, O worshipful one;

3025    And (in the case of) the penitence which you have felt for (having committed) an evil deed, you have been led (into the right path) through your power of choice.

The entire *Qur'án* consists of commands and prohibitions and threats (of punishment): who (ever) saw commands given to a marble rock?

Does any wise man, does any reasonable man, do this? Does he show anger and enmity to brickbats and stones?—

Saying, 'I told you to do thus or thus: why have ye not done it, O dead and helpless ones?'

How should reason exercise any authority over wood and stone? How should reason lay hold of the painted figure of a cripple,

3030    Saying, 'O slave with palsied hands and broken legs, take up the lance and come to battle'?

How, (then), should the Creator who is the Maker of stars and sky make commands and prohibitions like those of an ignorant person?

¹ *I.e.* deliberation on alternative courses of action.

You have removed from God the possibility of impotence, (but) you have (virtually) called Him ignorant and stupid and foolish.

(Divine) impotence does not follow from[1] the doctrine of Free-will; and even if[2] it do, ignorance is worse than impotence.

The Turcoman says graciously to the stranger-guest[3], 'Come to my door without a dog[4] and without a tattered cloak,

And hark, come in respectfully from such and such a quarter, 3035 in order that my dog may keep his teeth and mouth closed (and refrain) from (biting) thee.'

(But) you do the reverse of that and advance to the door: necessarily you are wounded by the violence of the dog.

(You must) advance in the same manner in which slaves have advanced, so that his dog may become gentle and affectionate.

(If) you take a dog or a fox with you, a dog will rage (at you) from the bottom of every tent.

If none but God have the power of choice, why do you become angry with one who has committed an offence (against you)?

Why do you gnash your teeth at a foe? Why do you regard 3040 the sin and offence as (proceeding) from him?

If a piece of timber break off from your house-roof and fall upon you and wound you severely,

Will you feel any anger against the timber of the roof? Will you ever devote yourself to taking vengeance upon it,

(And say), 'Why did it hit me and fracture my hand? It has been my mortal foe and enemy'?

Why do you beat little children (when they do wrong), since (in theory) you make out that adults are exempt from blame?

(In the case of) a man who steals your property, you say (to 3045 the magistrate), 'Arrest him, cut off his hand and foot, make him a captive';

And (in the case of) a man who visits your wife, a hundred thousand angers shoot up from you.

(On the contrary), if a flood come and sweep away your household goods, will your reason bear any enmity towards the flood?

And if the wind came and carried off your turban, when did your heart show any anger against the wind?

The anger within you is a clear demonstration of (the existence of) a power of choice (in Man), so that you must not excuse yourself after the fashion of Necessitarians.

If a camel-driver goes on striking a camel, the camel will 3050 attack the striker.

[1] Literally, "is not (a part or result) of."

[2] The reading ور گر appears to be correct. In this case گر is pleonastic; cf. إِنْ لَوْ in Arabic.

[3] See v. 2940 foll. The Turcoman represents God.

[4] I.e. the carnal soul.

The camel's anger is not (directed) against his stick: therefore the camel has got some notion of the power of choice (in Man).

Similarly a dog, if you throw a stone at him, will rush at you and become contorted[1] (with fury).

If he seize the stone, 'tis because of his anger against you; for you are far off and he has no means of getting at you[2].

Since the animal intelligence is conscious of the power of choice (in Man), do not thou, O human intelligence, hold this (Necessitarian doctrine). Be ashamed!

3055    This (power of choice) is manifest, but in his desire for the meal taken before dawn[3] that (greedy) eater shuts his eyes to the light.

Since all his desire is for eating bread, he sets his face towards the darkness, saying, 'It is not (yet) day.'

Inasmuch as greed causes the sun to be hidden (from him), what wonder if he turn his back on the convincing proof?

*A Story illustrating and confirming the view that mankind have the power of choice, and showing that Pre-ordination and Predestination do not annul the power of choice.*

A thief said to the magistrate, 'O (my) king, that which I have done was decreed by God.'

The magistrate replied, 'That which I am doing is also decreed by God, O light of my eyes[4].'

3060    If any one take a radish from a (greengrocer's) shop, saying, 'This is decreed by God, O man of understanding,'

You (the greengrocer) will give him two or three blows on the head with your fist, (as though to say), 'O detestable man, this (beating) is God's decree that you put it (the radish) back here.'

Since this excuse, O trifler, is not accepted (even) by a greengrocer in the case of (stealing) a single vegetable,

How are you placing (such) a reliance on this excuse and frequenting the neighbourhood of (such) a dragon?

By (making) an excuse like this, O ignoble simpleton, you sacrifice all—your life, your property, and your wife;

3065    (For) afterwards every one will pluck your moustache and offer (the same) excuse and make himself out to be acting under compulsion.

If 'the decree of God' seems to you a proper excuse, then instruct me and give me a canonical decision (on the point)[5];

For I have a hundred desires and lusts, (but) my hand is tied by fear and awe (of God).

---

[1] Literally, "bent double."        [2] Literally, "no hand over you."
[3] *I.e.* the last permissible meal during the time between sunset and dawn in the month of Ramaḍán, when the Moslem fasts from dawn to sunset.
[4] Literally, "O my two bright eyes," *i.e.* "my dear friend."
[5] This is said ironically.

Do me a favour, then: teach me the excuse, untie the knots from my hands and feet!

You have chosen a handicraft, (thereby) saying (virtually), 'I have a (certain) choice and a (certain) thought.'

Otherwise, how have you chosen that (particular) handicraft 3070 out of all the rest, O master of the house?

When the hour comes for the flesh and the passions (to be indulged), there comes to you as great a power of choice as is possessed by twenty men;

When your friend deprives you of a farthing of profit, the power to pick a quarrel (with him) is (at once) developed in your soul;

(But) when the hour comes for thanksgiving on account of (God's) benefactions, you have no power of choice and are inferior to a stone.

Assuredly this will be the excuse of your Hell[1], (namely), 'Consider me excused for this burning!'

Since no one holds you excusable on this plea, and (since) this 3075 (plea) does not keep you out of[2] the hands of the executioner,

(Clearly), then, the (present) world is arranged according to this rule[3], and the state of things in yonder world too is made known to you.

*Another Story in answer to the Necessitarian, confirming (Man's) power of choice and the validity of the (Divine) commands and prohibitions, and showing that the Necessitarian's excuse is not accepted in any religious sect or in any religion and that it does not save him from being duly punished for the (sinful) actions which he has committed, just as the Necessitarian Iblís was not saved (from punishment) by saying (to God), 'Because Thou hast made me to err.' And the little indicates the much.*

A certain man was climbing up a tree and vigorously scattering the fruit in the manner of thieves.

The owner of the orchard came along and said (to him), 'O rascal, where is your reverence for God? What are you doing?'

He replied, 'If a servant of God eat from God's orchard the dates which God has bestowed upon him as a gift,

Why do you vulgarly blame (him)? Stinginess at the table of 3080 the all-Rich Lord!'

'O Aybak,' said he, 'fetch that rope, that I may give my answer to Bu 'l-Ḥasan (to this fine fellow).'

Then at once he bound him tightly to the tree and thrashed him hard on the back and legs with a cudgel.

He (the thief) cried, 'Pray, have some reverence for God! Thou art killing me miserably who am innocent.'

---

[1] *I.e.* the Hell to which you will be consigned.    [2] Literally, "far from."
[3] Literally, "by means of this judge," *i.e.* the power of choice, which decides our actions for us.

He answered, 'With God's cudgel this servant of His is soundly beating the back of another servant.

3085    'Tis God's cudgel, and the back and sides belong to Him: I am (only) the slave and instrument of His command.'

He (the thief) said, 'O cunning knave, I make a recantation of Necessitarianism: there is free-will, there is free-will, (there is) free-will!'

His (God's universal) power of choice brought (our individual) powers of choice into existence: His power of choice is like a rider (hidden) beneath the dust (which he raises).

His (God's) power of choice makes our power of choice; His command is based on (is exercised in virtue of) a power of choice (in us).

Every created being has it in his power to exercise authority over the form (that is) without free-will[1],

3090    So that he (who is in possession of that power) drags (whither he pleases) the (lifeless) prey devoid of will, (or) so that having seized Zayd by the ear, he leads him away.

But (it is) the action of the Lord (that), without (using) any instrument, makes his free-will a noose for him (to catch Zayd)[2].

His (God's) free-will makes him a fetter for Zayd: God makes him (Zayd's captor) His prey without (the help of) dog or snare.

The carpenter has authority over a piece of wood, and the artist has authority over (the portrait of) a beauty;

The ironsmith is a superintendent of iron; the builder also is a ruler over his tools.

3095    This (matter) is extraordinary; for all this (human) free-will is bowing low, like a slave, in (homage to) His (God's) free-will.

When did the power forcibly exercised by you over inanimate objects deprive them of (their) inanimateness?

Similarly, His (God's) power over (our) acts of free-will does not deprive any act of free-will of that (quality).

Declare that His (God's) will is (exercised) in a complete manner, (but) without there being (involved in it) the attribution (to Him) of compulsion (*jabr*) and (responsibility for) error (disobedience to His commands).

Since you have said, 'My unbelief is willed by Him,' know that it is also willed by yourself;

3100    For without your will your unbelief does not exist at all: involuntary unbelief is a self-contradiction.

'Tis abominable and blameworthy to lay a command on one incapable (of obeying it); and anger (on account of his disobedience) is worse, especially from the Merciful Lord.

---

[1] *I.e.* either lacking volition or temporarily deprived of power to exercise it.
[2] *I.e.* his free-will is derived from, and subordinate to, the will and action of God.

An ox is beaten if he refuse the yoke: is an ox (ever) reduced to misery[1] because he will not fly?

Since the ox is not excused for frowardness, wherefore is the owner of the ox (to be held) excusable and infirm?[2]

Since you are not ill, don't bandage your head: you have free-will, don't laugh at your moustache[3].

Endeavour to gain freshness (spiritual grace) from God's cup (of love): then you will become selfless and volitionless.    3105

Then all volition will belong to that Wine, and you will be absolutely excusable, like a drunken man.

Whatsoever you beat will (then) be beaten by the Wine; whatsoever you sweep away will (then) be swept away by the Wine.

The drunken man who has quaffed wine from God's cup—how should he do aught but justice and right?

The magicians[4] said to Pharaoh, 'Stop! He that is drunken hath no care for his hands and feet.

The wine of the One (God) is our (real) hands and feet; the apparent hand is (but) a shadow and worthless.'    3110

*The meaning of 'whatever God willed came to be,' i.e. 'the will is His will and pleasure. Seek His pleasure, be not distressed by the anger of others and the disapproval of others.' Although the word 'kána' (came to be) denotes the past, yet there is no past or future in the action of God, for with God there is neither morn nor eve.*

The saying of (God's) servant[5], 'whatever God wills comes to pass' does not signify 'be lazy (inactive) in that (matter)[6]';

Nay, it is an incitement to entire self-devotion and exertion, meaning, 'Make yourself exceedingly ready to perform that service.'

If you are told, O sage, that what you wish (will come to pass, and that) you have full power to act according to your desire,

Then, if you are neglectful (in serving God), 'tis permissible; for what you wish and say will come to pass.

When (on the contrary) you are told that whatever God wills shall come to pass, and that to Him belongs the authority absolute and everlasting,    3115

Why, then, should not you move round Him like a slave, with the will of a hundred men to perform the devotions due to Him?

If you are told that what the vizier wishes (is law and that) his will is paramount in the exercise of authority,

Will you at once move round (pay court to) him with the zeal

---

[1] Literally, "made abject or sick and sorry (by blows)."
[2] *I.e.* incapacitated.
[3] *I.e.* "don't make a fool of yourself."
[4] Whose hands and feet Pharaoh threatened to cut off (*Qur'án*, VII, 121).
[5] *I.e.* the Prophet Mohammed.
[6] *I.e.* in the matter of serving God.

of a hundred men, that he may pour kindness and munificence on your head,

Or will you flee from the vizier and his palace? This (flight) is not the way to seek his help.

3120  You, inversely, have been made remiss by this saying[1]: you have been turned upside down in your apprehension and thought.

(Suppose you are told that) the command (supreme power) is vested in such and such a lord. Hark, what does this mean? It means, 'Do not sit (consort) with any one except him.

Move round (pay constant homage to) the lord, since the (power to) command belongs to him; for he slays his enemy and saves the life of his friend.

Whatsoever he wills, that same thing you will certainly obtain: do not go astray, prefer his service (to all else).'

(It does) not (mean), 'Since he is possessed of (supreme) authority, do not move round him (do not frequent his court), so that you may fall into his black books and be disgraced[2].'

3125  The interpretation that makes you ardent and hopeful and active and reverent is the true one;

And if it make you slack (in service), know the real truth to be this, that it is an alteration (of the right sense of the saying), not an interpretation.

This (saying) has come (down) in order to make (men) ardent (in serving God), that He may take the hands of those who have lost hope (and deliver them).

Ask the meaning of the Qur'án from the Qur'án alone, and from that one who has set fire to (and extinguished) his idle fancy,

And has become a sacrifice to the Qur'án and is (laid) low (in self-abasement), so that the Qur'án has become the essence of his spirit.

3130  The oil that has wholly devoted itself to the rose—smell either the oil or the rose as you please[3].

*And similarly (the Tradition), 'the Pen has dried' means that the Pen has dried after writing (the words), 'Obedience and dis-obedience (to God) are not on the same level, honesty and stealing are not on the same level.' The Pen has dried (after writing) that thanksgiving and ingratitude are not on the same level. The Pen has dried (after writing) that God does not let the reward of the righteous be lost[4].*

Likewise the (true) interpretation of 'the Pen has dried' (is that) it (this Tradition) is for the purpose of inciting to the most important work (of all).

---

[1] *I.e.* the saying that whatever God wills shall come to pass.
[2] Literally, "become yellow in face." Read درزیووی.
[3] *I.e.* both are equally fragrant.        [4] *Qur'án*, IX, 121.

Therefore the Pen wrote that every action has the effect and consequence appropriate to it.

The Pen has dried (after writing) that if you do wrong (in this world) you will suffer wrong (in the next)[1], and that if you act rightly (here) the result will be your felicity (there).

(If) you behave unjustly, you are damned: the Pen has dried (on that). If you show justice, you eat the fruit (of blessedness): the Pen has dried (on that).

When he (any one) steals, his hand goes[2]: the Pen has dried 3135 (on that). (When) he drinks wine, he becomes intoxicated: the Pen has dried (on that).

Do you deem it allowable, can it be allowable, that on account of the (eternally) prior decree God should come, like a person dismissed from office,

Saying, 'The affair has gone out of My hands: do not approach Me so often, do not entreat (Me) so much'?

Nay, the meaning is: 'the Pen has dried (on this that) justice and injustice are not equal in My sight.

I have laid down a distinction between good and evil; I have also laid down a distinction between the bad and the worse.'

If there be in you a single mote of self-discipline in excess of 3140 (that of) your companion, the grace of God will know,

And will bestow on you that mote's amount of superiority: the mote will step forth as (big as) a mountain (to meet you)[3].

A king before whose throne there is no distinction between the faithful (friend) and the seeker of iniquity—

Between him who trembles in fear of his (the king's) disapproval and him who intrigues against his fortune (empire)—

(So that) there is no difference, but both of them are one to him: he is not a king, may dark earth be on his head!

If your (devotional) labour exceed (that of another) by a single 3145 mote, it (that mote) will be weighed in God's balance.

You continually work yourself to death[4] in the service of these (worldly) kings, (yet) they are ignorant of (the difference between) treachery and honesty.

The words of a tale-bearer who speaks ill of you will cause your service (rendered) during (many) years to be wasted;

(But) the words of tale-bearers do not take their abode[5] in the presence of the King who is *hearing and seeing*.

All the tale-bearers are reduced to despair by Him: they come to us and increase (our) bondage.

They speak much abuse of the King before us, saying, 'Go! 3150

[1] Literally, "(if) you go wrong, wrong will come to you."
[2] *I.e.* his right hand is cut off. Cf. *Qur'án*, v, 42.
[3] *I.e.* on the Day of Judgement.
[4] Literally, "you give up the ghost (in the death-agony)."
[5] *I.e.* make no impression.

The Pen has dried (after writing your destiny). (Therefore) do not keep faith (with Him).'

How should the meaning of 'the Pen has dried' be (this), that acts of perfidy and acts of faithfulness are alike?

Nay, perfidy (in return) for acts of perfidy: the Pen has dried (on that); and faithfulness (in return) for those acts of faithfulness: the Pen has dried (on that).

(True), there may be pardon (for the sinner), but where (for him) is the glorious hope[1] that through piety the servant of God may be (spiritually) illumined?[2]

If a robber be pardoned, he saves his life, (but) how should he become a vizier and keeper of the treasury?

3155   Come, O godly Amínu'ddín[3], for every tiara and ensign[4] has grown from trustworthiness (amánat).

If the Sultan's son become a traitor to him, on that account his head will be severed from his body;

And if a Hindú slave show faithfulness, sovereignty will applaud him (and cry), 'Long may he live!'

What of a slave? If a dog is faithful (in keeping watch) at a door, there are a hundred feelings of satisfaction with him in the heart of the master (of the house).

Since, because of this (faithfulness), he kisses the mouth of a dog, if he (the faithful one) be a lion, how triumphant he will make him!

3160   (Robbers get nothing but pardon), except, to be sure, the robber who performs acts of service (to God) and whose sincerity uproots his (former) perfidy,

Like Fuḍayl[5], the brigand who played straight, because he ran with the strength of ten men towards repentance;

And as the magicians (who) blackened the face of Pharaoh by their fortitude and faithfulness.

They gave their hands and feet (to be cut off as a penalty) for the crime that entailed retaliation: how should that (degree of faithfulness) be attained by means of a hundred years' devotional service?

You who have served (Him) for fifty years, when have you brought into your possession such a sincerity as this?

---

[1] Literally, "the glory of the hope."
[2] Literally, "be white-faced."
[3] Literally, "trusted (guardian) of the (Mohammedan) religion."
[4] *I.e.* every pre-eminent mark of Divine favour.
[5] Fuḍayl ibn 'Iyáḍ, a celebrated Ṣúfí of Khurásán, who died in A.H. 187.

*Story of the dervish who saw at Herát the well-equipped slaves of the 'Amíd of Khurásán, mounted on Arab horses and wearing gold-embroidered coats, caps richly ornamented (with silver or gems), etc. He asked, 'What princes and what kings are these?' On being told that they were not princes, but the slaves of the 'Amíd of Khurásán, he turned his face to Heaven, crying, 'O God, learn from the 'Amíd how to take care of slaves!' There (in Khurásán) the State-accountant (Mustawfí) is called 'Amíd.*

A certain unmannerly (dervish) at Herát, when he saw a noble- 3165
man's slave

Going about in satin raiment with a belt of gold, would turn his face to Heaven[1],

And cry, 'O God, why dost not Thou learn from this bountiful Khwája how to keep (Thy) slave?

O God, let this *ra'ís* (high dignitary) and chosen (minister) of our king teach Thee how to care for Thy slave.'

He (the dervish) was needy and naked and without food: ('twas) in winter (and) he was trembling exceedingly from the (cold) air.

That man (who was) beside himself[2] (with cold and hunger) 3170 committed an impertinence[3]: from grossness (of disposition) he displayed an (impious) audacity.

He relied on the thousands (infinite number) of (God's) gifts, saying (to himself) that the gnostic has become God's booncompanion.

If the king's boon-companion take a liberty, (yet) do not thou behave so, who hast not the same support.

God gave the waist, and the waist is better than the belt: if any one give (thee) a tiara, (yet) He gave the head (that bears it).

(The dervish continued his reproaches) till a certain day when the king accused the Khwája (of dishonesty) and bound him hand and foot,

(While) he put those slaves to the rack, saying, 'Show (to me) 3175 at once the Khwája's buried treasure;

Tell me his secret, O ye rascals, or I will cut your throats and (cut out) your tongues.'

He tortured them during a (whole) month: ('twas) the rack, torment, and anguish by day and by night.

He rent them to pieces, but from their anxiety (for their master) not one slave betrayed the Khwája's secret.

A voice from Heaven said to him (the dervish) in his dream, 'O sir, do thou also learn how to be a slave, and (then) come (to Me).'

[1] Literally, "to the *qibla* (the place towards which a worshipper turns), namely, Heaven."
[2] Literally, "quit of himself."
[3] Literally, "freedom (of speech and manners)."

3180   O you who have torn the coats of the (spiritual) Josephs, know that it is your own fault[1] if the wolf tear you.

Wear, all the year round, (a garment) of that (cloth) which you are weaving; eat and drink, all the year round, of that (crop) which you are sowing.

These continual pangs (which you are suffering) are (the effect of) your own action: this is the meaning of 'the Pen has dried,'

(Namely, that God says), 'My Law (*Sunna*) does not turn aside from rectitude: good shall befall the good, evil the evil.'

Beware, do (good) works, for Solomon[2] is alive: so long as you are a devil, his sword is cutting;

3185   When he (the devil) becomes an angel, he is safe from the sword and has no dread of Solomon.

His (Solomon's) sway is over the devil, not (over) the angel: pain is on the earth, not above the sky.

Abandon this Necessitarianism, which is very empty (of good), in order that you may know what is the inmost secret[3] of Necessity.

Abandon this Necessitarianism of the idle party[4], in order that you may gain knowledge of the Necessity that is (dear) as the soul.

Abandon the state of being loved (by men) and adopt the practice of loving (God), O you who think that you are excellent and pre-eminent.

3190   O you who really are more silent than Night[5], how long will you seek a purchaser for your words?

They (your hearers) nod their heads in your presence for (the purpose of assenting to) you: your time is wasted in the passionate desire of (attracting) them.

You say to me, 'Don't indulge in[6] envy,' (but) how should any one feel envy in consequence of losing naught?[7]

O impudent man, instruction given to the worthless is like drawing a little design on a clod of earth.

Instruct thyself in love (of God) and (spiritual) insight; for that is like a design (engraved) on a solid mass of stone.

3195   Your own self is the (only) pupil that is (really) faithful to you: (all) the others perish: where will you seek them, where?

In order that you may make others erudite and eminent, you are making yourself evil-natured and empty (of true knowledge).

---

[1] Literally, "it is from yourself."
[2] Solomon, to whom the devils were subject, stands here as a type of the Divine vengeance.
[3] Literally, "the secret of the secret."
[4] Literally, "the party of the idlers," *i.e.* those who deny that a man has any power over his actions.
[5] *I.e.* "what you say has no spiritual value."
[6] Literally, "become implicated in."
[7] *I.e.* "you possess nothing that could excite my envy."

(But) when your heart is united with that Eden (of Reality), hark, speak on, and be not afraid of becoming empty.

Hence the (Divine) command, '*Speak!*' came to him (the Prophet), saying, 'O righteous one, it will not fail: this is an (infinite) ocean.'

(God said), '*Be ye silent,*' that is, 'do not waste your water in idle talk, for the orchard is dry-lipped (thirsty).'

This discourse hath no end, O father: leave this discourse and 3200 consider the end.

I am not jealous that they (your pupils) stand (listening) in your presence: they are (really) mocking you, they are not lovers.

Behold your (true) lovers behind the veil of the (Divine) Bounty, crying aloud for you continually.

Be the lover of those unseen lovers: do not cherish[1] the lovers who last (no more than) five days;

For they have devoured you by means of a (great) deceit and attraction (exerted upon you), and during (many) years you have never seen a grain (of profit) from them.

How long will you set up a show on the public road? You are 3205 footsore[2] (with travel), and no desire (of yours) has been fulfilled.

When you enjoy good health all of them are your friends and comrades, (but) in the hour of pain and sorrow where is any familiar friend but God?

In the hour of eye-ache or toothache will any one take your hand (to help) except Him who comes at the cry of distress?

Therefore (always) recollect that sickness and pain: take warning (from it), like Ayáz from that sheepskin jacket.

Your experience of pain is the sheepskin jacket which Ayáz took into his hand."

*How the Necessitarian infidel again replied to the Sunni who was inviting him to accept Islam and abandon his belief in Necessity, and how the debate was prolonged on both sides; for this difficult and controversial matter cannot be decided except by the real love that has no further interest in it—"and that is God's grace: He bestows it on whom He pleases."*

The Necessitarian infidel began his reply, by which that 3210 eloquent man (the Sunní) was confounded;

But if I relate all those answers and questions, I shall be unable to get on with this Discourse.

We have things of greater importance to say, whereby your understanding will obtain a better clue.

We have told (only) a little of that disputation, O fierce de-

---

[1] Literally, "carve, hew into shape"; hence "make an idol of."
[2] Literally, "you have wounded your foot."

bater, (but) from a little (part) the principle of the whole is evident.

Similarly, there is a disputation, (which will continue) till mankind are raised from the dead, between the Necessitarians and the partisans of (absolute) Free-will.

3215    If he (the disputant of either party) had been incapable of refuting his adversary, their (respective) doctrines would have fallen out of sight (would have failed to maintain themselves).

Since (in that case) they (the disputants) would not have had the means of escape (which consists) in replying (to their opponents), they would therefore have recoiled from the way of perdition (from their erroneous doctrines);

(But) inasmuch as their continuance in that course was (Divinely) destined, God feeds them with (logical) proofs,

In order that he (the disputant) may not be silenced by his adversary's difficult objection, and that he may be prevented from seeing his adversary's success,

So that these two-and-seventy sects may always remain in the world till the Day of Resurrection.

3220    Since this is the world of darkness and occultation, the earth[1] is necessary for (the existence of) the shadow[2].

These two-and-seventy (sects) will remain till the Resurrection: the heretic's talk and argument will not fail.

The high value of a treasury is (shown by the circumstance) that there are many locks upon it.

The greatness of the (traveller's) goal, O well-tried man, is (shown by) the intricate windings of the way and the mountain-passes and the brigands (infesting them).

The greatness of the Ka'ba and its assembly-place is (shown by) the brigandage of the Beduins and the length of the desert (traversed by the pilgrims).

3225    Every (religious) doctrine, every tenet, that is not praise-worthy is (like) a mountain-pass and a barrier and a brigand.

This doctrine has become the adversary and bitter enemy of that, so that the imitator (who adopts the beliefs of others) is in a dilemma[3];

(For) he sees that both the opponents are firm in their doctrine: every sect is pleased with its own path.

If it has no reply (to the arguments brought against it), it will cling obstinately to the same formula[4] till the Day of Resurrection,

Saying, "Our great authorities know the reply to this[5], although the right method (of answering) is hidden from us."

The only muzzle for evil suggestions (of doubt) is Love; else, 3230 when has any one (ever) stopped (such) temptation?

---

[1] *I.e.* the heresies.    [2] *I.e.* doubts which obscure the Truth.
[3] Literally, "is perplexed at the two roads."
[4] Literally, "breath," "utterance."    [5] Literally, "know this reply."

Become a lover, seek a fair minion, hunt a waterfowl from river to river.

How will you get water (spirituality) from that one who takes your water away? How will you apprehend (the truth) from that one (who) consumes your (spiritual) apprehension?

In Love, (which is) glorious and resplendent, you will find intelligible things other than these intelligible things.

To God belong intelligences other than this intelligence of yours, (intelligences) by which the mediate celestial things are ruled;

For by this (individual) intelligence you procure the means of 3235 subsistence, (while) by that other (universal intelligence) you make the tiers of Heaven a carpet (under your feet).

When you gamble away (sacrifice) your intelligence in love of the Lord, He gives you *ten like unto it* or seven hundred.

Those women (of Egypt), when they gambled away (sacrificed) their intelligences, sped onward to the pavilion of Joseph's love.

(Love which is) the cupbearer of life took away their intelligence in one moment: they drank their fill of wisdom all the rest of their lives.

The beauty of the Almighty is the source of a hundred Josephs: O you who are less than a woman, devote yourself to that beauty!

O (dear) soul, Love alone cuts disputation short, for it (alone) 3240 comes to the rescue when you cry for help against arguments.

Eloquence is dumbfounded by Love: it dare not[1] engage in altercation;

For he (the lover) fears that, if he answer back, a pearl (his inner experience) may fall out of his mouth.

He closes his lips tight against (uttering) good or evil (words) lest the pearl should fall from his mouth (and be lost),

Even as the Companion of the Prophet said, "Whenever the Prophet recited sections (of the *Qur'án*) to us,

At the moment of munificence that chosen Messenger would 3245 demand of us attentiveness and a hundred reverences."

'Tis as when a bird is (perched) on your head, and your soul trembles for fear of its flitting,

So you dare not stir from your place, lest your beautiful bird should take to the air;

You dare not breathe, you suppress a cough, lest that *humá* should fly away;

And if any one speak sweet or sour (words) to you, you lay a finger on your lip, meaning, "Hush!"

Bewilderment is (like) that bird: it makes you silent: it puts 3250 the lid on the kettle and fills you with the boiling (of love).

---

[1] Literally, "it has not the gall-bladder (stomach) to."

14

*How the King (Maḥmúd) purposely asked Ayáz, "(Why) art thou telling all this sorrow and joy to a rustic shoe and a sheepskin jacket, which are inanimate?" (His purpose was) that he might induce Ayáz to speak.*

(The King said), "O Ayáz, pray, why are these marks of affection, like (those of) a lover to his adored one, (shown by thee) to a rustic shoe?

Thou hast made a rustic shoe (the object of) thy devotion and religion, as Majnún (made) of his Laylá's face (an object of the same kind).

Thou hast mingled thy soul's love with two old articles (of dress) and hung them both in a chamber.

How long wilt thou speak new words to (those) two old things and breathe the ancient secret into a substance devoid of life?

3255    Like (the poets among) the Arabs, O Ayáz, thou art drawing out long and lovingly thy converse with the (deserted) abodes and the traces of former habitation.

Of what Áṣaf are thy shoon the abode? One would say that thy sheepskin jacket is the shirt of Joseph."

(This is) like (the case of) the Christian who recounts to his priest a year's sins—fornication and malice and hypocrisy—

In order that the priest may pardon his sins, for he regards his (the priest's) forgiveness as forgiveness from God.

The priest has no (real) knowledge of sin and pardon; but love and firm belief are mightily bewitching.

3260    Love and imagination weave (create) a hundred (forms beautiful as) Joseph: in sooth they are greater sorcerers than Hárút and Márút.

They cause a form (of phantasy) to appear in memory of him (your Beloved): the attraction of the form leads you into (conversation with it).

You tell a hundred thousand secrets in the form's presence, just as a friend speaks (intimately) in the presence of a friend.

No (material) form or shape is there; (yet) from it proceed a hundred (utterances of the words) "*Am not I* (thy Beloved)?" and (from you) a hundred "*Yeas.*"

('Tis) as when a mother, distraught (with grief) beside the grave of a child newly dead,

3265    Utters heart-felt words earnestly and intensely: the inanimate (corpse) seems to her to be alive.

She regards that dust as living and erect, she regards that rubbish as (having) an eye and an ear.

To her, at the moment when she is crazed (with grief), every atom of the earth in the grave seems to have hearing and intelligence.

She believes with all her might that the earth is hearkening (to her): look well at this Love that works magic!

Fondly 'and with tears she lays her face, time after time, on the fresh earth of the grave in such wise

As during his life she never laid her face on the son who was 3270 so dear to her;

(But) when some days pass in mourning, the fire of her love sinks to rest.

Love for the dead is not lasting: keep your love (fixed) on the Living One who increases spiritual life.

Afterwards, indeed, from that grave (nothing) comes to her (but) slumber (indifference and oblivion): from an insensible object is born in her the same insensibility,

Because Love has carried off his enchantment and gone away: as soon as the fire is sped, (only) ashes remain.

The (wise) Elder (*Pír*) beholds in the (iron) brick all that the 3275 (ignorant) young man beholds in the mirror.

The Elder is thy love, not (the owner of) a white beard. 'Tis he (Love) that gives a helping hand to thousands who are in despair.

In (the hour of) separation Love fashions forms (of phantasy); in the hour of union the Formless One puts forth his head,

Saying, "I am the ultimate origin[1] of sobriety and intoxication: the beauty in (all) forms is reflected from Me.

At this moment I have removed the veils: I have raised Beauty on high without intermediaries.

Because thou hast been much occupied with My reflexion, 3280 thou hast gained the power to contemplate My essence denuded[2] (of the forms by which it is veiled).

When My pull is set in motion (begins to be exerted) from this side, he (the Christian) does not see (is not conscious of) the priest intervening (between him and Me)."

(At that time) he is craving forgiveness for his sins and trespasses from the grace of God behind the veil.

When a fountain gushes from a rock, the rock disappears in the fountain.

After that, no one calls it "stone," seeing that such a pure substance has gushed forth from the rock.

Know that these forms are (like) bowls and acquire excellence 3285 through that which God pours into them.

[1] Literally, "the origin of the origin."
[2] Literally, "to denude My essence."

*How the kinsfolk of Majnún said to him, "The beauty of Laylá is limited, it is not so very great: in our city there are many fairer than she. We will show unto thee one or two or ten: take thy choice, and deliver us (from reproach) and thyself (from affliction)"; and how Majnún answered them.*

The fools in their ignorance said to Majnún, "The beauty of Laylá is not so very great, it is of slight account.

There are thousands of moon-like sweethearts[1] fairer than she in our city."

He replied, "The (outward) form is a pot, and beauty is the wine: God is giving me wine from her form.

He gave you vinegar from her pot, lest love of her should pull you by the ears."

3290    The hand of God, the Almighty and Glorious, gives poison or honey to every one from the same pot.

Thou seest the pot, but the wine does not show itself[2] to the wrong eye.

Spiritual experience is (like) *the women who look modestly*[3]: it shows no sign but to its possessor.

That wine is (like) *the women who look modestly*, while these vessels screening it (from view) are like *the tents*[4].

The great river (too) is (like) a tent, wherein is life for the duck, but death for crows.

3295    Venom also is the snake's food and provision, (but) its venom is anguish and death to others.

The form of every blessing and affliction is a Hell to this one, a Paradise to that one.

Therefore (though) *ye see* all bodies and things, and there is food and poison in them (all)—*ye see (it) not.*

Every body resembles a bowl or a pot, wherein is both food and a (cause of) heart-burning.

The bowl is visible, the plenty (contained) in it is hidden: (only) he who tastes it (the contents) knows what he is eating or drinking from it.

3300    The form of Joseph was like a beauteous cup: from it his father drank a hundred exhilarating wines.

Again, to his brethren (the draught they took) from it was poisoned water which was increasing in them anger and hatred.

Again, to Zalíkhá (the draught she took) from it was (sweet as) sugar: she was quaffing a different opiate from (the hand of) Love.

The nutriment which came from Joseph to that fair one was other than that which came to Jacob[5].

___

[1] Literally, "heart-captivating ones."      [2] Literally, "its face."
[3] Literally, "*the women who restrict their eyes (to looking at their husbands),*" *i.e.* the houris in Paradise.
[4] See *Qur'án*, LV, 72.
[5] *I.e.* Zalíkhá's love for Joseph was sensual, while Jacob's love was spiritual.

The sherbets are various, but the pot is one, in order that no doubt may remain in thee concerning the wine of the Unseen.

The wine belongs to the Unseen, the pot to this world: the 3305 pot is apparent, the wine in it is very hidden:

Very hidden from the eyes of the uninitiated, but manifest and evident to the adept.

O my God, our eyes have been intoxicated. Forgive us: our burdens have been made heavy.

O concealed One who hast filled (the world) from East to West (with Thy radiance) and art exalted above the light of the Orient and the Occident[1],

Thou art an inmost Ground of consciousness revealing our inmost thoughts, Thou art a bursting (Force) that causes our (dammed-up) rivers to burst forth.

O Thou whose Essence is hidden while Thy gifts are sensible, 3310 Thou art as the water and we as the millstone.

Thou art as the wind and we as the dust: the wind is hidden while the dust blown by it is plainly visible.

Thou art the Spring, we are fair as the verdant orchard: it (the Spring) is hidden while its bounty is manifest.

Thou art as the spirit, we are like hand and foot: the closing and opening of the hand is due to the spirit.

Thou art as the reason, we are like this tongue: this tongue hath its (power of) expression from the reason.

Thou art like the joy, and we are the laughter, for we are the 3315 result of (Thy) blessed joy.

(All) our movement (action) is really a continual profession of faith[2] which bears witness to the Eternal Almighty One.

The turning of the millstone in agitation is a profession of faith in the existence of the waterbrook.

O Thou who art beyond my conception and utterance, dust be on the head of me and my similes!

Thy servant cannot refrain from depicting Thy beauty[3]: every moment he says to Thee, "May my soul be Thy carpet!"

(He is) like the shepherd who used to say, "O God, come to 3320 Thy shepherd and lover,

That I may seek out the lice in Thy smock and stitch Thy shoon and kiss Thy skirt[4]."

There was none equal to him[5] in passion and love, but he fell short in glorification and (respectful) speech.

His love pitched its tent on the sky: the (beloved) Soul became the dog (guardian) of that shepherd's tent.

When the sea of Divine Love surged up, it struck upon his heart; it struck (only) upon your ear.

[1] Literally, "the place of sunrise and the place of sunset."
[2] Literally, "an 'I testify.'"
[3] Literally, "from the fair picture of Thee."
[4] See Book II, v. 1720 foll.   [5] Literally, "coupled with him."

*Story of Júḥí, who put on a chádar[1], went to hear the sermon[2], seated himself amongst the women, and behaved in such a way that a certain woman knew he was a man and screamed.*

3325　There was a preacher, very fine in his exposition, under whose pulpit a great number of men and women were assembled.

Júḥí went (to hear him): he got a *chádar* and veil and entered amongst the women without (his sex) being recognised.

Some one asked the preacher secretly[3] num pili in pube precibus sollennibus detrimentum faciant.

The preacher replied, "Quo tempore pili in pube longi fiunt, tum noxa est ob illos in precibus sollennibus.

Vel psilothro vel novacula illos tonde, in order that your ritual prayer may be perfect and excellent and seemly."

3330　The questioner said, "Ad quem modum pervenire oportet eorum longitudinem ut preces meae detrimentum capiant?"

He replied, "Cum longitudine tanti evaserint quantum hordei unum granum, relligio est ut tondeas, O multa rogitans."

At once Júḥí said (to the woman beside him), "O soror, in-spice piline in pube mea hujusmodi facti sint.

Deo ut placeas, manum affer, (tenta) num illi usque ad modum noxae pervenerint."

Mulier manum in bracas viri demisit: penis ejus impegit manum mulieris.

3335　Thereupon the woman gave a loud scream: the preacher said, "My discourse has smitten her heart."

He (Júḥí) answered, "Minime: cor ejus non percussit, manum percussit. O si cor percussisset, vir sapientissime!"

(When) it (Divine Love) struck a little upon the hearts of the magicians (of Pharaoh), staff and hand became one to them[4].

O king[5], if you take away the staff from an old man, he will be more grieved than that party (the magicians) were (grieved) by (the amputation of) their hands and feet.

The cry, "*No harm*[6]," reached Heaven: (they said to Pharaoh), "Hark, cut (them) off, for our souls are delivered from the agony.

3340　We have come to know (that) we are not this body: beyond the body we are living through God."

Oh, blest is he that has recognised his (real) essence and built (for himself) a palace in everlasting security.

A child weeps for walnuts and raisins; those are very trifling things in the view of a reasonable man.

(So) in the spirit's view the body is (like) walnuts and raisins, (but) how should (one who is) a child (in spiritual matters) attain to the knowledge possessed by (spiritual) men?

---

[1] A long mantle worn by women.　　[2] Literally, "and at the sermon."
[3] *I.e.* by writing a note and handing it to him.
[4] *I.e.* they lost all power of discrimination.
[5] *I.e.* "O excellent reader."　　　　[6] *Qur'án*, xxvi, 50.

Whoever is veiled (from God) is really a child: the man is he who is beyond (all) uncertainty.

Siquis barba et testiculis vir esset, every he-goat has a beard 3345 and plenty of hair.

That goat is a bad leader: he is taking his followers quickly along to the butcher.

He has combed his beard, saying, "I am the foremost." (Yes); thou art the foremost, but in the direction of death and anguish.

Hark, adopt (as thy vocation) travelling (on the Way of righteousness) and abandon thy beard: abandon this egoism and troubled thought,

That thou mayst become like the scent of the rose to (God's) lovers (and mayst be) their leader and guide to the Rose-garden.

Who (what) is the scent of the rose? The breath (voice) of 3350 reason and intelligence (which is) a sweet guide on the way to the Kingdom Everlasting.

*How the King (Maḥmúd) once more commanded Ayáz, saying, "Give a clear explanation concerning thy rustic shoon and sheepskin jacket in order that thy fellow-servants may be admonished by that indication; for (the Prophet has said), 'Religion consists in (giving) sincere counsel.'"*

"O Ayáz, declare the mystery of the rustic shoon and why in the presence of the shoon thou showest all this humility,

So that thy (fellow-servants) Sunqur and Bakyáruq may hear the inmost secret[1] of thy sheepskin jacket and rustic shoon.

O Ayáz, slavery hath gained lustre from thee: thy lustre hath sped from lowliness towards heaven.

Servitude has become an object of regret to the free[2], since thou hast given life (and splendour) to servitude.

The true believer is he by whose true belief amidst the ebb 3355 and flow (of fortune) the infidel is made regretful."

*Story of the infidel whom, in the time of Abá Yazíd[3] (Báyazíd), they invited to become a Moslem; and how he answered them.*

There was a certain infidel in the time of Báyazíd: a blessed Moslem said to him,

"How would it be if you profess Islam, so that you may gain a hundred salvations and sovereignties?"

He replied, "If this Faith (of thine), O disciple, is (the same as) that which is held by Báyazíd, the Shaykh (spiritual Director) of the world,

---

[1] Literally, "the secret of the secret."
[2] *I.e.* they regret that they are not slaves.
[3] The spelling Abá (instead of Abú) is supported by the authority of the oldest MSS.

I cannot endure the glowing heat thereof, which is too great for (all) the strivings of my soul (to attain unto it).

3360   Although I feel no certainty as regards the Faith and Religion (of Islam), yet I believe mightily in his Faith.

I hold the faith that that (Faith of his) is higher than all (others): 'tis very beautiful, resplendent, and glorious.

Inwardly I am a believer in his Faith, though a seal is set firmly on my mouth.

Again, if indeed the Faith (which thou wouldst have me embrace) is your Faith, I have no inclination or desire for it.

He that feels a hundred inclinations to believe—that (inclination) languishes as soon as he sees you (Moslems),

3365   Because he sees a (mere) name and no meaning in it, like calling the desert *mafáza* (a safe place).

When he looks upon your Faith, his love is chilled (and shrinks) from professing it."

*Story of the harsh-voiced muezzin who called (the Moslems) to prayer in the land of the infidels and to whom a certain infidel offered presents.*

A certain muezzin had a very harsh voice: he called (the Moslems to prayer) in the land of the infidels.

They said to him several times, "Do not give the call to prayer, for (otherwise) fighting and acts of hostility (against us) will be prolonged."

He defied (them), and then without showing (any) caution he gave the call to prayer in the land of the infidels.

3370   The (Moslem) folk were in fear of a general insurrection; however, an infidel came up (to them) with a robe.

He brought (with him) candles and *ḥalwá* and such a (fine) robe as gifts, and approached in a friendly manner,

Asking again and again, "Tell me, where is this muezzin, whose call and cry increases my pleasure?"

"Eh, what pleasure was there from such a harsh voice?" He replied, "His voice penetrated into the church.

I have a comely daughter of very high estate: she was desiring (to marry) a true believer.

3375   Never would this passion go out of her head, (though) so many infidels were exhorting her.

Love of the Faith had grown up in her heart: this grief was like a censer and I like the aloes-wood (burning in it).

I was in torment and anguish and continually on the rack lest her passion should lead her (to embrace Islam)[1].

I knew no remedy for it until this muezzin chanted the *adhán* (call to prayer).

---

[1] Literally, "lest her chain (the passion by which she was being dragged along) should move (towards Islam)."

(Then) my daughter said, 'What is this detestable noise? It grates on my ear[1].

Never in all my life have I heard such a harsh voice in this 3380 Christian convent and church.'

Her sister said to her, 'This chant, namely the *adhán*, gives (the Moslems) notice (of prayer-time) and is the watchword of the Faithful.'

She would not believe it, and asked some one else: that person too said, 'Yes, (it is true), O father[2].'

When she became sure (of this), her face turned pale and her heart grew cold (averse) to Islam.

I was delivered from anxiety and torment: last night I slept sound in a peaceful[3] sleep.

This was the pleasure (that came) to me from his voice: in 3385 gratitude I bring (these) gifts: where is the man?"

When he saw him (the muezzin), he said, "Accept the gift, for thou hast been my protector and saviour.

(On account of) the benefit and kindness that thou hast done to me, I have become thy slave perpetually.

If I were eminent in respect of property, possessions, and riches, I would fill thy mouth with gold."

"The Faith of you (Moslems) is hypocrisy and falsehood[4]: like that call to prayer, it waylays (the seeker and prevents him from embracing Islam);

But many a regret has come into my heart and soul from (my 3390 admiration for) the Faith and sincerity of Báyazíd."

Tanquam illa femina[5] quae, cum concubitum asini videret, dixit: "Eheu, quid est hic admissarius egregius?

Si concubitus hoc est, hi asini (praemium) abstulerunt: cacant super vulvis nostris hi mariti."

Báyazíd paid all that is due to (fulfilled every obligation of) the Faith: blessings be on such a peerless lion!

If a single drop of his Faith enter into the ocean, the ocean will be submerged in his drop,

As (when) a mote of fire (falls) amidst forests, the (whole) 3395 forest passes away in that mote;

(Or) as (when) a phantasy (appears) in the heart of a king or his army, (a phantasy which) destroyed his enemies in war.

A star[6] (of Divine illumination) appeared[7] in Mohammed, so that the substance of (the beliefs of) Magian and Jew passed away.

---

[1] In *v.* 3703 *infra* دو چار دانگ signifies "worthless." Here, according to the commentators, it is equivalent to ثقیل و قبیح, "harsh and abominable."

[2] پدر ("father") is often used as a title of respect; its application to a young girl must be humorous or ironical.          [3] Literally, "fearless."

[4] Here the speaker is the infidel of the preceding story.

[5] See *v.* 1333 foll.          [6] Read یك ستاره.

[7] Literally, "showed its face."

He that received the Faith entered into security; the infidelities of the rest became (a matter on which there were) two opinions.

At any rate, their first pure (entire) unbelief did not remain (with them): it (the star of Mohammed) planted (in them) either (formal acceptance of) Islam or a (great) dread (of it).

3400 This (description of the Faith of Báyazíd) is a (mere) makeshift varnishing[1]: these similes are not equivalent to the mote of (Divine light).

A mote is only a paltry bodily thing: a mote is not the indivisible Sun.

Know that (my) calling it (the Sun) a mote has a purpose hidden (from thee, for) thou art not familiar with the Sea: at present thou art (but) the foam.

If the luminous sun of the Shaykh's Faith should display itself from the Orient of the Shaykh's spirit,

All below, down to the moist clay (beneath the earth's crust), would gain (abundant) treasure, and all above would gain a verdant Paradise.

3405 He hath a spirit of resplendent light, he hath a body of despicable earth.

Oh, I wonder whether he is this or that. Tell (me), uncle, for I am left (helpless) in this difficulty.

O brother, if he is this, (then) what is that?—for the Seven Heavens are filled with its light—

And if he is that (spirit), (then) what is this body, my friend? Oh, I wonder which of these twain he is and who?

*Story of the woman who told her husband that the cat had eaten the meat, (whereupon) the husband put the cat in the balance (in order to weigh her). (Finding that) her weight amounted to half a "mann", he said, "O wife, the meat weighed half a 'mann' and more. If this is the meat, where is the cat? Or if this is the cat, where is the meat?"*

There was a man, a householder, who had a very sneering, dirty, and rapacious wife.

3410 Whatever (food) he brought (home), his wife would consume it, and the man was forced to keep silence.

(One day) that family man brought home, for a guest, (some) meat (which he had procured) with infinite pains[2].

His wife ate it up with *kabáb* and wine: (when) the man came in, she put him off with useless words.

The man said to her, "Where is the meat? The guest has arrived: one must set nice food before a guest."

---

[1] Literally, "a making water and oil (varnish) by contrivance."
[2] Literally, "with two hundred prolonged exertions."

"This cat has eaten the meat," she replied: "hey, go and buy some more meat if you can!¹"

He said (to the servant), "O Aybak, fetch the balance: I will 3415 weigh the cat².

He weighed her. The cat was half a *mann*. Then the man said, "O deceitful wife,

The meat was half a *mann* and one *sitír* over; the cat is just half a *mann*, my lady.

If this is the cat, then where is the meat? Or, if this is the meat, where is the cat? Search (for her)!"

If Báyazíd is this (body), what is that spirit? And if he is that spirit, who is this (bodily) image?

'Tis bewilderment on bewilderment. O my friend, (the solu- 3420 tion of) this (problem) is not your affair, nor is it mine either.

He is both (spirit and body), but in the corn-crop the grain is fundamental, while the stalk is derivative.

(The Divine) Wisdom has bound these contraries together: O butcher, this fleshy thigh-bone goes along with the neck³.

The spirit cannot function without the body; your body is frozen (inanimate) and cold (inert) without the spirit.

Your body is visible, while your spirit is hidden from view: the business of the world is conducted by means of them both.

If you throw earth at (some one's) head, his head will not be 3425 broken; if you throw water at his head, it will not be broken.

If you wish to break his head, you bring the earth and the water into contact with each other (and make a lump of clay).

When you have broken your head⁴, its water (the spirit) re- turns to its source, and earth returns to earth on the day of separation.

The providential purpose that God had—namely, humble supplication or obstinate contumacy⁵—was fulfilled by means of the marriage (of body and spirit).

Then (afterwards) there are other marriages that no ear hath heard and no eye hath seen.

If the ear had heard, how should the ear have remained (in 3430 action) or how should it have apprehended words any more?

If the snow and ice⁶ were to behold the sun⁷, they would de- spair of (retaining their) iciness;

They would become water (formless and) devoid of roots and

---

¹ Literally, "if it may be (possible)."
² Literally, "I will put the cat (in it) to compare her weight (with that of the meat)."
³ A proverb alluding to the Persian butcher's habit of giving his customers a cut partly from the thigh and partly from the neck.
⁴ *I.e.* "when you die."
⁵ *I.e.* the manifestation of faith or infidelity.
⁶ *I.e.* the sensual man.  ⁷ *I.e.* Divine Love.

knobs[1]: the air, David-like[2], would make of the water a mail-coat (of ripples),

And then it (the water) would become a life-giving medicine for every tree: every tree (would be made) fortunate by its advent.

(But) the frozen ice that remains (locked) within itself cries to the trees, *Touch me not!*[3]

3435   Its body makes none its friend nor is it made a friend by any: its portion is naught but miserly selfishness.

It is not wasted (entirely), the heart[4] is refreshed by it; but it is not the herald and lord of (the vernal) greenery.

"O Ayáz, thou art a very exalted star[5]: not every sign of the zodiac is worthy of its transit.

How should thy lofty spirit be satisfied with every loyalty? How should thy pureness choose (to accept) every sincerity?"

*Story of the Amír who bade his slave fetch some wine: the slave went off and was bringing a jug of wine, (when) an ascetic (who) was on the road admonished him that he should act righteously and threw a stone and smashed the jug; the Amír heard (of this) and resolved to punish the ascetic. That happened in the epoch of the religion of Jesus[6], on whom be peace, when wine had not yet been declared unlawful; but the ascetic was showing an abhorrence (for worldly pleasure) and preventing (others) from indulging themselves.*

There was an Amír of merry heart, exceedingly fond of wine: (he was) the refuge[7] of every drunkard and every resourceless person.

3440   (He was) a compassionate man, kind to the poor and just; a jewel (of bounty), gold-lavishing, ocean-hearted;

A king of men and commander of the Faithful; a keeper of the Way and a knower of secrets and a discerner of friends.

'Twas the epoch of Jesus and the days of the Messiah: he (the Amír) was beloved of the people and unoppressive and agreeable.

Suddenly one night, another Amír, a person of good principles (who was) congenial to him, came seeking his hospitality.

They wanted wine in order to enjoy themselves[8]: at that period wine was permissible and lawful;

3445   (But) they had no wine, so he (the Amír) said to his slave, "Go, fill the jug and fetch us wine

---

[1] *I.e.* pure spirit.
[2] Literally, "the David of the air." For David as a maker of mail-coats see *Qur'án*, xxi, 80.
[3] Like Sámirí (*Qur'án*, xx, 97).          [4] Literally, "the liver."
[5] The speaker is Sultan Maḥmúd.
[6] *I.e.* in the early Christian era.          [7] Literally, "cave."
[8] Literally, "to harmonise their state of mind."

From such-and-such a Christian ascetic who has choice wine, that the soul (in us) may win release from high and low."

One draught from the Christian ascetic's cup has the same effect as thousands of wine-jars and wine-cellars.

In that (Christian's) wine there is a hidden (spiritual) substance, even as (spiritual) sovereignty is (hidden) in the dervish-cloak.

Do not regard (merely) the tattered cloak, for they have put black on the outside of the gold[1].

On account of the evil eye he (the dervish) becomes (apparently) reprobate, and that (spiritual) ruby is tarnished with smoke on the outside. 3450

When are treasures and jewels (exposed to view) in the rooms of a house? Treasures are always (hidden) in ruins.

Since Adam's treasure was buried in a ruin, his clay became a bandage over the eye of the accursed (Iblís).

He (Iblís) was regarding the clay with the utmost contempt, (but) the spirit (of Adam) was saying, "My clay is a barrier to thee."

The slave took two jugs and ran with goodwill: (almost) immediately he arrived at the monastery of the Christian monks.

He paid gold and purchased wine like gold: he gave stones and bought jewels in exchange. 3455

('Twas) a wine that would fly to the head of kings and put a golden tiara on the crown of the cupbearer's head.

(By it) troubles and commotions are aroused, slaves and emperors are mingled together;

Bones vanish and become spirit entirely; throne and bench at that moment become alike.

They (the drinkers), when sober, are as water and oil[2]; when intoxicated, they are as the spirit in the body.

They become like a *harísa*[3]: no difference exists there: there is no difference that is not submerged there. 3460

The slave was carrying a wine of this sort to the palace of the Amír of good renown,

(When) an ascetic met him, one who had suffered anguish, whose brain was dry, and who was (writhing) in the coils of affliction;

His body melted by the fires of his heart; the house (of his heart) emptied of all but God.

The chastisement of pitiless tribulation (had seared him with) brands on brands, (ever) so many thousands.

Every hour saw his heart (engaged) in the struggle: by day and night he was firmly attached to (intent upon) the struggle. 3465

---

[1] *I.e.* the black woollen cloak worn by the dervish conceals his spiritual worth like the black pigment with which gold is disguised.
[2] *I.e.* contrary and different.
[3] A pottage of boiled wheat and meat pounded together.

During years and months he had been mixed up with dust and blood: (on seeing the slave) at midnight, his patience and forbearance fled (from him).

"What is that in the jugs?" asked the ascetic. "Wine," replied the slave. "Whose wine?" said he.

He (the slave) answered, "It belongs to so-and-so, the most honourable Amír." Said he, "Is the seeker's work like this?

(To be) a seeker of God, and then (indulge in) pleasure and drinking! (To drink) the Devil's wine, and then be (even) semi-intelligent!"

3470  (Even) without wine your intelligence is so shabby (that other) intelligences must be tied (added) to your (present) intelligence.

Consider, (then), what your intelligence will be at the time when you are intoxicated, O you who like a bird have fallen a prey to the snare of intoxication.

*Story of Ẓiyá-yi Dalq, who was very tall, while his brother, the Shaykh of Islam Táj of Balkh, was exceedingly short; and this Shaykh of Islam was ashamed of his brother Ẓiyá. (One day) Ẓiyá came to (hear) his brother's lecture, at which all the leading men of Balkh were present. Ẓiyá made a bow (to his brother) and passed on. The Shaykh of Islam half rose (from his seat) in a negligent manner, (whereupon) he (Ẓiyá) said, " Yes, you are very tall: take a bit off (your height)!"*

Ẓiyá-yi Dalq was a man of goodly inspiration: he was the brother of Táj, the Shaykh of Islam.

Táj, the Shaykhu 'l-Islám of the imperial city of Balkh, was short of stature and small as a chick.

Though he was learned and eminent and accomplished, (his brother) this Ẓiyá was superior in wit.

3475  He (Táj) was very short, while Ẓiyá was tall beyond measure: the Shaykh of Islam had a hundred arrogances and haughty airs.

He felt ashamed of this brother and disgraced (by him); yet Ẓiyá was a preacher in the way of salvation[1].

On the day of congregation Ẓiyá came in: the hall was filled with cadis and men distinguished (for piety).

In his complete arrogance the Shaykh of Islam (only) half rose (from his seat), in such a (careless) fashion, to (salute) his brother.

He (Ẓiyá) said to him, "Thou art very tall: take a little off thy cypress-like stature in order to gain the (Divine) reward."

3480  (The ascetic said), "How, then, have you the intelligence, how have you the (necessary) understanding to drink wine, O enemy of knowledge?

(If) your face is very beautiful, put some indigo on it (as an

───────
[1] Literally, "(endowed by God) with right guidance."

ornament); (but) indigo on the face of an Abyssinian (negro) would be a laughing-stock.

When did any (spiritual) light enter into you, O misguided man, that you should become a seeker of unconsciousness and darkness?

'Tis the (approved) rule to seek the shadow during the day; (but) you seek the shadow on a cloudy night.

If it (wine) is lawful as sustenance for the common folk, (yet) it is unlawful to those who seek the Beloved.

The wine for the lovers (of God) is their heart's blood: their 3485 eyes are (fixed) upon the Way and upon the Destination.

In this Way across the terrible wilderness the guide, Reason, suffers a hundred eclipses.

(If) you throw dust in the eyes of the guides, you will cause the caravan to perish and lose the way.

In sooth, barley bread is unlawful and injurious to the carnal soul: set (only) bread made of bran before it.

Keep in abject submission the enemy on the Way to God: do not place a pulpit for the robber, (but) keep him on the gibbet.

Deem the amputation of the robber's hand desirable: if you 3490 are unable to cut his hand off, bind it.

Unless you bind his hand, he will bind yours; unless you break his leg, he will break yours.

You give the enemy wine and sugar-cane—for what reason? Bid him laugh venomously and eat earth."

In his indignation he (the ascetic) hurled a stone at the jug and broke it: he (the slave) let the jug fall and sprang away from the ascetic.

He went to the Amír, who said to him, "Where is the wine?" He (the slave) related in his presence all that had happened, point by point.

### How the enraged Amír set out to punish the ascetic.

The Amír became like fire and jumped straight up. "Show 3495 me," he cried, "where the ascetic's house is,

That I may pound his head with this heavy club—his ignorant whoreson head.

What should he know about enjoining (others) to do right? He is currishly seeking notoriety and fame,

In order that by means of this hypocrisy he may make a position for himself and somehow make himself conspicuous;

For in truth he has no talent save this alone, that he plays the hypocrite to all and sundry[1].

[1] Literally, "to this one and that one."

3500    If he is mad and bent on mischief[1], the cure for a madman is an ox-hide whip[2],

So that the devil may go forth from his head: how should an ass go (forward) without the ass-drivers' blows?"

The Amír dashed out, with a mace in his hand: at midnight he came, half-intoxicated, to the ascetic.

In his rage he wished to kill the ascetic, (but) the ascetic hid beneath (some) wool.

The ascetic, hidden under the wool belonging to certain rope-makers, heard that (threat) from the Amír.

3505    He said (to himself), "(Only) the mirror that has made its face hard can tell a man to his face that he is ugly.

It needs a steel face, like a mirror, to say to thee, 'Behold thy ugly face.'"

### Story of Dalqak's checkmating the Sayyid, the Sháh of Tirmid.

The Sháh was playing chess with Dalqak: he (Dalqak) check-mated him: immediately the Sháh's anger burst out.

He (Dalqak) cried, "Checkmate, checkmate!" and the haughty monarch threw the chessmen, one by one, at his head,

Saying, "Take (it)! Here is 'checkmate' for you, O scoundrel." Dalqak restrained himself and (only) said, "Mercy!"

3510    The Prince commanded him to play a second game: he (Dalqak) was trembling like a naked man in bitter cold.

He played the second game, and the Sháh was defeated: (when) the time and moment for saying "checkmate, check-mate" arrived,

Dalqak jumped up and ran into a corner and in his fear hastily flung six rugs over himself.

(There) he lay hidden beneath (several) cushions and six rugs, that he might escape from the Sháh's blows.

The Sháh exclaimed, "Hi, hi! what have you done? What is this?" He replied, "Checkmate, checkmate, checkmate, check-mate, O excellent Sháh!

3515    How can one tell the truth to thee except under cover, O wrathful man who art wrapped in fire,

O thou who art defeated (by me), while I, defeated by thy Majesty's blows, am crying 'checkmate, checkmate' under thy house-furnishings?"

When the (whole) quarter became filled with the furious shouts of the Amír and his kicking the (ascetic's) door and holding and seizing[3],

The people quickly rushed out from left and right, crying, "O Prince, 'tis the hour for pardon and grace.

---

[1] Literally, "digging up (searching for) mischief."
[2] Literally, "veretrum tauri."        [3] *I.e.* violent behaviour.

His brain is dry, and at this time his intelligence is inferior to the intelligence and understanding of children.

Asceticism and old age have come on the top of each other, 3520 and no (spiritual) revelation[1] has been given to him in his asceticism.

He has suffered the pain but never seen the gain (that comes) from the Beloved: he has done (many) works (of devotion) but never seen the wages for his work.

Either the essential thing was not in his work at all, or by (Divine) decree the hour for the reward has not yet arrived.

Either his labour has been like the labour of the Jews, or the recompense has been connected with (deferred till) the appointed season.

For him 'tis sorrow and misfortune enough that he is without any one (to succour him) in this vale full of blood.

His eyes are painful, and he sits in a corner, sour-faced and 3525 chop-fallen.

There is no oculist to sympathise with him, nor has he any intelligence that he should find the way to a collyrium.

He is making a (great) effort with (the help of) conjecture and opinion: the matter rests in 'maybe' till it turn out well[2].

Far is the road he must travel ere he sees[3] the Beloved, because he does not seek the head; his desire is headship.

At one time he is (engaged) in reproach, saying (to God), 'The portion allotted to me from this calculation (of mine) is (nothing but) pain.'

At another time he is (engaged) in a quarrel with his own luck, 3530 saying, 'All (the others) are flying, and we have our wings cut off.'"

Whoever is imprisoned in scent and colour[4], his spirit is oppressed[5], (even) though he is (occupied) in (the practice of) asceticism.

Until he come forth from this narrow resting-place[6], how should his spirit[7] be happy and his breast expanded (with joy)?

One should never give a knife or razor to ascetics (living) in solitude before (they have gained the spiritual) revelation,

Since the anguish of disappointments and the grief (which they feel) would cause them to rip their bellies asunder from (uncontrollable) agitation of mind.

[1] Literally, "opening" (by way of ecstasy, illumination, vision, etc.).
[2] *I.e.* he has no more than a possibility of success.
[3] Literally, "far is his road till (he gains) the sight of."
[4] *I.e.* worldly vanities.
[5] Literally, "his disposition is contracted."
[6] Literally, "a place where camels lie down (at night)."
[7] Literally, "disposition."

15

*How Muṣṭafá (Mohammed), on whom be peace, (was about to) cast*
*himself down from Mount Ḥirá because of his distress at the long*
*delay of Gabriel, on whom be peace, in appearing; and how*
*Gabriel, on whom be peace, showed himself to him, saying, "Do*
*not cast (thyself down), for (great) fortunes are in front of*
*thee."*

3535    Whenever (the sense of) separation (from God) overpowered[1]
Muṣṭafá, he would be on the point of casting himself down from
the mountain,
    Until Gabriel would say to him, "Hark, do it not, for great
fortune is (coming) to thee from the Command, *Be!*[2]"
    (Then) Muṣṭafá would desist from casting (himself down),
(till) separation again made an attack (upon him).
    (Then) again, from grief and sorrow, he would be on the point
of throwing himself headlong from the mountain,
    And once more Gabriel would appear in person, saying, "Do
it not, O thou peerless (spiritual) king!"
3540    Even thus he would continue until the veil was lifted, so that
he gained the pearl (of his desire) from the bosom (of his inmost
consciousness).
    Since people kill themselves on account of any affliction, this
(separation from God) is the root of (all) afflictions: how should
they endure it?
    Men are amazed at the Fidá'í[3], (but) every one of us is a
Fidá'í in his behaviour.
    Oh, blest is he that has sacrificed his body for the sake of that
for which it is worth while to sacrifice one's self.
    Inasmuch as every one is devoted to some calling wherein he
spends his life and is killed[4]—
3545    Is killed[5] somewhere (either) in the West or in the East,
at which time neither the desiring subject nor the desired object
remains (in existence)—
    After all, this fortunate man[6] is devoted to the calling wherein
a hundred lives are (gained) in being killed;
    Its lover and beloved and love are everlastingly prosperous
and renowned in both worlds.
    O my generous friends, have pity on the votaries of passion:
'tis their business to go down to destruction after destruction.
    (The people said), "O Amír, pardon his (the ascetic's)
violence: consider his sorrow and ill-fortune,

    [1] Literally, "raised (him to the height of despair)."
    [2] *I.e.* the Creative Word of God.
    [3] The Fidá'í's (Assassins) were those members of the Ismáʿílí sect who were
trained to sacrifice their lives in blind obedience to the command of their
Grand Master.
    [4] Literally, "wherein is a spending of life and a killing."
    [5] Literally, "a killing."                [6] Referring to *v.* 3543.

In order that God may pardon thy sins likewise and heap for- 3550 giveness on thy faults.

Thou hast heedlessly broken many a jug and set thy heart on the hope of pardon.

Pardon, that thou mayst win pardon in return: the (Divine) decree splits hairs (is exceedingly scrupulous) in (giving every one his) deserts."

*How the Amír answered those neighbours of the ascetic who inter-ceded for him: " Why," said he, " did he behave (so) impudently and why did he break my jug (of wine)? I will not listen to inter-cession in this matter, for I have sworn to punish him as he deserves."*

The Amír said, "Who is he that he should throw a stone at my jug and break it?

When the fierce lion passes through my quarter, he passes in great affright and with a hundred precautions.

Why did he vex the heart of my slave and put me to shame 3555 before my guests?

He spilt a beverage that is better than his (own) blood, and now he has fled from me, like women.

But how shall he save his life from my hand? (Even) suppose that he flies up on high like a bird,

I will shoot the arrow of my vengeance at his wings, I will tear out his good-for-nothing wings and feathers.

If he enter the hard rock (to escape) from my pursuit[1], I will drag him forth from the heart of the rock just now.

I will inflict on his body such a blow as will be a warning to 3560 base scoundrels[2].

Hypocrisy to all and even to me! I will give him and a hun-dred like him their due at this moment."

His (the Amír's) bloodthirsty wrath had become a rebel[3]: a fire (of rage) was coming up from his mouth.

*How the neighbours of the ascetic, who were interceding for him, kissed the hands and feet of the Amír and humbly entreated him a second time.*

At the breath of his clamour those intercessors kissed his hands and feet several times,

Saying, "O Amír, it does not beseem thee to exact vengeance: if the wine is gone, (yet) thou art delicious without wine.

Wine derives its original substance from thy goodliness; the 3565 goodliness of water regrets (its lack of) thy goodliness.

---

[1] Literally, "effort."
[2] Literally, "vile pimps or wittols."     [3] *I.e.* beyond control.

Act royally, forgive him, O merciful one, O generous son of a generous sire and grandsire.

Every wine is the slave of this (comely) figure and (fair) cheek (of thine): all the drunken feel envy of thee.

Thou hast no need of rosy wine: take leave of (its) rosiness[1], thou (thyself) art (its) rosiness.

O thou whose Venus-like countenance is (bright as) the morning sun, O thou of whose colour (all) rosinesses are beggars,

3570 The wine that is bubbling invisibly in the jar bubbles thus from longing for thy face.

O thou who art the whole sea, what wilt thou do with dew? And O thou who art the whole of existence, why art thou seeking non-existence?

O resplendent Moon, what wilt thou do with the dust, O thou beside whose face the moon is pallid?

Thou art lovely and beautiful and the mine (source) of every loveliness: why indeed shouldst thou lay thyself under obligations to wine?

The tiara of *We have honoured* (*the sons of Adam*) is on the crown of thy head; the collar of *We have given thee* hangs on thy breast.

3575 Man is the substance, and the celestial sphere[2] is his accident; all things are (like) a branch or the step of a ladder[3]: he is the object.

O thou to whom reason and foresight[4] and intelligence are slaves, how art thou selling thyself so cheaply?

Service to thee is imposed on all existence as a duty: how should a substance beg for help from an accident?

Thou seekest knowledge from books—oh, ridiculous! Thou seekest pleasure from *ḥalwá* (sweetmeats)—oh, ridiculous!

Thou art the sea of knowledge hidden in a dewdrop; thou art the universe hidden in a body three ells long.

3580 What is wine or music or sexual intercourse that thou shouldst seek delight and profit therefrom?

('Tis as though) the sun sought to borrow (light) from a mote, (or) a Zuhra[5] begged for a cup (of wine) from a small jar.

Thou art the unconditional spirit imprisoned in conditionality, thou art the sun imprisoned in the (descending) node[6]: here's a pity[7]!"

### How the Amír answered them again.

He replied, "Nay, nay, I am the fellow for that wine: I am not content with tasting this delight (of which ye speak).

I desire such (wine), that, like the jasmine, I may ever be reeling crookedly (now) that way, now this,

---

[1] Literally, "rouge."　　　　　　　　　[2] *I.e.* the world.
[3] *I.e.* secondary and subsidiary.　　　[4] Literally, "proposings."
[5] The planet Venus, which is associated with minstrelsy and festivity.
[6] *I.e.* eclipsed.　　　　　　　　　　　[7] *I.e.* what a shame!

And, having been delivered from all fear and hope, I may be 3585 swaying to every side, like the willow,

Swaying to left and right like the willow-bough, which is made to dance all sorts of dances by the wind."

He that is accustomed to the joy of (spiritual) wine, how should he be satisfied with this delight, Khwája, eh?

The prophets abandoned[1] this delight because they were steeped in the Divine delight;

Since their spirit had experienced that delight, these delights seemed to them (mere) play.

When any one has been united with a living object of adora- 3590 tion, how should he embrace a dead one?

*Commentary on the Verse* " And lo, the After-home is the (real) life, if they but knew." *The gates and walls and area of that World and its water and pitchers and fruits and trees, all are living and speaking and hearing; and on that account Muṣṭafá (Mohammed), on whom be peace, has said that the present world is a carcase and those who seek it are curs. If the next world had no life, the next world too would be a carcase: a carcase is so called because of its being dead, not because of its evil smell and its foulness.*

Since every atom of that World is living and able to under-stand discourse and eloquent,

They (the prophets) have no rest in the dead world, for this (worldly) fodder is only fit for cattle.

Whoever has the rose-garden to feast and dwell in, how should he drink wine in the bath-stove?

The abode of the pure spirit is 'Illiyyín[2]; 'tis the worm that has its home in dung.

The cup that purifies is for those intoxicated with God; this 3595 briny water is for these blind birds.

In the eyes of any one to whom the justice of 'Umar has not displayed its power[3], the murderous Ḥajjáj is just.

A dead (lifeless) doll is given to (young) girls, for they are ignorant of the play (dalliance) of living (men).

A wooden sword is better suited to children (young boys), since they have not the strength and power (that comes) from manhood.

Infidels are content with the figures of the prophets which are painted (and kept) in churches;

(But) as we have (enjoy) a bright period (of inward illumina- 3600 tion) from those moons[4], we have no care for a shadow-figure.

The one figure of him (the prophet) is seated in the (sub-lunary) world, while his other figure is in heaven, like the moon.

---

[1] Literally, "went forth from."    [2] The Seventh Heaven or Paradise.
[3] Literally, "hand."    [4] *I.e.* the prophets.

This mouth of him is speaking on subtle points (of religion) to those sitting beside him, while the other (mouth) is (engaged) in discourse with God and intimate (with Him).

His outward ear is apprehending these (external) words, while his spiritual ear is drawing (into itself) the mysteries of (the Creative Word) *Be*.

His outward eye is apprehending human forms and features, while his inward eye is dazzled in (the glory of) *the eye did not stray*.

3605     His outward feet stand evenly in the row (of worshippers) in the mosque, while his spiritual feet are (engaged) in circum-ambulation above the sky.

Reckon up every member of him (and judge of it) in like fashion: this (bodily part) is within Time, while that (spiritual part) is beyond Time.

This which is in Time endures till death, while the other is the associate of everlastingness and the peer of eternity.

One name of him is "owner of the two empires"; one description of him is "Imám of the two *qiblas*."

The religious seclusion and the forty days' fast are no longer incumbent on him: no cloud is overclouding him any more.

3610     His solitary cell[1] is (resplendent as) the sun's orb: how should alien night throw a veil over it?

Sickness and abstinence are gone, the crisis is past: his infidelity has become faith, and disbelief is no more.

Like (the letter) *alif*, he has taken the foremost place because of his straightness (rectitude)[2]: he retains nothing of his own qualities.

He has become separated from the garment of his own dispositions: his spirit has gone, naked, to Him who gives it increase of spirituality.

Inasmuch as it went naked into the presence of the incomparable King, the King made for it a raiment of holy qualities.

3615     It put on a robe of the King's qualities: it flew up from the pit to the palace of majesty.

Such is the case: when dregs become pure, they rise from the bottom of the bowl to the top.

Although it (the spirit) remained like dregs at the bottom of the bowl owing to the ill-luck of mixing with particles of earth, (this was not in accordance with its nature).

Its disagreeable companion had tied its wings and plumes; else (it would have risen, for) originally it was very soaring[3].

---

[1] *I.e.* his heart.
[2] *Alif*, the first letter of the Arabic alphabet, has the form of a straight perpendicular line.
[3] Literally, "one that leaped up."

When they[1] uttered the rebuke *Get ye down*[2], they suspended it, head first, like Hárút.

Hárút was one of the angels of Heaven: on account of a 3620 (Divine) rebuke he was suspended thus.

He was (suspended), head downwards, because he remained far aloof from the Head and made himself the head and advanced alone.

When the basket saw itself to be full of water, it behaved with independence and parted from the sea.

(Afterwards, when) not a single drop of water remained inside it[3], the sea showed mercy and called it back.

From the (Divine) Sea comes an uncaused undeserved mercy[4] in a blessed hour.

For God's sake, for God's sake, frequent[5] the Seashore, 3625 though those who dwell on the seashore are pale,

In order that the grace of a Benefactor may come (to thee) and that thy pale face may be reddened by a jewel[6].

Yellowness (paleness) of face is the best of complexions, because it is in expectation of that meeting (with God);

But the redness on a face that is beaming appears (there) because his (its owner's) soul is content;

For (mere) hope makes him lean, pale, and wretched: he is not ill with bodily ailment.

The reason of even (a physician like) Galen becomes dis- 3630 traught when it sees a pale face without (unaccompanied by any symptom of) disease.

When thou hast fixed thy hope on the Light of Him (God), Muṣṭafá (Mohammed) says (concerning such an one), "His carnal self is abased."

The shadeless light is beautiful and lofty; the one enclosed in network is (only) the shadow of a sieve.

Amatores corpus volunt nudum; enervatis nil interest vestisne sit an corpus.

The (delicious) bread and dishes of food are (reserved) for the fasters; for the horse-fly what difference is there between the soup and the trivet?

---

[1] *I.e.* God.
[2] Referring to the Fall of Adam and Eve from Paradise.
[3] Literally, "on its liver."
[4] Literally, "a mercy without any cause and without any service."
[5] Literally, "wander round."
[6] *I.e.* in order that thy sorrow may be turned into rapture by the attainment of union with God.

*How the King (Maḥmúd) requested Ayáz for the second time,*
*saying, "Explain thy case and solve the difficulty felt by the*
*incredulous and censorious; for it is not (like thy) generosity to*
*leave them in perplexity."*

3635     This topic is beyond limit and measure. "Now, O Ayáz, tell
of thy 'states.'

Thy 'states' are from the mine of novelty: how shouldst thou
be satisfied with these (vulgar) 'states'?

Hark, tell the story of those goodly 'states'—dust (be thrown)
upon the 'states' and lessons of the five (elements) and the six
(directions)!"

If the inward "state" is not to be told, (yet) I will tell thee
the outward "state" in a word or two[1],

(Namely), that by grace of the Beloved the bitternesses of
death were made sweeter than sugar-cane to the soul.

3640     If the dust from that sugar-cane should enter the sea, all the
bitterness of the sea would become sweet.

Even so a hundred thousand "states" came (hither) and went
back to the Unseen, O trusted one.

Each day's "state" is not like (that of) the day before: (they
are passing) as a river that hath no obstacle in its course.

Each day's joy is of a different kind, each day's thought makes
a different impression.

*Comparison of the human body to a guest-house and of the diverse*
*thoughts to the diverse guests. The gnostic, acquiescing in those*
*thoughts of sorrow or joy, resembles a hospitable person who*
*treats strangers with kindness, like Khalíl (Abraham); for*
*Khalíl's door was always open to receive his guest with honour—*
*infidel and true believer and trusty and treacherous alike; and*
*he would show a cheerful face to all his guests.*

This body, O youth, is a guest-house: every morning a new
guest comes running (into it).

3645     Beware, do not say, "This (guest) is a burden to me[2]," for
presently he will fly back into non-existence.

Whatsoever comes into thy heart from the invisible world is
thy guest: entertain it well!

*Story of the guest concerning whom the wife of the master of the*
*house said, "The rain has set in, and our guest is left on our hands[3]."*

A guest came to a certain man at a late hour: he (the master
of the house) made him (at home) like a collar on the neck[4].

He brought trays of food and showed him every courtesy; on
that night there was a feast in their parish.

[1] Literally, "in odd and even."        [2] Literally, "remained on my neck."
[3] Literally, "on our neck."        [4] *I.e.* treated him with great consideration.

The man spoke secretly to his wife, saying, "To-night, mistress, make two beds."

Lay our bed towards the door, and lay a bed on the other side 3650 for the guest."

The wife replied, "I will do (this) service, I shall be glad (to do it). To hear is to obey, O light of mine eyes![1]"

The wife laid both the beds and (then) went off to the circumcision feast and stayed there (a long time).

The worthy guest and her husband remained (in the house): the host[2] set before him a dessert of fruit and wine[3].

Both the excellent men related (to each other) their good and bad experiences (and sat) chatting[4] till midnight.

Afterwards the guest, being sleepy and tired of talking[5], went 3655 to the bed that was on the opposite side to the door.

From (a feeling of) shame (delicacy) the husband did not tell him anything or say, "My dear friend[6], your bed is on this side;

I have had the bed for you to sleep in laid over there, most noble sir."

(So) the arrangement which he had made with his wife was altered, and the guest lay down on the other side (of the room).

During the night it began to rain violently in that place, (and continued so long) that they were astonished at the thickness of the clouds.

(When) the wife came (home), she thought[7] her husband was 3660 sleeping towards the door, and the uncle[8] on the other side.

The wife immediately undressed and went to bed[9] and kissed the guest fondly several times.

"O worthy man," said she, "I was afraid (of this), and now that very thing has happened, that very thing has happened, that very thing!

The mud and rain have stranded thy guest (here): he is left on thy hands[10] like Government soap[11].

How can he set out in this rain and mud? He will become a tax upon thy head and soul."

The guest at once jumped up and said, "O woman, leave off! 3665 I have boots, I don't mind the mud.

I depart. May good be with you! May your spirit during its (earthly) journey never rejoice (even) for a moment,

So that it may the sooner go towards its native home! for this (worldly) pleasure waylays (the traveller) on his journey."

---

[1] Literally, "Hearing and obedience, O my two bright eyes."
[2] Literally, "they."                    [3] Literally, "of dry and wet."
[4] Literally, "in chat."                  [5] Literally, "from sleep and talk."
[6] Literally, "O soul."                   [7] Literally, "in the opinion that."
[8] *I.e.* the guest.                      [9] Literally, "went naked to bed."
[10] Literally, "on thee."
[11] This probably means "like an impost from the payment of which there is no escape."

When the distinguished guest started up and went off, the wife was sorry for (having spoken) those unsympathetic words.

Many a time the wife said to him, "Why, O Amír, if I made a merry jest[1], don't take offence."

3670 The wife's supplication and lament were of no avail: he departed and left them to grieve.

Afterwards the husband and wife clad themselves in blue[2]: they deemed his (radiant) form to be a candle without a basin[3].

He was going (on his way), and by that man's candle-light the desert was isolated, like Paradise, from the darkness of night.

He (the husband) made his house a guest-house in sorrow and shame for this (calamitous) event.

In the hearts of them both[4], (coming) by the hidden way, the phantom of the guest was saying continually,

3675 "I am the friend of Khaḍir: I would have scattered a hundred treasures of munificence (over you), but 'twas not your appointed portion."

*Comparing the daily thoughts that come into the heart with the new guests who from the beginning of the day alight in the house and behave with arrogance and ill-temper towards the master of the house; and concerning the merit of treating the guest with kindness and of suffering his haughty airs patiently.*

Every day, too, at every moment a (different) thought comes, like an honoured guest, into thy bosom.

O (dear) soul, regard thought as a person, since (every) person derives his worth from thought and spirit.

If the thought of sorrow is waylaying (spoiling) joy, (yet) it is making preparations for joy.

It violently sweeps thy house clear of (all) else, in order that new joy from the source of good may enter in.

3680 It scatters the yellow leaves from the bough of the heart, in order that incessant green leaves may grow.

It uproots the old joy, in order that new delight may march in from the Beyond.

Sorrow pulls up the crooked rotten (root), in order that it may disclose the root that is veiled from sight.

Whatsoever (things) sorrow may cause to be shed from the heart or may take away (from it), assuredly it will bring better in exchange,

Especially for him who knows with certainty (intuitively) that sorrow is the servant of the possessors of (intuitive) certainty.

---

[1] Literally, "if I made a jest in good (merry) humour."
[2] *I.e.* mourning garb.
[3] *I.e.* a spirit without a body. The candle is placed in a basin which serves as a receptacle for the melted wax.
[4] The husband and wife.

Unless the clouds and the lightning show a frowning aspect[1], 3685
the vines will be burnt by the smiles of the sun[2].

Good and ill fortune become guests in thy heart: like the star
(planet), they go from house to house[3].

At the time when it (the auspicious or inauspicious star) is
residing in thy mansion, adapt thyself to it and be agreeable,
like its ascendant[4],

So that, when it rejoins the Moon, it may speak gratefully of
thee to the Lord of the heart.

Job, the (prophet who was) patient and well-pleased (with
God), showed sweetness to God's guest during seven years
(spent) in tribulation,

To the end that when the stern-visaged tribulation should 3690
turn back (on its way to God), it might give thanks to him in
God's presence in a hundred fashions,

Saying, "From love (of Thee) Job never for one moment
looked sourly on me, the killer of that which is loved."

From his loyalty and his shame before God's knowledge, he
(Job) was like milk and honey (in his behaviour) towards
tribulation.

(Whenever) the thought (of sorrow) comes into thy breast
anew, go to meet it with smiles and laughter[5],

Saying, "O my Creator, preserve me from its evil: do not
deprive me, (but) let me partake, of its good!

*O my Lord, prompt me* to give thanks for that which I see 3695
(receive): do not let me feel any subsequent regret, if it (the
benefit received) shall pass away."

Pay watchful regard to the sour-looking thought: deem that
sour one to be sweet as sugar.

If the cloud apparently has a sour face, (yet) the cloud is the
bringer-on of the rose-garden and the destroyer of the nitrous
(barren) soil.

Know that the thought of sorrow is like the cloud: do not look
so sourly on the sour!

It may be that the pearl (of thy desire) is in its hand: en-
deavour that it may depart from thee well-pleased.

And if the pearl be not (in its hand) and it be not rich, (yet) 3700
thou wilt increase (strengthen) thy sweet habit.

Thy habit will profit thee on another occasion: some day thy
need will suddenly be fulfilled.

The thought that hinders thee from joy comes by the com-
mand and wise purpose of the Maker.

---

[1] Literally, "sourness of face."
[2] Literally, "of the Orient."
[3] *I.e.* from one sign of the zodiac to another.
[4] *I.e.* "let thy attitude and relation to good or evil fortune be as harmonious
as the relation between a star and its ascendant."
[5] Literally, "laughing, laughing."

O youth, do not call it worthless: it may be a (happy) star and endowed with imperial fortune[1].

Do not say it is a branch: take it to be the root, in order that thou mayst always be master of thy object of desire;

3705 For if thou take it to be (merely) a branch (derivative) and pernicious, thine eye will be waiting to see the root.

Waiting to see is poison to (spiritual) perception[2]: by that method thou wilt remain perpetually in death.

Recognise it as the root, clasp it to thy bosom, and be for ever delivered from the death of waiting to see.

### How the Sultan (Maḥmúd) showed favour to Ayáz.

"O Ayáz, who art full of humbleness and sincere in all thy ways, thy sincerity is mightier than sea and mountain.

For thee there is no stumbling in the hour of lust, so that thy reason, which resembles a mountain (in solidity), should go (hither and thither) like a straw;

3710 Nor in the hour of anger and vengeance do thy powers of long-suffering fail to hold fast and firm."

Virilitas haec virilitas est, barba et penis non est; sin minus, rex virorum esset veretrum asini.

Whom has God in the Qur'án called men? How should there be room for this body there?

What worth has the animal soul? O father, come now, pass through the market of the butchers,

(And you will see) a hundred thousand (sheeps') heads laid on paunches (tripe), of which (heads) the value is less than (that of) the fat caudal part and tail.

3715 Meretrix est (quaevis femina) cui penis impetu mens (tanquam) mus fiat, libido tanquam leo.

### How a father enjoined his daughter to take care lest she should become with child by her husband.

There was a Khwája who had a daughter with cheeks like (those of) Venus, a face like the moon, and a breast (white) as silver.

(When) she reached maturity, he gave his daughter to a husband: as regards social rank[3] the husband was not a (good) match for her.

When a melon is ripe it becomes watery and goes to waste and ruin unless you slice it.

Since it was (a case of) necessity, he gave his daughter to one

---

[1] Literally, "the lord of the planetary conjunction."
[2] Literally, "taste."
[3] Literally, "in respect of (social) equality."

who was not (socially) her match, in fear of the evil (that might ensue).

He said to his daughter, "Guard thyself from this new 3720 bridegroom, do not become with child;

For thy marriage to this beggar was (dictated) by necessity; there is no constancy in this vagabond fellow[1].

Of a sudden he will jump off and leave all behind: his child will remain on thy hands[2] as a wrong (for which there is no redress)."

The daughter replied, "O father, I will do service (to thee): thy counsel is acceptable and prized."

Every two or three days the father would enjoin his daughter to take precautions;

(Nevertheless) she suddenly became with child by him (her 3725 husband): how should it be (otherwise when) both the wife and the husband are young?

She kept it (the child) hidden from her father, (till) the child was five or six months old.

(Then) the discovery was made. "What is this?" asked her father; "did not I tell thee to adopt (the practice of) withdrawal from him?

These injunctions of mine were (mere) wind, forsooth! My counsel and exhortations have been of no use to thee."

"Father," said she, "how should I guard myself? Man and wife, beyond doubt, are (as) fire and cotton.

What means has the cotton of guarding itself from the fire, or 3730 when is there (any) carefulness and caution in the fire?"

He replied, "I said, 'noli te viro admovere, noli semen ejus recipere.

Tempore summae voluptatis et emissionis et deliciarum te corpus ab eo retrahere oportet.'"

She said, "Quando sit ejus emissio quomodo intelligam? hoc enim occultum et valde difficile est."

He replied, "Cum res eo redierit ut oculi ejus volvantur, intellige id esse tempus emissionis."

She said, "Eo usque donec oculi ejus volvantur, hi mei oculi 3735 caeci occaecati sunt."

Not every despicable understanding remains steadfast in the hour of desire and anger and combat.

---

[1] Literally, "this man who is to be reckoned as a wandering stranger."
   Literally, "on thee."

*Description of the pusillanimity and weakness of the Ṣúfí who has
been brought up in ease¹ and has never struggled with himself or
experienced the pain and searing anguish of (Divine) love, and
has been deluded by the homage and hand-kissing of the vulgar
and their gazing on him with veneration and pointing at him with
their fingers and saying, "He is the (most famous) Ṣúfí in the
world to-day"; and has been made sick by vain imagination, like
the teacher who was told by the children that he was ill². In the
conceit of being a (spiritual) warrior and regarded as a hero in
this (spiritual) Way, he goes on campaign with the soldiers
engaged in the war against the infidels. "I will show my valour
outwardly too," says he; "I am unparalleled in the Greater
Warfare: what difficulty, forsooth, should the Lesser Warfare
present to me?³" He has beheld the phantasm of a lion and
performed (imaginary) feats of bravery and become intoxicated
with this bravery and has set out for the jungle to seek the lion.
(But) the lion says with mute eloquence, "Nay, ye will see!⁴ and
again, nay, ye will see!⁵"*

A Ṣúfí went with the army to fight the infidels: suddenly came
the clangours and din of war.

The Ṣúfí stayed behind with the baggage-train and tents and
invalids, (while) the horsemen rode into the line of battle.

The earth-bound heavies remained in their place; *the foremost
in the march, the foremost in the march*, rode on.

3740    After the combat, they came (back) victorious: they returned
in possession of profit and (laden) with spoils.

They gave (him) a present (from the battle-field), saying,
"Thou too, O Ṣúfí!" (but) he cast it out (of the tent) and would
not take anything.

Then they said to him, "Why art thou angry?" He answered,
"I have been deprived of (my share in) the fighting."

The Ṣúfí was not at all pleased with that act of kindness,
because he had not drawn the sword in the holy war.

So they said to him, "We have brought prisoners in: do thou
take that one to kill.

3745    Cut off his head, in order that thou too mayst be a holy
warrior." (Thereupon) the Ṣúfí was somewhat pleased and
encouraged;

For, though in the ritual ablution water has a hundred
excellences⁶, (yet) when it is not (obtainable) one must make
use of sand.

¹ Literally, "in the shade."
² See Book III, v. 1522 foll.
³ Literally, "what position, forsooth, should the Lesser Warfare hold in
my esteem?"
⁴ Literally, "ye will come to know."        ⁵ *Qur'án*, CII, 3–4.
⁶ Literally, "splendours."

The Ṣúfí led the pinioned prisoner behind the tent in order to wage the holy war.

The Ṣúfí tarried with the prisoner a long while; the party (of soldiers) said, "The dervish has made a long stay there.

An infidel with both hands tied! (Surely) he is ready for killing: what is the cause of this delay in slaughtering him?"

One of them went after him to investigate: he found the infidel on the top of him (the Ṣúfí), 3750

Tanquam mas super femina, and the infidel couching upon the dervish like a lion.

With his hands tied, he was gnawing the Ṣúfí's throat in obstinate strife.

The infidel was gnawing his throat with his teeth: the Ṣúfí lay beneath, senseless.

The pinioned infidel, (fierce) as a cat, had wounded his throat without (using) a lance.

The prisoner had half-killed him with his teeth: his beard was soaked in blood from the throat of the dervish. 3755

(This is) like you, who under the violence[1] of your pinioned[2] fleshly soul have become as senseless and abject as that Ṣúfí.

O you whose religion is incapable of (climbing) a single hillock, there are a hundred thousand mountains in front of you.

You are dead with fear of a ridge of this (small) size: how will you climb up precipices (big) as a mountain?

The warriors, (moved) by (religious) zeal[3], at that very instant ruthlessly put the infidel to the sword.

They sprinkled water and rose-water on the face of the Ṣúfí, that he might recover[4] from his unconsciousness and the sleep (of his senses). 3760

When he came to himself, he saw the party (of soldiers), and they asked him how it had happened,

(Saying), "God! God![5] what is the matter, O worshipful one? By what thing wert thou made so senseless?

Was a half-killed pinioned infidel the cause of thy falling into such a senseless and abject plight?"

He replied, "When I attempted (to cut off) his head in anger, the impudent fellow looked at me queerly.

He opened his eyes wide at me: he rolled his eyes, and consciousness vanished from my body. 3765

The rolling of his eyes seemed to me an army: I cannot describe how terrible it was.

(Let me) cut the story short: from (fright at) those eyes I became so beside myself and fell to the ground."

[1] Literally, "hand."
[2] *I.e.* held in restraint by the religious law of Islam.
[3] *I.e.* in their indignation at seeing a Moslem so maltreated.
[4] Literally, "come to his senses."
[5] Equivalent to "Good Heavens!"

*How the champions (of Islam) counselled him, saying, " Since thou
has so little heart (courage) and stomach (pluck) that thou art
made senseless by the rolling of a captive and pinioned infidel's
eyes, so that the dagger drops from thy hand, take heed, take
heed! Keep to the kitchen of the Ṣúfí convent and do not go to
battle lest thou incur public disgrace!"*

The party (of soldiers) said to him, "With such a stomach[1]
as thou hast, do not approach the (field of) battle and war.

Since thou wert sunk and thy ship wrecked by the eye of that
pinioned prisoner,

3770    How, then, amidst the onset of the fierce lions (champions),
to whose swords the head (of an enemy) is like a ball[2],

Canst thou swim in blood, when thou art not familiar with
the warfare of (brave) men?—

For the pounding noise made by fullers is banal in comparison
with the clang of (swords when) smiting necks (on the battle-
field).

(There thou wilt see) many a headless body that is (still)
quivering, many a bodiless head (floating) on blood, like
bubbles.

In war, hundreds of death-dealing (heroes) are drowned under
the legs[3] of the horses in (a sea of) death.

3775    How will wits like these (of thine), which flew away from (fear
of) a mouse, draw the sword in that battle-line?

'Tis war, not (a matter of) supping wheat-broth (*ḥamza*), that
thou shouldst turn up thy sleeve to sup it.

'Tis not (like) supping wheat-broth; here (on the field of
battle) eye the sword! In this battle-line one needs a Ḥamza[4]
of iron.

Fighting is not the business of any faint-heart who runs away
from a spectre (hallucination), like a (flitting) spectre.

'Tis the business of Turks (*Turkán*), not of (women like)
Tarkán. Begone! Home is the place for Tarkán: go home!"

---

[1] Literally, "gall-bladder."
[2] *I.e.* it is sent flying like a ball driven by a polo-bat.
[3] Literally, "hands and feet," *i.e.* forelegs and hindlegs.
[4] The Prophet's uncle, who was a doughty warrior.

*Story of 'Iyáḍí, may God have mercy on him, who had taken part in seventy campaigns against the infidels and had always fought with his breast bare (unprotected by armour), in the hope that he might become a martyr; and how, despairing of that, he turned from the Lesser Warfare to the Greater Warfare and adopted the practice of (religious) seclusion; and how he suddenly heard the drums of the holy warriors, and the fleshly soul within him urged him violently to take the field[1]; and how he suspected (the motives of) his fleshly soul in desiring this.*

'Iyáḍí said, "Ninety times I came (into battle) unarmed[2], 3780 that perchance I might be (mortally) wounded.

I went unarmed to meet the arrows, in order that I might receive a deep-seated[3] (deadly) arrow-wound.

None but a fortunate martyr attains unto (the happiness of) receiving an arrow-wound in the throat or any vital spot.

No place in my body is without wounds: this body of mine is like a sieve from (being pierced with) arrows;

But the arrows never (once) hit a vital spot: this is a matter of luck, not of bravery or cunning.

When (I saw that) martyrdom was not the lot of my spirit, 3785 I went immediately into (religious) seclusion and (entered on) a forty days' fast.

I threw myself[4] into the Greater Warfare (which consists) in practising austerities and becoming lean.

(One day) there reached my ear the sound of the drums of the holy warriors; for the hard-fighting[5] army was on the march.

My fleshly soul cried out to me from within: at morningtide I heard (its voice) with my sensuous ear,

(Saying), 'Arise! 'Tis time to fight. Go, devote thyself[6] to fighting in the holy war!'

I answered, 'O wicked perfidious soul, what hast thou to do 3790 with the desire to fight?[7]

Tell the truth, O my soul! This is trickery. Else (why wouldst thou fight)?—the lustful soul is quit of obedience (to the Divine command).

Unless thou tell the truth, I will attack thee, I will squeeze (torment) thee more painfully (than before) in maceration.'

Thereupon my soul, mutely eloquent[8], cried out in guile from within me,

[1] Literally, "tugged its chain furiously towards the holy war."
[2] Literally, "bare-bodied."
[3] Literally, "occupying a (fixed) place."
[4] Literally, "my body."
[5] Literally, "striving in war."
[6] Literally, "make thyself a pledge."
[7] Literally, "whence the desire to fight (and) whence thou?"
[8] Literally, "with eloquence without mouth."

16

'Here thou art killing me daily, thou art putting my (vital) spirit (on the rack), like the spirits of infidels.

3795 No one is aware of my plight—how thou art killing me (by keeping me) without sleep and food.

In war I should escape from the body at one stroke, and the people would see my manly valour and self-sacrifice.'

I replied, 'O wretched soul, a hypocrite thou hast lived and a hypocrite thou wilt die: what (a pitiful thing) art thou!

In both worlds thou hast been a hypocrite, in both worlds thou art such a worthless creature.'

I vowed that I would never put my head outside of (come out of) seclusion, seeing that this body is alive,

3800 Because everything that this body does in seclusion it does with no regard to man or woman.

During seclusion the intention of (all) its movement and rest is for God's sake only."

This is the Greater Warfare, and that (other) is the Lesser Warfare: both are (fit) work for (men like) Rustam and Ḥaydar ('Alí).

They are not (fit) work for one whose reason and wits fly out of his body when a mouse's tail moves.

Such a one must stay, like women, far off from the battle-field and the spears.

3805 That one a Ṣúfí and this one (too) a Ṣúfí! Here's a pity! That one is killed by a needle, while the sword is this one's food.

He (the false Ṣúfí) is (only) the figure of a Ṣúfí: he has no soul (life); accordingly, the (true) Ṣúfís get a bad name from Ṣúfís such as these.

Upon the door and wall of the body moulded of clay God, in His jealousy, traced the figures of a hundred Ṣúfís (of this sort),

To the end that by means of magic those figures should move and that Moses' rod should be hidden.

The truth of the rod swallows up the figures, (but) the Pharaoh-like eye is filled with dust and gravel (and cannot see).

3810 Another Ṣúfí entered the battle-line twenty times for the purpose of fighting

Along with the Moslems when they attacked the infidels; he did not fall back with the Moslems in their retreat.

He was wounded, but he bandaged the wound which he had received, and once more advanced to the charge and combat,

In order that his body might not die cheaply at one blow and that he might receive twenty blows in the battle.

To him it was anguish that he should give up his soul at one blow and that his soul should escape lightly from the hand of his fortitude.

*Story of the (spiritual) warrior who every day used to take one
dirhem separately from a purse containing (pieces of) silver and
throw it into a ditch (full of water) for the purpose of thwarting
the greed and cupidity of his fleshly soul; and how his soul tempted
him, saying, " Since you are going to throw (this money) into the
ditch, at least throw it away all at once, so that I may gain
deliverance, for despair is one of the two (possible) reliefs[1]"; and
how he replied, "I will not give thee this relief either."*

A certain man had forty dirhems in his hand: every night he 3815
would throw one (of them) into the sea-water,

In order that the long agony suffered in (the process of)
deliberation might become grievous to the illusory soul[2].

He (the valiant Ṣúfí) advanced with the Moslems to attack
(the infidels), (but) in the hour of retreat he did not fall back
in haste before the enemy.

He was wounded again, (but) he bound up those (wounds)
too: twenty times were the spears and arrows (of the enemy)
broken by him.

After that, no strength remained (in him): he fell forward
(and expired in) *the seat of truth*[3] because his love was true.

Truth consists in giving up the soul (to God). Hark, try to 3820
outstrip (the others) in the race! Recite from the *Qur'án* (the
words) *men who have been true.*

All this dying is not the death of the (physical) form: this body
is (only) like an instrument for the spirit.

Oh, there is many a raw (imperfect) one whose blood was shed
externally, but whose living fleshly soul escaped to yonder side[4].

Its instrument was shattered, but the brigand was left alive: the
fleshly soul is living though that on which it rode has bled to death[5].

His (the rider's) horse was killed before his road was traversed:
he became naught but ignorant and wicked and miserable.

If a martyr were made by every (mortal) bloodshed, an 3825
infidel killed (in battle) also would be a Bú Saʿíd[6].

Oh, there is many a trusty martyred soul that has died (to self)
in this world, (though) it is going about like the living.

The brigand (animal) spirit has died, though the body, which
is its sword, survives: it (the sword) is (still) in the hand of that
eager warrior.

The sword is that (same) sword, the man is not that (same)
man; but this appearance (of identity) is a cause of bewilderment
to you.

---

[1] *I.e.* "you can relieve me either by gratifying my desire or by removing
all hope of its being gratified."

[2] *I.e.* the soul that belongs to the world of illusion.

[3] *I.e.* he died and went to Paradise.        [4] *I.e.* to the world hereafter.

[5] Literally, "has scattered its blood."

[6] The great mystic, Abú Saʿíd ibn Abi 'l-Khayr (*ob.* A.D. 1049).

When the soul is transformed, this sword, namely, the body, remains in the hand of (is wielded by) the action of the Beneficent (God).

3830 The one (whose fleshly soul is dead) is a man whose food is entirely (Divine) love; the other is a man hollow[1] as dust.


*How an informer described a girl and exhibited the picture of her on paper, and how the Caliph of Egypt fell in love with it and sent an Amír with a mighty army to the gates of Mawṣil (Mosul) and made great slaughter and devastation for the purpose (of obtaining the girl).*

An informer said to the Caliph of Egypt, "The King of Mawṣil is wedded to a houri.

He holds in his arms a girl like whom there is no (other) beauty in the world.

She does not admit of description, for her loveliness is beyond (all) limits: here is her portrait on paper."

When the Emperor saw the portrait on the paper, he became distraught and the cup dropped from his hand.

3835 Immediately he despatched to Mawṣil a captain with a very mighty army,

Saying, "If he will not give up that moon (beauty) to thee, rase his court and palace to the ground[2];

But if he give her up, leave him alone and bring the moon (hither), that on the earth I may embrace the moon."

The captain set out towards Mawṣil with his retinue and with thousands of heroes[3] and drums and banners.

(With an army) like innumerable locusts (gathered) round the crops, he resolved to destroy the inhabitants of the city.

3840 On every side he brought into hostile action a mangonel (ballista) like Mount Qáf.

Wounds (were inflicted) by arrows and by stones from the mangonel; swords (flashed) amidst the dust, like lightning from a lightning-cloud.

During a (whole) week he wrought such carnage in hot fight: stone towers became unsteady as soft wax.

The King of Mawṣil saw the terrible combat: then (at last) he sent an envoy from within (the city) to him (the captain),

To say, "What do you wish (to obtain) by shedding the blood of true believers? They are being killed in this grievous war.

3845 If your object is to gain possession of the city of Mawṣil, look now, it is achieved without (any more) bloodshed like this.

I will go forth from the city: here it is for you, enter in, lest the blood of the oppressed lay hold of you (and demand vengeance);

---

[1] Literally, "empty within."
[2] Literally, "dig up...from the foundation."    [3] Literally, "Rustams."

And if your object is riches and gold and jewels, this is even more easy than to take possession of the city."

*How the lord of Mawṣil surrendered the girl to the Caliph in order that there might be no more shedding of Moslem blood.*

When the envoy came to the captain, he (the captain) gave him the paper on which the features (of the girl) were depicted[1],

(Saying), "Look on the paper: this (is what) I require. Hark, give (her up), or else (I will take her by force, for) I am the conqueror."

On the return of the envoy, that manly King said, "Take no account of a (mere) form, lead her away at once. 3850

I am not an idolater in the epoch of the true Faith: 'tis more fit that the idol should be in the hands of the idolater."

When the envoy brought her (to him), the captain straightway fell in love with her beauty.

Love is an (infinite) ocean, on which the heavens are (but) a flake of foam: (they are distraught) like Zalíkhá in desire for a Joseph.

Know that the wheeling heavens are turned by waves of Love: were it not for Love, the world would be frozen (inanimate).

How would an inorganic thing disappear (by change) into a plant? How would vegetive things sacrifice themselves to become (endowed with) spirit? 3855

How would the spirit sacrifice itself for the sake of that Breath by the waft whereof a Mary was made pregnant?

Each one (of them) would be (as) stiff and immovable[2] as ice: how should they be flying and seeking like locusts?

Every mote is in love with that Perfection and hastening upward like a sapling.

Their haste is (saying implicitly) *"Glory to God!"* They are purifying the body for the sake of the spirit.

The captain deemed (what was really) a pit to be like a (safe) road: to him the sterile soil appeared goodly, (so) he sowed seed (in it). 3860

Dormiens cum (aliquis) simulacrum (amatae) in somnio videret, cum eo coivit et aqua (seminis) effusa est.

Postquam somnium abscessit et ipse extemplo experrectus est, sensit illam pupam sibi jam vigilanti coram non adesse.

Dixit: "Eheu, aquam meam nihilo ingessi; eheu, dolosi illius (simulacri) dolum expertus sum."

Fuit ille dux (nonnisi) corporis imperator, revera vir non fuit: virilitatis semen in ejusmodi arena sevit.

The steed of his love tore up a hundred bridles: he (the captain) was shouting, "I care naught for death. 3865

[1] Literally, "in it the picture and sign."
[2] Literally, "compact in the (same) place."

What should I care about the Caliph? (Since I am) in love, my life and death are the same to me."

Prithee, do not sow with such ardour and heat: take counsel with a (spiritual) master.

(But) where is counsel, where is reason, (when) the torrent of cupidity has extended its talons to destroy (them)?

*A barrier in front and a barrier behind*; (but) he that is fascinated by a (lovely) cheek does not see (what is) before or behind.

3870    The black torrent comes to take his life, so that a fox may hurl a lion into the well (of destruction).

Something (materially) non-existent causes a phantom to appear in a well, in order that it (the phantom) may cast into it lions (strong) as mountains.

Do not have any one intimate with thy womenfolk, for these two (the man and the woman) may be compared to cotton and sparks of fire.

It needs a fire quenched by God's water, one that like Joseph holds fast (to God) in (the hour of) evil temptation,

To withdraw itself (bravely) as lions from a charming Zalíkhá tall and slender as a cypress[1].

3875    He (the captain) turned back from Mawṣil and went on his way till he encamped in a wooded meadowland[2].

The fire of his love was blazing in such wise that he could not distinguish earth from heaven.

He sought to embrace that moon (beauty) in her tent: where (at that time) was his reason and his dread of the Caliph?

When lust beats the drum (of victory) in this vale[3], what is thy reason? A (worthless) radish and the son of a radish.

To his fiery eye a hundred Caliphs seemed at that moment less than a gnat.

3880    Postquam ille feminarum cultor bracas exuit et inter crura mulieris recubavit,

Quo tempore penis ejus ad sedem suam recte ibat, tumultus ingens et clamor militum exortus est.

Exsiliit et nudo podice in aciem (currebat), grasping a fiery (flashing) scimitar in his hand.

He saw that a fierce black lion from the jungle[4] had suddenly rushed upon the centre of the army;

(That) the Arab horses were demoniacally excited, (that) every stable and tent was in confusion;

3885    (And that) the fierce lion from the covert was bounding twenty ells into the air, like billows of the sea.

The captain was manful and intrepid: he advanced, like a furious lion, to meet the lion.

---

[1] Literally, "like the cypress in stature."
[2] Literally, "a forest and place of meadows."
[3] *I.e.* the world.        [4] Literally, "reed-bed."

He smote (it) with his sword and clove its head; (then) at once he hastened (back) to the tent of the beauty.

Ubi sese puellae formosissimae ostendit, penis ejus itidem erectus erat.

Pugna congressus erat cum tali leone: penis ejus erectus manebat nec languore jacuerat.

Illa diva, facie venusta lunae simili praedita, virilitatis ejus 3890 admiratione obstupuit.

Protinus cum eo magna cupidine coivit: illae duae animae statim unitae evaserunt.

Through the union of these two souls with one another, there will come to them from the Unseen World another soul.

It will appear by the road of birth, if there be naught to waylay (prevent) its conception.

Wherever two persons unite in a love or hate[1], a third will certainly be born;

But those forms[2] are born in the Unseen World: when you go 3895 thither, you will see them in (clear) view.

That progeny is born of your associations: beware, do not rejoice too soon in any associate.

Remain in expectation of the appointed time (of meeting): recognise the truth of the (Divine) promise that the offspring shall join (their parents)[3];

For they are born of action and causes: each one hath form and speech and dwelling-place.

Their cry is coming (to you) from those delightful bowers[4]—
"O thou who hast forgotten us, hark, come with all speed!"

The soul (spiritual result) of (every) man and woman is 3900 waiting (for them) in the Unseen: why are you delaying? Step forward at once (on the way).

He (the captain) lost his way and, (beguiled) by that false dawn, fell like a gnat into the pot of buttermilk.


*How that military chief repented of the sin which he had committed and adjured the girl not to tell the Caliph anything of what had happened.*

He was absorbed in that (love-affair) for a while, (but) afterwards he repented of that grievous crime,

And adjured her, saying, "O thou whose face is like the sun, do not give the Caliph any hint of what has passed."

---

[1] *I.e.* love or hate each other.
[2] *I.e.* the qualities and dispositions produced in each of the two by their mutual relation.
[3] See *Qur'án*, LII, 21. Here "the offspring" denotes the results of good or evil action.
[4] *I.e.* "the results of your good actions, which assume the form of houris in Paradise, are calling you."

When the Caliph saw her he became distraught (with love), and then too his secret was exposed to all[1].

3905   He saw (her to be) a hundred times as beautiful as he (the informer) had described her: how in sooth should seeing be like hearing?

Description is a picture (drawn) for the eye of intelligence: know that the (sensible) form belongs to the eye, not to the ear.

A certain man asked an eloquent person, "What are truth and falsehood, O man of goodly discourse?"

He took hold of his ear and said, "This is false: the eye is true and possesses certainty."

The former is relatively false as compared with the latter: most sayings are relative, O trusty one.

3910   If the bat screens itself from the sun, (yet) it is not screened from the fancy (idea) of the sun.

Even the fancy (idea) of it (the sun) puts fear into it (the bat): that fancy leads it towards the darkness.

That fancy (idea) of the light terrifies it and causes it to become attached to the night of gloom.

'Tis from the fancy (idea) and the picture (thou hast formed) of thy enemy that thou hast become attached to thy comrade and friend.

O Moses, the revelation given to thee illumined[2] the mountain[3], (but) the fancy-conceiving (mountain) could not endure thy real experience (of the revelation).

3915   Hark, be not deluded by (the belief) that thou art able to conceive the fancy (idea) thereof and by this means canst attain (to the reality).

No one was ever terrified by the (mere) fancy (idea) of war: there is no bravery before (actual) war. Know this, and 'tis enough.

(Possessed) with the fancy (idea) of war, the poltroon makes, in his thoughts, a hundred heroic attacks (on the enemy)[4].

The antagonist[5] (conceived) in the mind of every raw (weakling) is the picture of Rustam that may be (found) in a bath-house.

When this fancy (idea) derived from hearing becomes (actually) visible, what of the poltroon? (Even) a Rustam (hero) is compelled (to submit).

3920   Endeavour that it (the fancy) may pass from thine ear into thine eye, and that what has (hitherto) been unreal may become real.

After that, thine ear will become connatural with thine eye: the two ears, (gross) as wool, will become of pure substance (and subtle);

---

[1] Literally, "his basin fell from the roof."
[2] Literally, "raised gleams upon."
[3] *I.e.* Mt Sinai. See *Qur'án*, VII, 139.
[4] Literally, "a hundred advances and retreats, like Rustams."
[5] Read اَلهَه for اَلهَه.

Nay, thy whole body will become like a mirror: it will become all eye and pure spiritual substance[1].

The ear rouses a fancy, and that fancy is the go-between (that leads) to union with that Beauty.

Endeavour that this fancy may increase, so that the go-between may become a guide for Majnún[2].

That foolish Caliph, too, was mightily infatuated for awhile 3925 with that girl.

Suppose the (monarch's) empire is the empire of the West and the East[3]: since it will not remain, deem it to be (as fleeting as) a lightning-flash.

O thou whose heart is slumbering (heedless), know that the kingdom that does not remain unto everlasting is (but) a dream.

Consider what thou wilt do with (all) that vanity and vain-glory[4]; for (ultimately) it will grip thy throat like an executioner.

Know that even in this world there is a safe refuge: do not listen to the hypocrite who says there is none.

*The argument of those who disbelieve in the after-life, and a demonstration of the weakness of that argument, since their argument amounts to " We do not see any other (world) than this."*

This is his (the hypocrite's) argument: he says at every 3930 moment, "If there were anything else, I should have seen it."

If a child does not see the various aspects of reason, will a rational person ever abandon[5] reason?

And if a rational person does not see the various aspects of Love, (yet) the auspicious moon of Love does not wane.

Joseph's beauty was not seen by the eyes of his brethren, (but) when did it (ever) disappear from the heart of Jacob?

The (physical) eye of Moses regarded the staff (rod) as wood; the eye of the Invisible[6] beheld (in it) a serpent[7] and (cause of) panic.

The eye of the head was in conflict with the eye of the heart: 3935 the eye of the heart prevailed (over the other) and displayed the proof.

The (physical) eye of Moses regarded his hand as a hand, (but) to the eye of the Invisible it was a manifest light[8].

This matter hath no limit in perfection[9], (yet) it seems like a fancy to every one that is deprived (of the reality).

[1] Literally, "the pure substance of the breast (heart)."
[2] *I.e.* may bring the lover (Majnún) to the Beloved (Laylá).
[3] *I.e.* world-wide.
[4] Literally, "wind and moustache (bluster)."
[5] Literally, "migrate from."
[6] *I.e.* the inward eye.          [7] Literally, "viper."
[8] An allusion to "the white hand" of Moses. See *Qur'án*, VII, 105; XXVI, 32; and Exodus iv. 6.
[9] *I.e.* it is perfectly and infinitely real.

Since to him the reality is the pudendum and the gullet, do not expound the mysteries of the Beloved to him.

To us the pudendum and the gullet are a (mere) fancy; consequently the (Beloved) Soul displays His beauty (to us) at every moment.

3940　Any one whose custom and habit is (addiction to) the pudendum and the gullet, for him (the fit answer) is " *Unto you (your) religion and unto me (my) religion*[1]."

Cut short thy talk with such (incarnate) scepticism: do not converse, O Aḥmad[2], with the ancient infidel.

### *Venit Khalīfa ad puellam formosam concubitus causa.*

Ille Khalīfa concubitum sibi proposuit, illam feminam coitus causa adivit.

Eam recordatus penem erexit, animum intendit ut concubitu[3] cum ea quae amorem augebat frueretur.

Cum inter crura mulieris recubavit, tum venit (Dei) decretum, ei viam voluptatis occlusit.

3945　Ad aures pervenit sonus tenuis quem mus facere solet: penis ejus languit, libido tota decessit;

Putabat enim illum susurrum ab angue exortum esse qui sese e storea vehementer sublevaret.

### *Puellam risus occupat propter libidinem Khalīfae debilem et libidinem illius ducis validissimam. Khalīfa puellae risum animadvertit.*

Femina languorem ejus vidit; rem mirando in cachinnos ivit: risus eam occupavit.

Venit in mentem virilitas ducis fortissimi qui leonem interfecit dum membrum (virile) ejus tale est.

The woman's laughter overpowered (her) and was prolonged: she tried hard (to suppress it) but her lips would not shut.

3950　She kept laughing violently like beng-eaters[4]: her laughter overpowered (all considerations of) gain or loss.

Everything that she thought of (only) increased her laughter, as (when) a flood-gate is suddenly opened.

Weeping and laughter and sorrow and joy of heart—know that each one (of them) has an independent source.

Each one has a (particular) store-house: know, O brother, that the key thereof is in the hand of the Opener.

Her laughter was never ceasing: then the Caliph became enraged and fierce.

---

[1] *Qur'án*, CIX, 6, slightly altered.
[2] *I.e.* "O thou of whom Aḥmad (Mohammed) is the ideal type."
[3] Literally, "recubando et exsurgendo."
[4] Beng (Indian hemp, *cannabis indica*), a powerful intoxicant, which when smoked or swallowed may produce the same effect as "laughing-gas."

He quickly drew his scimitar from its sheath and said, 3955
"Declare the secret cause of thy laughter, O foul (woman)!

From this laughter a suspicion has come into my heart: tell
the truth, thou canst not cajole me.

And if thou deceive me with falsehoods[1] or idly utter[2] glib
excuses,

I shall know, (for) there is light in my heart: thou must tell
everything that ought to be told.

Know that in the heart of kings there is a mighty moon,
though sometimes it is overclouded[3] by forgetfulness.

In the heart there is a lamp with which one goes about (as a 3960
rule)[4]; at times of anger and concupiscence it is put[5] under the
basin.

That clairvoyance accompanies me just now: unless thou tell
that which 'tis thy duty to tell,

I will sever thy neck with this scimitar: evasion will not avail
thee at all.

And if thou tell the truth, I will set thee free: I will not violate
the duty I owe to God, I will make thee glad."

At the same moment he placed seven *Qur'áns* one on the top
of another and swore an oath and thus confirmed (his promise).

*How the girl disclosed the secret to the Caliph in fear of (having her*
*head cut off by) a blow of the sword, and how she was forced (to*
*speak) by the Caliph (who said), "Give a true account of the*
*cause of thy laughter or else I will kill thee."*

When the woman became (found herself) helpless, she related 3965
what had happened (concerning) the manliness of that Rustam
who was the son of a hundred Záls[6].

She described to the Caliph, point by point, the bride-chamber
that was (prepared for her) on the route (of the march),

His killing the lion and returning to the tent pene erecto
tanquam cornu rhinocerotis;

Contra, hujus (membri) ambitiosi debilitatem quod ob unum
muris susurrum succidit.

God is ever making the hidden things manifest: since they
will grow up, do not sow bad seed.

Rain and clouds and fire and this sun are ever bringing up the 3970
hidden things from the earth.

---

[1] Literally, "against the truth."
[2] Literally, "bring forward with (mere) breath," *i.e.* talk devoid of
sincerity.
[3] Literally, "it is (hidden) beneath the clouds."
[4] Literally, "at the time of going about," *i.e.* every one carries such a lamp
about with him.
[5] Literally, "comes."
[6] *I.e.* that heroic son of a hundred heroes. Zál was the father of Rustam.

This new springtide after the fall of the leaves is a proof of the existence of the Resurrection.

In spring the secrets are revealed: whatsoever this Earth has eaten is exposed to view.

It shoots up from her mouth and lips in order that she may bring to light her hidden mind and way.

The secret of the root of every tree and its nutriment—the whole of that is plainly shown forth on its (leafy) top.

3975 Every sorrow whereby thou art (made) sore in heart is the headache arising from the wine[1] that thou hast drunk;

But how shouldst thou know from which wine that headache has arisen (and become) manifest?

This crop-sickness (headache) is the blossom of that seed: (only) he that is sagacious and wise will recognise it.

The bough and its blossom do not resemble the seed: how should semen resemble the body of man?

The matter (of which anything is composed) does not resemble the product: when did the seed (ever) resemble the tree (that sprang from it)?

3980 Semen is (the product) of bread, (but) how should it be like bread? Man is (the product) of semen, (but) how should he be like it?

The Jinní is (created) from fire, (but) how should he resemble fire? The cloud is (produced) from vapour, but it is not like vapour.

Jesus was produced from the breath of Gabriel, (but) when was he (ever) like him in form or comparable (to him in that respect)?

Adam is (made) of earth, (but) how should he resemble earth? No grape resembles the vine.

How should robbery look like the foot of the gallows? How should piety be like the everlasting abode (Paradise)?

3985 No origin resembles its product; therefore thou canst not know the origin of (thy) pain and headache.

But this punishment is not without an origin: how should God inflict pain without any sin (having been committed)?

That which is the origin and bringer-on of that (painful) thing—if it (the painful thing) does not resemble it, still it is (produced) from it.

Know, then, that thy pain is the result of some lapse (and that) this woe with which thou art stricken[2] arises from some lust.

If thou canst not discern that sin by means of consideration, at once make humble entreaty and seek pardon (from God).

3990 Prostrate thyself a hundred times and keep saying, "O God, this pain is nothing but my due and desert.

O Thou who art transcendent in holiness and free from (all) injustice and oppression, how shouldst Thou inflict grief and pain upon the soul when it has not sinned?

[1] Literally, "is (the result) of the crop-sickness produced by the wine."
[2] Literally, "the calamity of this affliction of thine."

I do not know my sin definitely, but (I know that) there must be a sin (to account) for the anguish.

Since Thou hast concealed the cause from my consideration, do Thou always keep my sin concealed (from others);

For it would be retribution to disclose my sin, so that my thievery (rascality) should be made manifest by punishment."

*How the monarch, on being acquainted with that act of treachery, resolved to conceal and pardon it and give her (the slave-girl) to him (the captain), and recognised that the tribulation was a punishment inflicted on him and was (the result of) his attempt (to obtain the slave-girl) and the wrong which he had done to the lord of Mawṣil; for "and whoso doeth evil, it is against himself" and "lo, thy Lord is on the watch"; and how he feared that, if he should avenge himself, the vengeance would recoil on his own head, as this injustice and greed (of his) had (already) recoiled upon him.*

The monarch came to himself. He asked pardon (of God) 3995 and confessed[1] his sin and lapse and persistence (in wrong-doing).

He said to himself, "The retribution for what I did to certain persons[2] has reached (overtaken) my soul.

From (pride of) power I made an attempt on the concubine of another[3]: that (injustice) recoiled upon me and I fell into the pit (which I had dug).

I knocked at the door of another person's house: consequently he knocked at the door of my house."

Whoever seeks to commit adultery with (other) people's wives, know that he is a pimp to his own wife;

For that (adultery) is requited by the like[4], since the retribu- 4000 tion for an evil act is an act like unto it[5].

Inasmuch as you have made a cord and pulled one like it towards yourself[6], you are a wittol and worse.

"I took the king of Mawṣil's concubine from him by force, (so) she was soon taken by force from me too.

My treacherous deeds made a traitor of him who was my trusted friend and servant.

'Tis no time to inflict punishment (for the injury) and avenge myself: I prepared the disaster[7] with my own hand.

[1] Literally, "made mention of."
[2] *I.e.* the king of Mawṣil.
[3] Literally, "others."
[4] Literally, "for the like of that (adultery) becomes the retribution for it."
[5] Cf. *Qur'án*, XLII, 38.
[6] *I.e.* you have been the cause of an injury which drew a like injury upon yourself.
[7] Literally, "I made the affair raw (futile and unsuccessful)."

4005    If I wreak vengeance on the Amír and the woman, that trespass also will come (recoil) on my head,

Just as this (other) one has (already) come (upon me) in retribution: I have tried Him (God), I will not try Him again.

The grief of the lord of Mawṣil has broken my neck: I dare not wound this other man as well.

God hath given us information concerning retribution: He hath said, '*If ye repeat it (the offence), We shall repeat it (the punishment).*'

Since in this case it is useless to commit excess (to transgress further), nothing but patience and mercy is praiseworthy.

4010    *O our Lord, verily we have done wrong*, a fault has occurred: perform an act of mercy, O Thou whose mercifulnesses are mighty!

I have pardoned (him), do Thou also pardon me—(pardon) the new sin and the old lapses!"

He said, "Now, O girl, do not relate (to any one) this tale which I have heard from thee.

I will unite thee with the Amír: for God's sake, for God's sake, do not breathe a word of this story,

Lest he become ashamed to face me; for he has done one bad deed and a hundred thousand good.

4015    (Many) times have I put him to the test: I have entrusted him with (girls) fairer than thou art.

I (always) found him perfect in fidelity; (so I know that) this too was a (Divine) judgement resulting from things done by me."

Then he summoned his Amír to his presence: he extinguished in himself the wrath that meditates a violent revenge[1].

He made an agreeable excuse to him, saying, "I have become disinclined to this slave-girl,

Because the mother of my children is terribly agitated[2] by jealousy and envy of the girl.

4020    The mother of my children has many claims (on me): she does not deserve (to suffer) such injustice and unkindness.

She is nursing envy and jealousy, she is suffering anguish[3], she is feeling great bitterness on account of this girl.

Since I wish to give this girl to some person, 'tis most fitting (that I should give her) to thee, O dear friend;

For thou didst hazard thy life for the sake of (obtaining) her: it would not be fair to give her to any one but thee."

He gave her in marriage and handed her over to him: he crushed anger and cupidity to atoms.

---

[1] Literally, "subjection (and abasement of an enemy)."
[2] Literally, "has a hundred (inward) boilings (or sounds of boiling)."
[3] Literally, "is drinking blood."

*Explaining that the words* "We have apportioned" *mean that He (God) bestows on one the lust and (physical) strength of asses and on another the intelligence and (spiritual) strength of the prophets and the angels.*

"To turn the head away from sensual desire is (a mark of) nobility[1]; to abandon sensual desire is (a mark of) the (spiritual) strength that belongs to prophethood."

"The seeds that are not sown in lust[2]—their fruit only appears at the Resurrection[3]."

If he (the Caliph) was deficient in the masculinity of asses, 4025 (yet) he possessed the manliness of the prophets.

It is (true) manliness and the nature of prophethood to abandon anger and lust and greed.

Let the masculinity of the ass be lacking in his nature, (what of that?): God calls him the great Beylerbey[4].

(If) I be a dead man and (if) God look on me (with favour), (my case is) better than (that of) the living man who is far (from God) and rejected (by Him).

Recognise this (abandonment of sensuality) to be the kernel of manliness, and that (indulgence in sensuality) to be the husk: the latter leads to Hell, the former to Paradise.

(The Tradition) "Paradise is encompassed with things dis- 4030 liked" has come (down to us); "Hell-fire is encompassed with sensual desire" has been declared.

"O Ayáz[5], fierce demon-killing lion, (thou in whom) the man-liness of the ass is inferior (subjugated), the manliness of Reason superior (predominant),

That which so many eminent persons did not apprehend was to thee child's play: lo, here is the (true) man!

O thou who hast felt the delight of (obeying) my command and hast loyally devoted thy life for the sake of my command,

Now hearken to the tale of the savour and relish of (obeying) the (Divine) command (as related) in the (following) spiritual exposition thereof."

---

[1] Literally, "princeliness."
[2] Literally, "connected with lust."
[3] Literally, "is only associated with the Resurrection."
[4] A Turkish word meaning "the chief Bey" (governor-general of a pro-vince), here equivalent to "spiritual sovereign."
[5] Formally the speaker is Sultan Maḥmúd of Ghazna, but as the following story of Maḥmúd and Ayáz is related by the poet himself, it seems likely that "Ayáz" is a type of the perfect saint, as in *v.* 4148.

*How the King (Maḥmúd), in the midst of (the company present in)
the Díwán and assembly-place, put a pearl in the hand of the
Vizier and asked him what it was worth; and how the Vizier
gave an extremely high estimate of its value; and when the King
commanded him to break it, answered, "How should I break it?"
and so forth[1].*

4035    One day the King hastened to the Díwán: in the Díwán he
found all the courtiers (assembled).

He produced a radiant pearl and immediately put it in the
palm of the Vizier.

"How about this pearl?" he asked, "and what is it worth?"
He replied, "It is worth more than a hundred ass-loads of gold."

He said, "Break it!" "How should I break it?" he replied:
"I am a well-wisher to thy treasury and riches.

How should I deem it allowable that a priceless pearl like this
should go to waste?"

4040    "Well said!" exclaimed the King and presented him with a
dress of honour; the generous King took the pearl from him,

(But) the munificent monarch bestowed on the Vizier every
garment and robe that he wore.

For a while he engaged them (the courtiers) in conversation
concerning new event and old mystery[2].

Afterwards he put it (the pearl) into the hand of a chamber-
lain, saying, "What is it worth to a would-be purchaser?[3]"

He replied, "It is worth half a kingdom: may God preserve
it from destruction!"

4045    "Break it," said he. "O thou whose sword is like the sun[4],"
he replied, "alas, 'tis a great pity to break it.

Let alone its value, mark its splendour and brilliancies: this
(shining) daylight has become second to it.

How should my hand make a movement to break it? How
should I be an enemy to the King's treasure-house?"

The King gave him a robe of honour and increased his stipend,
and then opened his mouth in praise of his (the chamberlain's)
intelligence.

After a short time he who was making the trial[5] again handed
the pearl to the Minister of Justice (*Mír-i dád*).

4050    He said the same, and all the (other) Amírs said the same:
he (the King) bestowed a costly robe of honour on every one
(of them).

The King was raising their salaries, (but in truth) he brought

[1] Literally, "and (so on) to the end of the story."
[2] *I.e.* on various topics.          [3] Literally, "to a seeker."
[4] *I.e.* "O thou whose flashing sword spreads the light (of Islam) over the
whole world."
[5] *I.e.* Sultan Maḥmúd.

those base wretches from the Way (of salvation) to the pit (of perdition).

All the fifty or sixty Amírs, one by one, spoke like this in imitation of the Vizier.

Though imitation is the pillar of the (present) world, (yet) every imitator is disgraced on being put to the trial.

*How the pearl, (passing) from hand to hand, came round at last to Ayáz; and (concerning) the sagacity of Ayáz, and how he did not act in conformity with them and was not beguiled by the King's giving them goods and riches and increasing their robes of honour and salaries and praising the intelligence of those erring men; for one ought not to regard the imitator as a Moslem: he may be a Moslem, but it rarely happens that he holds fast to his faith and comes off safely from the trials (to which he is exposed) —for he lacks the steadfastness of the clairvoyant—except (in the case of) those whom God preserves; because the Truth is one, and its contrary is very deceptive and like unto it (in appearance). Since the imitator does not know the contrary (so as to distinguish it from the Truth), on that account he cannot have known the Truth; but when, notwithstanding his ignorance, God preserves him by favour, that ignorance does him no harm.*

"Now, O Ayáz, wilt not thou say how much a pearl of this splendour and excellence is worth?"

He replied, "More than I am able to say." He (the King) 4055 said, "Now break it immediately into small fragments."

He (Ayáz) had (two) stones in his sleeve: he quickly reduced it to dust[1], (for) that seemed to him the right course.

Or (perhaps) that entirely sincere man had dreamed of this[2] and put the two stones under his arm,

Like Joseph to whom at the bottom of the well his ultimate fortune[3] was revealed by God.

To whomsoever He (God) has announced victory and triumph —to him success and unsuccess are one.

To whomsoever the favour of the Friend has become a surety 4060 —what fear should he have of defeat and (painful) combat?

When it has become certain to him that he will checkmate (his opponent), the loss of his horse (knight) and elephant (bishop) is a trifle to him.

If his horse be taken by any one who desires to take the horse, let the horse go; (for) is not he (by God's help) the winner?[4]

---

[1] Literally, "made it small (fragments)."
[2] The later MSS. add a verse giving "good luck" as the alternative explanation of Ayáz having the stones with him.
[3] Literally, "the end of his affair."
[4] Literally, "the foremost."

17

How should there be an affinity between a man and a horse?
His love for the horse is (only) for the purpose of getting in
front (of others).

Do not endure all this anguish for the sake of (mere) forms:
grasp the reality without (suffering) headache on account of a form.

4065 The ascetic feels anxiety concerning his latter end: (he con-
siders) what will be his plight on the Day of Reckoning;

(But) the gnostics, having become conscious of the beginning[1],
are free from anxiety and (care for) the ultimate conditions.

(Formerly) the gnostic had the same fear and hope (as the
ascetic), (but) his knowledge of the past devoured both those
(feelings).

He perceived that in the past he had sown pulse: he knows
what the produce[2] will be.

He is a gnostic and has been delivered from fear and dread:
the sword of God has cut lamentation[3] asunder[4].

4070 (Formerly) he had from God (feelings of) fear and hope: the
fear has passed away and the hope has come into clear view.

When he (Ayáz) broke that choice pearl, thereupon from the
Amírs arose a hundred clamours and outcries—

"What recklessness is this! By God, whoever has broken this
luminous pearl is an infidel"—

And (yet) the whole company (of Amírs) in their ignorance and
blindness had broken the pearl of the King's command.

The precious pearl, the product of love and affection—why
was it (ever) veiled from hearts like those?

### How the Amírs reviled Ayáz, saying, "Why did he break it?" and how Ayáz answered them.

4075 Ayáz said, "O renowned princes, is the King's command
more precious or the pearl?

In your eyes is the command of the sovereign or this goodly
pearl superior? For God's sake (tell me that)!

O ye whose gaze is (fixed) upon the pearl, not upon the King,
the ghoul is your object of desire, not the highway.

I will never avert my gaze from the King, I will not turn my
face towards a stone, like the polytheist.

Devoid of the (spiritual) pearl[5] is the soul that prefers a
coloured stone and puts my King behind."

4080 Turn thy back towards the rose-coloured doll[6], lose[7] thy
reason in Him who bestows the colour.

---

[1] *I.e.* having attained to knowledge of their eternally pre-ordained destiny.
[2] Literally, "the stack of threshed corn."
[3] Literally, "(cries of) *háy hú*."          [4] Literally, "in two halves."
[5] *I.e.* devoid of faith and knowledge of God.
[6] Worldly gauds.
[7] Literally, "make dumbfounded, stupefy."

Come into the river (of reality), dash the pitcher (of phenomenal form) against the stone, set fire to (mere) scent and colour.

If thou art not one of the brigands on the Way of the Religion, do not be addicted, like women, to colour and scent.

Those princes cast down their heads, craving with (all) their soul to be excused for that (act of) forgetfulness.

At that moment from the heart of each one (of them) two hundred·sighs were going (up), like a (great) smoke, to heaven.

The King made a sign to the ancient executioner, as though 4085 to say, " Remove these vile wretches from my seat of honour.

How are these vile wretches worthy of my seat of honour, when they break my command for the sake of a stone?

For the sake of a coloured stone my command is held contemptible and cheap by evil-doers like these."

*How the King was about to kill the Amírs, and how Ayáz made intercession before the royal throne, saying, "'Tis better to forgive."*

Then Ayáz, who was abounding in love, sprang up and ran to the throne of that mighty Sultan.

He made a prostration and spoke with bated breath[1], saying, "O Emperor at whom the celestial sphere is astounded,

O Humá[2] from whom (all) humá's have (their) auspiciousness, 4090 and every generous man (his) generosity,

O Noble One before whose self-sacrifice (all) acts of nobility in the world are hidden (eclipsed) and disappear,

O Lovely One whom the red rose beheld and tore its shirt in shame,

Forgiveness (itself) is fully content with thy forgivingness: because of thy pardon the foxes prevail over the lion.

Whosoever treats thy command with insolence, whom should he have to support him except thy pardon?

The heedlessness and irreverence of these sinners arise from 4095 the abundance of thy pardon (clemency), O mine of pardon."

Heedlessness always grows up from irreverence, for (only) reverence will remove the inflammation from the eye[3].

The heedlessness and wicked forgetfulness (which) he (the sinner) has learned will be consumed by the fire of reverence.

Awe (of God) will bestow on him wakefulness and keenwittedness: negligence and forgetfulness will leap forth from his heart.

Folk do not fall asleep at the time of a raid, lest any one should carry off his (the sleeper's) cloak.

Since sleep is banished by[4] fear for one's cloak, how should 4100

---

[1] Literally, "choked his windpipe."
[2] See translation of Book III, p. 91, note 2.
[3] *I.e.* will enable the spiritual eye to see clearly.
[4] Literally, "is fleeing because of."

the sleep of forgetfulness be (possible when accompanied) with fear for one's throat?[1]

(The text) *do not punish (us) if we forget* is evidence that forgetfulness too, in a certain way, is sinful,

Because he (who was forgetful) did not attain to complete reverence, or else forgetfulness would not have assailed him[2].

Although (his) forgetfulness was necessary and inevitable, (yet) he was a free agent in employing the means (by which it was produced);

For he showed remissness in his feelings of reverence, so that forgetfulness was born or negligence and trespass.

4105 ('Tis) like (the case of) the drunken man who commits sins and says, "I was excused from (responsibility for) myself."

"But," says he (the other) to him, "the cause (of your sin), (consisting) in the loss of that power to choose, proceeded from you, O evil-doer.

Your senselessness did not come of itself, you invited it; your power to choose did not go of itself, you drove it away.

If an intoxication had come (upon you) without exertion on your part, the spiritual Cup-bearer would have kept your covenant (inviolate).

He would have been your backer and intercessor: I am devoted to the sin of him who is intoxicated by God."

4110 (Ayáz said), "The forgivenesses of the whole world are (but) a mote—the reflexion of thy forgiveness, O thou from whom comes every fortune.

(All) forgivenesses sing the praise of thy forgiveness: there is no peer to it. O people, beware (of comparing it)!

Grant them their lives, neither banish them from thyself: they are (the objects of) thy sweet desire, O thou who bringest (all thy) desire to fruition.

Have mercy on him that beheld thy face: how shall he endure the bitter separation from thee?

Thou art speaking of separation and banishment: do what thou wilt but do not this!

4115 A hundred thousand bitter sixtyfold deaths are not like (comparable) to separation from thy face.

Keep the bitterness of banishment aloof from males and females, O thou whose help is besought by sinners!

'Tis sweet to die in hope of union with thee; the bitterness of banishment from thee is worse than[3] fire."

Amidst Hell-fire the infidel is saying, "What pain should I feel if He (God) were to look on me (with favour)?"

---

[1] *I.e.* fear of spiritual perdition.
[2] Literally, "would not have waged war (against him)."
[3] Literally, "is above."

For that look makes (all) pains sweet: it is the blood-price (paid) to the magicians (of Pharaoh) for (the amputation of) their hands and feet.

*Commentary on the Saying of Pharaoh's magicians in the hour of their punishment,* " *'Tis no harm, for lo, we shall return unto our Lord*[1]."

Heaven heard the cry, "*'Tis no harm*": the celestial sphere 4120 became a ball for that bat[2].

(The magicians said), "The punishment inflicted by Pharaoh is no harm to us: the grace of God prevails over the violence of (all) others.

If thou shouldst (come to) know our secret, O misleader, (thou wouldst see that) thou art delivering us from pain, O man whose heart is blind.

Hark, come and from this quarter behold this organ pealing '*Oh, would that my people knew!*'

God's bounty hath bestowed on us a Pharaohship, (but) not a perishable one like thy Pharaohship and kingdom.

Lift up thy head and behold the living and majestic kingdom, 4125 O thou who hast been deluded by Egypt and the river Nile.

If thou wilt take leave of this filthy tattered cloak, thou wilt drown the (bodily) Nile in the Nile of the spirit.

Hark, O Pharaoh, hold thy hand from (renounce) Egypt: there are a hundred Egypts within the Egypt of the Spirit.

Thou sayest to the vulgar, 'I am a Lord[3],' being unaware of the essential natures of both these names[4].

How should a Lord be trembling (with hope or fear) for that which is lorded over? How should one who knows 'I' be in bondage to body and soul?

Lo, we are (the real) 'I,' having been freed from (the unreal) 4130 'I,' from the 'I' that is full of tribulation and trouble.

To thee, O cur, that 'I'-hood was baleful, (but) in regard to us it was irreversibly ordained felicity.

Unless thou hadst had this vindictive 'I'-hood, how should such fortune have bidden us welcome?[5]

In thanksgiving for our deliverance from the perishable abode we are (now) admonishing thee on this gallows.

The gallows (*dár*) on which we are killed is the Buráq on which we ride (to Heaven)[6]; the abode (*dár*) possessed by thee is delusion and heedlessness.

---

[1] *Qur'án*, XXVI, 50.    [2] *I.e.* was thrown into commotion by that cry.
[3] The exact words attributed to Pharaoh are, "I am your Lord the Supreme."
[4] *I.e.* "I" and "Lord."
[5] Or, reading خوش اقبال, "how should such delectable fortune have befallen us?"
[6] Literally, "the Buráq (heavenly steed) of our journey."

4135  This (gallows) is a life concealed in the form of death, while that (abode) is a death concealed in the husk of life.

(Here) light seems as fire, and fire as light: else, how should this world have been the abode of delusion?"

Beware, do not make (too much) haste: first become naught, and when you sink (into non-existence) rise from the radiant East!

The heart was dumbfounded by the eternal "I"-hood: this (unreal) "I"-hood became insipid and opprobrious (in its sight).

The spirit was made glad by that "I"-hood without "I" and sprang away from the "I"-hood of the world.

4140  Since it has been delivered from "I," it has now become "I": blessings on the "I" that is without affliction;

For it is fleeing (from its unreal "I"-hood), and (the real) "I"-hood is running after it, since it saw it (the spirit) to be selfless.

(If) you seek it (the real "I"-hood), it will not become a seeker of you: (only) when you have died (to self) will that which you seek become your seeker.

(If) you are living, how should the corpse-washer wash you? (If) you are seeking, how should that which you seek go in search of you?

If the intellect could discern the (true) way in this question, Fakhr-i Rází[1] would be an adept in religious mysteries;

4145  But since he was (an example of the saying that) whoso has not tasted does not know, his intelligence and imaginations (only) increased his perplexity.

How should this "I" be revealed by thinking? That "I" is revealed (only) after passing away from self (faná).

These intellects in their quest (of the real "I") fall into the abyss of incarnation (ḥulúl) and ittiḥád[2].

O Ayáz[3] who hast passed away (from self) in union (with God) like the star in the beams of the sun—

Nay, (but rather) transmuted, like semen, into body—thou art not afflicted with ḥulúl and ittiḥád.

4150  "Forgive[4], O thou in whose coffer Forgiveness is (contained) and by whom all precedents of mercy are preceded.

Who am I that I should say 'Forgive,' O thou who art the sovereign and quintessence of the command Be?

Who am I that I should exist beside thee, O thou whose skirt all 'I's' have clutched?

---

[1] Fakhru'ddín of Rayy, a celebrated theologian and philosopher (ob. A.D. 1209).

[2] The heretical doctrine that the creature becomes one with the Creator.

[3] I.e. the perfect saint.

[4] This and the following verses are addressed by Ayáz to Sultan Maḥmúd.

[*How Ayáz deemed himself culpable for thus acting as intercessor and begged pardon for this offence and deemed himself culpable for begging pardon; and this self-abasement arises from knowledge of the majesty of the King; for (the Prophet hath said), 'I know God better than you and fear Him more than you,' and the High God hath said, 'None fears God but those of His servants that are possessed of knowledge.'*]

How should I bring (plead for) mercy to thee who art moved with anger, and point out the path of clemency to thee who art endued with knowledge?

If thou subject me to the indignity of (receiving) cuffs, I am deserving of a hundred thousand cuffs.

What should I say in thy presence? Should I give thee in- 4155 formation or recall to thy mind the method of lovingkindness?

What is that which is unknown to thee? And where in the world is that which thou dost not remember?

O thou who art free from ignorance and whose knowledge is free from (the possibility) that forgetfulness should cause (anything) to be hidden from it,

Thou hast deemed a nobody to be somebody and hast exalted him, like the sun, with (thy) light.

Since thou hast made me somebody, graciously hearken to my supplication if I supplicate (thee);

For, inasmuch as thou hast transported me from the form 4160 (of self-existence), 'tis (really) thou that hast made that intercession unto thyself.

Since this home has been emptied of my furniture, nothing great or small[1] in the house belongs to me.

Thou hast caused the prayer to flow forth from me like water: do thou accordingly give it reality and let it be granted.

Thou wert the bringer (inspirer) of the prayer in the beginning: be thou accordingly the hope for its acceptance in the end,

In order that I may boast that the King of the world pardoned the sinners for his slave's sake.

(Formerly) I was a pain, entirely self-satisfied: the King made 4165 me the remedy for every sufferer from pain.

(Formerly) I was a Hell filled with woe and bale: the hand of his grace made me a Kawthar.

Whomsoever Hell has consumed in vengeance, I cause him to grow anew from his body."

What is the work of (that) Kawthar by which every one that has been burned (in Hell) is made to grow and becomes redintegrated?

Drop by drop it proclaims its bounty, saying, "I restore that which Hell has consumed."

---

[1] Literally, "wet or dry."

4170   Hell is like the cold of autumn; Kawthar is like the spring, O rose-garden.

Hell is like death and the earth of the grave; Kawthar resembles the blast of the trumpet (of Resurrection).

O ye whose bodies are consumed by Hell, the kindness (of God) is leading you towards Kawthar.

Since Thy mercy, O Self-subsistent Living One, said, "I created the creatures that they might profit by Me[1],"

(And since Thy saying) "Not that I might profit by them" is (the expression of) Thy munificence, by which all defective things are made whole,

4175   Pardon these body-worshipping slaves: pardon from (Thee who art) the ocean of pardon is more worthy.

Creaturely pardon[2] is like a river and like a torrent: (all) the troop (of such pardons) run towards their ocean.

Every night from these individual hearts[3] the pardons come to Thee, O King, like pigeons.

At the hour of dawn Thou causest them to fly away again, and imprisonest them in these bodies till nightfall.

Once more, at eventide, flapping their wings they fly off in passionate longing for that palace and roof.

4180   In order that they may snap the thread that unites them with the body, they come before Thee, for by Thee they are endowed with fortune—

Flapping their wings, secure from falling back headlong, (soaring) in the (spiritual) air and saying, "*Verily unto Him we are returning.*"

From that Bounty comes the call, "Come! After that returning (unto Me) desire and anxiety are no more.

As exiles in the world ye suffered many indignities[4]: ye will have learned to value Me, O nobles.

Hark now, stretch your legs beneath the shade of this tree of Mine in the intoxication of delight,

4185   (Stretch) your legs, (which are) fatigued by (travel on) the Way of Religion, resting for ever on the bosoms and hands of the houris,

(While) the houris amorously and fondly say[5], 'These Ṣúfís have returned from their travels.

The Ṣúfís pure as the light of the sun, who for a long time had fallen into (the world of) earth and filth,

Have (now) come back stainless and undefiled, as the sunlight to the lofty orb (of the sun).'"

---

[1] Literally, "that profit might be made on Me."
[2] *I.e.* qualities of mercy and clemency.
[3] Literally, "these bits of heart (spirit)."
[4] Literally, "Ye suffered from the world many things such as strangers suffer."
[5] Literally, "have become ogling and fond, saying."

(Ayáz said), "This company of sinners likewise, O glorious (King)—all their heads have come against a wall[1].

They have become aware of their fault and sin, although they 4190 were defeated by the King's two dice[2].

Now they turn their faces towards thee, uttering cries of lamentation. O thou whose clemency is making way for sinners,

Speedily grant the defiled ones admission into the Euphrates of (thy) pardon and the fountain (which is) a (cool) *washing-place*,

That they may wash themselves clean of that prolonged sin and join in prayer among the ranks of the purified—

Among those innumerable ranks plunged in the light of '*We are they that stand in line.*'"

When the discourse reached the description of this (exalted) 4195 state, at once the pen broke and the paper tore.

Did any saucer measure the sea? Did a lamb ever carry off a lion?

If you are veiled, go forth from enveilment, that you may behold the marvellous sovereignty (of God).

Although the drunken fellows broke Thy cup, (yet) there is an excuse for him that is intoxicated by Thee.

Is not their intoxication with fortune and riches (the result) of Thy wine, O Thou whose actions are sweet?

O Emperor, they are intoxicated with Thy election (of them): 4200 pardon him that is intoxicated with Thee, O Pardoner!

The delight of being elected (singled out) by Thee at the moment of Thy addressing them has an effect that is not produced by a hundred jars of wine.

Since Thou hast intoxicated me, do not inflict a penalty: the Law does not see fit to inflict a penalty on the intoxicated.

Inflict it (only) at the time when I become sober; for indeed I shall never become sober (again).

Whoso has drunk of Thy cup, O Gracious One, is for ever delivered from self-consciousness and from the infliction of penalties.

Their intoxication consists in a state of unconsciousness of self 4205 (*faná*), (in which they are) abiding for ever: he that passes away from self in love for Thee[3] will not arise[4].

Thy grace saith to our heart, "Go, O thou who hast become in pawn to the buttermilk of My love.

Thou hast fallen, like a gnat, into My buttermilk: O gnat, thou art not intoxicated, thou art the wine (itself).

O gnat, the vultures become intoxicated by thee, when thou ridest on the ocean of honey.

[1] *I.e.* they are overcome with contrition.
[2] *I.e.* although the King played a game with them and beguiled them by seeming to approve of what they did.
[3] Literally, "you" (plural of majesty).
[4] *I.e.* will not come to himself again.

The mountains are tipsy with thee (and dance) like motes;
the point and the compass and the line are in thy hand (control).

4210   The torment at which they tremble is trembling at thee: every
costly pearl is cheap to thee."

If God gave me five hundred mouths, I would sing in
description (praise) of thee, O (my) soul and world[1];

(But) I have (only) one mouth, and even that one is crushed
with shame before thee, O knower of the mystery.

In sooth I am not more crushed than non-existence, from the
mouth of which (all) these peoples have come (forth).

A hundred thousand impressions of the Unseen World are
waiting to spring forth graciously and kindly from non-existence.

4215   Because of thy urgency my head is reeling: oh, I am dead in
the presence of that bounty.

Our desire (for thee) arises from thy urgency: wherever there
is a wayfarer, 'tis the pull of God (that draws him on).

Does the dust leap upward without a wind? Does a ship
voyage[2] without the sea?

None (ever) died in the presence of the Water of Life:
compared with thy water the Water of Life is (mere) dregs.

The Water of Life is the goal of those to whom life is dear:
by water the garden is (made) verdant and smiling.

4220   (But) those who quaff the cup of death are living through His
love: they have torn their hearts away from life and the Water of
Life.

When the water of Thy love gave us its hand (was gained by
us), the Water of Life became worthless in our sight.

Every soul derives freshness from the Water of Life, but Thou
art the Water (Source) of the Water of Life.

Thou didst bestow on me a (spiritual) death and a resurrection
continually, that I might experience the conquering power of
that bounty (of Thine).

This (bodily) dying became (as unformidable) to me as
sleeping, from my confidence that Thou, O God, wouldst raise
me from the dead.

4225   If the Seven Seas become a mirage at every moment, Thou
wilt take it (the water) by the ear and bring it (back), O Water
(Source) of the water.

Reason is trembling with fear of death, but Love is bold: how
should the stone be afraid of rain as the clod (is)?

This is the Fifth of the Scrolls (Books) of the *Mathnawí*: it is
like the stars in the zodiacal signs of the spiritual sky.

Not every sense can find its way by the star: (none can do so)
except the mariner acquainted with the star.

---

[1] This and the following verses are probably addressed to Ḥusámu'ddín,
who represents the God-intoxicated and "deified" saint.
[2] Literally, "set foot on the way."

The lot of the others is naught but looking (at it): they are ignorant of its auspiciousness and (fortunate) conjunction.

During the nights till daybreak make thyself familiar with 4230 devil-burning stars like these,

Every one (of which) is hurling naphtha from the fortress of Heaven to drive away the evil-thinking devil.

To the devil the stars are (noxious) as a scorpion, (but) to the buyer (of Truth) it (the star) is the next of kin (the nearest and dearest).

If the Bow (Sagittarius) pierce the devil with an arrow, (yet) the Bucket (Aquarius) is full of water for the crops and fruit.

Though the Fish (Pisces) wreck the ship of error, (yet) for the friend (of Truth) it is (ploughing and) sowing like the bull[1].

If the Sun rend Night to pieces, like a lion[2], (yet) there comes 4235 from it a satin robe of honour for the ruby[3].

Every existence that emerged from non-existence is poison to one and sugar to another.

Be a friend (of Truth) and become quit of unsweet qualities, so that you may eat sugar even from a jar of poison.

A (deadly) poison did no harm to Fárúq ('Umar) because to him the antidote, discrimination (*fárúqí*), was (sweet as) candy.

---

[1] *Thawr* (bull) also signifies the constellation Taurus.
[2] *Asad* (lion) also signifies the constellation Leo.
[3] Alluding to the belief that rubies derive their colour from the sun.

BOOK VI

IN THE NAME OF GOD THE COMPASSIONATE, THE MERCIFUL.

The Sixth Volume of the Books of Rhymed Couplets (*Mathnawí*) and Spiritual Evidences, which are a Lamp in the darkness of imagination and perplexity and phantasies and doubt and suspicion. And this Lamp cannot be perceived by the animal sense, because the state of animality is *the lowest of the low*, since they (the animals) have been created to keep in good order the outward form of the lower world; and about their senses and perceptive faculties there has been drawn a circle beyond which they may not pass: *that is the measurement* (*ordainment*) *of* (*God*) *the Mighty, the Wise, i.e.* He hath made manifest the limited measure of their action and the (confined) range of their speculation, just as every star has a certain measure (orbit) and sphere of work to which its action reaches in the sky; or as the ruler of a city whose authority is effective within that city, but beyond that city's dependencies he does not rule. May God preserve us from His imprisoning and sealing and from that wherewith He has veiled those who are veiled! Amen, O Lord of created beings.

IN THE NAME OF GOD THE COMPASSIONATE, THE MERCIFUL.

O Life of the heart, Ḥusámu'ddín, desire for (the composition of) a Sixth Part has long been boiling (within me).

Through the attraction (influence) of a Sage like thee, a Book of Ḥusám has come into circulation in the world.

(Now), O spiritual one, I bring to thee as an offering the Sixth Part to complete the *Mathnawí*.

From these Six Books give light to the Six Directions, in order that any one who has not performed the circumambulation may (now) perform it (round the *Mathnawí*).

5    Love hath naught to do with the five (senses) and the six (directions): its goal is only (to experience) the attraction exerted by the Beloved.

Afterwards, maybe, permission will come (from God): the secrets that ought to be told will be told,

With an eloquence that is nearer (to the understanding) than these subtle recondite allusions.

The secret is partner with none but the knower of the secret; in the sceptic's ear the secret is no secret (at all).

But (the command) to call (the people to God) comes down from the Maker: what has he (the prophet or saint) to do with (their) acceptance or non-acceptance?

10    Noah continued to call (the people to God) for nine hundred years: the unbelief of his folk was increasing from moment to moment.

Did he ever pull back the rein of speech? Did he ever creep into the cave of silence?

He said (to himself), "Does a caravan ever turn back from a journey on account of the noise and clamour of dogs?

Or on a night of moonlight is the running of the full-moon in its course retarded by the dog's outcry?

The moon sheds light and the dog barks: every one proceeds according to his nature.

15    (The Divine) Destiny hath allotted to every one a certain service, suitable to his essential nature, (to be performed) in (the way of) probation.

Since the dog will not leave off his pestilent howling, I (who am the moon, how should I abandon my course?"

Inasmuch as the vinegar increases acidity, therefore it is necessary to increase the sugar.

Wrath is (like) vinegar, mercy like honey; and these twain are the basis of every oxymel.

If the honey fail to withstand (be overpowered by) the vinegar, the oxymel will be spoilt.

The people were pouring vinegar on him (Noah), and the 20
Ocean (of Divine Bounty) was pouring more sugar for Noah.

His sugar was replenished from the Sea of Bounty, therefore
it was exceeding the vinegar of (all) the inhabitants of the world.

Who is a single one like a thousand? That Saint. Nay, that
Servant of the High (God) is (equivalent to) a hundred genera-
tions.

The great rivers kneel (in homage) before the jar into which
there comes a channel from the sea,

Especially this Sea (of Reality); for all the (other) seas, when
they heard this (imperial) mandate and (mighty) tumult[1]—

Their mouths became bitter with shame and confusion because 25
the Greatest Name had been joined with the least.

At the conjunction of this world with yonder world this world
is recoiling in shame.

This (manner of) expression is narrow (inadequate) and
deficient, for what resemblance exists between the vile and the
most elect?

(If) the crow caws in the orchard, (yet) how should the
nightingale cease its sweet song?

Every one, then, has his separate customer in this bazaar of
*He doeth what He pleases*.

The dessert provided by the thornbrake is nutriment (fuel) 30
for the fire; the scent of the rose is food for the intoxicated brain.

If filth is disgraceful in our opinion, (yet) it is sugar and
sweetmeat to the pig and the dog.

If the filthy ones commit these foulnesses, (yet) the (pure)
waters are intent on purification.

Though the snakes are scattering venom and though the sour
people are making us distressed,

(Yet) in mountain and hive and tree the bees are depositing
a sugar-store of honey.

However much the venoms show venomousness, the antidotes 35
quickly root them out.

When you consider, this world is all at strife, mote with mote,
as religion (is in conflict) with infidelity.

One mote is flying to the left, and another to the right in
search.

One mote (flies) up and another down: in their inclination
(movement) behold actual strife.

The actual strife is the result of the hidden strife: know that
that discord springs from this discord.

The strife of the mote that has been effaced in the sun is 40
beyond description and calculation.

Since the (individual) soul and breath have been effaced from
the mote, its strife now is only the strife of the sun,

---

[1] *I.e.* the infusion of Divine grace into Noah.

18

(Its) natural movement and rest have gone from it—by what (means)? By means of *Verily unto Him we are returning*.

We have returned from ourselves to Thy sea and have sucked from the source that suckled us.

O thou who, on account of the ghoul, hast remained in the derivatives (unessentials) of the Way, do not boast of (possessing) the fundamental principles (thereof), O unprincipled man.

45  Our war and our peace is in the light of the Essence: 'tis not from us, 'tis between the two fingers (of God).

War of nature, war of action, war of speech—there is a terrible conflict amongst the parts (of the universe).

This world is maintained by means of this war: consider the elements, in order that it (the difficulty) may be solved.

The four elements are four strong pillars by which the roof of the present world is (kept) upright.

Each pillar is a destroyer of the other: the pillar (known as) water is a destroyer of the flames (of fire).

50  Hence the edifice of creation is (based) upon contraries; consequently we are at war for weal and woe[1].

My states (of mind and body) are mutually opposed: each one is mutually opposite in its effect.

Since I am incessantly waylaying (struggling with) myself, how should I act in harmony with another?

Behold the surging armies[2] of my "states," each at war and strife with another.

Contemplate the same grievous war in thyself: why, then, art thou engaged in warring with others?

55  Or (is it because thou hast no means of escape) unless God shall redeem thee from this war and bring thee into the uni-coloured world of peace?

That world is naught but everlasting and flourishing, because it is not composed of contraries.

This reciprocal destruction is inflicted by (every) contrary on its contrary: when there is no contrary, there is naught but everlastingness.

He (God) who hath no like banished contraries from Paradise, saying, "Neither sun nor its contrary, intense cold, shall be there."

Colourlessness is the origin of colours, peaces are the origins of wars.

60  That world is the origin of this dolorous abode, union is the origin of every parting and separation.

Wherefore, sire, are we thus in opposition, and wherefore does unity give birth to these numbers?

---

[1] Literally, "from (the motive of inflicting) injury and (gaining) advantage."      [2] Literally, "the waves of the armies."

Because we are the branch and the four elements are the stock: in the branch the stock has brought its own nature into existence.

(But) since the substance, (which is) the spirit, is beyond ramifications, its nature is not this (plurality); it is the nature of (the Divine) Majesty.

Perceive that wars which are the origins of peaces are like (the war of) the Prophet whose war is for God's sake.

He is victorious and mighty in both worlds: the description 65 of this victor is not contained in the mouth.

Still, if it is impossible to drain (drink) the Oxus, one cannot deny one's self[1] as much (water) as will slake thirst.

If you are thirsting for the spiritual Ocean, make a breach in the island of the *Mathnawi*.

Make such a great breach that at every moment you will see the *Mathnawi* to be only spiritual.

When the wind sweeps away the straw from the (surface of) the river-water, the water displays its unicolouredness.

Behold the fresh branches of coral, behold the fruits grown 70 from the water of the spirit!

When it (the *Mathnawi*) is made single (and denuded) of words and sounds and breaths, it leaves all that (behind) and becomes the (spiritual) Ocean.

The speaker of the word and the hearer of the word and the words (themselves)—all three become spirit in the end.

The bread-giver and the bread-receiver and the wholesome bread become single (denuded) of their forms and are turned into earth,

But their reality, in the three (above-mentioned) categories, is both differentiated in (these) grades and permanent.

In appearance they have become earth, in reality they have 75 not; if any one say that they have, say to him, "No, they have not."

In the spiritual world all three are waiting (for the Divine command), sometimes fleeing from form and sometimes taking abode (in it).

(When) the (Divine) command comes—"Enter into forms"— they enter (into them); likewise at His command they become divested (of form).

Know, therefore, that (in the text) *to Him belongs the creation and to Him the command* "the creation" is the form and "the command" is the spirit riding upon it.

(Both) the rider and the ridden are under the authority of the King: the body is at the portal and the spirit in the audience-chamber.

When the King desires the water to come into the pitcher, 80 He says to the spirit-army, "Ride!"

[1] Literally, "cut one's self off from."

Again, when He calls the spirit aloft, there comes from the overseers the cry, "Dismount!"

The discourse, (if continued) after this (point), will become subtle: diminish the fire, do not put more faggots on it,

Lest the small pots boil (too) quickly: the pot of the perceptions is small and low.

The Holy Transcendent One who makes the apple-orchard[1] conceals them (the apples) in a mist of words.

85   From this mist of sound and words and talk (arises such) a screen that naught of the apple comes (into perception) save the scent.

At least draw (inhale) this scent in greater quantity with (the nostrils of) your intelligence, that taking you by the ear it may lead you towards your origin.

Preserve the scent and beware of the rheum: protect your body from the cold wind (breath) and being of the vulgar,

Lest by the effect (thereof) it stop up your nose: oh, their air is colder than winter.

They are like lifeless matter and frozen and stout of body: their breaths issue from a snow-hill.

90   When the earth (of your being) is covered with a shroud of this snow, brandish the sunbeam-sword of Ḥusámu'ddín[2].

Hark, lift up the sword of Allah from the east: with (the radiance of) that east make this portal hot[3].

That Sun smites the snow with a dagger: it causes the torrents to pour from the mountains upon the (frozen) earth,

For it is neither of the east nor of the west: by day and by night it is at war with the astronomer,

Saying, "Why in thy baseness and blindness hast thou made a *qibla* other than me of stars that give no true guidance?

95   Displeasing to thee are the words of that trusty one[4] in the *Qur'án*—'*I love not them that set.*'

(Prompted) by Quzaḥ[5], thou hast girt thyself (for service) before the moon: hence thou art vexed by (the sign announced in the Verse) *and the moon shall be split asunder*[6].

Thou disbelievest that *the sun shall be folded up*[7]: in thy opinion the sun is of the highest degree.

Thou deemest change of weather to be caused by the stars: thou art displeased with (the text) *when the star shall fall*[8].

Verily, the moon produces no greater effect than bread: O many a loaf of bread that severs the vein of life!

---

[1] *I.e.* the world of reality.
[2] *I.e.* the *Mathnawí* and the illuminating spiritual truths contained in it.
[3] *I.e.* "melt the hardness of your heart."
[4] Abraham. See *Qur'án*, VI, 76.
[5] A demon associated with clouds and the rainbow.
[6] *Qur'án*, LIV, 1.
[7] *Qur'án*, LXXXI, 1.                [8] *Qur'án*, LIII, 1, slightly altered.

Verily, (the planet) Venus produces no greater effect than 100 water: O many a water that has destroyed the body!

Love of those (stars) is (implanted) in thy soul, and the advice of thy friend strikes (only) on the outer skin of thy ear.

(If) our advice takes no hold of thee, O great man, know that neither does thy advice take any hold of us.

(Thy ears are closed) unless, perchance, the special (sovereign) key (to open them) come from the Friend to whom belong *the keys of the heavens.*"

This discourse is like the stars and the moon (in splendour), but without the command of God it makes no impression.

The impression made by this star[1] (which is) beyond locality 105 strikes (only) on ears that seek inspiration,

Saying, "Come ye from (the world of) locality to the world without spatial relations, in order that the wolf may not tear you to pieces in checkmate (utter discomfiture)."

Since its pearl-scattering radiance is such (as has been mentioned), the sun of the present world may be described as its bat[2].

The seven blue (celestial) spheres are in servitude to it; the courier moon is fevered and wasted away by it.

Venus lays her hand[3] upon it to beseech (its favour); Jupiter[4] comes forward to offer to it the ready money[5] of his soul.

Saturn is eager to kiss its hand, but he does not regard himself 110 as worthy of that honour.

On account of it, Mars has inflicted so many wounds on his hands and feet; and on account of it Mercury has broken a hundred pens[6].

All these stars (planets) are at war with the astronomer, saying, "O thou who hast let the spirit go and hast preferred colour (vanity),

It[7] is the spirit, and we all are (mere) colour and designs: the star (spark) of every thought in it is the soul of the (material) stars."

Where is thought (in relation to it)? There all is pure light: this word "thought" is (used only) for thy sake, O thinker.

Every (material) star hath its house on high: our star is not 115 contained in any house.

How should that which burns (transcends) place (spatial relations) enter into space? How should there be a limit for the illimitable light?

[1] *I.e.* the essential nature of the *Mathnawi.*
[2] Literally, "is in quality its bat," *i.e.* "is dazzled by it."
[3] This can also mean "plays her harp." Venus (Zuhra) is the celestial harpist.
[4] *Mushtari,* which also means "purchaser."
[5] Literally, "with the ready money."
[6] Mercury, the celestial scribe, cannot write the mysteries of the *Mathnawi.*
[7] *I.e.* the Reality of which the *Mathnawi* is the expression.

But they (the mystics) use a comparison and illustration, in order that a loving feeble-minded man may apprehend (the truth).

'Tis not a simile, but 'tis a parable for the purpose of releasing (melting) the frozen intellect.

The intellect is strong in the head but weak in the legs[1], because it is sick[2] of heart (spiritually decayed) though sound of body (materially flourishing).

120 Their (the unspiritual men's) intellect is deeply involved in the dessert (pleasures) of this world: never, never do they think of abandoning sensuality.

In the hour of pretension their breasts are (glowing) like the orient sun, (but) in the hour of pious devotion their endurance is (brief) as the lightning.

A learned man who shows self-conceit in (displaying) his talents is faithless as the world at the time for keeping faith[3].

At the time when he regards himself (with pride) he is not contained in the world: he has become lost in the gullet and belly, like bread.

(Yet) all these (evil) qualities of theirs may become good: evil does not remain when it turns to seeking good.

125 If egoism is foul-smelling like semen, (yet) when it attains unto the spirit (spirituality) it gains light.

Every mineral that sets its face towards (aspires to evolve into) the plant (the vegetative state)—life grows from the tree of its fortune.

Every plant that turns its face towards the (animal) spirit drinks, like Khiẓr, from the Fountain of Life.

Once more, when the (animal) spirit sets its face towards the (Divine) Beloved, it lays down its baggage (and passes) into the life without end.

*How an inquirer asked (a preacher) about a bird that was supposed to have settled on the wall of a city—"Is its head more excellent and estimable and noble and honourable or its tail?"—and how the preacher gave him a reply suited to the measure of his understanding.*

One day an inquirer said to a preacher, "O thou who art the pulpit's most eminent expounder,

130 I have a question to ask. Answer my question in this assembly-place, O possessor of the marrow (of wisdom).

A bird has settled on the city-wall: which is better—its head or its tail?"

---

[1] *I.e.* it has no strength to search after spiritual things.
[2] Literally, "ruined."
[3] *I.e.* when the time comes for him to make good his pretensions.

He replied, "If its face is to the town and its tail to the country, know that its face is better than its tail;

But if its tail is towards the town and its face to the country, be the dust on that tail and spring away from its face."

A bird flies to its nest by means of wings: the wings of Man are aspiration, O people.

(In the case of) the lover who is soiled with good and evil, do 135 not regard the good and evil; (only) regard the aspiration.

If a falcon be white and beyond compare, (yet) it becomes despicable when it hunts a mouse;

And if there be an owl that has desire for the king, it is (noble as) the falcon's head: do not regard the hood[1].

Man, no bigger than[2] a kneading-trough (scooped in a log), has surpassed (in glory) the heavens and the aether (the empyrean).

Did this heaven ever hear (the words) *We have honoured*[3] which this sorrowful Man heard (from God)?

Did any one offer to earth and sky (his) beauty and reason and 140 eloquence[4] and fond affection?

Didst thou ever display to heaven thy beauty of countenance and thy sureness of judgement in (matters of) opinion?

Didst thou ever, O son, offer thy silvery limbs to the pictured forms in the bath-house?

(No); thou leavest those houri-like figures and displayest thyself to a half-blind old woman.

What is there in the old woman that was not in them, so that she rapt thee away from those figures (and attracted thee) to herself?

(If) thou wilt not say (what it is), I will tell (thee) plainly: 145 'tis reason and sense and perception and consideration and soul.

In the old woman there is a soul that mingles (with the body): the pictured forms in the hot-baths have no (rational) spirit.

If the pictured form in the hot-bath should move, it would at once separate thee from the old woman.

What is soul? (Soul is) conscious of good and evil, rejoicing on account of kindness, weeping on account of injury.

Since consciousness is the inmost nature and essence of the soul, the more aware one is the more spiritual is he.

Awareness is the effect of the spirit: any one who has this in 150 excess is a man of God.

Since there are consciousnesses beyond this (bodily) nature, in that (spiritual) arena these (sensual) souls are (like) inanimate matter.

---

[1] *I.e.* the bodily form which masks its spiritual nature.
[2] Literally, "with the stature of."
[3] *Qur'án*, XVII, 72.
[4] Literally, "expressions (of speech)," "phrases."

The first soul is the theatre of the (Divine) court[1]; the Soul of the soul is verily the theatre of God (Himself)[2].

The angels were entirely reason and spirit (till) there came a new Spirit[3] of which they were the body[4].

When, by happy fortune, they attached themselves to that Spirit, they became subservient to that Spirit[5], as the body (is subservient to the spirit dwelling in it).

155 Hence Iblís (Satan) had turned his head away from the Spirit: he did not become one with it because he was a dead limb.

Since he had it not, he did not become devoted to it: the broken hand does not obey the spirit (which rules the body).

(But) the Spirit is not impaired though its limb is broken, for that (limb) is in its power, and it can bring it to life.

There is another mystery (to be told), (but) where is another ear? Where is a parrot capable of (eating) that sugar?

For the elect parrots there is a profound (occult) candy: to that food the eyes of the vulgar parrots are closed.

160 How should one who has (only) the appearance of a dervish taste of that purity? It is spiritual reality, not (mere) *fa'úlun fá'ilát* (amphibrachs and cretics)[6].

Candy is not withheld from the ass of Jesus by him (Jesus), but the ass is naturally pleased with straw.

If candy had roused delight in the ass, he would have poured hundredweights of sugar in front of the ass.

Know that this is the (inner) meaning of *We seal their mouths*: this (knowledge) is important for the traveller on the Way,

That perchance, by (his following) the Way of the Seal of the prophets, the heavy seal may be lifted from his lips.

165 The seals which the (former) prophets left were removed by the religion of Aḥmad (Mohammed).

The unopened locks had remained (as they were): they were opened by the hand of *Lo, We have opened (unto thee)*.

He is the intercessor in this world and in yonder world—in this world (for guidance) to the (true) religion, and yonder (for entrance) to Paradise.

In this world he says, "Do Thou show unto them the Way," and in yonder world he says, "Do Thou show unto them the Moon."

It was his custom in public and in private (to say), "Guide my people: verily they know not."

170 By his breath (powerful intercession) both the Gates were opened: in both worlds his prayer is answered.

---

[1] *I.e.* the unregenerate soul belongs to the phenomenal world.
[2] *I.e.* the soul of the perfect Man is the mirror of the Divine Essence.
[3] The spirit of Adam.
[4] *I.e.* to which they were subordinate.
[5] Referring to the worship of Adam by the angels.
[6] *I.e.* versification. *Fa'úlun* (⏑ – –) and *fá'ilát* (– ⏑ –) are used in Arabic prosody to represent metrical feet.

He has become the Seal (of the prophets) for this reason that there never was any one like him in munificence nor ever shall be.

When a master surpasses (all others) in his craft, don't you say (to him), "The craft is sealed on thee"?[1]

In the opening of seals thou (O Mohammed) art the Seal[2]: in the world of the givers of spiritual life[3] thou art the Ḥátim[4].

The purport (is this, that) the indications (esoteric teachings) of Mohammed are wholly revelation within revelation within revelation.

A hundred thousand blessings on his spirit and on the advent 175 and cycle of his sons!

Those fortunate Caliph-born sons of his are born of the substance of his soul and heart.

Whether they be of Baghdád or Herát or Rayy, they are his progeny without admixture of water and earth.

Wherever the rose-bough blossoms, 'tis still the (same) rose; wherever the wine-jar bubbles, 'tis still the (same) wine.

If the sun uplift its head (rise) from the west, 'tis the same sun, not anything else.

O Maker, by means of Thy veiling grace keep the fault- 180 pickers blind to this (mystic) utterance.

God said (in answer to my prayer), "I have blindfolded the eyes of the evil-natured bat (so as to prevent it) from (seeing) the peerless Sun.

From the glances of the infirm and feeble bat even the stars of that Sun are concealed."

*In blame of the rotten (worthless) reputations which prevent spiritual experience of the Faith and point to insincerity and stand in the way of hundreds of thousands of fools; as (for example) the (flock of) sheep stood in the way of a certain effeminate person, and he durst not pass, so he asked the shepherd, "Will these sheep of yours bite me, I wonder?" "If you are a man," he replied, "and the root of manhood is in you, they all are devoted to you; but if you are effeminate, each one of them is a dragon to (destroy) you." There is another (kind of) effeminate person who, when he sees the sheep, immediately turns back and does not dare to ask (the shepherd); for he is afraid that, if he asks, the sheep will fall upon him and bite him.*

Come, O Radiance of God, Ḥusámu'ddín, O polisher of the spirit and sovereign of the Way to salvation,

Give the *Mathnawí* a free and open course, endow the outward form of its parables with the spirit (of life),

---

[1] *I.e.* "has been brought by thee to the highest possible perfection."
[2] *I.e.* "thou art the supreme hierophant."    [3] The prophets and saints.
[4] *I.e.* the most bounteous. The generosity of Ḥátim of Ṭayy is proverbial.

185    That all its words may become reason and soul and may fly towards the soul's everlasting abode.

('Twas) through thy efforts (that) they came from the (world of) spirits into the trap of words and were confined (there).

May thy life in the world be like (that of) Khaḍir, soul-increasing and help-giving and perpetual!

Like Khaḍir and Ilyás, mayst thou remain in the world (for ever), that by thy grace earth may become heaven!

I would declare a hundredth part of thy grace, were it not for the vainglory of the evil eye;

190    But from the evil venomous[1] eye I have suffered spirit-crushing strokes.

(Therefore) I will not give an eloquent description of thy state except allusively, by telling of the state of others.

(Really, however) this pretext too is one of the lures of the heart whereby the feet of the heart are (caught) in a mire.

Hundreds of hearts and souls are in love with the Maker, (but) the evil eye or the evil ear has hindered (them from seeking union with Him).

One (of them), indeed, (is) Bú Ṭálib, the Prophet's uncle: to him the revilement of the Arabs seemed terrible,

195    For (he thought), "What will the Arabs say of me? (They will say), 'At the bidding of his nephew[2] he has changed the (traditional) custom on which we rely.'"

He (the Prophet) said to him, "O uncle, pronounce once the profession of faith, that I may plead with God for thee."

He (Bú Ṭálib) said, "But it will be spread abroad by hearsay: every secret that passes beyond the two (who share it) becomes common talk.

I shall remain (a laughing-stock) on the tongues of these Arabs: because of this I shall become despicable in their sight."

But if the predestined grace had been (granted) to him, how should this faint-heartedness have existed (simultaneously) with God's pull (towards Himself)?[3]

200    O Thou who art the Help of those who seek help, help (me to escape) from this pillory of wicked acts of free-will.

By the heart's deceit and guile I have been so discomfited that I am left unable (even) to lament.

Who am I? Heaven, with its hundred (mighty) businesses, cried out for help against this ambush of free-will,

Saying, "Deliver me from this pillory of free-will, O gracious and long-suffering Lord!

The one-way pull on *the straight Path* is better than the two ways of perplexity, O gracious One.

---

[1] Literally, "poison-breathing."    [2] Literally, "child."
[3] *I.e.* if he had been predestined to salvation, God would have drawn him on and no fear of reproach would have affected him.

Although Thou art the entire (only) goal of these two ways, 205 yet indeed this duality is agonising to the spirit.

Although the destination of these two ways is unto Thee alone, yet the battle is never like the banquet."

Hearken to the explanation thereof given by God in the Qur'án, (namely) the Verse *they shrank from bearing it*[1].

This perplexity in the heart is like war: (when a man is perplexed he says, "I wonder) whether this is better for my case or that."

In perplexity the fear (of failure) and the hope of success are always in conflict with each other, (now) advancing and (now) retreating.

*A prayer and a seeking refuge with God from the temptation of free-will and from the temptation of those things that minister to free-will; for the heavens and the earths dreaded and feared free-will and the things that minister to it, while the nature of Man is addicted to seeking free-will and all that ministers to his free-will; as (for example) if he is sick he feels himself to have little free-will and desires health, which ministers to free-will, in order that his free-will may be increased; and he desires high office in order that his free-will may be increased. And it was excess of free-will and of whatever ministers to it that caused the wrath of God to fall upon the peoples of the past. No one ever saw Pharaoh destitute.*

From Thee first came this ebb and flow within me; else, 210 O glorious One, this sea (of mine) was still.

From the same source whence Thou gavest me this perplexity, graciously (now) make me unperplexed likewise.

Thou art afflicting me. Ah, help (me), O Thou by whose affliction men are (made weak) as women.

How long (will) this affliction (continue)? Do not (afflict me), O Lord! Bestow on me one path, do not make me follow ten paths!

I am (like) an emaciated camel, and my back is wounded by my free-will which resembles a pack-saddle.

At one moment this pannier weighs heavily on this side, at 215 another moment that pannier sags to that side.

Let the ill-balanced load drop from me, that I may behold the meadow of the pious.

(Then), like the Fellows of the Cave, I shall browse on the orchard of Bounty—not *awake, nay, they are asleep*[2].

I shall recline on the right or on the left, I shall not roll save involuntarily, like a ball,

[1] *Qur'án*, XXXIII, 72. Heaven and earth refused the "trust" (of free-will) which God offered to them, but Man accepted it.
[2] *Qur'án*, XVIII, 17, slightly altered.

Just as Thou, O Lord of the Judgement, turnest me over either to the right or to the left.

220    Hundreds of thousands of years I was flying (to and fro) involuntarily, like the motes in the air.

If I have forgotten that time and state, (yet) the migration in sleep (to the spiritual world) recalls it to my memory.

(Every night) I escape from this four-branched cross and spring away from this (confined) halting-place into the (spacious) pasture of the spirit.

From the nurse, Sleep, I suck the milk of those bygone days of mine, O Lord.

All the (people in the) world are fleeing from their free-will and (self-)existence to their drunken (unconscious) side.

225    In order that for awhile they may be delivered from sobriety (consciousness), they lay upon themselves the opprobrium of wine and minstrelsy.

All know that this existence is a snare, that volitional thought and memory are a hell.

They are fleeing from selfhood into selflessness either by means of intoxication or by means of (some engrossing) occupation, O well-conducted man.

Thou (O God) drawest the soul back from that state of not-being because it entered into unconsciousness without Thy command.

Neither for the Jinn (genies) nor for mankind is it (possible) to pierce through the prison of the regions of the temporal world[1].

230    There is no piercing through the cavities of the highest heavens save by the power of Guidance.

There is no guidance save by a power that preserves the spirit of the devout from the keepers of the shooting stars.

There is no way (admittance) for any one, till he become naughted, into the audience-chamber of (Divine) Majesty.

What is the means of ascension to Heaven? This not-being. Not-being is the creed and religion of the lovers (of God).

From self-abasement in the way of Love the fur jacket and rustic shoon became the prayer-niche of Ayáz.

235    Even though he was beloved by the king (Mahmúd), and was charming and beauteous outwardly and inwardly—

(For) he had become devoid of any arrogance or ostentation or malice, and his face was a mirror for the beauty of the king—

(Yet 'twas only) because he was far removed from his (self-)existence, (that) the end of his affair was praiseworthy.

The steadfastness of Ayáz was all the firmer forasmuch as he was taking (those) precautions in fear of arrogance.

He had been purified, and he had come and smitten the neck of (had beheaded) arrogance and selfishness.

---

[1] *Qur'án*, LV, 33.

He was practising these devices either for the purpose of 240
instructing (others) or for the sake of some principle of wisdom
far removed from fear;

Or (perhaps) the sight of his rustic shoon pleased him because
(self-)existence is a shutter against the breeze of not-being[1],

(And he looked at them) in order that the charnel-house which
is (built) on not-being might open, and that he might feel the
breeze of vitality and life.

The wealth and riches and silks of this travellers' halt are a
chain on the light-footed spirit.

The spirit espied the golden chain and was beguiled: it
remained in the hole of a dungeon (far) from the open country.

Its (the world's) appearance is (that of) Paradise, (but) in 245
reality it is a hell; it is a viper full of venom, though its figure is
(that of) a rose-cheeked (beauty).

Although Hell-fire does no injury to the true believer, yet
'tis still better to pass on from that place (and leave it behind).

Although Hell keeps its torment far from him, yet in any case
Paradise is better for him.

O ye deficient (in understanding), beware of this rose-cheeked
one who at the time of intercourse becomes (like) a hell.

*Story of the Hindú slave who had secretly fallen in love with his
master's daughter. On learning that the girl was betrothed to the
son of a nobleman, the slave sickened and began to waste away.
No physician could diagnose his malady, and he (the slave) durst
not tell.*

A certain Khwája had a Hindú slave whom he had educated
and enlivened (with knowledge).

He had taught him science and all polite accomplishments; 250
he had lighted the candle of erudition in his heart.

That beneficent man had brought him up indulgently from
childhood in the lap of kindness.

This Khwája had also a fair daughter, silver-limbed, lovely,
and of excellent disposition.

When the girl had almost reached womanhood, the suitors
(for her hand) were offering heavy dowries,

And there was continually coming to him (the Khwája) from
every nobleman a wooer to ask for the girl (in marriage).

The Khwája said (to himself), "Wealth has no permanence: 255
it comes in the morning, and at night it goes in all directions
(is scattered to the winds).

Physical beauty too has no importance, for a (rosy) face is
made yellow (pale) by a single thorn-scratch.

Noble birth also is of small account, for he (such an one) is
befooled by money and horses."

---

[1] *I.e.* pride is an obstacle to self-abandonment.

Oh, there is many a nobleman's son who in riot and mischief has disgraced his father by his wicked deeds.

Do not court a man full of talent either, (even) if he be exquisite (in that respect), and take a warning from (the example of) Iblís.

260 He (Iblís) had knowledge, (but) since he had not religious love, he beheld in Adam nothing but a figure of clay.

Though you may know (all) the minutiae of knowledge, O trustworthy (scholar), not by that (means) will your two (inward) eyes that discern the invisible be opened.

He (the scholar) sees nothing but a turban and beard: he asks the announcer (for information) about his (the stranger's) merits and demerits[1].

(But) you, O knower (of God), have no need of the announcer: you see for yourself, for you are the rising light.

The (only) thing that matters is fear of God and religion and piety, of which the result is happiness in both worlds.

265 He (the Khwája) chose a pious son-in-law who was the pride of the whole clan and stock.

Then the women said, "He has no riches, he has neither nobility nor beauty nor independence."

He replied, "Those things are secondary to asceticism and religion: he (the pious man), (though) without gold, is a treasure on the face of the earth."

When it became known that the girl was going to be married in earnest, (as was proved by) the hand-promise[2], the tokens, and the wedding-outfit,

The little slave, who was in the house, immediately became ill and weak and poorly.

270 He was wasting away like one suffering from phthisis: no physician could recognise his ailment.

Reason declared that the malady had its source in his heart (and that) medicine for the body is useless for heart-ache.

The little slave breathed no word of his (real) state and did not tell what was the cause of the pangs in his breast[3].

One night the husband said to his wife, "Ask him privately what is the matter with him.

You are in the place of a mother to him: maybe he will disclose his trouble to you."

275 When the mistress heard these words, next day she went to the slave.

Then the dame combed his head very fondly[4] with many endearments and signs of friendliness.

---

[1] Literally, "his plus and minus."

[2] *I.e.* the marriage-contract.

[3] Literally, "from what cause the sharp point was coming (down) on him (and plunging) into his breast."

[4] Literally, "with two hundred fondnesses."

In the fashion of fond mothers she soothed him until he began to explain,

Saying, "I did not expect this from you—that you would give your daughter to a cross-grained stranger.

She is my master's child, and I am heart-sick: is it not a shame that she should go elsewhere (as a bride)?"

The mistress, (impelled) by the anger that rose in her[1], was about to strike him and hurl him down from the roof, 280

Saying (to herself), "Who is he, a whoreson Hindú, that he should desire a Khwája's daughter?"

(But) she said, "Patience is best," and restrained herself; (afterwards) she said to the Khwája, "Listen to this wonderful thing!

Such a wretched slave a traitor! (And) we thought he could be trusted!"

*How the Khwája bade the girl's mother be patient, saying, "Don't scold the slave: without scolding him I will make him abandon[2] this desire in such a way that neither will the spit be burnt nor the meat be left uncooked[3].*

"Have patience," said the Khwája: "tell him, 'We will break off (the match) with him (the prospective bridegroom) and give her to you,'

That perchance I may banish this (hope) from his mind: watch and see how I will thwart him. 285

Gladden his heart and say, 'Know for sure that our daughter is really your (destined) spouse.

O goodly wooer, we didn't know (that you desired her): (now), since we know (that), you are the most worthy.

Our fire is in our own hearth[4]: Laylá (the bride) is ours, and you are our Majnún (bridegroom).'

(Tell him this) in order that happy fancies and thoughts may affect him: sweet thoughts make a man fat.

An animal is made fat, but (only) by fodder; man is fattened by honour and eminence. 290

Man is fattened through his ear; an animal is fattened through its gullet and by eating and drinking."

The mistress said, "Such a vile disgrace! How indeed shall my lips move in this matter?

Why should I talk drivel like this for his sake? Let the devilish traitor die!"

"Nay," replied the Khwája, "have no fear, but wheedle him[5],

[1] Literally, "came to her."
[2] Literally, "I will turn him back from."
[3] *I.e.* the business will be settled without loss to us.
[4] *I.e.* the marriage is a family affair.
[5] Literally, "give him (empty) breath."

in order that his illness may depart from him by virtue of this sweet flattery.

295 Charge me with the task of thwarting him[1], O beloved, and let that spinner of fine yarns regain his health."

When the mistress had spoken in this strain to the invalid, on account of his swagger there was no room for him on the earth.

He grew stout and fat and red(-cheeked), and bloomed like a red rose and gave a thousand thanks.

Now and again he would say, "O my mistress, (I am afraid) lest this may be a deception and trick."

The Khwája gave a party and a feast, saying (to his guests), "I am making a match for Faraj,"

300 So that the company chaffed and quizzed (him) and said, "May your marriage be blessed, O Faraj!"

With the result that the promise seemed to Faraj more sure, and his illness vanished entirely and radically[2].

Afterwards, on the wedding-night, he (the Khwája) artfully dyed (the hands and feet of) a youth with henna, like (those of) a woman.

He decorated his fore-arms like (those of) a bride: then he displayed to him (Faraj) a hen, but (actually) he gave him a cock;

(For) he dressed the sturdy youth in the veil and robes of beautiful brides.

305 Quo tempore mos est sponsam cum conjuge in thalamo relinquere, (paterfamilias) candelam statim exstinxit: manebat Indus coram tali adulescente robusto et aspero.

Indulus clamorem et ululatum tollebat, (sed) tympanistarum causa nemo extra (thalamum) audiebat.

Tympana pulsata, manus complosae, virorum et feminarum clamores clamorem illius (pueri) clamitantis celabant.

(Adulescens) istum Indulum comprimebat usque ad diluculum: coram cane quid fiat sacco farinae?

At morning they brought the wash-basin and a big package (of clothes, etc.), and according to the custom of bridegrooms Faraj went to the bath.

310 He went to the bath, sorely troubled in soul, laceratus culum tanquam panni fornacatorum (bath-stokers).

From the bath he returned to the bridal chamber, a laughing-stock (to all): beside him sat the (Khwája's) daughter (dressed) like a bride.

Her mother (too) was sitting there to keep watch, lest he should make any attempt in the daytime.

He eyed her sulkily for awhile: then with both hands (spread) he gave her the ten (fingers)[3].

[1] Literally, "Write down against me (the obligation) to thwart him."
[2] Literally, "from the root and foundation."
[3] A gesture of malediction and repudiation.

"May no one," he exclaimed, "live in wedlock with a nasty evil-doing bride like thee!

By day thy face is the face of fresh young ladies; noctu penis 315 tuus turpis pejor est quam veretrum asini."

Even so all the pleasures of this world are very delightful (when viewed) from a distance before the (actual) test.

Seen from a distance they appear (like refreshing) water, (but) when you approach (them) they are a mirage.

She (the World) is a stinking hag, though by reason of her great blandishments she displays herself like a young bride.

Hark! Do not be deceived by her rouge, do not taste her sherbet which is mixed with poison!

Have patience (self-restraint), for patience is the key to joy, 320 lest like Faraj you fall into a hundred (grievous) straits.

Her (the World's) bait is visible, (but) her trap is hidden: at first (sight) her favours seem sweet to you.


*Explaining that this self-delusion was not (peculiar) to that Hindú alone; on the contrary, every human being is afflicted with a similar self-delusion at every stage (of the journey), except those whom God has preserved.*

Since you are attached to those (worldly goods), oh, beware! How often (afterwards) will you sob piteously in repentance!

The names "princehood," "vizierate," and "kingship" (are enticing, but) hidden beneath them is death and pain and giving up the ghost.

Be a slave (of God) and walk on the earth like a horse (under the rider), not like a bier which is carried on the necks (of the bearers).

The ungrateful (worldly) man wishes all people to carry him: 325 they bring him, like a dead rider, to the grave.

If you dream of any one (being carried) on a bier, he will become a high-stirruped rider of (will rise to high eminence in) office.

Inasmuch as the coffin is a burden on the people (who carry it), these grandees have laid the burden (of their rank and riches) on (the necks of) the people (whom they oppress).

Do not lay your burden on any one, lay it on yourself: do not seek eminence, 'tis best to be poor.

Do not be perpetually riding on the necks of people, lest gout attack[1] your feet.

The vehicle[2] which you will curse[3] in the end, saying, "Thou 330 resemblest a (flourishing) city, but thou art (really) a ruined village"—

[1] Literally, "come into."      [2] *I.e.* worldly fortune.
[3] See note on *v.* 313.

19

Curse it now when it (still) appears to you like a city, in order that (ultimately) you may not have to unload in the wilderness.

Curse it now when you (still) possess a hundred gardens, lest you become unable (to renounce it) and (become) devoted to the wilderness (of worldly fortune).

The Prophet said, " If thou desirest Paradise from God, desire nothing from any one (else).

When thou desirest nothing (from any one), I am thy surety for *the Garden of resort*[1] and the vision of God."

335 Because of this suretyship that Companion (of the Prophet) became so independent (of others) that one day when he had mounted (his horse),

And the whip fell right out of his hand, he himself dismounted and did not ask any one to give it to him.

He (God), from whose gifts no evil cometh, knows (your want) and Himself will give it without any asking.

But if you ask by God's command, that is right: such asking is the way followed by the prophets.

When the Beloved has signified (that you should do so and so), 'tis evil no more: infidelity (itself) becomes faith when the infidelity is for His sake.

340 Any evil deed prompted by His command surpasses (all) the good deeds in the world.

Even if the skin (exterior) of the oyster-shell be damaged, do not curse it, for within it there are a hundred thousand pearls.

This topic hath no end. Return to the King (God) and become endued with the nature of[2] the falcon.

Like pure gold, return to the mine, in order that your hands may be delivered from (the necessity of) giving the ten (fingers)[3];

(For) when they (worldlings) admit a phenomenal form into their hearts, in the end they curse it in contrition.

345 The repentance they show is like that of the moth: (soon) forgetfulness draws them back again to the (same) work.

Like the moth, he (such a one) deems the fire (seen) from a distance to be light, and packs off[4] (sets out) towards it.

As soon as he comes (to the fire), it burns his wings, and he flees; and (then) again he falls, like (greedy) children (in a hurry), and spills the salt[5].

Once more, thinking and hoping to profit, he quickly dashes himself on the fire of that candle.

[1] *I.e.* Paradise (*Qur'án*, LIII, 15).
[2] Literally, "of the same temperament as." The royal falcon, having caught its prey, always returns to the king.
[3] *I.e.* from the necessity of spurning the phenomenal illusions to which you are attached.
[4] Literally, "binds the load (on the beast of burden)."
[5] *I.e.* he relapses into his old ways and spoils his good resolutions.

Once more he is scorched and recoils; (then) again the greed of his heart makes him forgetful and intoxicated.

At the moment when he recoils on being scorched, he gives 350 the ten (fingers), like the Hindú (slave), to the candle[1],

Saying, "Oh, thy face is splendid as the night-illuming moon, but oh, in (actual) intercourse thou art false and destructive to him that is duped (by thee)."

(Then) again his repentance and moaning go out of his memory, for God hath made the stratagems of the liars to be feeble.

*Concerning the interpretation, in a general sense, of the Verse:*
"*as often as they kindle a fire for war.*"

As often as they kindle the fire of (spiritual) warfare, God quenches their fire so that it is put out (entirely).

He (such an one) makes a resolution, saying, "O (my) heart, do not stay there![2]" (but soon) he becomes forgetful, for he is not (really) resolute.

Since there was no seed of sincerity sown by him, God has 355 caused him to forget that (resolution)[3].

Though he strikes the match[4] of his heart, the Hand of God is always extinguishing the star (spark).

### *A Story in further exposition of this.*

A man of trust heard a sound of footsteps (in his house) during the night: he took up the fire-lighter to strike a flame.

At that (same) moment the thief came and sat down beside him, and whenever the tinder caught (fire) he put it out,

Laying the tip of his finger on the place, in order that the fiery star (spark) might vanish.

The Khwája thought it was dying of itself: he didn't see that 360 the thief was extinguishing it.

The Khwája said, "This tinder was moist: on account of its wetness the star (spark) is dying at once."

As there was great mirk and darkness in front (of him), he didn't see a fire-extinguisher beside him.

(So) the infidel's eye, because of (its) dimness, does not see a similar fire-extinguisher in his heart.

How is the heart of any knowing person ignorant (that) with the moving (object) there is (necessarily) a mover?

Why don't you say (to yourself), "How should day and night 365 come and go of themselves without a Lord?"

[1] *I.e.* he curses the candle. See *v.* 313.
[2] *I.e.* "do not remain attached to worldly pleasures."
[3] Literally, "has set over him (has made him subject to) forgetfulness of that (resolution)."
[4] Literally, "the (steel-and-flint) fire-lighter."

You are conversant with[1] intelligibles; (but) see what a lack of intelligence is shown by you (in this matter)[2], O despicable man!

Is a house more intelligible with a builder or without a builder? Answer, O man of little knowledge!

Is writing more intelligible with a writer or without a writer? Think, O son!

How should the *jím* of the ear and the *'ayn* of the eye and the *mím* of the mouth be (formed) without a Writer[3], O suspect?

370    Is the bright (lighted) candle without one who lights it or with a skilful lighter?

Is it more reasonable to expect good craftsmanship[4] from the hand of one who is palsied and blind or from[5] one who has control (of his hands) and can see?

Since, therefore, you have apprehended (the fact) that He (God) will overpower you and beat the mace of tribulation on your head,

Like a Nimrod, repel Him by war (if you can)! Launch an arrow of (hard) poplar-wood into the air against Him!

Like the Mongol soldiery, shoot an arrow at Heaven to prevent your soul being torn (from your body)!

375    Or flee from Him, if you can, and go (your way); (but) how can you go, since you are a pawn in His hand?

(When) you were in non-existence, you did not escape from His hand: how will you escape from His hand (now), O helpless[6] one?

To seek (one's own) desire is to flee (from God) and shed the blood of piety in the presence of His justice.

This world is a trap, and desire is its bait: flee from the traps, quickly turn your face (towards God).

When you have gone this way, you have enjoyed a hundred (spiritual) blessings; when you have gone the opposite way, you have fared ill.

380    Therefore the Prophet said, "Consult your hearts, though the mufti outside gives you advice in[7] (worldly) affairs."

Abandon desire, in order that He may have mercy (on you): you have found by experience that such (renunciation) is required by Him.

Since you cannot escape, do service to Him, that you may go from His prison into His rose-garden.

When you keep watch (over your thoughts and actions)

---

[1] Literally, "are moving round."
[2] Literally, "see such a lack of intelligence on your part."
[3] Because of their resemblance in shape these Arabic letters are often used to describe the ear, eye, and mouth respectively.
[4] Literally, "is good craftsmanship more suitable...?"
[5] Literally, "to."        [6] Literally, "easy to catch."
[7] Literally, "tells you about."

continually, you are always seeing the (Divine) justice and the (Divine) Judge, O misguided man;

And if you shut your eyes because you have veiled yourself (in heedlessness), (yet) how should the sun relinquish its work?

*How the King (Maḥmúd) revealed to the Amírs and those who were intriguing against Ayáz the reason of his superiority to them in rank and favour and salary, (explaining it) in such a manner that no argument or objection was left for them (to bring forward).*

When the Amírs boiled over with envy (of Ayáz), at last they 385 taunted their King,

Saying, "This Ayáz of thine has not thirty intellects: how should he consume the salary of thirty Amírs?"

The King, accompanied by the thirty Amírs, went out to hunt in the desert and mountain-land.

The monarch descried a caravan in the distance: he said to an Amír, "Go, man of weak judgement,

Go and ask that caravan at the custom-house[1] from what city they are arriving."

He went and asked and returned, saying, "From Rayy." 390 "Whither bound?" asked the King. He (the Amír) was unable (to reply).

(Then) he said to another (Amír), "Go, noble lord[2], and ask whither the caravan is bound."

He went and returned and said, "For Yemen." "Ha," said the King, "what is their merchandise, O trusty one?"

He (the Amír) remained (silent) in perplexity. (Then) the King said to another Amír, "Go and inquire (what is) the merchandise of those people."

He came back and said, "It is of every sort; the greater part consists of cups made in Rayy."

He (the King) asked, "When did they set out from the city 395 of Rayy?" The dull-witted[3] Amír remained (silent) in perplexity.

So (it went on) till thirty Amírs and more (had been tested): (all were) feeble in judgement and deficient in (mental) power[4].

(Then) he said to the Amírs, "One day I put my Ayáz to the test separately,

Saying, 'Inquire of the caravan (and find out) whence it comes.' He went and asked all these questions (just) right.

Without instructions, without a hint (from me), he apprehended everything concerning them, point by point, without any uncertainty or doubt."

Everything that was discovered by these thirty Amírs in thirty 400 stages was completed by him (Ayáz) in one moment.

---

[1] Where toll was paid by travellers.    [2] Literally, "father of eminence."
[3] Literally, "weak-sinewed."    [4] Literally, "in advance and retreat."

*How the Amírs endeavoured to rebut that argument by the
Necessitarian error and how the King answered them.*

Then the Amírs said, "This is a branch (species) of His
(God's) providential favours: it has nothing to do with (personal)
effort.

The fair face of the moon is bestowed on it by God, the sweet
scent of the rose is the gift of Fortune."

"Nay," said the Sultan, "that which proceeds from one's self
is the product of (one's own) remissness and the income derived
from (one's own) labour[1].

Otherwise, how should Adam have said unto God, '*O our
Lord, verily we have wronged ourselves*'?

405    Surely he would have said, '*This sin was from Fate: since it
was destiny, what does our precaution avail?*'

Like Iblís, who said, '*Thou hast led me astray*: Thou hast
broken the cup and art beating me.'"

Nay, (the Divine) destiny is a fact and the slave's (man's)
exertion (of power) is a fact: beware, do not be blind of one eye[2],
like the tatterdemalion Iblís.

We are left vacillating between two (alternative) actions: how
should this vacillation be without (unaccompanied by) free-will?

How should he whose hands and feet are chained say, "Shall
I do this or shall I do that?"

410    Can there ever be in my head such a dilemma as this[3],
(namely), "Shall I walk on the sea or shall I fly aloft?"

(No); there is (only) this (kind of) vacillation, (namely),
"Shall I go to Mosul (for trade) or shall I go to Babylon for (the
study of) magic?"

Vacillation, then, must have (in connexion with it) a power to
act; otherwise, it would be a (mere) mockery[4].

Do not put the blame[5] on Destiny, O youth: how can you
lay upon others (responsibility for) your own sin?

Does Zayd commit murder, and the retaliation for which he
is liable fall upon 'Amr? Does 'Amr drink wine, and the penalty
for wine(-drinking) fall upon Aḥmad?

415    Circle round yourself and perceive your sin: perceive that the
movement proceeds from the sun and do not regard it as pro-
ceeding from the shadow;

For the Lord's retribution will not err: that sagacious Lord
knows the guilty one[6].

When you have eaten (too much) honey, the fever (caused by

---

[1] *I.e.* human actions are the result of personal defects and personal merits.
[2] *I.e.* seeing only one side of the truth.
[3] Literally, "in my head this vacillation."
[4] Literally, "a laughing at the moustache."
[5] Literally, "the pretext."        [6] Literally, "the adversary."

it) does not come to (does not attack) another; your day's wages do not come at nightfall to another.

In what (work) have you exerted yourself without its returning to you (in some form)? What have you sown without the produce of the seed coming (back to you)?

Your action that is born of your soul and body clings to your skirt, like your (own) child.

In the Unseen World the action is given a form (corresponding 420 to its nature): is not a gallows erected (in retribution) for the act of robbery?

How should the gallows resemble robbery? But that is the form given (to robbery) by God who knoweth things unseen,

Since God inspired the prefect's heart to make such a form for justice' sake.

So long as you are wise and just, how should Destiny deal justice and give retribution not in accordance (with your actions)?

Since a judge does this in the case of a virtuous[1] man, how (then) will *the most Just of* these *judges*[2] give judgement?

When you sow barley nothing except barley will grow up: 425 (if) you have borrowed, from whom (but yourself) will you require the security[3]?

Do not lay (responsibility for) your sin upon any one else: give your mind and ear to this retribution.

Lay the sin upon yourself, for you yourself sowed (the seed): make peace with the recompense and justice of God.

The cause of (your) affliction is some evil deed: acknowledge that evil is done by you, not by Fate.

To look at Fate (alone) makes the eye asquint: it makes the dog[4] be attached to the kennel and lazy.

Suspect yourself, O youth; do not suspect the recompense of 430 (Divine) justice.

Repent like a man, turn your head into the (right) Way, *for whoso doeth a mote's weight (of good or evil) shall see it.*

Do not be duped by the wiles of the carnal soul, for the Divine Sun will not conceal a single mote.

These material motes, O profitable man, are visible in the presence of this material sun.

(So too) the motes consisting of ideas and thought are manifest in the presence of the Sun of Realities.

---

[1] Literally, "choice, excellent."
[2] God is so described in *Qur'án*, XI, 47.
[3] *I.e.* "if you incur a debt you must make yourself responsible for its repayment."
[4] *I.e.* the carnal soul.

*Story of the fowler who had wrapped himself in grass and drawn over his head a handful of roses and red anemones, like a cap, in order that the birds might think he was grass. The clever bird had some little notion that he was (really) a man, and said (to itself), "I have never seen grass of this shape"; but it did not wholly apprehend (the truth) and was deceived by his guile, because at the first view it had no decisive argument[1], (whereas) on its second view of the trick it had a decisive argument, namely, cupidity and greed, (which are) especially (potent) at the time of excessive want and poverty. The Prophet—God bless and save him!—has said that poverty is almost infidelity[2].*

435   A bird went into a meadow: there was a trap (set) for the purpose of fowling.

Some grain had been placed on the ground, and the fowler was ensconced there in ambush.

He had wrapped himself in leaves and grass, that the wretched prey might slip off from the path (of safety).

A little bird approached him in ignorance (of his disguise): then it hopped round[3] and ran up to the man,

And said to him, "Who are you, clad in green in the desert amidst (all) these wild animals?"

440   He replied, "I am an ascetic severed (from mankind): I have become content (to live) here with some grass.

I adopted asceticism and piety as my religion and practice because I saw before me the appointed end of my life.

My neighbour's death had given me warning and upset my (worldly) business and shop.

Since I shall be left alone at the last, it behoves me not to become friendly with every man and woman.

I shall turn my face to the grave at the last: 'tis better that I should make friends with the One (God).

445   Since my jaw[4] will (ultimately) be bound up[5], O worshipful one[6], 'tis better that I should jaw[7] little (now).

O thou who hast learned to wear a gold-embroidered robe and a belt, at the last there is (only) the unsewn garment[8] for thee (to wear).

We shall turn our faces to the earth whence we have sprung: why (then) have we fixed our hearts on creatures devoid of constancy (permanence)?

The four 'natures[9]' are our ancestors and kinsfolk from of old, (yet) we have fixed our hopes on a borrowed (temporary) kinship.

---

[1] *I.e.* nothing to convince it that its suspicions were correct.
[2] Because stress of poverty drives a man to commit great sins.
[3] Literally, "made a circuit."    [4] Literally, "chin."
[5] Before burial.    [6] Literally, "idol."
[7] Literally, "ply the chin," *i.e.* talk.    [8] The shroud.
[9] *I.e.* the natural properties of the four elements, viz. heat, cold, moisture, and dryness.

During (many) years the body of Man had companionship and intimacy with the elements.

His spirit, indeed, is from the (world of) souls and intelli- 450 gences, (but) the spirit has forsaken its origins.

From the pure souls and intelligences there is coming to the spirit a letter, saying, 'O faithless one,

Thou hast found (some) miserable five-day friends and hast turned thy face away from thy friends of old.'

Although the children are happy in their play, (yet) at night-fall they are dragged off and taken home.

At play-time the little child strips: suddenly the thief carries off his coat and shoes.

He is so hotly engaged in play that his cap and shirt are 455 forgotten.

Night falls, and his play becomes helpless (impossible): he has not the face to go home.

Have not you heard (the Verse) *the present life is only a play*? You have squandered[1] your goods and have become afraid.

Look for your clothes ere night comes on: do not waste the day in (idle) talk.

I have chosen a (place of) seclusion in the desert: I have perceived that mankind are stealers of clothes.

Half of life (is lost) in desire for a charming friend[2]; (the other) 460 half of life (is lost) in anxieties caused by foes.

That (desire) has carried off (our) cloak, this (anxiety) has carried off (our) cap, (while) we have become absorbed in play, like a little child.

Lo, the night-time of death is near. Leave this play: you have (played) enough, do not return (to it).

Hark, mount (the steed of) repentance, overtake the thief, and recover your clothes from him.

The steed of repentance is a marvellous steed: in one moment it runs from below up to heaven.

But always keep the steed (safe) from him who secretly stole 465 your coat.

Lest he steal your steed also, keep watch over this steed of yours incessantly."

*Story of the person whose ram was stolen by some thieves. Not content with that, they stole his clothes too by means of a trick.*

A certain man had a ram (which) he was leading along behind him: a thief carried off the ram, having cut its halter.

As soon as he (the owner) noticed, he began to run to left and right, that he might find out where the stolen ram was.

Beside a well he saw the thief crying, "Alas! Woe is me!"

[1] Literally, "you have given to the wind."
[2] Literally, "one who captivates the heart."

470 "O master," said he, "why are you lamenting?" He replied, "My purse (full) of gold has fallen into the well.

If you can go in and fetch it out, I will give you a fifth (of the money) with pleasure.

You will receive the fifth part of a hundred dinars in your hand." He (the owner of the ram) said (to himself), "Why, this is the price of ten rams.

If one door is shut ten doors are opened: if a ram is gone, God gives a camel in compensation."

He took off his clothes and went into the well: at once the thief carried away his clothes too.

475 A prudent man is needed to find the way to the village: (if) prudence be absent, cupidity brings calamity[1].

He (the Devil) is a mischievous thief: like a phantom, he has (he appears in) a (different) shape at every moment.

None but God knows his cunning: take refuge with God and escape from that impostor[2].

*The bird's debate with the fowler concerning monasticism and about the meaning of the monasticism which Muṣṭafá (Mohammed), on whom be peace, forbade his community to practise, saying, "There is no monkery in Islam."*

The bird said to him, "O Khwája, don't stay in (monastic) seclusion: monasticism is not good in regard to the religion of Aḥmad (Mohammed).

The Prophet has forbidden monasticism: how have you embraced a heresy, O trifler?

480 The conditions (imposed by Islam) are: (to take part in) the Friday worship and the public prayers, to enjoin good and shun evil,

To bear patiently[3] affliction caused by the ill-natured, and to confer benefit on (God's) creatures as (bounteously as) the clouds.

O father, the best of the people is he who benefits the people: if you are not a stone, why are you consorting with the clod?

Live amongst the community that is the object of (Divine) mercy: do not forsake the religion of Aḥmad (Mohammed), be ruled (by his practice)."

He (the fowler) replied, "Any one whose intelligence is infirm, *he* in the opinion of the intelligent is like a stone and clod.

485 One whose (only) wish is for bread resembles an ass: companionship with him is the essence of monkery.

(Do not associate with him), for all except God crumbles away, (and) everything that is coming after a time will (inevitably) come.

[1] Literally, "pestilence."    [2] Or, "imposture."
[3] Literally, "under patience."

His predicament is the same as that of his *qibla* (object of desire): call him 'dead' inasmuch as he seeks the dead[1].

Any one who lives with these (worldly) people is a monk, for his companions are (like) clods and stones.

In sooth, (actual) clods and stones never waylaid (and ruined) any one, (while) from *those* clods come a hundred thousand corruptions."

The bird said to him, "(Well), then, the *Jihád* (spiritual war) 490 is (waged) at the time when a brigand like this is on the road.

The valiant man enters on the unsafe road for the purpose of protecting and helping and fighting.

The root (innate quality) of manhood (only) becomes apparent at the time when the traveller meets his enemies on the road.

Since the Messenger (of Allah) was the Prophet of the sword, (the people of) his community are heroes[2] and champions.

In our religion the right thing is war and terror; in the religion of Jesus the right thing is (retirement to) cave and mountain."

He (the fowler) said, "Yes; if one has help (from God) and 495 strength to make a mighty attack on evil and mischief.

(But) when there is no strength, 'tis better to abstain: spring easily away in flight from what cannot be endured."

It (the bird) replied, "Firmness of heart is needed for achievement, but a (firm) friend does not lack friends.

Be a (firm) friend, that you may find friends innumerable; for without friends you will be left helpless.

The Devil is a wolf, and you are like Joseph: do not let go Jacob's skirt, O excellent one.

Generally the wolf seizes (his prey) at the moment when a 500 year-old sheep strays alone by itself from the flock.

He who has abandoned (the performance of) the Sunna with the (Moslem) community, has not he drunk his own blood (exposed himself to destruction) in such a haunt of wild beasts?

The Sunna is the (safe) road, and the community are like (your) companions (on the road): without the road and without comrades you will fall into (sore) straits;

(But) not the fellow-traveller who is an enemy to Reason and seeks an opportunity to carry off your clothes,

(And only) goes about with you in order to find a mountain-pass where he can plunder you!

Nor one who has the (timorous) heart of a camel and, when 505 he feels afraid, instructs (you) to turn back on the road!

By his camel's courage he frightens his comrade: know that such a fellow-traveller is an enemy, not a friend.

---

[1] *I.e.* the world is like a carcase, and those who desire it are (spiritually) dead.

[2] Literally, "cleavers of the ranks (of battle)."

The road (to God) is self-sacrifice, and in every thicket is a bane to drive back any one whose soul is (brittle) as a glass bottle.

The road of religion is full of trouble and bale for the reason that it is not the road for any one whose nature is effeminate.

On this road (men's) souls are tried by terror[1] as a sieve (is used) for sifting bran.

510 What is the road? Full of footprints. What is the comrade? The ladder whereby minds ascend.

I grant that, through (your) taking precautions, the wolf may not find you, (but) without company you will not find that (spiritual) alacrity.

He who cheerfully goes alone on a journey—(if he goes) with companions his progress is increased a hundredfold.

Notwithstanding the grossness of the ass, it (the ass) is exhilarated, O dervish, by comrades (of its own kind) and becomes capable of (exerting) strength.

To any ass that goes alone (and away) from the caravan the road is (made) a hundredfold (longer) by fatigue.

515 How many more goadings and cudgellings does it suffer that it may cross the desert (unaccompanied and) alone!

That ass is saying to you (implicitly), 'Take good heed! Don't travel alone like this, unless you are an ass!'

Beyond doubt he who cheerfully goes alone into the custom-house[2] will go more cheerfully (when he is) with companions.

Every prophet (that walked) on this straight road produced evidentiary miracles and sought fellow-travellers.

Were it not for the help given by the walls, how should houses and magazines arise?

520 If each wall be separated (from the others), how shall the roof remain suspended in the air?

If no help be given by ink and pen, how shall the writing come on to the surface of the paper?[3]

If this rush-mat which some one is spreading were not joined together (interwoven), the wind would carry it away.

Since God created pairs of every kind, therefore (all) results are produced by means of union."

He (the fowler) spoke (on one side) and it (the bird) spoke (on the other side): their debate on this subject was prolonged by the vehemence (with which they argued).

525 Make the *Mathnawí* nimble and pleasing to the heart: abridge and shorten (their) controversy[4].

Afterwards, it (the bird) said to him, "Whose is the wheat?" He replied, "It is the deposit of an orphan who has no guardian.

---

[1] Literally, "terror is the (means of applying) tests to souls."
[2] Cf. *v.* 389 *supra*.
[3] Read كاغذها رقم.
[4] This verse is addressed by the poet to himself or to his amanuensis.

It is orphans' property, deposited with me because people deem me trustworthy."

The bird said, "I am driven by necessity and in a sore plight: (even) carrion is lawful to me at this moment.

Hark, with your permission I will eat of this wheat, O trusty and devout and venerable one."

He replied, "You are the judge of (your) necessity: if you eat 530 without necessity, you will commit a sin;

And if the necessity exists, yet 'tis better to abstain; or if you do eat, at any rate give a guarantee for (payment of) it."

Thereupon the bird pondered deeply[1], (but) its restive steed took its head (recoiled) from the pull of the rein[2].

When it had eaten the wheat, it remained in the trap: it recited several times (the chapters of the *Qur'án* entitled) *Yásín* and *al-An'ám*.

What is (the use of crying) "Alas" and "Ah me" after being left helpless? This black smoke[3] ought to have been (exhaled) before that (calamity).

At the time when greed and desire have stirred (in the heart), 535 at *that* time keep saying, "(Help me), O Thou who comest at the cry for help!"

For that time is prior to the devastation of Baṣra, and it may be that Baṣra will still be saved from that overthrow.

O thou that wilt weep for me, O thou that wilt be bereft of me, weep for me before the demolition of Baṣra and Mawṣil (Mosul).

Mourn for me and smear thyself with dust before my death; do not mourn for me after my death, but bear (the loss of me) with patience.

Weep for me before my destruction in (the flood of) decease: after the flood of decease leave off weeping.

At the time when the Devil was waylaying (you), at *that* time 540 you ought to have recited (the Súra entitled) *Yásín*.

O watchman, use your rattle before the caravan is ruined (by the robbers).

*Story of the watchman who kept silence till the robbers had carried off the entire stock of the merchants, but afterwards made an outcry and did the duty of a watchman.*

A certain watchman fell asleep. The robbers carried off the goods and secreted the (various) articles under any piece of earth.

(When) it was day, the caravaneers awoke: they saw that stock and money and camels were gone.

Then they said to him, "O watchman, tell (us) what has happened. Where are this stock and these goods?"

---

[1] Literally, "went far down into itself."
[2] *I.e.* its carnal soul refused to follow the guidance of reason.
[3] *I.e.* these heavy sighs.

545 He replied, "The robbers came unexpectedly, and hastily carried off the stock from before me."

The party (of merchants) said to him, "O man (weak) as a sandhill, what were you doing, then? Who are you, O recreant?"

"I was (only) one," said he, "and they were a band, armed and brave and formidable."

He (the spokesman of the merchants) said, "If you had no hope (of overcoming them) in battle, (why didn't you) shout, 'Gentlemen, spring up (from your beds)?'"

He replied, "At that moment they produced knives and swords, crying, 'Silence! or we will kill you ruthlessly.'

550 At that time I shut my mouth in terror; at this time (I can utter) screams and calls for help and cries of distress.

At that time my breath was stopped from breathing a word: at this time I will scream as much as you please."

After the Devil who exposes (sinners) to disgrace has carried off your life, it is foolish (to cry) "*I take refuge (with God)*" and (to recite) the *Fátiḥa*;

(But) though 'tis foolish to moan now, (yet) assuredly heedlessness is (even) more foolish than that (tardy supplication).

Continue to sob thus, even foolishly, crying, "Regard the base (sinners), O Almighty One!

555 Whether it be late or early, Thou art omnipotent: when did anything escape Thee, O God?"

The King of (*that ye*) *may not grieve for what hath escaped you* —how should the object of (your) desire vanish from (the range of) His power?

*How the bird attributed its being caught in the trap to the artifice and cunning and hypocrisy of the ascetic; and how the ascetic answered the bird.*

The bird said, "This is a fit punishment for one who listens to the beguiling talk of ascetics."

"Nay," said the ascetic; "it is a fit punishment for the greedy wretch[1] who incontinently devours the property of orphans."

Afterwards it (the bird) began to lament in such wise that the trap and the fowler trembled at the grief (which it displayed),

560 Crying, "My back is broken by the contradictions (conflicting motives) in my heart: come, O Beloved, rub Thy hand on my head.

Under Thy hand my head hath a (great) relief (from pain): Thy hand is a miracle in bestowing favour.

Do not take away Thy shadow (protection) from my head: I am restless, restless, restless.

(All) sorts of sleep have quitted mine eye in my passion for Thee, O Thou who art envied by the cypress and the jasmine.

---

[1] Literally, "one who sops bread in soup before it is served."

Though I am not deserving (of Thy favour), what matter if for a moment Thou ask after an unworthy one (who is) in a (great) anguish?"

What right (to Thy favour), forsooth, had Not-being, to which 565 Thy grace opened such doors?

(Thy) bounty touched (embraced) the mangy earth and put in its bosom ten pearls of the light of sensation—

Five outward senses and five inward senses—whereby the dead semen was made Man.

Repentance without Thy blessing, O sublime Light, what is it but to laugh at the beard of repentance?

Thou dost tear the moustaches of repentance piecemeal: repentance is the shadow and Thou art the shining moon.

O Thou by whom my shop and dwelling is ruined, how shall 570 not I wail when Thou rackest my heart?

How shall I flee (from Thee), since without Thee none liveth, and without Thy lordship no slave hath existence?

Take my life, O Source of my life, for without Thee I have become weary of my life.

I am in love with the art of madness, I am surfeited with wisdom and sagacity.

When (the veil of) shame is rent asunder, I will publicly declare the mystery: how much (more) of this self-restraint and griping pain and tremor?

I have become concealed in shame, like the fringe (sewn on 575 the inside of a garment): I will spring forth of a sudden from beneath this coverlet.

O comrades, the Beloved has barred the ways: we are lame deer and He a hunting lion.

(For one who is) in the clutch of a fierce bloodthirsty lion where is any resource except resignation and acquiescence?

He, like the sun, hath neither sleep nor food: He makes the spirits (also) to be without food and sleep,

Saying, "Come, be Me or one with Me in nature, that thou mayest behold My Face when I unveil Myself.

And if thou hadst not beheld it[1], how shouldst thou have 580 become so distraught? Thou wert earth, (and now) thou hast become one who seeks to be quickened (with spiritual life)."

If He has not given you provender from the (world that is) without spatial relations, how has your spiritual eye remained (fixed) on that region?

The cat became intent on (watching) the (mouse)-hole because she had (formerly) provisioned herself from that hole.

Another cat prowls on the roof because she (formerly) obtained food by preying on birds.

One man's *qibla* (object of attention) is the weaver's craft,

[1] *I.e.* in the state of pre-existence.

while another is a guardsman for the sake of the (king's) allowance;

585 And another is unemployed, his face (turned) towards (the world of) non-spatiality because Thou (formerly) gavest him spiritual food from that quarter.

He has the (real) work who has become desirous of God and for His work's sake has severed himself from every (other) work.

The rest are like children playing, these few days, till the departure at nightfall.

The drowsy one who awakes and springs up[1], him the nurse, evil suggestion, beguiles,

Saying, "Go to sleep, my darling[2], for I will not let any one arouse thee from (thy heedless) slumber."

590 You yourself (if you are wise) will tear up your slumber by the roots, like the thirsty man who heard the noise of the water.

(God says to you), "I am the noise of the water in the ears of the thirsty: I am coming like rain from heaven.

Spring up, O lover, exhibit agitation: noise of water and (you) thirsty, and then to fall asleep!"

*Story of the lover who, in hope of the tryst promised (to him) by his beloved, came at night to the house that he had indicated. He waited (there) part of the night; (then) he was overcome by sleep. (When) his beloved came to fulfil his promise and found him asleep, he filled his lap with walnuts and left him sleeping and returned (home).*

In the days of old there was a lover, one who kept troth in his time.

For years (he had been) checkmated (irretrievably caught) in the toils of (seeking) his fair one's[3] favour and mated by his king.

595 In the end the seeker is a finder, for from patience joy is born.

One day his friend said, "Come to-night, for I have cooked haricot beans for thee.

Sit in such and such a room till midnight, that at midnight I may come unsought."

The man offered sacrifice and distributed loaves, since the moon (of good fortune) had appeared to him from beneath the dust (of ill-luck).

At night the passionate lover seated himself in the room in hope of the tryst promised by that loyal friend[4].

600 (Just) after midnight his friend, the charmer of his heart, arrived (punctually) like those who are true to their promise.

He found his lover lying asleep; (thereupon) he tore off a little piece of his (the lover's) sleeve

---

[1] Literally, "springs up from wakefulness."        [2] Literally, "soul."
[3] Literally, "moon's."              [4] Literally, "that friend of the Cave."

And put some walnuts in his lap, saying, "Thou art a child: take these and play a game of dice."

When at dawn the lover sprang up from sleep, he saw the (torn) sleeve and the walnuts.

He said, "Our king is entirely truth and loyalty: that (disgrace) which is coming upon us is from ourselves alone."

O sleepless heart, we (true lovers) are secure from this: we, 605 like guardsmen, are plying our rattles on the roof.

Our walnuts are crushed in this mill: whatever we may tell of our anguish, 'tis (but) little[1].

O railer, how long (will you continue to give) this invitation to (join in) the business (of the world)? Henceforth do not give advice to a madman.

I will not listen to deceitful talk of separation (from the Beloved): I have experienced it: how long shall I experience it?

In this Way everything except derangement and madness is (a cause of) farness and alienation (from Him).

Hark, put that fetter on my leg, for I have torn the chain of 610 (rational) consideration to pieces.

Though you bring two hundred fetters, I will snap (them all) except the curls of my auspicious Beauty.

Love and reputation, O brother, are not in accord: do not stand at the door of reputation, O lover.

The time is come for me to strip, to quit the (bodily) form and become wholly spirit.

Come, O Enemy of shame and anxious thought, for I have rent the veil of shame and bashfulness.

O Thou who by Thy magic hast spell-bound the spirit's 615 sleep, O hard-hearted Beloved that Thou art in the world,

Hark, grip the throat of self-restraint and strangle it, in order that Love's heart may be made happy, O Cavalier!

How should His heart be made happy till I burn? Oh, my heart is His home and dwelling-place.

(If) Thou wilt burn Thy house, burn it! Who is he that will say, "'Tis not allowed"?

Burn this house well (and thoroughly), O furious Lion! The lover's house is better so.

Henceforth I will make this burning my *qibla* (aim), for I am 620 (like) the candle: I am (made) bright by burning.

Abandon sleep to-night, O father: for one night traverse the district of the sleepless.

Look on these (lovers) who have become frenzied and been killed, like moths, by (their) union (with the Beloved).

Look on this ship of (God's) creatures (and see how it is) sunk in Love: you would say that Love's throat has become a dragon (to swallow it)—

---

[1] *I.e.* only a small part of it admits of description.

20

An invisible heart-ravishing dragon: it is a magnet[1] to draw (towards itself) the reason that is (firm) like a mountain.

625   Every druggist whose reason became acquainted with Him (Love) dropped the trays (containing drugs and perfumes) into the water of the river[2].

Go, for you will not emerge from this river (of Love) unto everlasting: in truth *there is none to be compared with Him.*

O false pretender, open your eye and see! How long will you say, "I know not that or this[3]"?

Ascend from the plague of hypocrisy and deprivation: enter the world of Life and Self-subsistence[4],

So that "I see not" may become "I see" and these "I know not's" of yours may be (turned into) "I know."

630   Pass beyond intoxication and be one who bestows intoxication (on others): move away from this mutability into His permanence.

How long will you take pride in this intoxication? 'Tis enough: there are so many intoxicated (like you) at the top of every street.

If the two worlds were filled with those whom the Friend has intoxicated, they all would be one (spirit), and that one is not despicable.

This (spirit) is nowise rendered despicable by (the appearance of) multitude. Who is despicable? A body-server (sensualist) of fiery nature.

Though the world is filled with the sun's light, how should that splendour of beauteous flame be despicable?

635   But, notwithstanding all this, mount[5] higher, since *God's earth is spacious* and delightful.

Although this intoxication is (excellent) like the white falcon, (yet) in the earth of (Divine) Transcendence there is (something) superior to it.

Go, become an Isráfíl (Seraphiel) in (your) distinction (preeminence)—(become) an inspirer of spirituality and intoxicated and an intoxicator (of others).

Since the intoxicated man's heart is occupied with thoughts of merriment, it has become his practice (to say repeatedly) "I don't know this" and "I don't know that."

What is the purpose of (saying) "I don't know this" and "I don't know that"? (It is) in order that you may say who He is whom we know[6].

[1] Literally, "the attractor of straw," *i.e.* amber.
[2] This verse alludes to Shaykh Farídu'ddín 'Aṭṭár (the Druggist and Perfumer) of Níshápúr.
[3] *I.e.* "how long will you remain in the state of *faná* or *sukr* (mystical intoxication)?"
[4] *I.e.* the state of *baqá* or *ṣaḥw* ("sobriety after intoxication").
[5] Literally, "walk with a proud gait."
[6] *I.e.* "in order that you may affirm the Absolute Being of God, as we do."

In discourse negation is (employed) for the purpose of affirma- 640
tion: cease from negating and begin to affirm.

Come, leave off (saying) "this is not" and "that is not":
bring forward that One who is Real Being.

Leave negation and worship only that Real Being: learn this,
O father, from (the story of) the drunken Turk.

*How a drunken Turkish Amír summoned a minstrel at the hour of
the morning-drink; and a commentary on the Tradition, "Verily,
God most High hath a wine that He prepared for His friends:
when they drink it they become intoxicated, and when they become
intoxicated they are purified," to the end of the Tradition.*

*"The wine is bubbling in the jars of the mysteries in order that any
one who is denuded (of self-existence) may drink of that wine."*

*God most High hath said,* "Lo, the righteous shall drink."

*"This wine that thou drinkest is forbidden; we drink none but a
lawful wine."*

*"Endeavour through non-existence (of self) to become (really)
existent and to be intoxicated with God's wine."*

A barbarian Turk came to his senses at dawn and, (suffering)
from crop-sickness caused by wine, desired the minstrel (to
divert him).

The spiritual minstrel is the bosom-friend of those intoxicated
(with God): he is the dessert and food and strength of the
drunken.

The minstrel led them on to intoxication; then again, he (the 645
intoxicated one) quaffed intoxication from the song of the
minstrel.

That one (the mystic) fetches God's wine (to drink) because
of that (spiritual) minstrel, while this one (the sensualist)
imbibes the bodily wine from this (sensual) minstrel.

Though both (minstrels) have one name in discourse, yet
there is a vast difference between this Ḥasan and that Ḥasan[1].

There is a verbal resemblance in enunciation, but what (real)
relation has heaven (*ásmán*) to a rope (*rísmán*)?

The participation of a word (in several meanings) is always
obstructive[2] (to the understanding): the participation of the
infidel with the true believer is in the body (alone).

Bodies are like pots with the lids on: look and see what is in 650
each pot.

The pot of that body is filled with the Water of Life; the pot
of this body is filled with the poison of death.

If you keep your eye fixed on its contents, you are a (spiritual)
king; but if you regard its vessel, you are misguided.

---

[1] Alluding to the story of the poet and the two viziers, each of whom was
called Ḥasan (Book IV, *v.* 1156 foll.).

[2] Literally, "a highway robber."

Know that words resemble this body and that their inward meaning resembles the soul.

The bodily eye is always seeing the body; the spiritual eye sees the artful (elusive) soul.

655   Therefore the man of appearance is misled by the form of the expressions used in the *Mathnawí*, while they guide the man of reality (to the Truth).

He (God) hath said in the *Qur'án*, "This *Qur'án* with all its heart leads some aright and others astray."

God, God! When the gnostic speaks of "wine," how in the gnostic's eyes should the (materially) non-existent be a (material) thing?

Since your understanding is (only of) the Devil's wine, how should you have any conception of the wine of the Merciful (God)?

These twain—the minstrel and the wine—are partners: this one quickly leads to that, and that one to this.

660   They that are full of crop-sickness feed on the song of the minstrel: the minstrels bring them to the tavern.

That one (the minstrel) is the beginning of the (lover's) course, and this (tavern) is the end thereof: the witless (lover)[1] is like a ball in (the sway of) his polo-bat.

The ear goes (inclines) to that which is in the head: if there is yellow bile in the head, it becomes black bile[2].

Afterwards, these twain (the minstrel and the lover) pass into unconsciousness: there the begetter and the begotten become one.

When joy and sorrow made peace (with each other)[3], our Turk awakened the minstrels.

665   The minstrel began (to sing) a slumberous verse—"Hand me the cup, O Thou whom I see not.

Thou art my face: no wonder that I see it not: extreme proximity is a mystifying veil.

Thou art my reason: no wonder if I see Thee not, on account of the abundance of the intricate perplexities (of thought).

Thou hast come nearer to me than my neck-artery: how long shall I say 'Oh'? 'Oh' is a call to one who is far off.

Nay, but I dissemble with them when I call (to Him) in the deserts, in order that I may conceal Him who is beside me from those who excite my jealousy."

---

[1] Literally, "he whose mind is gone."
[2] *I.e.* the lover will not listen to anything but songs of love which inflame his passion.
[3] *I.e.* when his intoxication had carried him beyond the world of opposites.

*How a blind man entered the house of Muṣṭafá (Mohammed), on
whom be peace, and how ʿÁʾisha, may God be pleased with her,
fled from the presence of the blind man, and how the Prophet, on
whom be peace, asked, "Why art thou running away? He cannot
see thee"; and the answer given by ʿÁʾisha, may God be pleased
with her, to the Prophet—God bless and save him!*

A blind man came into the presence of the Prophet, saying, 670
"O thou who suppliest fuel to every oven of dough[1],
O thou who art the lord of the Water (of Life), while I
am suffering from dropsy—help, help[2], O giver of drink to
me!"
When the blind man came in hastily by the door, ʿÁʾisha ran
away to conceal herself (from him),
Because that chaste lady was aware of the resentfulness of the
jealous Prophet.
The more beautiful any one is, the greater his jealousy, for
jealousy arises from (the possession of) loveliness, O sons.
Since foul hags are aware of their ugliness and old age, they 675
let their husbands take a concubine.
When has there (ever) been in the two worlds a beauty like
that of Aḥmad (Mohammed)? Oh, may the Divine Glory aid
him!
To him belong (all) the charms of both worlds: it beseems
that hundredfold Sun to be jealous,
Saying, "I have thrown my (resplendent) orb over Saturn:
beware, O stars, and cover your faces!
Be naughted in my incomparable radiance; else ye will be put
to shame before my light.
For kindness' sake, I disappear every night; (but) how should 680
I depart? I only make a show of departing,
That for a night ye may fly without me like bats, flapping
your wings, around this flying-place;
And that, like peacocks, ye may display a (gorgeous) wing,
and then become intoxicated and haughty and self-conceited.
Look at your uncouth feet, like the rustic shoon that were (as)
a candle to Ayáz[3].
At dawn I show my face to reprimand you, lest from egoism
ye become (included) among the people of the left hand[4]."
Leave that (topic), for that topic is lengthy: (he[5] who is the 685
final cause of) the command "*Be!*" hath forbidden lengthiness.

---

[1] *I.e.* "who dost increase the ardour of every (seeker's) heart."
[2] Literally, "(I beseech) Thee from whom help is sought."
[3] *I.e.* they were placed before him, like a candle, to remind him of the low
estate from which he had risen.
[4] *I.e.* those doomed to Hell.
[5] *I.e.* the Prophet.

*How Muṣṭafá (Mohammed), on whom be peace, made trial of* ʿA'isha, may God be pleased with her, and said, " Why art thou hiding? Do not hide, for the blind man cannot see thee," in order that it might appear whether ʿA'isha was acquainted with the secret thoughts of Muṣṭafá, on whom be peace, or whether she was (merely) one who would follow his expressed wishes.*

The Prophet said by way of trial, " He cannot see thee: do not hide."

ʿA'isha made a sign with her hands (as though to say), "(If) he does not see (me), yet I see him."

Reason's jealousy of the beauty of the Spirit is (the cause of) this sincere admonition[1] being full of similitudes and allegories.

Notwithstanding that this Spirit is so hidden, why is Reason so jealous of Him?

690　O jealous one, from whom art thou hiding Him whose face is concealed by His light?

This Sun goes with face uncovered: His face is veiled by the excess of His light.

From whom art thou hiding Him, O jealous one? The sun (itself) cannot see a trace of Him.

(Reason says), "The jealousy in my body is (all) the greater because I desire to hide Him even from myself.

On account of the fire of fell[2] jealousy I am at war with my own eyes and ears."

695　Since thou hast such a (mighty) jealousy, O my soul and heart, close thy mouth and leave off speaking.

(Reason says), " If I keep silence, I fear that that Sun will rend the veil and (display Himself) from another quarter."

In (keeping) silence our (inward) speaking (of Him) is (only) made more evident, since the desire (for manifestation) is increased by suppression.

If the Sea roar, its roaring turns to foam and becomes the surge of " I desired to be known[3]."

To utter words (concerning Him) is to shut the window (through which He reveals Himself): the very act of expression is the concealment (of Him).

700　Sing, like nightingales, in the presence of the Rose, in order that you may divert them[4] from the scent of the Rose,

So that their ears will be engaged in (listening to) the song, and their attention will not fly to the face of the Rose.

Before this Sun, which is exceedingly radiant, every guide is in reality a highway robber[5].

---

[1] *I.e.* the *Mathnawí.*
[2] Literally, " having a serious and formidable purpose."
[3] Referring to the famous tradition, " I was a Hidden Treasure, etc."
[4] The lovers of God.
[5] *I.e.* all the proofs of God's existence and nature are so many stumbling-blocks on the Way to Him.

*Story of the minstrel who began to sing this ode at the banquet of the*
  *Turkish Amír:*
*"Art Thou a rose or a lily or a cypress or a man? I know not.*
*What dost Thou desire from this bewildered one who has lost his*
  *heart? I know not"—and how the Turk shouted at him, "Tell*
  *of that which you know!"—and the minstrel's reply to the*
  *Amír.*

In the presence of the drunken Turk the minstrel began (to
sing of) the mysteries of *Alast*[1] under the veil of melody—
  "I know not whether Thou art a moon or an idol, I know not
what Thou desirest of me.

I know not what service I shall pay Thee, whether I shall keep 705
silence or express Thee in words.

'Tis marvellous that Thou art not separate from me, (and yet)
where am I, and where Thou, I know not.

I know not how Thou art drawing me: Thou drawest me now
into Thy bosom, now into blood."

In this fashion he opened his lips (only) to say "I know not":
he made a tune of "I know not, I know not."

When (the refrain) "I know not" passed beyond bounds, our
Turk was amazed and his heart became[2] sick of this ditty.

The Turk leaped up and fetched an iron mace to smite the 710
minstrel's head with it[3] on the spot[4];

(But) an officer seized the mace with his hand, saying, "Nay;
'tis wicked to kill the minstrel at this moment."

He (the Turk) replied, "This endless and countless repetition
of his has pounded my nerves[5]: I will pound his head.

O cuckold, (if) you don't know, don't talk nonsense[6]; and if
you do know, play (a tune) to the purpose.

Tell of that which you know, O crazy fool: don't draw out
(repeat continually) 'I know not, I know not.'

(Suppose) I ask, 'Where do you come from, hypocrite, eh?' 715
you will say, 'Not from Balkh, and not from Herát,

Not from Baghdád and not from Mosul and not from Ṭiráz':
you will draw out a long journey in (saying) 'not' and 'not.'

Just say where you come from and escape (from further
discussion): in this case it is folly to elaborate the point at issue.

Or (suppose) I asked, 'What had you for breakfast?' you
would say, 'Not wine and not roast-meat,

---

[1] Referring to the Primal Covenant between God and Man in the state of
pre-existence (*Qur'án*, VII, 171).
[2] Literally, "from amazement our Turk's heart became."
[3] Literally, "that it might come on the minstrel's head."
[4] علیها is said to be used colloquially in this sense.
[5] Literally, "nature," "humour."
[6] Literally, "don't eat dung."

Not *qadíd*[1] and not *tharíd*[2] and not lentils': tell me what you did eat, only (that) and no more.

720 Wherefore is this long palaver?[3]" "Because," said the minstrel, "my object is recondite.

Before (until) you deny (all else), affirmation (of God) evades (you): I denied (everything) in order that you might get a scent of (perceive the means of attaining to) affirmation.

I play the tune of[4] negation: when you die, death will declare the mystery.

[*Commentary on his (the Prophet's) saying—peace be upon him!—*
'*Die before ye die.'*
'*O friend, die before thy death if thou desirest life; for by so dying Idrís became a dweller in Paradise before (the rest of) us*[5].']

You have suffered much agony, but you are (still) in the veil, because dying (to self) was the fundamental principle, and you have not fulfilled it.

Your agony is not finished till you die: you cannot reach the roof without completing the ladder.

725 When two rungs out of a hundred are wanting, the striver will be forbidden to (set foot on) the roof.

When the rope lacks one ell out of a hundred, how should the water go from the well into the bucket?

O Amír, you will not experience the wreck of this ship (of self-existence) till you put into it the last *mann*[6].

Know that the last *mann* is fundamental, for it is (like) the (piercing) star that rises at night[7]: it wrecks the ship of evil suggestion and error.

The ship of (self-)consciousness, when it is utterly wrecked, becomes (like) the sun in the blue vault (of heaven).

730 Inasmuch as you have not died, your agony has been prolonged: be extinguished in the dawn, O candle of Tiráz![8]

Know that the Sun of the world is hidden till our stars have become hidden.

Wield the mace against yourself: shatter egoism to pieces, for the bodily eye is (as) cottonwool in the ear[9].

You *are* wielding the mace against yourself, O base man: this egoism is the reflexion of yourself in (the mirror of) my actions.

You have seen the reflexion of yourself in (the mirror of) my form and have risen in fury[10] to fight with yourself,

---

[1] Dried meat cut in strips.       [2] Bread soaked in gravy.
[3] Literally, "chewing of words."
[4] Literally, "I tune this instrument (of mine) with."
[5] He was taken alive to Paradise.
[6] A weight varying from half a stone or less to a stone and a half.
[7] *Qur'án*, LXXXVI, 1–3.       [8] *I.e.* "O beauteous one."
[9] *I.e.* an obstacle to spiritual perception.
[10] Literally, "have boiled up."

Like the lion who went down into the well; (for) he fancied 735
that the reflexion of himself was his enemy[1]."

Beyond any doubt, negation (not-being) is the opposite of
(real) being, (and this is) in order that by means of the
(one) opposite you may gain a little knowledge of the (other)
opposite.

At this time there is no (means of) making (God) known
except (by) denying the opposite: in this (earthly) life no moment
is without a snare[2].

O you who possess sincerity, (if) you want that (Reality)
unveiled, choose death and tear off the veil—

Not such a death that you will go into a grave, (but) a death
consisting of (spiritual) transformation, so that you will go into
a Light.

(When) a man grows up, his childhood dies; (when) he 740
becomes a (fair-complexioned) Greek, he washes out the dye
(swarthy colour) of the Ethiopian.

(When) earth becomes gold, its earthly aspect remains not;
(when) sorrow becomes joy, the thorn of sorrowfulness remains
not.

Hence Muṣṭafá (Mohammed) said, "O seeker of the mysteries,
(if) you wish to see a dead man living—

Walking on the earth, like living men; (yet he is) dead and his
spirit is gone to heaven;

(One) whose spirit hath a dwelling-place on high at this
moment, (so that) if he die, his spirit is not translated,

Because it has been translated before death: this (mystery) is 745
understood (only) by dying, not by (using one's) reason;

Translation it is, (but) not like the translation of the spirits of
the vulgar: it resembles a removal (during life) from one place
to another—

If any one wish to see a dead man walking thus visibly on
the earth,

Let him behold Abú Bakr, the devout, (who) through being
a true witness (ṣiddíq) became the Prince of the Resurrected.

In this (earthly) life look at the Ṣiddíq (Abú Bakr), that you
may believe more firmly in the Resurrection."

Mohammed, then, was a hundred (spiritual) resurrections[3] 750
here and now[4], for he was dissolved (naughted) in dying to
(temporal) loosing and binding.

Aḥmad (Mohammed) is the twice-born in this world: he was
manifestly a hundred resurrections.

They asked him concerning the Resurrection, saying, "O (thou

[1] See Book I, v. 1304 and foll.
[2] I.e. all temporal things are conditioned by "otherness," and attachment
to them is incompatible with spiritual freedom.
[3] This appears to be an echo of "I am the Resurrection and the Life."
[4] Literally, "in cash."

who art the) Resurrection, how long is the way to the Resurrection?"

And often he would say with mute eloquence[1], "Does any one ask (me who am) the Resurrection concerning the Resurrection?"

Hence the Messenger of good tidings said, (speaking) symbolically, "Die before ye die, O nobles,

755    Even as I have died before death and brought from Yonder this fame and renown."

Do thou, then, become the (spiritual) resurrection and (thereby) see (experience) the resurrection: this (becoming) is the necessary condition for seeing (knowing and experiencing the real nature of) anything.

Until thou become it, thou wilt not know it completely, whether it be light or darkness.

(If) thou become Reason, thou wilt know Reason perfectly; if thou become Love, thou wilt know Love's (flaming) wick.

I would declare plainly the proof of this assertion, if there were an understanding fit to receive it.

760    Figs are very cheap in this vicinity[2], if a fig-eating bird should arrive as a guest.

(All), whether men or women, in the whole world are continually in the death-agony and are dying.

Regard their words as the (final) injunctions which a father gives at that moment to his son,

That thereby consideration and pity may grow (in thy heart), so that the root of hatred and jealousy and enmity may be cut off.

Look on thy kinsman with that intention, so that thy heart may burn (with pity) for his death-agony.

765    "Everything that is coming will come": deem it (to have come) here and now, deem thy friend to be in the death-agony and in the act of losing (his life).

And if (selfish) motives debar (thee) from this insight, cast these motives out of thy bosom;

And if thou canst not (cast them out), do not stand inertly in a state of incapacity: know that with (every) incapable there is a goodly Incapacitator.

Incapacity is a chain: He laid it upon thee: thou must open thine eye to (behold) Him who lays the chain.¯

Therefore make humble entreaty, saying, "O Guide (in the ways) of life, I was free, (and now) I have fallen into bondage: what is the cause of this?

770    I have planted my foot in evil more firmly (than ever), for

---

[1] Literally, "with the tongue of his inward state"; *i.e.* although he made no reply in words, those who realised his essential nature were virtually answered.
[2] *I.e.* "my store of mystic knowledge is abundant and easily accessible."

through Thy omnipotence *verily* I am (engaged) *in a losing business* all the time.

I have been deaf to Thy admonitions: while professing to be an idol-breaker, I have (really) been an idol-maker.

Is it more incumbent (on me) to think of Thy works or of death? (Of death): death is like autumn, and Thou art (the root which is) the origin of the leaves."

For years this death has been beating the drum, (but only when it is) too late is your ear moved (to listen).

In his agony he (the heedless man) cries from his (inmost) soul, "Alas, I am dying!" Has Death made you aware of himself (only) now?

Death's throat is exhausted with shouting: his drum is split 775 with the astounding blows (with which it has been beaten).

(But) you enmeshed yourself in trivialities: (only) now have you apprehended the mystery of dying.

*Comparison of (the behaviour of) the heedless man who wastes his life and (only) begins to repent and ask pardon (of God) when he lies in extreme distress on his death-bed to the yearly mourning of the Shí'ites of Aleppo at the Antioch Gate (of the city) during the 'Áshúrá[1]; and how a poet, who was a stranger, arrived (there) on his journey and asked what was the cause of these shrieks of mourning.*

On the Day of 'Áshúrá all the people of Aleppo gather at the Antioch Gate till nightfall,

Men and women, a great multitude, and keep up a constant lamentation for the (Holy) Family[2].

During the 'Áshúrá the Shí'ites wail and lament with tears and sobs on account of Karbalá[3].

They recount the oppressions and tribulations which the 780 (Holy) Family suffered at the hands of Yazíd and Shimr.

They utter shrieks[4] mingled with cries of woe and grief: the whole plain and desert is filled (with their cries).

A stranger, (who was) a poet, arrived from the road on the Day of 'Áshúrá and heard that lamentation.

He left the city and resolved (to go) in that direction: he set out to investigate (the cause of) those shrill cries.

He went along, asking many questions in his search—"What is this sorrow? Whose death has occasioned this mourning?[5]

It must be a great personage who has died: such a concourse 785 is no small affair.

[1] The 10th of Muḥarram.
[2] *I.e.* Ḥusayn, the Prophet's grandson, and his family.
[3] See Book III (translation), p. 8, note 1.
[4] Literally, "their shrieks are going (forth)."
[5] Literally, "for whom has this mourning taken place?"

Inform me of his name and titles, for I am a stranger and ye belong to the town.

What is his name and profession and character? (Tell me) in order that I may compose an elegy on his gracious qualities.

I will make an elegy—for I am a poet—that I may carry away from here some provision and morsels of food."

"Eh," said one (of them), "are you mad? You are not a Shí'ite, you are an enemy of the (Holy) Family.

790 Don't you know that the Day of 'Áshúrá is (a day of) mourning for a single soul that is more excellent than a (whole) generation?

How should this anguish (tragedy) be lightly esteemed by the true believer? Love for the ear-ring[1] is in proportion to love for the ear[2].

In the true believer's view the mourning for that pure spirit is more celebrated than a hundred Floods of Noah."

### *The poet's subtle discourse in criticism of the Shí'ites of Aleppo.*

"Yes," said he; "but where (in relation to our time) is the epoch of Yazíd? When did this grievous tragedy occur? How late has (the news of) it arrived here!

The eyes of the blind have seen that loss, the ears of the deaf have heard that story.

795 Have ye been asleep till now, that (only) now ye have rent your garments in mourning?

Then, O sleepers, mourn for yourselves, for this heavy slumber is an evil death.

A royal spirit escaped from a prison: why should we rend our garments and how should we gnaw our hands?

Since they[3] were monarchs of the (true) religion, 'twas the hour of joy (for them) when they broke their bonds.

They sped towards the pavilion of empire, they cast off their fetters and chains.

800 'Tis the day of (their) kingship and pride and sovereignty, if thou hast (even) an atom of knowledge of them.

And if thou hast not (this) knowledge, go, weep for thyself, for thou art disbelieving in the removal (from this world to the next) and in the assembly at the Last Judgement.

Mourn for thy corrupt heart and religion, for it (thy heart) sees naught but this old earth.

Or if it is seeing (the spiritual world), why is it not brave and supporting (others) and self-sacrificing and fully contented?

In thy countenance where is the happiness (which is the effect) of the wine of (true) religion? If thou hast beheld the Ocean (of Bounty), where is the bounteous hand?

805 He that has beheld the River does not grudge water (to the thirsty), especially he that has beheld that Sea and (those) Clouds."

[1] *I.e.* Ḥusayn.     [2] *I.e.* the Prophet.     [3] Ḥusayn and his family.

*Comparison of the covetous man, who does not see the all-providingness of God and the (infinite) stores of His mercy, to an ant struggling with a single grain of wheat on a great threshing-floor and showing violent agitation and trembling and dragging it hurriedly along, unconscious of the amplitude of the threshing-floor.*

The ant trembles for a grain (of wheat) because it is blind to the goodly threshing-floors.

It drags a grain along greedily and fearfully, for it does not see such a noble stack of winnowed wheat (as is there).

The Owner of the threshing-floor is saying (to the ant), "Hey, thou who in thy blindness deemest nothing something,

Hast thou regarded that (alone) as belonging to My threshing-floors, so that thou art devoted[1] with (all) thy soul to that (single) grain?"

O thou who in semblance art (insignificant as) a mote, look at 810 Saturn; thou art a lame ant: go, look at Solomon.

Thou art not this body: thou art that (spiritual) Eye. If thou hast beheld the spirit, thou art delivered from the body.

Man (essentially) is eye: the rest (of him) is (mere) flesh and skin: whatsoever his eye has beheld, he is that thing.

A jar will submerge a mountain with (its) water when the eye of the jar is open to the Sea.

When from the soul (interior) of the jar a channel is made to the Sea, the jar will overwhelm[2] the Jayhún (Oxus).

For that reason whatsoever the speech (voice) of Aḥmad 815 (Mohammed) may utter, the words are (really) uttered by the Sea.

All his words were pearls of the Sea, for his heart had a passage into the Sea.

Since the bounty of the Sea is (poured) through our jar, what wonder (that) the Sea (itself) should be (contained) in a Fish?[3]

The sensual eye is fixed on the form of the thoroughfare[4]: thou art regarding it as a thoroughfare, but he (the Perfect Man) as a permanent abode.

This dualism is characteristic of the eye that sees double; but (in reality) the first is the last and the last is the first.

Hark, by what means is this made known (to thee)? By means 820 of the (spiritual) resurrection. Seek to experience (that) resurrection: do not dispute concerning (that) resurrection.

The (necessary) condition of (experiencing) the Day of Resurrection is to die first, for (the word) *ba'th* (resurrection) is (signifies) "to raise to life from the dead."

[1] Literally, "wrapped up."
[2] Literally, "start a violent quarrel with," "inflict violence on."
[3] *I.e.* in a Perfect Man (prophet or saint).
[4] *I.e.* on the phenomenal aspect of things.

Hence all the world have taken the wrong way, for they are afraid of non-existence, though it is (really) the refuge (in which they find salvation).

Whence shall we seek (true) knowledge? From renouncing (our false) knowledge. Whence shall we seek (true) peace? From renouncing peace (with our carnal selves).

Whence shall we seek (real) existence? From renouncing (illusory) existence. Whence shall we seek the apple (of Truth)? From renouncing the hand (of self-assertion and self-interest).

825 O best Helper, only Thou canst make the eye that regards the non-existent to regard that which is (really) existent.

The eye that was produced from non-existence regarded the Essence of (real) Being as wholly non-existent;

(But), if (thy) two eyes are transformed and illumined, this well-ordered world becomes the scene of the Last Judgement[1].

These realities are shown forth imperfectly (here) because the apprehension of them is forbidden to these raw (ignorant) ones.

Although God is munificent, the enjoyment of the delightful gardens of Paradise is forbidden to him who is destined for Hell.

830 The honey of Paradise becomes bitter in his mouth, since he was not (destined to be) one of them that faithfully keep the covenant of everlasting life.

Ye (worldly folk) also (who are engaged) in commerce—how should your hands move (to sell anything) when there is no buyer?

How should (idle) looking-on be capable of buying? The fool's looking-on is (not for buying, but merely for) loitering.

(He strolls about) continually asking, "How much is this?" and "How much is that?" for the sake of pastime and mockery.

('Tis only) from boredom (that) he asks you (to show him) your goods: that person is not a buyer and customer[2].

835 He inspects the article a hundred times and hands it back (to you): when did he (ever) measure a piece of cloth? He measured wind (and nothing else).

What a distance between[3] the approach and bargaining[4] of a purchaser and the pleasantries of a silly joker?

Since there is not a mite in his possession, how should he seek (to buy) a coat except in jest?

He has no capital for trading: what, then, is the difference between his ill-favoured person and a shadow?

The capital (required) for the market of this world is gold; there (in the next world) the capital is love and two eyes wet (with tears).

---

[1] *I.e.* "thou wilt see all things in the world *sub specie aeternitatis.*"
[2] Literally, "seeker of goods."
[3] Literally, "where is...and where is...?"
[4] Literally, "the advance and retreat."

Whoever went to market without any capital, his life passed 840 and he speedily returned in disappointment.

"Oh, where hast thou been, brother?" "Nowhere." "Oh, what hast thou cooked to eat?" "No (good) soup."

Become a buyer, that my hand may move (to sell to thee), and that my pregnant mine may bring forth the ruby.

Though the buyer is slack and lukewarm, (yet) call (him) to the (true) religion, for the (command to) call hath come down (from God).

Let the falcon fly and catch the spiritual dove: in calling (to God) take the way of Noah.

Perform an act of service for the Creator's sake: what hast 845 thou to do with being accepted or rejected by the people?

*Story of the person who was giving the drum-call for the sahúr[1] at the gate of a certain palace at midnight. A neighbour said to him, "Why, it is midnight, it is not (yet) dawn; and besides, there is no one in this palace: for whose sake are you drumming?"—and the minstrel's reply to him.*

A certain man was drumming at a certain gate to announce the *sahúr*: 'twas a court-house and the pavilion of a grandee.

(Whilst) he was beating his drum vigorously at midnight, some one said to him, "O thou who art seeking (the means of) support,

Firstly, give this call to the *sahúr* at daybreak: midnight is not the time for (making) this disturbance;

And secondly, observe, O man of vain desire, whether in fact there is any one inside this house at midnight.

There is nobody here except demons and spirits: why art thou 850 trifling thy time away?

Thou art beating thy tambourine for the sake of an ear: where is the ear? Intelligence is needed in order to know (thy purpose): where is the intelligence?"

He replied, "You have said (your say): (now) hear the answer from your (humble) servant, that you may not remain in bewilderment and confusion.

Although in your opinion this moment is midnight, in my view the dawn of delight is near at hand.

In my sight every defeat has been turned to victory, in my eyes all nights have been turned to day.

To you the water of the river Nile seems blood; to me it is not 855 blood, 'tis water, O noble one[2].

In regard to you, that (object) is iron or marble, (but) to the prophet David it is (soft as) wax and tractable[3].

[1] The meal taken just before daybreak during the month of Ramadán.
[2] See Book IV (translation), p. 461.
[3] Referring to David's skill as an iron-smith (*Qur'án*, XXI, 80).

To you the mountain is exceedingly heavy (solid) and inanimate, (but) to David it is a master-musician[1].

To you the gravel is silent; to Aḥmad (Mohammed) it is eloquent and making supplication (to God)[2].

To you the pillar of the mosque is a dead thing; to Aḥmad it is (like) a lover who has lost his heart[3].

860 To the vulgar all the particles of the world seem dead, but before God they are possessed of knowledge and submissive (to His commands).

As for your saying, 'There is nobody in this house and palace: why art thou beating this drum?'—

(I reply that) this (Moslem) people are giving (large) sums of gold for God's sake, founding hundreds of pious institutions and mosques,

And, like intoxicated lovers, gladly risking their property and lives[4] on their way to (perform) the distant Pilgrimage:

Do they ever say, 'The House (Ka'ba) is empty'? Nay, (they know that) the Lord of the House is the Spirit invisible.

865 He that is illumined by the Light of God deems the House of the Beloved[5] to be full (of Him).

In the eyes of those who see the end, many a palace filled with a crowd and throng (of people) is empty.

Seek in the (spiritual) Ka'ba whomsoever you please, that he may at once grow (rise into view) before your face.

How should the form (of the Perfect Man), which is splendid and sublime, (ever) be absent from the House of God?

He is (always) present (there), exempt from exclusion, (while) the rest of mankind (are there only) on account of (their occasional) need.

870 Do they (the pilgrims) ever say, 'We are crying *Labbayka* without (receiving) any response. Pray, why (is this)'?

Nay, the Divine blessing which causes (their cries of) *Labbayka* is (in truth) a response (coming) from the One (God) at every moment[6].

I know by intuition[7] that this pavilion and palace is the banquet of the soul, and that its dust is an elixir.

I will strike my copper on its elixir unto everlasting in the mode of treble and bass[8],

That, from (my) playing the *saḥúr* tune in this fashion, the seas (of Divine mercy) may surge (and be roused) to scatter (their) pearls and (lavish their) bounty.

---

[1] See Book III (translation), p. 239.
[2] See Book I (translation), p. 117.
[3] *Ibid.* p. 115.       [4] Literally, "body."       [5] *I.e.* the heart.
[6] See translation of Book III, *v.* 189 foll.       [7] Literally, "scent."
[8] *I.e.* "I will strike every chord (employ every means) in seeking spiritual transmutation, like the lute-player whose plectrum moves up and down the strings." The elixir was supposed to turn copper into gold.

Men hazard their lives in the line of battle and in fighting for 875 the Creator's sake.

One is like Job in tribulation; another like Jacob in patience.

Hundreds of thousands of people, thirsty and sorrowful, are doing some sore toil for God's sake in desire (of pleasing Him).

I too, for the merciful Lord's sake and in hope of Him, am drumming the *sahúr*-call at the gate."

(If) you want a customer from whom you will get gold, how should there be a better customer than God, O (my) heart?

He buys a dirty bag from your (stock of) goods, and gives (you 880 in return) an inner light that borrows (its splendour from Himself).

He receives the (dissolving) ice of this mortal body, and gives a kingdom beyond our imagination.

He receives a few tear-drops, and gives a Kawthar[1] (so delicious) that sugar shows jealousy (of its sweetness).

He receives sighs full of melancholy and vaporous gloom[2], and gives for every sigh a hundred gainful dignities.

Because of the wind of sighs that drove onward the tearful cloud[3], He hath called a Khalíl (Abraham) *awwáh* (sighful)[4].

Hark, sell your old rags in this brisk incomparable market, and 885 receive the sterling (real and genuine) kingdom (in exchange).

And if any doubt and suspicion waylay (assail) you, rely upon the (spiritual) traders, (namely), the prophets.

Inasmuch as the (Divine) Emperor increased their fortune exceedingly, no mountain can carry their merchandise.

*The Story of Bilál's crying " One! One!" in the heat of the Ḥijáz,*
   *from his love for Muṣṭafá (Mohammed), on whom be peace, in*
   *the forenoons when his master, (impelled) by Jewish fanaticism,*
   *used to flog him with a thorny branch under the (blazing) sun of*
   *the Ḥijáz; and how at (each) blow the blood spurted from*
   *Bilál's body, and (the words) "One! One!" escaped (from his*
   *lips) involuntarily, just as sobs escape involuntarily from others*
   *stricken with grief, because he was (so) full of the passion of love*
   *(that) there was no room for any care about relieving the pain of*
   *the thorns to enter (his heart). (His case was) like (that of)*
   *Pharaoh's magicians and Jirjís and others (who are) innumerable*
   *and beyond computation.*

That Bilál was devoting his body to the (scourge of) thorns: his master was flogging him by way of correction,

Saying, "Why dost thou celebrate Aḥmad (Mohammed)? Wicked slave, thou disbelievest in my religion!"

He was beating him in the sun with thorns (while) he (Bilál) 890 cried vauntingly "One!"

[1] A river in Paradise.                     [2] Literally, "smoke."
[3] *I.e.* produced a flood of tears.         [4] *Qur'án,* IX, 115; XI, 77.

21

Till (at last) those cries of "One!" reached the ears of the
Ṣiddíq (Abú Bakr), who was passing in that neighbourhood.

His eyes became filled with tears and his heart with trouble,
(for) from that "One!" he caught the scent of a loving friend
(of God).

Afterwards he saw him (Bilál) in private and admonished him,
saying, "Keep thy belief hidden from the Jews.          '

He (God) knows (all) secrets: conceal thy desire." He (Bilál)
said, "I repent before thee, O prince."

895    Early next day, (when) the Ṣiddíq was going quickly in that
district on account of some affair,

He again heard (cries of) "One!" and (the sound of) blows
inflicted by the (scourge of) thorns: flames and sparks of fire
were kindled in his heart.

He admonished him once more, and once more he (Bilál)
repented; (but) Love came and consumed his repentance.

There was much repenting of this sort, (till) at last he became
quit of repentance,

And proclaimed (his faith) and yielded up his body to tribula-
tion, crying, "O Mohammed, O enemy of vows of repentance,

900    O thou with whom my body and (all) my veins are filled—how
should there be room therein for repentance?—

Henceforth I will banish repentance from this heart (of mine):
how should I repent of the life everlasting?"

Love is the All-subduer, and I am subdued by Love: by
Love's bitterness[1] I have been made sweet as sugar.

O fierce Wind, before Thee I am (but) a straw: how can
I know where I shall fall? .

Whether I am (stout as) Bilál or (thin as) the new moon
(hilál)[2], I am running on and following the course of Thy sun.

905    What has the moon to do with stoutness and thinness? She
runs at the heels of the sun, like a shadow.

Any one who offers to make a settlement with (the Divine)
destiny is mocking at his own moustache.

A straw in the face of the wind, and then (the idea of) a
settlement! A Resurrection (going on), and then the resolve
to act (independently)!

In the hand of Love I am like a cat in a bag, now lifted high
and now flung low by Love.

He is whirling me round His head: I have no rest either below
or aloft.

910    The lovers (of God) have fallen into a fierce torrent: they have
set their hearts on (resigned themselves to) the ordinance of Love.

---

[1] Literally, "saltiness"; but there is also an allusion to the ordinary
meaning of شور, "tumultuous agitation."

[2] Or, "(thin as) Hilál." Hilál is the name of a slave whose story is related
in this Book (v. 1111 foll.).

(They are) like the millstone turning, day and night, in (continual) revolution and moaning incessantly.

Its turning is evidence for those who seek the River, lest any one should say that the River is motionless.

If thou seest not the hidden River[1], see the (perpetual) turning of the celestial water-wheel[2].

Since the heavens have no rest from (being moved by) Him (Love), (be) thou, O heart, like a star, (and) seek no rest.

If thou lay hold of a branch, how should He let (thee cling 915 to it)? Wherever thou makest an attachment, He will break it.

If thou seest not the revolutionary action of the (Divine) decree, look at the surging and whirling (that appears) in the (four) elements;

For the whirling of the sticks and straws and foam are caused by the boiling of the noble Sea (of Love).

See the giddy wind howling; see the billows surging at His command.

The sun and moon are two mill-oxen, going round and round and keeping watch (over the world).

The stars likewise run from house to house (in the sky) and 920 convey every good and evil fortune.

Hark, though the stars of heaven are far away and thy senses are (too) dull and slack (to apprehend their motions),

(Yet ask thyself) where are *our* stars—eye, ear, and mind—at night, and where (are they) when we are awake?

Now (they are) in good luck and union and happiness; now in ill-luck and separation and insensibility.

Since the moon of heaven is (engaged) in making this circuit, she is sometimes dark and sometimes bright.

Sometimes 'tis spring and summer, (delicious) as honey and 925 milk; sometimes (the world is) a place of punishment by snow and piercing cold.

Seeing that before Him (God) universals are like a ball, subject (to Him) and prostrating themselves before His bat,

How shouldst thou, O heart, which art (but) one of these hundred thousand particulars, not be in restless movement at His decree?

Be at the disposal of the Prince, like a horse (or mule), now confined in the stable, now going (on the road).

When He fastens thee to a peg, be fastened (quiet and submissive); when He looses thee, go, be exultant (prance and bound).

(But keep on the right road, for when) the sun in heaven 930 jumps crookedly, He causes it to be eclipsed in black disgrace[3],

---

[1] *I.e.* the action of the Divine Beloved.
[2] *I.e.* the revolution of the heavens.
[3] Literally, "blackness of face."

Saying, "Avoid the (Dragon's) Tail[1]: hark, take heed, lest thou become black of face like a cooking-pot."

The cloud, too, is lashed with a whip of fire[2], (as though to say), "Go that way, do not go this way!

Rain upon such and such a valley, do not rain in this quarter": He reprimands it, saying, "Give ear!

Thy reason is not superior to a sun: do not stay in (dally with) a thought that has been forbidden.

935     O Reason, do not thou too step crookedly, lest that eclipse of (the bright) face befall (thee).

When (thy) sin is less, thou wilt see half the sun eclipsed and half radiant,

For I punish thee in proportion to thy sin: this is the principle laid down for justice and retribution.

Whether (thou art) good or bad or open or secret, I am *He that overheareth and overseeth* all things."

Leave this topic, O father: New Year's Day is come: the creatures have had their mouths made sweet[3] by the Creator.

940     The spiritual Water (of Life) has returned into our river-bed, our King has returned into our street.

Fortune is strutting and (proudly) trailing her skirt and beating the drums (as a signal) to break vows of repentance.

Once more the flood-water has swept repentance away: the opportunity has arrived, the watchman is overcome by sleep.

Every toper has drunk the wine and is intoxicated: to-night we will pawn all our belongings.

From (drinking) the ruby wine of the life-increasing Spirit we are ruby within ruby within ruby.

945     Once more the assembly-place has become flourishing and heart-illuminating: arise and burn rue-seed to keep off the evil eye.

The cries of the joyous drunken (lovers) are coming to me: O Beloved, I want it (to continue) like this unto everlasting.

Lo, a new moon (*hilálí*) has been united with a Bilál: the blows of the (scourge of) thorns have become (delightful) to him (as) roses and pomegranate-flowers.

(Bilál said), "If my body is (full of holes, like) a sieve from the blows of the (scourge of) thorns, (yet) my soul and body are a rose-garden of felicity.

My body is exposed to the blows of the Jew's (scourge of) thorns, (but) my spirit is intoxicated and enravished by that Loving One.

---

[1] One of the two points at which the moon's apparent **path** intersects the ecliptic, thus causing eclipse.

[2] *I.e.* lightning.

[3] *I.e.* have been presented with delicious (spiritual) gifts.

The scent of a (beloved) Soul is coming towards my soul: the 950
scent of my loving Friend is coming to me."

(When) Muṣṭafá (Mohammed) came (to earth) from the
Ascension, (he pronounced) on his Bilál (the blessing), "How
dear to me (art thou), how dear!"

On hearing this (ecstatic utterance) from Bilál, in whose speech
there was no guile[1], the Ṣiddíq (Abú Bakr) washed his hands of
urging him to repent[2].


*How the Ṣiddíq (Abú Bakr), may God be pleased with him,*
*recalled (to his mind) what had happened to Bilál, may God be*
*pleased with him, and his maltreatment by the Jews and his crying*
*"One! One!" and the Jews becoming more incensed (against him);*
*and how he told the story of the affair to Muṣṭafá (Mohammed),*
*on whom be peace, and consulted him as to buying him (Bilál)*
*from the Jews.*

Afterwards the Ṣiddíq related to Muṣṭafá the plight of the
faithful Bilál,

Saying, "That heaven-surveying nimble (spirit) of blessed
wing is at this time in love (with thee) and in thy net.

The Sultan's falcon is tormented by those owls; that grand 955
treasure is buried in filth.

The owls are doing violence to the falcon: they are tearing
out his plumes and feathers though he is innocent.

His only crime is this, that he is a falcon: after all, what is
Joseph's crime except (that he had) beauty?

The owl's origin and existence is (in) the wilderness; that is
the cause of their Jewish (fanatical) anger against the falcon.

(They say), 'Why art thou (always) making mention of
yonder land, or of the palace and wrist of the Emperor?

Thou art behaving impudently in the owls' village, thou art 960
introducing dissension and disturbance (amongst us).

Our dwelling-place, which is the envy of the empyrean, thou
callest a wilderness and givest it the name of "vile."

Thou hast employed hypocrisy in order that our owls may
make thee (their) king and leader.

Thou art instilling[3] into them a vain imagination and a mad
fancy: thou art giving the name "ruin" to this Paradise.

We will beat thy head so long, O (bird) of evil qualities, that
thou wilt renounce this hypocrisy and nonsense.'

They (the Jews) are crucifying him (Bilál), his face to the 965
East, and flogging his naked body with a thorny branch.

---

[1] Literally, "the righteous in speech."
[2] Literally, "of his repentance."
[3] Literally, "weaving."

The blood is spurting from his body in a hundred places, (whilst) he is crying 'One!' and bowing his head (in resignation).

I admonished him often, saying, 'Keep thy religion hidden, conceal thy secret from the accursed Jews.'

(But) he is a lover: to him the (spiritual) resurrection has come, so that the door of repentance has been shut on him."

Loverhood and[1] repentance or (even) the possibility of patience—this, O (dear) soul, is a very enormous absurdity.

970    Repentance is a worm, while Love is like a dragon: repentance is an attribute of Man, while that (other) is an attribute of God.

Love is (one) of the attributes of God who wants nothing: love for aught besides Him is unreal,

Because that (which is besides Him) is (but) a gilded beauty: its outside is (shining) light, (but) 'tis (like dark) smoke within.

When the light goes and the smoke becomes visible, at that moment the unreal love is frozen up[2].

That beauty returns to its source; the body is left—foul-smelling, shameful, and ugly.

975    The moonlight is returning to the moon: its reflexion goes off the black (dark) wall;

And then, (when) the water and clay (of the wall) are left without that ornament, the wall, (being) moonless, becomes (hideous) as a devil.

When the gold flies from the surface of the base coin, that gold returns to its (original) mine and settles (there);

Then the shamefully exposed copper is left (looking black) like smoke, and its lover is left looking blacker[3] than it.

(But) the love of them that have (spiritual) insight is (fixed) on the gold-mine; necessarily it is (grows) greater every day,

980    Because the mine hath no partner in aureity. Hail, O Gold-mine (of Reality), Thou concerning whom there is no doubt!

If any one let a base coin become a sharer with the Mine (in his affection), the gold goes back to the Mine (which is) beyond locality,

(And then) the lover and his beloved are dead (left to die) in agony: the fish is left (writhing), the water is gone from the whirlpool.

The Divine Love is the Sun of perfection: the (Divine) Word[4] is its light, the creatures are as shadows.

When Muṣṭafá (Mohammed) expanded with joy on (hearing) this story, his (the Ṣiddíq's) desire to speak (of Bilál) increased also.

----

[1] *I.e.* accompanied by.          [2] *I.e.* is extinguished.
[3] *I.e.* in worse disgrace.        [4] Literally, "command."

Since he found a hearer like Muṣṭafá, every hair of him 985
became a separate tongue.

Muṣṭafá said to him, "Now what is the remedy?" He (the
Ṣiddíq) replied, "This servant (of God) is going to buy him.

I will buy him at whatever price he (the Jew) may name:
I will not regard the apparent loss (of money) and the extortion;

For he is God's captive on the earth, and he has become
subjected to the anger of God's enemy."

*How Muṣṭafá (Mohammed), on whom be peace, enjoined the Ṣiddíq,
may God be pleased with him, saying, "Since thou art going to
purchase Bilál, they (the Jews) will certainly raise his price by
wrangling (with thee): make me thy partner in this merit, be my
agent, and receive from me half the purchase-money."*

Muṣṭafá said to him, "O seeker of (spiritual) fortune, I will
be thy partner in this (enterprise).

Be my agent, buy a half share (in him) on my account, and 990
receive the payment from me."

He replied, "I will do my utmost to serve thee[1]." Then he
went to the house of the merciless Jew.

He said to himself, "From the hands of children one can buy
pearls very cheaply, O father."

From these foolish children the ghoul-like Devil is buying
their reason and faith in exchange for the kingdom of this world.

He decks out the carcase so finely that (with it) he buys from
them two hundred rose-gardens.

By magic he produces such moonshine that by means of (his) 995
magic he carries off from worthless folk a hundred purses (of
money)[2].

The prophets taught them to trade (in the spiritual market)
and lighted the candle of the (true) religion before them;

(But) by means of magic and in despite the devilish and
ghoulish Magician caused the prophets to appear ugly in their
eyes.

By (his) sorcery the Foe causes ugliness (to appear), so that
divorce takes place between the wife and (her) husband.

Their eyes have been sealed by a (mighty) enchantment, so
that they have sold such a (precious) pearl for rubbish.

This pearl is superior to both the worlds: hark, buy (it) from 1000
this ignorant child, for he is an ass.

To the ass a cowrie and a pearl are alike: the ass has a (great)
doubt concerning the (spiritual) pearl and the Sea.

He disbelieves in the Sea and its pearls: how should an animal
be a seeker of pearls and adornments?

[1] Literally, "I will do a hundred services."
[2] See translation of Book III, *vv*. 1163-4.

God has not put it into the animal's head to be engrossed with rubies and devoted to pearls.

Have you ever seen asses with ear-rings? The ear and mind of the ass are (set) on the meadow.

1005 Read in (the Súra entitled) *Wa'l-Tín* (the words), (*We created Man*) *in the best proportion*[1], for the spirit, O friend, is a precious pearl.

(That spirit created) *in the best proportion* surpasses the empyrean: (that spirit created) *in the best proportion* is beyond (the range of) thought.

If I declare the value of this inaccessible (pearl), I shall be consumed, and the hearer too will be consumed.

At this point close thy lips and proceed no further[2]. This Siddíq went to those asses (the Jews).

He knocked the door-ring, and when the Jew opened the door he (the Siddíq) went into his house, beside himself (with indignation).

1010 He sat down, beside himself and furious and full of fire: from his mouth leaped many bitter words—

"Why art thou beating this friend of God? What hatred is this, O enemy of the Light?

If thou art steadfast in thy own religion, how is thy heart consenting to maltreat him who is steadfast (in his religion)?

O thou effeminate in Judaism, who dost impute this (same effeminacy) to a (spiritual) prince!

Do not view all (things) in the distorting mirror of thy self-hood, O thou who art banned with an everlasting curse!"

1015 If I should tell what burst from the lips of the Siddíq at that moment, you would lose (both) foot and hand[3].

(Coming) from (the world) beyond spatial relations, the fountains of wisdom (copious) as the Euphrates were running from his mouth,

As from the rock whence gushed a (great) water[4], (the rock) having no source of supply in (its own) side or interior;

(For) God made that rock a shield (veil) for Himself and opened (a way for) the blue crystalline water,

Even as He hath caused the light to flow from the fountain of your eye without stint or abatement:

1020 It has no source of supply either in the fat (the white of the eye) or in the coating (retina); (but) the Beloved made (these) a veil (for Himself) when bringing (the light) into existence.

The attracting[5] air in the cavity of the ear apprehends that which is spoken, (whether) true or false.

[1] *Qur'án*, xcv, 4.
[2] Literally, "do not drive the ass in this direction."
[3] *I.e.* "you would be lost in amazement."
[4] Referring to the rock which Moses smote with his rod (*Qur'án*, ii, 57).
[5] *I.e.* drawing the spoken words to itself.

What is that air within that little bone, (that air) which receives the words and sounds uttered by the story-teller?

The bone and the air are only a veil: in the two worlds there is none except God.

He is the hearer, He is the speaker, (whom mystics behold) unveiled; for the ears belong to the head[1], O you who have merited the Divine recompense.

He (the Jew) said, "If thou art feeling pity for him, give (me) 1025 gold and take him (in exchange), O man of generous disposition.

Since thy heart is burning (with sympathy), ransom him from me: thy difficulty will not be solved without expense."

He replied, "I will perform a hundred services (on his behalf) and five hundred prostrations (in thanksgiving for success). I have a handsome slave, but (he is) a Jew;

He has a white body, but a black heart: take (him), and give (me) in exchange that one whose body is black but whose heart is illumined."

Then the chieftain (Abú Bakr) sent (a messenger) to fetch him: in sooth that slave was exceedingly comely,

So that the Jew was dumbfounded: at once his stony heart 1030 inclined (towards him)[2].

This is what happens to form-worshippers: their stone is (made) waxen[3] by a (beauteous) form.

(Then) again he wrangled and would not be satisfied, saying, "Without any evasion, (thou must) give more than this."

He offered him in addition a *nişáb* (two hundred dirhems) of silver, so that the Jew's cupidity was satisfied.

### *How the Jew laughed and imagined that the Şiddíq had been swindled in this bargain.*

The stony-hearted Jew guffawed jeeringly and mockingly in malice and spite.

The Şiddíq said to him, "Why this laughter?" In reply to 1035 the question he laughed more loudly,

And said, "Had it not been for the (extraordinary) earnestness and ardour shown by thee in the purchase of this black slave,

I would not have wrangled excitedly[4]: indeed I would have sold him for a tenth of this (sum),

For in my opinion he is not worth half a *dáng*; (but) thou mad'st his price heavy by (thy) clamour."

Then the Şiddíq answered him, "O simpleton, thou hast given away a pearl in exchange for a walnut, like a (silly) boy;

[1] *I.e.* human sight and hearing are related to God's sight and hearing as the part to the whole.
[2] Literally, "went from its place."
[3] *I.e.* their hard hearts are melted.
[4] Literally, "I would not have become excited in wrangling."

1040     For in my opinion he is worth the two worlds: I am regarding his spirit, thou his colour.

He is red gold that has been made (like) black polished iron on account of the enviousness of this abode of fools.

The eye that sees these seven bodily colours cannot perceive the spirit because of this veil.

If thou hadst haggled in the sale more (excessively than thou didst), I would have given the whole of my property and riches;

And if thou hadst (then) increased thy demands[1], I would have borrowed a skirtful of gold in my anxiety (to purchase him).

1045     Thou gavest (him) up easily because thou gottest (him) cheap: thou didst not see the pearl, thou didst not split the casket.

Thy folly gave (me) a sealed[2] casket: thou wilt soon see what a swindle has befallen thee.

Thou hast given away[3] a casket full of rubies and, like the negro, thou art rejoicing in thy blackness of face (disastrous plight).

In the end thou wilt utter many a 'woe is me!' Does any one, forsooth, sell (his) fortune and felicity?

Fortune came (to thee) in the garb of a slave, (but) thy unlucky eye saw only the surface.

1050     He showed unto thee his slavery (alone): thy wicked nature practised cunning and deceit with him.

(Now), O driveller, take idolatrously this (slave) whose secret thoughts are black though his body is white.

This one for thee, that one for me: we (both) have profited. Hark, *unto you (your) religion and unto me (my) religion*, O Jew."

Truly this is meet for idolaters[4]: his (the idolater's) horse-cloth is (of) satin (while) his horse is made of wood.

It (the object of his worship) is like the tomb of infidels—full of smoke and fire (within), (while) on the outside it is decked with a hundred (beautiful) designs and ornaments;

1055     (Or) like the wealth of tyrants—fair externally, (but) within it (intrinsically) the blood of the oppressed and (future) woe;

(Or) like the hypocrite (who) externally (is engaged in) fasting and prayer, (while) inwardly (he resembles) black loam without vegetation;

(Or) like a cloud empty (of rain), full of thunderclaps, wherein is neither benefit to the earth nor nourishment for the wheat;

(Or) like a promise (full) of guile and lying words, of which the end is shameful though its beginning is splendid.

Afterwards he (the Ṣiddíq) took the hand of Bilál, who was (thin) as a toothpick from the blows inflicted by the tooth of tribulation.

---

[1] Literally, "haggling."      [2] Literally, "fastened at the top."
[3] Literally, "given to the wind."
[4] *I.e.* those who are attached to phenomenal existence.

He became (like) a toothpick and found his way into a mouth: 1060
he was hastening towards a man of sweet tongue[1].

When that (sorely) wounded one beheld the face of Muṣṭafá
(Mohammed), *he fell down* in a swoon[2], he fell on his back.

For a long time he remained unconscious and beside himself:
when he came to himself, he shed tears for joy.

Muṣṭafá clasped him to his bosom: how should any one know
the bounty that was bestowed on him?

How is it with a piece of copper that has touched the elixir?
How with an insolvent who has hit upon an ample treasure?

('Twas as though) a fish parched (for want of water) fell into 1065
the sea, (or) a caravan that had lost its way struck the right road.

If the words which the Prophet addressed (to him) at that
moment should fall upon (the ears of) Night, it (Night) would
cease from being night;

Night would become day radiant as dawn: I cannot express
(the real meaning of) that mystic allocution.

You yourself know what (words) a sun, in (the sign of) Aries,
speaks to the plants and the date-palms;

You yourself, too, know what the limpid water is saying to
the sweet herbs and the sapling.

The doing of God towards all the particles of the world is 1070
like the words (spells) breathed by[3] enchanters.

The Divine attraction holds a hundred discourses with the
effects and secondary causes, without (uttering) a word or
(moving) a lip.

Not that the production of effects by the Divine decree is not
actual; but His production of effects thereby is inconceivable to
reason.

Since reason has learned by rote (from the prophets) in regard
to the fundamentals, know, O trifler, that it (also) learns by rote
in regard to the derivatives.

If reason should ask how the aim[4] may be (attained), say, " In
a manner that thou knowest not, and (so) farewell!"

*How Muṣṭafá (Mohammed), on whom be peace, reproached the
Ṣiddíq, may God be pleased with him, saying, " I enjoined thee
to buy in partnership with me: why hast thou bought for thyself
alone?" and his (the Ṣiddíq's) excuse.*

He (the Prophet) said, " Why, O Ṣiddíq, I told thee to make 1075
me the partner in (thy) generosity."

He replied, " We[5] are two slaves in thy street: I set him free
for thy sake.

---

[1] *I.e.* the Prophet.　　　　[2] An allusion to *Qur'án*, VII, 139.
[3] Literally, " the breath and words (uttered) by."
[4] *I.e.* union with God.　　　　[5] *I.e.* " Bilál and I."

Keep me as thy slave and loyal friend[1]: I want no freedom, beware (of thinking so)!

For my freedom consists in being thy slave: without thee, tribulation and injustice are (inflicted) on me.

O thou who through being the chosen (Prophet) hast brought the (whole) world to life and hast made the common folk to be the elect, especially me,

1080    In my youth my spirit used to dream that the orb of the sun salaamed to me,

And lifted me up from earth to heaven: by mounting (so) high I had become its fellow-traveller.

I said (to myself), 'This is an hallucination and absurd: how should absurdity ever become actuality?[2]'

When I beheld thee I beheld myself: blessings on that mirror goodly in its ways!

When I beheld thee, the absurd became actual for me: my spirit was submerged in the Glory.

1085    When I beheld thee, O Spirit of the world, verily love for this (earthly) sun fell from mine eye.

By thee mine eye was endowed with lofty aspiration: it looks not on the (earthly) garden save with contempt.

I sought light: verily I beheld the Light of light. I sought the houri: verily (in thee) I beheld an object of envy to the houri.

I sought a Joseph comely and with limbs (white as) silver: in thee I beheld an assembly of Josephs.

I was (engaged) in searching after Paradise: from every part of thee a Paradise appeared (to me).

1090    In relation to me this is praise and eulogy; in relation to thee this is vituperation and satire,

Like the praise given to God by the simple shepherd in the presence of Moses the *Kalím*[3]—

'I will seek out Thy lice, I will give Thee milk, I will stitch Thy shoon and lay them before Thee.'

God accepted his vituperation as an expression of praise: if thou also have mercy, 'twill be no marvel.

Have mercy upon the failure of (our) minds (to comprehend thee), O thou who art beyond (all) understandings and conceptions."

1095    O lovers, new fortune has arrived from the old World that makes (all things) new[4],

From the World that is seeking a remedy for them that have no remedy: hundreds of thousands of wonders of the (present) world are (contained) in it.

---

[1] Literally, "friend in the Cave."
[2] Literally, "become the description of an (actual) state."
[3] See Book II, *v.* 1720 foll.    [4] *I.e.* the World of Reality.

Rejoice, O people, since the relief has come; be glad, O people:
the distress is removed.

A Sun[1] went into the hut of the new-moon[2], making urgent
demands and saying, "Refresh us, O Bilál![3]

From fear of the foe thou wert wont to speak under thy
breath: (now), to his confusion, go up into the minaret and
speak (aloud)."

The announcer of glad news[4] is shouting in the ear of every 1100
sorrowful one, "Arise, O unlucky man, and take the road to
fortune.

O thou that art in this prison and amidst this stench and these
lice, beware lest any one hear! Thou hast escaped (from
prison): be silent!"

How shouldst thou keep silence now, O my beloved, when
a drummer has appeared from the root of every hair (in thy
body)?

The jealous foe has become so deaf (that) he says, "Where is
the sound of all these drums?"

The fresh sweet basil is touching his face, (but) in his blindness
he says, "What is this annoyance?"

The houri is nipping his hand and drawing (him towards her): 1105
the blind man is distraught and says, "Wherefore is he (some
one) hurting me?

What is this (painful sense of) having my hand and body
pulled hither and thither? I am asleep, let me sleep awhile."

He whom thou seekest in thy slumbers, this is He! Open
thine eye, (thou wilt see) 'tis that auspicious Moon.

Tribulations were (laid) more (heavily) upon (His) dear ones
because the Beloved showed more coquettishness towards the
beauteous (lovers).

He sports with the beauteous ones in every path; sometimes,
too, he throws the blind into frenzy.

For a moment He gives Himself to the blind, so that a great 1110
uproar arises from the street of the blind.

[1] The Prophet.
[2] Bilál.
[3] *I.e.* by chanting the *adhán* (call to prayer).
[4] *I.e.* the muezzin.

*Story of Hilál, who was a devoted servant to God. (He was)*
*possessed of spiritual insight and (in his religion) was not a mere*
*imitator (of others). He had concealed himself in (the disguise of)*
*being a slave to (God's) creatures, not from helplessness but for*
*good reason, as Luqmán and Joseph and others (did, who were*
*slaves) in appearance. He was a groom in the service of a certain*
*Amír, and that Amír was a Moslem, but (spiritually) blind.*
*" The blind man knows that he has a mother, but he cannot conceive*
*what she is like."*
*If, having this knowledge, he show reverence towards his mother,*
*it is possible that he may gain deliverance from blindness, for (the*
*Prophet has said that) when God wills good unto a servant (of*
*His) He opens the eyes of his heart, that He may let him see the*
*Invisible (World) with them.*

Since you have heard some of the (excellent) qualities of
Bilál, now hear the story of the emaciation of Hilál.

He was more advanced than Bilál in the Way (to God): he
had mortified his evil nature more.

(He was) not a backslider like you, for at every moment you
are farther back: you are moving away from the state of the
(precious) pearl towards the state of the (worthless) stone.

'Tis like the case of the guest who came to a certain Khwája:
the Khwája inquired concerning his days and years.

1115    He asked, "How many years hast thou lived, my lad? Say
(it) out and don't hide (it) away but count up (correctly)."

He replied, "Eighteen, seventeen, or sixteen, or fifteen,
O adoptive brother."

"(Go) backward, backward," said he, "O giddy-headed one";
"keep going back usque ad cunnum matris tuae!"

*Story in exposition of the same topic.*

A certain man begged an Amír to give him a horse: he said,
"Go and take that grey horse."

He replied, "I don't want that one." "Why not?" he asked.
"It goes backward and is very restive," said he;

1120    "It goes back, back very hard in the direction of its rump."
He replied, "Turn its tail towards home!"

The tail of this beast you are riding, (namely), your carnal
soul, is lust; hence that self-worshipper goes back, back.

O changer, make its (carnal) lust, which is the tail, to be
entirely[1] lust for the world hereafter.

When you bind its lust (and debar it) from the loaf, that lust
puts forth its head from (is transformed into) noble reason,

---

[1] Literally, "from the root," "fundamentally."

As, when you lop off a (superfluous) branch from a tree, vigour is imparted to[1] the well-conditioned[2] branches.

When you have turned its (the carnal steed's) tail in that  1125 direction, if it goes backward, it goes to the place of shelter[3].

How excellent are the docile horses which go forward, not backward, and are not given over to restiveness,

Going hot-foot, like the body of Moses the *Kalím*, to which (the distance) to *the two seas* (was) as the breadth of a blanket!

Seven hundred years is the duration of the journey on which he set out in the path of Love, (the journey that lasted) *for an age*[4].

Since the aspiration (that carried him) on his journey in the body is (as immense as) this, his journey in the spirit must be (even) unto the highest Paradise.

The kingly cavaliers[5] sped forward in advance (of all); the  1130 boobies[6] unloaded (their beasts of burden) in the stable-yard.

### Parable.

'Tis like (the tale of) the caravaneers (who) arrived and entered a village and found a certain door open.

One (of them) said, "During this spell of cold weather[7] let us unload (alight) here for a few days."

A voice cried, "Nay, unload outside, and then come indoors!

Drop outside everything that ought to be dropped: do not come in with it, for this assembly-place is of high dignity."

Hilál was a spiritual adept and a man of illumined soul,  1135 (though he was) the groom and slave of a Moslem Amír.

The youth served as a groom in the stable, but (he was really) a king of kings and a slave (only) in name.

The Amír was ignorant of his slave's (real) condition, for he had no discernment but of the sort possessed by Iblís.

He saw the clay, but not the treasure (buried) in it: he saw the five (senses) and the six (directions), but not the source of the five.

The colour of clay is manifest, the light of religion is hidden: such was (the case of) every prophet in the world.

One (person) saw the minaret, but not the bird (perched) upon  1140 it, (though) upon the minaret (was) a fully accomplished royal falcon;

And a second (observer) saw a bird flapping its wings, but not the hair in the bird's mouth (beak);

---

[1] Literally, "puts forth its head from."
[2] Literally, "good-fortuned."          [3] *I.e.* the spiritual world.
[4] *Qur'án*, XVIII, 59.          [5] *I.e.* the prophets and saints.
[6] Literally, "big geese," *i.e.* stupid worldlings.
[7] Literally, "old woman's cold." The term is properly applied to a "cold spell" which lasts about a week and ends shortly before the vernal equinox.

But that one who was seeing by the light of God was aware both of the bird and of the hair,

And said (to the other), "Pray, direct thine eye towards the hair: till thou see the hair, the knot will not be untied."

The one saw in the mud (only) figured clay, while the other saw clay replete with knowledge and works.

1145    The body is the minaret, knowledge and obedience (to God) are like the bird: suppose three hundred birds (to be perched on it) or (only) two birds, whichever you please.

The middle man[1] sees the bird only: neither before nor behind (him) does he see anything but a bird.

The hair is the hidden light belonging to the bird, whereby the soul of the bird is enduring (for ever).

The works of the bird in whose beak is that hair are never counterfeit.

Its knowledge gushes perpetually from its soul: it (this bird) has nothing that is borrowed (from others) and (owes) no debt.

*How this Hilál fell ill, and how his master was unaware of his being ill, because he despised him and did not recognise (his real worth); and how the heart of Muṣṭafá (Mohammed), on whom be peace, came to know of his illness and his state (of weakness), and how the Prophet, on whom be peace, inquired after this Hilál and went to see him.*

1150    By (Divine) destiny Hilál became ill and weak: inspiration acquainted Muṣṭafá with his condition.

His master was unaware of his illness, for in his eyes he (Hilál) was worth little and without importance.

(Such) a well-doer[2] lay (ill) in the stable for nine days, and none took notice of his plight.

(But) he[3] who was a personage and the Emperor of (all) personages, he whose oceanic[4] mind reaches every place—

To him came the (Divine) inspiration: God's Mercy sympathised (with Hilál), saying (to the Prophet), "Such-and-such an one who longs for thee is fallen sick."

1155    (Thereupon) Muṣṭafá went thither to pay a visit to the noble Hilál.

The (Prophetic) Moon was running behind the Sun of inspiration, while the Companions followed behind him, like the stars.

The Moon is saying, "My Companions are stars—a model for (those who follow them in) the night-journey, and missiles[5] hurled at the disobedient."

---

[1] *I.e.* the second of the three mentioned above.
[2] *I.e.* one who worships God as though he were seeing Him.
[3] *I.e.* the Prophet.
[4] Literally, "resembling a hundred Red Seas."
[5] *I.e.* shooting stars, with which the angels are supposed to pelt the devils.

(When) the Amír was told of the arrival of that (spiritual) Sultan, he sprang up, beside himself[1] with joy;

He clapped his hands joyously, thinking that the (spiritual) Emperor had come on his account[2].

When the Amír came down from the upper chamber, he was 1160 ready to lavish[3] his soul on the messenger as a reward (for the news he had brought).

Then he kissed the earth (before the Prophet) and gave the salaam (with great ceremony): in his delight he made his countenance like a rose.

"In God's name," he said, "bestow honour on the house (by entering it), so that this assembly-place may become a Paradise,

And that my palace may surpass heaven (in glory), saying, 'I have seen the Pole on which Time revolves.'"

The venerable (Prophet) said to him by way of rebuke, "I have not come to visit you."

He replied, "My spirit belongs to thee—what, indeed, is my 1165 spirit (before thee)? Oh, say on whose account is this solicitude?—

That I may become dust for the feet of the person who is planted[4] in the orchard of thy favour."

Then he (the Prophet) said to him, "Where is that New-moon (*Hilál*) of the highest heaven? Where is he that in his humility is spread as moonbeams (like a carpet on the ground)?—

That king who is disguised as a slave and has come (down) to this world for the purpose of spying?

Do not say, 'He is my slave and stableman': know this, that he is a treasure (buried) in ruins.

Oh, I wonder to what state he has been reduced by sickness— 1170 that New-moon by which thousands of full-moons are trodden underfoot."

He (the Amír) said, "I have no knowledge of his illness, but he has not been at the palace-gate for several days.

He keeps company with the horses and mules: he is a groom, and this stable is his dwelling-place."

*How Muṣṭafá, on whom be peace, came into the Amír's stable to see the sick Hilál, and how he caressed Hilál, may God be pleased with him!*

The Prophet went eagerly into the stable (to look) for him and began to search.

The stable was dark, foul, and dirty, (but) all this vanished (from Hilál's mind) when friendship arrived.

---

[1] Literally, "without heart and soul."
[2] Literally, "on account of that Amír."
[3] Literally, "he was scattering (as coins and the like)."
[4] Literally, "has a planting-place."

22

1175    That fierce (spiritual) lion scented the Prophet just as the scent of Joseph was perceived by his father (Jacob).

Miracles are not the cause of religious faith; 'tis the scent of homogeneity that attracts (to itself) qualities (of the same kind).

Miracles are (wrought) for the purpose of subjugating the foe: the scent of homogeneity is (only) for the winning of hearts.

A foe is subjugated, but not a friend: how should a friend have his neck bound?

He (Hilál) was awakened from sleep by his (the Prophet's) scent: he said (to himself), "A stable full of dung¹, and this kind of scent within it!"

1180    (Then) through the legs of the riding-beasts he saw the holy skirt of the peerless Prophet,

And that (spiritual) hero came creeping out of a corner in the stable and laid his face upon his (the Prophet's) feet.

Then the Prophet laid his face against his (Hilál's) face and kissed his head and eyes and cheeks².

"O Lord," he cried, "what a hidden pearl art thou! How art thou, O heavenly stranger? Art thou better?"

He (Hilál) said, "One whose sleep was disturbed (with grief), how forsooth is he when the Sun (of Prophecy) comes into his mouth?

1185    The thirsty man who eats clay (to slake his thirst), how is he (when) the Water (of Life) lays him on its head (surface) and bears him happily along?

[*Explanation of (the following Tradition), that Muṣṭafá (Moham-med), on whom be peace, hearing that Jesus, on whom be peace, walked on the water, said, 'If his faith had increased, he would have walked on the air.*']

(How is he) whom the vast river³ takes on its head (surface), like Jesus, saying, 'In the Water of Life thou art safe from drowning'?"

Aḥmad (Mohammed) says, "Had (his) faith been greater, even the air would have carried him safely⁴,

Like me, who rode upon the air on the night of the Ascension and sought communion (with God)."

He (Hilál) said, "How is a blind filthy dog that sprang up from sleep and found itself to be a lion?—

1190    Not such a lion as any one could shoot; nay, but (such an one that) by the terror of it sword and javelin would be shattered.

The blind man, (who was) going on his belly, like a snake— (how is he when) he has opened his eyes in the garden and in spring?"

¹ Literally, "a receptacle for dung."
² Literally, "face."          ³ Literally, "the Euphrates."
⁴ Literally, "would have been his vehicle and safe (for him)."

How is the "how" (contingent being) that has been freed from "how-ness" (conditionedness) and has attained unto the abounding life[1] of "how-lessness"?

He has become a dispenser of "how-ness" in the world beyond locality: all "how's" are (gathered) round his table, like dogs.

He gives (throws) to them a bone from (the table of) "how-lessness." Do thou, (being) in the state of pollution, keep silence: do not recite this Súra (of the *Qur'án*).

Until thou wash thyself entirely clean of "how-ness," do not 1195 put thy hand on this (Holy) Book, O youth.

Whether I am dirty or clean, O (spiritual) princes, if I do not recite this, then what in the world shall I recite?

You say to me, "For the sake of the (Divine) reward, do not go into the water-tank without having washed";

(But) outside of the tank there is nothing but earth: no one who does not enter the tank is clean.

If the waters have not the grace to receive filth continually,

Alas for the longing lover and his hope! Oh, sorrow for his 1200 everlasting sorrow!

(Nay, but) the water hath a hundred graces, a hundred (noble) pities[2], for it receives the defiled ones (and purifies them)—and peace (be with thee)!

O thou Radiance of God, Husámu'ddín, the Light is thy protector from the worst of flying creatures[3].

The Light and its ascent are thy protector, O Sun who art concealed from the bat.

The veil before the face of the Sun, what is it but excess of brilliance and intensity of splendour?

The veil over the Sun is just the Light of the Lord: the bat 1205 and the night have no lot therein.

Inasmuch as both (of them) have remained far (from the Sun) and veiled (from it), they have remained either black-faced (like Night) or cold (like the bat).

Since thou hast written part of the story of the New-moon (*Hilál*), (now) put into words the tale of the Full-moon.

The New-moon[4] and the Full-moon[5] have oneness (with each other): they are far from duality and from imperfection and corruption.

The new-moon is inwardly free from imperfection: its apparent imperfection is (due to its) increasing gradually.

Night by night it gives a lesson in gradualness, and with 1210 deliberation it produces relief (for itself).

[1] Literally, "the place abounding with life."
[2] Literally, "feelings of shame and respect (for others)."
[3] *I.e.* the bat.
[4] The disciple.
[5] The Perfect Man (saint and spiritual Director).

With deliberation it says, "O hasty fool, (only) step by step can one mount to the roof."

Let the cooking-pot boil gradually, as a skilful (cook) does: the stew boiled in a mad hurry is of no use.

Was not God able to create heaven in one moment by (the word) "*Be*"? Without any doubt (He was).

Why, then, O seeker of instruction, did He extend (the time) for it to six days, every day (being as long as) a thousand years?[1]

1215   Wherefore is the creation of a child (completed) in nine months? Because gradualness is a characteristic of (the action of) that King.

Why was (the time occupied in) the creation of Adam forty mornings? (Because) He (God) was adding (perfections) to that clay little by little,

Not like you, O foolish one, who have rushed forward just now: you are a child, and you have made yourself out to be an Elder.

You have run up, like a gourd, to the top of all, (but) where is the (spiritual) warfare and combat to sustain you?

You have rested on trees and walls for support: you have climbed up like a pumpkin, O little baldhead.

1220   If at first you mounted on a tall cypress, yet in the end you are dry and pulpless and empty.

Your green (fresh) colour soon turned yellow (faded), O pumpkin, for it was derived from rouge, it was not original.

*Story of the old woman who used to depilate and rouge her ugly face, though it could never be put right and become pleasing.*

There was a decrepit old woman aged ninety years, her face covered with wrinkles and her complexion (yellow as) saffron.

Her face was in folds like the surface of a traveller's food-wallet, but there remained in her the passionate desire for a husband.

Her teeth had dropped out and her hair had become (white) as milk: her figure was (bent) like a bow, and every sense in her was decayed.

1225   Her passion for a husband and her lust and desire were (there) in full (force): the passion for snaring (was there), though the trap had fallen to pieces.

(She was like) a cock that crows at the wrong time[2], a road that leads nowhere[3], a big fire beneath an empty kettle;

(Like one who is) exceedingly fond of the race-course, but has no horse and no means of running[4]; (or) exceedingly fond of piping, but having neither lip nor pipe.

---

[1] Cf. *Qur'án*, XXII, 46.     [2] Literally, "an untimely bird."
[3] Literally, "a wayless way," *i.e.* a blind alley.     [4] Literally, "no foot."

May (even) Jews have no (such) cupidity in (their) old age!
Oh, (how) miserable is he on whom God hath bestowed this
cupidity!

A dog's teeth drop out when it grows old: it leaves people
(alone) and takes to (eating) dung;

(But) look at these sexagenarian dogs! Their dog-teeth get 1230
sharper at every moment.

The hairs drop from the fur of an old dog; (but) see these old
(human) dogs clad in satin!

See how their passionate desire and greed for women and gold,
like the progeny of dogs, is increasing continually!

Such a life as this, which is Hell's stock-in-trade, is a shambles
for the butchers (executioners) of (the Divine) Wrath;

(Yet) when people say to him, "May your life be long!" he is
delighted and opens his mouth in laughter.

He thinks a curse like this is a benediction: he never uncloses 1235
his (inward) eye or raises his head once (from the slumber of
heedlessness).

If he had seen (even as much as) a hair's tip of the future
state, he would have said to him (who wished him long life),
"May *thy* life be like this!"


*Story of the dervish who blessed a man of Gílán, saying, "May
God bring thee back in safety to thy home and household!"*

One day a sturdy beggar, (who was) very fond of bread and
carried a basket (about with him), accosted a Khwája of Gílán.

On receiving some bread from him, he cried, "O Thou (God)
whose help is besought, bring him back happy to his home and
household!"

He (the Khwája) said, "If the house is the one that I have
seen (recently), may God bring *thee* there, O squalid wretch!"

Worthless folk humiliate every story-teller: if his words are 1240
lofty, they make them low;

For the tale is (lofty or low) in proportion to (the understanding
of) the hearer: the tailor cuts the coat according to the Khwája's
(customer's) figure.

### [Description of the old woman.]

Since the audience is not free from such reproach, there is no
means of avoiding low and undignified talk.

Hark, redeem this topic (of discourse) from pawn[1]: return to
the tale of the old woman.

When he (any one) has become advanced in years and is not
a man (adept) in this Way, bestow the name of "aged crone"
upon him.

[1] *I.e.* take up the story again at the point where it was left.

1245    He has neither (any spiritual) capital and basis, nor is he capable of receiving (such a) stock-in-trade.

He is neither a giver nor a receiver of (spiritual) delight; in him there is neither reality nor (the power of) absorbing reality.

(He has) neither tongue nor ear nor understanding and insight nor consciousness nor unconsciousness nor reflections;

Neither humble supplication nor any beauty (with which) to show pride: his (whole interior), coat on coat, is stinking, like an onion.

He has not traversed any path, nor (has he) the foot for (any power to traverse) the path: that shameless one[1] has neither (inward) glow nor burning (passion) and sighs.


*Story of the dervish to whom, whenever he begged anything from a certain house, he (the owner) used to say, "It is not (to be had here)."*

1250    A beggar came to a house and asked for a piece of dry bread or a piece of moist (new) bread.

The owner of the house said, "Where is bread in this place? Are you crazy? How is this (house) a baker's shop?"

"At least," he begged, "get me a little bit of fat." "Why," said he, "it isn't a butcher's shop."

He said, "O master of the house, give me a pittance of flour." "Do you think this is a mill?" he replied.

"Well then," said he, "give me some water from the reservoir." "Why," he replied, "it isn't a river or a watering-place."

1255    Whatever he asked for, from bread to bran, he (the householder) was mocking and deriding him.

The beggar went in and drew up his skirt: in ea domo voluit consulto cacare.

He (the householder) cried, "Hey, hey!" "Be quiet, O morose man," said he, "ut in hoc loco deserto alvum exonerem.

Since there is no means of living (zístan) here, upon a house like this cacare (rístan) oportet."

Since you are not a falcon, so as to (be able to) catch the prey, (a falcon) hand-trained for the King's hunting;

1260    Nor a peacock painted with a hundred (beautiful) designs, so that (all) eyes should be illumined by the picture which you present;

Nor a parrot, so that when sugar is given to you, (all) ears should bend to (listen to) your sweet talk;

Nor a nightingale to sing, like a lover, sweetly and plaintively in the meadow or the tulip-garden;

[1] Literally, "harlot."

Nor a hoopoe to bring messages[1], nor are you like a stork to make your nest on high—

In what work are you (employed), and for what (purpose) are you bought? What (sort of) bird are you, and with what (digestive) are you eaten?

Mount beyond this shop of hagglers to the shop of Bounty 1265 where *God is the purchaser.*

(There) that Gracious One hath purchased the piece of goods that no people would look at on account of its shabbiness.

With Him no base coin is rejected, for His object in buying is not (to make a) profit.

### *Return to the tale of the old woman.*

Since that (crone who was faded as) autumn desired to be wed[2], that lustful one[3] plucked out the hair of her eyebrows.

The old woman took the mirror (and held it) before her face, that she might beautify her cheeks and face and mouth.

She rubbed (them) gleefully (with) rouge several times, (but) 1270 the creases[4] of her face did not become more concealed,

(So) that filthy (hag) was cutting out portions of the Holy Book and sticking them on her face,

In order that the creases of her face might be hidden, and that she might become the bezel in the ring of fair (women).

She was putting (these) bits of the Book all over her face, (but) they always dropped off when she put on her *chádar* (veil);

Then she would stick them on again with spittle on all sides of her face,

And once more that bezel (paragon of beauty) would arrange 1275 her veil, and (again) the bits of the Book would fall from her face to the ground.

Since they always dropped off though she tried many an artifice, (at last) she exclaimed, "A hundred curses on Iblís!"

Immediately Iblís took (visible) shape and said (to her), "O luckless[5] dried-up[6] harlot,

In all my life I have never thought of this: I have never seen this (impiety practised) by any harlot except thee.

Thou hast sown unique seed in (the field of) infamy: thou hast not left a single Scripture (*Qur'án*) in the world.

Thou art a hundred Devils, troop on troop: let me alone, 1280 O foul hag!"

---

[1] Referring to the hoopoe that brought news to Solomon (*Qur'án*, XXVII, 22).
[2] Literally, "to go to the wedding."
[3] Literally, "lati praeputii avida."
[4] Literally, "crumpled table-cloth."    [5] Literally, "without advent."
[6] Literally, "(slit like) *qadíd*," *i.e.* flesh cut in strips and dried in the sun.

How long will you steal portions of the lore of the Book, in order that your face may be coloured like an apple?[1]

How long will you steal the words of the men of God, that you may sell (them) and obtain applause[2] (from the crowd)?

The daubed-on colour never made you (really) rosy; the tied-on bough never performed the function of the (fruit-bearing) stump (from which the dates are cut off).

At last, when the veil of death comes over you, these bits of the Book drop away from your face.

1285　When the call comes to arise and depart[3], thereafter (all) the arts of disputation vanish.

The world of silence comes into view. Stop (talking)! Alas for him that hath not a familiarity (with silence) within him!

Polish your breast (heart) for a day or two: make that mirror[4] your book (of meditation),

For from (seeing) the reflexion of the imperial[5] Joseph old Zalíkhá became young anew.

The chilly temperature of "the old woman's cold spell[6]" is changed (into heat) by the sun of Tamúz (July).

1290　A dry-lipped bough is changed into a flourishing palm-tree by the burning (anguish) of a Mary[7].

O (you who are like the) old woman, how long will you strive with the (Divine) destiny? Seek the cash now: let bygones be.

Since your face hath no hope of (acquiring) beauty, you may either put rouge (on it) or, if you wish, ink.

### Story of the sick man of whose recovery the physician despaired.

A certain sick man went to a physician and said, "Feel my pulse, O sagacious one,

That by (feeling) the pulse you may diagnose the state of my heart, for the hand-vein is connected with the heart."

1295　Since the heart is invisible, if you want a symbol of it, seek (it) from him who hath connexion with the heart.

The wind is hidden from the eye, O trusty (friend), (but) see it in the dust and in the movement of the leaves,

(And observe) whether it is blowing from the right or from the left: the movement of the leaves will describe its condition to you.

(If) you know not intoxication of the heart (and ask) where (it is), seek the description of it from the inebriated (languid) eye[8].

---

[1] I.e. "in order that you may be honoured and venerated."
[2] Literally, "welcome."
[3] Literally, "when the 'Arise, arise' of that departure comes."
[4] I.e. the illumined heart.
[5] Literally, "lord of the conjunction (of two planets)."
[6] See note on v. 1132 supra.
[7] Qur'án, XIX, 22 foll.　　　　[8] Literally, "narcissus."

Since you are far from (knowing) the Essence of God, you may recognise the description of the Essence in the Prophet and (his) evidentiary miracles.

Certain secret miracles and graces (proceeding) from the elect 1300 (Ṣúfí) Elders impress the heart (of the disciple);

For within them (those Elders) there are a hundred immediate (spiritual) resurrections, (of which) the least is this, that their neighbour becomes intoxicated;

Hence that fortunate (disciple) who has devoted himself to[1] a blessed (saint) has become the companion of God.

The evidentiary miracle that produced an effect upon something inanimate (is) either (like) the rod (of Moses) or (the passage of) the sea (by the Israelites) or the splitting of the moon.

If it (the evidentiary miracle) produces an immediate effect upon the soul, (the reason is that) it (the soul) is brought into connexion (with the producer of the effect) by means of a hidden link.

The effects produced upon inanimate objects are (only) 1305 accessory: they are (really) for the sake of the fair invisible spirit,

In order that the inmost heart may be affected by means of that inanimate object. (But) how (much more) excellent is bread (produced) without the substance (of bread), (namely), dough!

How excellent is the Messiah's table of food without stint![2] How excellent is Mary's fruit (that was produced) without an orchard![3]

Miracles (proceeding) from the spirit of the perfect (saint) affect the soul of the seeker as life (bestowed on the dead).

The miracle is (like) the sea, and the deficient (heedless) man is (like) the land-bird (which perishes in the sea); (but) the water-bird is safe from destruction there.

It (the miracle) bestows infirmity on any one that is un- 1310 initiated, but it bestows power on the spirit of an intimate.

Since you do not feel this bliss in your inmost heart, then continually seek the clue to it from outside,

For effects are apparent to the senses, and these effects give information concerning their producer.

The virtue of every drug is hidden like magic and the art of any sorcerer;

(But) when you regard its action and effects, you bring it to light (even) though it is hidden.

The potency that is concealed within it is clearly seen and 1315 made manifest when it comes into action.

Since all these things are revealed to you by means of effects, how is not God revealed to you by the production of effects?

[1] Literally, "has carried his baggage to the side of."
[2] Qur'án, v, 112 foll.  [3] Qur'án, III, 32.

Causes and effects, (both) kernel and husk—are not the whole (of them), when you investigate, effects produced by Him?

You make friends with things because of the effect (which they produce): why, then, are you ignorant of Him who produces (all) effects?

You make friends with people on the ground of a phantasy: why do not you make friends with the King of west and east?

1320     This topic hath no end. O (spiritual) emperor, may there be no end to our desire for this (mystic knowledge)!

### Returning to the Story of the sick man.

Return (from the digression) and tell the story of the sick man and the wise physician whose nature was to palliate.

He felt his pulse and ascertained his state (of health): (he saw) that it was absurd to hope for his recovery.

He said, "Do whatever your heart desires, in order that this old malady may quit your body.

Do not withhold anything that your inclination craves, lest your self-restraint and abstinence turn to gripes.

1325     Know that self-restraint and abstinence are injurious to this disease: proffer to your heart whatever it may desire.

O uncle, (it was) in reference to a sick man like this (that) God most High said, '*Do what ye will.*"

He (the sick man) said, "(Now) go; look you, my dear nephew[1], I am going for a walk on the bank of the river."

He was strolling beside the water, as his heart desired, in order that he might find the door to health opened to him.

On the river-bank a Ṣúfí was seated, washing his hands and face and cleansing himself more and more[2].

1330     He saw the nape of his (the Ṣúfí's) neck and, like a crazy man, felt a longing to give it a slap;

(So) he raised his hand to inflict a blow on the nape of the pottage-worshipping Ṣúfí,

Saying (to himself), "The physician told me it would make me ill if I would not let my desire have its way.

I will give him a slap in quarrel, for (God hath said), '*Do not cast yourselves with your own hands into destruction.*'

O such-and-such[3], this self-restraint and abstinence is (thy) destruction: give him a good blow, do not keep quiet like the others."

1335     When he slapped him, there was the sound of a crack: the Ṣúfí cried, "Hey, hey, O rascally[4] pimp!"

The Ṣúfí was about to give him two or three blows with his

---

[1] Literally, "O soul of thy uncle."
[2] Literally, "and increasing (his) cleanliness."
[3] The sick man addresses himself.     [4] Literally, "undutiful."

fist and tear out his moustache and beard piecemeal (but refrained from doing so).

Mankind are (like) sufferers from phthisis and without a remedy (for their disease), and through the Devil's deception they are passionately addicted to slapping (each other).

All (of them) are eager to injure the innocent and are seeking (to find) fault behind each others' backs.

O you who strike the napes of the guiltless, don't you see the retribution (that is coming) behind you?

O you who fancy that (indulgence of) desire is your (right) 1340 medicine and inflict slaps on the weak,

He who told you that this is the cure (for your disease) mocked at you: 'tis he that guided Adam to the wheat[1],

Saying, "O ye twain who implore help, eat this grain as a remedy that *ye may abide (in Paradise) for ever*."

He caused him (Adam) to stumble and gave him a slap on the nape: that slap recoiled and became a (penal) retribution for him (the Devil).

He caused him (Adam) to stumble terribly in backsliding, but God was his (Adam's) support and helper.

Adam was (like) a mountain: (even) if he was filled with 1345 serpents (of sin), he is a mine of the antidote (to snake-poison) and was unhurt.

You, who do not possess an atom of the antidote, why are you deluded by your (hope of) deliverance?

Where, in your case, is trust in God like (the trust of) Khalíl (Abraham), and whence will you get the (Divine) grace like (that bestowed upon) Kalím (Moses),

So that your knife should not cut (the throat of) Ismá'íl (Ishmael) and that you should make the depths of the Nile a (dry) highway?

If a blessed one fell from the minaret (and) was saved by the wind filling[2] his raiment,

Why have you, O good man, committed yourself to the wind 1350 when you are not sure of that (same) fortune?

From this minaret hundreds of thousands (of peoples) like 'Ád fell down and gave to the wind (lost) their lives and souls[3].

Behold those who have fallen headlong from this minaret, hundreds of thousands on thousands!

(If) you have no sure skill in rope-dancing, give thanks for your feet and walk on the ground.

Don't make wings of paper and fly from the (top of a) mountain, for many a head has gone (to destruction) in this craze.

Although the Ṣúfí was afire with anger, yet he cast his eye on 1355 the consequence.

---

[1] *I.e.* the forbidden fruit.    [2] Literally, "falling into."
[3] Literally, "their heads and hearts."

The highest success belongs permanently to him[1] who does not take the bait and sees (the danger of) imprisonment in the trap.

How excellent are two noble end-discerning eyes that preserve the body from corruption!

That (foresight) was (derived) from the vision of the end that was seen by Ahmad (Mohammed), who even here (in the present life) saw Hell, hair by hair[2],

And saw the Throne (of God) and the Footstool and the Gardens (of Paradise), so that he rent the veil of (our) forgetfulnesses.

1360    If you desire to be safe from harm, close your eye to the beginning and contemplate the end,

That you may regard all (apparent) nonentities as (really) existent and look upon (all) entities, (so far as they are) perceived by the senses, as of low degree[3].

At least consider this, that every one who possesses reason is daily and nightly in quest of the (relatively) non-existent.

In begging, he seeks a munificence that is not in being[4]; in the shops he seeks a profit that is not in being.

In the cornfields he seeks an income (crop) that is not in being; in the plantations he seeks a date-palm that is not in being.

1365    In the colleges he seeks a knowledge that is not in being; in the Christian monasteries he seeks a morality that is not in being.

They (the intelligent) have thrown the (actually) existent things behind them and are seekers of, and devoted to, the (relatively) non-existent things,

Because the mine and treasury of God's doing is not other than non-existence in (process of) being brought into manifestation.

We have previously given some indication of this (matter)[5]: regard this (present discourse) and that (former discourse) as one, not as two.

It was stated (formerly) that every craftsman who appeared (in the world) sought the abode of (relative) non-existence in (exercising) his craft.

1370    The builder sought an unrepaired place that had become ruined and (where) the roofs (were) fallen in.

The water-carrier sought a pot with no water in it, and the carpenter a house with no door.

At the moment of pursuing (their object) they rushed into (relative) non-existence; then (afterwards) they all are fleeing from non-existence.

---

[1] Literally, "the first place in the rank remains with success on him."
[2] *I.e.* in every detail.      [3] *I.e.* lacking reality.
[4] *I.e.* potentially, but not actually, existent.     [5] See Book I, *v.* 3204 foll.

Since your hope is (in) non-existence, why (this) avoidance of it? Why (this) strife with what is congenial to your desire?

Since that non-existence is congenial to your desire, why this avoidance of nonentity and non-existence?

O (dear) soul, if you are not inwardly congenial to non- 1375 existence, why are you waiting in ambush for non-existence?

You have torn your heart away from all that you own, you have cast the net of your heart into the sea of non-existence.

Wherefore, then, (this) flight from this sea of (heart's) desire that has put hundreds of thousands of prey into your net?

Wherefore have you given the name "death" to (what is really) provision (for the spirit)? Observe the sorcery that has caused the provision (*barg*) to seem to you death (*marg*).

The magic of His (God's) doing has bound both your eyes, so that desire for the (worldly) pit has come over your soul.

Through the contrivance of the Creator, in its (your soul's) 1380 fancy all the expanse above the pit is (full of) poison and snakes;

Consequently it has made the pit a refuge (for itself), so that (fear of) death has cast it into the pit.

(Having heard) what I have said concerning your mis-apprehensions, O dear friend, hear also the utterance of 'Aṭṭár on this same (subject).

### Story of Sultan Maḥmúd and the Hindú boy.

He, God have mercy upon him, has told it: he has strung together[1] the tale of King Maḥmúd, the *Ghází*[2]—

How, amongst the booty of his campaign in India, (there was) a boy (who) was brought into the presence of that sovereign.

Afterwards he made him his vicegerent and seated him on the 1385 throne and gave him preferment above (the rest of) the army and called him "son."

Seek the length and breadth and all particulars[3] of the story in the discourse of that prince of the Faith[4].

In short, the lad was seated on this throne of gold beside the King-emperor.

He wept and shed tears in burning grief. The King said to him, "O thou whose day (fortune) is triumphant,

Wherefore shouldst thou weep? Has thy fortune become disagreeable to thee? Thou art above kings, (thou art) the familiar companion of the Emperor.

Thou art (seated) on this throne, while the viziers and 1390 soldiers are ranged in file before thy throne, like the stars and the moon."

---

[1] Literally, "has bored (the pearls of) the tale."
[2] *I.e.* champion of Islam against the infidels.
[3] Literally, "description, fold by fold."    [4] The *Muṣíbat-náma* of 'Aṭṭár.

The boy said, "The cause of my weeping bitterly is that in yonder city and country my mother

Was always threatening me with thee, (saying), 'May I see you in the hands of the lion, Maḥmúd!'

Then my father would wrangle with my mother (and say) in reply, 'What wrath and torment is this (that you would inflict on him)?

Cannot you find any other curse lighter than this deadly curse?

1395 You are very pitiless and exceedingly hard-hearted, for you are (virtually) killing him with a hundred swords.'

I used to be dismayed by the talk of both: a (great) terror and pain would come into my heart,

(Thinking), 'Oh, wonderful! What a hellish person Maḥmúd must be, since he has become proverbial for woe and anguish!'

I used to tremble in fear of thee, being ignorant of thy gracious treatment and high regard.

Where is my mother, that she might see me now (seated) on the throne, O King of the world?"

1400 (Spiritual) poverty is your Maḥmúd, O man without affluence: your (sensual) nature is always making you afraid of it.

If you come to know the mercifulness of this noble Maḥmúd, you will cry joyously, "May the end be praised (maḥmúd)!"

Poverty is your Maḥmúd, O craven-hearted one: do not listen to this mother, namely, your misguiding nature.

When you become a prey to poverty, you will certainly shed tears (of delight), like the Hindú boy, on the Day of Judgement.

Although the body is (like) a mother in fostering (the spirit), yet it is more inimical to you than a hundred enemies.

1405 When your body falls ill it makes you seek medicine; and if it grows strong it makes you an outrageous devil.

Know that this iniquitous body is like a coat of mail: it serves neither for winter nor summer[1].

(Yet) the bad associate[2] is good (for you) because of the patience (which you must show in overcoming its desires), for the exercise of patience expands the heart (with spiritual peace).

The patience shown by the moon to the (dark) night keeps it illumined; the patience shown by the rose to the thorn keeps it fragrant.

The patience shown by the milk (chyle) betwixt the faeces (in the intestine) and the blood[3] enables it to rear the camel-foal till he has entered on his third year[4].

1410 The patience shown by all the prophets to the unbelievers

---

[1] *I.e.* it is like a useless garment.
[2] *I.e.* the body.   [3] See *Qur'án*, xvi, 68.
[4] Literally, "makes it a rearer of the male camel that has entered on his third year."

made them the elect of God and lords of the planetary con-
junction[1].

When you see any one wearing goodly raiment, know that he
has gained it by patience and work.

If you have seen any one naked and destitute, that is a testi-
mony of his lack of patience.

Any one who feels lonely and whose soul is full of anguish
must have associated with an impostor.

If he had shown patience and loyal friendship (to God), he
would not have suffered this affliction[2] through being separated
from Him.

He would have consorted with God as honey with milk,  1415
saying, "*I love not them that set*[3]."

(Then) assuredly he would not have remained alone, even as
a fire left on the road by caravaneers.

(But) since from lack of patience he associated himself with
others (than God), in separation from Him he became sorrowful
and deprived of good.

Since your friendship is (precious) as pure gold, how are
you placing it in trust with a traitor?

Consort with Him with whom your trusts are safe from loss[4]
and violation.

Consort with Him who created (human) nature and fostered[5]  1420
the natures of the prophets.

(If) you give (Him) a lamb, He will give you back a (whole)
flock (of sheep): verily the Lord is the fosterer of every (good)
quality.

Will you entrust the lamb to the wolf? (Nay), do not tell the
wolf and Joseph[6] to travel in company with each other.

If the wolf show foxiness towards you (fawn upon you),
beware, do not believe (him), for no goodness comes from
him.

If a churl show sympathy towards you, (yet) in the end he
will inflict blows upon you because of his churlishness.

Ille duo instrumenta[7] habet et androgynus est: amborum  1425
effectus sine dubio apparet.

Penem oculis feminarum subtrahit ut sese earum sororem
faciat.

Vulvam ne viri videant manu obtegit, ut sese de genere
virorum faciat.

Dixit Deus, "Ex ejus cunno occulto scissuram[8] in naso ejus
faciemus[9],

---

[1] *I.e.* mighty and victorious spiritual emperors.
[2] Literally, "blow on the nape."          [3] *Qur'án*, VI, 76.
[4] Literally, "setting."      [5] *I.e.* developed and brought to perfection.
[6] See *Qur'án*, XII, 13 foll.
[7] *I.e.* membra genitalia utriusque sexus.
[8] Literally, "vulvam."
[9] See *Qur'án*, LXVIII, 16.

In order that Our seers may not be entrapped by the artfulness of that ogler."

1430 The gist (of the matter) is that masculinity does not come from every male: beware of the ignorant man if you are wise.

Do not listen to the friendliness of the fair-spoken ignorant man, for it is like old (virulent) poison.

He says to you, "O soul of thy mother![1] O light of my eye![2] " (but) from those (endearments) only grief and sorrow are added to you.

That (foolish) mother says plainly to your father, "My child has grown very thin because of (going to) school.

If thou hadst gotten him by another wife, thou wouldst not have treated him with such cruelty and unkindness."

1435 (Your father replies), "Had this child of mine been (born) of another (wife), not of thee, that wife too would have talked this (same) nonsense."

Beware, recoil from this mother and from her blandishments: your father's slaps are better than her sweetmeat.

The mother is the carnal soul, and the father is noble reason: its beginning is constraint, but its end is a hundred expansions (of the spirit).

O Giver of (all) understandings, come to my help: none wills (aught) unless Thou will (it).

Both the desire (for good) and the good action (itself) proceed from Thee: who are we? Thou art the First, Thou art the Last.

1440 Do Thou speak and do Thou hear and do Thou be! We are wholly naught notwithstanding all this hewing[3].

Because of this resignation (to Thy will) do Thou increase our desire for worship (of Thee): do not send (upon us) the sloth and stagnation[4] of necessitarianism.

Necessitarianism is the wing and pinion of the perfect; necessitarianism is also the prison and chains of the slothful.

Know that this necessitarianism is like the water of the Nile— water to the true believer and blood to the infidel[5].

Wings carry falcons to the king; wings carry crows to the graveyard.

1445 Now return to the description of non-existence, for it (non-existence) is like bezoar, though you think it is poison.

Hark, O fellow-servant, go and, like the Hindú boy, be not afraid of the Maḥmúd of non-existence.

Be afraid of the existence in which you are now: that phantasy of yours[6] is nothing and you (yourself) are nothing.

[1] The ignorant man is compared to a foolish mother.
[2] Literally, "O (my) bright eye."      [3] I.e. effort and exertion.
[4] Literally, "extinction (of a fire)."
[5] See translation of Book IV, v. 3431 foll.
[6] I.e. the illusion of your existence.

One nothing has fallen in love with another nothing: has any naught ever waylaid (and attacked) any other naught?

When these phantasies have departed from before you, that which your understanding hath not conceived becomes clear to you.

*Those who have passed away do not grieve on account of death;*
*their only regret is to have missed the opportunities (of life).*

That captain of mankind[1] has said truly that no one who has 1450 passed away from this world

Feels sorrow and regret and disappointment on account of death; nay, but he feels a hundred regrets for having missed the opportunity,

Saying (to himself), "Why did not I make death my object —(death, which is) the store-house of every fortune and every provision—

(And why), through seeing double, did I make the lifelong object of my attention those phantoms that vanished at the fated hour?"

The grief of the dead is not on account of death; it is because (so they say) "we dwelt upon the (phenomenal) forms,

And this we did not perceive, that those are (mere) form and 1455 foam, (and that) the foam is moved and fed by the Sea."

When the Sea has cast the foam-flakes on the shore, go to the graveyard and behold those flakes of foam!

Then say (to them), "Where is your movement and gyration (now)? The Sea has cast you into the crisis (of a deadly malady)"—

In order that they may say to you, not with their lips but implicitly, "Ask this question of the Sea, not of us."

How should the foam-like (phenomenal) form move without the wave? How should the dust rise to the zenith without a wind?

Since you have perceived the dust, namely, the form, perceive 1460 the wind; since you have perceived the foam, perceive the ocean of Creative Energy[2].

Come, perceive (it), for insight (is the only thing) in you (that) avails: the rest of you is a piece of fat and flesh, a weft and warp (of bones, muscles, etc.).

Your fat never increased the light in candles, your flesh never became roast-meat for any one drunken with (spiritual) wine.

Dissolve the whole of this body of yours in vision: pass into sight, pass into sight, into sight!

One sight perceives (only) two yards of the road; another sight has beheld the two worlds and the Face of the King.

[1] The Prophet.
[2] Literally, "the action of bringing into existence."

**23**

1465   Between these twain there is an incalculable difference: seek
the collyrium—and God best knoweth the things occult.

Since you have heard the description of the sea of non-
existence, continually endeavour to stand (depend) upon this
sea.

Inasmuch as the foundation of the workshop is that non-
existence which is void and traceless and empty,

(And inasmuch as) all master-craftsmen seek non-existence
and a place of breakage for the purpose of exhibiting their skill,

Necessarily the Lord (who is) the Master of (all) masters—
His workshop is non-existence and naught.

1470   Wherever this non-existence is greater, (the more manifest)
in that quarter is the work and workshop of God.

Since the highest stage is non-existence, the dervishes have
outstripped all (others),

Especially the dervish that has become devoid of body and
(worldly) goods: poverty (deprivation) of body is the (important)
matter, not beggary.

The beggar is he whose (worldly) goods have melted away;
the contented man is he who has gambled away (sacrificed) his
body.

Therefore do not now complain of affliction, for it is a smooth-
paced horse (carrying you) towards non-existence.

1475   We have said so much: think of the remainder, (or) if thought
be frozen (unable to move), practise recollection (of God).

Recollection (of God) brings thought into movement: make
recollection to be the sun for this congealed (thought).

(God's) pulling is, indeed, the original source; but, O fellow-
servant, exert yourself, do not be dependent on that pulling;

For to renounce exertion is like an act of disdain: how should
disdain be seemly for a devoted lover (of God)?

O youth, think neither of acceptance nor refusal: regard
always the (Divine) command and prohibition.

1480   (Then) suddenly the bird, namely, the (Divine) attraction, will
fly from its nest (towards you): put out the candle as soon as you
see the dawn.

When the eyes have become piercing, 'tis its (the dawn's)
light (that illumines them): in the very husk it (the illumined
eye) beholds the kernels.

In the mote it beholds the everlasting Sun, in the drop (of
water) it beholds the entire Sea.

*Returning once more to the Story of the Ṣúfí and the Cadi.*

The Ṣúfí said (to himself), " It does not behove me blindly to
lose my head by taking retaliation for a single slap on the nape.

My putting on the (Ṣúfí's) mantle of resignation has made it
easy for me to suffer blows."

The Ṣūfí observed that his adversary was exceedingly frail: 1485
he said (to himself), "If I give him a hostile blow with my fist,

At my first[1] blow he will crumble like lead, and then the king
will punish me and exact retaliation.

The tent is ruined and the tent-pin broken: it (the tent) is
seeking (the least) excuse to fall in.

It would be a pity, a (great) pity, that on account of this (virtu-
ally) dead man retaliation should fall upon me under the sword."

Since he durst not give his adversary a fisticuff, he resolved
to take him to the Cadi,

Saying (to himself), "He (the cadi) is God's scales and 1490
measure, he is the means of deliverance from the deceit and
cunning of the Devil.

He is the scissors for (cutting off) enmities and wranglings, he
is the decider of the quarrels and disputes of the two litigants.

His spells put the Devil in the bottle, his legal ruling makes
dissensions cease.

When the covetous adversary sees the scales (of justice), he
abandons rebelliousness and becomes submissive;

But if there are no scales, (even) though you give him more
(than his fair share) his shrewdness will never be satisfied with
the portion (allotted to him)."

The cadi is a mercy (bestowed by God) and the means of 1495
removing strife: he is a drop from the ocean of the justice of the
Resurrection.

Though the drop be small and short of foot, (yet) by it the
purity of the ocean's water is made manifest.

If you keep the (outer) veil (coat of the inward eye) free from
dust, you will see the Tigris in a single drop (of water).

The parts bear witness to the state of (their) wholes, so that
the afterglow of sunset has become an informer concerning the
sun.

God applied that oath, (namely), His Words[2] *Verily (I swear)
by the afterglow of sunset*[3], to the body of Aḥmad (Mohammed).

Wherefore should the ant have been trembling (in desire) for 1500
the grain (of corn), if from that single grain it had known (in-
ferred) the (existence of) the stack?

Come (now) to the topic (in hand), for the Ṣūfí is distraught
(has lost control of his reason) and is making haste to exact
redress for the injury (inflicted on him).

O thou that hast committed deeds of injustice, how art thou
(so) glad at heart? Art thou unaware of the demand (that will
be made upon thee) by him who exacts the penalty?

Or hast thou forgotten those deeds of thine, since heedlessness
has let down curtains (of oblivion) over thee?

[1] Literally, "one."
[2] Literally, "that which He hath said."     [3] *Qur'án*, LXXXIV, 16.

If there were no litigations pursuing thee[1], the celestial orb
would envy thy happiness;

1505   But on account of those just claims (against thee) thou art
embarrassed. Little by little, (therefore), beg to be excused for
thy unrighteousness.

Lest the Inspector suddenly arrest thee, now (at once) make
thy (turbid) water clear (make full amends and wipe out thy
injustice) towards the lover (of God).

The Ṣúfí went to the man who had slapped him, and laid hold
of his skirt like a plaintiff.

Haling him along, he brought him to the Cadi, saying,
"Mount this asinine miscreant[2] on an ass (and parade him
through the streets),

Or punish him with blows of the whip, according as thy
judgement may deem fitting;

1510   For (in the case of) one who dies under thy chastisement, no
fine is (imposed) on thee in vengeance (for him): that (death) is
unpenalised."

When any one has died under the punishment and flagellation
of the cadi[3], no responsibility lies on the cadi, for he (the cadi)
is not a person of small account.

He is God's deputy and the shadow of God's justice, the
mirror (that displays the real nature) of every plaintiff and
defendant;

For he inflicts correction for the sake of one who has been
wronged, not for the sake of his honour or his anger or his
income (profit).

Since it is (done) for the sake of God and the Day (of Judge-
ment) hereafter, if a mistake is made (by him) the blood-wit falls
upon the (dead man's) kinsmen on the father's side.

1515   He who strikes (and kills) for his own sake is (held) responsible,
while he who strikes (and kills) for God's sake is secure.

If a father strikes his son and he (the son) dies, the father must
pay the blood-price,

Because he struck him for his own benefit, (since) it is the duty
of the son to serve him (the father).

(But) when a teacher strikes a boy and he (the boy) perishes
(is killed by the blows), nothing (in the way of penalty) is
(imposed) on the teacher; no fear![4]

For the teacher is a deputy (of God) and a trustee; and the
case of every trustee is the same as this[5].

1520   It is not his (the boy's) duty to serve his master (teacher):
therefore in chastising him the master was not seeking benefit
(for himself);

---

[1] Literally, "behind thee."          [2] Literally, "this luckless ass."
[3] *I.e.* to which the cadi has sentenced him.     [4] Literally, "do not fear."
[5] *I.e.* the same rule is applicable to every trustee.

But if his father struck him, he struck for his own sake: consequently he was not freed from (responsibility for) paying the blood-price.

Behead (your) selfhood, then, O (you who resemble the sword) Dhu 'l-faqár: become a selfless naughted one like the dervish.

When you have become selfless, everything that you do (is a case of) *thou didst not throw when thou threwest*, (and) you are safe.

The responsibility lies on God, not on the trustee: 'tis set forth plainly in (books of) jurisprudence.

Every shop has a different (kind of) merchandise: the 1525 *Mathnawí* is the shop for (spiritual) poverty, O son.

In the shoemaker's shop there is fine leather: if you see wood (there), it is (only) the mould for the shoe.

The drapers have (in their shops) silk and dun-coloured cloth: if iron be (there), it is (only to serve) for a yard-measure.

Our *Mathnawí* is the shop for Unity: anything that you see (there) except the One (God) is (only) an idol[1].

Know that to praise an idol for the purpose of ensnaring the vulgar is just like (the Prophet's reference to) "the most exalted Cranes[2]."

He recited it (those words) quickly in the Súra (entitled) 1530 *Wa'l-Najm*, but it was a temptation (of the Devil), it was not (really) part of the Súra.

Thereupon all the infidels prostrated themselves (in worship): 'twas a mystery (of Divine Wisdom), too, that they knocked their heads upon the door[3].

After this there is a perplexing and abstruse argument[4]: stay with Solomon and do not stir up the demons!

Hark, relate the story of the Ṣúfí and the Cadi and the offender who was (so) feeble and wretchedly ill.

The Cadi said (to the Ṣúfí), "Make the roof firm, O son, in order that I may decorate it with good and evil[5].

Where is the assailant? Where is that which is subject to 1535 vengeance? This man in (consequence of) sickness has become a (mere) phantom.

The law is for the living and self-sufficient: where (how) is the law (binding) upon the occupants of the graveyard?"

The class (of men) who are headless (selfless) because of (their spiritual) poverty are in a hundred respects more naughted than those dead (and buried).

The dead man is naughted (only) from one point of view,

---

[1] *I.e.* a means of attraction.
[2] These words originally came in *Qur'án*, LIII, immediately after *v.* 21.
[3] *I.e.* performed the ritual act of prostration.
[4] *I.e.* further discussion of this question would take us into deep waters.
[5] *I.e.* "first prove your case, then I will give judgement."

(namely), as regards loss (of bodily life); the Ṣúfís have been naughted in a hundred respects.

(Bodily) death is a single killing, while this (spiritual death) is three hundred thousand (killings), for each one of which there is a blood-price beyond reckoning.

1540    Though God hath killed these folk many a time, (yet) He hath poured forth (infinite) stores (of grace) in payment of the blood-price.

Every one (of these martyrs) is inwardly like Jirjís (St George): they have been killed and brought to life (again) sixty times.

From his delight in (being smitten by) the spear-point of the (Divine) Judge, the killed one is ever burning (in rapture) and crying, "Strike another blow!"

(I swear) by God, from love for the existence that fosters the spirit, the killed one longs (still) more passionately to be killed a second time.

The Cadi said, "I am the cadi for the living: how am I the judge of the occupants of the graveyard?

1545    If to outward seeming this man is not laid low in the grave, (yet) graves have entered into his household[1].

You have seen many a dead man in the grave: (now), O blind one, see the grave in a dead man.

If bricks from a grave have fallen on you, how should reasonable persons seek redress from the grave?

Do not concern yourself with[2] anger and hatred against a dead man: beware, do not make war on (one who is as dead as) the pictures in a bath-house.

Give thanks that a living one[3] did not strike you, for he whom the living one rejects is rejected of God.

1550    The anger of the living ones is God's anger and His blows, for that pure-skinned one is living through God.

God killed him and breathed on his trotters and quickly, like a butcher, stripped off his skin.

The breath remains in him till (he reaches) the final bourn: the breathing of God is not as the breathing of the butcher.

There is a great difference between the two breathings: this is wholly honour, while that (other) side is entirely shame.

This (the latter) took life away from it (the slaughtered beast) and injured it, while by the breathing of God that (spiritual) life was made perpetual.

1555    This (Divine) breath is not a breath that can be described: hark, come up from the bottom of the pit to the top of the palace.

'Tis not a sound legal decision to mount him (the defendant) on an ass (and parade him): does any one lay upon an ass a (mere) picture of firewood?

---

[1] *I.e.* his spiritual faculties are dead and, as it were, entombed in his body.
[2] Literally, "do not revolve round."    [3] *I.e.* a saint.

The back of an ass is not his proper seat: the back of a bier is more fitting for him.

What is injustice? To put (a thing) out of its proper place: beware, do not let it be lost (by putting it) out of its place."

The Ṣúfí said, "Then do you think it right for him to slap me without (my taking) retaliation, and without (his paying) a farthing?

Is it right that a big rascally bear should inflict slaps on Ṣúfís for nothing?" 1560

The Cadi said (to the defendant), "What (coins) have you, larger or smaller?" He replied, "I have (only) six dirhems in the world."

Said the Cadi, "Spend three dirhems (on yourself) and give the other three to him without (any further) words.

(For," he thought to himself), "he (the defendant) is weak and ill and poor and infirm: he will need three dirhems for vegetables and loaves."

His (the defendant's) eye fell on the nape of the Cadi's neck: it was better (more inviting) than the nape of the Ṣúfí.

He raised his hand to slap it, saying (to himself), "The retaliation (penalty) for my slap has been made cheap." 1565

He approached the Cadi's ear (as though) for the purpose of (whispering) a secret, and dealt the Cadi a (severe) blow with his palm.

"O my two enemies," he cried, "take all the six dirhems: (then) I shall be free (from care and) without trouble and anxiety."

### How the Cadi was incensed by the slap of the poor (sick) man and how the Ṣúfí taunted the Cadi.

The Cadi was incensed. "Hey," cried the Ṣúfí, "your decision is just, no doubt (about it): there is no error.

O Shaykh of the (Mohammedan) religion, how can you approve for a brother (Moslem) what you disapprove for yourself, O man of trust?

Don't you know this, that (if) you dig a pit for me you will at last let yourself fall into the same pit? 1570

Haven't you read in the Traditions (of the Prophet), 'Whoever digs a pit (for his brother will fall into it)'? Practise what you have read, O soul of your father!

This one judicial decision of yours was like this, for it has brought you a slap on the nape.

Alas for your other (unjust) decisions! (Consider) what (penalty) they will bring upon your head and feet.

From kindness you take pity on a wrong-doer, saying, 'Mayst thou have three dirhems to spend (on food)!'

1575    Cut off the wrong-doer's hand: what occasion is there for you
to put the control and reins in his hand?
        O you from whom justice is unknown, you resemble the goat
that gave her milk to the wolf-cub.''

### The Cadi's reply to the Ṣúfí.

The Cadi said, "It is our duty to acquiesce, whatever slap or
cruelty the (Divine) destiny may bring to pass.
        I am inwardly pleased with the decision (inscribed) in the
(Heavenly) Scrolls, though my face has become sour—for
Truth is bitter.
        This heart of mine is an orchard, and my eye is like the cloud:
(when) the cloud weeps the orchard laughs joyously and
happily.
1580    In a year of drought the orchards are reduced to death and
agony by the sun laughing unconscionably.
        You have read in God's Commandment (the words) *and weep
ye much*: why have you remained grinning like a roast (sheep's)
head?
        You will be the light of the house, like the candle, if like the
candle you shed showers of tears.
        The mother's or father's sourness of face preserves the child
from every harm.
        You have experienced the pleasure of laughing, O inordinate
laugher: (now) experience the pleasure of weeping (and re-
cognise) that it is a mine of sugar.
1585    Since thinking of Hell causes weeping, therefore Hell is
better than Paradise.
        In tears there are laughters concealed: seek treasure amidst
ruins, O simple (sincere) man.
        Pleasure is (concealed) in pains: the track has been lost, the
Water of Life has been taken away into the (Land of) Darkness.
        On the way to the Caravanseray the shoes are upside down[1]:
make your (two) eyes to be (as) four in precaution (against being
deceived).
        Make your (two) eyes to be (as) four in careful consideration:
join to your own eye (eyes) the two eyes of the Friend.
1590    Read in the pages (of the *Qur'án*) *their affair is a matter for
consultation*: be (devoted) to the Friend and do not say to him
disdainfully, 'Fie!'
        The Friend is the support and refuge on the Way: when you
consider well, (you will see that) the Friend is the Way.
        When you come into a company of friends, sit silent: do not
make yourself the bezel in that ring.
        At the Friday prayer-service look well and attentively: (you

_____
[1] *I.e.* the appearance is contrary to the reality.

will see that) all are concentrated and possessed by a single thought and silent.

Direct your course[1] towards silence: when you seek the marks (of the Way), do not make yourself a mark (for attention).

The Prophet said, 'Know that amidst the sea of cares (my) 1595 Companions are (as) stars in respect of guidance.'

Fix your eye on the stars, seek the Way; speech is a cause of confusion to the sight: do not speak.

If you utter two true words, O such-and-such, the dark (false) speech will begin to flow in their train.

Haven't you read that (your) talk concerning (your) griefs, O frenzied (lover), is drawn along by the draw (tide) of talk?

Beware, do not begin (to speak) those right words, for words quickly draw (other) words (after them).

When you have (once) opened your mouth, they are not in your 1600 control: the dark (falsehood) flows on the heels of the pure (truth).

He (alone) may open (his mouth) who is preserved (from error) in the way of (Divine) inspiration: 'tis permissible, since he is entirely pure;

For *a prophet does not speak from self-will*: how should self-will proceed from him who is preserved by God?

Make yourself one that speaks eloquently from ecstatic feeling, lest you become a slave to argumentation, like me."

### How the Ṣúfí questioned the Cadi.

The Ṣúfí said, "Since (all) the gold is from a single Mine, why is this beneficial and that other harmful?

Since the whole (Creation) has come from a single Hand, why 1605 has this one come sober and that one intoxicated?

Since (all) these rivers flow from a single Sea, why is this one honey and that one poison in the mouth?

Since all lights are (derived) from the everlasting Sun, wherefore did the true dawn and the false dawn rise?

Since the blackness of every seeing person's eye is (derived) from a single Collyrium, wherefore did true sight and strabism come (into being)?

Since God is the Governor of the Mint, how is it that (both) good and spurious coins are struck?

Since God has called the Way 'My Way,' wherefore is this 1610 one a trusty escort and that one a brigand?

How can (both) the (noble) freeman and the (base) fool come from a single womb, since it is certain that the son is (the expression of) his father's inmost nature?

Who (ever) saw a Unity with so many thousand (numbers), (or) a hundred thousand motions (proceeding) from the essence of Rest?"

[1] Literally, "convey your baggage."

### The Cadi's reply to the Ṣúfí.

The Cadi said, "O Ṣúfí, do not be perplexed: hearken to a parable in explanation of this (mystery).

('Tis) just as the disquiet of lovers is the result of the tranquillity of the one who captivates their hearts.

1615   He stands immovable, like a mountain, in his disdain, while his lovers are quivering like leaves.

His laughter stirs (them to) tears, his glory causes their glories to fade.

All this conditionality[1] is tossing like foam on the surface of the unconditioned Sea.

In its (the Sea's) essence and action there is neither opposite nor like: by it (alone) are (all) existences clothed in robes (of existence).

How should an opposite bestow being and existence on its opposite? Nay, it flees and escapes from it.

1620   What is (the meaning of) nidd? The like (mithl), the like of (something) good or bad. How should a like make its own like?

When there are two likes, O God-fearing man, why should this one be more fit than that one for (the purpose of) creating?

Opposites and likes, in number as the leaves of the orchard, are (but) as a flake of foam on the Sea that hath no like or opposite.

Perceive that the victory and defeat of the Sea[2] are unconditioned: how, (then), should there be room for conditionality in the essence of the Sea?

Your soul is the least of its playthings; (yet) how can the quality and description of the soul be ascertained?

1625   Such a Sea, then, with every drop whereof the intellect and the spirit are more unfamiliar[3] than the body—

How should it be contained in the narrow room of quantity and quality? There (even) Universal Reason is one of the ignorant.

Reason says to the body, 'O lifeless thing, hast thou ever had a scent of the Sea whither all return?'

The body replies, 'Assuredly I am thy shadow: who would seek help from a shadow, O soul of thy uncle?'

Reason says, 'This is the house of bewilderment, not a house where the worthy is bolder than the unworthy.'

1630   Here the resplendent sun pays homage to the mote, like a menial.

In this quarter the lion lays his head (in submission) before

---

[1] Literally, "all this 'how?' and 'of what sort?'"
[2] I.e. the opposite attributes of God.
[3] Literally, "greater upstarts," i.e. more uninitiated and uninformed. The ignorance of the intellect and spirit concerning the Essence of God is more profound than the ignorance of the body concerning themselves.

the deer; here the falcon lays (droops) his wings before the partridge.

(If) you cannot believe this, (then) how is it that Muṣṭafá (Mohammed) seeks a blessing from the lowly poor?

If you reply that it was for the purpose of teaching (his followers), in what respect was his leaving them in absolute ignorance (of the reason for his action) a means of causing them to understand?

Nay, but he knows that the King deposits the royal treasure in ruined places.

Evil thoughts (about the saint) are (due to) his presenting an 1635 appearance contrary to the reality[1], though (in fact) every part of him is his spy (informing him of Divine mysteries).

Nay, the Truth is absorbed in the Truth; hence seventy, nay, a hundred sects have arisen.

(Now) I will talk to you of matters indifferent[2]. Hark, O Ṣúfí, open your spiritual ear very wide.

Whatever blow may come to you from Heaven, always be expecting (to receive) a gift of honour after it;

For He is not the king to slap you and then not give you a crown and a throne on which to recline.

The whole world has (but) the value of a gnat's wing; (but) 1640 for one slap there is an infinite reward.

Nimbly slip your neck out of this golden collar, (which is) the world, and take the slaps (that come) from God.

Since the prophets suffered those blows on the nape, in consequence of that affliction they have lifted their heads (high).

But (always) be present (attentive and ready) in yourself, O youth, in order that He may find you at home.

Else He will take back His gift of honour, saying, 'I found nobody in the house.'"

### How the Ṣúfí again questioned the Cadi.

The Ṣúfí said, "How would it be if this world were to unknit 1645 the eyebrow of mercy for evermore!

If it were not to bring on some trouble at every moment and produce anguish by its (incessant) changes!

If Night were not to steal the lamp of Day, and if December were not to sweep away the orchard that has learned to delight (in its fresh beauty)!

If there were no stone of fever to shatter the cup of health, and if fear did not bring anxieties for (one's) safety!

How, indeed, would His munificence and mercy be diminished if in His bounty there were no torment?"

---

[1] Literally, "his inverted shoe."
[2] *I.e.* trifles in comparison with the arcana of mystical theology.

*The Cadi's answer to the questions of the Ṣúfí, and how he adduced the Story of the Turk and the Tailor as a parable.*

1650    The Cadi said, "You are a very idle vagabond Ṣúfí: you are devoid of intelligence, (you are) like the Kúfic *káf*[1].

Haven't you heard that a certain sugar-lipped (story-teller) used to tell at nightfall of the perfidy of tailors,

Setting forth to the people old stories concerning the thievery of that class (of men)?

To that one and this one he would relate tales of their snatching (stealing) pieces of cloth while cutting it,

And during the night-talk he would read aloud a book on (the tricks of) tailors, when a throng had gathered round him.

1655    Since he found eager listeners among those who came (to hear him), all parts of him had become the story (that he was telling)[2].

*The Prophet, on whom be peace, said, 'Verily God teaches wisdom by the tongues of the preachers according to the measure of the aspirations of those who hear them.'*

If any one have suave eloquence, hearing draws it out: the teacher's enthusiasm and energy are (derived) from the boy (whom he teaches).

When the harpist who plays the four-and-twenty (musical modes) finds no ear (to listen), his harp becomes a burden;

Neither ditty nor ode comes into his memory: his ten fingers will not get to work.

If there were no ears to receive (the message from) the Unseen, no announcer (prophet) would have brought a Revelation from Heaven;

1660    And if there were no eyes to see the works of God, neither would the sky have revolved nor would the earth have smiled (been gay with verdure).

The declaration *lawláka* (but for thee)[3] means this, that the (whole) affair (of creation) is for the sake of the piercing eye and the seer.

How should the vulgar, in their love for bedfellow and dishes (of food), have any care for love of God's work?

You do not pour *tutmáj* broth into a trough till there are a number of greedy dogs to drink it.

Go, be the Cave-dog[4] of His Lordship in order that His election (of you) may deliver you from this trough.

---

[1] *I.e.* empty, referring to the loop of the letter ﻙ which in Kúfic script has nothing inside it.

[2] *I.e.* he was entirely absorbed in the tale.

[3] Referring to the Holy Tradition, "But for thee (Mohammed) I would not have created the heavens."

[4] Referring to the faithful dog of the "Men of the Cave" (the Seven Sleepers).

When he (the story-teller) related the pitiless thefts which 1665
those tailors commit in secret,

A Turk from Khiṭá (who was) amongst the crowd (audience)
was exceedingly annoyed by that exposure[1].

At night-time he (the story-teller) was exposing those secrets
(of the tailors) for the benefit of the intelligent (listeners), as
(plainly as secrets shall be exposed) on the Day of Resurrection.

Wherever you come to close quarters with a wrangle, you will
see there two enemies (engaged) in exposing (each other's)
secret.

Know that that hour (of quarrel) is (like) the (hour of the)
Last Judgement mentioned (in the *Qur'án*), and know that the
throat which tells the secret is (like) the trumpet (of Isráfíl);

For God hath provided the motives of anger and (thus) hath 1670
caused those shameful things to be divulged[2].

When he (the story-teller) had related many instances of the
perfidy of tailors, the Turk became annoyed and angry and
aggrieved,

And said, 'O story-teller, in your city who is the greatest
expert in this (kind of) deceit and fraud?'

[*How the Turk boasted and wagered that the tailor would not
be able to steal anything from him.*]

He replied, 'There is a tailor named Pír-i Shush who beats[3]
(all other) folk in light-fingeredness and thievery.'

'I warrant,' said he (the Turk), 'that (even) with a hundred
efforts he will not be able to take away a coil of thread in my
presence.'

Then they told him, 'Cleverer persons than you have been 1675
checkmated by him: do not soar (too high) in your pretensions.

Go to, be not so deluded by your intelligence, else you will be
lost in his wiles.'

The Turk became (still) hotter and made a wager there (and
then) that he (the tailor) would not be able to rob (him of any-
thing) either old or new.

Those who flattered his hopes made him hotter (than before):
immediately he wagered and declared the stakes,

Saying, 'I will pay this Arab horse of mine as a forfeit if he
artfully steals my stuff;

And if he cannot rob (me) I shall receive a horse from you (as 1680
an equivalent) for the first stake[4].'

Because of his anxiety sleep did not overcome the Turk (all)
that night: he was fighting with the phantom of the thief.

---

[1] Literally, "the removal of that lid."
[2] Literally, "hath let those shameful things fall into the street."
[3] Literally, "kills."　　　　[4] *I.e.* "for my horse."

In the morning he put a piece of satin under his arm, went to the bazaar, and (entered) the shop of that cunning rogue.

Then he saluted him warmly, and the master(-tailor) sprang up from his seat and opened his lips to bid him welcome.

He inquired (after his health, etc.) with a cordiality exceeding (even) that of the Turk, so that he planted in his (the Turk's) heart (feelings of) affection for him.

1685    When he (the Turk) heard[1] from him a song like the nightingale's, he threw down before him the piece of Stamboul satin,

Saying, 'Cut this into a coat for the day of battle: (let it be) wide below my navel and tight above it—

Tight above, to show off my body (figure); wide below, so as not to hamper my legs.'

He replied, 'O kindly man, I will do (you) a hundred services,' and in (token of) accepting it (the commission) he laid his hand upon his eye.

Then he measured (the satin) and inspected the working surface (of it) and, after that, opened his lips in idle chat.

1690    Of stories about other Amírs and of the bounties and gifts of those persons

And about the misers and their (mean) economies—(of all this) he gave a sample for the purpose of (exciting) laughter.

In a flash[2] he whipped out a pair of scissors and went on cutting while his lips were full of tales and beguiling talk.

*How the tailor told laughable jests, and how the narrow eyes of the Turk were closed by the violence of his laughter, and how the tailor found an opportunity (to steal).*

The Turk began to laugh at the stories, and at that moment his narrow eyes closed.

He (the tailor) filched a shred (of satin) and put it under his thigh, (where it was) hidden from all living beings except God.

1695    God saw it, but He is disposed to cover up (sins); yet when you carry (them) beyond bounds He is a tell-tale.

From his delight in his (the tailor's) anecdotes the Turk's former boast went out of his head[3].

What satin? What boast? What wager? The Turk is intoxicated with the jokes of the pasha[4].

The Turk implored him, crying, 'For God's sake go on telling jokes, for they are meat to me.'

(Then) the rascal told such a ridiculous story that he (the Turk) fell on his back in an explosion of laughter.

---

[1] Literally, "saw."          [2] Literally, "(quick) as fire."
[3] Literally, "heart."
[4] The reading اخی (guildsman) is plausible, but the best MSS. have which is supported by v. 4576 *infra*.

He (the tailor) swiftly clapped a shred of satin to the hem of 1700
his under-breeches, while the Turk was paying no attention and
greedily sucking in (absorbing) the jests.

Still (continuing his entreaties), the Turk of Khiṭá said for the
third time, 'Tell me a joke for God's sake!'

He (the tailor) told a story more laughable than (those which
he had related) on the two previous occasions, and made this
Turk entirely his prey.

His eyes shut, his reason flown, bewildered, the boastful Turk
was intoxicated with guffaws.

Then for the third time he (the tailor) filched a strip from the
coat (which he was cutting), since the Turk's laughter gave him
ample scope (for his dexterity)[1].

When for the fourth time the Turk of Khiṭá was demanding 1705
a jest from the master(-tailor),

The master took pity on him and put aside (abandoned)
artfulness and injustice.

He said (to himself), 'This infatuated man has a great desire
for these (facetious tales), not knowing what a loss and swindle
they are (for him).'

(Nevertheless) he (the Turk) showered kisses on (the face
and eyes of) the master, crying, 'For God's sake tell me a
story!'

O thou who hast become a story and (art) dead to (useful)
existence, how long wilt thou wish to make trial of stories?

No story is more laughable than thou (thyself): stand (and 1710
meditate) on the edge of thine own ruinous grave!

O thou who hast gone down into the grave of ignorance and
doubt, how long wilt thou seek (to hear) the jests and tales of
Time?[2]

How long wilt thou listen to the blandishments of this world
that leave neither thy mind underanged nor thy spirit?[3]

The jests of Time, this mean and petty boon-companion, have
robbed of honour a hundred thousand like thee.

This Universal Tailor is ever tearing and stitching the gar-
ments of a hundred travellers silly as children.

If his jests conferred a gift on the orchards (in spring), when 1715
December came they (his jests) gave that gift to the winds.

The old children sit down beside him to beg that he will jest
(and amuse them) by (giving them) fortunes good or bad.

---

[1] Literally, "since from his (the Turk's) laughter he gained a wide field."
[2] *Falak* or *charkh*, the celestial sphere, is often best rendered by "Time."
[3] Literally, "so that neither thy mind nor thy spirit continues (to function)
regularly."

*How the tailor said to the Turk, "Hey, hold your tongue: if I tell
any more funny stories the coat will be (too) tight for you."*

The tailor said, 'Begone, unmanly fellow![1] Woe to you if I
make another jest;

(For) then, after that, the coat will be (too) tight for you:
does any one practise this (fraud) on himself?

What laughter (is this)? If you had an inkling (of the truth)[2],
instead of laughing you would weep (tears of) blood.'

*Explaining that the idle folk who wish (to hear) stories are like the
Turk, and that the deluding and treacherous World is like the
tailor, and that lusts and women are (like) this World's telling
laughable jokes, and that Life resembles the piece of satin placed
before this Tailor to be made into a coat of eternity and a garment
of piety.*

1720  The Tailor, (who is) Worldly Vanity, takes away the satin of
your life, bit by bit, with his scissors, (which are) the months.

You wish that your star might always jest and your happiness
continue for ever.

You are very angry with its quartile aspects and its disdain
and enmity and mischiefs;

You are very annoyed with its silence and inauspiciousness
and severity and its endeavour to show hostility,

Saying, 'Why doesn't the merry Venus dance?' Do not
depend on its good luck and auspicious dance.

1725  Your star says, 'If I jest any more, I shall cause you to be
swindled entirely.'

Do not regard the counterfeiting of these stars[3]: regard your
love for the counterfeiter[4], O despicable man.

### Parable.

A certain man was on the way to his shop (when) he found the
road in front of him barred by women.

He was hurrying along hot-foot[5], and the way was blocked by
a crowd of women (beautiful) as the moon.

He turned his face to one woman and said, 'O vile (creature),
how numerous you are, little girls, eh!'

1730  The woman turned towards him and replied, 'O man of trust,
do not think it dreadful that there are so many of us.

Consider that notwithstanding the multitude of us on the
earth you (men) find it insufficient for your enjoyment[6].

---

[1] Literally, "eunuch."     [2] Literally, "if you knew a hint."
[3] The poet represents Fortune as a maker of adulterated coin.
[4] *I.e.* the World.
[5] Literally, "his feet were burning with haste."
[6] Literally, "(the range of) enjoyment seems to you (men) restricted."

Propter paucitatem feminarum inciditis in paedicationem:
infamissimi in mundo sunt agens et patiens.'

(O Șūfí)[1], do not regard these happenings of Time which
(proceed) from heaven (and) come to pass intolerably here.

Do not regard the (anxious) husbanding of (one's) daily bread
and livelihood and this dearth (of food) and fear and trembling,

(But) consider that in spite of all its (the World's) bitternesses 1735
ye are mortally enamoured of it and recklessly devoted to it.

Deem bitter tribulation to be a (Divine) mercy, deem the
kingdom of Merv and Balkh to be a (Divine) vengeance.

That Ibráhím[2] fled not from destruction and remained (safe),
while this Ibráhím[3] fled from (worldly) honour and rode away.

That one is not burnt[4], and this one is burnt[5]. Oh, wonderful!
In the Way of search (for God) everything is upside down[6]."

### How the Șūfí repeated his questions.

The Șūfí said, "He (God) whose help is invoked hath the
power to make our trading free from loss.

He who turns the fire (of Nimrod) into roses and trees[7] is also 1740
able to make this (World-fire) harmless.

He who brings forth roses from the very midst of thorns is
also able to turn this winter[8] into spring.

He by whom every cypress is made 'free' (evergreen) hath
the power if He would turn sorrow into joy.

He by whom every non-existence is made existent—what
damage would He suffer if He were to preserve it for ever?

He who gives the body a soul that it may live—how would
He be a loser if He did not cause it to die?

What, indeed, would it matter if that Bounteous One should 1745
bestow on His servant the desire of his soul without (painful)
toil,

And keep far off from poor (mortals) the cunning of the flesh
and the temptation of the Devil (which lurk) in ambush?"

### The Cadi's reply to the Șūfí.

The Cadi said, "Were there no bitter (stern) Commandment
(from God) and were there no good and evil and no pebbles and
pearls,

And were there no flesh and Devil and passions, and were
there no blows and battle and war,

---

[1] This is the Cadi's reply to the questions put by the Șūfí in vv. 1645–9.
[2] Abraham, who let himself be cast into the fire by Nimrod.
[3] Ibráhím son of Adham, who gave up the kingdom of Balkh to become
a Șūfí.
[4] I.e. by Nimrod's fire.          [5] I.e. in the fire of Divine Love.
[6] Literally, "(it is a case of) inverted shoes."
[7] See Qur'án, XXI, 69.          [8] Literally, "December."

24

Then by what name and title would the King call His servants, O abandoned man?

1750 How could He say, 'O steadfast one' and 'O forbearing one'? How could He say, 'O brave one' and 'O wise one'?

How could there be *steadfast and sincere and spending*[1] men without a brigand and accursed Devil?

Rustam and Ḥamza and a catamite would be (all) one; knowledge and wisdom would be annulled and utterly demolished.

Knowledge and wisdom exist for the purpose of (distinguishing between) the right path and the wrong paths[2]: when all (paths) are the right path, knowledge and wisdom are void (of meaning).

Do you think it allowable that both the worlds should be ruined for the sake of this briny (foul) shop of the (sensual) nature?

1755 I know that you are pure (enlightened), not raw (foolish), and that these questions of yours are (asked) for the sake of (instructing) the vulgar.

The cruelty of Time (Fortune) and every affliction that exists are lighter than farness from God and forgetfulness (of Him),

Because these (afflictions) will pass, (but) that (forgetfulness) will not. (Only) he that brings his spirit (to God) awake (and mindful of Him) is possessed of felicity."

*A Story setting forth that patience in bearing worldly affliction is easier than patience in bearing separation from the Beloved.*

A certain woman said to her husband, "Hey, O you who have finished with[3] generosity once and for all,

Why have you no care for me? How long shall I dwell in this abode[4] of misery?"

1760 The husband replied, "I am doing my best[5] to earn money; though I am destitute, I am moving hand and foot.

O beloved[6], it is my duty (to provide you with) money and clothes: you get both these from me and they are not insufficient."

The wife showed (him) the sleeve of her chemise: the chemise was very coarse and dirty.

"It is so rough[7]," said she, "it eats (wounds) my body: does any one get a garment of this kind for any one?"

He said, "O wife, I will ask you one question. I am a poor man: this is all I know (how to do)[8].

1765 This (chemise) is rough and coarse and disagreeable, but think (well), O thoughtful (anxious) wife!

[1] *I.e.* not stingy.   [2] Literally, "the path and pathlessness."
[3] Literally, "folded up."   [4] Literally, "pasture."
[5] Literally, "using (every) means."
[6] Literally, "O (my) idol."   [7] Literally, "because of its roughness."
[8] *I.e.* in the way of providing for you.

Is this (chemise) rougher and nastier, or divorce? Is this (chemise) more odious to you, or separation?"

Even so, O Khwája who art reviling on account of affliction and poverty and distress and tribulations,

No doubt this renunciation of sensuality gives bitter pain, but 'tis better than the bitterness of being far from God.

If fighting (against the flesh) and fasting are hard and rough, yet these are better than being far from Him who inflicts tribulation.

How should pain endure for a single moment when the Giver 1770 of favours says to thee, "How art thou, O My sick one?"

And (even) if He say (it) not, because thou hast not the understanding and knowledge (needed) for it, yet thy inward feeling (of supplication) is (equivalent to His) inquiring (after thee).

Those beauteous ones who are spiritual physicians turn towards the sick to inquire (after them);

And if they be afraid of (incurring) disgrace and (loss of) reputation, they devise some means and send a message;

Or if not, that (care for the sick) is pondered in their hearts: no beloved is unaware (forgetful) of his lover.

O thou who desirest (to hear) a wondrous tale, read the story 1775 of them that play the game of love.

Thou hast been boiling mightily during (all) this long time, (and yet), O dried meat, thou hast not even become half-cooked[1].

During a (whole) life-time thou hast seen the justice and jurisdiction (of God), and then (after all) thou art more ignorant[2] than the blind.

Whoever serves Him as a pupil becomes a master, (but) thou hast gone backwards, O blind fool!

Verily thou hast learned nothing from thy parents, nor hast thou taken a lesson from night and day.

## Parable.

A (Ṣúfí) gnostic asked an old Christian priest, "Sire, art thou 1780 the more advanced in age, or thy beard?"

He replied, "Nay; I was born before it: I have seen much of the world without a beard."

He (the Ṣúfí) said, "Thy beard has turned white, it has changed, (but) thy evil disposition has not become good."

It (thy beard) was born after thee and (yet) it has surpassed thee: thou art so dry (vain and unprofitable) because of thy passion for *tharíd*[3].

---

[1] Literally, "meat boiled by Turcomans (and eaten half-raw)."
[2] See note on *v.* 1625 *supra*.          [3] Bread soaked in gravy.

Thou art (still) of the same complexion with which thou wast born: thou hast not taken one step forward.

1785     Still thou art (as) sour buttermilk in the churn[1]: in sooth thou hast not extracted any oil (butter) from it.

Still thou art (as) dough in the jar of clay, though thou hast been a (whole) life-time in the fiery oven.

Thou art like a herb on a hillock: (thy) foot (is fixed immovably) in the earth, though thy head is tossed (to and fro) by the wind of passion.

Like the people of Moses in the heat of the Desert, thou hast remained forty years in (the same) place, O foolish man.

Daily thou marchest rapidly till nightfall and findest thyself (still) in the first stage of thy journey.

1790     Thou wilt never traverse this three hundred years' distance so long as thou hast love for the calf.

Until the fancy (illusion) of the calf went out of their hearts, the Desert was to them like a blazing whirlpool.

Besides this calf which thou hast obtained from Him (God), thou hast experienced infinite graces and bounties.

Thou hast the nature of a cow; hence in thy love for this calf (those) mighty benefits have vanished from thy heart.

Prithee now, ask each part of thee: these dumb parts have a hundred tongues

1795     To recall the bounties of the World-Provider which are hidden in the pages of Time.

By day and night thou art eagerly seeking (to hear) stories, while each several part of thee is telling thee the story (of His bounties).

(Ever) since each several part of thee grew up from non-existence, how much joy have they experienced and how much pain!

For without pleasure no part will grow; on the contrary, at every spasm (of pain) the part (affected) becomes thin (dwindles).

The part remained (in being), but the pleasure vanished from memory; nay, it did not vanish, (though) it became concealed from the five (senses) and the seven (members of the body).

1800     ('Tis) like summer, from which cotton is born: the cotton remains, the summer is no more remembered;

Or like the ice which is born of winter: winter disappears, but the ice is with us.

The ice is a souvenir of the hardships (of winter), and in December these fruits are a souvenir of summer.

Similarly, O youth, every single part in thy body is telling the story of a (past) bounty,

As, (in the case of) a woman who has twenty children, each (child) is telling of a (past) delight.

---

[1] Literally, "source," "place of production."

There is no pregnancy without (past) rapture and amorous 1805
sport: how should the orchard produce (fruit) without a Spring?

The pregnant (trees) and the children[1] on their laps are
evidence of dalliance with the Spring.

Every tree (engaged) in suckling its children is impregnated,
like Mary, by a King unseen.

Although in (boiling) water the heat of fire is concealed (from
view), a hundred thousand bubbles froth upon it,

And though the fire works[2] very secretly, the froth indicates
(its presence) with ten fingers.

In like manner (all) the parts of those intoxicated with union 1810
are pregnant with the (ideal) forms of (ecstatic) feelings and
words.

Their mouths remain gaping (in amazement) at the beauty of
(that) ecstasy, (while) their eyes are absent (withdrawn) from the
forms of this world.

Those (spiritual) progenies are not (produced) by means of
these four (elements); consequently they are not seen by these
eyes.

Those progenies are born of (Divine) illumination; conse-
quently they are covered (from sight) by a pure veil.

We said "born," but in reality they are not born, and this
expression is only (used) in order to guide (the understanding).

Hark, be silent that the King of *Say*[3] may speak: do not play 1815
the nightingale[4] with a Rose of this kind.

This eloquent Rose is full of song[5] and cry: O nightingale, let
thy tongue cease, be (all) ear!

Both (these) kinds[6] of pure ideal forms are valid (trustworthy)
witnesses to the mystery of union.

Both (these) kinds of subtle and delectable beauty are witnesses
to (spiritual) pregnancies and growing big (with child)[7] in the past,

Like ice that in the brilliant[8] (month of) Tamúz is ever telling
the story of winter

And recalling the cold winds and intense frost in those hard 1820
days and times;

(Or) like fruit that in winter-time tells the story of God's
lovingkindness

And the tale of the season when the sun was smiling and
embracing[9] the brides of the orchard.

The ecstasy is gone but thy (every) part remains as a souvenir:
either inquire of it, or thyself recall (the ecstasy) to mind.

---

[1] *I.e.* the leaves and fruit.    [2] Literally, "weaves."
[3] *I.e.* God who speaks through the prophets and saints.
[4] Literally, "do not sell (offer for sale and display) the quality (song) of
the nightingale."    [5] Literally, "(sound of) boiling."
[6] *I.e.* feeling and words.    [7] Literally, "(the process of) raising to life."
[8] Literally, "made new," "renovated."
[9] Literally, "contactu et coitu fruebatur."

When grief takes possession of thee, if thou art a fit (alert and capable) person thou wouldst question that moment of despair[1]

1825　And wouldst say to it, "O Sorrow that deniest implicitly the allowance of favours (bestowed upon thee) by that Perfection,

If Spring and (its) fresh gladness are not always thine, (then) of what is thy body, (which is) like a heap of roses, the storehouse?

Thy body is a heap of roses, thy thought is like rose-water; the rose-water denies the rose: lo, here is a marvel!"

(Even) straw is refused to those who apishly show ingratitude, (while) sun and cloud (sunshine and rain) are lavished on those who resemble the prophets in disposition.

That obstinacy in (showing) ingratitude is the rule followed by the ape, while that thankfulness and gratitude is the way of the prophet.

1830　(See) what was done to the apish by their deeds of shame; (see) what was done to those of prophetic complexion by their acts of piety![2]

In well-cultivated places[3] there are curs and biting (dogs); in ruined places[4] there is the treasure of glory and light.

If this (spiritual) moonlight[5] had not been in eclipse, so many philosophers would not have lost the (right) way.

Through losing their way the acute and intelligent saw the brand of foolishness on their noses[6].

*The remainder of the Story of the fakir[7] who desired (to receive) his daily bread without (having recourse to) work as a means (of earning it).*

In his grief that wretched pauper, who suffered a thousand agonies[8] on account of indigence,

1835　Used to beseech (God) in prayer and invocation, crying, "O Lord and Guardian of (them that are) the shepherds (of their people),

Thou didst create me without any exertion (on my part): give me daily bread from this mansion (the world) without contrivance (on my part).

Thou gavest me the five jewels[9] in the casket of my head, and also five other occult senses.

These gifts of Thine are not to be numbered or computed; in setting them forth I am tongue-tied and shamefaced.

---

[1] Literally, "that moment which causes thee to despair."
[2] *I.e.* consider the ultimate result in each case.
[3] *I.e.* prosperous worldlings.　　　　[4] *I.e.* the poor afflicted (saints).
[5] Literally, "moonrise."
[6] *I.e.* found themselves branded as fools.
[7] Apparently this refers to the story which is told in *vv.* 1758–66 *supra.*
[8] Literally, "drank a thousand poisons."
[9] *I.e.* the five physical senses.

Since Thou art alone (without partner) in my creation, do Thou adjust (accordingly)[1] the matter of providing me with daily bread."

For years this prayer was frequently uttered by him, and at 1840 last his supplication took effect,

As (in the case of) the person who used to beg God to grant him a lawful livelihood without labour and fatigue,

(Till) at length the cow brought him happiness: ('twas in) the epoch of David whose justice was divinely inspired[2].

This thrall of love, too, made piteous entreaties, and he like-wise carried off the ball from the field of (favourable) response[3].

(Yet) while praying he would at times become distrustful[4] on account of the postponement of the recompense and reward;

(And then) again the gracious Lord's deferment (of his hopes) 1845 would bring a message of joy to his heart and become a surety (for their fulfilment).

Whenever in (the course of his) earnest supplication[5] weariness caused him to despair, he would hear from the Presence of God (the call) "Come!"

This (Divine) Maker is He who abaseth and exalteth: without these two (attributes) no work is accomplished.

Consider the lowness of the earth and the loftiness of the sky: without these two (attributes) its (the sky's) revolution is not (possible), O such-and-such.

The lowness and loftiness of this earth are of another sort: for one half of the year it is barren and for (the other) half (it is) green and fresh.

The lowness and loftiness of distressful Time are of another 1850 sort: one half day and (the other) half night.

The lowness and loftiness of this blended (bodily) tempera-ment (of ours) are now health and now sickness that causes (us) to cry out (in pain).

Know that even so are all the changing conditions of the world—famine and drought and peace and war—(which arise) from (Divine) probation.

By means of these two wings this world is (kept up like a bird) in the air; by means of these twain (all) souls are habitations of fear and hope,

To the end that the world may be (always) trembling like a leaf in the north-wind and simoom of resurrection and death,

(And) that (ultimately) the vat of the unicolority of our Jesus[6] 1855 may destroy the value of the vat containing a hundred dyes[7];

[1] *I.e.* put on the same footing.
[2] This story is related in Book III, *v.* 1450 foll.
[3] *I.e.* he was successful in his petition.
[4] Literally, "thinking evil."          [5] Literally, "exertion."
[6] *I.e.* the spiritual world of Unity and Reality.
[7] *I.e.* the world of plurality.

For that world (of Unity) is like a salt-mine: whatever has gone thither has become exempt from coloration (dyeing with various colours).

Look at earth: it makes many-coloured (diverse) humankind to be (all) of one colour in their graves.

This is the salt-mine for visible (material) bodies, (but) in sooth the salt-mine for ideal (supersensible) things is different.

The salt-mine for ideal things is ideal (spiritual and real): it remains new[1] from eternity unto everlasting.

1860 This (earthly) newness has oldness as its opposite, but that newness (belonging to the world of Reality) is without opposite or like or number.

'Tis (even) as by the polishing action of the Light of Muṣṭafá (Mohammed) a hundred thousand sorts of darkness became radiant.

Jew and polytheist and Christian and Magian—all were made of one colour by that Alp Ulugh (great hero).

A hundred thousand shadows short and long became one in the light of that Sun of mystery.

Neither a long (shadow) remained nor a short nor a wide: shadows of every kind were given in pawn to (absorbed in) the Sun.

1865 But the unicolority that is (everywhere) at the Resurrection is (then) revealed and (made) manifest to the evil and the good (alike);

For in that world ideas are endued with form, and our (visible) shapes become congruous with our (moral and spiritual) qualities.

The (secret) thoughts will then become (materialised in) the form of the books (recording good and evil actions): this lining will become the working surface of the garments.

During this (present) time (men's) inward beliefs are (as variegated) as a piebald cow, and in the (different) religious sects the spindle of speech is spinning (threads of) a hundred colours.

'Tis the turn (reign) of many-colouredness and many-mindedness: how should the one-coloured world become unveiled?

1870 'Tis the turn (reign) of the Ethiopian; the Greek is hidden (from view): this is night, and the sun is in pawn.

'Tis the turn (reign) of the wolf, and Joseph is at the bottom of the well; 'tis the turn (reign) of the Egyptians, and Pharaoh is king.

(Such is the Divine purpose), in order that for a few days these curs may have their allotted portion of the unstinted and deluding[2] (worldly) provision.

---

[1] Literally, "is in the state of newness."
[2] Literally, "laughing recklessly (with intent to deceive)."

(But) within the jungle (of this world) are lions (righteous and holy men), waiting for the command "Come!" to be spread abroad.

Then those lions will come forth from the (worldly) pasture, and God will show (unto them) their income and expenditure[1] without any veil (disguise).

The (spiritual) essence of Man will encompass land and sea, 1875 (while) the piebald cattle will be killed as victims on the Day of Slaughter.

The terrible Day of Slaughter at the Resurrection is a festival for the true believers and (the hour of) destruction for the cattle.

On that Day of Slaughter all the water-birds (will be) sailing along like ships on the surface of the Sea.

(This Day is ordained) to the end that *they who perish may perish by a clear proof*[2], and that they who are saved and have sure knowledge thereof[3] may be saved (by a clear proof),

And that the falcons may go to the Sultan and that the crows may go to the graveyard;

For in this world the dessert of the crows was bones and pieces 1880 of dung like bread.

How remote is the sugar of wisdom from the crow! How remote is the dung-beetle from the orchard!

It is not suitable for an effeminate man to go to fight against the carnal soul: aloes-wood and musk are not suitable for the arse of an ass.

Since women are not at all adapted for fighting[4], how should they be adapted for that (fight) which is the greater holy war?[5]

A Rustam may (sometimes) have been concealed in a woman's body, as (was the case with) a Mary; (but) only seldom[6].

Similarly, women are (sometimes) concealed in men's bodies, 1885 and they (such men) are (virtually) female because of (their) faintness of heart.

In that world, if any one has not found in his manhood the capacity (for spiritual combat), his femininity takes (visible) shape.

The Day (of Judgement) is justice, and justice consists in giving (to every one) what is proper: the shoe belongs to the foot, and the cap belongs to the head.

(This is) in order that every seeker may attain to the object of his search, and that everything destined to set may go to its point of setting.

---

[1] *I.e.* the result of their dealings with Him.
[2] *Qur'án*, VIII, 44.
[3] *I.e.* know for certain that their salvation or perdition depends on the Divine Providence.
[4] Literally, "since fighting gives no hand to women."
[5] *I.e.* the struggle against the flesh and the passions.
[6] Literally, "(it does not occur) except rarely."

No object of search is withheld from the seeker: the sun is paired with heat and the cloud with water.

1890    The present world is the Creator's penitentiary: since you have chosen (to incur) punishment, suffer punishment!

Contemplate the bones and hair of the punished ones (whom) the sword of (Divine) punishment overthrew on sea and land.

Consider the bird's feathers and feet (lying) around the trap and silently expounding (the nature of) God's punishment.

He (the worldling) dies and leaves a (sepulchral) vault to occupy his place; and (in the case of) one who has lain for ages (in the earth)[1], even the vault has disappeared.

The justice of God hath mated every one (with one of his own kind)—elephant with elephant and gnat with gnat.

1895    The familiar associates of Aḥmad (Mohammed)[2] were the Four Friends[3], (while) the familiars of Bú Jahl were 'Utba[4] and Dhu 'l-Khimár[5].

The Ka'ba of Gabriel and the (celestial) spirits is a Lotus-tree[6]; the qibla of the belly-slave is a table-cloth (covered with dishes of food).

The qibla of the gnostic is the light of union (with God); the qibla of the philosopher's intellect is phantasy.

The qibla of the ascetic is the Gracious God; the qibla of the flatterer is a purse of gold.

The qibla of the spiritual is patience and long-suffering; the qibla of form-worshippers is the image of stone.

1900    The qibla of those who dwell on the inward is the Bounteous One; the qibla of those who worship the outward is a woman's face.

Similarly reckon up new and old (instances); and if you are weary (of doing so), go about your business.

Our provision (from God) is wine in a golden cup, while those curs have the tutmáj broth and the trough.

(God says), "To him on whom We have bestowed a (particular) disposition We have sent the appropriate provision accordingly.

We have made it that one's disposition to be passionately fond of bread, We have made it this one's disposition to be intoxicated with the Beloved."

1905    Since you are pleased and happy with your disposition, then why are you fleeing from that which is appropriate to your disposition?

---

[1] Literally, "has grown old."
[2] Literally, "the familiars of Aḥmad in the place where people sat together.'
[3] Abú Bakr, 'Umar, 'Uthmán, and 'Alí.
[4] 'Utba ibn Rabí'a.
[5] I.e. "the man with the veil." His name is al-Aswad 'Ayhala ('Abhala) ibn Ka'b.
[6] See Qur'án, LIII, 14.

(If) feminality pleases you, get a *chádar*; (if) the prowess of Rustam pleases you, get a dagger.

This topic hath no end, and (meanwhile) the fakir has been sorely wounded by the blows of penury.

*Story of the treasure-scroll (in which it was written), "Beside a certain domed building turn your face towards the qibla (Mecca) and put an arrow to the bow and shoot: the treasure is (buried) at the spot where it falls."*

One night he dreamed—but where was sleep? The vision without sleep is familiar to the Ṣúfí—

(That) a heavenly voice said to him, "O you who have seen trouble, search among the (loose) leaves of handwriting sold (as models) by stationers for a certain scroll.

Unobserved by the stationer who is your neighbour, bring 1910 your hand into touch with his papers.

It is a scroll of such a shape and such a colour: then (as soon as possible) read it in privacy, O sorrowful one.

When you steal it from the stationer, my lad, then go out of the crowd and the noise and turmoil,

And read it by yourself in some lonely place: beware, do not seek any partnership in reading it.

But even if it (the secret) be divulged, do not be anxious, for none but you will get (so much as) half a barley-corn thereof.

And if it (the affair) be long drawn out, beware and take heed! 1915 Make (the text) *do not ye despair* your litany at every moment."

The (heavenly) announcer of the good news said this and put his hand on his (the fakir's) heart, saying, "Go, endure the toil."

When the youth came back to himself after the absence, on account of his joy he could not be contained in the world.

Had it not been for the tender care and protection and favour of God, his gall-bladder would have burst from agitation.

One (cause of) joy was this, that after (having passed through) six hundred veils his ear had heard the answer (to his prayer) from the (Divine) Presence.

When his auditory sense had pierced through the veils, he 1920 raised his head aloft and passed beyond the skies,

(Thinking) that maybe, by taking the lesson to heart, his sense of sight would also find a passage through the veil of the Unseen,

And that when (both) his senses had passed through the veil, his vision and allocution (from God) would then be continuous.

(So) he came to the stationer's shop and (for some time) was laying his hand here and there on his (the stationer's) models for writing.

Suddenly that piece of script, with the distinctive marks which the heavenly voice had mentioned, caught his eye.

1925 He slipped it under his arm and said, "Good-bye, Khwája: I will come back presently, O master."

He went into a solitary nook and read it and remained lost in bewilderment and amazement,

(Wondering) how a priceless treasure-scroll of this sort had fallen and been left among the (stationer's) papers.

(Then) again the thought darted into his mind, that God is the guardian for everything,

(And) how should the Guardian, in (His) circumspection, let any one recklessly carry off anything?

1930 Though the desert be filled with gold and (silver) money, not a single mite can be taken away without God's approval;

And though you read a hundred volumes without a pause, you will not remember a single point (of argument) without the Divine decree;

But if you serve God and do not read a single book, you will learn rare sciences from your (own) bosom.

The hand of Moses was spreading from his bosom a radiance that surpassed the moon in the sky,

Saying (implicitly), "That which thou wert seeking from the terrible celestial sphere hath uprisen, O Moses, from thy own bosom,

1935 In order that thou mayst know that the lofty heavens are the reflexion of the perceptive (rational) faculties of Man."

Is it not (the case) that the hand of the Glorious God created Reason first (of all), before (the creation of) the two worlds?

This discourse is clear (to some) and exceedingly recondite (to others), for the fly is not intimate with the 'Anqá.

O son, return once more to the tale: bring the tale of the treasure and the fakir to an end.

### Conclusion of the Story of the fakir and (a description of) the signs indicating the position of the treasure.

This is what was written in the scroll—"Know that outside of the town a treasure is buried.

1940 (Go to) such-and-such a domed building in which there is a martyr's shrine, with its back to the town and its gate towards the desert.

Turn your back to it and face the qibla (Mecca) and then let loose an arrow from your bow.

When you have shot the arrow from your bow, O fortunate one, dig up the place where your arrow fell."

Thereupon the youth fetched a strongbow and let fly an arrow into the expanse of (aerial) space,

And quickly and with great joy brought a pick-axe and mattock and dug up the spot where his arrow had fallen;

(But) both he and the mattock and pick-axe were worn out 1945 (in vain efforts), and he found not even a trace of the hidden treasure.

Every day in like fashion he was shooting arrows, but never getting to know the situation of the treasure.

Since he made this his continual practice, a whispered rumour arose in the city and (among) the people.

### How the news of this treasure became known and reached the ears of the king.

Then the party (of informers) who lay in ambush gave information of this to the king,

And submitted the matter (to him) secretly, saying that such-and-such an one had found a treasure-scroll.

When this person (the fakir) heard that it had come to (the 1950 knowledge of) the king, he saw no remedy but resignation and acquiescence;

(So), ere he should suffer (torture on) the rack by order of the Emperor, that person laid the note (of the treasure) before him,

Saying, "(Ever) since I found this scroll, I have seen no treasure but (only) infinite trouble.

Not even a single mite of treasure has been discovered, but I have writhed very much, like a snake.

During a (whole) month I have been in bitter distress like this, for loss or gain (accruing) from this (treasure-scroll) is forbidden to me.

Maybe thy fortune will disclose (to thee) this mine (of riches), 1955 O king (who art) victorious in war and the conqueror of fortresses."

For six long months and more the king shot arrows and dug pits (where the arrows fell).

Wherever an energetic drawer of the strongbow was (to be found), he (the king) gave (him) arrows to shoot and searched for the treasure in every direction.

(The result was) nothing but vexation and grief and futilities: as (in the case of) the 'Anqá, the name (of the treasure) was known to all, but the essence (reality) was non-existent.

### How the king despaired of finding the treasure and became weary of searching for it.

When he met with obstacles (to success) in (all) the breadth and length (of his enterprise), the king became sick at heart and weary.

(After) the king (had) dug pits in the deserts, yard by yard, 1960 he threw the scroll wrathfully before him (the fakir).

"Take this scroll," said he, "which has no (good) effects; you are the fittest (owner) for it, since you have no work.

It is no use for one who has work (to do) that he should burn the rose and go about (busy himself with) the thorn.

'Tis singular (how) the victims of this melancholy madness expect grass to grow from iron.

This specialty needs a man of stout heart like you: do you, who have a stout heart, search for this (treasure).

1965   If you cannot find it, you will never weary (of seeking); and if you find it, I grant you the right of possession."

How should Reason wend the way of despair? 'Tis Love that runs on its head in that direction.

Love is reckless, not Reason: Reason seeks that from which it may get some profit.

(The lover is) fierce in onset and body-consuming and unabashed: in tribulation, like the nether millstone;

A hard-faced one that has no back: he has killed in himself the seeking of self-interest.

1970   He gambles (everything) clean away, he seeks no reward, even as he receives (everything) clean (as a free gift) from Him (God).

God gives him his existence without any cause: the devoted (lover) yields it up again without cause;

For devotion consists in giving without cause: gambling (one's self) clean away (pure self-sacrifice) is outside of (transcends) every religion.

Forasmuch as religion seeks (Divine) grace or salvation, those who gamble (everything) clean away are (God's) chosen favourites.

Neither do they put God to any test, nor do they knock at the door of any profit or loss.

### How the king gave back the treasure-scroll to the fakir, saying, *" Take it: we are quit of it."*

1975   When the king handed over to that grief-stricken man the treasure-scroll (which was) fraught with commotion,

He (the fakir) became secure from rivals and annoyance, (so) he went and wrapped himself in his melancholy madness.

He made sad-thoughted Love his friend: a dog licks his own sore himself.

Love hath none to help him in his torment: there is not in the village one inhabitant familiar with him.

None is more mad than the lover, (yet) Reason is blind and deaf to his melancholia,

1980   Because this is no common madness: in these cases Medicine cannot give right guidance.

If frenzy of this kind overtake a physician, he will wash out (obliterate) the book of Medicine with (tears of) blood.

The Medicine of all intellects is (but) a picture of him (Love); the faces of all sweethearts are (but) a veil of him.

O votary of Love, turn thy face towards thine own face: thou hast no kinsman but thyself, O distraught one.

He (the fakir) made a *qibla* of his heart and began to pray: *man hath naught but that for which he laboureth.*

Ere he had heard any answer (to his prayer) he had (already) 1985 been engaged in praying for (many) years.

He was always praying intently without (receiving) any (overt) response, (but) he was hearing *Labbayka* in secret from the (Divine) grace.

Since that sickly man was always dancing without the tambourine, in reliance upon the bounty of the Almighty Creator,

(Though) neither a heavenly voice nor a (Divine) messenger was (ever) beside him, (yet) the ear of his hope was filled with *Labbayka*;

His hope was always saying, without tongue, "Come!" and that call was sweeping (all) weariness from his heart.

Do not call the pigeon that has learned (to haunt) the roof: 1990 drive it away (if you can), for its wings are stuck (to the roof).

Do thou, O Radiance of God, Husámu'ddín, drive him (such an one) away (if thou canst), for ('tis) through meeting with thee (that) his spirit has grown up in him.

If thou unconscionably drive away the bird, his spirit, it will still circle about thy roof.

All its grain and food is on thy roof: (while) flying in the zenith, it is (still) intoxicated with (love for) thy snare.

If for one moment the spirit stealthily (secretly) disbelieve in rendering thanks to thee, O (thou who art bestowing) victory and favour (upon it),

Love, the magistrate who exacts vengeance repeatedly, will 1995 lay the fiery cauldron (of separation) on its breast,

Saying, "Come to the Moon and leave the dust behind; Love, the King, calls thee: return with all speed!"

I am flying ecstatically, like a pigeon, about this roof and pigeon-house.

I am Love's Gabriel, and thou art my Lotus-tree[1]; I am the sick man, and thou art (my) Jesus son of Mary.

Let that pearl-shedding sea (of thine) break into surge: to-day ask kindly after this ailing one.

When thou hast become his, the sea (of spiritual mysteries) 2000 is his, even though this is the hour of his crisis.

This (*Mathnawí*) is only the wailful music that he has uttered; (as for) that which is (kept) hidden (within him), (have) mercy, O Lord![2]

We have two vocal mouths, like the reed: one mouth is hidden in his lips.

---

[1] See *Qur'án*, LIII, 13–18.    [2] *I.e.* do not reveal it.

One mouth is wailing unto you: it lets (many) a shrill note fall on the air;

But every one who hath insight knows that the lamentation (issuing) at *this* end is (inspired) from *that* end.

2005    The noise of this reed is from his breaths: the spirit's outcry ⁱs from his outcry.

If the reed had no converse with his lip, the reed would not the world with (music sweet as) sugar.

With whom hast thou slept and from what (whose) side hast thou risen, that thou art so full of agitation, like the sea?

Or hast thou recited (the words of the Prophet), "I pass the night with my Lord," and plunged into the heart of the sea of fire?

The shout (of God), "*O fire, be cool*[1]," became a protection to thy spirit, O exemplar (for all).

2010    O Radiance of God, Ḥusám (Sword) religious and spiritual, how can a sun be daubed over with clay?

These lumps of clay (thy detractors) attempted (in vain) to cover up thy sun.

The rubies in the mountain's heart are brokers (advertisers) of thee; the orchards in (their) laughter (full-blown beauty) are filled to the brim with thee.

For one familiar (as I am) with thy manhood, where is a Rustam that I might tell (him) a single barley-corn (thereof) out of (thy) hundred stacks?

When I wish to sigh forth thy secret, like 'Alí I put my head down into a well.

2015    Since his brethren have vindictive hearts, the bottom of the well is (the) best (place) for my Joseph.

I have become intoxicated, I will set about making a row: what of the well? I will pitch my tent in the open plain.

Put the fiery wine in my hand, and then behold the pomp and glory that is enjoyed by the drunken!

Bid the fakir wait (though he is still) without the treasure, for at this moment we are drowned in the syrup (of union).

Now, O fakir, seek refuge with God: do not seek help from me who am drowned;

2020    For I have no concern with lending support (to you): I have no recollection of myself and my own beard.

How should there be room for wind of the moustache (self-assertion) and water of the face (personal reputation) in the wine in which there is no room for a single hair (of self-existence)?

Hand (him) a heavy (large) goblet, O cup-bearer: deliver the Khwája from his beard and moustache.

His arrogance is (contemptuously) curling a moustache at us, but he is (really) tearing out his beard in envy of us.

[1] *Qur'án*, XXI, 69.

(He is) mated by Him (God), mated by Him, mated by Him, for we are acquainted with his impostures.

The Pír is seeing distinctly, hair by hair, what will become of 2025 him (the Khwája) after a hundred years.

What does the common man see in the mirror that the Pír does not see in the crude brick (of iron)?

That which the bushy-bearded man never saw in his own house is apparent at once to him who has but a few hairs on his chin.

Go to the Sea of whose fish thou art born: how hast thou fallen, like rubbish, into the beard?

Thou art not rubbish—far be it from thee! Thou art an object of envy to the pearl: thou hast the best right (to dwell) amidst the waves and the sea.

'Tis the Sea of Unity: there is no fellow or consort: its pearls 2030 and fishes are not other than its waves.

Oh, absurd, absurd to make (aught) its partner. Far be it from that Sea and its pure waves!

In the Sea there is no partnership or perplexity; but what can I say to him that sees double? Nothing, nothing.

Since we are the mates of those who see double, O idolater, 'tis necessary to speak in the fashion of him who attributes a partner (to God).

That Unity is beyond description and condition: nothing comes into the arena (domain) of speech except duality.

Either, like the double-seeing man, drink in (absorb and be 2035 satisfied with) this duality, or close your mouth and be very silent;

Or (do both) in turns, now silence, now speech: (in the company of the uninitiated) beat the drum like him that sees double, and peace (be with you)!

When you see a confidant, declare the mystery of the Spirit: (if) you see the rose, sing loud like nightingales.

(But) when you see (one who resembles) a water-skin full of deceit and falsehood, shut your lips and make yourself like a (dry-lipped) jar;

(For) he is an enemy to the water (of spiritual life): in his presence do not move (your lips), else the stone of his ignorance breaks the jar.

Patiently endure the punishments inflicted by the ignorant 2040 man: give him fair words and dissemble (towards him) with the reason that is divinely inspired.

Patience (shown) to the unworthy is the means of polishing (purifying) the worthy: wherever a heart exists, patience purifies it.

The fire of Nimrod was the means of making pure (resplendent) the (inward) mirror of Abraham in (the process of) polishing.

25

The iniquitous unbelief of Noah's people and the patience of Noah were instrumental in polishing the mirror of Noah's spirit.

### Story of the disciple of Shaykh (Abú) Ḥasan Kharraqání, may God sanctify his spirit!

A dervish went from the town of Ṭálaqán because of the fame of Abu 'l-Ḥusayn of Kháraqán.

2045  He traversed the mountains and the long valley to visit the Shaykh who was endowed with sincerity and fervent supplication.

Although the afflictions and injuries which he suffered on the road are deserving (of mention), I will abridge (the story).

When the young man reached the end of his journey, he asked to be directed to the house of that (spiritual) king.

As soon as he knocked at his door with a hundred reverences, the (Shaykh's) wife put forth her head from the door of the house,

Saying, "What do you want? Tell (me), kind sir." He replied, "I have come with the intention of paying a visit (to the Shaykh)."

2050  The wife gave a (loud) laugh. "Ha, ha," she exclaimed, "look at your beard[1], look at this undertaking of a journey and (all) this trouble!

Was there nothing for you to do in the place (where you come from), that you should idly set out upon this expedition?

Did you feel a craving to indulge in foolish sight-seeing[2], or were you overcome by disgust with your home?

Or, perchance, the Devil laid on you a two-forked barnacle[3] and let loose upon you the temptation to travel."

She uttered unseemly and foul and silly words: I cannot relate all of them.

2055  The disciple was thrown into a painful state of dejection by her parables and countless mockeries.

### How the new-comer asked the Shaykh's wife, "Where is the Shaykh? Where shall I look for him?" and the rude answer given by the Shaykh's wife.

Tears burst from his eyes, and he said, "Nevertheless, where is that (spiritual) king of sweet name?"

She replied, "That vain hypocritical impostor, a trap for fools and a noose for (leading into) error—

Hundreds of thousands of callow simpletons like you have fallen, through him, into a hundred rebelliousnesses.

[1] See translation of Book II, v. 544, note.
[2] Literally, "to wander about foolishly."
[3] Such as farriers put on the nose of horses and asses when shoeing them.

If you should not see him and return (home) in safety, it will be good (luck) for you: you will not be led astray by him.

A braggart, a lick-platter, a parasite: the noise of his drum has 2060 reached the remotest parts of the world.

These folk (who follow him) are (like) Israelites and worshippers of the (golden) calf: why do they fondle[1] such a cow?

Any one who is duped by this parasite is a carcase[2] by night and a good-for-nothing by day.

These folk have abandoned a hundred kinds of knowledge and perfection and have embraced a deceit and imposture, saying, 'This is ecstasy.'

Alas, where are the family of Moses that now they might shed the blood of the calf-worshippers

(Who) have cast religion and piety behind their backs? Where 2065 is 'Umar? Where is a stern command to act righteously?

For the licence practised by these people has become notorious: 'tis an indulgence enjoyed by every scoundrelly evil-doer.

Where is the Way of the Prophet and his Companions? Where are his ritual prayer and rosary and (religious) observances?"

*How the disciple answered that railing woman and bade her refrain from her unbelief and idle talk.*

The youth cried out at her and said, "Enough! In bright daylight where did the night-patrol come from?[3]

The splendour of the (holy) men has overspread the East and the West: the heavens have bowed low in amazement.

The Sun of God has risen from (the sign of) the Ram: the 2070 (material) sun has gone, shamefaced[4], under the veil.

How should the bletherings of a devil like you turn me back from the dust of this abode?

I have not (been impelled to) come by a wind (of vain desire) like a cloud, that I should be turned back from this (holy) presence by a dust (of foolish words).

By virtue of that Light the calf becomes a *qibla* of (Divine) grace; without that Light the *qibla* becomes (a symbol of) infidelity and an idol.

The licence that comes from self-will is error; the licence that comes from God is perfection.

In that quarter where the illimitable Light has shone, in- 2075 fidelity has become faith and the Devil has attained unto Islam.

He (the saint) is a theatre for the manifestation of the (Divine)

---

[1] Literally, "rub their hands on."    [2] *I.e.* sunk in heavy slumber.
[3] *I.e.* what is the use of the night-patrol in the day-time?
[4] Literally, "from shame."

Glory, and he is the real beloved (of God): he has carried off the prize from (taken precedence over) all the Cherubim.

The worship of Adam (by the angels) is clear evidence of his superiority: the husk always bows down (pays homage) to the kernel.

O old woman, (if) you puff (try to put out) God's candle, you will be burnt, you and your head at the same time, O foul-mouthed one.

How should the sea be defiled by a dog's muzzle? How should the sun be extinguished by a puff?

2080 Even if you judge (only) by appearances, tell (me), what is more apparent than this Light?

In comparison with this appearance all apparent things are in the utmost degree of imperfection and default.

If any one puff at God's candle, how should the candle be extinguished? His jaws and nose will be burnt.

Bats like you often dream that this world will be left orphaned (deprived) of the Sun.

The fierce waves of the seas of the Spirit are a hundred times as many as was (the multitude of waves in) the Flood of Noah;

2085 But hair grew (and formed an obstruction) in the eye of Canaan: he forsook Noah and the Ark and sought the mountain.

Then half a wave swept the mountain and Canaan down into the abyss of dishonour.

The moon scatters her light and the dog bays: how should the dog feed on the light of the moon?

Those who travel by night and move swiftly with the moon on her way, how should they relinquish their journey because of the dog's yelping?

The part is speeding like an arrow towards the Whole: how should it stop on account of any old hag?

2090 The gnostic is the soul of religion and the soul of piety: gnosis is the result of past asceticism.

Asceticism is the labour of sowing; gnosis is the growth of the seed.

Therefore the (ascetic's) hard struggle and his firm religious conviction are like the body, (while) the soul of this sowing is the growth (of the seed) and its harvesting.

He (the gnostic) is both the command to do right and the right (itself); he is both the revealer of mysteries and that which is revealed.

He is our king to-day and to-morrow: the husk[1] is for ever a slave to his goodly kernel.

2095 When the Shaykh (Halláj) said 'I am God' and carried it through (to the end), he throttled (vanquished) all the blind (sceptics).

[1] *I.e.* the phenomenal world.

When a man's 'I' is negated (and eliminated) from existence, then what remains? Consider, O denier.

If you have an eye, open it and look! After '*not*,' why, what else remains?

Oh, (may) the lips and throat and mouth (be) cut off that spit at the moon or the sky!

Without any doubt his spittle will recoil upon his face: spittle can find no path to heaven.

Spittle from the Lord rains upon him till the Resurrection, 2100 just as (the perdition denoted by) *tabbat* (rains) upon the spirit of Bú Lahab[1].

Drum (*tabl*) and banner are the (rightful) possession of the (spiritual) king: any one who calls him a parasite (*tabl-khwár*) is a cur.

The heavens are a slave to his moon: the whole East and West is begging him for bread;

For *lawláka* (but for thee)[2] is (inscribed) on his (imperial) sign-manual: all are (included) in his bounty and distribution.

If he did not exist, Heaven would not have gained circling motion and light and (the dignity of) being the abode of the angels;

If he did not exist, the seas would not have gained the awe 2105 (which they inspire) and fish and regal pearls;

If he did not exist, the earth would not have gained treasure within and jasmine (flowers and verdure) without.

(Our) means of sustenance are eating the means of sustenance bestowed by him: the fruits are dry-lipped (thirsty) for his rain.

Take heed, for in the (Divine) command (to give alms) this knot is (tied) upside down[3]. Give alms to him[4] who gives alms to yourself.

All (your) gold and silk comes to you from the (apparently) poor man: hark, give an alms to the (really) rich man, O you who are (really) poor.

A disgrace (an infamous creature) like thee, married to that 2110 man whose spirit is accepted (by God), resembles the unbelieving wedded wife of Noah.

Were it not for thy relationship to this (blessed) house, I would tear thee to pieces at this moment.

I would deliver that Noah from thee, in order that I might be ennobled (by being slain) in retaliation.

[1] See *Qur'án*, CXI, I.
[2] Referring to the Tradition, "But for thee (O Mohammed), I would not have created the heavens."
[3] *I.e.* the appearance is contrary to the reality.
[4] *I.e.* the saintly dervish, a type of the Perfect Man, whose spiritual riches are infinite and by whom all bounties are conferred.

But such a disrespect to the house of the emperor of the world cannot be shown by me.

Go and thank God[1] that thou art the dog of this dwelling-place, (for) otherwise I would do now what ought to be done."

*How the disciple turned back from the Shaykh's house and questioned the people (in the neighbourhood), and how they directed him, saying, "The Shaykh has gone to such and such a forest."*

2115  Afterwards he began to inquire of every one and sought the Shaykh for a long while in every quarter.

Then (at last) somebody said to him, "That Quṭb (Pivot) of the world has gone to fetch faggots from the hilly country."

The disciple, whose thoughts were (like) Dhu 'l-faqár (a sharp sword), ran quickly to the forest in eager desire for the Shaykh.

(But) the Devil was introducing to the (young) man's mind an evil suggestion, in order that the (spiritual) Moon might be concealed by dust,

Namely, "Why should this Shaykh of the (true) religion keep in his house a woman like this as his mate and companion?

2120  Whence (this) familiarity between opposite and opposite? Whence (comes it that) a *nasnás* (anthropoid ape) is (associated) with the Imám of mankind?"

Then again he was exclaiming fervidly, "God help me![2] My impugning him (the Shaykh) is infidelity and enmity.

Who am I, in view of God's exercising (absolute) control (over everything he does), that my carnal soul should raise difficulties and objections?"

But soon his carnal soul was returning to the attack—(for) in consequence of this acquaintance[3] (there was) smoke in his straw-like heart[4]—

Saying, "What affinity has (this woman like) the Devil with (a saint like) Gabriel, that she should be his bedfellow in (connubial) intercourse?

2125  How can Khalíl (Abraham) agree with Ázar? How can a guide agree with a brigand?"

*How the disciple gained his wish and met the Shaykh near the forest.*

He was (absorbed) in this (perplexity) when suddenly the renowned Shaykh appeared before him, riding on a lion.

The roaring lion carried his faggots, while that blessed one sat on the top of them.

---

[1] Literally, "offer a prayer (of thanksgiving)."

[2] Literally, "he was uttering a fiery *lá ḥawl* (there is no power except in God)."

[3] *I.e.* with the Shaykh's wife.

[4] The heart inflamed by suspicion is compared to straw which smokes as it burns.

Because of the honour (in which God held him) his whip was a fierce serpent: he had grasped the serpent in his hand, like an ass-goad.

Know for certain that likewise every Shaykh that exists is riding on a furious lion.

Although that (riding) and this (lion) are not perceived by the 2130 senses, yet 'tis not concealed from the spiritual eye.

Under their (the saints') thighs a hundred thousand lions carrying faggots are (present) before the eye that knows the Unseen;

But God has (sometimes) made them visible singly, in order that even he who is not a (holy) man may behold them.

That (spiritual) prince saw him (the disciple) from afar and laughed and said (to him), " O you who are tempted, do not listen to it (the evil suggestion) from the Devil."

The venerable (saint) knew his secret thought by the light of the heart: yea, 'tis an excellent guide (to knowledge of the occult).

(Then) the master of (mystical) sciences recited to him in 2135 detail all that had befallen him (the disciple) on his journey until now.

Afterwards that man of sweet discourse opened his mouth (to speak) on the difficult matter of his wife's disbelief,

Saying, " My long-suffering is not from (the motive of) sensual desire; that (suspicion) is a vain fancy of your carnal soul: do not take that standpoint[1].

Unless my patience had endured the burden of (supporting) my wife, how should the fierce lion have endured the labour of (carrying) me?

I am (like) Bactrian camels, (speeding) in advance (of the caravan), intoxicated and beside myself under the panniers of God.

I am not half-raw (imperfect) in (fulfilling) the (Divine) order 2140 and command, that I should take any thought of revilement by the public.

My public and my private (object) is His command: my spirit is running on its face in search of Him.

My being single or wedded is not on account of sensual desire: my spirit is like a die in the hand of God.

I endure the disdain of that foolish (woman) and a hundred like her, neither from love of colour nor passion for scent.

This much, indeed, is (only) the lesson learned by my disciples; (but) unto what place (attains) the forward and back-ward movement of my battle!

Unto what place? Unto the place where Place (itself) finds 2145 no admittance, and where nothing exists save the lightning-flash of the Moon of Allah.

---

[1] Literally, " do not stand there."

('Tis) far beyond all conceptions and imaginations, ('tis) the Light of light of light of light of light of light."

If I have made my discourse low for your sake, (it is) in order that you may put up with an ill-natured companion,

And smilingly and cheerfully bear the burden of distress, because patience is the key to relief from pain.

When you put up with the vileness of these vile folk you will attain unto the light of the (Prophetic) *sunnas* (ways and practices);

2150 For the prophets have often suffered affliction from the vile: often have they writhed in anguish on account of such snakes.

Since in eternity it was the will and decree of God, the Forgiver, to reveal and manifest Himself,

(This involves contrariety, for) nothing[1] can be shown without a contrary; and there was no contrary to that incomparable King.

### The (Divine) purpose in (saying), "Lo, I will place a viceroy in the earth."

Therefore He made a viceroy, one having a heart[2], to the end that he might be a mirror for His sovereignty;

So He endowed him with infinite purity (spiritual light), and then set up against him a contrary (in the form) of darkness.

2155 He made two banners, white and black: one (was) Adam, the other (was) the Iblís (Devil) of the Way (to Him).

Between those two mighty camps (there was) combat and strife, and there came to pass what came to pass.

Likewise in the second period Hábíl (Abel) arose, and Qábíl (Cain) became the antagonist of his pure light.

Even so (were) these two banners of justice and iniquity (continuing to be raised) till in the course of time the period of Nimrod arrived.

He became the antagonist and adversary of Abraham, and those two armies waged war (against each other) and sought battle.

2160 (At last) when He was displeased with the prolongation of the strife, His fire became the (means of) decision between the twain.

So He caused a fire to be His arbiter and servant, in order that the difficulty (controversy) of those two persons might be solved.

These two (contrary) parties (carried on the struggle) from period to period and from generation to generation, down to (the time of) Pharaoh and God-fearing Moses,

Between whom there was war for (many) years. When it passed (all) bounds and was causing excessive weariness,

God made the water of the sea His arbiter, that it might be left (to the sea to decide) which of these two should prevail.

---

[1] Literally, "no contrary."  [2] Literally, "breast."

So (it went on) till the period and time of Muṣṭafá (Moham- 2165
med), (who contended) with Abú Jahl, the general of the army
of iniquity.

Moreover He (God) appointed a servant for (the destruction
of) Thamúd, (namely), the (awful) Cry that took away their
lives.

Moreover He appointed a servant for (the destruction of) the
people of 'Ád, one that rises quickly and moves rapidly, that is
(to say), the Wind.

Moreover He appointed a discerning servant for (the de-
struction of) Qárún (Korah): He endued the graciousness of the
Earth with enmity,

So that the graciousness of the Earth turned entirely to
wrath, and she bore Qárún and his treasure down to the abyss.

In the case of the food that is a pillar (support) for this body, 2170
bread is like a breastplate to repel the sword of hunger;

(Yet) when God puts a (motive of) wrath into your bread,
that bread will stick in your gullet (and choke you) like a
quinsy.

This garment that protects you from the cold—God gives it
the temperature of intense frost,

So that this greatcoat on your body becomes cold as ice and
biting as snow.

(This He does) in order that you may flee from the fox-fur
and silk and take refuge from them with the intense cold.

You are not the (statutory) two *qullas* (ewers), you are (only) 2175
one ewer[1]: you have forgotten the (Divine) chastisement inflicted
by an overshadowing cloud[2].

In town and village, to (every) house and wall came the
command of God, "Give no shade!

Do not ward off the rain and the (heat of the) sun!" so that
the people went in haste to that Apostle (Shu'ayb),

Crying, "We are dead for the most part: mercy, O Prince!"
Read the rest of it in the book of commentary (on the *Qur'án*).

Since that deft-handed One made the rod (of Moses) a serpent,
that instance is enough if you have any intelligence.

You possess (the faculty of) consideration, but it does not go 2180
deep (into the subject)[3]: it is a frozen spring and has stopped
(flowing).

Hence the (Divine) Artist who depicts thoughts is saying,
"Consider deeply, O (My) servant."

He does not mean (to say), "Beat cold iron[4]," but (what He

---

[1] *I.e.* "your knowledge is incomplete." The metaphor is taken from a
Tradition regarding the quantity of water sufficient to ensure that the ritual
ablution shall be performed with "pure" water.

[2] *Qur'án*, XXVI, 189.

[3] Literally, "it has not profundity (*im'án*)."

[4] *I.e.* waste your time in the pursuit of speculative knowledge.

means is) "O (thou who art hard as) steel, devote thyself to[1] David[2]."

If your body is dead, resort to Isráfíl[3]; if your heart is frozen, repair to the sun of the Spirit.

Inasmuch as you have wrapped yourself in the garment of phantasy, lo, you will (soon) reach (the position of) the evil-minded sophist (sceptic).

2185    Verily he was dispossessed of the kernel (which is) Reason: he was dispossessed of (true) perception and deprived of (immediate) experience.

Hark, O mouther, 'tis the hour for mumbling: if thou speak (clearly) to the people, 'tis a shameful exposure.

What is (the meaning of) *im'án*? (It means) causing the spring to flow: when the spirit (*ján*) has escaped from the body, they call it *rawán*[4].

The philosopher whose spirit was delivered from the bondage of the body and began to wander (*rawán*) in the garden (of Reality)

Bestowed two (different) titles on these two (spirits)[5] in order to distinguish (the one from the other). Oh, may his spirit be blest!

2190    (Now hear a story) showing that if he who walks according to the (Divine) command wishes a rose to become a thorn, it will become that.

*The evidentiary miracle of Húd, on whom be peace, in the deliverance of the true believers of the community at the moment when the Wind descended.*

All the true believers, (seeking refuge) from the violence of the pernicious Wind, seated themselves in the circle (drawn by Húd).

The Wind was (like) the Flood, and His (God's) grace was the ship (Ark): He hath many such arks and floods.

God makes a king to be (as) an ark (for his subjects), to the end that he, (impelled) by selfishness, may assault the ranks (of his enemies).

The king's aim is not that the people should become safe; his aim is that his kingdom should become (like) a fetter (on his foot)[6].

2195    The ass that turns the mill is running along: its aim is (to

---

[1] Literally, "turn upon (the pivot of)."
[2] As David was a worker in iron (*Qur'án*, XXI, 80), his name is aptly used here as a type of the perfect saint.
[3] The angel who calls the dead to life at the Resurrection.
[4] *Rawán* means (1) "going" or "flowing," (2) "spirit." Cf. Shelley's "the pure spirit shall flow Back to the burning fountain whence it came."
[5] *I.e.* the animal (vital) spirit and the rational spirit.
[6] *I.e.* tied fast to him.

obtain) release, so that it may gain refuge from blows at that moment.

Its aim is not to draw some water or thereby (by turning the mill) to make sesame into oil.

The ox hurries for fear of (receiving) hard blows, not for the purpose of taking the cart and baggage (to their destination);

But God put such fear of pain in him, to the end that good results might be achieved in consequence (of his fear).

Similarly, every shopkeeper works for himself, not for the improvement of the world.

Every one seeks a plaster for his pain, and in consequence of 2200 this a whole world is set in order.

God made of fear the pillar (support) of this world: because of fear every one has devoted himself to work.

Praise be to God that on this wise He has made a fear to be the architect and (means for the) improvement of the world.

All these (people) are afraid of (losing) good and (suffering) evil: none that is afraid is himself frightened by himself.

In reality, then, (the creator of their fear and) the ruler over (them) all is that One who is near, though He is not perceived by the senses.

He is perceived in a certain hiding-place (the heart), but not 2205 perceived by the sense of this house (the body).

The sense to which God is manifested is not the sense of this world; it is another.

If the animal sense perceived those (Divine) forms (ideas) an ox or an ass would be the Báyazíd of the time.

He who made the body to be the theatre in which every spirit is manifested, He who made the Ark to be the Buráq (steed) of Noah,

He, if He will, makes (what is) a very ark in (its ordinary) character to be a (destructive) flood for you, O seeker of light.

At every moment, O man of little means, He has conjoined 2210 with your grief and gladness an ark (to save you) and a flood (to destroy you).

If you do not perceive the ark and the sea (flood) before you, (then) consider (whence come) the tremors in all your limbs.

Since his (the trembling man's) eyes do not perceive the source of his fear, he is affrighted by diverse kinds of phantasy.

(For example), a drunken boor strikes a blind man with his fist: the blind man thinks it is a kicking camel,

Because at that moment he heard a camel's cry: the ear, not the eye, is the mirror for the blind.

(But) then again the blind man says, "No, it was a stone 2215 (which some one threw at me), or perhaps it was (a brick) from an echoing dome."

It was neither this nor that nor that: He who created fear produced these (phantasies).

Certainly fear and trembling are (produced) by another: nobody is frightened by himself, O sorrowful man.

The miserable philosopher calls fear "imagination" (*wahm*): he has wrongly understood this lesson.

How should there be any imagination without reality? How should any false coin pass (into circulation) without a genuine one?

2220    How should a lie fetch a price (have value) without truth? Every lie in both worlds has arisen from truth.

He (the liar) saw the currency and prestige enjoyed by truth: he set going (circulated) the lie in hope of (its enjoying) the same.

O (incarnate) lie, whose fortune is (derived) from veracity, give thanks for the bounty and do not deny the truth!

Shall I speak of the philosopher and his mad fancy, or of His (God's) ships (arks) and seas (floods)?

Nay, (I will speak) of His arks, which are the spiritual counsel (given by the saints); I will speak of the whole: the part is included in the whole.

2225    Know every saint to be a Noah and captain of the Ark; know companionship with these (worldly) people to be the Flood.

Do not flee from lions and fierce dragons, (but) beware of friends and kinsmen.

They waste your time (when you are) face to face (with them), and your recollections of them devour (the time of) your absence (from them).

Like a thirsty ass, the image of each one (in your phantasy) is licking up the sherbet of (spiritual) thought from the flagon of the body.

The (mental) image of those talebearers has sucked out of you the dew that you have (derived) from the Sea of Life.

2230    The sign, then, of the absorption (drying up) of the water (sap) in the boughs is that they are not moved to sway (to and fro).

The limb of him who is free (detached from the world) is (like) a moist fresh bough: (if) you pull it in any direction, it is (easily) pulled.

If you want a basket, you can make it (a basket); you can also make its neck a hoop[1];

(But) when it has been sucked dry by the draining of (the sap from) its root, it does not come (readily) in the direction to which (your) command is pulling it.

Recite, then, from the *Qur'án* (the words) *they stand up languidly*, when the bough gets no medicinal (curative) treatment from its root.

---

[1] *I.e.* bend its extremity into the shape of a hoop (the curved handle of a basket).

This symbol (allegory) is fiery, (but) I will cut it short and 2235
resume (the story of) the fakir and the treasure and the circum-
stances connected with it.

You have seen the fire that burns every (dry) sapling; (now)
see the fire of the Spirit by which phantasy is burnt.

Neither for phantasy nor for reality is there any protection
against a fire like this which flamed forth from the Spirit.

He is the adversary of every lion and every fox: *everything is
perishing except His Face.*

Go into His aspects (attributes) and Face (Essence), become
spent (emptied of self): go in, become enveloped (suppressed),
like the *alif* in *bism*.

In *bism* the *alif* has stayed hidden: it is in *bism* and also it is 2240
not in *bism*.

Such is the case with all the letters that disappear[1] when they
are elided for the purpose of (effecting) conjunctions.

It (the suppressed *alif* in *bism*) is a *ṣila* (means of conjunction)
and through it the *b* and the *s* have attained to union: the union
of the *b* and the *s* could not bear the (external intervention of the)
*alif*.

Since this union cannot bear (the intervention of) a single
letter, it behoves me to cut short the discourse.

Since a single letter is the cause of separation between the *s*
and the *b*, here silence is a most urgent duty[2].

When the *alif* has passed away from self(-existence), taking 2245
shelter (in self-abandonment), the *b* and the *s* say " *alif*" without
it[3].

(The words) *thou didst not throw when thou threwest* are (an
utterance spoken) without him (the Prophet); likewise (the
words) *God said* sprang from his silence.

So long as a drug exists (independently), it has no effect; it
removes diseases (only) when it has perished (has been dissolved
and assimilated).

(Even) if (all) the forest should become pens and (all) the
ocean ink, (yet) there is no hope of bringing the *Mathnawi* to an
end.

So long as the Brick-maker's mould is (filled with) earth, the
scansion of its (the *Mathnawi's*) poetry, too, will be kept up.

When earth remains no more and He (God) dries (withers and 2250
destroys) its existence, His sea when it foams will make (fresh)
earth.

When the forest remains no more and disappears (from
existence), (other) forests will raise their heads from the essence
of the Sea.

[1] Literally, "have become dead."
[2] *I.e.* mystical union demands self-effacement.
[3] *I.e.* the real meaning of "*alif*" is only expressed when "*alif*" ceases to
exist as a phenomenal individualisation.

Hence that Lord of relief (from sorrow)[1] said, "Relate Traditions (drawn) from our Sea, since there is no harm (in doing so)."

(Now) turn back from the Sea and set thy face towards dry land: talk only of the plaything, for it is better (more suitable) for the child,

So that in his boyhood, (advancing) little by little beyond the plaything, his spirit may become acquainted with the ocean of Reason.

2255    By means of that play the boy is (gradually) acquiring reason, though superficially it (his play) is repugnant (to reason).

How can a demented child play? There must be (in the child) a part (of reason) in order that it (the part) may attain to the whole.

### Returning to the Story of the dome and the treasure.

Lo, the idea of that fakir with (his cries) "Come! come!" has rendered me unfeignedly (really) unable (to resist his appeal).

You do not hear his cry, (but) I hear it, because I am his confidant in my inmost thoughts.

Do not regard him as a seeker of the treasure; he is the treasure himself: how should the lover in reality be other than the beloved?

2260    At every moment he is bowing down (in worship) to himself: the bowing is (performed) in front of the mirror for the sake of (beholding) the face.

If he saw in the mirror a single mite without any phantasy, nothing would be left of him.

Both his phantasies and he (himself) would vanish: his knowledge would be obliterated in nescience.

From our nescience another knowledge would rise into clear view, saying, "*Lo, I am (God)*."

The (Divine) call was coming (to the angels)—"*Bow down to Adam*, for ye are (essentially) Adam, and for a moment see yourselves to be (identical with) him."

2265    He (God) removed strabism from their eyes, so that the earth became identical with the azure heavens.

He said, "*There is no god*," and He said, "*except God*": not (*any god*) became *except God*, and Unity blossomed forth (was revealed).

The time has come for that righteous beloved and dear friend (of God)[2] to pull my ear (and lead me)

Towards the fountain (of Unity), saying, "Wash thy mouth clean of these things: do not tell that which we have concealed from the people.

And if thou tell (it), it will not become manifest, (yet) thou wilt be guilty of attempting to reveal it.

[1] *I.e.* the Prophet.        [2] Ḥusámu'ddín.

But, mark, I am compassing them about: I am at once the 2270 speaker and the hearer of this (mystery).

Tell (only) of the (outward) form of the dervish and the picture (external description) of the treasure. These folk are addicted to (worldly) trouble: tell (them) of trouble.

The fountain of Mercy has become unlawful to them: they are drinking cup after cup of deadly poison.

Having filled their skirts with clods, they are taking them along in order to make a dam[1] for these fountains.

How should this fountain, which is replenished by the Sea, be stopped up by this good or bad folk's handful of earth?

But it (the fountain) says, 'With you, I am closed; without 2275 you, I continue (to flow) unto everlasting.'"

The (worldly) folk are perverted in their appetites: (they are) eating earth and have left the water (untasted).

The people (of the world) have a nature opposite to that of the prophets: the people deem the dragon (the world) an object of reliance.

Inasmuch as you have known (from the *Qur'án*) the eye-bandage whereby God seals (the sight), do you know at all to what you have shut your eyes?

To what instead have you opened these eyes (of yours)? (Whatever it be), know that in every respect it is a bad exchange for you.

But (nevertheless) the sun of (Divine) favour has shone 2280 (forth) and has graciously succoured them that despair.

He (God) in His mercy has played a very marvellous game of backgammon: He has made the essence of ingratitude to be a turning in repentance (towards Him).

Even from this ill-fatedness (unrighteousness) of the people (of the world) that Bounteous One has caused two hundred fountains of love to burst.

He gives to the rose-bud a source (of growth) in the thorn; He gives to the snake-stone, (though obtained) from the snake, an ornamental quality.

He brings forth day from the blackness of night and makes ease (opulence) to grow (flow) from the hand of him who suffers hardship (penury).

He makes sand into flour for Khalíl (Abraham); the mountain 2285 becomes an accompanist to David.

The solitary mountain amidst that cloud of darkness opens the music of the harp and (the tones of) treble and bass,

(Singing), "Arise, O David, thou shunner of the people! Thou hast abandoned that (society): receive compensation from me."

---

[1] Literally, "dry-bandage."

*How the seeker of the treasure, after having searched much and having been reduced to helplessness and despair, turned to God most High, saying, "O Thou to whom manifestation belongs, do Thou make this hidden thing evident!"*

The dervish said, "O Knower of the secret, I have run about in vain for the sake of this treasure.

The devil of greed and cupidity and hurry sought neither deliberation nor calmness.

2290 I have not gained a morsel from any pot: I have (only) blackened my hand and burnt my mouth.

Verily, I did not say (to myself), 'Since I have no certainty in this (matter), I will untie this knot by (the help of) Him who ties (all) knots.'"

Seek the exposition of God's Word from God: do not talk nonsense (derived) from (your own) opinion, O hard-faced (impudent) man.

The knot which He tied He also will loose: the die which He cast (on the board) He (Himself) will take off.

Although words of that sort seemed to you to be easy, how should the esoteric (Divine) symbols be easy (to understand)?

2295 He (the fakir) said, "O Lord, I repent of this haste: since Thou hast shut the door, do Thou also open the door.

(It behoves me) to go (betake myself) once more to the patched frock (of the dervish): even in making (my) invocation (to God) I was devoid of merit.

How have I any independent merit or personality or heart? All these are the reflexion of Thee, and Thou Thyself art (all).

Every night in sleep my forethought and knowledge become like a ship overwhelmed by the water (of the sea).

Neither do I myself remain nor that merit (of mine): my body lies unconscious like a carcase.

2300 The whole night until dawn that exalted King is Himself uttering an '*Alast*' ('Am not I...?') and (answering) '*Yea.*'

Where is any one to say '*Yea*'? The flood (of slumber) has swept them all away, or a leviathan has swallowed them all piecemeal.

At morningtide, when He draws His sheeny sword from the scabbard of the darkness of night,

And the orient sun rolls up (makes an end of) night, this leviathan spews out all that it swallowed,

And we, delivered like Jonah from the belly of that leviathan, are dispersed into (the world of) scent and colour.

2305 Like Jonah, the people give praise (to God), because they were restful in that darkness.

At the hour of dawn each one says, when he comes forth from the belly of the (great) Fish, Night,

'O Gracious One who dost deposit in lonesome (fearful) Night the treasure of Mercy and all these delicious experiences!

By means of Night, which resembles the scaly leviathan, the eye (is made) keen, the ear fresh, and the body nimble.

Henceforth, with One like Thee (beside us), we will never flee from positions of fearful aspect.

Moses deemed that (which he saw) to be fire, but it was 2310 (really) light: we regarded Night as a (hideous) negro, but it was (really) a houri.

After this, we beg of Thee (only) the eye (that sees truly), in order that sticks and straws may not conceal the Sea (from us).'

When the eyes of (Pharaoh's) magicians were delivered from blindness, they were clapping their hands (joyfully), (though) deprived of these (bodily) hands and feet.

What bandages the people's eyes is nothing but means (secondary causes): whoever trembles (in anxiety) for (the loss of) means is not one of the Comrades.

But, O my comrades, God has opened the door to the Comrades and led them to the high-seat in the palace.

Through His hand the unworthy and the worthy are freed by 2315 Mercy from the bonds of servitude.

During (our) non-existence how were we worthy to attain to this spirituality and knowledge?

O Thou who hast made every stranger (Thy) friend, and O Thou who hast given the rose as a robe of honour to the thorn,

Sift our dust a second time, make (our) nothing to be something once more!

Thou didst command this invocation (of Thee) from the beginning; else how should a creature of dust have dared (to do) this?

Since—oh, wonder!—Thou didst command us to invoke 2320 Thee, cause this invocation of Thee to be answered favourably.

Night has wrecked the ship of (my) understanding and senses: no hope is left, nor fear nor despair.

God has borne me into the sea of Mercy: (I know not) with what specialty He will fill me and send me (back to the world).

He fills one with the light of Majesty, while He fills another with (vain) imagination and fancy.

If I had any judgement and skill by myself, my judgement and forethought would be under my control;

At night my consciousness would not go (from me) without 2325 my bidding, and my birds (senses and faculties) would be under my trap.

I should be aware of the stages (of the journey) of the soul (both) at the time of sleep and unconsciousness and (at the time of) tribulation.

Inasmuch as my hand is (made) empty by this (sovereign)

26

power of His to loose and bind, oh, I wonder, from whom comes this self-conceit of mine?

I have even deemed that what I saw was not seen (by me)[1], and (like a beggar) I have again held up the basket of invocation.

Like *alif*, I possess nothing, O Gracious One, except a heart more constricted with anguish than the eye of *mím*.

2330    This *alif* and this *mím* are the mother (*umm*) of our existence: the *mím* of *umm* is narrow (distressful), and the *alif* is (begging for deliverance) from it (like) a sturdy beggar.

(The state denoted by) 'alif possesses nothing' is forgetfulness (unconsciousness); the distressful *mím* is (denotes) the time of rationality (consciousness).

During the time of unconsciousness I am nothing at all; during the time of consciousness I am in torment.

Do not lay another nothing[2] upon a nothing like this; do not put the name of '(worldly) fortune' upon a torment like this.

Truly (the state of) 'I possess nothing' suits me better, since these hundred troubles arise from imagining that I possess (something).

2335    Just in (the state where) I possess nothing do Thou act in sovereign fashion towards me. I have suffered pain: do Thou increase my pleasure.

I will just stand naked in (a flood of) tears at Thy gate, since I have no sight[3].

Do Thou bestow on the tears of Thy sightless slave a verdure and vegetation from this (bountiful) pasture;

And if I leave no tears (in my eyes), do Thou give me tears (flowing abundantly) from an eye like the two streaming eyes of the Prophet.

Since he, with all that high fortune and majesty and pre-eminence, sought tears from the bounty of God,

2340    How should not I, an empty-handed destitute lick-platter, spin fine webs of blood-stained tears?

Inasmuch as an eye like that (of the Prophet) is enamoured of tears, it behoves my tears to be (like) a hundred great rivers."

A single drop of those (tears) is better than these two hundred great rivers, for by that single drop mankind and the Jinn were saved.

Since that Garden of Paradise sought rain, how should not the foul briny soil seek water?

O comrade, do not refrain from invoking (God): what business have you with His acceptance or rejection (of your prayer)?

---

[1] *I.e.* "I have abandoned my dream of riches and have fixed all my hopes on poverty."
[2] *I.e.* worldly goods.          [3] *I.e.* "since I am blinded by weeping."

Since bread (worldliness) was the barrier and obstacle to this 2345
water (tears), you must quickly wash your hands of that bread.

Make yourself harmonious and congruous and balanced[1]: let
your bread be baked well with (burning) tears.

*How the Voice from heaven called to the seeker of the treasure
and acquainted him with the truth of the mysteries thereof.*

He was (engaged) in this (prayer) when inspiration came to
him and these difficulties were solved for him by God,

Saying, "It (the Divine intimation) told you to put an arrow
to the bow, (but) when were you told to pull the bowstring
(hard)?

It did not tell you to draw the bow hard: it bade you put (the
arrow) to the bow, not 'shoot with your full strength.'

You, from (motives of) vanity, raised the bow aloft and brought 2350
to a high pitch the art of archery.

Go, renounce this skill in drawing the strongbow: put the
arrow to the bow and do not seek to draw to the full extent (of
your power).

When it (the arrow) falls, dig up the spot and search: abandon
(trust in) strength and seek the gold by means of piteous
supplication."

That which is real is nearer than the neck-artery; you have
shot the arrow of thought far afield.

O you who have provided yourself with bow and arrows, the
prey is near and you have shot far.

The farther one shoots, the farther away and more separated 2355
is he from a treasure like this.

The philosopher killed (exhausted) himself with thinking: let
him run on (in vain), for his back is turned towards the treasure.

Let him run on: the more he runs, the more remote does he
become from the object of his heart's desire.

That (Divine) King said, "*(those who) have striven in (for) Us*":
He did not say, "*(those who) have striven away from Us*,"
O restless one,

As (was the case with) Canaan, who in disdain of Noah went
up to the top of that great mountain.

The more he sought deliverance (by turning) towards the 2360
mountain, the more was he separated from the place of refuge,

Like this dervish (who) for the sake of the treasure and the
mine (of riches) sought (to draw) the bow more strongly every
morning,

And the more strongly he gripped the bow each time, the
worse luck he had in respect of (finding) the treasure and
(hitting) the mark.

[1] *I.e.* in full accord with the Divine will.

This parable is of vital import (to the soul) in the world: the soul of the ignorant is worthy of pain (deserves to suffer).

Inasmuch as the ignoramus disdains his teacher, consequently he goes and opens a new shop.

2365 O (you who are vain and specious as a) picture, that shop, (set up) over the teacher, is stinking and full of scorpions and snakes.

Quickly lay waste that shop and turn back to the greenery and the rose-trees and the watering-place;

Not like Canaan, who from pride and ignorance made of the "protecting" mountain a ship (ark) of safety.

His (the fakir's) knowledge of archery became a veil (barrier) to him, while (all the time) he had that object of desire present in his bosom.

Oh, how often have knowledge and keen wits and understandings become as (deadly as) the ghoul or brigand to the wayfarer!

2370 Most of those destined for Paradise are simpletons (simple-minded), so that they escape from the mischief of philosophy.

Strip yourself of (useless) learning and vanity, in order that (the Divine) mercy may descend on you at every moment.

Cleverness is the opposite of abasement and supplication: give up cleverness and sort with stupidity.

Know that cleverness is a trap for (a means of) gaining victory and (indulging) ambition and a scarecrow (such as is used by fowlers): why should the pure devotee wish to be clever?

The clever ones are content with an ingenious device; the simple ones have gone (away) from the artifice to rest in the Artificer,

2375 Because at breakfast time a mother will have laid the little child's hands and feet (in repose) on her bosom.

*Story of the three travellers—a Moslem, a Christian, and a Jew—who obtained (a gift of) some food at a hostelry. The Christian and the Jew had already eaten their fill, so they said, "Let us eat this food to-morrow." The Moslem was fasting, and he remained hungry because he was overpowered (by his companions).*

Here listen to a story, O son, in order that you may not suffer affliction in (relying upon) talent.

As it happened, a Jew and a true believer and a Christian travelled together on a journey.

A true believer travelled along with two miscreants, like reason (associated) with a carnal soul and Devil.

In travel the man of Merv and the man of Rayy meet one another as companions on the road and at table.

2380 Crow and owl and falcon come (as captives) into the (same) cage: the holy and the irreligious become mates in prison.

At night Easterners and Westerners and Transoxanians make their abode in the same caravanseray.

Small and great (folk) remain together for days in the caravanseray because of frost and snow.

As soon as the road is opened and the obstacle removed, they separate and every one goes in a (different) direction.

When sovereign Reason breaks the cage, all the birds fly away, each one to a (different) quarter.

Before this (deliverance) each one, full of longing and lament[1], 2385 spreads its wings towards its destination, in desire for its mate.

At every moment it spreads its wings with tears and sighs, but it has no room or way to fly.

(As soon as) way is made, each one flies like the wind towards that in remembrance of which it spread its wings.

Its way, when it gains the opportunity, is towards the region whither its tears and sighs were (directed).

Consider your own body: from what places were these corporeal parts (elements and faculties) collected in the body—

Watery and earthen and airy and fiery, celestial and terrestrial, 2390 (some) of Rúm and (some) of Kash[2].

In this (bodily) caravanseray one and all, from fear of the snow, have closed their eyes to the hope of returning (to their final destination).

The various snows are (symbolise) the congelation of every inanimate thing in the winter of farness from that Sun of justice.

(But) when the heat of the angry Sun flames (forth), the mountain becomes now (like) sand and now (like) wool.

The gross inanimate things dissolve, like the dissolution of the body at the hour of the spirit's departure.

When these three fellow-travellers arrived at a certain 2395 hostelry, a man of fortune brought them (some) *halwá* (sweetmeat) as a gift.

A benefactor brought to the three strangers (some) *halwá* from the kitchen of *Lo, I am near.*

One who had expectation of (earning) the (Divine) reward brought (to them) warm bread and a dish of *halwá* made with honey.

Intelligence and culture are characteristic of townsmen; hospitality and entertainment (of guests) are characteristic of tent-dwellers.

The Merciful (God) has implanted hospitality to strangers and entertainment (of guests) in the villagers (countryfolk).

Every day in the villages (countryside) there is a new guest 2400 who has none to help him except God.

Every night in the villages (countryside) are new-comers who have no refuge there save God.

[1] Literally, "wind."
[2] The town of Kash (Kish) was situated about 50 miles south of Samarcand.

The two aliens (the Jew and the Christian) were surfeited with food and suffering from indigestion; the true believer, as it happened, was fasting (all) day.

At the (time of) the evening prayer, when the *halwá* arrived, the true believer was reduced to extreme hunger.

The two (others) said, "We have eaten our fill: let us put it away to-night and eat it to-morrow.

2405      To-night let us practise self-denial and refrain from food; let us hide (reserve) the dainty for to-morrow."

The true believer said, "Let this (sweetmeat) be eaten to-night; let us put away self-denial till to-morrow."

Then they said to him, "Your purpose in this wisdom-mongering is that you may eat it (all) by yourself."

"O my friends," said he, "are not we three persons? Since disagreement has occurred, let us share.

Let him who wishes take his own share to his heart (enjoy it); let him who wishes put his share in hiding."

2410      The two (others) said to him, "Abandon (the thought of) sharing: give ear to (the words) 'The sharer is in Hell-fire' from the Traditions (of the Prophet)."

He replied, "The sharer (referred to) is he that has shared himself between sensuality and God."

Thou art God's property and His share entirely: (if) thou givest the share (of God) to another, thou art a dualist.

This lion[1] would have prevailed over the curs[2], if it had not been the turn of those evil-natured ones (to prevail).

'Twas their intention that the Moslem should suffer pain and pass the night[3] in want of food.

2415      He was overpowered: he said, with resignation and acquiescence, "My friends, I hear and obey."

So they slept (all) that night, and in the morning they rose and dressed themselves,

And washed their faces and mouths; and each one had a (different) method and practice in his devotions.

For a while each one applied himself[4] to his devotions, seeking favour from God.

True believer and Christian, Jew and Guebre and Magian— the faces of them all are (turned) towards that mighty Sultan.

2420      Nay, stone and earth and mountain and water have their invisible recourse to God.

This topic is infinite. At that time the three companions looked on one another[5] friendlily,

And one (of them) said, "Let each (of us) relate what he dreamed last night.

---

[1] The Moslem.          [2] The Jew and the Christian.
[3] Literally, "that the night should pass over him."
[4] Literally, "turned his face towards."
[5] Literally, "put their faces together."

Let him who had the best dream eat this (sweetmeat): let the most excellent carry off the share of every one that is excelled (by him)."

He who mounts highest in (the scale of) reason—his eating is (equivalent to) the eating of all (his inferiors).

His luminous spirit is supreme: 'tis enough for the rest of 2425 them to tend (cherish) him.

Since those endowed with (perfect) reason endure for ever, in reality this world is enduring for ever[1].

Then the Jew related his dream (and told them) whither his spirit had wandered during the night.

He said, "Moses met me on the way, (according to the adage) 'the cat sees a fat sheep's tail in her dreams.'

I followed Moses to Mt Sinai: in the Light (of the Divine Epiphany) all three of us[2] vanished.

All (our) three shadows disappeared in the Sun; after that, 2430 there came from the Light an opening of the door (revelation).

From the heart of that Light another Light sprang up, and then the second (Light) quickly sought to transcend it.

Both I and Moses and also Mt Sinai, we were lost, all three, in that effulgence of the (second) Light.

After that, I saw the mountain break into three pieces when the Light of God surged[3] upon it.

When the Attribute of Majesty was revealed to it, it burst asunder in every direction.

One piece of the mountain fell towards the sea, and the water 2435 bitter as poison was made sweet.

One piece thereof sank into the earth, and a medicinal spring of running water gushed forth,

So that its water became a cure for all the sick by the blessedness of the goodly revelation.

The other (third) piece flew at once to the neighbourhood of the Ka'ba where 'Arafát was (situated).

When I came back to myself out of that swoon, Sinai was in its place, neither greater nor less (than before);

But under the foot of Moses it was (inwardly) melting like ice: 2440 no spur or peak of it remained.

The mountain was levelled to the earth by terror: it was turned upside down by that awful Majesty.

After that scattering (of my senses) I came to myself again and saw that Sinai and Moses were unchanged,

And that the desert skirting the mountain was filled from end to end with people resembling Moses in (the illumination of) their faces.

---

[1] Because the Perfect Man is the life and soul of the world.
[2] *I.e.* Moses, Mt Sinai, and himself.
[3] Literally, "blew hard."

Their (staves and) mantles were like his staff and mantle: all (of them) were speeding[1] joyously towards Sinai.

2445 All had lifted their hands in prayer and struck up together the tune of *let me see (Thee)*.

Again, as soon as the trance departed from me, the form of each one seemed to me to be diverse.

They were the prophets endowed with love (of God): (thus) the (spiritual) unity of the prophets was (clearly) apprehended by me.

Again, I beheld some mighty angels: their outward form was (composed) of bodies of snow;

And (I saw) another circle of angels asking help (of God): their outward form was wholly of fire."

2450 On this wise did the Jew tell (his dream): there is many a Jew whose end was praiseworthy.

Do not regard any infidel with contempt, for there may be hope of his dying a Moslem.

What knowledge have you of the close of his life that you should once (and for all) avert your face from him?

Afterwards the Christian began to speak, saying, "The Messiah appeared to me in my dream.

I went with him to the Fourth Heaven, (which is) the centre and abode of the sun of this world.

2455 Verily, the marvels of the citadels of Heaven have no relation (cannot be compared) to the wonders of the (lower) world.

Every one knows, O pride of the sons (of Adam), that the artifice of the celestial sphere exceeds (that of) the earth."

*Story of the camel and the ox and the ram who found a bunch of grass on the road, and each said, "I will eat it."*

Whilst a camel, ox, and ram were going along, they found a bunch of grass in front of (them on) the road.

The ram said, "If we divide this, certainly none of us will get his fill of it;

But whichever of us has lived longest has the best right to this fodder[2]: let him eat;

2460 For (the injunction) to give the foremost place to the seniors has come from Muṣṭafá (Mohammed) among the practices observed by him,

Although, at this time when vile men hold sway, the vulgar put forward the elders on two occasions (only),

Either in (tasting) food that is burning hot, or on a bridge that is (damaged) by cracks (and) in a state of ruin.

---

[1] Literally, "trailing their skirts."
[2] Literally, "this fodder is most fit for him."

The vulgar do not pay homage to a venerable Shaykh and leader without some mischievous idea associated (with their homage).

This is their good: what must their evil be? Distinguish their (inward) foulness from their (outward) fairness."

### *Parable.*

A king was going to the congregational mosque, and the 2465 marshals and mace-bearers were beating the people off.

The wielder of the stick would break the head of one and tear to bits the shirt of another.

A poor wretch amidst the throng received ten blows with the stick without (having committed) any offence. "Begone," they cried, "get out of the way!"

Dripping blood, he turned his face to the king and said, "Behold the manifest iniquity: why ask of that which is hidden?

This is thy good: (thou doest this whilst) thou art going to the mosque; what must thy evil and burden (of sin) be, O misguided one?"

The Pír (Elder) never hears a salaam from a base fellow 2470 without being exceedingly tormented by him in the end.

(If) a wolf catch a saint, it is better than that the saint should be caught by the wicked carnal soul,

Because, though the wolf does great violence, yet it has not the same knowledge and craft and cunning;

Else how should it fall into the trap? Cunning is complete (attains to perfection) in man.

The ram said to the ox and the camel, "O comrades, since such a (lucky) chance has come to us,

Let each (of us) declare the date (antiquity) of his life: the 2475 oldest has the best right, let the others suffer (disappointment) in silence.

In those times," said the ram, "my pasturage was (shared) with the ram that was sacrificed for Ismá'íl (Ishmael)."

The ox said, "I am the (most) advanced in years, (I was) coupled with the ox that Adam yoked.

I am the yoke-fellow of the ox with which Adam, the forefather of mankind, used to plough the earth in sowing."

When the camel heard the ox and the ram (make these assertions) he was amazed: he lowered his head and picked up that (bunch of grass).

Promptly, without any palaver, the Bactrian camel raised the 2480 bunch of fresh barley in the air,

Saying, "I, in sooth, need no (support from) chronology, since I have such a (stout) body and high neck.

Indeed every one knows, O father's darling, that I am not smaller than you.

Whoever is one of those possessed of intelligence knows this,
that my nature is superior to yours."

(The Christian said), "All know that this lofty heaven is a
hundred times as great as this low earth.

2485    How can the wide expanse of the celestial domains be com-
pared with the (limited) character of the terrestrial regions?"

*How the Moslem in reply told his companions, the Jew and the
Christian, what he had seen (in his dream), and how they were
disappointed.*

Then the Moslem said, "O my friends, to me came Muṣṭafá
(Mohammed), my sovereign,

And said to me, 'That one (the Jew) has sped to Sinai with
him (Moses) to whom God spake, and has played the game of
love (with God);

And the other (the Christian) has been carried by Jesus, the
Lord of happy star, to the zenith of the Fourth Heaven.

Arise, O thou who hast been left behind and hast suffered
injury, at least eat up the sweetmeat and comfit!

2490    Those (two) talented and accomplished men have pushed
forward and have read the book of fortune and honour.

Those two eminent men have attained to their (proper)
eminence and because of their talents have mingled with the
angels.

Hark, O foolish simpleton who hast been left behind, jump
up and seat thyself beside the bowl of *ḥalwá*!'"

Thereupon they said to him, "Then, you greedy fellow, have
you made a meal of the *ḥalwá* and *khabíṣ*?[1] Oh, (what) an
astonishing thing!"

He replied, "When that sovereign who is obeyed (by all) gave
the order, who was I that I should resist it?

2495    Will you, Jew, rebel against the command of Moses if he
summon you (either) in a fair cause or a foul?

Can you, Christian, ever spurn[2] the command of Christ
(whether) for good or evil?

How, (then), should I rebel against the Glory of the prophets?
I have eaten the *ḥalwá* and now I am happy."

Then they said to him, "By God, you have dreamed a true
dream, and 'tis better than a hundred dreams of ours.

Your dreaming is waking, O gleeful one, for its effect (reality)
is made evident by (your) waking (and eating the sweetmeat)."

2500    Abandon eminence and (worldly) energy and skill: what
matters is service (rendered to God) and a goodly disposi-
tion.

----

[1] A kind of *ḥalwá*.
[2] Literally, "turn the head away from."

For this (object) God brought us forth (from non-existence):
"*I did not create mankind except to serve Me.*"

How did that knowledge (of his) profit Sámirí, whom the skill
(shown in making the golden Calf) banished from God's
door?

What did Qárún gain by his alchemy? See how the earth bore
him down to its abyss.

What, after all, did Bu 'l-Ḥakam (Abú Jahl) get from (in-
tellectual) knowledge? On account of his unbelief he went
headlong into Hell.

Know that (true) knowledge consists in seeing fire plainly, not 2505
in prating that smoke is evidence of fire.

O you whose evidence in the eyes of the Sage is really more
stinking than the evidence of the physician,

Since you have no evidence but this, O son, eat dung and
inspect urine!

O you whose evidence is like the staff in your hand (which)
indicates that you suffer from blindness[1],

(All this) noise and pompous talk and assumption of authority
(only means), "I cannot see: (kindly) excuse me."

*How the Sayyid, the King of Tirmid, proclaimed that he would
give robes of honour and horses and slave-boys and slave-girls and
a large sum in gold to any one who would go on urgent business to
Samarcand (and complete the journey) in three or four days;
and how Dalqak, having heard the news of this proclamation in
the country (where he then was), came post-haste to the king,
saying, " I, at all events, cannot go."*

The sagacious Dalqak was the buffoon (court-jester) of the 2510
Sayyid of Tirmid, who reigned in that place (city).

He (the king) had an urgent affair in Samarcand, and wanted
a courier in order that he might conclude it.

(Therefore) he proclaimed that he would bestow (his)
treasures on any one who should bring him news from there in
five days.

Dalqak was in the country and heard of that (proclamation):
he mounted (a horse) and galloped to Tirmid.

Two horses dropped (dead) on the way because of his gal-
loping in that (furious) manner.

Then, (fresh) from the dust of the road, he ran into the 2515
council-chamber and demanded admission to the king at an
untimely hour.

A whispered rumour arose in the council, and a (feeling of)
agitation came into the mind of the Sultan.

The hearts of the nobles and populace of the city were stricken

---

[1] Literally, "indicates the defect of blindness."

with panic[1], (for they wondered) what disturbance and calamity had occurred,

(Saying), "Either a conquering enemy is about to attack us or a deadly calamity has emerged from the Unseen,

For Dalqak, riding hard from the country, has killed several Arab horses on the way."

2520 The people gathered at the king's palace, wondering why Dalqak had come in such a hurry.

Because of his (hot) haste and the enormity of his exertions, tumult and commotion arose in Tirmid;

One man (was) beating both hands against his knee, while another, from presentiment of evil, was uttering woeful cries.

On account of the hubbub and distraction and the dread of punishment every heart went to (wander in) a hundred streets (haunts) of phantasy.

Every one was taking an omen (predicting) by conjecture (and trying to guess) what had set the rug on fire[2].

2525 He (Dalqak) sought admission and the king at once granted it to him. When he kissed the earth (in homage), the king said to him, "Hey, what's the matter?"

Whenever any one asked that sour-faced man for some particulars, he laid his hand on his lips as though to say "Hush!"

(Their) apprehension was increased by his gravity: all were perplexed and dumbfounded by him.

Dalqak made a gesture, as though to say, "O gracious king, let me have a moment to take breath,

That my wits may once come back to me, for I am fallen into a marvellous state (of exhaustion)."

2530 After a little while, during which both the throat and the mouth of the king were made bitter by (anxious) foreboding and surmise—

Because he had never seen Dalqak like this; for there was no companion more agreeable to him than he;

He was always bringing up stories and jests and keeping the king in merriment and laughter.

When sitting (with him) he used to make him laugh so (heartily) that the king would grip his belly with both hands;

And (many a time) his body sweated from the violence of his laughter and he would fall on his face with laughing.

2535 (How strange, then, that) to-day, on the contrary, he (Dalqak), pale and grim like this, is laying his hand on his lips as though to say, "Hush, O King!"

Foreboding on foreboding and fancy on fancy (occurred) to

---

[1] Literally, "got out of hand (control)."
[2] Literally, "what fire had fallen on the rug," *i.e.* "what was the cause of the trouble."

the king (as he wondered) what chastisement would come (upon him),

For the king's heart was anxious and alarmed because the Khwárizmsháh was very bloodthirsty,

And that perverse (tyrant) had killed many kings in that region either by craft or violence.

This King of Tirmid was apprehensive of (being attacked by) him, and his apprehension was increased by the artifice of Dalqak.

He said, "Be quick! Tell (me) what is the matter. Who is the 2540 cause of your being so perturbed and agitated?"

He replied, "I heard in the country that the king had proclaimed on every highway

That he required some one to run to Samarcand in three days and would bestow (his) treasures (on the courier).

I hurried to you in order to say that I am not able to do it.

For one like me such agility is impossible: at all events do not expect this of me[1]."

"Curse your hurry!" cried the king; "for (in consequence of 2545 it) a hundred[2] confusions have arisen in the city.

(Is it only) for this trifle[3], O half-baked fool, (that) you have set fire to this meadow and hay?"

(This is) like (the behaviour of) these raw (ignorant) persons (who come) with drum and banner, saying, "We are couriers (speeding) in (the path of spiritual) poverty and non-existence,"

(Who) boast far and wide[4] of being Shaykhs and make out that they have (attained to) the rank of Báyazíd,

And, having (as they claim) travelled away from themselves and become united (with God), open a conventicle (for disciples) in the abode of pretension.

(While) the bridegroom's house is full of turmoil and trouble, 2550 the girl's family know nothing about it.

(The bridegroom's people raise) an outcry, saying, "Half the affair is concluded: the conditions that are (necessary) on our side have been fulfilled.

We have swept and garnished the rooms and have risen up (from our labour) intoxicated and glad with this ardent desire (to receive the bride)."

Has any message come from over there? "No." Has any bird come hither from that roof? "No."

After (all) these missives (which ye have sent) one on the top of another[5], has any answer reached you from that neighbourhood?

[1] Literally, "do not weave on (attach to) me this hope."
[2] Literally, "two hundred."
[3] Literally, "(small) amount."
[4] Literally, "let fall into the world (spread abroad) the boast."
[5] Literally, "addition upon addition."

2555  "No; but our Friend is acquainted with this (matter), because inevitably there is a way from heart to heart."

Why, then, is the way devoid of (any) answer to (your) letter from the Friend who is (the object of) your hope?

There are a hundred signs (of response), (both) secret and manifest; but desist, do not lift the curtain from this door[1].

Return to the story of that foolish Dalqak who brought tribulation on himself by his silly meddling.

Afterwards the vizier said to him (the king), "O Pillar of the Truth, hear a word from thy humble slave.

2560  Dalqak came from the country on some (wicked) enterprise; (but now) his mind is changed and he has repented.

He is making the old (corruption) new with water and oil (varnish), he is evading (punishment) by means of buffoonery.

He has displayed the scabbard and concealed the sword: he must be tortured without mercy.

Unless you break the pistachio or walnut, it will neither reveal its heart (kernel) nor give any oil.

Do not listen to this skilful defence[2] of his; look at his trembling and his (pallid) colour.

2565  God hath said, '*Their mark is on their faces*,' for the mark is an informer and tell-tale.

This ocular evidence is opposed to that story (told by Dalqak), for this (whole race of) mankind are moulded of evil."

"O Ṣáḥib," cried Dalqak, wailing and sobbing, "do not endeavour to shed the blood of this miserable wretch.

Many a thought and fancy that is not real and true comes into the mind, O Prince.

*Verily, some suspicion is a sin*, O Vizier: injustice is not right, especially (when it is done) to a poor man.

2570  The king does not chastise one who vexes him: wherefore should he chastise one who makes him laugh?"

The words of the Ṣáḥib (vizier) impressed[3] the king, and he resolved to clear up this deceit and imposture.

"Take Dalqak to prison," he said, "and pay no attention to[4] his wheedling and hypocrisy.

Beat him, empty-bellied like a drum (as he is), that like a drum he may give us information.

(Whether) the drum is wet or dry or full or empty, its sound informs us of everything.

2575  (Beat him) in order that he may be compelled to declare the secret, so that these (apprehensive) hearts will be reassured.

---

[1] *I.e.* do not further expose their hypocrisy.
[2] Literally, "defence and skill."
[3] Literally, "took abode with (established themselves in the mind of) the king."
[4] Literally, "do not buy."

Since the shining truth is (a cause of) tranquillity, the heart
will not be calmed by lying words.

Falsehood is like a (piece of stick or) straw, and the heart like
a mouth: a straw never becomes (quietly) hidden in the mouth.

So long as it is there, he (who is annoyed by it) keeps moving
his tongue, in order that thereby he may eject it from his mouth.

Especially, when a straw (blown) by the wind falls into the eye,
the eye begins to water and shut and open.

We, therefore, now kick (out) this (man of) straw[1], in order 2580
that our mouth and eye may be delivered from (the disquiet
caused by) this straw."

Dalqak said, "O King, be calm: do not scratch the face of
clemency and forgiveness.

Why such an excessive haste to take revenge? I cannot fly
away, I am in thy hand (power).

'Tis not right to be hasty in (the case of) correction that is
(inflicted) for God's sake;

(But as regards) that (of) which (the motive) is (ill) humour
and casual anger, he (the corrector) is in a hurry (for fear) lest
he should become content (reconciled).

He is afraid that, if contentment come and his anger go, his 2585
revenge and the pleasure of (taking) it will be lost.

False appetite makes haste to (devour) the food for fear of
missing the pleasure: that is sickness indeed.

(If) the appetite be true, 'tis better to delay, in order that it
(the food) may be digested without difficulty[2].

Wilt thou beat me for the purpose of averting a (dreaded)
calamity, to the end that thou mayst see the crevice and block
it up,

So that the calamity will not issue from that crevice? Destiny
hath many a crevice besides that one.

Violence is not the means of averting calamity: the means is 2590
beneficence and pardon and kindness.

He (the Prophet) said, 'Alms is a means of averting calamity:
cure thy diseased ones by (giving) alms, O youth.'

'Tis not alms-giving to burn a poor man (in the fire of anger)
and to blind the eye that meditates on forbearance."

The king replied, "Charity and the occasion for it are ex-
cellent (things), but (only) when you perform an act of charity
in its (proper) place.

(If) you put the king in the rook's place, 'tis ruin (to the
game); likewise, (if you put) the horse (knight) in the king's
place, 'tis the act of an ignoramus.

Both bounty and severity are (sanctioned) in the religious 2595
Law: ('tis) for the king (to sit on) the throne, ('tis) for the horse
(to stand at) the gate.

---

[1] *I.e.* Dalqak.          [2] Literally, "without knot."

What is justice? To put (a thing) in its (right) place. What is injustice? To put it in its wrong place.

Nothing is vain that God created, (whether it be) anger or forbearance or sincere counsel or guile.

None of these things is absolutely good, nor is any of them absolutely evil.

The usefulness and harm of each depend on the place (occasion): for this reason knowledge is necessary and useful.

2600   Oh, many a punishment inflicted on a poor fellow is more meritorious[1] than (a gift of) bread and sweetmeat,

For sweetmeat (when eaten) unseasonably causes yellow bile, (whereas) slaps purge him of wickedness.

Give the poor fellow a slap in season: it will save him from beheading (afterwards).

The blow is really inflicted because of (his) evil disposition: the stick falls on the dust (in the garment of felt), not on the felt (itself).

Every Bahrám (emperor) has a banquet(-hall) and a prison: the banquet is for the sincere (friend) and the prison for the half-baked (churl).

2605   (If) a sore wants lancing and you apply a poultice to it, you will (only) establish the pus in the sore,

So that it will eat away the flesh underneath: (the result) will be a half (a mere fraction) of profit and fifty losses."

Dalqak said, "I am not saying, 'Let (my offence) pass'; I am saying, 'Take some care to investigate.'

Hark, do not bar the road of patience and deliberation: be patient, reflect for a few days.

In (the course of) deliberation thou wilt hit upon a certainty, (and then) thou wilt chastise me with a sure conviction (of knowing the truth)."

2610   Why, indeed, (be one who) *walks falling (on his face)* in wayfaring, when it behoves him to walk in an upright posture?

Take counsel with the company of the righteous: note the (Divine) command (given) to the Prophet, "*Consult them.*"

(The words) *their affair is (a matter for) consultation* are to this (the same) purpose, for owing to consultation mistakes and errors occur less (frequently).

These (human) intellects are luminous like lamps: twenty lamps are brighter than one.

There may happen to be amongst them a lamp that has become aflame with the light of Heaven,

2615   (For) the jealousy of God has produced a veil (of concealment) and has mingled the low and the lofty together.

He hath said, "*Travel*": always be seeking in the world and trying your fortune and (destined) lot.

---

[1] Literally, "better in regard to the Divine recompense."

In (all) assembly-places always be seeking amidst the intellects such an intellect as is (found) in the Prophet,

For the only heritage from the Prophet is that (intellect) which perceives the unseen things before and behind (future and past).

Amidst the (inward) eyes, too, always be seeking that (inward) eye which this epitome[1] has not the power to describe.

Hence the majestic (Prophet) has forbidden monkery and 2620 going to live as a hermit in the mountains,

In order that this kind of meeting (with saints) should not be lost; for to be looked on by them[2] is fortune and an elixir of immortality.

Amongst the righteous there is one (who is) the most righteous: on his diploma (is inscribed) by the Sultan's hand a *ṣaḥḥ*[3],

(Indicating) that the prayer (uttered by him) is (inseparably) linked with acceptance, (and that) the greatest of men and Jinn are not his peers.

(When) those who are sweet or sour (engage) in contention with him, in God's sight their argument is null,

For (God says), "As We have exalted him by (grace of) 2625 Ourselves, We have done away with (every) plea and argument (against him)."

Since the Hand of God has made the *Qibla* manifest, henceforth deem searching to be disallowed.

Hark, avert your face and head from searching, now that the Destination and Dwelling-place has come into view.

If you forget this *Qibla* for one moment, you will become in thrall to every worthless *qibla* (object of desire).

When you show ingratitude to him that gives you discernment, the thought that recognises the *Qibla* will dart away from you.

If you desire benefit and (spiritual) wheat from this Barn, do 2630 not part, even for half an hour, from those who sympathise,

For at the moment when you part from this helper you will be afflicted with *an evil comrade*.

*Story of the attachment between the mouse and the frog: how they tied their legs together with a long string, and how a raven carried off the mouse, and how the frog was suspended (in the air) and lamented and repented of having attached himself to an animal of a different species instead of sorting with one of his own kind.*

As it happened, a mouse and a faithful frog had become friends on the bank of a river.

Both of them were bound to (keep) a (daily) tryst: every morning they would come into a nook,

---

[1] *I.e.* the *Mathnawí.*        [2] Literally, "that look."
[3] The Arabic word *ṣaḥḥ*, meaning "it is correct," certifies that the document which bears it is genuine and valid.

27

(Where) they played heart-and-soul[1] with one another and emptied their breasts of evil (suspicious) thoughts.

2635 The hearts of both swelled (with joy) from meeting: they recited stories and listened to each other,

Telling secrets with and without tongue, knowing how to interpret (the Tradition), "A united party is a (Divine) mercy."

Whenever the exultant (mouse) consorted with the merry (frog), a five years' tale would come into his mind.

Flow of speech from the heart is a sign of (intimate) friendship; obstruction of speech arises from lack of intimacy.

The heart that has seen the sweetheart, how should it remain bitter? (When) a nightingale has seen the rose, how should he remain silent?

2640 At the touch of Khaḍir the roasted fish came to life and took its abode in the sea[2].

To the friend, when he is seated beside his Friend, a hundred thousand tablets of mystery are made known.

The brow of the Friend is a Guarded Tablet: to him (his friend) it reveals plainly the secret of the two worlds.

The Friend is the guide on the way during (his friend's) advance: hence Muṣṭafá (Mohammed) said, "My Companions are (like) the stars."

The star shows the way in (desert) sands and on the sea: fix thine eye on the (spiritual) Star, for he is the one to be followed.

2645 Keep thine eye always paired with (unseparated from) his face: do not stir up dust by way of discussion and argument,

Because the Star will be hidden by that dust: the eye is better than the stumbling tongue.

(Be silent) in order that he may speak whose innermost garment[3] is (Divine) inspiration which lays the dust and does not stir up trouble.

When Adam became the theatre of (Divine) inspiration and love, his rational soul revealed (to him) the knowledge of the Names[4].

His tongue, (reading) from the page of his heart, recited the name of everything as it (really) is.

2650 Through his (inward) vision his tongue was divulging the properties and quiddities of all things.

(It was bestowing) such a name as fits the things (named), not so as to call a catamite a lion (hero).

Nine hundred years Noah (walked) in the straight way, and every day he had a new sermon to preach.

His ruby (lip) drew its eloquence from[5] the corundum

---

[1] Literally, "played the backgammon of the heart."
[2] See Qur'án, XVIII, 59 foll.
[3] Or, "badge (characteristic mark)."
[4] Literally, "revealed He (God) taught (Adam) the Names" (Qur'án, II, 29).
[5] Literally, "was speaking from."

(precious jewel) in the hearts (of prophets): he had not read (mystical books like) the *Risála*[1] or the *Qútu 'l-qulúb*[2].

He had never learned to preach from (studying) commentaries; nay, (he learned) from the fountain of revelations and from the exposition (set forth) by the spirit—

From the wine that (is so potent that) when it is quaffed the 2655 water of speech gushes from (the mouth of) the dumb,

And the new-born child becomes an eloquent divine and, like the Messiah (Christ), recites (words of) mature wisdom.

The prophet David learned a hundred odes (melodies) from the mountain that gained from that wine (the gift of) sweet song[3].

All the birds left off chirping and joined their voices with King David as accompanists.

What wonder that a bird should be enraptured by him, since (even) iron obeyed the call of his hand?[4]

A roaring wind became murderous to (the people of) 'Ád, 2660 (but) to Solomon it became (serviceable) as a carrier.

A roaring wind carried on its head the throne of the king (Solomon) a month's journey every morn and eve.

It became both a carrier and a spy for him, making the talk of the absent to be apprehended by him.

The waft of air that caught the words of the absent would hasten to the ear of the king,

Saying, "Such-and-such an one said so-and-so just now, O mighty Solomon of auspicious fortune!"

*How the mouse made an arrangement with the frog, saying, "I cannot come to you in the water when I want (to see you). There must be some means of communication between us, so that when I come to the river-bank I may be able to let you know, and when you come to the mouse-hole you may be able to let me know, etc."*

This topic is endless. One day the mouse said to the frog, 2665 "O lamp of intelligence,

At times I wish to talk with you in secret, and you are gambolling in the water.

I am on the river-bank, crying aloud for you, (but) you in the water do not hear the wailing of lovers.

(When we meet) at this appointed time, O brave (frog), I never become weary of conversing with you."

The (ritual) prayer is five times (daily), but the guide for lovers is (the Verse), (*they who are*) *in prayer continually*[5].

---

[1] By Qushayrí.                    [2] By Abú Ṭálib al-Makkí.
[3] Literally, "gained the quality of the sweet-lipped."
[4] *I.e.* became plastic under his hand. See *Qur'án*, XXXIV, 10.
[5] *Qur'án*, LXX, 23, slightly altered.

2670  The wine-headache that is in those heads is not relieved by five (times) nor by five hundred thousand.

"Visit once a week" is not the ration for lovers; the soul of the sincere (lovers) has an intense craving to drink.

"Visit once a week" is not the ration for (those) fishes, since they feel no spiritual joy without the Sea.

Notwithstanding the crop-sickness of the fishes, the water of this Sea, which is a tremendous place, is but a single draught (too little to satisfy them).

To the lover one moment of separation is as a year; to him a (whole) year's uninterrupted union is a (fleeting) fancy.

2675  Love craves to drink and seeks him who craves to drink: this (Love) and that (lover) are at each other's heels, like Day and Night.

Day is in love with Night and has lost control of itself; when you look (inwardly), (you will see that) Night is (even) more in love with it.

Never for one instant do they cease from seeking; never for one moment do they cease from pursuing each other.

This one has caught the foot of that one, and that one the ear of this one: this one is distraught with that one, and that one is beside itself for this one.

In the heart of the beloved the lover is all: Wámiq is always in the heart of 'Adhrá.

2680  In the lover's heart is naught but the beloved: there is nothing to separate and divide them.

These two bells are on one camel: how, then, in regard to these twain should (the injunction), "Visit once a week," be admissible?

Did any one (ever) pay recurring visits to himself? Was any one (ever) a companion to himself at regular intervals?

That (of which I speak) is not the (sort of) oneness that reason apprehends: the apprehension of this (oneness) depends on a man's dying (to self);

And if it were possible to perceive this (oneness) by means of reason, wherefore should self-violence have become a duty?

2685  How, with such (infinite) mercy as He hath, would the King of intellect say unnecessarily "Kill thyself"?[1]

*How the mouse exerted himself to the utmost in supplication and humble entreaty and besought the water-frog to grant him access (at all times).*

He (the mouse) said, "O dear and affectionate friend, without (seeing) thy face I have not a moment's rest.

By day thou art my light and (power of) acquisition and strength; by night thou art my rest and comfort and sleep.

_____

[1] *I.e.* "practise self-mortification, die to self."

It would be a generous act if thou wouldst make me happy and kindly remember me early and late[1].

During (the period of) a (whole) day and night thou hast allowed me (only) breakfast-time for access (to thee), O well-wisher.

I feel in my liver five hundred cravings for drink, and bulimy 2690 (morbid hunger) is conjoined with every craving.

Thou, O prince, art unconcerned with my passion: pay the poor-tax on thy high estate, look (kindly) on (this) poor wretch.

This poor unmannerly wretch is not worthy (of thy favour); but thy universal grace is superior to (regard for) that.

Thy universal grace requires no support (reason to justify it): a sun strikes (with its beams) on (all) ordures.

Its light suffers no loss thereby, and the ordure is made dry and[2] (fit for) fuel,

So that the ordure goes into a bath-furnace, is converted into 2695 light, and illumines the door and wall of a bath-house.

(Formerly) it was a defilement, now it has become an adornment, since the sun chanted that spell (exerted that powerful influence) upon it.

The sun also warms the belly of the earth, so that the earth consumes the remaining ordures.

They become a part of the earth, and herbage springs up from them: even so doth God wipe out evil actions.

To ordure, which is the worst (of things), He does this (favour), that He makes it herbage and narcissus and eglantine.

(Judge, then), what God bestows in (the way of) recompense 2700 and bounty on the eglantines (good works) of devotion[3] (performed) faithfully.

Since He confers such a robe of honour on the wicked, (consider) what He bestows on the righteous in the place where He waits (for them).

God gives them that which no eye hath beheld, that which is not comprehensible in any tongue or language.

Who are we to (aspire to) this? Come, my friend, make my day bright with (thy) goodly disposition.

Do not regard my ugliness and hatefulness, though I am as venomous[4] as a mountain-snake.

Oh, I am ugly and all my qualities are ugly: since He planted 2705 me as a thorn, how should I become a rose?

Bestow on the thorn the springtide of the rose's beauty: bestow on this snake the loveliness of the peacock!

---

[1] Literally, "in time and out of time."
[2] Literally, "on account of a dryness becomes."
[3] Literally, "religious observances."
[4] Literally, "for through being full of venom I am."

I have reached the limit in perfection of ugliness: thy grace has reached the limit in excellence and accomplishment.

Do thou grant the boon sought by this consummate one from that consummate one, O thou who art the envy of the tall cypress.

When I die, thy bounty, though it is exempt from need, will weep for kindness' sake.

2710   It will sit beside my grave a long while: tears will gush from its gracious eye.

It will mourn for my deprivation (of beauty), it will shut its eyes to my abjectness.

Bestow a little of those favours now, put a few of those (kind) words as a ring into my ear!

That which thou wilt say (hereafter) to my dust—strew it (now) upon my sorrowful perception!"

*How the mouse humbly entreated the frog, saying, "Do not think of pretexts and do not defer the fulfilment of this request of mine, for 'there are dangers in delay,' and 'the Ṣúfí is the son of the moment.'" A son (child) does not withdraw his hand from the skirt of his father, and the Ṣúfí's kind father, who is the "moment," does not let him be reduced to the necessity of looking to the morrow (but) keeps him all the while absorbed, unlike the common folk, in (contemplation of) the garden of his (the father's) swift (immediate) reckoning. He (the Ṣúfí) does not wait for the future. He is of the (timeless) River, not of Time, for "with God is neither morn nor eve": there the past and the future and time without beginning and time without end do not exist: Adam is not prior nor is Dajjál (Antichrist) posterior. (All) these terms belong to the domain of the particular (discursive) reason and the animal soul: they are not (applicable) in the non-spatial and non-temporal world. Therefore he is the son of that "moment" by which is to be understood only a denial of the division of times (into several categories)¹, just as (the statement) "God is One" is to be understood as a denial of duality, not as (expressing) the real nature of unity.*

A certain Khwája, accustomed to scatter (pieces of) silver, said to a Ṣúfí, "O you for whose feet my soul is a carpet,

2715   Would you like one dirhem to-day, my king, or three dirhems at breakfast-time to-morrow?"

He replied, "I am more pleased with (the possession of) half a dirhem yesterday than with (the promise of) this (one dirhem) to-day and a hundred dirhems to-morrow."

(The mouse said), "A slap (given) in cash (immediately) is better than a donation (paid) on credit (hereafter): lo, I put the nape of my neck before thee: give (me) the cash!

¹ *I.e.* present, past, future, etc.

Especially as the slap is from thy hand, for both the nape and the slap inflicted on it are intoxicated (enraptured) with thee.

Hark, come, O soul of my soul and (O thou who art the soul) of a hundred worlds[1], gladly take the opportunity of (seizing) the cash of this (present) moment.

Do not stealthily remove thy moon-like face from the night- 2720 travellers, do not withdraw thyself[2] from this river-bed, O flowing water,

(But flow) in order that the river-bank may laugh (may be made to blossom) by the running water, and that jasmines may rear their heads on each brim of the river."

When you see that verdure is fresh[3] on the river-brim, then (you may) know (even) from afar that water is there.

The Maker hath said, "*Their mark is (on) their faces,*" for the verdant orchard tells a tale of rain.

If it rains during the night, no one sees (the rain), for (then) every soul and breath is asleep;

(But) the freshness of every beauteous rose-garden is (clear) 2725 evidence of the rain (that was) hidden (from view).

(The mouse said), "O comrade, I am of the earth, thou art of the water; but thou art the king of mercy and munificence.

By way of (conferring) bounty and dispensing (favour) so act that I may attain to (the privilege of) serving thee early and late.

I am always calling thee on the river-bank with (all) my soul, (but) I never experience the mercy of response.

Entrance into the water is barred against me because my (bodily) frame has grown from a piece of earth.

Use the aid either of a messenger or a token to make thee 2730 aware of my (piteous) cry."

The two friends debated on this (matter): at the close of the debate it was settled

That they should procure a long string, in order that by pulling the string the secret should be revealed.

(The mouse said), "One end must be tied to the foot of this slave (who is bent) double, and the other (end) to thy foot,

That by this device we two persons may come together and mingle as the soul with the body."

The body is like a string (tied) on the foot of the soul, drawing 2735 it (down) from Heaven to earth.

When the frog-like soul escapes from the mouse-like body into the water, (which is) the sleep of unconsciousness, it enters into a happy state;

(But) the mouse-like body pulls it back with that string: how much bitterness does the soul taste from this pulling!

[1] Or, "(O thou who art) a hundred worlds (to me)."
[2] Literally, "thy head."          [3] Literally, "intoxicated."

Were it not for the pulling of the scatter-brained[1] mouse, the frog would have enjoyed himself in the water.

You will hear the rest of it from the light-giving (illumination) of the Sun when you rise from slumber on the Day (of Resurrection).

2740    (The mouse said), "Knot one end of the string on my foot and the other end on thine,

That I may be able to pull thee to this dry land: lo, the end of the string (the object of my plan) is (now) clear (to thee)."

This news (proposal) was disagreeable to the heart of the frog, (who thought to himself), "This wicked fellow will bring me into a tangle."

Whenever a feeling of repugnance comes into the heart of a good man, 'tis not devoid of some significance[2].

Deem that (intuitive) sagacity to be a Divine attribute, not a (vain) suspicion: the light of the heart has apprehended (by intuitive perception) from the Universal Tablet.

2745    (For example) the refusal of the Elephant to march against the House (of Allah) notwithstanding the driver's efforts and cries of "Come on!"

In spite of all blows the Elephant's feet would not move, either much or little, towards the Ka'ba.

You would have said that its legs were paralysed or that its impetuous spirit was dead.

(But) whenever they turned its head towards Yemen, the fierce Elephant would begin to stride (forward) with the speed of a hundred horses.

(Since) the Elephant's perception was aware of the blow (coming) from the Unseen, how (much more) must the perception of the saint (endowed) with (the Divine) afflatus[3] be (aware)!

2750    Is it not (the case) that the prophet Jacob, that man of holy nature, (said) for Joseph's sake to all his (Joseph's) brethren—

When the brothers begged their father to give him to them, that they might take him to the country for a while,

(And) they all said to him, "Do not be afraid of harm (befalling him): give him one or two days' time, O father;

For why wilt not thou entrust thy Joseph to us in going about and travelling (for pleasure),

That we may play together in the meadows? In (making) this request we are trustworthy and beneficent"—

2755    Did not he (Jacob) say (to them), "I know this, that (the thought of) his being removed from me is kindling grief and sickness in my heart;

This heart of mine never lies, for my heart is illumined by the light of the highest heaven"?

---

[1] Literally, "having a putrid kernel," an epithet applied to one who talks idly and boastfully.

[2] Literally, "some (useful) knowledge" or "some (peculiar) art."

[3] Or, "the blessed saint." Cf. v. 1277 supra.

That (foreboding) was a decisive proof of (their) wickedness, but by (Divine) destiny he took no account (of it).

An intimation like that passed away from him (from his mind), because Destiny was at that moment (engaged) in (putting into operation the Divine) philosophy.

'Tis no wonder that a blind man should fall into a pit, (but) the falling of one who can see the way is beyond all wonder[1].

This Destiny employs diverse shifts: its eye-binding spell is 2760 *God doeth what He pleaseth.*

The heart knows and yet knows not its (Destiny's) artfulness: its (hard) iron becomes (soft) as wax for the seal.

'Tis as though[2] the heart should say (to itself), "Since its (Destiny's) inclination is turned to (bringing) this (to pass), whatever may happen, let it come!"

Accordingly it makes itself heedless of this (happening) and binds its soul fast in the shackle thereof[3].

If that exalted one (the prophet or saint) is checkmated (worsted) in this (matter), 'tis not (really) checkmate, 'tis tribulation.

A single tribulation redeems him from a hundred tribulations, 2765 a single fall takes him (high) up on the ladders (of spiritual ascent).

The half-baked saucy fellow, whom the wine (of Love) has relieved from the surfeit of intoxication with a hundred thousand wicked half-baked (persons like himself),

Finally becomes mature and adept: he escapes from enslavement to this world and is made free.

He is made drunken with the everlasting wine, he becomes (spiritually) discerning, and is delivered from created beings,

From their weak conventional faith and from the illusions of their unseeing eyes.

Oh, what device can their mental perception employ, I wonder, 2770 against the ebb and flow of the trackless Sea?

From that Desert came (all) these signs of cultivation and prosperity; (thence) came (all) empires and kingships and vizierates.

Yearning with desire they (phenomenal ideas) come in troops from the Desert of Non-existence into the visible (material) world.

Caravan on caravan, they arrive from this Desert every evening and morning.

They come and seize our houses in distraint[4], (each one) saying, "I have arrived, 'tis my turn, do thou begone!"

When the son has opened the eye of reason (attained to years 2775 of discretion), the father at once puts his (own) baggage in the cart.

---

[1] Literally, "is the father of wonder."    [2] Literally, "you might say."
[3] *I.e.* submits to the inevitable.    [4] *I.e.* occupy our hearts.

'Tis (like) the King's highway—(travellers) departing and arriving, one going in this direction, another in that direction.

Consider well! We, (though apparently) sitting still, are (really) marching: don't you see that we are bound for a new place (of abode)?

You do not get (and spend) your capital for any present need; nay, but (you keep it) for your ultimate purposes.

The traveller, then, O devotee of the Way, is he whose march and face are towards the future,

2780 Even as the troops of Phantasy are at every moment arriving (and passing) unweariedly through the curtains of the heart.

If (these) ideas are not (sprung) from one (and the same) Plantation, how are they coming to the heart on each other's heels?

Company after company, the army of our ideas, (impelled) by thirst, is speeding towards the fountain of the heart.

They fill their jars and go: they are continually appearing and vanishing.

Regard (your) thoughts as stars of the sky (which are) revolving in the sphere of another heaven.

2785 (If) you have experienced good fortune (spiritual thoughts), give thanks (to God) and do works of charity; (if) you have experienced bad fortune (sensual thoughts), give alms and ask pardon (of God).

Who am I in relation to this?[1] Come, O my King, make my ruling star auspicious and wheel once (towards me)[2].

Illumine my spirit with moonbeams, for my soul is blackened (eclipsed) by contact with the (Dragon's) Tail[3].

Deliver it from fancy and vain imagination and opinion, deliver it from the well and the tyranny of the rope,

In order that through Thy goodly lovingkindness a heart (such as mine) may lift its wings and soar up from a (body of) water and earth.

2790 O Prince of Egypt and faithful keeper of thy promise, the wronged Joseph is in thy prison.

Quickly dream a dream of his release, for *God loveth the beneficent.*

The seven noxious lean kine are devouring its (the spirit's) seven fat kine.

The seven dry, ugly, and unapproved ears of corn are feeding on its fresh ears.

Famine has arisen in its Egypt, O mighty Potentate: hark, O King, do not continue to sanction this.

[1] *I.e.* "I am helpless before the Divine destiny, which brings good or evil fortune to every one."

[2] *I.e.* "let Thy favour descend upon me."

[3] One of the two places where the moon's apparent path intersects the ecliptic.

Let my Joseph sit in Thy prison, O King: come, deliver me 2795
from the wiles of the women.

My mother's lust caused me to fall from the highest heaven
which was my tethering-place (stable), for (God said), *Fall ye
down!*

So by the artfulness of a crone I fell from (a state of) complete
perfection into the prison of the womb.

She brings the spirit from the highest heaven to the (corporeal)
*Ḥatīm* (enclosure): great must be the craft of women.

(Both) my first and my last fall were caused by woman[1], since
I was spirit—and how have I become body?

Hearken to this lament of Joseph in his lapse (from grace), 2800
or take pity on that distraught Jacob.

Shall I complain of my brethren or of the women who have
cast me, like Adam, from the gardens (of Eden)?

I am withered like leaves in December because I have eaten
the wheat[2] from the Paradise of union.

When I saw Thy graciousness and kindness and Thy greeting
of peace and Thy message,

I produced rue (to burn as a charm) against the evil eye; (but)
the evil eye reached even my rue.

('Tis) only Thy languishing eyes (that) are able to avert every 2805
evil eye (whether) in front or behind.

Thy good eye, O King, defeats and extirpates the evil eye:
how excellent it is as a remedy!

Nay, from Thine eye come (wondrous) alchemies (trans-
mutations): they turn the evil eye into the good eye.

The King's eye hath smitten the eye of the falcon-heart, and
its falcon-eye hath become mightily aspiring,

So that, because of the great aspiration which it has gained
from the (King's) look, the royal falcon will (now) catch (hunt)
nothing but the fierce lion.

What (of the) lion? The spiritual royal falcon is Thy quarry 2810
and at the same time Thou art its prey.

The call uttered by the falcon-soul in the meadow of devotion
is cries of "*I love not them that set.*"

From Thy infinite bounty there came an (inward) eye to the
falcon-soul that was flying for Thy sake.

From Thee its nose gained (the inward sense of) smell, and
its ear the (inward) hearing: to each sense was allotted a portion
(of the spiritual sense that was) distributed (amongst them
all).

Since Thou givest to each sense the means of access to the
Unseen, that (spiritual) sense is not subject to the frailty of
death and hoary eld.

---

[1] *I.e.* "firstly by Eve and lastly by my own mother."
[2] *I.e.* the forbidden fruit.

2815 Thou art the Lord of the kingdom: Thou givest to the (spiritual) sense something (peculiar to itself), so that that sense exercises sovereignty over (all) the senses.

*Story of the night-thieves with whom Sultan Maḥmúd fell in during the night (and joined them), saying, "I am one of you"; and how he became acquainted with their affairs, etc.*

While King Maḥmúd was roaming about alone at night he encountered a band of thieves.

Thereupon they said to him, "Who art thou, O honest man?" "I am one of you," replied the King.

One (of the thieves) said, "O company practised in cunning, let each of us declare his (special) talent;

Let him tell his comrades in the night-talk what (eminent) skill he possesses in his nature."

2820 One said, "O ye fellows who are exhibiting (your) cleverness, my specialty lies in my two ears.

(It is this), that I know what a dog is saying when it barks." The (rest of the) party replied, "Two *dángs* of a *dínár*[1]."

Another (thief) said, "O company of gold-worshippers, my specialty lies wholly in my eyes.

If I see any one in the world by night, I know him by day without (having any) doubt (as to his identity)."

Another said, "My specialty lies in my arm: I make tunnels (through walls) by strength of hand."

2825 Another said, "My specialty lies in my nose: my business is to detect the (characteristic) smell in (different) earths (soils).

The secret of 'men are mines' has yielded itself (to me), so that (I know the reason) why the Prophet has said it.

From (smelling) the earth of the body I know how much good ore is (hidden) therein and what (sort of) mine it holds.

In one mine is contained gold immeasurable, while (in the case of) another the revenue (derived) from it is less than the expenditure (cost of working it).

Like Majnún, I smell the soil and detect the soil (abode) of Laylá without mistake.

2830 I smell and know from (the scent of) every shirt whether 'tis (belongs to) a Joseph or an Ahriman (devil).

Like Aḥmad (Mohammed), who catches scent from Yemen, this nose of mine has gained (been endowed with) some portion of that (spiritual faculty),

(So that I can smell) which soil is a neighbour of gold, or which soil is empty and poor."

Another said, "Look here, my specialty lies in my fist: I can throw a lasso to the height of a mountain,

[1] Equivalent to "twopence in the pound," *i.e.* "your talent is of very small account."

Like Aḥmad (Mohammed), whose spirit threw a lasso so (high) that his lasso bore him to Heaven,

And God said to him, 'O thrower of the lasso (of thy aspira- 2835 tion) at the (celestial) House, deem that (act of throwing) to be from Me: *thou didst not throw when thou threwest.*'"

Then they (the thieves) asked the King, saying, "O man of authority, in what may thy special talent consist?"

He replied, "My specialty lies in my beard: I can save criminals from punishment.

When criminals are handed over to the executioners, as soon as my beard moves they are saved.

When I move my beard in mercy, they (the executioners) put an end to the killing and (all) the trouble."

The company said to him, "Thou art our *quṭb* (supreme 2840 chief), for thou wilt be the (means of our) deliverance on the day of tribulation."

[Afterwards they all set out together and went towards the palace of the fortunate King[1].]

When a dog barked on the right, (one of them) said, "It says 'The Sultan is with you.'"

Another smelt the ground from (the top of) a hill and said, "This belongs to the house of a widow."

Then the skilful master of the lasso threw his lasso, so that (by means of it) they got over the lofty wall.

When he (the thief who had previously smelt from the hill) 2845 smelt the earth in this other place, he said, "'Tis the earth (site) of the treasury of a peerless king."

The tunneller made a tunnel and reached the treasury: every one carried off some goods from the treasury.

The band took away much gold and gold-embroidered cloth and big pearls and quickly concealed them.

The King saw distinctly their lodging-place and (noticed) their personal appearance and names and (where they took) refuge and (what) way (they went).

He stole away from them and returned (to the palace), and (next) day related his adventure (to the ministers) in council.

Thereupon furious officers rushed away to arrest and pinion 2850 the thieves.

They (the thieves) came handcuffed into the council-chamber, and they were trembling in fear for their lives.

When they stood before the King's throne, that moon-like King was their (last) night's companion.

He (the thief) who could without hesitation recognise by day any one on whom he had cast his eye by night

---

[1] The two oldest MSS. omit this verse. There can be little doubt that it is spurious.

Saw the King on the throne and said, "This man was going about with us last night and was our comrade.

2855    He who has such a great talent in his beard—our arrest is the result of his enquiry."

His (the thief's) eye was a knower of the King: consequently he opened his lips (to speak) of (mystic) knowledge to his followers.

He said, "This King was (the subject of) *and He is with you*: he was seeing our actions and hearing our secret.

My eye made its way (to him), recognised the King by night, and all night long played the game of love with his moon-like face.

I will beg (forgiveness for) my people from him, for he never averts his face from the knower.

2860    Deem the eye of the knower to be the salvation of the two worlds, whereby every Bahrám (sovereign) obtained help.

Mohammed was the intercessor for every brand (of disgrace) because his eye *did not swerve* for aught except God.

In the night of this world, where the sun (of Reality) is veiled, he was beholding God, and (all) his hope was in Him.

His eyes received collyrium from *Did not We expand (thy breast)?* He saw that which Gabriel could not endure.

The orphan to whom (to whose eyes) God applies collyrium becomes the orphan (unique) pearl endowed with (Divine) guidance.

2865    Its light overpowers (that of all other) pearls, (because) it desires such an (exalted) object of desire.

(All) the (spiritual) stations (attainments) of God's servants were visible to him (the Prophet): consequently God named him 'The Witness.'

The weapons of the Witness[1] are a trenchant (veracious) tongue and a keen eye, whose nightly vigil no secret can elude.

Though a thousand pretenders (false witnesses) may raise their heads, the Judge turns his ear towards the Witness.

This is the practice of judges in dealing justice: to them the (truthful) witness is (like) two clear eyes.

2870    The words (testimony) of the Witness are equivalent to the eye because he has seen the secret (of Reality) with a disinterested eye.

The pretender (false witness) has seen it (too), but with self-interest: self-interest is a veil upon the eye of the heart.

God desires that you should become an ascetic (*záhid*) in order that you may abandon self-interest and become a Witness (*sháhid*);

For these motives of self-interest are a veil upon the eye: they enfold (muffle) the sight, like a veil.

---

[1] *I.e.* the Perfect Man.

Therefore he (the self-interested man) does not see the whole in (all its) various aspects[1]: your love of (created) things makes you blind and deaf.

Since the (Divine) Sun caused a light to dwell in his (the 2875 Witness's) heart, the stars no longer had any values for him.

Therefore he beheld the mysteries without veil: (he beheld) the journey of the spirit of the true believers and the infidels.

God hath not (created) in the earth or in the lofty heaven anything more occult than the spirit of Man.

God hath unfolded (the mystery of all things) moist or dry, (but) He hath sealed (the mystery of) the spirit: '(*it is*) *of the amr of my Lord*[2].'

Therefore, since the august eye (of the Witness) beheld that spirit, nothing remains hidden from him.

He is the absolute witness in every dispute: his word crushes 2880 the crop-sickness (which is the cause) of every headache[3].

God is named 'the Just,' and the Witness belongs to Him: for this reason the just Witness is the eye of the Beloved.

The object of God's regard in both worlds is the (pure) heart, for the king's gaze is fixed upon the favourite[4].

God's love and the mystery of His dallying with His favourite were the origin of all His veil-making (creation of phenomena).

('Twas) on that account, then, (that) in meeting (the Prophet) on the night of the Ascension our (Lord who is) fond of dalliance said, 'But for thee (I would not have created the heavens).'

This (Divine) Destiny rules (everything) good and evil: does 2885 not the Witness become the ruler of Destiny?

The bondsman of Destiny became the Commander of Destiny: hail to thee, O keen-sighted one who art pleasing (to God)!

The knower made many a petition to the Known, saying, 'O Thou who watchest over us in heat and cold,

O Thou who givest us intimations in weal and woe, (though) our hearts are unaware of Thy intimations,

O (Lord) who daily and nightly seest us and whom we see not, (our) regarding the secondary cause (instead of the Causer) has muffled our eyes.

My eye has been chosen above (all other) eyes, so that the 2890 (Divine) Sun was beheld by me in the night (of material existence).

That was (through) Thy well-known grace, O Beauteous One;

---

[1] Literally, "with (all its) much and little."

[2] *Qur'án*, XVII, 87. In this verse the meaning of *amr* ("command" or "affair") is uncertain.

[3] *I.e.* the intoxication of worldliness, with all its painful consequences.

[4] Here and in the following verses the word *sháhid* (witness) is used in its erotic sense (minion).

and (as the proverb says), 'The perfection of kindness consists in making it complete.'

O Lord, *make our light complete* in the plain of Resurrection and deliver us from shameful and overwhelming indignities!

Do not let Thy night-companion be banished (from Thy presence) in the day-time, do not inflict farness (separation) on the soul that has experienced nearness (union).

Absence from Thee is a grievous and tormenting death, especially the absence that comes after enjoyment of Thy favour.

2895 Do not put him that hath seen Thee in the position of one that hath not seen (Thee): sprinkle water on his verdure that has sprung up.

I have not acted recklessly (heedlessly) while faring (on Thy Way): do not Thou either act recklessly (ruthlessly) in pricking (inflicting pain upon me).

Oh, do not drive far from Thy face him who once beheld Thy face!

To behold the face of any one but Thee is (like the torture of) an iron collar for the throat: everything except God is vain.

They are vain, but they show me the right way because vanity attracts (only) the vain.

2900 Each one of the atoms on atoms which exist in this earth and heaven is like amber (a magnet) for its congener.

The belly attracts bread to its resting-place; the heat of the liver attracts water.

The eye is an attractor of beautiful persons from these (different) quarters of the town; the brain (nose) is seeking (to attract) scents from the rose-garden,

Because the sense peculiar to the eye is an attractor of colour, while the brain and nose attract sweet perfumes.

O Lord who knowest the secret, do Thou preserve us from these attractions by the attraction of Thy grace!

2905 Thou, O Purchaser[1], art dominant over (all) attractors: it would be fitting if Thou redeem the helpless."

He turned his face to the King as a thirsty man to a cloud— he who on the Night of Power was the Full-moon's own.

Since his tongue and his spirit were His (the King's), (he was not afraid, for) he who is His may converse with Him boldly.

He said, "We have been bound (in chains) like the spirit in its prison of clay: Thou art the Sun (illuminator) of the spirit on the Day of Judgement.

O King whose course is concealed (from view), the time is come for Thee graciously to make a movement (sign) with Thy beard in clemency.

2910 Each one (of us) has displayed his specialty: all those talents have (only) increased (our) ill-fortune.

---

[1] See *Qur'án*, IX, 112.

Those talents have bound our necks, by those high attainments[1] we are (thrown) headlong and (laid) low.

(Our) talent is *a cord of palm-fibre on our neck*: there is no help (to be gained) from those accomplishments on the day of death."

(None of them avails) save only the specialty of that man endowed with goodly perceptions whose eye was recognising the Sultan in the (darkness of) night.

All those talents were (as) ghouls (waylaying travellers) on the road, except (that of) the eye which was aware of the King.

On the day of audience the King was ashamed (to refuse the 2915 petition) of him whose gaze was (fixed) on the King's face at night.

And the dog that is acquainted with the loving King—even him you must entitle "the Dog of the Cave."

Excellent, too, is the specialty (residing) in the ear; for he (who possesses it) by (hearing) the bark of a dog is made aware of the Lion.

When the dog is awake during the night, like a watchman, he is not ignorant of the nightly vigil of the (spiritual) kings.

Hark, you must not disdain them that have a bad name[2]: you must set your mind on their inward parts (spiritual qualities).

Whoever has once got a bad name must not seek (to win) a 2920 (good) name and (thereby) become half-baked.

Oh, many a (piece of) gold is made (like) black polished iron in order that it may be saved from pillage and calamity.

*Story of the sea-cow[3]: how it brings up the royal pearl from the depths of the ocean and at night lays it on the seashore and feeds in the resplendence and lustre thereof; and how the trader comes forth from his hiding-place and, when the cow has gone some distance away from the pearl, covers the pearl with loam and black clay and runs off and climbs a tree; and so on to the end of the story and exposition.*

The water-cow fetches a pearl out of the sea, lays it on the meadow, and grazes around it.

In the radiance of the light of the pearl the water-cow feeds hurriedly on hyacinths and lilies.

The excrement of the water-cow is ambergris because its food is narcissus and nenuphar.

Any one whose food is the Light of (Divine) Majesty, how 2925 should not lawful magic (wondrous eloquence) spring from his lips?

Any one who, like the bee, has been given (Divine) inspiration as a prize, how should not his house be full of honey?

---

[1] Literally, "positions of eminence."
[2] *I.e.* those who have no regard for worldly reputation.
[3] The dugong.

The cow grazes in the light of the pearl; (then) suddenly it moves some distance away from the pearl.

A trader (appears and) puts black loam on the pearl, so that the meadow and verdant ground becomes dark.

Then the trader takes refuge on a tree, while the cow seeks the man with its hard horn.

2930    Twenty times the cow runs about the meadow, in order to impale[1] its enemy on its horn.

When the fierce cow despairs of (finding) him, it comes to the place where the pearl was laid

And sees the loam (spread) over the royal pearl; then it runs away from the clay, like Iblís.

(Since) Iblís is blind and deaf to the gist (spiritual content) of the clay (of Adam), how should the cow know that the pearl is in the clay?

(The Divine command) *fall ye* cast the spirit into abasement[2]: this menstruation excluded it from prayer (communion with God).

2935    O comrades, beware of this resting-place and of that (idle) talk: verily, sensuality is the menstruation of men.

(The Divine command) *fall ye* cast the spirit into the body, that the pearl of Aden might be hidden in clay.

The trader knows it, but the cow does not: the spiritual know, but not any clay-digger.

Every piece of clay in the heart of which there is a pearl—its pearl can tell the secrets of another (piece of) clay[3];

While the clay that has not been illumined by God's sprinkling (of light) cannot bear the companionship of the pieces of clay that are filled with pearls.

2940    This topic is endless, (and meanwhile) our mouse on the bank of the river is (waiting) on our ear (attention).

*Return to the Story of the mouse seeking the frog on the river-bank and pulling the string in order that the frog in the water might become aware of his seeking him.*

That (creature) moulded of love is pulling the string in hope of being united with the righteous frog.

He is perpetually harping on the heart-string, saying, "I have got the end of the string in my paw.

My heart and soul have become as (frail as) a thread in contemplation, ever since the end of the string (the prospect of success) showed itself[4] to me."

But suddenly the raven of separation came to chase the mouse and carried it off from that spot.

[1] Literally, "roll up."          [2] Literally, "low ground."
[3] *I.e.* the heart of the mystic can recognise others like itself.
[4] Literally, "showed a face."

When the mouse was taken up into the air by the raven, the 2945 frog too was dragged from the bottom of the water.

The mouse (was) in the raven's beak, and the frog likewise (was) suspended in the air, (with) its foot (entangled) in the string.

The people were saying, "How could the raven make the water-frog its prey by craft and cunning?

How could it go into the water, and how could it carry him off? When was the water-frog (ever) the raven's prey?"

"This," said the frog, "is the fit punishment for that one who, like persons devoid of honour, consorts with a rascal."

Oh, alas, alas for the sorrow caused by a base friend! O sirs, 2950 seek ye a good companion.

Reason complains bitterly of the vicious carnal soul: (they are as discordant) as an ugly nose on a beautiful face.

Reason was saying to him (the frog), "'Tis certain that congeniality is spiritual in origin[1] and is not (derived) from water and clay (the outward form)."

Take heed, do not become a worshipper of form and do not say this. Do not seek (to discover) the secret of congeniality in the (outward) form.

Form resembles the mineral and the stone: an inorganic thing has no knowledge of congeniality.

The spirit is like an ant, and the body like a grain of wheat 2955 which it (the ant) carries to and fro continually.

The ant knows that the grains of which it has taken charge[2] will be changed and become homogeneous with it[3].

One ant picks up (a grain of) barley on the road, another ant picks up a grain of wheat and runs away.

The barley does not hurry to the wheat, but the ant comes to the ant; yes (it does).

The going of the barley to the wheat is (merely) consequential: ('tis) the ant, mark you, (that) returns to its congener.

Do not say, "Why did the wheat go to the barley?" Fix your 2960 eye on the holder, not on that which he holds in pawn.

(As when) a black ant (moves along) on a black felt cloth: the ant is hidden (from view), (only) the grain is visible on its way,

(But) Reason says, "Look well to your eye: when does a grain ever go along without a grain-bearer?"

('Twas) on this account (that) the dog came to the Companions (of the Cave): the (outward) forms are (like) the grains, while the heart (spirit) is (like) the ant.

Hence Jesus goes (ascends) to the holy ones of Heaven: the

---

[1] Literally, "is by way of spiritual nature."
[2] Literally, "received in pawn."
[3] *I.e.* they will be eaten and assimilated.

cages (bodies) were diverse, (but) the young birds (spirits) were of the same kind.

2965   This cage is visible, but the young bird in it is hidden (from sight): how should the cage be moving without a cage-carrier?

Oh, blessed is the eye that is ruled by reason, (the eye) that discerns the end and is wise and cool.

Get (learn) the distinction between evil and good from reason, not from the eye that tells (only) of black and white.

The eye is beguiled by the verdure on dunghills, (but) reason says, "Put it to my touchstone."

The eye that sees (only) its (object of) desire is the bird's bane; reason, which sees the trap, is the bird's means of deliverance.

2970   (But) there was another trap which reason did not perceive; hence the inspiration which beholds the unseen sped in this direction[1].

By reason you can recognise congener and non-congener: you ought not to run at once to (outward) forms.

My being your congener is not in respect of (outward) form: Jesus, in the form of man, was (really) homogeneous with the angels.

The celestial Bird (Gabriel) carried him up above this dark-blue fortress (vault) as the raven (carried) the frog.

*Story of 'Abdu 'l-Ghawth and his being carried off by the peris and staying among them for years, and how after (many) years he returned to his (native) town and his children, but could not endure to be parted from the peris, because he was really their congener and spiritually one with them.*

'Abdu 'l-Ghawth was a congener of the peri: for nine years he was flying about invisibly, like a peri.

2975   His wife had offspring by another husband, and his ('Abdu 'l-Ghawth's) orphans used to talk of his death,

Saying, "A wolf or a brigand (must have) attacked him, or (perhaps) he fell into a pit or ambush."

All his children were passionately absorbed in (worldly) occupations: they never said (thought) that they had a father (who might be alive).

After nine years he came (back) temporarily: he appeared and (then) disappeared again.

He was the guest of his children for one month, and after that nobody saw any more of him[2].

2980   (Inward) homogeneity with the peris carried him off, just as a spear-thrust ravishes the spirit (from the body).

---

[1] *I.e.* the prophets were sent to inform us.
[2] Literally, "of his colour (external qualities)."

Since one who is destined for Paradise is (inwardly) homo-
geneous with Paradise, on account of homogeneity he also
becomes a worshipper of God.

Has not the Prophet said, "Know that liberality and virtue[1]
are (drooping) branches of (the trees in) Paradise (and have)
come (have been let down) into this world"?

Declare all loves to be homogeneous with (Divine) Love;
deem all wraths to be homogeneous with (Divine) Wrath.

The reckless man gets a reckless man (as his comrade),
because they are congenial in respect of their understanding.

The congeniality (spiritual affinity) in Idrís was (derived) from   2985
the stars: for eight years he was coming along with Saturn.

He was his (Saturn's) companion in the East and in the West;
(he was) his partner in conversation and familiar with his
characteristics.

When after his absence (from the body) he arrived (on earth),
on the earth he was always giving lessons in astronomy.

The stars gladly ranged themselves in ranks before him: the
stars attended his lectures,

So that the people (present), nobles and commons alike, would
hear the voices of the stars.

The attraction exerted by homogeneity (spiritual affinity)   2990
drew the stars down to the earth and caused them to speak
plainly before him.

Each one declared its name and its circumstances and ex-
pounded to him (the science of) astronomical observation.

What is (real) homogeneity? A species of insight whereby
people gain admission into (the minds and feelings of) one
another.

When God endows you with the same insight which He has
hidden in him (another person), you become his congener.

What draws a body (person) in any direction? Insight. How
should the conscious attract the unconscious?

When He (God) implants in a man the nature of a woman, fit   2995
catamitus et coitum dat.

When God implants in a woman the masculine nature, illa
femina feminam cupit et cum ea rem habet.

When He implants in you the qualities of Gabriel, you will
seek the way up to the air, like a young bird,

Gazing exspectantly, your eye fixed upon the air, estranged
from the earth and enamoured of heaven.

When He implants in you the asinine qualities, (even) if you
have a hundred wings (expedients) you will fly to the stable.

The mouse is not despised for its (outward) form: it becomes   3000
a helpless victim of the kite[2] because of its villainous character.

[1] Literally, "a praiseworthy quality or action."
[2] Literally, "mouse-eater."

It is a (greedy) food-seeker and a traitor and a lover of dark-
ness, besotted with cheese and pistachio nuts and syrup.

When the white falcon has the nature of a mouse, it is an
object of contempt to the mice and a disgrace to the wild animals.

O son, when the nature of Hárút and Márút was changed and
He (God) bestowed on them the nature of man,

They fell from (the eminence of) *verily, we are they that stand
in rows*[1] into the pit at Babylon (where they remain) shackled
head-foremost.

3005 The Guarded Tablet was removed from their sight: sorcerer
and ensorcelled became their tablet[2].

The same arms, the same head, the same figure—(yet) a
Moses is celestial (in his nature), while a Pharaoh is contemptible.

Be always in quest of the (inward) nature and consort with
him whose nature is good: observe how rose-oil (otto) has
received (imbibed) the nature (of the rose).

The earth of the grave is ennobled by the (holy) man (buried
there), so that the (owner of an illumined) heart lays his face and
hands on his grave.

Since the earth (of the grave) is ennobled and made fortunate
by the neighbourhood of the pure body,

3010 Do thou too, then, say, "(First) the neighbour, then the
house[3]": if thou hast a heart, go, seek a sweetheart.

His dust (body) is endued with the character of his soul: it
becomes a collyrium for the eyes of those who are dear (to God).

Oh, many a one sleeping like dust in the grave is superior in
usefulness and open-handedness to a hundred living.

He has taken away (from us) his shadow (body), but his dust
is overshadowing (blessing and protecting us): hundreds of
thousands of the living are in his shadow (under his protection).

*Story of the man who had an allowance from the Police Inspector
of Tabríz and had incurred (large) debts in expectation of that
allowance, since he was unaware of his (the Inspector's) death.
The gist (of the story is that) his debts were paid, not by any
living person, but by the deceased Inspector, (for) as has been said,
"He that died and found peace is not dead: the (real) dead one
is the man (spiritually) dead among the (materially) living."*

A certain dervish, who was in debt, came from the outlying
provinces to Tabríz.

3015 His debts amounted to nine thousand pieces of gold. It
happened that in Tabríz was (a man named) Badru'ddín 'Umar.

He was the Police Inspector, (but) at heart he was an ocean

---

[1] *I.e.* the angels in heaven.
[2] *I.e.* they turned their attention to studying and teaching the science of
magic.
[3] *I.e.* "before buying a house, make sure that you will have good neigh-
bours."

(of bounty): every hair's tip of him was a dwelling-place (worthy) of Ḥátim.

Ḥátim, had he been (alive), would have become a beggar to him and laid his head (before him) and made himself (as) the dust of his feet.

If he had given an ocean of limpid water to a thirsty man, such was his generosity that[1] he would be ashamed of (bestowing) that gift;

And if he had made a mote (as full of splendour as) a place of sunrise, (even) that would (seem) to his lofty aspiration (to) be an unworthy action.

That poor stranger came (to Tabríz) in hope of him, for to poor strangers he was always (like) a kinsman and relative. 3020

That poor stranger was familiar with his door and had paid innumerable debts from his bounty.

In reliance upon that generous (patron) he ran into debt, for the (poor) man was confident of (receiving) his donations.

He had been made reckless by him (the Inspector) and eager to incur debts in hope of (being enriched by) that munificent sea.

His creditors looked sour, while he was laughing happily, like the rose, on account of that garden (abode) of generous souls[2].

(When) his (the Moslem's) back is warmed by the Sun of the Arabs[3], what does he care for the moustache (vain bluster) of Bú Lahab? 3025

When he has a covenant and alliance with the rain-cloud, how should he grudge water to the water-carriers?

How should the magicians who were acquainted with God's Hand (Power) bestow (the name of) hands and feet upon these hands and feet?[4]

The fox that is backed by those lions will break the skulls of the leopards with his fist.

*How Jaʿfar, may God be well-pleased with him, advanced alone to capture a fortress, and how the king of the fortress consulted (his vizier) as to the means of repelling him, and how the vizier said to the king, " Beware!  Surrender (it) and do not be so foolhardy as to hurl thyself upon him; for this man is (Divinely) aided and possesses in his soul a great collectedness (derived) from God," etc.*

When Jaʿfar advanced against a certain fortress, the fortress (seemed) to his dry palate (to be no more than) a single gulp.

Riding alone, he charged up to the fortress, so that they (the garrison) locked the fortress-gate in dread. 3030

---

[1] Literally, "in (his) generosity."
[2] *I.e.* Tabríz. Cf. *v.* 3109.        [3] *I.e.* the Prophet.
[4] *I.e.* how should they attach any value to their own hands and feet which Pharaoh threatened to cut off?

No one dared to meet him in battle: what stomach have the ship's crew (to contend) with a leviathan?

The king turned to his vizier, saying, "What is to be done in this crisis, O Counsellor?"

He replied, "(The only remedy is) that you should bid farewell to pride and cunning, and come to him with sword and shroud[1]."

"Why," said the king, "is not he a single man (and) alone?" He (the vizier) replied, "Do not look with contempt on the man's loneliness.

3035    Open your eye: look well at the fortress: it is trembling before him like quicksilver.

He sits (alone) on the saddle, (but) his nerve is just as un-shaken as if an (army of the) East and West were accompanying him.

Several men rushed forward, like Fidá'ís (desperate assassins), and flung themselves into combat with him.

He felled each of them with a blow of his mace (so that they were hurled) headlong at the feet of his steed.

God's (creative) action had bestowed on him such a collected-ness that he was attacking a (whole) people single-handed.

3040    When mine eye beheld the face of that (spiritual) emperor, (all) plurality vanished from my sight."

The stars are many; though the sun is one, (yet) on his appearance their foundation is demolished.

If a thousand mice put forth their heads, the cat feels no fear or apprehension of danger.

How should mice advance (to the attack), O such-and-such? They have no collectedness in their souls.

The collectedness (that consists) in outward forms is a vain thing: hark, beg from the Creator collectedness of spirit.

3045    Collectedness is not the result of bodily multitude: know that body, like name, is built on (empty) air.

If there were any collectedness in the heart of the mouse, a number of mice would be collected (united) by a feeling of indignation,

And, rushing up like assassins, they would throw themselves on a cat without (giving her) any respite.

One would tear out her eyes in conflict (with her), while another would rip her ears with its teeth,

And another make a hole in her side: there would be no way of escape for her[2] from the united party.

3050    But the soul of the mouse has no collectedness: at the miaul of a cat (all) its wits fly out of its soul.

The mouse is paralysed by the wily cat, (even) if the numbers of the mice amount to a hundred thousand.

---

[1] I.e. "throw yourself on his mercy."
[2] Literally, "her way of escape would be lost."

What cares the butcher for the numerous flock (of sheep)? How can abundance of consciousness prevent (the approach of) slumber?

He (God) is the Lord of the kingdom: He gives collectedness to the lion, so that he springs on the herd of onagers.

A hundred thousand savage[1] and courageous onagers are as naught before the onset of the lion.

He is the Lord of the kingdom: He gives to a Joseph the 3055 kingdom of Beauty, so that he is (lovely) as the water of white clouds.

He bestows upon one face the radiance of a star, so that a king becomes the slave of a girl.

He bestows upon another face His own Light, so that at midnight it sees everything good and evil.

Joseph and Moses fetched light from God into their cheeks and countenances and into their *inmost bosoms*.

The face of Moses shot forth a flashing beam: he hung a veil[2] in front of his face.

The splendour of his face would have dazzled (men's) eyes as 3060 the emerald (blinds) the eyes of the deaf adder.

He besought God that the veil[2] might become a covering for that powerful Light.

He (God) said, "Hark, make a veil[2] of thy felt raiment, for the garment of gnosis can be trusted (to keep it safe),

Because that robe has become inured to[3] the Light: the Light of the Spirit shines through its warp and woof.

Nothing will be a (safe) repository (for it) except a mantle like this: nothing else can endure Our Light.

If Mt Qáf should come forward as a barrier (to it), the Light 3065 would rend it asunder like Mt Sinai[4]."

Through the (Divine) omnipotence the bodies of (holy) men have gained ability to support the unconditioned Light.

His (God's) power makes a glass vessel the dwelling-place of that (Light) of which Sinai cannot bear (even) a mote.

A lamp-niche and a lamp-glass[5] have become the dwelling-place of the Light by which Mt Qáf and Mt Sinai are torn to pieces.

Know that their (the holy men's) bodies are the lamp-niche and their hearts the glass: this lamp illumines the empyrean and the heavens.

Their (the heavens') light is dazzled by this Light and vanishes 3070 like the stars in this radiance of morning.

[1] Literally, "ten-horned," *i.e.* exceedingly strong, fierce, and untamable.
[2] Literally, "nose-bag."
[3] Literally, "has gained from (permeation by) that Light a (great power of) endurance."
[4] See *Qur'án*, VII, 139.
[5] See *Qur'án*, XXIV, 35.

Hence the Seal of the prophets has related (the saying) of the everlasting and eternal Lord—

"I am not contained in the heavens or in the void or in the exalted intelligences and souls;

(But) I am contained, as a guest, in the true believer's heart, without qualification or definition or description,

To the end that by the mediation of that heart (all) above and below may win from Me sovereignties and fortune.

3075 Without such a mirror neither Earth nor Time could bear the vision of My beauty.

I caused the steed of (My) mercy to gallop over the two worlds: I fashioned a very spacious mirror.

From this mirror (appear) at every moment fifty (spiritual) wedding-feasts: hearken to the mirror, but do not ask (Me) to describe it."

The gist (of the discourse) is this, that he (Moses) made a veil of his raiment, since he knew the penetrativeness of (the light of) that Moon.

Had the veil been (made) of anything except his raiment, it would have been torn to shreds, (even) if it had been (like) a solid[1] mountain.

3080 It (the Light) would penetrate through iron walls: what contrivance could the veil employ against the Light of God?

That veil had become glowing: it was the mantle of a gnostic in the moment of ecstasy.

The fire is deposited (becomes immanent) in the tinder because it (the tinder) is already familiar with the fire.

And in sooth Ṣafúrá[2], from desire and love for that Light of true guidance, sacrificed[3] both her eyes.

At first she closed one eye and beheld the light of his (Moses') face (with the other); and that eye was lost[4].

3085 Afterwards she could no longer restrain herself and (therefore) she opened the other (eye) and spent it on that Moon.

Even so the (spiritual) warrior (first) gives away his bread; (but) when the light of devotion strikes on him, he gives away his life.

Then a woman said to her, "Art thou grieving for the jonquil-like eye that thou hast lost?[5]"

"I am grieving," she replied, "(to think) would that I had a hundred thousand eyes to lavish (on that Moon)!

The window, (which is) mine eye, has been ruined by the Moon; but the Moon is seated (there) like the (buried) treasure in the ruin.

---

[1] Literally, "two-ply."
[2] The daughter of Shu'ayb and the wife of Moses.
[3] Literally, "gave to the winds."
[4] Literally, "flew away."
[5] Literally, "that is gone out of thy hand."

How should the treasure let this ruin of mine have (any 3090
regretful) memory of my porch and house?"

The light of Joseph's face, when he was passing by, used to
fall on the latticed windows of every villa,

And the people within the house would say, "Joseph is taking
a walk in this quarter and passing by";

For they would see the radiance on the wall, and then the
landlords (inmates) would understand (the cause of it).

The house that has its window in that direction is ennobled
by that Joseph's walking for recreation.

Hark, open a window towards Joseph[1] and begin to delight 3095
yourself by looking at him through the aperture.

The business of love is to make that window (in the heart), for
the breast is illumined by the beauty of the Beloved.

Therefore gaze incessantly on the face of the Beloved! This
is in your power. Hearken, O father!

Make a way for yourself into the innermost parts: banish the
perception that is concerned with other (than God).

You possess an elixir: treat your (vile) skin (with it), and by
means of this art (alchemy) make your enemies your friends[2].

When you have become beauteous you will attain unto the 3100
Beauteous One who delivers the spirit from friendlessness.

His moisture (grace) is nourishment for the garden of spirits;
His breath revives him that has died of anguish.

He does not (only) bestow (on you) the entire kingdom of
the base world; He bestows a hundred thousand kingdoms of
diverse kinds.

God gave him (Joseph), in addition to the kingdom of beauty,
the kingdom of interpretation (of dreams) without his having
studied and taken lessons (in that science).

The kingdom of beauty led him to prison[3]; the kingdom of
knowledge led him to Saturn[4].

Because of his knowledge and skill (in interpretation) the 3105
King (of Egypt) became his slave: the kingdom of knowledge is
more praiseworthy than the kingdom of beauty.

*Return to the Story of the man who incurred (great) debts and his
coming to Tabríz in hope of (enjoying) the favour of the Inspector
of Police.*

The poor stranger, (who was) afflicted with fear on account
of his debts, set out on the way to that *Abode of Peace.*

He went to Tabríz and the rose-garden district: his hope was
reclining (luxuriously)[5] on roses[6].

[1] *I.e.* "open your heart to God."
[2] *I.e.* "transmute your evil qualities into good ones."
[3] In consequence of the false charge brought against him by Potiphar's wife.
[4] *I.e.* raised him to eminence.   [5] Literally, "lying supine."
[6] *I.e.* he was perfectly at ease as to the fulfilment of his hopes.

From the glorious imperial city of Tabríz darted (beams of) light upon light (and shed radiance) on his hope.

His spirit was laughing for (joy in) that orchard of (noble) men and the fragrant breeze (blowing) from Joseph and the Egypt of union.

3110 He cried, "O cameleer, let my camel kneel for me (to alight): my help is come and my need is flown.

Kneel down, O my camel! All goes well[1]: verily, Tabríz is the place where princes alight (and abide).

Graze, O my camel, round the meadows: verily Tabríz is for us the most excellent source of bountifulness.

O camel-driver, unload the camels: 'tis the city of Tabríz and the district of the rose-garden.

This garden hath the splendour of Paradise: this Tabríz hath the brilliance of Heaven.

3115 At every moment of time joy-enkindling odours diffused by the Spirit (are floating down) from above the empyrean upon the inhabitants of Tabríz."

When the poor stranger sought the Inspector's house, the people told him that the loved one had passed away.

"The day before yesterday," they said, "he removed from this world: (every) man and woman is pale (with grief) for the calamity that has overtaken him.

That celestial peacock went to Heaven, when the scent (intimation) of Heaven reached him from invisible messengers.

Although his shadow was the refuge of people (seeking protection), the Sun rolled it up very quickly.

3120 He pushed off his boat from this beach the day before yesterday: the Khwája had become sated with this house of sorrow."

The (poor) man shrieked and fell senseless: you would say that he too had given up the ghost (and followed) on the heels (of his friend).

Then they threw julep and water on his face: his fellow-travellers wept and bewailed his plight.

He remained unconscious till nightfall, and then his soul returned, half-dead, from the Unseen.

*How the poor stranger was informed of the Inspector's death and begged God to pardon him for having relied upon a created being and having rested his hopes upon the bounty of a created being; and how he remembered the blessings he had received from God, and turned to God and repented of his sin: "then those who disbelieve equal (Him with others)."*

When he came to his senses, he said, "O Maker, I am a sinner: I was setting my hopes on (Thy) creatures.

3125 Though the Khwája had shown great generosity, (yet) that was never a match for Thy bounty.

---

[1] Literally, "my affairs are flourishing."

He gave the cap, but Thou the head filled with intelligence; he gave the coat, but Thou the tall figure and stature (of its wearer).

He gave me gold, but Thou the hand that counts gold; he gave me the beast for riding, but Thou the mind that rides it.

The Khwája gave me the candle, but Thou the cool (bright and cheerful) eye; the Khwája gave me the dessert, but Thou the food-receiving (stomach).

He gave me the stipend, but Thou life and animate existence; his promise was gold, but Thy promise the pure things (of the spirit).

He gave me a house, but Thou the sky and the earth: in Thy 3130 house he and a hundred like him (grow) fat.

Gold is Thine: he did not create gold. Bread is Thine: bread came to him from Thee.

Thou also gavest him generosity and pity, and his joy was increased by (showing) that generosity.

I made him my *qibla* (object of desire): I let the original *qibla*-Maker fall (into neglect)."

Where were we when the Judge of Judgement (Day) was sowing reason in the water and clay (of Adam)?—

Since ('twas for us that) He was producing the sky from non- 3135 existence and spreading this carpet of earth,

And making lamps of the stars, and of the (four) natural properties a lock together with the keys (to open it)[1].

Oh, how many structures hidden (from sight) and plain to see has He enclosed in this roof (heaven) and this carpet (earth)!

Adam is the astrolabe of the attributes of (Divine) Sublimity: the nature of Adam is the theatre for His revelations.

Whatever appears in him (Adam) is the reflexion of Him, just as the moon is reflected in the water of the river.

The figures (cut) on the "spider" (uppermost tablet) on his 3140 astrolabe are there for the sake of (typifying) the Eternal Attributes,

In order that its "spider" may give lessons in exposition of the sky of the Unseen and the sun of the Spirit.

Without a (spiritual) astronomer (to explain their significance), the "spider" and this astrolabe which guides aright fall (uselessly) into the hands of the vulgar.

God bestowed (knowledge of) this (spiritual) astronomy on the prophets: for (the mysteries of) the Unseen an eye that observes the Unseen is necessary.

These (worldly) generations fell into the well of the present world: every one saw in the well his own reflexion.

Know that what appears to you in the well is (really) from 3145

---

[1] *I.e.* the material world with the intellectual and spiritual faculties by which it is apprehended.

outside; else you are (like) the lion that plunged into the well (and was drowned)[1].

A hare led him astray, saying, "O such-and-such, this furious lion (thy rival) is at the bottom of the well.

Go into the well and wreak vengeance on him: tear off his head, since thou art mightier than he."

That (blind) follower of authority was subjugated by the hare: he was filled with boiling (fury) by his own fancy.

He did not say, "This image is not produced by the water: this is not (produced) by anything except the changing activity of the (Divine) Changer."

3150   So when you, O slave to the six (directions), wreak vengeance on your enemy you are in error concerning all the six[2].

That enmity in him (your enemy) is reflected from God, for it is derived from the (Divine) attributes of Wrath (which are manifested) there;

And that sin in him is homogeneous with[3] your sin: you must wash that (evil) disposition out of your own nature.

Your evil character showed itself to you in him because he was (like) the surface of a mirror to you.

When you have seen your ugliness in the mirror, O Ḥasan, do not strike (a blow) at the mirror!

3155   A lofty star is reflected in the water, and you cast earth on the star's reflexion,

Saying, "This unlucky star has come into the water to overthrow my good luck."

You pour upon it the earth of subjection, because on account of the resemblance you deem it to be the star (itself).

(When) the reflexion becomes hidden (from sight) and disappears, you think that the star is no more;

(But) the unlucky star is in the sky: 'tis in that quarter it must be cured (of its ill-luck);

3160   Nay, you must fix your heart on that which is quarterless (illimitable): the ill-luck in this quarter is (only) the reflexion of the ill-luck in the realm where no quarters exist.

Know that (all) gifts are the gift of God and are His bounty: 'tis the reflexion of those gifts that appears in (the world of) the five (senses) and the six (directions).

Though the gifts of the base (worldlings) be more (in number) than the sands, (yet) you will die and they will be left behind as an inheritance.

After all, how long does a reflexion remain in view? Make a practice of contemplating the origin (of the reflexion), O you who look awry.

[1] See translation of Book I, p. 72.
[2] *I.e.* "everywhere you see only your own fancies and fail to perceive that all action is the manifestation of Divine energy."
[3] *I.e.* the reflexion of.

When God bestows bounty on those who supplicate Him in their need, together with His gift He bestows on them a long life.

(Both) the benefit and the beneficiary are made enduring for 3165 ever. 'Tis He that brings the dead to life, so repair unto Him.

The gifts of God are mingled with you like the spirit, in such wise that you are they and they are you.

If you have no more appetite for bread and water, He will give you goodly nourishment without these twain.

If your fatness is gone, God will give you from yonder a (spiritual) fatness concealed in (bodily) leanness.

Since He gives the peri nourishment from scent and gives every angel nourishment from spirit,

What is the (animal) soul that you should make a support of 3170 (should rely upon) it? God will make you living by His love.

Ask of Him the life of love and do not ask for the (animal) soul: ask of Him that (spiritual) provision and do not ask for bread.

Know that (the world of) created beings is like pure and limpid water in which the attributes of the Almighty are shining.

Their knowledge and their justice and their clemency are like a star of heaven (reflected) in running water.

Kings are the theatre for the manifestation of God's kingship; the learned (divines) are the mirrors for God's wisdom.

Generations have passed away, and this is a new generation: 3175 the moon is the same moon, the water is not the same water.

The justice is the same justice, and the learning is the same learning too; but those generations and peoples have been changed (supplanted by others).

Generations on generations have gone, O sire, but these Ideas (Divine attributes) are permanent and everlasting.

The water in this channel has been changed many times: the reflexion of the moon and of the stars remains unaltered.

Therefore its foundation is not in the running water; nay, but in the regions of the breadth (wide expanse) of Heaven.

These attributes are like Ideal stars: know that they are 3180 stablished in the sphere of the Ideas (Realities).

The beauteous are the mirror of His beauty: love for them is the reflexion of the desire of which He is the (real) object.

This cheek and mole goes (back) to the Source thereof: how should a phantom continue in the water for ever?

The whole sum of pictured forms (phenomena) is a (mere) reflexion in the water of the river: when you rub your eye, (you will perceive that) all of them are really He.

Again, his (the debtor's) reason said (to him), "Abandon this seeing double: vinegar is grape-syrup and grape-syrup is vinegar.

Since, from defect (of vision), you have called the Khwája 3185 'other' (than God), be ashamed (contrite) before the jealous King, O man of double sight.

Do not suppose the Khwája, who has passed beyond the aether (the ninth celestial sphere), to be homogeneous with these mice of darkness.

Regard the Khwája as spirit, do not regard him as gross body: regard him as marrow, do not regard him as bone.

Do not look at the Khwája with the eye of Iblís the accursed, and do not relate him (refer his origin) to clay.

Do not call the fellow-traveller of the Sun 'a bat': do not call him who was worshipped (by the angels) a worshipper (of the material).

3190   This (Khwája) resembles the (other) reflexions; but (in reality) 'tis not a reflexion, 'tis the appearance of God in the likeness of a reflexion.

He beheld a Sun and remained frozen no more: the oil of roses was no longer (mingled with) oil of sesame.

Since the *Abdál* (Lieutenants)[1] of God have been transmuted, they are not (to be reckoned) among created beings: turn over a (new) leaf![2]

How should the *qibla* (object of worship), namely, the (Divine) Unity, be two? How should earth be worshipped by the angels?[3]

When a man sees the reflexion of apples in this river, and the sight of them fills his skirt with (real) apples,

3195   How should that which he saw in the river be a phantom, when a hundred sacks have been filled by his vision?

Do not regard the body, and do not act like those *dumb and deaf men (who) disbelieved in the Truth when it came to them.*

The Khwája is (the God-man of whom God said) *Thou didst not throw when thou threwest*: to see him is to see the Creator.

To serve him is to serve God: to see this window[4] is to see the Daylight[5];

Especially (as) this window is resplendent of itself: nothing (no light) is deposited (therein) by the sun and the Farqad (stars).

3200   From that (Divine) Sun, too, (beams) strike upon a window, but not in the ordinary way and direction.

Between the Sun and this window there is a way; (but) the (other) windows are not acquainted with it,

So that, if a cloud arise and cover the sky, in this window its (the Sun's) light will (still) be coruscating.

There is familiarity between the window and the Sun, otherwise than (by) the way of this atmosphere and the six directions.

---

[1] An exalted class of Ṣúfí saints.    [2] *I.e.* "discard this false opinion."
[3] *I.e.* in worshipping Ádam the angels really worshipped God.
[4] *I.e.* the Perfect Man.        [5] *I.e.* The Light of God.

To praise and glorify him (the Perfect Man) is to glorify God: the fruit[1] is growing out of the essential nature of this tray[2].

Apples grow from this basket in fine variety: 'tis no harm if 3205 you bestow on it the name 'tree.'

Call this basket 'the Apple-tree,' for between the two there is a hidden way.

That which grows from the fruit-bearing Tree—the same kind of fruit grows from this basket.

Therefore regard the basket as the Tree of Fortune and sit happily under the shade (protection) of this basket.

When bread produces looseness (acts as a laxative), why call it bread, O kindly man? Call it scammony.

When the dust on the road illumines the eye and the spirit, 3210 regard its dust as collyrium and know that it is collyrium.

When the sunrise shines forth from the face of this earth, why should I lift up my face to (the star) 'Ayyúq?

He (the Khwája) is naughted: do not call him existent, O bold-eyed (impudent) man! How should the sod remain dry in a River like this?

How should the new-moon shine in the presence of this Sun? What is the strength of a decrepit old woman (zál) against such a Rustam?

The (only real) Agent is seeking and prevailing (over all), to the end that He may utterly destroy (all unreal) existences.

Do not say 'two,' do not know 'two,' and do not call 'two': 3215 deem the slave to be effaced in his master.

The Khwája likewise is naughted and dead and checkmated and buried in the Khwája's Creator.

When you regard this Khwája as separate from God, you lose both the text and the preface[3].

Hark, let your (inward) eye and your heart pass beyond (transcend) the (bodily) clay! This is One Qibla (object of worship): do not see two qiblas.

When you see two you remain deprived of both sides (aspects of the One): a flame falls on the touchwood, and the touchwood is gone[4]."

---

[1] I.e. Divine attributes.
[2] I.e. the spirit of the Perfect Man.
[3] I.e. the inward and outward aspects of the One Reality.
[4] I.e. when God reveals Himself in His glory, the illusion of self-existence disappears.

29

*Parable of the man who sees double. (He is) like the stranger in the town of Kásh (Káshán), whose name was 'Umar. Because of this (name) they[1] (refused to serve him and) passed him on from one shop to another. He did not perceive that all the shops were one in this respect that they (the shopkeepers) would not sell bread to (a person named) 'Umar; (so he did not say to himself), "Here (and now) I will repair my error (and say), 'I made a mistake: my name is not 'Umar.' When I recant and repair my error in this shop, I shall get bread from all the shops in the town; but if, without repairing my error, I still keep the name 'Umar and depart from this shop (to another), (then) I am deprived (of bread) and seeing double, for I (shall) have deemed (all) these shops to be separate from each other."*

3220   If your name is 'Umar, nobody in the town of Kásh will sell you a roll of bread (even) for a hundred *dángs*.

When you say at one shop, "I am 'Umar: kindly sell bread to this 'Umar,"

He (the baker) will say, "Go to that other shop: one loaf from that (shop) is better than fifty from this."

If he (the customer) had not been seeing double, he would have replied, "There is no other shop";

And then the illumination produced by not seeing double would have shot (rays) upon the heart of him (the baker) of Kásh, and 'Umar would have become 'Alí.

3225   This (baker) says, (speaking) from this place (shop) to that (other) baker, "O baker, sell bread to this 'Umar";

And he too, on hearing (the name) 'Umar, withholds bread (from you) and sends (you) to a shop some way off,

Saying, "Give bread to this 'Umar, O my partner," *i.e.* "apprehend the secret (my real meaning) from (the tone of) my voice."

He also will pass you on from there (to another baker), (saying to him), "Hark, 'Umar is come to get some bread."

When you have been 'Umar in one shop, go (your way) and do not expect to obtain bread[2] in all Káshán.

3230   But if you have said in one shop, "(I am) 'Alí," (then you may) obtain bread from this place (shop) without being passed on (to another shop) and without trouble.

Since the squinter who sees two (instead of one) is deprived of the enjoyment of delicious food, (your case is worse, for) you are seeing ten, O you who would sell your mother!

Because of seeing double, wander (to and fro) like 'Umar in this Káshán of earth, since you are not 'Alí.

In this ruined monastery the man who sees double is (con-

---

[1] Literally "he," *i.e.* the baker whose shop he first visited.
[2] Literally, "and be deprived of bread."

tinually) removing from one nook to another, O (you who say to yourself), "The good (which I seek) is (to be found) there."

But if you get two eyes that can recognise God, (you will) see (that) the (entire) expanse of both worlds (is) full of the Beloved,

(And so) you escape from being transferred from place to 3235 place in this Káshán (which is) filled with fear and hope.

(If) you have seen buds or trees (reflected) in this River[1], do not suppose that they are a phantom (illusion) like (those of) any (ordinary) river;

For by means of the very reflexion of these images God is made real to you and sells (to you) the fruit (of reality).

By means of this Water the eye is freed from seeing double: it sees the reflexion, and the basket is filled (with fruit).

Therefore this (Water) is really an orchard, not water: do not, then, like Bilqís[2], strip yourself from (fear of being splashed by) the waves.

Diverse loads are (laid) upon the backs of asses: do not drive 3240 (all) these asses with one (and the same) stick.

One ass is laden with rubies and pearls, another with (common) stones and marble.

Do not apply this (uniform) principle to all rivers; in this River behold the Moon (itself), and do not call it a (mere) reflexion.

This is the Water of Khiẓr, not the water drunk by herbivorous animals and beasts of prey: everything that appears in it is Real.

From the bottom of this River the Moon cries, "I am the Moon, I am not a reflexion: I am conversing and travelling with (the River).

That which is (in the world) above is in this River: take 3245 possession of it either (in the world) above or in that (River) as you please.

Do not assume this River to be of (the same class as) other rivers: know that this ray of the moon-faced (Beauty) is the Moon (itself).

This topic is endless. The poor stranger wept exceedingly: he was heart-broken by grief for (the death of) the Khwája.

*How the (Inspector's) bailiff sought subscriptions in all parts of the city of Tabríz, and how (only) a small amount was collected, and how the poor stranger went to visit the Inspector's tomb and related this (pitiful) tale on his grave by the method of concentrating the mind on prayer (for his help), etc.*

The calamity of his debts became notorious, and the bailiff was distressed by his grief.

He (the bailiff) went round the city to collect subscriptions and everywhere, in hope (of exciting compassion), he told all that had happened;

[1] *I.e.* the Perfect Man.　　　　[2] See *Qur'án*, xxvii, 44.

3250 (But) that devoted beggar obtained by means of begging no more than a hundred dinars.

(Then) the bailiff came to him and took his hand and went (with him) to (visit) the grave of that very wonderful generous man.

He said, "When a servant (of God) gains the Divine favour so that he entertains a fortunate man,

And gives up his own wealth for his sake and sacrifices his own dignity for the sake of (conferring) dignity on him,

Gratitude to him (the benefactor) is certainly (the same as) gratitude to God, since (it was) the Divine favour (that) caused him to show beneficence[1].

3255 To be ungrateful to him is to be ungrateful to God: beyond doubt his right (to gratitude) is consequent on (that of) God.

Always give thanks to God for His bounties, and always give thanks and praise to the Khwája (your benefactor) too.

Though a mother's tenderness is (derived) from God, (yet) 'tis a sacred duty and a worthy task to serve her.

For this reason God hath said, '*Do ye bless him* (*the Prophet*),' for Mohammed was one to whom (the attributes of Divine Providence) were transferred.

At the Resurrection God will say to His servant, 'Hark, what have you done with that which I bestowed on you?'

3260 He will reply, 'O Lord, I gave thanks to Thee with (all) my soul, since the source of my daily provision and bread was in Thee.'

(Then) God will say to him, 'Nay, you did not give thanks to Me, inasmuch as you did not give thanks to him who made a practice of generosity.

You have done wrong and injustice to a generous man: did not My bounty come to you by his hand?'"

When he (the debtor) arrived at the tomb of his benefactor, he began to weep bitterly and broke into loud lamentation.

He said, "O thou who wert the support and refuge of every noble (righteous) man and the hope and helper of wayfarers,

3265 O thou on whose heart the care for our means of livelihood (lay constantly), O thou whose beneficence and charity were (like) the universal provision of sustenance,

O thou who wert (as) kinsfolk and parents to the poor in (paying) their taxes and expenses and in discharging their debts,

O thou who, like the sea, gavest pearls for those near (to thee) and (didst send) rain as a gift to those afar,

Our backs were warmed by thee, O sun (who wert) the splendour in every palace and the treasure in every ruin.

---

[1] Literally, "associated him with beneficence."

O thou in whose eyebrow none ever saw knots (wrinkles),
O thou (who wert) generous and bountiful as (the archangel)
Michael,

O thou whose heart was connected with the Sea of the Unseen, 3270
O thou who wert the invisible 'Anqá on the Qáf (mountain) of
munificence,

Who never tookest thought how much of thy wealth had gone,
and the roof of the azimuth (amplitude) of thy magnanimity was
never cloven[1],

O thou to whom in (every) month and year I and a hundred
like me had become a family (tenderly cared for) like thine own
children,

Thou wert our ready money and our movables and our furni-
ture, our fame and our glory and our fortune.

Thou art not dead; (but) our luxury and fortune are dead,
our happy life is dead and the sustenance that was provided in
full measure.

(Thou wert) a single person like (equivalent to) a thousand in 3275
warfare and in generosity; (thou wert) as a hundred Ḥátims in
the hour of lavishing bounties unselfishly.

If Ḥátim bestows dead (worldly goods) on the (spiritually)
dead (worldlings), he (is like one who) bestows a certain number
of walnuts (on children).

Thou at every moment art bestowing a life that, because of its
preciousness, cannot be contained in breath (words).

Thou art bestowing a life exceedingly enduring, real gold coin
exempt from depreciation and beyond count.

There exists no heir (even) to one (noble) disposition of thine,
O thou to whose abode Heaven is bowing in worship.

Thy grace is the shepherd of all who have been created, 3280
(guarding them) from the wolf of pain—a loving shepherd like
God's *Kalím* (Moses)."

One sheep fled from God's *Kalím*: the feet of Moses were
blistered (in following it) and his shoes dropped off.

(He continued) searching after it till nightfall, and (mean-
while) the flock had vanished from his sight.

The (lost) sheep was enfeebled and exhausted by fatigue:
then God's *Kalím* shook the dust off it,

And stroked its back and head with his hand, fondling it
lovingly like a mother.

Not (even) half a mite of irritation and anger, nothing but 3285
love and pity and tears!

He said (to the sheep), "I grant you (naturally) had no pity
on me, (but) why did your nature show (such) cruelty to itself?"

At that moment God said to the angels, "So-and-so is
suitable for prophethood."

[1] Read نَكَفْتٌ.

Muṣṭafá (Mohammed) himself has said that every prophet herded sheep[1] as a young man or boy,

(And that) without his having been a shepherd and (having undergone) that trial, God did not bestow on him the leadership of the world.

3290   A questioner said, "Even thou, O man of might?" "I too," he replied, "was a shepherd for a long while."

In order that their (the prophets') calmness and fortitude should be displayed, God made them shepherds before (investing them with) prophethood.

Every prince who performs the task of shepherding mankind in such wise that he obeys the Commandments (of God),

(And) in tending them with foresight and understanding shows a forbearance like that of Moses,

Inevitably God will bestow on him a spiritual shepherd's office (exalted) above the sphere of the moon,

3295   Even as He raised the prophets from this herding (of sheep) and gave them the task of tending the righteous.

"Thou, in short, O Khwája, hast performed in thy shepherding (of the poor) that which causes him that hates thee to become blind (utterly confounded).

I know that God will give thee yonder an everlasting sovereignty in compensation.

In hope of thy (open) hand as (bountiful as) the ocean and (in reliance) upon thy giving (me) a stipend and discharging (my obligations) in full,

I recklessly incurred debts (amounting to) nine thousand pieces of gold: where art thou, that these dregs may become clear?

3300   Where art thou, that laughing like the (verdant) garden thou mayst say, 'Receive that (sum) and ten times as much from me'?

Where art thou, that thou mayst make me laughing (flourishing) and show favour and beneficence as lords (are wont to do)?

Where art thou, that thou mayst take me into thy treasury and make me secure from debt and poverty?—

(Whilst) I am saying continually, 'Enough!' and thou, my bounteous friend, replying, 'Accept this too for my heart's sake.'

How can a world (microcosm) be contained under the clay (of the body)? How should a Heaven be contained in the earth?

3305   God forfend! Thou art beyond this world both in thy lifetime and at the present hour.

A bird is flying in the atmosphere of the Unseen: its shadow falls on a piece of earth.

The body is the shadow of the shadow of the shadow of the heart: how is the body worthy of the (lofty) rank of the heart?

---

[1] Literally, "shepherded it (the sheep)."

A man lies asleep: his spirit is shining in Heaven, like the sun, while his body is in bed.

His spirit is hidden in the Void, like the fringe (sewn inside a garment): his body is turning to and fro beneath the coverlet.

Since the spirit, being *from the command of my Lord*, is in- 3310 visible, every similitude that I may utter (concerning it) is denying (the truth of the description).

Oh, where, I wonder, is thy sugar-shedding ruby (lip) and those sweet replies and mysteries of thine?

Oh, where, I wonder, is that candy-chewing cornelian (lip), the key to the lock of our perplexities?

Oh, where, I wonder, is that breath (keen) as Dhu 'l-faqár[1], that used to make our understandings distraught?

How long, like a ringdove seeking her nest, (shall I cry) 'where (*kú*) and where and where and where and where and where?'

Where (is he now)? In the place where are the Attributes of 3315 (Divine) Mercy, and (the Divine) Power and Transcendence, and (celestial) Intelligence.

Where (is he now)? In the same place where his heart and thought always dwelt, like the lion in his jungle.

Where (is he now)? In that place whither the hope of (every) man and woman turns in the hour of anguish and sorrow.

Where (is he now)? In the place to which in time of illness the eye takes wing in hope of (regaining) health—

In that quarter where, in order to avert a calamity, you seek wind for (winnowing) the corn or (speeding) a ship (on its way);

In that quarter which is signified by the heart when the tongue 3320 utters the expression ' *Yá Hú*[2].'

He is always with God (and) beyond 'where? where?[3]' (*kú, kú*). Would that like weavers I might have said *má kú*![4]

Where is our reason, that it should (be able to) perceive the spiritual West and East (the universal Divine epiphany) flashing forth a hundred kinds of splendour?

His (the Khwája's) ebb and flow was caused by a (great) foaming Sea: (now) the ebb has ceased and (only) the flow remains.

I am nine thousand (dinars) in debt and have no resources: there are (only) a hundred dinars, (resulting) from this sub-scription.

God hath withdrawn thee (from this world) and I am left in 3325 agony: I am going (hence) in despair, O thou whose dust is sweet!

[1] The name of a sword belonging to the Prophet.
[2] *I.e.* 'O He (who is the only real Being).'
[3] *I.e.* beyond all spatial relations.
[4] The poet plays on the words *mákú* (a weaver's shuttle) and *má kú* (where are we?).

Keep in thy mind a prayer for thy grief-stricken (mourner),
O thou whose face and hands and prayers are auspicious.

I come to the spring and the source of (all) fountains: I find
in it instead of water blood.

The sky is the same sky, (but) 'tis not the same moonlight:
the river is the same river, (but) the water is not the same
water.

There are benefactors, (but) where is that one who was found
(by all) to be (supremely) good? There are stars, (but) where is
that sun?

3330 Thou hast gone unto God, O venerated man: I too, therefore,
will go unto God."

God is the assembly-place where the generations (of mankind)
are mustered under His banner: *all are brought before Us.*

The pictures (phenomenal forms), whether unconscious or
conscious (of it), are (always) present in the hand of the Painter.

Moment by moment that traceless One is setting down (what
He will) on the page of their thought and (then) obliterating
it.

He is putting anger (there) and taking acquiescence away: He
is putting stinginess (there) and taking generosity away.

3335 Never for (even) half a wink at eve or morn are my ideas
exempt from this (process of) imprinting (on the mind) and
obliterating.

The potter works at the pot to fashion it: how should the pot
become broad and long of itself?

The wood is kept constantly in the carpenter's hand: else how
should it be hewn and put into right shape?

The garment (while being made) is in the hands of a tailor:
else how should it sew and cut of itself?

The water-skin is with the water-carrier, O adept: else how
should it become full or empty by itself?

3340 You are being filled and emptied at every moment: know,
then, that you are in the hand of His working.

On the Day when the eye-bandage falls from the eye, how
madly will the work be enamoured of the Worker!

(If) you have an eye, look with your own eye: do not look
through the eye of an ignorant fool.

(If) you have an ear, hearken with your own ear: why be
dependent on[1] the ears of blockheads?

Make a practice of seeing (for yourself) without blindly
following any authority: think in accordance with the view of
your own reason.

[1] Literally, "in pawn to."

*How the Khwárizmsháh, may God have mercy upon him, while riding for pleasure, saw an exceedingly fine horse in his cavalcade; and how the king's heart fell in love with the beauty and elegance of the horse; and how the 'Imádu 'l-Mulk caused the horse to appear undesirable to the king[1]; and how the king preferred his (the 'Imádu 'l-Mulk's) word to his own sight, as the Ḥakím (Saná'í), may God have mercy upon him, has said in the Iláhi-náma:*

*"When the tongue of envy turns slave-dealer (salesman), you may get a Joseph for an ell of linen."*

*Owing to the envious feelings of Joseph's brethren when they acted as brokers (in selling him), (even) such a great beauty (as his) was veiled from the heart (perception) of the buyers and he began to seem ugly (to them), for "they (his brethren) were setting little value on him."*

A certain Amír had a fine horse: there was no equal to it in the Sultan's troop. 3345

Early[2] (one morning) he rode out in the royal cavalcade: suddenly the Khwárizmsháh observed the horse.

Its beauty and colour enraptured the king's eye: till his return (home) the king's eye was following the horse.

On whichever limb he let his gaze fall, each seemed to him more pleasing than the other.

Besides elegance and beauty and spiritedness, God had bestowed on it (other) exquisite qualities.

Then the king's mind sought to discover what it could be that waylaid (and overpowered) his reason, 3350

Saying, "My eye is full and satisfied and wanting naught: it is illumined by two hundred suns[3].

Oh, the rook of (other) kings is (but) a pawn in my sight, (and yet) a demi-horse[4] enraptures me without any justification.

The Creator of witchery has bewitched me: 'tis a (Divine) attraction (exerted upon me), not the peculiar virtues of this (horse)."

He recited the *Fátiḥa* and uttered many a *lá ḥawl*, (but)-the *Fátiḥa* (only) increased the passion in his breast,

Because the *Fátiḥa* itself[5] was drawing him on: the *Fátiḥa* is unique in drawing on (good) and averting (evil). 3355

If (aught) other (than God) appear (to you), 'tis (the effect of) His illusion; and if (all) other (than God) vanish from sight, 'tis (the effect of) His awakening (you to the reality).

Then it became certain to him (the king) that the attraction

---

[1] Literally, "cold in the king's heart."     [2] Read دلان.

[3] *I.e.* two hundred splendid horses.

[4] *I.e.* "a bit of horseflesh." In Persian chess "the horse" corresponds to our "knight."

[5] *I.e.* God, in whom the *Fátiḥa* subsists as an eternal attribute.

was from Yonder: the action of God is producing marvels at every moment.

Because of the (Divine) probation a stone horse (or) a stone cow becomes, through God's deception, an object of worship.

In the eyes of the infidel (idolater) the idol has no second (is without parallel), (though) the idol has neither glory nor spirituality.

3360     What is the attracting power, hidden in the hiddenmost, that shines forth in this world from (its source in) the other world?

The intellect is barred, and the spirit also, from (access to) this ambush; I cannot see it: see it (if) you can!

When the Khwárizmsháh returned from his ride, he conferred with the nobles of his kingdom.

Then he immediately ordered the officers to fetch the horse from that (Amír's) household.

(Quick) as fire, the party (of officers) arrived (there): the Amír who was like a mountain (in pride and stubbornness) became (soft and weak) as a piece of wool.

3365     He almost expired[1] from the anguish and defraudment: he saw no (means of) protection except the 'Imádu 'l-Mulk;

For the 'Imádu 'l-Mulk was the foot of the banner to which every victim of injustice and every one stricken by distress would flock for refuge.

In sooth there was no chief more revered than he: in the eyes of the Sultan he was like a prophet.

He was unambitious, strong-minded, devout, ascetic, one who kept vigils and was (like) Ḥátim in generosity;

Very felicitous in judgement, endowed with foresight, and sage: his judgement had been proved in everything that he sought to attain.

3370     (He was) generous both in self-sacrifice and in sacrificing wealth: (he was) always seeking the Sun of the invisible world, like the new-moon.

In his (worldly) princedom he felt strange and embarrassed: he was clad (inwardly) in the attributes of (spiritual) poverty and love (of God).

He was like a father to every one in need: before the Sultan he was an intercessor and the means of averting harm.

To the wicked he was a covering (to palliate their offences), like the clemency of God: his nature was opposite to (that of other) created beings and apart (from theirs).

Many a time he would have gone alone to the mountains (in order to seclude himself), (but) the Sultan prevented (dissuaded) him by (making) a hundred humble entreaties.

3375     If at every moment he had interceded for a hundred sins, the Sultan's eye would have been abashed before him.

        [1] Literally, "his soul reached his lips."

He (the Amír) went to the noble 'Imádu 'l-Mulk: he bared his head and fell on the ground,

Saying, "Let him (the king) take my harem together with all that I possess! Let any raider seize my (entire) revenue!

(But) there is this one horse—my soul is devoted to it: if he take it, I will surely die, O lover of good.

If he take this horse out of my hands, I know for certain that I shall not live (long).

Since God has bestowed (on thee) a (spiritual) connexion 3380 (with Himself), stroke my head at once with thy hand, O Messiah!

I can bear the loss of my women and gold and estates: this is not pretence nor is it an imposture.

If thou dost not believe me in this (matter)[1], try me, try me in word and deed!"

Weeping and wiping his eyes, the 'Imádu 'l-Mulk ran, with agitated mien, into the presence of the Sultan.

He closed his lips and stood before the Sultan, communing with God *the Lord of (all) His slaves.*

He stood and listened to the Sultan's intimate talk, while 3385 inwardly his thought was weaving this (prayer)—

"O God, if that young man (the Amír) has gone the wrong way, for 'tis not fitting to make any one except Thee a refuge,

(Yet) do Thou act in Thine own (generous) fashion and be not offended with him although he beseech any (poor) prisoner (like me) to deliver him,

Because all these creatures (of Thine) are in need (of Thee): take (it that) all (are alike in this respect) from a beggar to the Sultan (himself)."

To seek guidance from candle and wick when the perfect Sun is present,

To seek light from candle and lamp when the smoothly- 3390 rolling Sun is present,

Doubtless 'tis irreverence on our part, 'tis ingratitude and an act of self-will,

But most minds in (their) thinking are lovers of darkness, like the bat.

If the bat eats a worm during the night, (yet it is) the Sun (that) fosters the life of the worm.

If the bat is intoxicated with (the pleasure of eating) a worm during the night, (yet it is) by the Sun (that) the worm has been caused to move.

The Sun whence radiance gushes forth is giving food to his 3395 enemy.

But (in the case of) the royal falcon which is not a bat and whose falcon-eye is seeing truly and is clear,

---

[1] Reading گر می‌نداری.

If it, like the bat, seek increase (of sustenance) during the night, the Sun will rub its ear (chastise it) in correction,

And will say to it, "I grant that the perverse bat has an infirmity, (but) anyhow what is the matter with you?

I will chastise you severely with affliction, in order that you may not again turn your head away from the Sun."

*How Joseph the Ṣiddíq (truthful witness)—the blessings of God be upon him!—was punished with imprisonment* "for several years" *because of his seeking help from another than God and saying (to him),* "Mention me in thy lord's presence," *together with the exposition thereof.*

3400 That is like Joseph's (asking help) of a (fellow-)prisoner, a needy abject groundling[1].

He besought him for help and said, "When you come out (of prison), your affairs will prosper[2] with the king.

Make mention of me before the throne of that mighty prince, that he may redeem (release) me also from this prison."

(But) how should a prisoner in captivity[3] give release to another imprisoned man?

All the people of this world are prisoners (waiting) in expectation of death in the abode that is passing away;

3405 Except, to be sure, in the rare case of one who is single (*fardání*), one whose body is in the prison (of this world) and his spirit like Saturn (in the seventh heaven).

Therefore, in retribution for having regarded him (the fellow-prisoner) as a helper, Joseph was left in prison *for several years*.

The Devil erased from his mind the recollection of Joseph and removed from his memory those words (which Joseph had spoken).

In consequence of the sin which proceeded from that man of goodly qualities (Joseph), he was left in prison for several years by the (Divine) Judge,

Who said, "What failure was shown by the Sun of justice that thou shouldst fall, like a bat, into the blackness (of night)?

3410 Hark, what failure was shown by the sea and the cloud that thou shouldst seek help from the sand and the mirage?

If the vulgar are bats by nature and unreal (unspiritual), thou, at least, O Joseph, hast the eye of the falcon.

If a bat went into the blind and blue (the world of darkness and misery), ('tis no wonder, but) after all what ailed the falcon that had seen the Sultan?"

Therefore the (Divine) Master punished him for this sin, saying, "Do not make thy prop of rotten wood";

---

[1] Literally, "akin to the *saʿdán*," a prickly shrub on which camels browse.
[2] Literally, "will be set on a sound footing."
[3] Literally, "in the state of being made a prey."

But He caused Joseph to be engrossed with Him, to the end that his heart should not be pained by that imprisonment.

God gave him such intimate joy and rapture that neither the 3415 prison nor the mirk (of his dungeon) remained (visible) to him.

There is no prison more frightful than the womb—noisome and dark and full of blood and unhealthy;

(Yet), when God has opened for you a window in His direction, your body (hidden) in the womb grows more (and more) every moment,

And in that prison, from the immeasurable delight (which you feel therein), the senses blossom happily from the plant, your body.

'Tis grievous to you to go forth from the womb: you are fleeing from her (your mother's) pubes towards her back.

Know that the way of (spiritual) pleasure is from within, not 3420 from without: know that it is folly to seek palaces and castles.

One man is enraptured and delighted in the nook of a mosque, while another is morose and disappointed in a garden.

The palace (body) is nothing: ruin your body! The treasure lies in the ruin, O my prince.

Don't you see that at the wine-feast the drunkard becomes happy (only) when he becomes ruined (senseless)?

Although the (bodily) house is full of pictures, demolish it: seek the treasure, and with the treasure put it (the house) into good repair.

'Tis a house filled with pictures of imagination and fancy, and 3425 these forms (ideas) are as a veil over the treasure of union (with God).

'Tis the radiance of the Treasure and the splendours of the (spiritual) gold that cause the forms (ideas) to surge up in this breast.

'Tis from the purity and translucence of the noble Water that the particles of foam have veiled the face of the Water.

'Tis from the purity and (ceaseless) agitation of the precious Spirit that the bodily figure has veiled the face of the Spirit.

Hearken, then, to the adage that issued from the mouths (of men)—"this which is (cast) upon us, O brother, is (derived) from us."

Because of this veil, these thirsty ones who are (so) fond of the foam have got out of reach of the pure Water.

"O (Divine) Sun, notwithstanding (that we have) a *qibla* 3430 (object of adoration) and Imám like Thee, we worship the night and behave in the manner of bats.

Make these bats to fly towards Thee and redeem them from this bat-like disposition, O Thou whose protection is implored!

This youth (the Amír), by (committing) this sin, has gone astray and trespassed (against Thee), for he came to me (for help); but do not chastise him."

In the 'Imádu 'l-Mulk these thoughts were raging like a lion (rushing) through the jungles.

3435 His exterior (person) stood before the Sultan, (but) his soaring spirit was in the meadows of the Unseen.

Like the angels, he was momently being intoxicated with fresh draughts (of spiritual wine) in the realm of *Alast*;

Inwardly (merry as) a wedding-feast, but outwardly like a man filled with sorrow; a delectable world (concealed) in a tomb-like body.

He was in this (state of) bewilderment and waiting to see what would appear from the (world of) things occult and mysterious,

(When) at that time the officers brought the horse along into the presence of the Khwárizmsháh.

3440 Verily beneath this azure sky there was no (other) colt like that in (tallness and comeliness of) figure and in fleetness.

Its colour (splendid appearance) dazzled every eye: (all would exclaim), "Hail to the (steed) born of the lightning and the moon!"

It moved as swiftly as the moon and Mercury: you might say that its fodder was the *ṣarṣar* wind, not barley.

The moon traverses the expanse of heaven in one night during a single journey and course.

Since the moon traversed the signs of the zodiac in one night, wherefore wilt thou disbelieve the Ascension (of the Prophet)?

3445 That wondrous orphan Pearl is as a hundred moons, for at a nod from him the moon became (split in) two halves.

(Even) the marvel which he displayed in splitting the moon was only according to the measure of the weakness of the perception possessed by the (common) people.

The work and business of the prophets and (Divine) messengers is beyond the skies and the stars.

Do thou also go beyond (transcend) the skies and the revolving (orb), and then contemplate that work and business.

(Whilst) thou art inside the egg, like chicks, thou canst not hear the glorification of God by the birds of the (supermundane) air.

3450 The miracles (of the Prophet) will not be set forth here: tell of the horse and the Khwárizmsháh and what happened.

Whatsoever the sun of God's grace shines upon, whether it be dog or horse, gains (is endowed with) the glory of the Cave[1];

Yet deem not the radiance of His grace to be uniform: it has given a sign (distinctive character) to the pebble and the ruby.

From that (radiance) the ruby has a borrowed treasure, (while) the pebble has only heat and brightness.

(The radiance of) the sun falling on a wall is not the same as (when it is reflected) from water and quivering movement.

3455 After the peerless king had been astounded by (gazing at) it

---

[1] *I.e.* the Divine protection.

(the horse) for a moment, he turned his face to the 'Imádu 'l-Mulk,

Saying, "O vizier, is not this an exceedingly beautiful horse? Surely it belongs to Paradise, not to the earth."

Thereupon the 'Imádu 'l-Mulk said to him, "O emperor, a demon is made angelic by thy (fond) inclination.

That on which thou lookest (fondly) becomes (appears) good (to thee). This steed is very handsome and graceful, and yet

The head is a blemish in its (elegant) form: you might say that its head is like the head of an ox."

These words worked on the heart of the Khwárizmsháh and 3460 caused the horse to be cheap in the king's sight.

When prejudice becomes a go-between and describer (of beauty), you may get (buy) a Joseph for three ells of linen.

When the hour arrives for the spirit's parting (from the body), the Devil becomes a broker (depreciator) of the pearl of Faith,

And then in that (moment of) sore distress the fool hastily sells his faith for a jug of water;

But 'tis a (mere) phantom and not (really) a jug: the aim of the broker (the Devil) is naught but trickery.

At this (present) time, when you are healthy and fat, you are 3465 giving up the Truth for a phantom.

You are constantly selling the pearls of the (spiritual) mine and taking walnuts (in exchange), like a child;

Therefore it is no wonder if you act in this (same) way in the (mortal) sickness of your day of doom (death).

You have concocted an idea (a vain notion) in your fancy: when you are rattled (tested) like a walnut, you are (proved to be) rotten.

In the beginning that phantom resembles the full-moon, but in the end it will become like the new-moon.

If you regard its first (state) as being (really) like its last (state), 3470 you will be quit of its feeble deception.

This world is a rotten walnut: O man of trust, do not make trial of it, (but) behold it from afar.

The king viewed the horse with regard to the present, while the 'Imádu 'l-Mulk (viewed it) with regard to the future.

The king's eye, because of (its) distortion, saw (only) two ells, (but) the eye of him who regarded the end saw fifty ells.

What a (wondrous) collyrium is that which God applies (to the spiritual eye), so that the spirit discerns the truth behind a hundred curtains!

Since the Chief's (the Prophet's) eye was ever fixed on[1] the 3475 end, by reason of (seeing with) that eye he called the world a carcase.

On hearing only this single (word of) blame from him (the

[1] Literally, "associated with."

'Imádu 'l-Mulk), the love (that was) in the king's heart for the horse became chilled.

He abandoned his own eye and preferred his (the 'Imádu 'l-Mulk's) eye: he abandoned his own intelligence and hearkened to his (the other's) words.

This (speech of the 'Imádu 'l-Mulk) was (only) the pretext, and (in reality) at (his) entreaty the unique Judge caused it (the horse) to be cold (despicable) in the king's heart.

He (God) shut the door on its beauty (made its beauty invisible) to the eye (of the king): those words (of the 'Imádu 'l-Mulk) intervened (between the king's eye and the horse) like the sound of the door.

3480 He (God) made that cryptic saying a veil over the king's eye, a veil through which the moon appears to be black.

Pure (transcendent) is the Builder who in the unseen world constructs castles of speech and beguiling talk.

Know that speech is the sound of the door (coming) from the palace of mystery: consider whether it is the sound of opening or shutting.

The sound of the door is perceptible, but the door (itself) is beyond perception: *ye see* (are aware of) this sound, but the door *ye see not*.

When the harp of wisdom breaks into melody, (bethink yourself) what door of the Garden of Paradise has been opened.

3485 When the sound of evil speech becomes loud, (bethink yourself) what door of Hell is being opened.

Since you are far from its door, hearken to the sound of the door: oh, blest is he whose eye has been opened (so that he can recognise the wicked).

When you are aware of doing a good action, you obtain a (feeling of spiritual) life and joy;

And when a fault and evil deed issues (from you), that (feeling of) life and rapture disappears.

Do not abandon your own eye (judgement) from regard for the vile, for these vultures will lead you to the carcase.

3490 You close your narcissus-like eye, saying, "What (is it)? Hey, sir, take my stick (and show me the way), for I am blind";

But if you would only look, (you would see that) the guide whom you have chosen for the journey is (even) blinder than you.

Grasp in a blind man's fashion *the rope of Allah*: do not cling to aught but the Divine commandments and prohibitions.

What is *the rope of Allah*? To renounce self-will, for this self-will was a roaring wind (of destruction) to (the people of) 'Ád.

'Tis from self-will that folk are sitting in gaol, 'tis from self-will that the (trapped) bird's wings are tied.

'Tis from self-will that the fish is (cooked) in a hot pan, 'tis 3495
from self-will that shame (bashfulness) is gone from the modest.

The anger[1] of the police magistrate is a fiery spark from self-
will; crucifixion and the awfulness of the gallows are (the con-
sequence) of self-will.

You have seen the magistrate (who carries out the punish-
ment) of bodies on the earth: (now) see also the magistrate who
executes judgements against the soul.

Verily tortures are inflicted on the soul in the world invisible,
but until you escape (from self-will) the torture is concealed
(from view).

When you are freed you will behold the torture and perdition
(of the soul), because contrary is made manifest by contrary.

He that was born in the well (of the material world) and the 3500
black water, how should he know the pleasantness of the open
country and (distinguish it from) the pain of (being in) the well?

When, from fear of God, you have relinquished self-will, the
goblet (of drink) from God's Tasním[2] will arrive.

Do not in your self-will make a way: ask of God's Majesty the
way to Salsabíl[2].

Be not submissive to self-will (and yielding) like hay: in sooth
the shade of the Divine Throne is better than the summer-house
(of the world).

The Sultan said, "Take the horse back (to the Amír) and with
all speed redeem (deliver) me from (committing) this wrong."

The King did not say in his heart, "Do not (seek to) deceive 3505
the lion so greatly by means of the head of an ox.

You (the 'Imádu 'l-Mulk) drag in the ox in order to cheat
(me): begone, God does not stick the horns of an ox upon a
horse."

This renowned Master-builder observes great congruity in
His workmanship: how should He attach to a horse's body part
of (the body of) an ox?

The Master-builder has made (all) bodies congruously: He
has constructed moving palaces,

(With) balconies in them and cisterns (distributing water)
from this (part of the palace) to that;

And within them an infinite world: all this (vast) expanse (is 3510
contained) in a single tent.

Now He causes (one beautiful as) the moon to seem like an
incubus (nightmare), now He causes the bottom of a well to
have the semblance of a garden.

Inasmuch as the closing and opening of the eye of the heart
by the Almighty is continually working lawful magic,

For this reason Muṣṭafá (Mohammed) entreated God, saying,
"Let the false appear as false and the true as true,

---

[1] Read خَشم شـه.      [2] A fountain in Paradise.

So that at last, when Thou turnest the leaf, I may not (be stricken) by sorrow (and) fall into agitation."

3515 ('Twas) the Lord of the Kingdom (that) guided the peerless 'Imádu 'l-Mulk to the deception which he practised.

God's deception is the fountainhead of (all) these deceptions: the heart is between the two fingers of the (Divine) Majesty.

He who creates deception and (false) analogy in your heart can (also) set the sackcloth (of deception) on fire.

*Return to the Story of the bailiff and the poor debtor: how they turned back from the Khwája's grave, and how the bailiff saw the Khwája in a dream, etc.*

This goodly episode is endless (too long to relate in full). When the poor stranger turned back from the Khwája's grave,

The bailiff took him to his house and handed over to him the purse of a hundred dinars.

3520 He fetched viands for him and told him stories, so that from the (feeling of) hope (with which the bailiff inspired him) a hundred roses blossomed in his heart.

He (the bailiff) opened his lips to relate the ease (prosperity) which he had experienced after difficulty (adversity).

Midnight passed, and (he was still) narrating: (then) sleep transported them to the meadow where the spirit feeds.

On that night the bailiff dreamed that he saw the blessed Khwája (seated) on the high-seat in the (heavenly) palace.

The Khwája said, "O excellent bailiff, I have heard what you said, point by point,

3525 But I was not commanded to answer, and I durst not open my lips without being directed.

Now that we have become acquainted with the conditions and degrees (of the spiritual world), a seal has been laid upon our lips,

Lest the mysteries of the Unseen should be divulged and (thereby) the life and livelihood (of mortals) be destroyed,

And lest the veil of forgetfulness should be entirely rent and (the meat in) the pot of tribulation be left half-raw.

We are all ear, (though) the (material) form of the ear has become deaf: we are all speech, but our lips are silent.

3530 We now see (the result of) everything that we gave (during our life in the world): this (material) world is the veil, and that (spiritual) world is the vision.

The day of sowing is the day of concealment and scattering seed in a piece of earth.

The season of reaping and the time of plying the sickle is the day of recompense and manifestation.

[*How the Khwája disclosed to the bailiff in his dream the means of
paying the debts incurred by the friend who had come (to visit
him); and how he indicated the spot where the money was
buried, and sent a message to his heirs that on no account should
they regard that (sum of money) as too much (for the debtor) or
withhold anything (from him), and that (even) though he were
to refuse the whole or a part of it they must let it remain in the
place (where it was accessible), in order that any one who wished
might take it away; 'for,' said he, 'I have made vows to God
that not one mite of that money shall come back again to me and
those connected with me,' etc.*]

Now hear the bounty (which I have reserved) for my new
guest. I foresaw that he would arrive,

And I had heard the news of his debt, (so) I packed up two
or three jewels for him,

Which are (enough for) the full payment of his debt, and 3535
more: (this I did) in order that the heart of my guest should not
be wounded (torn with anxiety).

He owes nine thousand (pieces) of gold: let him discharge his
debt with some of these (jewels).

There will be a great many of them left over: let him expend
(this surplus) and include me too in a benediction.

I wished to give them (to him) with my own hand: (all) these
assignments are written in such-and-such a note-book.

Death, however, did not allow me time to hand over to him
secretly the pearls of Aden.

Rubies and corundums for (the payment of) his debt are 3540
(stored) in a certain vessel on which his name is written.

I have buried it in a certain vault: I have shown solicitude for
my ancient friend.

None but kings can know the value of that (treasure): take
care, then, that they (the purchasers) do not cheat you in the sale.

In sales (commercial transactions), for fear of being swindled,
behave in the same manner as the Prophet, who taught (his
followers to demand) three days' option.

Do not be afraid of it (the treasure) depreciating and do not
fall (into anxiety), since the demand for it will never decline.

Give my heirs a greeting from me and rehearse to them this 3545
injunction, point by point,

In order that they may not be deterred by the largeness of the
(sum of) gold, but may deliver it to that guest (of mine) without
reluctance.

And if he say that he does not want so much, bid him take it
and bestow it on whom he will.

I will not take back a jot of what I have given: the milk never
comes back to the teat.

According to the Prophet's saying, he who reclaims a gift will have become like a dog devouring his vomit.

3550 And if he shut the door and (declare that he) has no need of the gold, let them pour the bounty at his door,

(So that) every one who passes may carry gold away: the gifts of the sincere are never taken back.

I laid it in store for him two years ago and vowed to the Almighty (that it should be his).

And if they (my heirs) deem it permissible to take aught (for themselves), verily twentyfold loss will befall them.

If they vex my spirit, a hundred doors of tribulation will at once be opened for them.

3555 I have good hope of God that He will cause the due (payment) to reach the person who has the right to it."

He (the Khwája) unfolded two other matters to him (the bailiff), (but) I will not open my lips in mention of them,

In order that (these) two matters may remain secret and mysterious, and also that the *Mathnawí* may not become so very long.

He (the bailiff) sprang up from sleep, (joyously) snapping his fingers, now singing love-songs and now making lament.

The guest (the debtor) said, "In what mad fits are you (plunged)? O bailiff, you have risen intoxicated and merry.

3560 I wonder what you dreamed last night, O exalted one, that you cannot be contained in city or desert.

Your elephant has dreamed of Hindustán, for you have fled from the circle of your friends."

He replied, "I have dreamed a mad dream: I have beheld a sun in my heart.

In my dream I saw the wakeful Khwája, who gave up his life for vision (of God).

In my dream I saw the Khwája, the giver of things desired, (who was) one man like (equal to) a thousand if any (grave) affair happened."

3565 Drunken and beside himself, he continued to recount in this fashion till intoxication bereft him of reason and consciousness.

He fell (and lay) at full length in the middle of the room: a crowd of people gathered round him.

(When) he came to himself, he said, "O Sea of bliss, O Thou who hast stored (transcendental) forms of consciousness in unconsciousness,

Thou hast stored a wakefulness in sleep, Thou hast fastened (attached) a dominion over the heart to the state of one who has lost his heart.

Thou dost conceal riches in the lowliness of poverty, Thou dost fasten the necklace of wealth to the iron collar of poverty."

Contrary is secretly enclosed in contrary: fire is enclosed in 3570
boiling water.

A (delightful) garden is enclosed in Nimrod's fire: revenues
grow from giving and spending;

So that Muṣṭafá (Mohammed), the King of prosperity, has
said, "O possessors of wealth, munificence is a gainful trade."

Riches were never diminished by alms-giving: in sooth, acts
of charity are an excellent means of attaching (wealth) to one's
self.

In the poor-tax is (involved) the overflow and increase of
(one's) gold: in the ritual prayer is (involved) preservation from
lewdness and iniquity.

The poor-tax is the keeper of your purse, the ritual prayer is 3575
the shepherd who saves you from the wolves.

The sweet fruit is hidden in boughs and leaves: the ever-
lasting life is (hidden) under death.

Dung, by a certain manner (of assimilation), becomes nutri-
ment for the earth, and by means of that food a fruit is born to
the earth.

An existence is concealed in non-existence, an adorability in
the nature of adoration.

The steel and flint are dark externally, (but) inwardly a
(resplendent) light and a world-illuminating candle.

In a single fear (danger) are enclosed a thousand securities; in 3580
the black (pupil) of the eye ever so many brilliancies.

Within the cow-like body there is a prince, a treasure de-
posited in a ruin,

To the end that an old ass, Iblís to wit, may flee from that
precious (treasure) and may see (only) the cow and not (see) the
king.

*Story of the King who enjoined his three sons, saying, "In this
journey through my empire establish certain arrangements in such-
and-such a place and appoint certain viceroys in such-and-such
a place, but for God's sake, for God's sake, do not go to such-and-
such a fortress and do not roam around it."*

There was a King, and the King had three sons: all three (were)
endowed with sagacity and discernment.

Each one (was) more praiseworthy than another in generosity
and in battle and in exercising royal sway [1].

The princes, (who were) the delight of the King's eye, stood 3585
together, like three candles, before the King,

And the father's palm-tree was drawing water by a hidden
channel from the two fountains (eyes) of the son.

So long as the water of this fountain is running swiftly from
the son towards the gardens of his mother and father,

[1] Or "in advance and retreat," *i.e.* "in warlike prowess."

His parents' gardens will always be fresh: their fountain is made to flow by (the water from) both these fountains.

(But) when from sickness the (son's) fountain fails, the leaves and boughs of the (father's) palm-tree become withered.

3590　　The withering of his palm-tree tells plainly that the tree was drawing moisture from the son.

How many a hidden conduit is connected in like fashion with your souls, O ye heedless ones!

O thou who hast drawn stocks (of nourishment) from heaven and earth, so that thy body has grown fat,

(All) this is a loan: thou need'st not stuff (thy body) so much, for thou must needs pay back what thou hast taken—

(All) except (that of which God said) "*I breathed*," for that hath come from the Munificent. Cleave to the spirit! The other things are vain.

3595　　I call them vain in relation to the spirit, not in relation to His (their Maker's) consummate making.

*Explaining that the gnostic seeks replenishment from the Fountain-head of everlasting life and that he is relieved of any need to seek replenishment and draw (supplies) from the fountains of inconstant water; and the sign thereof is his holding aloof from the abode of delusion; for when a man relies on the replenishments drawn from those fountains, he slackens in his search for the Fountain everlasting and permanent.*

*"A work done from within thy soul is necessary, for no door will be opened to thee by things given on loan.*

*A water-spring inside the house is better than an aqueduct that comes from outside."*

How goodly is the Conduit which is the source of (all) things! It makes you independent of these (other) conduits.

You are quaffing drink from a hundred fountains: whenever any of those hundred yields less, your pleasure is diminished;

(But) when the sublime Fountain gushes from within (you), no longer need you steal from the (other) fountains.

Since your eye is rejoiced by water and earth, heart's sorrow is the payment for this joy.

3600　　When (the supply of) water comes to a fortress from outside, it is more than enough in times of peace;

(But) when the enemy forms a ring round that (fortress), in order that he may drown them (the garrison) in blood,

The (hostile) troops cut off the outside water, that (the defenders of) the fortress may have no refuge from them.

At that time a briny well inside (the walls) is better than a hundred sweet rivers outside.

The Cutter of cords (Death) and the armies of Death come, like December, to cut the boughs and leaves (of the body),

(And then) there is no succour for them in the world from 3605
Spring, except perchance the Spring of the Beloved's face in the
soul.

The Earth is entitled "the Abode of delusion" because she
draws back her foot (and deserts you) on the day of passage.

Before that (time) she was running right and left, saying,
" I will take away thy sorrow"; but she never took anything away.

In the hour of anxieties she would say to you, "May pain be
far from thee, and (may) ten mountains (stand) between (pain
and thee)!"

When the army of Pain arrives, she holds her breath: she will
not even say, "I have seen (and been acquainted with) thee."

God made a parable concerning the Devil on this wise: "He 3610
leads you into battle by his cunning tricks,

Saying, 'I will give thee help, I am beside thee, I will run
before thee in the perils (of war);

I will be thy shield amidst the arrows[1] of *khadang* wood,
I will be thy refuge in the hour of distress;

I will sacrifice my life for thee in raising thee to thy feet. Thou
art a Rustam, a lion: come on, be manful!'"

By means of these wiles that bag of deceit and cunning and
craft leads him (whom he makes his dupe) to infidelity.

As soon as he sets foot (therein) and falls into the moat (of 3615
fire), he (the Devil) opens his lips with a loud ha, ha.

(The dupe cries), "Hey, come! I have hopes of thee." He
(the Devil) says, "Begone, begone, for I am quit of thee.

Thou didst not fear the justice of the Creator, (but) I fear (it):
keep thy hands off me!"

(Then) God says (to the Devil), "He (thy dupe), indeed, is
parted from felicity, and how shouldst thou be saved by these
hypocrisies?"

On the Day of Reckoning et faciens et pathicus infames sunt
lapidationisque consortes.

Assuredly, by the decree and just dispensation (of God), 3620
(both) the waylaid and the waylayer are in the pit of farness
(from God) and in *an evil resting-place.*

(Both) the fool and the ghoul who deceived him must ever
endure to be deprived of salvation and felicity.

Both the ass and he that caught the ass are (stuck) in the mud
here: here (in this world) they are forgetful of (God) and there
(in the next world) they are sunk (in woe)—

(All) except those who turn back from that (deception) and
come (forth) from the autumn (of sensuality) into the springtide
of (Divine) grace,

And who repent, for God is ready to accept repentance, and
cleave to His command, for a goodly Commander is He!

[1] Literally, "at the time of the arrow."

3625  When, (moved) by sorrow, they raise a piteous cry, the highest
Heaven trembles at the moaning of the sinners.

It trembles even as a mother for her child: it takes them by
the hand and draws them upward,

Saying, "O ye whom God hath redeemed from delusion,
behold the gardens of (Divine) grace and behold the forgiving
Lord!

Henceforth ye have everlasting provision and sustenance from
God's air, not from the gutter (on the roof)."

Inasmuch as the Sea is jealous of intermediaries, he that is
thirsty as a fish takes leave of the water-skin.

*How the princes, having bidden the King farewell, set out on a
journey through their father's empire, and how the King repeated
his injunctions at the moment of farewell.*

3630  The (King's) three sons set out, in the fashion of (men
equipped for) travel, to (visit) their father's (distant) possessions,

And to make a tour of his cities and fortresses for the purpose
of regulating the administrative and economic conditions[1].

They kissed the King's hand and bade him farewell; then the
King, (who is) obeyed (by all), said to them:

"Direct your course whithersoever your heart (inclination)
may lead you, go (your way) under the protection of God,
waving your hands (dancing joyously).

(Go anywhere) except to one fortress, the name of which is
'the robber of reason': it makes the coat tight for[2] wearers of
the tiara.

3635  For God's sake, for God's sake, keep far away from that castle
adorned with pictures, and beware of the peril!

The front and back of its towers and its roof and floor are all
(covered with) images and decorations and pictures,

Like the chamber of Zalíkhá (which she made) full of pictures
in order that Joseph should look upon her willy-nilly.

Since Joseph would not look at her, she cunningly filled the
room with portraits of herself,

So that, wherever the fair-cheeked (youth) looked, he might
see her face without having the power to choose.

3640  The peerless God hath made (all) the six directions a theatre
for the display of His signs to the clairvoyant,

In order that, whatever animal or plant they look upon, they
may feed on the meadows of Divine Beauty.

Hence He said unto the company (of mystics), '*Wheresoever
ye turn, His Face is there.*

If in thirst ye drink some water from a cup, ye are beholding
God within the water.'

---

[1] Literally, "the government bureaux and the means of livelihood."
[2] *I.e.* "reduces to sore straits," "causes anguish to."

He that is not a lover (of God) sees in the water his own image,
O man of insight;

(But) since the lover's image has disappeared in Him (the 3645
Beloved), whom now should he behold in the water? Tell (me
that)!

Through the working of the Jealous One, they (the mystics)
behold the beauty of God in the faces of the houris, like the
moon (reflected) in water.

His jealousy is (directed) against a lover and sincere (adorer);
His jealousy is not (directed) against a (human) devil and
beast;

(But) if the devil become a lover (of God), he has carried off
the palm[1]: he has become a Gabriel and his devilish nature is
dead.

(The meaning of) 'the Devil became a true believer' is made
manifest on the occasion when by His (God's) grace a Yazíd
becomes a Báyazíd.

This topic is endless. Beware, O company (of travellers), 3650
keep your faces (safe) from that fortress!

Oh, let not vain desire waylay you, or ye will fall into ever-
lasting misery.

'Tis a bounden duty to abstain from peril: hear disinterested
advice from me.

In seeking relief (from sorrow) 'tis better that one's wits
should be sharp: 'tis better to abstain from (falling into) the
ambuscade of tribulation."

If their father had not spoken these words and had not warned
them against that fortress,

Their party would never have approached the fortress, their 3655
desire would never have inclined towards it;

For it was not well-known: it was exceedingly remote and
aloof from the (other) fortresses and the highways.

(But) when he (the King) uttered that prohibition, their
hearts were thrown by his speech into vain desire and into the
quarter of phantasy,

And, because of this prohibition, a craving arose in their
hearts to investigate the secret of that (fortress).

Who is (to be found) that will refrain from the forbidden
thing, since man longs eagerly for what is forbidden?

The veto causes the devout to hate (that which is vetoed); 3660
the veto incites the sensual to covet it.

Therefore He (God) leads many folk astray by this means,
and by the same means He guides aright (many) a knowing heart.

How should the friendly dove be scared by the (fowler's)
pipe? Nay, (only) the (wild) doves in the air are scared by that
pipe.

---

[1] Literally, "the ball," a metaphor derived from the game of polo.

Then they (the princes) said to him (the King), "We will perform the services (required of us), we will be intent on hearing and obeying (thy commands).

We will not turn aside from thy commands: 'twould be ingratitude to forget thy kindness";

3665    But, because of their reliance upon themselves, 'twas far from them to pronounce the saving clause[1] and glorify God.

Mention of the saving clause and (of the need for) manifold precaution was made at the beginning of the *Mathnawí*[2].

If there are a hundred (religious) books, (yet) they are but one chapter[3]: a hundred (different) regions seek but one place of worship.

(All) these roads end in one House: (all) these thousand ears of corn are from one Seed.

All the hundred thousand sorts of food and drink are (only) one thing in respect (of their final cause).

3670    When you are entirely satiated with one (kind of food), fifty (other) foods become cold (displeasing) to your heart.

In hunger, then, you are seeing double, for you have regarded a single one as a hundred thousand.

We had (previously) told of the sickness of the handmaiden and (the story) of the physicians and also their lack of understanding[4]—

How those physicians were like an unbridled horse, heedless of the rider and having no profit (of him).

(Though) their palates were covered with sores made by the impact of the bit, and their hooves wounded by (continually) changing step,

3675    They had not become aware (of the truth and never said to themselves), "Lo, on our back is a nimble Trainer who displays masterly skill.

Our turning the head to and fro is not caused by this bit, but only by the control of a successful Rider.

We (are like those who) went into the gardens to gather roses: they seemed to be roses, but they were (really) thorns."

It never occurred to them to ask, (prompted) by reason, "Who is kicking (bruising) our throats?"

Those (worldly-wise) physicians (are) so enthralled by the secondary cause (that) they have become blind to[5] God's contrivance.

3680    If you tether an ox in a stall and then find an ass in the place of the ox,

'Twould be asinine carelessness, like (that of) a man in

---

[1] *I.e.* the words "if God will."
[2] See translation of Book I, *v.* 48 foll.
[3] *I.e.* the gist of them all is contained in one chapter.
[4] See Book I, translation, p. 6 foll.
[5] Literally, "veiled from (the sight of)."

slumber, not to inquire who is the secret agent (that has effected the substitution).

(Yet) you never said, "Let me see who this changer is: he is not visible; surely, he is a celestial being."

You have shot an arrow to the right and have seen your arrow go to the left.

You have ridden in chase of a deer and have made yourself the prey of a hog.

You have run after some gain for the purpose of stuffing 3685 yourself: the gain has not reached (you) and you have been cast into prison.

You have dug pits for others and have seen yourself fall into them.

Since the Lord has disappointed you in regard to the means (of obtaining your desire), then why do not you become suspicious of the means?

Many a one has become an emperor by dint of toil, while (many) another has been made destitute by that (same) toil.

Many a one has been made (rich as) Qárún by marriage, and many a one has been made bankrupt by marriage.

The means, then, is turning about, like the tail of an ass: 'tis 3690 better not to rely upon it.

And if you take the means, you should not take it boldly, for beneath it there are many hidden banes.

This prudence and precaution is the gist of the saving clause, for this (Divine) decree (often) makes the ass appear to be a goat.

Although he whose eye it (the Divine decree) has bandaged is clever, (yet) because of his seeing double, in his eyes the ass is a goat.

Since God is the Turner of eyes, who (else) should turn the heart and the thoughts?

(Hence) you deem a pit to be a pleasant house, you deem a 3695 trap to be a dainty bait.

This is not sophistry (scepticism), it is God's turning: it shows where the realities are.

He who denies the realities is wholly involved in a phantasy.

He does not say (to himself), "Thy thinking (that all is) phantasy (illusion) is also a phantasy: rub an eye (and see)!"

*How the Sultan's sons went to the forbidden fortress, inasmuch as man eagerly covets that which he is refused—*
"*We rendered our service, but thy evil nature could not buy the servant (could not profit by the service that we rendered).*"
*They trod all their father's injunctions and counsels underfoot, so that they fell into the pit of tribulation, and their reproachful souls (consciences) were saying to them,* "Did not a warner come to you?" *while they, weeping and contrite, replied,* "If we had been wont to hearken or understand we should not have been among those who dwell in the flaming Fire."

This discourse hath no end. The party (of travellers) took their way to seek that castle.

3700　They approached the tree of the forbidden fruit, they went forth from the file of the sincere.

Since they were made more ardent by their father's prohibition and veto, they raised their heads (rebelliously) towards that fortress.

In spite of the orders of the elect King (they advanced) to the fortress which is the destroyer of self-restraint and the robber of rationality.

Turning their backs on the (bright) day, they came in the dark night in defiance of counsel-bestowing Reason

Into the beautiful fortress adorned with pictures, (which had) five gates to the sea and five to the land—

3705　Five of those (gates), like the (external) senses, facing towards colour and perfume (the material world); five of them, like the interior senses, seeking the (world of) mystery.

By those thousands of pictures and designs and decorations they (the princes) were made mightily restless (so that they wandered) to and fro (in amazement).

Do not be intoxicated with these cups, which are (phenomenal) forms, lest thou become a carver of idols and an idolater.

Abandon the cups, namely, the (phenomenal) forms: do not tarry! There is wine in the cup, but it is not (derived) from the cup.

Open thy mouth wide to the Giver of the wine: when the wine comes, the cup will not be lacking.

3710　(God said), "O Adam, seek My heart-enthralling Reality: take leave of the husk and (outward) form of the (forbidden) wheat."

Since sand was turned into flour for the Friend (Abraham), know that the wheat is deposed from its office[1], O noble one.

Form is brought into existence by the Formless, just as smoke is produced by a fire.

The least blemish in the qualities of that which is endowed with form becomes annoying when you regard it continually;

---

[1] *I.e.* God can make flour without wheat.

(But) Formlessness throws you into absolute bewilderment: from non-instrumentality a hundred kinds of instruments are born.

Handlessness is weaving (fashioning) hands: the Soul of the 3715 soul makes a (fully) formed Man.

'Tis like as (when) from separation and union diverse fancies are woven (conceived) in the heart.

Does this cause ever resemble its effect? Does the cry (of pain) and lamentation ever resemble the loss (that caused it)?

The lamentation has a form, the loss is formless: they (the losers) gnaw their hands on account of a loss that has no hand.

This comparison, O seeker of guidance, does not fit (the case), (but) 'tis the best effort a poor man can make to explain it.

The formless working (of God) sows (the seed of) a form 3720 (idea), (whence) there grows up a body endowed with senses and a (rational) faculty,

So that the form (idea), whatever it be, according to its own nature brings the body into (a state of) good or evil.

If it be a form (idea) of beneficence, it (the body) turns to thanksgiving; if it be a form of deferment, it (the body) becomes patient;

If it be a form of mercy, it (the body) becomes flourishing; if it be a form of repulse, it (the body) becomes full of moans;

If it be the form of a city, it (the body) takes a journey (thither); if it be the form of an arrow, it (the body) takes a shield (in defence);

If it be the form of fair ones, it (the body) indulges in enjoy- 3725 ment; if it be a form of the unseen world, it (the body) practises religious seclusion.

The form of want leads (the body) to earn (the means of livelihood); the form of strength of arm leads (the body) to seize (the property of others) by force.

These (ideas) are boundless and immeasurable (in number): the motive to action (arises) from various sorts of (such) phantasy.

All the infinite ways of life and (all) the crafts are the shadow (reflexion) of the form of thoughts.

(For example, when) happy folk (are) standing on the edge of a roof, observe the shadow of each one on the ground.

The form of thought is on the lofty roof (of the spirit), while 3730 the (resultant) action appears, like a shadow, on the pillars (bodily limbs).

The action is (manifested) on the pillars, while the thought (that produces it) is concealed; but the two are combined in the correlation of cause and effect[1].

---

[1] Literally, "in effect and (logical) connexion."

The forms (ideas) that arise at a banquet from the festive cup have as their result unconsciousness and senselessness.

The forms (ideas) of man and woman and (amorous) sport and sexual intercourse—hinc nascitur perturbatio animi in coitu.

The (material) form of bread and salt, which is a benefit (conferred by God), has as its result (bodily) strength, which is formless.

3735　On the battle-field the (material) form of sword and shield has as its result a formless thing, *i.e.* victory.

(Attendance at) college and learning and the (various) forms thereof are (all) done with, as soon as they have reached (their goal, namely) knowledge.

Since these forms are the slaves of the Formless, why, then, are they denying their Benefactor?

These forms have their existence from the Formless: what means, then, their denial of Him who brought them into existence?

His (the sceptic's) disbelief is really manifested by Him: in truth this act of his is naught but a reflexion.

3740　Know that the form of the walls and roof of every dwelling-place is a shadow (reflexion) of the thought of the architect,

Even though in the seat of his thought there is no visible (material) stone and wood and brick.

Assuredly the Absolute Agent is formless: form is as a tool in His hand.

Sometimes the Formless One graciously shows His face to the forms from the concealment (veil) of non-existence,

In order that every form may thereby be replenished with some perfection and beauty and power.

3745　When, again, the Formless One has hidden His face, they come to beg in (the realm of) colour and perfume.

If one form seek perfection from another form, 'tis the quintessence of error.

Why, then, O worthless man, are you submitting your need to another needy (creature)?

Inasmuch as (all) forms are slaves (to God), do not say or deem that form is applicable to God: do not seek Him by *tashbíh* (likening Him to His creatures).

Seek (Him) in self-abasement and in self-extinction, for nothing but forms is produced by thinking.

3750　And if you derive no advantage (comfort) except from form, (then) the form that comes to birth within you involuntarily[1] is the best.

(Suppose it is) the form of a city to which you are going: you

---

[1] Literally, "without you," *i.e.* without conscious thought or imagination on your part.

are drawn (thither) by a formless feeling of pleasure, O dependent one[1];

Therefore you are really going to that which has no locality, for pleasure is (something) different from place and time.

(Suppose it is) the form of a friend to whom you would go: you are going for the sake of enjoying his society;

Therefore in reality you go to the formless (world), though you are unaware of that (being the) object (of your journey).

In truth, then, God is worshipped by all, since (all) wayfaring is for the sake of the pleasure (of which He is the source). 3755

But some have set their face towards the tail[2] and have lost the Head, although the Head is the principal;

But (nevertheless) that Head is bestowing on these lost and erring ones the bounty proper to Headship by way of the tail.

That one obtains the bounty from the Head, this one from the tail; another company (of mystics) have lost (both) foot and head.

Since all has been lost, they have gained all: through dwindling away (to naught) they have sped towards the Whole.

*How in the pavilion of the fortress adorned with pictures they (the princes) saw a portrait of the daughter of the King of China and how all three lost their senses and fell into distraction and made inquiries, asking, "Whose portrait is this?"*

This topic is endless. The company (of three) espied a 3760 beauteous and majestic portrait.

The (travelling) party had seen (pictures) more beautiful than that, but at (the sight of) this one they were plunged in the deep sea,

Because opium came to them in this cup: the cups are visible, but the opium is unseen.

The fortress, (named) the destroyer of reason, wrought its work: it cast them, all three, into the pit of tribulation.

Without a bow the arrow-like glances (of Love) pierce the heart—mercy, mercy, O merciless one!

(Adoration of) a stone image consumed the (past) generations 3765 and kindled a fire (of love for it) in their religion and their hearts.

When it (the image) is spiritual, how (ravishing) must it be! Its fascination changes at every moment.

Since love of the pictured form was stabbing the hearts of the princes like a spear-point,

Each (of them) was shedding tears, like a cloud, and gnawing his hands and crying, "Oh, alas!

Now we see (what) the King saw at the beginning. How often did that peerless one adjure us!"

[1] Literally, "O rhyme-letter." Cf. Book III, *v*. 1283.
[2] *I.e.* phenomenal form.

3770 The prophets have conferred a great obligation (on us) because they have made us aware of the end,

Saying, "That which thou art sowing will produce naught but thorns; and (if) thou fly in this (worldly) direction thou wilt find there no room to fly (beyond).

Get the seed from me, that it may yield a (good) crop; fly with my wings, that the arrow may speed Yonder.

(If) thou dost not recognise the necessity and (real) existence of that (flight to God), yet in the end thou wilt confess that it was necessary."

He (the prophet) is thou, but not this (unreal) "thou": (he is) that "thou" which in the end is conscious of escape (from the world of illusion).

3775 Thy last (unreal) "thou" has come to thy first (real) "thou" to receive admonition and gifts.

Thy (real) "thou" is buried in another (unreal "thou"): I am the (devoted) slave of a man who thus (truly) sees himself.

That which the youth sees in the mirror the Elder sees beforehand in the (crude iron) brick.

(The princes said), "We have transgressed the command of our King, we have rebelled against the favours of our father.

We have lightly esteemed the King's word and those incomparable favours.

3780 Lo, we all are fallen into the moat, killed and wounded by affliction without combat.

We relied on our own intelligence and wisdom, so that this tribulation has come to pass.

We regarded ourselves as being without disease and emancipated (from fear of death), just as one suffering from phthisis regards himself.

Now, after we have been made prisoners and a prey, the hidden malady has become apparent."

The shadow (protection) of the (spiritual) Guide is better than praising God (by one's self): a single (feeling of) contentment is better than a hundred viands and trays (of food).

3785 A seeing eye is better than three hundred (blind men's) staves: the eye knows (can distinguish) pearls from pebbles.

(Moved) by sorrows (pains of love) they began to make inquiry, saying, "Who in the world, we wonder, is she of whom this is the portrait?"

After much inquiry in (the course of their) travel, a Shaykh endowed with insight disclosed the mystery,

Not (verbally) by way of the ear, but (silently) by inspiration (derived) from Reason: to him (all) mysteries were unveiled.

He said, "This is the portrait of (her who is) an object of envy to the Pleiades: this is the picture of the Princess of China.

She is hidden like the spirit and like the embryo: she is (kept) 3790
in a secret bower and palace.

Neither man nor woman is admitted to her (presence): the
King has concealed her on account of her fascinations.

The King has a (great) jealousy for her (good) name, so that
not even a bird flies above her roof."

Alas for the heart that such an insane passion has stricken:
may no one feel a passion like this!

This is the retribution due to him who sowed the seed of
ignorance and held light and cheap that (precious) counsel,

And put a (great) trust in his own management, saying, " By 3795
dint of intelligence I will carry my affair to success."

Half a mite of the (King's) favour is better than three hundred
spells (expedients) devised by the intellect.

Abandon your own cunning, O Amír: draw back your foot
before the (Divine) favour and gladly die.

This is not (to be gained) by a certain amount of contrivance[1]:
nothing avails until you die to (all) these contrivings.


*Story of the Ṣadr-i Jahán of Bukhárá. (It was his custom that)
any beggar who begged with his tongue was excluded from his
universal and unstinted charity. A certain poor savant, for-
getting (this rule) and being excessively eager and in a hurry,
begged (alms) with his tongue (while the Ṣadr was passing)
amidst his cavalcade. The Ṣadr-i Jahán averted his face from
him, and (though) he contrived a new trick every day and disguised
himself, now as a woman veiled in a chádar and now as a blind
man with bandaged eyes and face, he (the Ṣadr) always had
discernment enough to recognise him, etc.*

It was the habit of that most noble lord in Bukhárá to deal
kindly with beggars.

His great bounty and immeasurable munificence were always 3800
scattering gold till nightfall.

The gold was wrapped in bits of paper: he continued to
lavish bounty as long as he lived.

(He was) like the sun and the spendthrift moon[2]; (for) they
give back (all) the radiance that they receive (from God).

Who bestows gold on the earth? The sun. Through him, gold
is in the mine and treasure in the ruin.

Every morning an allowance (was distributed) to a (different)
set of people, in order that no class should be left disappointed
by him.

On one day his gifts were made to those afflicted (by disease); 3805
next day the same generosity (was shown) to widows;

---

[1] *I.e.* by the limited powers of the intellect.
[2] Literally, "the moon that gambles (her light) clean away."

31

Next day to impoverished descendants of 'Alí together with poor jurists engaged in study (of the canon-law);

Next day to empty-handed common folk; next day to persons fallen into debt.

His rule (in giving alms) was that no one should beg for gold with his tongue or open his lips at all;

But the paupers stood in silence, like a wall, on the outskirts of his path,

3810   And any one who suddenly begged with his lips was punished for this offence by not getting from him[1] (even) a mite of money.

His maxim was "Those of you who keep silence are saved": his purses and bowls (of food) were (reserved) for the silent.

One day (it happened) extraordinarily (that) an old man said, "Give me alms, for I am hungry[2]."

He refused (alms) to the old man, but the old man importuned him: the people were astounded by the old man's importunity.

He (the Ṣadr) said, "You are a very shameless old man, O father." The old man replied, "Thou art more shameless than I,

3815   For thou hast enjoyed this world, and in thy greed thou wouldst fain take the other world (to enjoy it) together with this world[3]."

He (the Ṣadr) laughed and gave the old man some money: the old man alone obtained the bounty.

Except that old man none of those who begged (aloud) saw half a mite or a single farthing of his money.

On the day when it was the turn of the jurists (to receive alms), a certain jurist, (impelled) by cupidity, suddenly began to whine.

He made many piteous appeals, but there was no help (for him); he uttered every kind (of entreaty), but it availed him naught.

3820   Next day he wrapped his leg in rags (and stood) in the row of the sufferers (from illness), hanging his head.

He tied splints on his shank, left and right, in order that it might be supposed that his leg was broken.

He (the Ṣadr) saw and recognised him and did not give him anything. Next day he covered his face with a rain-cloak,

(But) the noble lord knew him still and gave him nothing because of the sin and crime (which he had committed) by speaking.

When he had failed in a hundred sorts of trickery, he drew a *chádar* over his head, like women,

---

[1] Literally, "because of this offence would not get from him."
[2] Literally, "consorting with hunger."
[3] *I.e.* "thou art making thy present munificence the means of ensuring thy future felicity."

And went and sat down amongst the widows, and let his head 3825 droop and concealed his hands.

Still he (the Ṣadr) recognised him and did not give him any alms: on account of the disappointment a (feeling of) burning grief came into his heart.

He went early in the morning to a purveyor of grave-clothes, saying, "Wrap me in a felt (shroud) and lay me out on the road.

Do not open thy lips at all, (but) sit down and look on till the Ṣadr-i Jahán passes here.

Maybe he will see (me) and suppose that I am dead and drop some money to cover the cost of the shroud.

I will pay thee half of whatever he may give." The poor man, 3830 desiring the (expected) present, did just as he was told.

He wrapped him in the felt and laid him out on the road. The Ṣadr-i Jahán happened to pass that way

And dropped some gold on the felt (shroud). He (the jurist) put forth his hand in his haste (and fear)

Lest the purveyor of the grave-clothes should seize the gift of money and lest that perfidious rascal should hide it from him.

The dead man raised his hand from beneath the felt (shroud), and, following his hand, his head (too) came forth from below.

He said to the Ṣadr-i Jahán, "(See) how I have received 3835 (it), O thou who didst shut the doors of generosity against me!"

He (the Ṣadr) replied, "(Yes), but until you died, O obstinate man, you got no bounty from me."

The mystery of "Die before death" is this, that the prizes come after dying (and not before).

Except dying, no other skill avails with God, O artful schemer.

One (Divine) favour is better than a hundred kinds of (personal) effort: (such) exertion is in danger from a hundred kinds of mischief.

And the (Divine) favour depends on dying: the trustworthy 3840 (authorities) have put this way (doctrine) to the test.

Nay, not even his (the mystic's) death is (possible) without the (Divine) favour: hark, hark, do not tarry anywhere without the (Divine) favour!

That (favour) is (like) an emerald, and this (carnal self) is (like) an old viper: without the emerald how should the viper be made blind?

*Story of two brothers, one of whom had a few hairs on his chin while the other was a beardless boy. They went to sleep in a house for celibates. One night, as it happened, the boy lateribus congestis nates obtexit. Denique paedicator adrepsit, lateres ab ejus tergo callide et molliter summovit. The boy awoke and began to quarrel, saying, "Where are these bricks? Where have you taken them to? Why did you take them?" He replied, "Why did you put these bricks there?" etc.*

A beardless boy and a youth with a few hairs on his chin came to a festive gathering, for there was an assembly-place in the town.

The select party remained busy (enjoying themselves) till the day was gone and a third of the night had passed.

3845 The two (brothers) did not leave that house for celibates: they lay down to sleep there for fear of (meeting) the night-patrol.

The youth had four hairs on his chin, but his face was like the full-moon (in beauty).

The beardless boy was ugly in appearance: post culum tamen viginti lateres posuit.

Paedicator quidam noctu in frequentia hominum adrepsit: lateres amovit vir libidinosus.

Cum manum ei injiceret exsiluit puer: "eho," inquit, "tu quis homo es, O canis[1] cultor?"

3850 Respondit: "Cur hos triginta lateres congessisti?" "Tu," inquit, "cur triginta lateres sustulisti?

I am a sick boy and because of my weakness I took precautions and made here a place to lie down."

He replied, "If you are ill with a fever, why didn't you go to the hospital

Or to the house of a kindly physician, in order that he might relieve you[2] of your malady?"

"Why," said he, "where can I go? for wherever I go, persecuted (as I am),

3855 Some foul ungodly miscreant like you springs up[3] before me like a wild beast.

The dervish-convent, which is the best place—not (even) there do I find safety for one moment.

A handful of (greedy) pottage-eaters direct their looks at me: oculi semine impleti dum pressant manibus testiculos;

And even he that has regard for decorum steals covert glances et penem fricat.

Since the convent is (like) this, what must the public market be like? A herd of asses and boorish devils!

---

[1] *I.e.* the carnal soul.  [2] Literally, "open a lock."
[3] Literally, "raises his head."

What has an ass to do with decorum and piety?  How should 3860
an ass know (anything about) reverence and fear and hope?

(Real) intelligence consists in being safe (from temptation)
and in the desire to act justly towards (every) woman and towards
(every) man; but where is (such) intelligence (to be found)?

And if I run away and go to the women, I should fall into
tribulation like Joseph.

Joseph suffered imprisonment and torment at the hands of a
woman: I should be divided amongst fifty gibbets.

Those women in their foolishness would attach themselves
to me, and (then) their nearest and dearest (relatives by blood
or marriage) would seek my life.

I have no means of escape either from men or women: 3865
what can I do, since I belong neither to these nor to those?"

After (making) that (complaint) the boy looked at the youth
and said, "He is quit of trouble by reason of the two (or three)
hairs (on his chin).

He is independent of the bricks and of quarrelling over the
bricks and of a wicked young ruffian like you who would sell
(prostitute) his own mother.

Three or four hairs on the chin as a notice are better than
triginta lateres circa culum."

One atom of the shade (protection) of (Divine) favour is better
than a thousand endeavours of the devout pietist,

Because the Devil will remove the bricks of piety: (even) if 3870
there are two hundred bricks he will make a way for himself.

If the bricks are numerous, (yet) they are laid by you, (while)
those two or three hairs are a gift from Yonder.

In reality each one of those (hairs) is (firm) as a mountain, for
it is a safe-conduct bestowed by an Emperor.

If you put a hundred locks on a door, some reckless fellow
may remove them all;

(But) if a police magistrate put a wax seal (on it), at (the sight
of) that (even) the hearts of doughty champions will quail.

Those two or three hair-threads of (Divine) favour form a 3875
barrier (strong) as a mountain (against evil), like majesty of
aspect in the faces (of potentates) [1].

Do not neglect (to lay) the bricks, O man of goodly nature;
but at the same time do not sleep (as though you were) safe from
the wicked Devil.

Go and get two hairs of that (Divine) grace, and then sleep
safe (sound) and have no anxiety.

The sleep of the wise (*álim*) is better than worship (performed
by the ignorant), (if it be) such a wisdom (*ilm*) as brings
(spiritual) awakening.

[1] Or, "like the majesty of the marks (caused by prostration in prayer) on
the faces (of the pious)." See *Qur'án*, XLVIII, 29.

The quiet of the (expert) swimmer in swimming is better than the exertion (violent movements) with hands and feet of one who is unable (to swim).

3880   He that cannot swim throws out his hands and feet (desperately) and drowns, (while) the (practised) swimmer moves quietly (with a steadiness) like (that of) pillars.

Knowledge ('ilm) is an ocean without bound or shore: the seeker of knowledge is (like) the diver in (those) seas.

Though his life be a thousand years, never will he become weary of seeking,

For the Messenger of God said in explanation (thereof) this (saying)—"There are two greedy ones who are never satisfied."

*Commentary on the Tradition that Muṣṭafá (Mohammed)—the blessings of God be upon him!—said, " There are two greedy ones who will never be satisfied: the seeker of the present world and the seeker of knowledge." This " knowledge" must be different from " knowledge of the present world," in order that there may be the two (separate) classes (mentioned in the Tradition); but " knowledge of the present world" is just the same (in effect) as " the present world," etc.; and if it (the double phrase used above) be equivalent to " the seeker of the present world and the seeker of the present world," that would be repetition, not division (into two categories). With the exposition thereof.*

(The two classes mentioned are) the seeker of the present world and its abundant opportunities for acquisition, and the seeker of knowledge and the considerations proper to it.

3885   Now, when you fix your attention on this division, (you will see that) this knowledge must be other than the present world, O father.

What, then, is other than the present world? The next world, (the knowledge of) which will take you away from here and be your guide (to God).

*How the three princes discussed the (best) plan to adopt in view of what had occurred.*

The three afflicted ones put their heads[1] together: all three felt the same grief and pain and sorrow.

All three were comrades in one meditation and one passion; all three were sick with one disease and one malady.

At the time of silence all three had one thought; at the time of speech, too, all three had one argument.

3890   At one moment they all were shedding tears and weeping[2] blood on the dining-table of calamity;

At another moment all three, from the fire in their hearts, heaved burning sighs as (hot as) a chafing-pan.

[1] Literally, "faces."          [2] Literally, "scattering."

*The discourse of the eldest brother.*

The eldest said, "O men of probity, were not we masculine (vigorous and bold) in giving counsel to others?

Whenever one of the (King's) retainers complained to us of affliction and poverty and fear and agitation,

We used to say, 'Do not bewail thy hardships: be patient, for patience (fortitude) is the key to relief from pain.'

What has become now of this key, (namely) fortitude? 3895 Wonderful! The rule (which we laid down for others) is null and void (for us): what has become of it?

Did not we always say, 'In the (hour of) struggle laugh happily like gold in the fire'?

We said to the soldiers at the time of conflict in battle, 'Hark, do not change colour (lose courage)!'

At the time when the ground trodden underfoot by the horses was entirely (composed of) severed heads,

We were shouting to our troops, 'On, on! Advance irresistibly like the spear-point!'

We preached[1] fortitude to all the world, because fortitude (we 3900 said) is a lamp and light in the breast.

Now it is our turn. Why have we become distracted and gone under the *chádar* (veil) like cowardly women?"

O heart that didst inspire all (others) with ardour[2], inspire thyself with ardour and be ashamed of thyself!

O tongue that wert a mentor to all (others), now 'tis thy turn: why art thou silent?

O reason, where is thy eloquent and persuasive[3] counsel? Now 'tis thy turn: what has become of thy (former) admonitions?[4]

O thou who hast removed a hundred anxieties from (other) 3905 hearts, now 'tis thy turn: wag thy beard![5]

If now, in thy vile poltroonery, thou hast (only) stolen a beard (art devoid of real manhood), formerly thou must have been laughing at thy beard (making a mock display of manly virtue).

When thou exhortest others, (thy cry is), "Come on! come on!" In thine own anguish (thou criest), "Alas, alas!" like women.

Since thou wert a cure for others' pain, (how is it that) thou art silent when pain has become thy guest?

'Twas thy fashion to shout at the soldiers (to encourage them): (now) shout (at thyself): why is thy voice choked?

For fifty years thou hast woven on (the loom of) thy intelli- 3910

---

[1] Literally, "indicated," "recommended."
[2] Literally, "didst make all (others) hot."
[3] Literally, "sugar-chewing."       [4] Literally, "cries of 'hey!'"
[5] *I.e.* "move thy jaws and exhort thyself."

gence: (now) put on an undervest of the fabric which thou thyself hast woven.

The ears of thy friends were delighted by thy song: (now) put forth thy hand and pull thine own ear[1].

(Formerly) thou wert always a head (leader): do not make thyself a tail, do not lose thy feet and hands and beard and moustache[2].

(Now) 'tis for thee to make a move on the (chess-)board: restore thyself to thy normal state (of spiritual health) and thy (natural) vigour.

*Anecdote of a king who brought a learned doctor into his banquet-hall by force and made him sit down. (When) the cup-bearer offered him wine and held out the goblet to him, the doctor averted his face and began to look sour and behave rudely. The king said to the cup-bearer, "Come, put him in a good humour." The cup-bearer beat him on the head several times and made him drink the wine, etc.*

(Whilst) a drunken king was feasting merrily, a certain jurist passed by his gate.

3915 He gave directions, saying, "Bring him into this hall and give him a drink of the ruby wine."

So they brought him to the king, (for) he had no choice (power to resist): he sat down in the hall, (looking) sour as poison and snakes.

(When) he (the cup-bearer) offered him wine, he angrily refused it and averted his eyes from the king and the cup-bearer,

Saying, "I have never drunk wine in my life: rank poison would please me better than wine.

Hey, give me some poison instead of the wine, that I may be delivered from myself and ye from this (impoliteness)."

3920 Without having drunk wine, he began to make a row and became as disagreeable to the company as death and (its) pangs.

(This is) like (the behaviour of) carnal earthly-minded people[3] in the world when they sit (associate) with spiritual folk.

God keeps His elect (ever) drinking[4] secretly the wine of the free.

They offer the cup to one who is veiled (uninitiated), (but his) perception apprehends naught thereof except the (literal) words.

He averts his face from their guidance because he does not see their gift with his eye.

3925 If there were a passage from his ear to his throat, the hidden

---

[1] *I.e.* "induce thyself to listen attentively."
[2] *I.e.* "do not lose thy former energy and authority and prestige."
[3] Literally, "followers of water and earth."
[4] Literally, "does not keep His elect save in (the state of) drinking."

meaning of their admonition would have entered his inward
parts.

Inasmuch as his spirit is wholly fire, not light, who would
throw anything but husks into a blazing fire?

The kernel remains outside and the husk, (consisting of mere)
words, goes (in): how should the stomach be made warm and
stout by husks?

The Fire of Hell torments only the husks: the Fire has nothing
to do with any kernel;

And if a fire should dart its flames at the kernel, know that 'tis
in order to cook it, not to burn it.

So long as God is the Wise, know that this law is perpetual 3930
(both) in the past and in the time that has not (yet) come.

The pure kernels and (also) the husks are pardoned by Him:
how, then, should He burn the kernel? Far (be it) from Him!

If in His grace He beat the head of him (who resembles the
husk), he (such an one) will feel an eager desire for the red wine;

And if He do not beat him, he will remain, like the jurist, with
his mouth closed against the potations and festivity of these
(spiritual) kings.

The king said to his cup-bearer, "O well-conducted (youth),
why art thou silent? Give (it him)[1] and put him in good humour."

Over every mind there is a hidden Ruler, (who) cunningly 3935
diverts from his purpose whomsoever He will.

The sun in the East and his radiance are bound like captives
in His chain.

He causes the (celestial) sphere to revolve immediately when
He chants half of a cunning spell in its brain.

The mind which dominates another mind has (obtains) the
dice (of victory) from Him: He is the Master-player[2].

He (the cup-bearer) gave him (the jurist) several cuffs on the
head, saying, "Take (the cup)!" The tormented man drained
it in dread of (receiving further) blows.

He became tipsy and merry and smiling (gay) as a garden: 3940
he began to act like a boon-companion and tell ridiculous stories
and make jokes.

He became pot-valiant and jolly and snapped his fingers: in
latrinam ivit ut mingéret.

Erat in latrina puella lunae similis, venustissima, una de regis
ancillis.

When he espied her, his mouth gaped (in amazement)[3], his
reason fled and his body was ready for violence.

Per aeva coelebs vixerat: extemplo cupidine et furore accensus
puellae manus injecit.

[1] I.e. "make him drink the wine."
[2] Literally, "the master (champion player) of backgammon."
[3] Literally, "remained open."

3945 Valde trepidavit puella et clamorem sustulit: ei non poterat resistere, operam perdidit.

Femina viro in manus tempore congressus tradita is like dough in the hands of a baker.

He kneads it now gently, now roughly, and makes it groan under (the thumps of) his fist;

Now he draws it out flat on a board (rolling-pin), now for a bit he rolls it up;

Now he pours water on it and now salt: he puts it to the ordeal[1] of oven and fire.

3950 Thus are the sought and the seeker intertwined: (both) the conquered and the conqueror are (engaged) in this sport.

This sport is not between husband and wife only: this is the practice of everything that is loved and loves.

A mutual embracing, like (that of) Wís and Rámín, is obligatory (Divinely ordained) between eternal and non-eternal and between substance and accident;

But the sport is of a different character in each case: the embracing is for a different reason in each instance.

This is said as a parable for husband and wife, meaning, "O husband, do not dismiss thy wife unkindly.

3955 On thy wedding-night did not the bridesmaid place her (the wife's) hand in thy hand as a goodly trust?

For the evil or good which thou doest unto her, O man worthy of confidence, God will do (the same) unto thee."

To resume, on this occasion this jurist was so beside himself that neither continence nor asceticism remained in him.

The jurist threw himself on the nymph: his fire caught hold of her cotton.

Anima cum anima conjuncta est, corpora mutuo amplexu implicata tanquam duae aves abscissis capitibus tremebant.

3960 What (to them) was the wine-party or the king or Arslán (the Turkish slave)? What (to them) was modesty or religion or fear and dread of (losing) their lives?

Their eyes were contorted like[2] (the letters) 'ayn and ghayn: here neither Ḥasan nor Ḥusayn is seen distinctly.

It (the jurist's absence) became protracted, and how could he return[3] (to the party)? The king's expectancy too passed beyond (all) bounds.

The king came to see what had happened: he beheld there (what resembled) the commotion (on the Day) of Calamity[4].

The jurist sprang up in terror and fled to the banquet-hall and hastily seized the wine-cup.

---

[1] Literally, "makes a touchstone for it."
[2] Literally, "fallen into (the shape of)."
[3] Literally, "where was the way of returning?"
[4] *I.e.* the Resurrection.

The king, full of fire and fury[1] like Hell, was thirsting for the 3965 blood of the guilty pair.

When the jurist saw his enraged and wrathful countenance, which had become bitter and murderous as a cup of poison,

He shouted to his cup-bearer, "O solicitous (attendant), why do you sit (there) dumbfounded? Give (him wine) and put him in good humour!"

The king laughed and said, "O sir, I am restored to my good humour: the girl is thine.

I am the king: my business is (to show) justice and bounty: I drink of that which my munificence bestowed on my friend.

How should I give friend and kinsman for food and drink 3970 what I (myself) would not (eat and) drink as (gladly as) honey?

I let my pages eat and drink of that which I eat and drink at my own private table.

I give my slaves the same food, cooked or raw, as I eat myself.

When I put on a robe of silk or satin, I clothe my retainers in the same (fabric), not in coarse woollen garments.

I feel reverence for the all-accomplished Prophet, who said, 'Clothe them in that wherewith ye clothe yourselves.'

Muṣṭafá (Mohammed) gave his (spiritual) sons this injunction 3975 —'Feed your dependents with what ye eat (yourselves).'"

You have often restored others to a good disposition: you have made them ready and willing to show fortitude.

(Now) manfully restore yourself too to (that) disposition: take the reason that meditates on fortitude as your guide.

When the guidance of fortitude becomes a wing for you, your spirit will soar to the zenith of the (Divine) Throne and Footstool.

See, when fortitude became a Buráq for him, how it carried Muṣṭafá (Mohammed) up to the top of the (celestial) spheres[2].

*How, after full discussion and debate, the princes set out for the province of China towards their beloved and the object (of their desire), in order that they might be as near as possible to that object; (for) although the way to union is barred, 'tis praiseworthy to approach as near as is possible.*

They said this and immediately set out: O my friend, every- 3980 thing that was (to be gained) was (gained) at that moment.

They chose fortitude (as their guide) and became true witnesses; then they set off towards the land of China.

They left their parents and kingdom, they took the way to the hidden beloved.

Like Ibráhím son of Adham, Love (banished them) from the throne (and) made them footless and headless and destitute.

[1] Literally, "sparks and (terrible) chastisement."
[2] Literally, "stages," *i.e.* concentric spheres set one above another.

Either, like Abraham who was sent (as a prophet), one intoxicated (with love) cast himself into a fire,

3985    Or, like the much-enduring and glorious Ismá'íl (Ishmael), offered a throat to Love and his dagger.

*Story of Imra'u 'l-Qays, who was the king of the Arabs and exceedingly handsome: he was the Joseph of his time, and the Arab women were desperately in love with him[1], like Zalíkhá (with Joseph). He had the poetic genius (and composed the ode beginning)—*
*"Halt, let us weep in memory of a beloved and a dwelling-place[2]."*
*Since all the women desired him with (heart and) soul, one may well wonder what was the object of his love-songs and lamentations. Surely he knew that all these (beauteous forms) are copies of a (unique) picture which have been drawn (by the Artist) on frames of earth. At last there came to this Imra'u 'l-Qays such a (spiritual) experience that in the middle of the night he fled from his kingdom and children and concealed himself in the garb of a dervish and wandered from that clime to another clime in search of Him who transcends all climes:* "He chooseth for His mercy whom He will"; *and so forth.*

Imra'u 'l-Qays was weary[3] of his empire: Love carried him away from the country of the Arabs,

So that he came and worked as a brick-maker at Tabúk. The king was told that a royal personage,

Imra'u 'l-Qays (by name), having fallen a prey to Love, had come thither and was making bricks by (his own) labour.

The king rose up and went to him at night and said to him, "O king of beauteous countenance,

3990    Thou art the Joseph of the age. Two empires have become entirely subject to thee—(one), of the territories (under thy sway), and (the other), of Beauty.

Men are enslaved by thy sword, while women are the chattels[4] of thy cloudless moon[5].

(If) thou wilt dwell with me, 'twill be my fortune: by union with thee my soul will be made (equal to) a hundred (enraptured) souls.

Both I (myself) and my kingdom are thine to hold as thine own, O thou who in high aspiration hast abandoned kingdoms!"

He reasoned[6] with him for a long time, and he₁(Imra'u 'l-Qays) kept silence, (till) suddenly he unveiled the mystery.

3995    Think what (secrets) of love and passion he (must have)

---

[1] Literally, "dead for him."
[2] The opening line of the *Mu'allaqa* of Imra'u 'l-Qays.
[3] Literally, "dry-lipped."            [4] Literally, "possessions."
[5] *I.e.* "thy resplendent beauty."    [6] Literally, "talked philosophy."

whispered into his ear! Immediately he made him a crazy wanderer like himself.

He (the king of Tabúk) took his hand and accompanied him: he too renounced his throne and (royal) belt.

These two kings went to distant lands: not once (only) has Love committed this crime.

It (Love) is honey for the grown-up and milk for children: for every boat it is (like) the last bale[1] (which causes the boat to founder).

Besides these two, many kings, (kings) beyond number, hath Love torn from their kingdoms and families.

The souls of these three princes also were roaming around 4000 China in every direction, like birds picking up grain.

They durst not open their lips to utter the thoughts hidden (in their hearts), because it was a perilous and grave secret.

A hundred thousand heads (go) for a farthing at the moment (when) Love strings his bow in anger.

Even without anger, at the time when he is well-pleased, Love is always accustomed to kill recklessly.

This is (his habit) at the moment when he is contented: how shall I describe (what he does) when he is angered?

But may the soul's pasture be the ransom for his (Love's) lion 4005 who is killed by this Love and his scimitar!

('Tis) a killing better than a thousand lives: (all) sovereignties are mortally enamoured of this servitude.

They (the princes) were telling each other their secrets allusively in low tones with a hundred fears and precautions.

None but God was the confidant of their secret, their sighs were breathed to Heaven alone[2].

They were using certain mystical terms among themselves in order to convey information.

The vulgar have learned this birds' language and (by means 4010 of it) have acquired prestige and authority.

That terminology is (only) the image (imitation) of the bird's voice: the uninitiated man is ignorant of the (inward) state of the birds.

Where is the Solomon who knows the birds' song? The demon, though he seize the kingdom (of Solomon), is an alien.

The demon in the likeness of Solomon stood (in Solomon's place): he knows how to deceive, but he does not possess (the knowledge denoted by the words) *we have been taught*[3].

Inasmuch as Solomon was rejoiced exceedingly by (the favour

---

[1] Literally, "the last *mann* (a weight of ten to thirty pounds)."
[2] Literally, "none but Heaven was sympathetic to their sighs."
[3] Referring to *Qur'án*, XXVII, 16: "And he (Solomon) said, 'O people, we have been taught the language of birds.'"

of) God, he had a birds' language (derived) from *we have been taught*.

4015 Understand that you are a bird of the (common) air because you have not beheld the esoteric birds.

The home of the Símurghs is beyond (Mt) Qáf: it is not (like) a hand-loom (easily accessible) to any imagination,

But only to the imagination that beholds it by chance and then, after the vision, is parted (from it)—

Not a parting that involves severance, (but a parting) for a wise purpose; for that high estate is secure from every (real) parting.

In order to preserve the spiritual body the (Divine) Sun for a time withdraws (His beams) from the snow.

4020 Seek good for thy soul from them (who have attained unto God): beware, do not steal mystical expressions from their language.

Zalíkhá had applied to Joseph the name of everything, from rue-seed to aloes-wood.

She concealed his name in (all other) names and made the inner meaning thereof known to (none but her) confidants.

When she said, "The wax is softened by the fire," this meant, "My beloved is very fond of[1] me."

And if she said, "Look, the moon is risen"; or if she said, "The willow-bough is green (with new leaves)";

4025 Or if she said, "The leaves are quivering mightily"; or if she said, "The rue-seed is burning merrily";

Or if she said, "The rose has told her secret to the nightingale"; or if she said, "The king has disclosed his passion for Shahnáz[2]";

Or if she said, "How auspicious is Fortune!" or if she said, "Give the furniture a good dusting[3]";

Or if she said, "The water-carrier has brought the water"; or if she said, "The sun is risen";

Or if she said, "Last night they cooked a potful of food" or "The vegetables are cooked to perfection[4]";

4030 Or if she said, "The loaves have no salt (savour)"; or if she said, "The heavenly sphere is going round in the contrary direction";

Or if she said, "My head aches"; or if she said, "My headache is better"—

If she praised, 'twas his (Joseph's) caresses (that she meant); and if she blamed, 'twas separation from him (that she meant).

[1] Literally, "hot towards."
[2] Literally, "has told the secret of Shahnáz." The name Shahnáz signifies "the king's delight."
[3] Literally, "shake up the furniture."
[4] Literally, "have been made uniform by cooking."

If she piled up a hundred thousand names, her meaning and intention was always Joseph.

Were she hungry, as soon as she spoke his name she would be filled (with spiritual food) and intoxicated by his cup.

Her thirst would be quenched by his name: the name of Joseph was a sherbet to her soul[1]; 4035

And if she were in pain, her pain would immediately be turned into profit by that exalted name.

In cold weather it was a fur to her. This, this (is what) the Beloved's name can do (when one is) in love.

The vulgar are always pronouncing the Holy Name, (but) it does not do this work (for them) since they are not[2] endowed with (true) love.

That (miracle)[3] which Jesus had wrought by (pronouncing) the Name of *Hú* (God) was manifested to her through the name of him (Joseph).

When the soul has been united with God, to speak of that (God) is (to speak of) this (soul), and to speak of this (soul) is (to speak of) that (God). 4040

She was empty of self and filled with love for her friend (Joseph), and (as the proverb says), "A pot[4] drips what is in it."

The scent of the saffron of union produces (happy) laughter; the smell of the onion of absence (produces) tears.

Every (other) one has in his heart a hundred objects of desire, (but) this is not the way of love and fondness.

Love's sun in the day-time is the (Face of the) Beloved: the sun is as a veil over that Face.

He that does not know (distinguish) the veil from the Face of the Beloved is a sun-worshipper: keep thy hand off (keep thyself aloof) from him. 4045

He is both the lover's day and daily bread, He is both the lover's heart and heart-burning.

(God's)[5] fishes receive directly[5] from the Essence of the Water their bread and water and clothes and drugs and sleep.

He (the lover) is like a child getting milk from the breast: he knows nothing in the two worlds except the milk.

The child knows the milk and yet he does not know it: (intellectual) consideration has no means of entrance here[6].

This circular (issued by Love) made the spirit crazy to find (both) the Opener and that which is opened (by Him). 4050

It (the spirit) is not crazy in going (on that quest); nay, (for) 'tis the Sea within it that bears it along, not a torrent or a river.

---

[1] Literally, "an inward sherbet."
[2] Literally, "he (such an one) is not."
[3] *I.e.* bringing the dead to life.      [4] Literally, "from the pot."
[5] Literally, "in cash."
[6] *I.e.* the reason cannot enter into the mystery of Divine grace.

How should it (the spirit) find (God)? He that finds (God) be-
comes lost (in Him): like a torrent he is absorbed in the Ocean.

The seed is lost (in the earth): (only) then does it become a
fig-tree. This is (the meaning of) "I did not give (you) the money
till you died[1]."

*How, after they had stayed in hiding and tarried patiently for a*
*long while in the capital of China, where the Emperor was*
*enthroned, the eldest (brother) lost patience and said, "Farewell!*
*I will go and present myself to the King.*
*Either my feet will bring me to the object of my quest, or I will lose[2]*
*my head there as (I have already lost) my heart"—*
*(The Persian translation of this Arabic verse is):*
*"Either my feet will bring me to the object of my quest and desire,*
*or I will give away my head there as (I have given away) my*
*heart"—*
*and how the good advice of his brothers was of no avail.*
*"O thou that chidest those in love, let them alone! How shouldst*
*thou direct a band which God has led astray?" And so forth.*

The eldest (brother) said, "O my brethren, from waiting (so
long) this soul of mine is on the verge (of leaving my body).

4055    I have become reckless, I can endure no more: this endurance
has set me on fire.

My strength is exhausted by this fortitude: my plight is a
warning to (all) lovers.

I am weary of my life in separation (from the beloved): 'tis
hypocrisy to be alive in separation.

How long will the anguish of separation from her be killing
me? Cut off my head, in order that Love may give me a (new)
head.

My religion is, to be (kept) alive by Love: life (derived) from
this (animal) soul and head is a disgrace to me.

4060    The sword (of Love) sweeps the dust away from the lover's
soul, because the sword is a wiper-out of sins.

When the bodily dust is gone, my moon shines: my spirit's
moon finds a clear sky.

For ages, O adored one, I have been beating the drum of love
for thee (to the tune of) 'Lo, my life depends on my dying.'

My spirit has boasted that it is a water-bird: how should it
lament the flood of tribulation?

What cares the duck for shipwreck? Her feet in the water are
ship enough.

4065    My soul and body are (kept) alive by this boast: how should
I refrain from making this boast?

I am dreaming but I am not asleep; I am a boaster but I am
not a liar.

---

[1] See v. 3836 *supra*.          [2] Literally, "cast away."

Though you behead me a hundred times, I am like a candle: I will burn brightly (still).

Though the stack (of my existence) catch fire (both) in front and behind, the stack (halo) of that Moon is enough for travellers in the night.

Joseph was hidden and concealed from Jacob the prophet by the trickery of his brethren.

They put him out of sight by an artifice, (but) at last his shirt 4070 gave an information."

The two (brothers of the eldest prince) admonished him in converse, saying, "Do not ignore the dangers.

Hark, do not put salt on our wounds! Beware, do not drink this poison rashly and in doubt (of the consequences).

How canst thou go without being counselled by a wise Shaykh, since thou hast not a discerning heart?

Woe to the unfledged bird that flies up to the zenith and falls into peril!"

Intelligence is wings and feathers to a man: when he lacks 4075 intelligence, (he must rely on) the intelligence of a guide.

Either be victorious or in search of a victor: either have insight or be in search of one endowed with insight.

Without (possession of) the key, namely, intelligence, this knocking at the door is prompted by self-will, not by right motives.

See a whole world ensnared by self-will and by wounds (harmful things) that look like remedies (beneficial things).

The snake, (terrible) as death, stands (raises itself) on its breast, with a big leaf in its mouth in order to catch its prey.

It stands erect, like a herb, amidst the herbage, (so that) the 4080 bird thinks it is the stalk of a plant.

When it (the bird) settles on the leaf for the purpose of eating, it falls into the mouth of the snake and (into the jaws of) death.

A crocodile opens its mouth: its teeth are surrounded by long worms.

The worms were produced by the residue of food left in its teeth; and it gave them lodging there.

The little birds see the worms and the food and imagine that coffin to be a meadow.

When its mouth is filled with birds, it suddenly swallows 4085 them and closes its mouth (again).

Know that this world full of dessert (viands) and bread is like the open mouth of the crocodile.

O thou who scrapest together the means of livelihood, (in thy desire) for worms and morsels do not feel secure from the artfulness of the crocodile, (which is) Time.

A fox falls (and lies) flat under his earth: above his earth are deceptive grains,

32

In order that the heedless crow may approach them and the crafty one cunningly seize her by the leg.

4090  Since there are a hundred thousand cunning tricks in animals, how (great) must be the cunning of Man who is superior (to all other animals)!

In his hand (he carries) a copy of the Holy Book as (though he were) Zaynu 'l-'Ábidín[1]; (but) in his sleeve a vengeful dagger.

He addresses thee smilingly—"O my lord," (while) in his heart there is a Babylon of sorcery and guileful spells.

(He is) deadly poison, (though) in appearance he is honey and milk. Beware, do not go (on thy way) save in company with a wise (spiritual) preceptor.

All selfish pleasures are a deceit and fraud: round the lightning-flash is a wall of darkness.

4095  The lightning is (but) a brief gleam, false and fleeting, surrounded by darkness; and thy way is long.

By its light thou canst neither read a letter nor ride to thy destination.

But, as a penalty for thy being enthralled[2] by the lightning, the beams of sunrise withdraw themselves[3] from thee.

Mile after mile through the night the lightning's deception leads thee on, without a guide, in a dark wilderness.

Now thou fallest on a mountain, now into a river; now thou wanderest in this direction, now in that.

4100  O seeker of worldly estate, thou wilt never find the guide; and if thou find him, thou wilt avert thy face from him,

Saying, "I have travelled sixty miles on this road, and (now) this guide tells me I have lost my way.

If I give ear to this marvel, I must begin my journey again[4] under his authority.

I have devoted my life to this journey: (I will pursue it) come what may. Begone, O Khwája!"

"(Yes), thou hast journeyed (far), but (only) in opinion (unsubstantial) as lightning: (come), make a tenth part of that journey for the sake of (Divine) inspiration (glorious) as the sunrise.

4105  Thou hast read (the Verse), *Opinion cannot serve instead of truth*, and (yet) by a lightning-flash like that thou hast been blinded to[5] a rising sun.

Hark, come into our boat, O wretched man, or (at least) tie that boat (of thine) to this boat (of ours)."

---

1 "The Ornament of the Devout," a title given to 'Alí, son of Ḥusayn, the fourth Imám of the Shí'ites.
2 Literally, "in pawn to."
3 Literally, "their face."
4 Literally, "take the road from the beginning."
5 Literally, "hast been left without."

He replies, "How should I abandon power and dominion? How should I follow thee blindly?"

A blind man is certainly better off with a guide than (when he goes) alone: in the former case there is (only) one ignominy, while in the latter there are a hundred.

Thou art fleeing from a gnat to a scorpion, thou art fleeing from a dewdrop into an ocean.

Thou art fleeing from thy father's unkindnesses into the midst 4110 of scoundrels and mischief and trouble.

Like Joseph, thou art fleeing from one sorrow to fall into a well (of woe) through (being beguiled by) "*let us frolic and play*[1]."

Because of this pastime thou fallest into a well, like him; but where is the (Divine) favour to help *thee* (as it helped him)?

Had it not been (done) by his father's leave, he would never have emerged from the well till the Resurrection;

(But) in order to please him[2] his father gave the permission and said, "Since this is thy desire, may good come (of it)!"

Any blind man who turns away in scorn from a Messiah will 4115 be left, like the Jews, without guidance;

(For) though he was blind, he was capable of receiving light; (but) from showing this aversion he becomes blind and blue (miserably lost).

Jesus says to him, "O blind man, cling to me with both hands: I have a precious collyrium.

If thou art blind, thou wilt obtain light from me and lay hold of the (sweet-scented) Joseph's shirt of the spirit."

The (real) fortune and highway (of success) lies in the business that comes to thee after utter defeat (self-abasement).

Give up the business that hath no foot or head (permanence): 4120 hark, old donkey, get for thyself a Pír!

May none but the Pír be (thy) master and captain!—not the Pír (old man) of the rolling sky[3], but the Pír of right guidance[4].

The devotee of darkness sees the light immediately as soon as he becomes subject to (the authority of) the Pír.

What is required is self-surrender, not long toil: 'tis useless to rush about in error.

Henceforth I will not seek the way to the Ether (the highest celestial sphere): I will seek the Pír, I will seek the Pír, the Pír, the Pír!

The Pír is the ladder to Heaven: by whom (what) is the arrow 4125 made to fly? By the bow.

Was it not Abraham that caused the gross Nimrod to (attempt the) journey to heaven by means of the vulture?

---

[1] Cf. translation of Book III, *v.* 416 foll.
[2] Literally, "for his heart's sake."
[3] *I.e.* "Father Time" or "Fortune."
[4] *I.e.* the spiritual director.

(Impelled) by self-will, he often went upward; but no vulture can fly to heaven.

Abraham said to him, "O traveller, I will be thy vulture: this is more seemly for thee.

When thou makest of me a ladder to go aloft, thou wilt ascend to heaven without flying"—

4130    As the heart (spirit), without provisions or riding-camel, travels (swiftly) as lightning to west and east;

As man's consciousness, wandering abroad whilst he is asleep, travels during the night to (remote) cities;

As the gnostic, sitting quietly (in one place), travels by a hidden track through a hundred worlds.

If he has not been endowed with power to travel like this, (then) from whom are (derived) these reports concerning that (spiritual) country?

Hundreds of thousands of Pírs are agreed upon (the truth of) these reports and these veracious narratives.

4135    Amongst these sources (authorities) there is no dispute, such as there is in (the case of) knowledge based on opinions.

That (knowledge based on opinion) is (like) searching (for the direction of the Ka'ba) in the dark night, while this (mystic knowledge) is (like) the presence of the Ka'ba and midday.

Arise, O (thou who resemblest) Nimrod, and seek wings from (holy) personages: thou wilt not get any ladder from these vultures.

The vulture is the particular (discursive) reason, O poor (-spirited) one: its wings are connected with the eating of carrion;

(But) the reason of the *Abdál* (exalted saints) is like the wings of Gabriel: it soars, mile by mile, up to the shade of the lote-tree (in Paradise).

4140    (It says), "I am a royal falcon, I am fair and auspicious, I have nothing to do with carrion: I am not a vulture.

Abandon the vulture, for I will be thy helper: a wing of mine is better for thee than a hundred vultures."

How long wilt thou gallop blindly? For (learning) a trade and business one needs a master.

Do not disgrace thyself in the capital of China: seek a sage and do not separate thyself from him.

Hark, whatever the Plato of the age bids thee do, give up thy self-will and act in accordance with that (counsel).

4145    All (who dwell) in China are saying in zeal for (the glory of) their King, "*He begetteth not.*

Never in sooth has our King begotten a child; nay, he has not allowed a woman to approach him."

When any king says of him something of this sort, he weds his (traducer's) neck to the cutting scimitar.

The King says (to such an one), "Since thou hast spoken these words, either prove that I have a wife and family—

And if thou prove that I have a daughter, thou art safe[1] from my keen sword—

Or else without any doubt I will cut thy throat: I will tear the   4150 mantle (thy body) off the Ṣúfí, thy spirit.

Thou wilt never save thy head from the sword, O thou that hast spoken vain and lying words!

O thou that hast foolishly spoken an untruth, behold a moat full of severed heads!—

A moat filled from its bottom to its mouth[2] with heads severed on account of this enormity.

All have been sacrificed to this (false) assertion: they have beheaded themselves with this assertion.

Beware! Regard this with a heedful eye: do not conceive or   4155 utter such an assertion!"

(The two princes said), "Thou wilt make our lives bitter to us: who is inducing thee to (act like) this, O brother?

If one who is ignorant should journey a hundred years in blindness, that is not reckoned as a journey.

Do not go into battle unarmed, do not go recklessly[3] into destruction."

They said all this (to him), but the impatient (prince) replied, "These words (of warning) inspire me with repugnance.

My bosom is full of fire, like a brazier: the crop is ripe, 'tis   4160 time for the sickle.

There was a (great) fortitude in my breast, (but) now it is no more: Love has set fire to the dwelling-place of fortitude.

My fortitude died on the night when Love was born: it has passed away—long live those who are present!

O thou that tellest (me) of (a stern) rebuke (from the King) and (terrible) punishments[4], I have passed beyond (all) that: do not beat a piece of cold iron!

I am (rushing) headlong: hey, let go my feet! Where in all my limbs is (any) understanding?

I am (like) a camel: I carry (my load) as long as I can, (but)   4165 when I fall down exhausted, I am glad to be killed.

If there are a hundred moats full of severed heads, 'tis an absolute pleasantry in comparison with my anguish.

Nevermore in fear and dread will I beat such a drum of passion under a blanket[5].

Now I will plant my banner in the open plain: (let my fate be) either to lose my head or (to behold) the face of my adored one!

[1] Literally, "thou hast gained security."
[2] Literally, "gullet."
[3] Literally, "like those who are without fear."
[4] Literally, "events," "calamities."
[5] *I.e.* "conceal my passion."

The throat that is not worthy of that wine—'tis best it should be cut by blows of the sword[1];

4170 The eye that is not (rejoiced) in abundance by union with her—such an eye is best white (with disease) and blind;

The ear that is not worthy of (hearing) her secret—tear it off, for it is no good on the head;

The hand in which there is not the (requisite) amount (to win her favour)—'tis best that it should be chopped off by the butcher's knife;

The foot by whose faring the spirit is not led into[2] her narcissus-plot—

Such a foot is best in iron (chains), for such a foot is ultimately (the cause of) headache (affliction).

[*Setting forth (the case of) the earnest seeker who does not refrain from exerting himself to the utmost, although he knows that the amplitude of God's bounty may cause the object of his desire to reach him from a different quarter and by means of work of a different kind which he has never imagined; but since all his thoughts and hopes are fixed on this particular method (of attaining his object), he continues to knock at this same door, (knowing that) maybe God most High will cause his appointed portion to reach him through some other door which he has not foreseen, 'and will provide for him from a quarter on which he does not reckon'—'Man proposes but God disposes.' And, (again), a slave (of God) may conceive, as beseems a slave, that although he keeps knocking at this (particular) door he will be supplied from another door; and (nevertheless) God most High may cause his portion to reach him through this very door (at which he is knocking). In short, all these (doors) are the doors of one Palace. And the exposition thereof.*]

4175 Either this desire of mine will be fulfilled on this journey or when I return home from the journey.

It may be that (the fulfilment of) my desire depends on going abroad and that after I have gone abroad I shall attain (to it) at home.

I will seek the Beloved with all my might and energy until I know whether I need not have sought (Him).

How should (the mystery of) His being with me enter my (spiritual) ear unless I wander round the world?

How should I apprehend the mystery of His being with me except after (making) long journeys?"

4180 God hath said that He is with us, but He hath sealed the heart in order that it (the real meaning) may enter the heart's ear contrariwise (indirectly), not directly.

---

[1] Literally, "by the sword and conflict."    [2] Literally, "joined to."

When he (the seeker) has made (many) journeys and per-
formed the duties of the Way, after that (and not before) the seal
is removed from his heart.

As (in the arithmetical method of) "the two errors[1]," the
excellent (successful) calculation (only) becomes clear[2] to him
after two mistakes.

After that, he says (to himself), "If I had known (the real
nature of) this being with God, how should I have searched for
Him?

(But) the knowledge thereof depended on journeying: that
knowledge is not to be gained by keenness of thought."

'Tis just as the payment[3] of the Shaykh's debts was contingent[4] 4185
and dependent on the weeping of that (young) creature[5].

(When) the confectioner's boy wept bitterly, the debts of the
venerable Shaykh were discharged.

That spiritual tale has already been related in the course of
the *Mathnawi*[6].

He (God) puts in thy heart the fear of (losing) a certain
position, in order that no other (position) may be an object of
hope to thee.

To thy hope (of gaining thy wish from that quarter) He
attaches another advantage (beneficial result)[7]; but He grants
thee thy wish from (the hands of) some one else.

O thou who hast fixed thy hopes firmly on one quarter, saying, 4190
"The fruit will come to me from that lofty tree,"

Thy hope will not be fulfilled from there; nay, the bounty will
come from another place.

Why, then, did He implant in thee that hope, since He would
not give thee the (desired) thing from that quarter?

('Tis) for a wise purpose and contrivance; and also in order
that thy heart may be in a state of bewilderment.

('Tis) that thy heart may be bewildered, O learner, (wondering)
from where the object of thy desire will come (to thee).

('Tis) that thou mayst know thy weakness and thy ignorance 4195
and that consequently thy faith in the Unseen may be increased;

And, moreover, that thy heart may be perplexed concerning
the source whence the (expected) benefit will arrive, and what
(result) the (Divine) Disposer will produce from this hope.

Thou hopest (to find) a means of livelihood in tailoring, so
that by working as a tailor thou mayst earn money all thy life;

(But) He causes thy daily bread to come to thee in the gold-

---

[1] *I.e.* the rule for finding unknown quantities which is now called "double
position."
[2] *I.e.* the mystery of Divine immanence is revealed.
[3] Literally, "the means (of paying)."
[4] Literally, "bound up (with)."          [5] Literally, "existence."
[6] See the translation of Book II, *v.* 376 foll.
[7] As explained in *vv.* 4193–4201.

smith's craft—a means of gain that was far from (entering) thy imagination.

Wherefore, then, were thy hopes set on tailoring, when He did not intend to let thy daily bread reach thee from that side?

4200    ('Twas) by reason of a marvellous providence in the knowledge of God—an edict which He wrote in the (eternal) past;

And also to the end that thy thoughts should be bewildered, so that bewilderment should be thy whole occupation.

(The eldest prince said), "My union with the Beloved will be achieved either by this effort or by some means outside of bodily effort.

I do not assert that my object will be gained in this (particular) way: I am palpitating (restlessly seeking) to ascertain from what quarter it will appear.

The decapitated bird tumbles in every direction to see in what direction its (vital) spirit may escape from its body.

4205    My desire will be attained either by this going forth (in quest of it) or through (the opening of) some other gateway by (the hand of) Heaven[1]."

*Story of the person who dreamed that his hopes of opulence would be fulfilled in Cairo, and that there was a treasure (buried) in a certain house in a certain quarter of that city. When he came to Cairo, some one said to him, " I have dreamed of a treasure in such and such a quarter and such and such a house in Baghdád"; and he named the quarter and house in which this person lived. The latter perceived, however, that the information concerning the treasure in Cairo had been given to him (in his dream) in order to make him realise that, (although) he must not seek anywhere but in his own house, this treasure would really and truly be gained only in Cairo.*

There was (once) a man who inherited money and estates: he squandered all and was left destitute and miserable.

Inherited wealth indeed does not remain constant (to its new owner), since it was parted against its will from the deceased one.

Just because he (the heir) got it easily, he does not know its value; for he never made haste to work and toil and earn it.

O such-and-such, you know not the value of your soul because God bountifully gave it to you for nothing.

4210    His ready money went and his furniture and houses went: he was left (alone) like owls in the deserts.

He cried, "O Lord, Thou gavest (me) provision: the provision is gone: either give (me) some provision or send death."

---

[1] Literally, "or from some other tower of the many-towered (heaven)." Cf. *Qur'án*, LXXXV, 1.

When he became empty, he began to call unto God: he started the tune of "O Lord!" and "O Lord, protect me!"

Since the Prophet has said that the true believer is (like) a lute (*mizhar*), (which) makes music (only) at the time when it is empty—

(For) as soon as it is filled, the minstrel lays it down—do not become full, for sweet is the touch of His hand.

Become empty and stay happily between (His) two fingers, 4215 for "where" is intoxicated with the wine of "nowhere[1]."

Frowardness departed (from him) and released the water (tears) from his eye: his tears watered (revived) the crops of devotion.

*The reason why the answer to the true believer's prayer is delayed.*

Oh, how many a sincere (worshipper) moans in prayer, so that the smoke of his sincerity ascends to Heaven,

And from the lamentation of the sinful the perfume of the censer[2] floats up beyond this lofty roof!

Then the angels beseech God piteously, saying, "O Thou who answerest every prayer and O Thou whose protection is invoked,

A faithful slave (of Thine) is making humble entreaty: he 4220 knows none but Thee on whom to rely.

Thou bestowest Thy bounty (even) on strangers: every ardent wisher gains his desire from Thee."

God saith, "'Tis not that he is despicable (in My sight); (nay), the very deferment of the bounty is (for the sake of) helping him.

Need caused him to turn towards Me from his (former state of) forgetfulness: it dragged him by the hair into My presence[3].

If I satisfy his need, he will go back and (again) become absorbed in that idle play.

Although he is (now) crying with (all) his soul, 'O Thou whose 4225 protection is invoked,' let him (continue to) moan with broken heart and wounded breast!

It pleases Me (to hear) his (piteous) voice and his cries of 'O Lord' and his secret (prayer),

And how in supplication and pleading (with Me) he would fain beguile Me with every sort (of persuasion)."

Parrots and nightingales are put into cages because they give pleasure by their sweet song;

(But) how should crows and owls be caged? This has never been recorded in story.

When two persons, one of them a decrepit old man and the 4230

---

[1] *I.e.* the spiritual world, which transcends all spatial relations.
[2] *I.e.* the contrite heart aglow with love and longing.
[3] Literally, "street," "quarter."

other a fair-chinned (youth), come to (a baker who is) an admirer of handsome boys,

And both ask for bread, he will at once fetch the unleavened bread and bid the old man take it;

But how should he (immediately) give bread to the other, by whose figure and cheeks (countenance) he is pleased? Nay, he will delay him

And say to him, "Sit down a (little) while, 'twill do (thee) no harm; for the new bread is baking in the house";

And when, after the work (of baking is finished), the hot bread is brought to him (the youth), he (the baker) will say to him, "Sit down, for *halwá* (sweetmeat) is coming."

4235	In this same fashion he is always detaining him and seeking covertly to make him his prey,

Saying, "I have some (important) business to do with thee: wait a moment, O beauty of the world!"

Know for sure that this is the reason why the true believers suffer disappointment (whether) in (seeking) good or (in avoiding) evil.

*Returning to the Story of the person who was given a clue to the treasure (buried) at Cairo, and setting forth his supplication to God on account of his poverty.*

When the man who received the inheritance had squandered it and become a pauper, he began to cry "O Lord!" and weep and lament.

Verily, who shall knock at this Door, from which mercy is showered, without gaining in response a hundred springs (seasons of spiritual refreshment)?

4240	He dreamed that he heard a Voice from heaven saying, "Thy fortune[1] will be found in Cairo;

Go to Cairo: there thy affair will be set right. He (God) hath accepted thy humble petition: He is the (only) Object of hope.

In such-and-such a spot is a great treasure: thou must go to Cairo in quest of it.

Hark, O wretched man, go without any delay from Baghdád to Cairo and the home of sugar-candy[2]."

When he departed from Baghdád (and came) to Cairo, at the sight of Cairo his courage was restored[3],

4245	(For he was) in hope of (the fulfilment of) the promise given by the heavenly Voice that he would find in Cairo the treasure to remove his trouble—

"In such and such a quarter and such and such a spot there is a buried treasure exceedingly rare and very choice."

---

[1] Literally, "wealth."
[2] Literally, "the place where sugar-candy grows."
[3] Literally, "his back became warm."

But of money for expenses, great or small, he had nothing left; and he was about to go and beg from the common folk,

But (feelings of) shame and honour held him back[1], (so that) he began to plant himself firmly on fortitude.

(Meanwhile), however, his soul fluttered (in distress) on account of hunger: he saw no means of escape from foraging and begging.

"At nightfall," he said (to himself), "I will slip out very 4250 quietly, in order that I may beg in the dark without feeling ashamed[2].

At night I will chant (litanies) and bawl like a night-mendicant, that half a *dáng* may come to me from the roofs."

Thus meditating, he went out into the street, and with these thoughts (in his head) he wandered to and fro.

At one moment shame and dignity prevented him (from begging), at another moment hunger said to him, "Beg!"

Till a third part of the night was gone, (he kept putting) one foot forward and one foot backward (hesitating and asking himself), "Shall I beg or shall I lie down to sleep with my lips dry?"

*How that person arrived at Cairo and at night came out into the street to play the mendicant and beg, and how he was arrested by the night-patrol and after having been soundly beaten succeeded through him in gaining his object. "And it may be that ye loathe a thing though it is better for you"; and as God most High hath (also) said, "God will surely vouchsafe after hardship ease"; and as God most High hath said, "Lo, with hardship goeth ease"; and as he (the Prophet), on whom be peace, hath said, "O year of drought, become severe, and then thou wilt pass away." And the whole of the Qur'án and all the Revealed Books confirm this.*

Suddenly the night-patrol seized him and, unable to restrain 4255 his anger[3], beat him with fist and cudgel.

As it happened, the people (of the city) had suffered losses in those dark nights from (the depredations of) night-thieves.

They were nights of alarm and disaster, and the police were searching for the thieves with all their might,

(So much so) that the Khalífa said, "Cut off the hand of any one who roams about by night, even if he is a kinsman of mine."

The king had terrified the police with threats, saying, "Why are you (so) merciful to the thieves?

[1] Literally, "took hold of his skirt."
[2] Literally, "in order that, by reason of the darkness, shame may not come over me in begging."
[3] Literally, "yellow bile."

4260  For what reason do you believe their blarney or why do you accept gold (bribes) from them?"

To show mercy to thieves and any sinister-handed (noxious) person is to inflict blows and have no mercy on the weak.

Beware, from sympathy with a particular (offender) do not let him go unpunished[1]: do not consider his sufferings, consider the sufferings of the public.

Amputate the snake-bitten finger to prevent (worse) mischief: keep in view the infection and (consequent) destruction of the (whole) body.

In those days, as it happened, the thieves, both expert and unskilled, had become numerous.

4265  He (the night-patrol) saw him (in the street) at such a time and gave him a sound drubbing and blows without number.

Shrieks and cries for mercy arose from the poor wretch: "Don't strike! let me tell the truth about it all!"

He replied, "Look now, I will give you time: speak, that I may learn how you came out into the streets by night.

You do not belong to this place, you are a stranger and unknown (to me): tell me truly what you are plotting (here).

The government officials have attacked the police, asking why there is now such a great number of thieves (in the city).

4270  It is owing to you and the likes of you that they are so numerous: first disclose (the names of) your wicked associates;

Otherwise I will exact from you the vengeance incurred by all of them, in order that every respectable person's money may be safe."

After taking many oaths he replied, "I am not a housebreaker or cutpurse.

I am no thief and criminal: I am a stranger in Cairo, I belong to Baghdád."

### Explaining the Tradition (of the Prophet), "Falsehood causes suspicion, while veracity inspires confidence."

He related the story of his dream and the treasure of gold, and from (under the influence of) his veracity the man's heart expanded (like a flower).

4275  From his (the treasure-seeker's) oaths (protestations) he scented the truth[2]: in him (both) the combustion and the rue-seed[3] were evident.

The heart is comforted by true words, just as a thirsty man is comforted by water—

Except the heart of one who is veiled (deprived of discern-

---

[1] Literally, "do not break away (refrain) from taking vengeance."
[2] Literally, "the scent of truth came to him."
[3] I.e. both his inward sincerity and his veracity. Rue-seed is burnt as a charm against the evil eye.

ment) and suffers from a (spiritual) malady, (so that) he cannot distinguish between a prophet and a dolt;

Or else, (if) the message that is (brought) from the place (of truth) were to descend upon the moon, it (the moon) would be split asunder.

The moon would be split, but not the heart of him who is veiled; for he is rejected (by God), he is not beloved.

The night-patrol's eye became (like) a fountain with wetting 4280 tears, not from the dry words, nay, but from the fragrance (of truth) in the heart.

One word comes to the lips from Hell, one word (comes) into the region of the lips from the Spiritual City.

There is the spirit-increasing sea and the distressful sea: these lips are where the two seas meet (but do not mingle)[1].

('Tis) like a great mart (situated) between towns: thither come goods from all directions:

Damaged, spurious, and swindling[2] commodities (and also) lucrative commodities highly esteemed, like pearls.

The shrewdest traders in this mart (carefully) inspect the 4285 genuine and spurious wares.

To him (such an one) the mart is a place of gain, while to others in their blindness it is a place of loss.

Every particle of the world, one by one, is a fetter for the fool and a means of deliverance for the wise.

It is (sweet as) candy for one and (bitter) as poison for another: it is (beautiful as) mercy for one and (terrible) as wrath for another.

Every inanimate thing tells a tale to the Prophet: the Ka'ba testifies to the pilgrim and is eloquent (on his behalf).

The mosque, too, bears witness to him who performs the 4290 ritual prayer, saying, "He came a long way to (visit) me."

The fire is (like) flowers and sweet basils and roses to (one like) Khalíl (Abraham); to those like Nimrod, on the contrary, it is death and anguish.

We have said this many a time, O Ḥasan: I will never be weary of setting it forth.

Many a time have you eaten bread to prevent (yourself from) getting thin: 'tis the same bread: why are not you surfeited?

(Because), in normal health, a new hunger comes to you, by which indigestion and satiety are consumed.

When one actually feels the pangs of hunger, a (sense of) 4295 refreshment is associated with every part (of the body).

The pleasure (of eating) is (derived) from hunger, not from new dessert (viands): hunger makes barley-bread more delicious than sugar.

That weariness, then, is caused by lack of hunger (ardour) and

---

[1] See *Qur'án*, xxv, 55.                [2] Literally, "cutpurse."

complete (spiritual) indigestion, not by repetition of the discourse.

How is it that you are not weary of your shop and of haggling and disputing in order to cheat people?

How is it that you have not been surfeited by speaking ill of men in their absence and backbiting them[1] for sixty years?

4300   Time after time, without wearying, you have gaily spoken false words of flattery in pursuit of a vile woman[2];

And the last time you utter them with fire and energy, a hundred times more ardently than the first time.

Passion makes the old medicine new; passion lops every bough of weariness.

Passion is the elixir that makes (things) new: how (can there be) weariness where passion has arisen?

Oh, do not sigh heavily from weariness: seek passion, seek passion, passion, passion!

4305   Vain remedies (only) beguile (true) passion: they are (like) brigands and those who extort money in the form of tolls.

A briny water is no remedy for thirst: (even) if it seem cold and delicious at the moment of drinking,

Yet it beguiles (you) and prevents (you) from seeking the sweet water by which a hundred plants are made to grow.

Likewise every piece of spurious gold prevents (you) from recognising the good (genuine) gold wherever it is (to be found).

It (the spurious gold) cuts off your feet and (clips) your wings by imposture, saying, "I am what you seek: take me, O seeker."

4310   It says, "I will remove thy passion," (but) in truth it is (worthless as) dregs: it is (really) checkmate (defeat) though it is victory in appearance.

Go, always be fleeing from the false remedy, in order that thy passion may be successful and rich in perfume[3].

He (the night-patrol) said, "You are not a thief and you are not a reprobate: you are a good man, but you are foolish and silly.

You make such a long journey, (relying) on a phantasy and (mere) dream: your intelligence has not the least spark[4] of brightness.

I have dreamed many times, continuously, that there is a concealed treasure at Baghdád,

4315   Buried in such-and-such a quarter and such-and-such a street"
—the name, in fact, was that of the street where this sorrowful man lived.

"It is in so-and-so's house: go and seek it!"—the enemy (the

---

[1] Literally, "eating their flesh."
[2] Literally, "vulva dirupta."
[3] Literally, "musk-diffusing."
[4] Literally, "a *tasú* (a very small weight)."

night-patrol) named the house and mentioned his (the treasure-seeker's) name.

"I myself have often dreamed that there is a treasure in the dwelling-place at Baghdád.

I never left my home[1] on account of this phantasy, (but) you in consequence of a single dream come (hither) without thinking of the fatigue[2].

The dreams of a fool are suitable to his intelligence: like it, they are worthless and good-for-nothing.

Know that a woman's dreams are inferior to those of a man 4320 because of her deficiency of intelligence and weakness of soul.

The dreams of one deficient in intelligence and foolish are of little value: what, then, must be the dreams produced by (entire) lack of intelligence? (Mere) wind!"

He (the treasure-seeker) said to himself, "The treasure is in my house: then why am I poverty-stricken and lamenting there?

(While living) over the treasure, I have (almost) died of beggary because I am heedless and blind[3]."

At this good news he was intoxicated (with joy): his sorrow vanished, and without (opening his) lips he chanted a hundred thousand praises to God.

He said, "My food (fortune) depended on (my suffering) 4325 these blows: the Water of Life was in my shop (all the time).

Begone, for I have met with a great piece of fortune, to confound the idea that I was destitute.

Deem me foolish or contemptible as you please: it (the treasure) is mine, say what you like.

Beyond doubt I have seen my wish (fulfilled): call me anything you please, O foul-mouthed one!

Call me sorrowful, O respected sir: in your view I am sorrowful, but in my view I am happy.

Alas, if the case[4] had been reversed (and if I had been like) 4330 a rose-garden in your view and miserable in my own!"

### Parable.

One day a base fellow said to a dervish, "Thou art unknown to any one here."

He replied, "If the vulgar do not know me, I know very well who I am.

Alas, if the pain and sore (the spiritual malady) had been reversed (bestowed contrariwise) and he (the vulgar man) had seen me (as I really am), while I was blind to myself!"

(The treasure-seeker said), "Suppose I am a fool, I am a lucky fool: luck is better than perversity and a hard (impudent) face.

---

[1] Or, "I was never disturbed."
[2] Or, "become careless of fatigue."        [3] Literally, "in the veil."
[4] Literally, "this flight," *i.e.* the course taken by each of us.

4335 These words (of yours) express (only) your (false) opinion[1]; for my luck at the same time endows me with all that belongs to (perfect) intelligence."

*How that person returned (to Baghdád) rejoicing and successful and giving thanks to God and prostrating himself (in prayer) and amazed at the wondrous indications vouchsafed (to him) by God and the coming to light of the interpretations thereof in a way that no mind and understanding can conceive.*

He returned from Cairo to Baghdád, prostrating himself and bowing (in prayer) and giving praise and thanks (to God).

All the way he was bewildered and intoxicated by this marvel, (namely), by the complete change[2] (which had taken place) as regards his daily bread (the treasure) and the method of seeking (it),

Saying (to himself), "Whence did He make me hopeful and whence did He shower money and profit upon me![3]

What wisdom was this, that the Object of (all) desire caused me to go forth from my home gladly on a fool's errand[4],

4340 So that I was hastening to lose the way and at every moment was being farther removed from that which I sought—

And then God in His munificence made that very aberration the means of (my) reaching the right road and gaining wealth!"

He maketh losing the way an avenue to (true) faith; He maketh going wrong a field for the harvest of righteousness,

To the end that no righteous man may be without fear[5], and that no traitor (sinner) may be without hope.

The Gracious One hath put an antidote in the poison in order that they may say He is the Lord of hidden grace.

4345 That (Divine) bounty is not mysterious in (the case of) piety; (but) the (Divine) Forgiveness bestows a robe of honour (even) in (the case of) sin.

The unbelievers sought to abase those (the prophets) who were worthy of trust: (that) abasement became exaltation and (the cause of) miracles being displayed.

In their unbelief they attempted to abase the (true) religion: that very abasement was turned to glory for the prophets.

Unless every wicked man had shown unbelief, wherefore should evidentiary miracles[6] have appeared?

How should a judge require (a litigant to give) evidence until his disbelieving opponent has demanded proof of his veracity?

---

[1] Literally, "leap forth (are uttered) in accordance with your opinion."
[2] Literally, "the inversion."
[3] *I.e.* "He gave me hopes of finding the treasure in Cairo, and then enriched me in Baghdád."
[4] Literally, "astray and glad."     [5] Literally, "shock (of terror)."
[6] Literally, "miracles and convincing evidence."

The miracle (performed by a prophet) is like an honest witness 4350 to the indubitable veracity of the claimant.

Since they (the prophets) were being attacked by every ignoramus, God bestowed on them the gift of miracles and showed them favour.

The plots of Pharaoh were three-hundredfold: all (of them) became (the means to) his abasement and subjugation.

He brought magicians, good and bad, into his presence in order that he might invalidate the miracles of Moses,

That he might nullify the rod (of Moses) and put it to shame and remove from (men's) hearts the respect (which they had) for it.

Those very plots only serve to manifest the veracity of Moses[1]: 4355 the prestige of his rod goes up.

He (Pharaoh) leads his army betimes to the neighbourhood of the Nile in order to waylay Moses and his people;

(But) it only serves to ensure the safety of the followers of Moses, (while) he (Pharaoh) goes under the earth and the plain (of sand).

If he (Moses) had stayed in Egypt, he (Pharaoh) would not have marched (against him): how, (then), would the Israelites have been relieved of dread?

He marched and caused the Israelites to be consumed (with terror); for (you must) know that safety is concealed in danger.

The hidden grace consists in this, that the Lord shows unto 4360 him (the recipient of grace) a (terrible) fire, but it is really a (gracious) light.

There is nothing mysterious in (God's) rewarding piety, (but) look at the reward bestowed on the magicians (of Pharaoh) after their sin!

There is nothing mysterious in the favour shown (by God) while cherishing (His lovers), (but) He bestowed His favour on the magicians in the amputation (of their hands and feet).

There is nothing mysterious in journeying with feet that move, but look at the journey of the magicians when their feet had been cut off!

The knowers of God are safe for ever because they have passed through a sea of blood.

Safety appeared to them from the very midst of terror; 4365 consequently they are always in a state of increase (of safety).

You have seen that safety is concealed in a (state of) fear (danger): O excellent man, observe also that fear (danger) is (lurking) in a (state of) hope.

A certain Amír cunningly shadows[2] Jesus: Jesus hides himself[3] in the house.

---

[1] Literally, "become a manifest sign of (the veracity of) Moses."
[2] Literally, "attends on," "follows closely."     [3] Literally, "his face."

He (the Amír) enters in order that he may (seize him and) wear the crown (of sovereignty): because of his likeness to Jesus he himself becomes the crown of[1] the gibbet.

(He cries out), "Oh, do not hang me: I am not Jesus, I am the Amír, I am well-disposed to the Jews."

4370    "Hang him on the gibbet," (cry the Jews), "with all speed, for he is Jesus: (he is) seeking to escape from our hands by personating another[2]."

How often does an army march (hoping) to enjoy the fruits (of victory): its equipment becomes spoil (for the enemy), and it is overthrown[3].

How often does a merchant go (from home) in hope of gain: he thinks it will be a feast ('íd), but he is consumed like aloes-wood ('úd).

How often in the world does it happen contrariwise to this: (for example) one fancies (something to be bitter as) poison when it is (really sweet as) honey.

Often, (when) soldiers have made up their minds to die, the splendours (of triumph) and victory appear.

4375    Abraha came with the elephant to dishonour the House (of Allah), that he might throw down the living (and leave them lying) as though dead,

And destroy the holy Ka'ba and cause all (the inhabitants) to wander forth from that place,

In order that all the pilgrims might gather round him and might all turn in worship to his Ka'ba,

And that he might take vengeance on the Arabs for the injury (inflicted by them), for "why," said he, "should they set my Ka'ba on fire?"

His efforts only turned to glory for the Ka'ba: they caused the (holy) House to be glorified.

4380    (Formerly) the glory of the Meccans had been one: (now) it became a hundred: their glory was now extending to the Resurrection.

He (Abraha) and his Ka'ba were eclipsed more (and more). Whence is this? From the favours of the (Divine) Decree.

Those poor Arabs were enriched by the equipment and baggage of (the host of) Abraha, (who was) like a wild beast.

He thought that he was bringing an army (against the Ka'ba): (in fact) he was bringing gold for the defenders of the House.

He (the treasure-seeker) was (occupied), every step of the way, in contemplating this (wondrous) annulment of fixed purposes and ambitions.

4385    (When) he came home, he discovered the treasure: by Divine grace his fortune was restored.

---

[1] I.e. is suspended on.         [2] Literally, "confusing (us)."
[3] Literally, "falls on its head."

*How the (two) brothers repeated their advice to the eldest, and how he was unable to endure it and ran away from them and went off, frenzied and beside himself, and rushed into the King's audience-chamber without asking permission; but (this was) from excess of passionate love, not from disrespect and recklessness, etc.*

The two (brothers) said to him, "In our souls are answers (to thy arguments), like stars in the sky.

Unless we (answer and) speak, the game will not come out right; and if we speak, thy heart will be grieved.

We are like frogs in the water: 'tis painful to speak, while the result of silence is suffocation and illness.

If we speak not, (our) friendship (with thee) has no light (of truth); and if we speak, 'tis without leave (from thee)."

Straightway he sprang up, crying, "Farewell, O kinsmen: 4390 verily this world and all therein is but a passing enjoyment,"

And darted away like an arrow from the bow, so that there was no opportunity (for them) to speak at that time.

He came intoxicated (with love) into the presence of the King of China and at once kissed the earth frenziedly (at his feet).

To the King their (his lovers') feelings, their passion and agitation, were (an) open (book) in every detail from first to last.

The sheep are busy in their pasture, but the shepherd knows all about the sheep.

(Any one of those of whom the Prophet said), "Each of you 4395 is a shepherd," knows which of the flock is feeding and which is (engaged) in combat.

Although apparently he was far from those ranks, yet he was (in their midst) like the tambourine at a wedding-feast.

(He was) well acquainted with the burning and flaming (passion) of those who came to his court, (but) in his wisdom he had ignored them and kept silence.

That exalted (monarch) was in the midst (depths) of their souls, but he had purposely feigned to be unfamiliar (with them).

The form (appearance) of the fire is beneath the kettle; the spirit (reality) of the fire is in the soul of the kettle.

Its form is outside and its spirit inside: the spirit (real nature) 4400 of the soul's Beloved is (in the soul) like blood in the veins.

The prince knelt before the King, (while) ten announcers gave a description of his state.

Although the King knew it all long ago, yet the announcer was performing the duties of his office.

O sincere man, a single atom of the light of (mystic) knowledge within (thee) is better than a hundred announcers.

To confine one's attention[1] to the announcer is a mark of being

---

[1] Literally, "to keep the ear in pawn."

debarred (from access to real knowledge) and of (being pre-occupied with) conjecture and (mere) opinion.

4405    He whose scout is his inward eye—his eye will behold with the very acme of clairvoyance.

His soul is not content with traditional authority; nay, his feeling of (absolute) certainty comes from the inward eye.

Then the announcer opened his lips to describe his (the eldest brother's) plight in the presence of the elect King.

He said, "O King, he is fallen a prey to thy beneficence: show kingly favour (to him), for he has no means of escape.

He has clutched the saddle-strap of this empire: stroke his distraught head with thy (royal) hand!"

4410    The King replied, "This youth will obtain (from me) every high dignity and sovereignty that he seeks.

I will bestow on him here (and now) twenty times as many kingdoms as he has relinquished, and myself into the bargain."

He (the announcer) said, "Since thy royal majesty sowed in him the seed of love, how could it leave (in him) any passion except passion for thee?

'Tis so agreeable to him to be thy slave that kingship has become cold comfort to his heart.

He has gambled away kingship and princedom: for thy sake he has put up with living in exile.

4415    He is a Ṣúfí: he has flung away his mantle in ecstasy: how should he turn again to his mantle?

To hanker for the given away mantle and repent (of having given it) is as much as to say, 'I have been swindled:

Put the mantle back here, O comrade, for that (ecstasy) was not worth it, that is, (not worth) this (mantle).'

Far be it from a lover that such a thought should occur to him; and if it do, dust ought to be (sprinkled) on his head.

Love is worth a hundred mantles like that of the body, which contains a (principle of) life and sensation and reason;

4420    Especially the mantle of worldly dominion, which is cut short (exiguous): a pennyworth[1] of intoxication with it is (results in) headache.

Worldly dominion is lawful (only) to those who indulge the body: we (lovers) are devoted to the everlasting kingdom of Love.

He (the prince) is Love's agent: do not deprive him of his employment, do not let him be employed in aught but loving thee.

The office (business) that veils me from (the sight of) thy face is the very essence of unemployment, though it is called 'office.'

The cause of (his) delay in coming hither was lack of capability and defect of skill."

---

[1] Literally, "five *dángs*."

(If) you go into a mine without (having) capability, you will 4425
not gain possession of a single grain (of gold),

Tanquam vir veneri inhabilis qui virginem emit: ea, etsi pectus
argenteum (candidum) sit, frui quo pacto poterit?

(The incapable man is) like a lamp without oil or wick that
gets neither much nor little from the (flaming) taper.

(If) one who cannot smell enter a garden, how should his
brain (nose) be delighted by the fragrant herbs?—

Tanquam formosa et venusta hospita viri debilis; (and) like
the sound of a harp or lute in the ears of the deaf;

(And) like the land-bird that falls into great waters: what 4430
should it find there but death and perdition?

(And) like one who, having no wheat, goes to a mill: nothing
will be given to him except the whitening of his beard and hair
(with flour).

The celestial mill bestows on those who have no wheat (only)
whiteness of hair and weakness in the loins;

But on those who bring wheat with them this mill bestows
empire and gives them sovereign power.

You must first be qualified for Paradise in order that from
Paradise the (everlasting) life may be born to you.

What pleasure has the new-born child in wine and roast-meat 4435
and palaces and domes?

These parables have no limit: do not seek (more) words (of
this kind): go and acquire capability!

(The announcer said), "He tarried until now for the sake of
capability (qualification), (but) ere it was acquired his longing
burst (all) bounds."

He (the prince) said, "Capability too is imparted by the King:
how should the body be made capable without (the intervention
of) the soul?"

(Then) the favours of the King did away with his anguish:
he had gone to hunt the King: he became the King's prey.

(The announcer said), "Whosoever goes in chase of a quarry 4440
like thee does not catch his quarry till he is himself caught."

'Tis certain that every seeker of princedom is thrown into
captivity before (he gains) it.

Know that what is depicted on this mundane frontispiece[1] is
preposterous: every slave to the world is named "lord of the
world."

O wrong-thinking perversely-acting body, thou that hast
enthralled a hundred thousand freemen,

Abandon this guileful plotting for a time: live free a few
moments ere thou die;

For if, like the (heavily-laden) ass, thou hast no way of 4445

[1] Literally, "preface" or "small piece of brocade." This world may be
regarded as the preface to the next.

attaining to freedom, thy movement, like that of the bucket[1], can only be (down) into the well.

Go, take leave of my spirit for awhile: go, seek another companion instead of me.

My turn is finished: set me free, espouse another, (beguile) some one else.

O body with thy hundred (worldly) concerns, bid me farewell: thou hast taken my life: (now) seek another (victim).

*How a cadi was infatuated with the wife of Júḥí and remained (hidden) in a chest, and how the cadi's deputy purchased the chest; and how next year (when) Júḥí's wife came again, hoping to play the same trick (which had succeeded) last year, the cadi said (to her), "Set me free and seek some one else"; and so on to the end of the story.*

Every year, on account of poverty, Júḥí would artfully turn to his wife and say, "O sweetheart,

4450  Since thou hast the weapons, go, catch some game in order that we may get milk (profit) from thy prey.

Wherefore has God given thee the bow of thine eyebrow, the arrow of thy amorous glance, and the snare of thy craftiness? For hunting.

Go, lay the snare for a big bird: show the bait, but do not let him eat it.

Show him his wish, but disappoint him: how can he eat the bait when he is imprisoned in the snare?"

His wife went to the cadi to complain, saying, "I appeal (to thee) for help against my faithless husband."

4455  (To) cut the tale short, the cadi fell a prey to the (pleading) words and beauty of the fair woman.

He said, "There is such a noise in the court of justice (that) I cannot understand this complaint;

(But) if you will come to my private house, O cypress-slender one, and describe to me the injurious behaviour of your husband"—

"In thy house," she replied, "there will be a (constant) coming and going of every sort of people, good and bad, for the purpose of making complaints."

(If) the house of the head be wholly filled with a mad passion, the breast will be full of anxiety and commotion.

4460  The rest of the (bodily) members are undisturbed by thinking, while those breasts are consumed by thoughts that return[2].

Take refuge in the autumn gale[3] of fear of God: let last year's flowers[4] be shed;

---

[1] Read همچو دلوت.    [2] Literally, "by returning ones."
[3] Literally, "the autumn and the gale."    [4] Literally, "peonies."

(For) these flowers[1] prevent the new buds (from blossoming), and it is (only) for the sake of their growth that the tree of the heart exists.

Put thyself to sleep (and escape) from this (vain) thinking: (then) lift up thy head from sleep into (spiritual) wakefulness.

Like the Men of the Cave (the Seven Sleepers), pass quickly, O Khwája, into (the state of those who are) *awake, though thou wouldst deem them asleep*[2].

"O adorable one," said the cadi, "what can be contrived?" 4465 She answered, "This (thy) handmaid's house is quite empty.

The enemy has gone into the country, and the caretaker is not there either: it is a very good place for meeting in private.

Come there to-night if possible: what one does by night is (done) without (the intention of) making (people) hear of it or see it;

(At that time) all the spies are intoxicated with the wine of sleep: all have been beheaded (and left as though lifeless) by the negro, Night."

The sugar-lipped (damsel) chanted wondrous spells over the cadi—and then with what (bewitching) lips!

How often did Iblís palaver with Adam!—but when Eve told 4470 him to eat, then (and not till then) did he eat.

The first blood (shed) in this world of iniquity and justice was shed by Qábíl (Cain) for the sake of a woman.

Whenever Noah was frying meat in the frying-pan[3], Wáhila (his wife) would throw stones at the frying-pan,

And his wife's plotting would defeat his (missionary) work, (so that) the clear water of his exhortation would become turbid;

(For) she used to send secret messages to the (unbelieving) folk, saying, "Preserve your religion from (being corrupted by) these erring men!"

*How the cadi went to the house of Júḥí's wife, and how Júḥí knocked angrily at the door, and how the cadi took refuge in a chest, etc.*

The guile of woman is infinite. The sagacious cadi went at 4475 night to the wife (of Júḥí) ut cum ea coiret.

The wife set two (lighted) candles and the dessert for his entertainment. "(I can do) without this drink," said he: "I am intoxicated (with love)."

At that moment Júḥí came and knocked at the door: the cadi looked for a place into which he could slink for refuge.

---

[1] Literally, "peonies."

[2] The *Qur'án*, XVIII, 17, has: "*asleep though thou wouldst deem them awake.*"

[3] *I.e.* seeking to inspire the stubborn hearts of the infidels with ardent faith in his religion.

He saw no hiding-place but a chest: in his fright the man went into the chest.

(Then) Júhí came in and said (to his wife), "O spouse, O thou who art my plague (both) in spring and autumn,

4480 What do I possess that is not sacrificed to thee: (why, then, is it) that thou art always crying out at me?

Thou hast let loose thy tongue at my dry crusts: now thou callest me 'pauper,' now 'cuckold.'

If, my dear, I suffer from these two maladies, one (the latter) comes from thee and the other from God.

What do I possess but that chest, which is a source of suspicion and a ground for (evil) surmise?

People think I keep gold in it, and because of these (false) opinions charity is withheld from me.

4485 The appearance of the chest is very pleasing, but it is quite empty of goods and silver and gold.

('Tis) like the person of a hypocrite, (one who is) handsome and dignified; (but) in the basket you will find nothing except a snake.

To-morrow I will take the chest into the street and burn it in the midst of the market at the cross-ways,

That true believer and Zoroastrian and Jew may see there was nothing in this chest but (cause for) cursing."

"O husband," cried the woman, "come now, give up this (idea)!" (However), he swore several times that he would do just as he had said.

4490 Early (next morning) he (went) like the wind, fetched a porter, and immediately put the chest on his back.

(He set off with it, while) the cadi inside the chest shouted in an agony (of terror), "O porter! O porter!"

The porter looked to the right and the left to see from what direction the shouts and warnings were coming.

"I wonder," said he, "is it a hátif, this voice which is calling me, or is it a peri (jinní) summoning me mysteriously?"

When the shouts followed one another in succession and increased, he said, "'Tis not a hátif," and recovered himself.

4495 At last he perceived that the shouts and cries for help came from the chest and that somebody was concealed in it.

The lover who has fallen passionately in love with an (earthly) object of affection has gone into the chest, though (in appearance) he is outside.

He has spent (wasted) his life in the chest on account of (worldly) cares: he can see nothing of the world except a chest.

The head that is not (raised) above the sky—know that it is (confined) in that chest by its vain desires.

When he (such an one) goes forth from the chest of the body, he will (only) go from one tomb to another tomb.

This topic is endless. The cadi said to him, "O porter, O carrier 4500 of the chest,

Give news of me to my deputy at the court of justice and acquaint him with all (the details of) this (affair) as quickly as possible,

In order that he may buy this (chest) with gold from this witless fellow and take it fastened, just as it is, to my house."

O Lord, appoint a spiritually endowed company to redeem us from the chest of the body!

Who but the prophets and apostles can redeem the people from confinement in the chest of guile?

Among thousands there is (only) one person of comely aspect, 4505 who knows that he is inside the chest.

He must formerly have beheld the (spiritual) world, so that by means of that contrary this contrary should be made evident to him.

Because "knowledge is the true believer's lost camel," he recognises his own lost camel and feels certain (that it is his).

(But) he that has never seen good fortune, how will he be perturbed in this calamity?

Either he fell into captivity in childhood, or was born a slave at first from his mother's womb.

His soul has never known the delight of (spiritual) freedom: 4510 the chest of (phenomenal) forms is his arena.

His mind is for ever imprisoned in forms: he (only) passes from cage into cage.

He has no means of passing beyond the cage (and going) aloft: he goes to and fro into (successive) cages.

In the *Qur'án* (is the text), "*If ye have the power, pass beyond*": these words came from Him (God) to the Jinn and mankind.

He said, "There is no way for you to pass beyond the sky save by (Divine) authority and by inspiration from Heaven."

If he (any one) go from chest to chest, he is not of Heaven, he 4515 is of the chest (the lower world)

The pleasure of changing his chest (only) stupefies him anew: he does not perceive that he is inside the chest.

If he is not deluded by (all) these chests, he seeks release and deliverance, like the cadi.

Know that the mark of one who apprehends this is his crying for help and being in terror[1].

Like the cadi, he will be quaking (with fear): how should a breath of joy rise from his soul?

[1] Literally, "that he is not without lamentation and terror."

### The arrival of the cadi's deputy in the bazaar and his purchase of the chest from Júḥí, etc.

4520    The deputy arrived and asked, "How much (do you want) for your chest?" "They are offering nine hundred pieces of gold and more," said he,

"(But) I will not come lower than a thousand: if you intend to buy, open your purse and produce (the money)."

He replied, "Have some shame, you in the short felt frock! The value of the chest is self-evident."

He (Júḥí) said, "To buy without seeing is an iniquity: our bargain is (being made) in the dark[1]: this is not right.

I will open (it): if it is not worth (the money), don't buy, lest you be defrauded, O father!"

4525    He (the deputy) said (addressing God), "O Veiler (of faults)[2], do not reveal the secret!" (Then he said to Júḥí), "I will buy it with the lid on: come to terms with me.

Veil (the faults of others) in order that (the like) veiling may be vouchsafed to you: do not deride any one till you see (yourself in) security.

Many like you have been left in this chest and have landed themselves in tribulation.

Inflict upon another (only) the pain and injury that you would wish and approve for yourself,

For God is lying in wait and in ambush, ready to give retribution before the Day of Judgement.

4530    All-encompassing is the Throne of Him who is throned in grandeur: over all souls is spread the Throne of His justice.

A corner of His throne is touching you: beware, do not move a hand to act impiously or unjustly.

Keep a careful watch over your own behaviour: observe that the honey is (contained) in justice and that after injustice comes the sting."

He (Júḥí) said, "Yes, what I did is wrong, but at the same time (you must) know (the proverb) that the aggressor is the more unjust (of the two)."

The deputy replied, "We are aggressors, every one of us, but notwithstanding our blackness of face we are happy,

4535    Like the negro who is happy and pleased, (for) he does not see his face, (though) others see it."

The altercation in bidding[3] (for the chest) was prolonged: (finally) he paid a hundred dinars and bought it from him.

O thou that findest wickedness agreeable, thou art always in the chest: the hátifs (voices from Heaven) and those who belong to the Unseen are redeeming thee.

---

[1] Literally, "under the blanket."
[2] Or, if the appeal is made directly to Júḥí, "O man who veilest (the faults of others)."     [3] Literally, "who will bid higher?"

*Expounding the Tradition that Muṣṭafá (Mohammed) said, the blessings of God be upon him: " When I am the protector of any one, 'Alí too is his protector," so that the Hypocrites asked sarcastically, " Was not he satisfied with the obedience and service rendered by us to himself that he bids us render the same service to a snivelling child?" etc.*

For this reason the Prophet, who laboured with the utmost zeal (in devotion), applied the name "protector" (*mawlá*) to himself and to 'Alí.

He said, "My cousin 'Alí is the protector and friend of every one who is under my protection."

Who is the "protector"? He that sets you free and removes 4540 the fetters of servitude from your feet.

Since prophethood is the guide to freedom, freedom is bestowed on true believers by the prophets.

Rejoice, O community of true believers: show yourselves to be "free" (pure and noble) as the cypress and the lily;

But do ye, like the gay-coloured garden, at every moment give unspoken thanks to the Water.

The cypresses and the green orchard mutely thank the water (that nourishes them) and show (silent) gratitude for the justice of Spring:

Clad in (fresh) robes and trailing their skirts, drunken and 4545 dancing and jubilant and scattering perfume;

Every part (of them) impregnated by royal Spring, their bodies as caskets filled with pearly fruit;

(Like) Maries, having no husband, yet big with a Messiah; silent ones, wordless and devoid of articulate expression,

(Saying implicitly), "Our Moon hath shone brightly (upon us) without speech: every tongue hath derived its speech from our beauty."

The speech of Jesus is (derived) from the (spiritual) beauty of Mary; the speech of Adam is a ray (reflexion) of the (Divine) Breath.

(This thanksgiving of the orchard is a lesson to you) in order 4550 that from (your) thanksgiving, O men of trust, increase (of spiritual glory) may accrue; (and if ye give thanks) then other plants are (springing up) amidst the herbage[1].

Here the reverse (of the well-known Tradition) is (applicable), (for) he that is content (with a modicum of thanksgiving) shall be abased; (and similarly), in this case, he that covets (excess of thanksgiving) shall be exalted.

Do not go so much into the sack of thy fleshly soul, do not be (so) forgetful of thy purchasers (redeemers).

---

[1] *I.e.* new blessings are added to those already received.

*How next year Júḥí's wife returned to the court of the cadi, hoping for the same contribution (of money) as last year, and how the cadi recognised her, and so on to the end of the story.*

After a year Júḥí, in consequence of the afflictions (of poverty), turned to his wife and said, "O clever wife,

Renew last year's contribution (to our household): complain of me to the cadi."

4555 The wife came before the cadi with (some other) women: she made a certain woman her interpreter,

Lest the cadi should recognise her by her speech and remember his past misfortune.

The coquettish glances of a woman are fascinating, but that (fascination) is increased a hundredfold by her voice.

Since she durst not raise (utter) a sound, the wife's ogling looks alone were of no avail.

"Go," said the cadi, "and fetch the defendant[1], that I may settle thy quarrel with him."

4560 (When) Júḥí arrived, the cadi did not recognise him at once, for at (their first) meeting he was in the chest.

He had (only) heard his voice outside, during the buying and selling and chaffering[2].

He said (to Júḥí), "Why won't you give your wife all the money she needs for expenses?" He replied, "I am devoted with (heart and) soul to the religious law,

But if I die I do not possess (enough to pay for) the shroud: I am bankrupt in this game, I have gambled everything away[3]."

From (hearing) these words the cadi, as it happened, recognised him and called to mind his roguery and the trick he had played.

4565 "You played that game[4] with me," he said: "last year you put me out of action[5].

My turn is past: this year try that gamble on some one else and keep your hands off me!"

The knower of God has been isolated from the six (directions) and the five (senses): (necessarily, therefore), he has become on his guard against the sixes and fives of the backgammon (played by the World and the Devil).

He has escaped from the five senses and the six directions: he has made you acquainted with (what lies) beyond all that.

His intimations are the intimations of Eternity: he has transcended all conceptions and withdrawn himself apart.

[1] Literally, "thy adversary."
[2] Literally, "the (asking) less and more."
[3] Literally, "I am one who throws the six and five."
[4] Literally, "(game of) sixes and fives."
[5] Literally, "you threw me into the *shashdara*," a metaphor taken from the game of *nard*.

Unless he is outside of this hexagonal well[1], how should he 4570
bring up a Joseph from the inside (of it)?

He is one who goes to draw water above the unpillared firmament, (while) his body, like a bucket, is (low down) in the well, helping (to rescue the fallen).

The Josephs cling to his bucket, escape from the well, and become kings of Egypt.

The other buckets seek water from the well: his bucket has no concern with the water, it seeks (only) friends (in trouble).

The (other) buckets plunge into the water for food: his bucket is the food and life of the soul of the fish.

The (other) buckets are attached to the lofty wheel (of 4575
Fortune): his bucket is (held) in two Almighty fingers.

What bucket and what cord and what wheel? This is a very weak comparison, O pasha.

(But) whence shall I get a comparison that is without frailty? One to match him (the knower of God) will not come, and never has come, (to hand).

(He is) a hundred thousand men concealed in a single man, a hundred bows and arrows enclosed in a single blow-pipe;

A (type of) *thou didst not throw when thou threwest*, a temptation (for the ignorant), a hundred thousand stacks (of grain) in a handful.

(He is) a sun hidden in a mote: suddenly that mote opens its 4580
mouth (and reveals the sun).

The heavens and the earth crumble to atoms before that Sun when he springs forth from ambush.

How is a spirit like this meet for (confinement in) the body? Hark, O body, wash thy hands of this spirit!

O body that hast become the spirit's dwelling-place, 'tis enough: how long can the Sea abide in a water-skin?

O thou who art a thousand Gabriels in (the form of) man, O thou who art (many) Messiahs inside the ass (of Jesus),

O thou who art a thousand Ka'bas concealed in a church, 4585
O thou who causest 'ifrít and devil to fall into error,

Thou art the spaceless Object of worship in space: the devils have their shop destroyed by thee,

(For they say), "How should I pay homage to this clay? How should I bestow on a (mere) form a title signifying (my) obedience (adoration)?"

He is not the form (in which he appears): rub thine eye well, that thou mayst behold (in him) the radiance of the light of (Divine) glory!

---

[1] *I.e.* the sensible world.

*Resuming the explanation of the Story of the (eldest) prince and*
*his constant attendance at the court of the King.*

The prince in the presence of the King was bewildered by
this (mystery): he beheld the Seven Heavens in a handful of
clay.

4590   Nowise was it possible (for him) to open his lips in discussion,
but never for a moment did soul cease to converse with soul.

It came into his mind that 'twas exceedingly mysterious—
"all this is reality: whence, then, comes the form (appearance)?"

('Tis) a form that frees thee from (the illusion of) form, a
sleeper that awakens every one who is asleep (to the Truth).

The words (spoken by him) deliver (thee) from words (of idle
disputation), and the sickness (of love inspired by him) lets thee
escape from the sickness (of sensuality).

Therefore the sickness of love is the (very) soul of health:
its pains are the envy of every pleasure.

4595   O body, now wash thy hands of this (animal) soul, or if thou
wilt not wash (thy hands of it), seek another soul than this!

In short, the King cherished him (the prince) fondly, and in
(the beams of) that Sun he was melting away like the moon.

The melting (wasting) away of lovers is (the cause of their
spiritual) growth: like the moon, he (the lover) hath a fresh
(shining) face whilst he is melting away.

All the sick hope to be cured, but this sick one sobs, crying,
"Increase my sickness!"[1]

I have found no drink sweeter than this poison: no state of
health can be sweeter than this disease.

4600   No act of piety can be better than this sin: years in comparison
with this moment are (but) an hour."

In this fashion he remained with this King for a long while,
his heart (roasted like) *kabáb* and his soul laid on the tray (of
self-devotion).

He said, "The King beheads every one once, (but) I am
sacrificed anew by the King at every instant.

I am poor in gold, but rich in heads (lives): my head (life) hath
a hundred heads to take its place.

No one can run in (the path of) Love with two feet: no one
can play (the game of) Love with one head;

4605   Yet every one has two feet and one head: the body with
thousands of feet and heads is a rarity."

On this account all (other) combats are (fought) in vain[2],
(while) this combat[3] (of Love) grows hotter every moment.

The source of its heat lies beyond the realm of space: the
seven Hells are (but) a smoke (rising) from the sparks of its fire.

---

[1] Literally, "make me more (sick)."
[2] Literally, "all (other) arenas come to naught."    [3] Literally, "arena."

*Setting forth how Hell will say, when the Bridge Ṣirāṭ is (laid) over it (at the Resurrection), "O believer, pass more quickly across the Ṣirāṭ! Quick, make haste, lest the greatness of thy light put out my fire," (according to the Tradition), "Pass, O believer, for lo, thy light hath extinguished my fire."*

For this reason, O sincere man, Hell is enfeebled and extinguished by the fire of Love.

It says to him (the believer), "Pass speedily, O respected one, or else my fire will be destroyed by thy flames."

Behold how this breath (of Love) dissolves infidelity, which 4610 alone is the brimstone of Hell!

Quickly entrust thy brimstone to this passion (of Love), in order that neither Hell nor (even) its sparks may assail thee.

Paradise (too) says to him, "Pass like the wind, or else all that I possess will become unsalable;

For thou art the owner of the (whole) stack, (while) I am (but) a gleaner: I am (but) an idol, (while) thou art (all) the provinces of China[1]."

Both Hell and Paradise are trembling in fear of him (the believer): neither the one nor the other feels safe from him.

His (the prince's) life sped away and he found no opportunity 4615 to cure (his passion): the waiting consumed him exceedingly and his soul could not endure it.

For a long time, gnashing his teeth, he suffered this (agony): ere he attained, his life reached its end.

The form (appearance) of the Beloved vanished from him: he died and was united with the reality of the Beloved.

He said (to himself), "Though his raiment was of silk and Shushtar cloth, his unscreened embrace is sweeter.

(Now) I am denuded of my body, and he of (the veil of) phantasy: I am advancing triumphantly in the consummation of union."

These topics may be discussed up to this point, (but) all that 4620 comes after this must be kept hid;

And if you would tell it and make a hundred thousand efforts, 'tis fruitless labour, for it will never become clear.

As far as the sea, 'tis a journey on horseback[2]: after this you (must) have a wooden horse.

The wooden horse is no good on the dry land: it carries exclusively those who voyage on the sea.

The wooden horse is this (mystical) silence: (this) silence gives instruction to the sea-folk.

Every (such) silent one who wearies you is (really) uttering 4625 shrieks of love Yonder.

---

[1] *I.e.* the origin and home of idols (images of Buddha painted by Chinese artists).

[2] Literally, "a journey of horse and saddle."

You say, "I wonder why he is silent"; he says (to himself),
"How strange! Where is his ear?

I am deafened by the shrieks, (yet) he is unaware (of them)."
The (apparently) sharp-eared are (in fact) deaf to this (mystical)
converse.

(For example), some one cries aloud in his dream and gives a
hundred thousand discussions and communications,

(While) this (other), sitting beside him, is unaware (of it): 'tis
really he who is asleep and deaf to (all) that turmoil and tumult.

4630 And he whose wooden horse is shattered and sunk in the
water (of the sea), he in sooth is the fish.

He is neither silent nor speaking: he is a marvel: there is no
name to describe his state.

He does not belong to these two (categories), (and yet) that
prodigy is (really) both: to explain this would transgress the
limits of due reverence.

This comparison is poor and unsuccessful, but in the sensible
(world) there was none better than this (to be found).


*The death of the eldest prince, and how the middle brother came to
his funeral—for the youngest was confined to his bed by illness;
and how the King treated the middle brother with great affection,
so that he too was crippled (captivated) by his kindness; (and
how) he remained with the King, and a hundred thousand spoils
(precious gifts), from the unseen and visible worlds, were conferred
upon him by the fortune and favour of the King; with an exposi-
tion of some part thereof.*

The youngest (brother) was ill, and (so) the middle one came
alone to the funeral of the eldest.

4635 (When) the King espied him, he said with a purpose, "Who
is this?—for he is of that sea, and he too is a fish."

Then the announcer said, "He is a son of the same father:
this brother is younger than that (deceased) brother."

The King greeted him affectionately, saying, "Thou art a
keepsake (from thy brother to me)"; and by this enquiry
(gracious attention) made him too his prey.

In consequence of the kindness shown (to him) by the King,
that wretched man, (who was) roasted (in the fire of love), found
in his body a soul other than the (animal) soul.

He felt within his heart a sublime emotion which the Ṣúfí does
not experience during a hundred *chilas*[1].

4640 Court-yard and wall and mountain woven of stone seemed to
split open before him like a laughing (bursting) pomegranate.

One by one, the atoms (of the universe) were momently
opening their doors to him, like tents, in a hundred diverse ways.

[1] *Chila* is the name given to a forty days' period of religious seclusion.

The door would become now the window, now the sunbeams; the earth would become now the wheat, now the bushel[1].

In (men's) eyes the heavens are very old and threadbare; in his eye 'twas *a new creation* at every moment.

When the beauteous spirit is delivered from the body, no doubt an eye like this will be conferred upon it by (Divine) destiny.

A hundred thousand mysteries were revealed to him: he 4645 beheld that which the eyes of the initiated behold.

He opened (the inward) eye (and gazed) on the (ideal) form of that which he had (only) read in books.

From the dust of the mighty King's horse he obtained a precious collyrium for his eyesight.

In such a garden of flowers he was trailing his skirt, while every part of him was crying, "*Is there any more?*"

The flowers that grow from plants are (living but) a moment; the flowers that grow from Reason are (ever) fresh.

The flowers that bloom from earth become faded; the flowers 4650 that bloom from the heart—oh, what a joy!

Know that (all) the delightful sciences known to us are (only) two or three bunches of flowers from that Garden.

We are devoted to these two or three bunches of flowers because we have shut the Garden-door on ourselves.

Alas, O (dear) soul, (that) on account of (thy greed for) bread such (admirable) keys are always dropping from thy fingers!

And if for a moment thou art relieved from preoccupation with bread, thou danglest about the *chádar*[2] and (givest thyself up to) thy passion for women;

And then, when (the sea of) thy dropsy (lust) breaks into 4655 billows, thou must needs have under thy sway a (whole) city full of bread and women.

(At first) thou wert (only) a snake: (now) indeed thou hast become a dragon. Thou hadst (only) one head: now thou hast seven heads.

Hell is a seven-headed dragon: thy greed is the bait and Hell the snare.

Pull the snare to pieces, burn the bait, open new doors in this (bodily) tenement!

O sturdy beggar, unless thou art a lover (of God), thou hast (only) an echo, like the unconscious mountain.

How should the mountain possess a voice of its own? The 4660 echo is reflected from another, O trusty man.

In the same fashion as thy speech is the reflexion of another, so all thy feelings are nothing but a reflexion.

Both thy anger and thy pleasure are (only) reflected from

---

[1] Literally, *ṣá'*, a corn-measure of varying capacity.
[2] A woman's mantle.

34

others, (like) the joy of the procuress and the rage of the night-patrol.

Pray, what (harm) did that poor fellow do to the night-patrol that he should punish and torment him in revenge?[1]

How long (wilt thou follow) the glittering phantom reflected (from another)? Strive to make this[2] (experience) actual for thyself,

4665    So that thy words will be (prompted) by thy immediate feelings, and thy flight will be made with thine own wings and pinions.

'Tis with alien feathers that the arrow captures its prey; consequently it gets no share of the bird's flesh;

(But) the falcon brings its quarry from the mountains itself; consequently the king lets it eat partridge and starling.

The speech that is not (derived) from (Divine) inspiration springs from self-will: it is like dust (floating) in the air and among the motes (in the sunbeams).

If this saying appear to the Khwája[3] to be erroneous, recite a few lines at the beginning of (the Súra) *Wa'l-Najm*[4]

4670    Down to (the words), Mohammed *does not speak from self-will: 'tis only (a speech) gained by inspiration*[5].

O Aḥmad (Mohammed), since thou despairest not of (receiving) inspiration, leave investigation and conjecture to the corporealists;

For in case of necessity a carcase is lawful (food), but there is no need to investigate[6] (when one is) in the Ka'ba of union.

Whosoever wilfully adopts a heresy without investigation and the utmost efforts to discover the right way,

The wind (of self-will) will lift him up and kill him, like (the people of) 'Ád: he is no Solomon that it should waft his throne along.

4675    For 'Ád (and those like them) the wind is a treacherous carrier: (they are) as a lamb in the hands of a glutton,

Which he lays in his lap as though it were his own child and carries away to slaughter like a butcher.

That wind was (the punishment) for 'Ád because of their pride: they indeed deemed it a friend, (but) it was (really) a stranger (foe).

When of a sudden it turned its coat, that *evil comrade* shattered them piecemeal.

Shatter (destroy) the wind—for the wind (of self-will) is a great temptation—ere it shatter thee, like 'Ád.

---

1  See *v.* 4255 foll., *supra.*
2  Literally, "that this may become."
3  *I.e.* the reader.          4  *Qur'án,* LIII.
5  For metrical reasons the text of the *Qur'án* has been altered here.
6  *I.e.* seek to determine the direction in which the Ka'ba lies.

Húd admonished them, saying, "O prideful folk, this wind 4680
will tear out of your hands the skirt (to which ye are clinging).

The wind is God's army, and (only) in hypocrisy (deceit) has
it embraced you for a few days.

Secretly it is loyal to its Creator: when the appointed term
arrives, the wind will throw up its hands (and desert you)."

See how the wind passes through the mouth, coming and
going at every moment in advance and retreat.

The throat and teeth are in no danger from it; (but) when God
commands, it attacks the teeth;

(And then) a (mere) atom of wind becomes (like) a mountain 4685
and heavy, and toothache keeps him (the sufferer) miserable and
ill.

This is the same wind that used to pass by harmlessly: it was
the life of the crops and it became the death of the crops.

The hand of the person who (formerly) kissed thy hand—in
the moment of anger that hand becomes a mace.

He (who has toothache) cries from his soul, "O Lord! O Lord!
Take away this wind, O Thou whose aid is besought (by all)!

O mouth, thou wert heedless of this wind: (now) go and
betake thyself to asking pardon of God with utter abasement[1]."

His hard eye (now) sheds tears like rain: (only) pain causes 4690
the unbelievers to call unto God.

Since thou hast not received the breath (inspiration) of (holy)
men from a (holy) man, hark, receive the Divine inspiration from
pain.

The wind says, "I am a messenger from the King of mankind:
now I bring good news, now calamitous and bad;

For I am subject to command, I am not in command of myself:
when am I forgetful, like thee, of my King?

If thy (spiritual) state resembled that of Solomon, I should
have carried thee as (I carried) Solomon.

I am (only) lent (to thee); I should have become a possession in 4695
thy hand: I should have made thee acquainted with my mystery.

But since thou art rebellious and I am (only) taken on loan to
serve thee for three or four days,

Therefore I will lay thee low, like 'Ád, and dash away in
revolt from thy army,

In order that thy faith in the Unseen may become firm at the
moment when thy faith is (only) a source of woe."

(For) at that moment, in sooth, all become believers: at that
moment even the (most) headstrong run on their heads[2].

At that moment they cry piteously and make humble supplica- 4700
tion, like robbers and brigands under the gibbet.

But if you become upright in (your faith in) the Unseen,

[1] Literally, "from the roots of the teeth."
[2] *I.e.* are eager to show devotion.

you are owner of the two worlds and a magistrate (exercising sovereign authority) over yourself.

The abiding (spiritual) magistracy and kingship is not (something) taken on loan for two days and ailing (perishable).

(Possessing that) you are delivered from strife and can act for yourself: you are king and at the same time beating your own drum.

When the World squeezes our throats tightly[1], would that our gullets and mouths had eaten (only) earth!

4705 This mouth, indeed, has (always) been an eater of earth; but an earth that has been coloured.

This roast-meat and this wine and this sugar are (merely) coloured and painted earth, O son.

When you have eaten or drunk (them) and they have become flesh and skin, He gives them the colour of flesh, but they are still the earth of (His) street.

'Tis from a bit of earth that He stitches the (body of) clay, and then makes the whole (fabric) a bit of earth again.

Hindús and Qifcháq (Turks) and Greeks and Abyssinians— all have quite the same colour in the grave.

4710 So you may know that all those colours and pictures are entirely a mask and deceit and borrowed (ephemeral).

The only lasting colour is *the dye of Allah*: know that all the rest are tied (stuck) on (superficially) like a bell.

The colour of sincerity and the colour of piety and intuitive faith will endure in the (devout) worshippers for evermore;

And the colour of doubt and the colour of ingratitude and hypocrisy will endure in the undutiful soul for evermore;

Like wicked Pharaoh's blackness of face, the colour whereof is enduring, though his body passes away.

4715 (And so with) the radiance and glory in the beauteous faces of the sincere (believers): their bodies pass away, but that remains till the Day of Judgement.

The only ugly one is that (eternally) ugly one; the only beautiful one is that (eternally) beautiful one: this one is always laughing and that one scowling.

He (God) gives to earth a certain colour and variety and value, and causes childish folk to wrangle over it.

(When) a piece of dough is baked in the shape of a camel or lion, (these) children bite their fingers (excitedly) in their greed for it.

The lion or camel turns to bread in the mouth, but it is futile[2] to tell this to children.

4720 The child is in a (state of) ignorance and fancy and doubt: at any rate, thank God, his strength is (but) little.

---

[1] *I.e.* on the approach of death.
[2] Literally, "does not take hold," "produces no effect."

The child is quarrelsome and very mischievous[1]: thank God for his lack of skill and strength.

(But) alas for these childish undisciplined elders who in their strength have become an affliction to every guardian!

When weapons and ignorance are brought together, he (such an one) becomes in his tyranny a world-consuming Pharaoh.

O poor man, thank God for thy deficiency (of means), for (thereby) thou art delivered from being a Pharaoh and ungrateful (for Divine blessings).

Thank God that thou art the oppressed, not the oppressor: 4725 thou art secure from acting like Pharaoh and from every temptation.

An empty belly never bragged of Divinity, for it has no faggots to feed its fire.

An empty belly is the Devil's prison, because anxiety for bread prevents him from plotting and deceiving.

Know that a belly full of viands is the Devil's market, where the Devil's merchants raise a clamour:

Merchants who practise sorcery and sell worthless goods and obfuscate (men's) wits by vociferation.

By a (trick of) sorcery they cause a vat to run like a horse and 4730 make a piece of linen out of moonshine and twilight.

They weave earth like silk and throw earth (dust) in the eyes of the discerning.

They give to a bit of (fragrant) sandal-wood the appearance of a piece of (common) wood; they put in us the envious desire for a clod.

(But) holy is He who giveth (mere) earth a (specious) colour and causes us to quarrel over it like children.

(The world is) a skirtful of earth, and we are like little children: in our sight the earth is as gold of the mine.

There is no room for a child beside (grown-up) men: how 4735 should God let a child sit with men?

If fruit become old, (yet) so long as it is immature and not ripe it is called *ghúra* (unripe grapes).

Though (one resembling) immature and sour (fruit) reach the age of a hundred years, he is (still) a child and unripe (*ghúra*) in the opinion of every sagacious person.

Though his hair and beard be white, he is still in the childish state of fear and hope,

Saying, "Shall I attain (to maturity), or am I (to be) left immature? Oh, I wonder, will the Vine bestow that bounty on me?

Notwithstanding such an incapacity and remoteness (from 4740 God), will He confer on these unripe grapes (*ghúra*) of mine a perfection like that of the ripe grape (*angúr*)?

---

[1] Literally, "has a hundred mischiefs."

I have no hopes from any quarter, but that (Divine) Bounty is saying to me, '*Do not ye despair!*'"

Our Ḳháqán (Emperor) has made a perpetual feast (for us): He is always pulling our ears (drawing us thither and saying), "*Do not lose hope!*"

Although we are in the ditch (and overwhelmed) by this despair, let us go dancing along since He has invited us.

Let us dance (along) like mettlesome horses galloping towards the familiar pasturage.

4745     Let us toss our feet, though no foot is there; let us drain the cup, though no cup is there,

Because all things there are spiritual: 'tis reality on reality on reality.

Form is the shadow, reality is the sun: the shadowless light is (only to be found) in the ruin[1].

When not a brick is left (resting) on a brick there, no ugly shadow remains in the moonlight.

(Even) if the brick be of gold it must be torn away, since (the removal of) the brick is the price paid for inspiration and light.

4750     In order to remove the shadow (of materiality) the mountain (Sinai) is rased to the ground: 'tis a small matter to fall to pieces for the sake of this light.

When the light of the Lord struck on the surface of the mountain, it (the mountain) fell to pieces in order that it (the light) should penetrate its interior too.

As soon as a loaf of bread touches the palm of a hungry man, his eyes and mouth open wide in desire (to eat it).

This (light) is worth (the price, namely) falling into a hundred thousand pieces: soar up through the (spiritual) heaven, O (thou who resemblest) earth,

That the light of heaven may consume thy shadow: the (dark) night is caused by thy shadow, O enemy of Day.

4755     This earth is like a cradle for babes: it cramps the movements[2] of grown-up men.

On account of the babes (who live in it) God hath called the earth a cradle (*mahd*), and He hath bestowed milk on the babes in their cradle.

The house is crowded with these cradles: let the babes grow up quickly, O King!

O cradle, do not incommode the house (but let there be room), so that the grown-up man can move freely.

---

[1] *I.e.* when material forms are eliminated.
[2] Literally, "keeps narrow the dwelling-place."

*(Concerning) the vicious distempered thoughts that arose in the prince in consequence of the (spiritual) self-sufficiency and illumination with which his heart had been endowed by the King: how he proceeded to show ingratitude and rebelliousness, and how the King, being made aware of it in an inspired and mysterious manner, was pained at heart and, though outwardly unconscious (of it), dealt his (the prince's) spirit a (mortal) wound, etc.*

When from the inward nature of the King the (spiritual) allowance was paid over, without sale or purchase, into his (the prince's) soul,

His moon-like soul was feeding on the light of the King's soul 4760 as the moon (feeds) on (the light of) the sun,

And the spiritual ration from the peerless King was arriving in his intoxicated soul at every moment.

'Twas not that (material food) which polytheists and Christians eat, (but) part of the (spiritual) food which the angels eat.

He felt self-sufficiency within himself, and from self-sufficiency emerged a feeling of insolent pride.

"Am not I," said he, "both a king and a king's son? How have I let this King take control of me?

Now that a resplendent moon has risen for me, why should 4765 I be following a (cloud of) dust?

The water is (running) in my river-bed, and 'tis time to show disdain: wherefore should I who want nothing endure disdain from another?

Why should I bandage my head when my headache is gone? The time for pale face and tearful eye is past.

Since my lips have become (sweet) as sugar and my cheeks (bright) as the moon, I must open another (independent) shop."

When his carnal soul began to spawn from this egoism, he began to chew a hundred thousand thistles (cherish absurd fancies).

Even the evil eye can traverse a hundred deserts to reach the 4770 object of its greed and envy[1]:

How, (then), should the sea of the King, to which every water returns, be ignorant of what is (contained) in torrent and river?

The King's heart was pained by his (the prince's) thoughts and the ingratitude (shown) for his virgin (ever new) munificence.

He said (to himself), "Prithee, O base ill-mannered fellow, was this what my bounty deserved? Marvellous!

(Look) how I have dealt with thee in (lavishing) this precious treasure! (Look) how thou hast dealt with me in thy mean-spiritedness!

---

[1] Literally, "reaches the place that lies a hundred deserts away from greed and envy."

4775    I have put in thy bosom a moon that will never set till the Day of Reckoning,

And in requital for that gift of pure light thou hast thrown thorns and earth in mine eye.

I have become for thee a ladder to Heaven, and thou hast become a bow and arrow in combat with me."

Pangs of jealousy arose in (the heart of) the King: the reflexion of the King's pangs entered into him (the prince).

The bird of his felicity fluttered violently in reproaching him and tore the veil (exposed the disgrace) of him who had sought seclusion (made himself independent of the King).

4780    When the comely youth felt within himself the dust and (disturbing) effects of his wicked behaviour,

(And saw that) the allowance of favour and bounty had failed and that the house of his joy was filled with sorrow,

He came to himself (recovered) from the intoxication caused by the wine (of egoism); (but) in consequence of that sin his head became the abode of crop-sickness.

He had eaten the wheat (the forbidden fruit), his celestial robe had been stripped off him, and Paradise had become for him a desert and sandy plain.

He perceived that that (intoxicating) draught had made him ill and that the poison of those egoistic pretensions had done its work.

4785    His soul that was (formerly) like a peacock in the (eternal) garden of delight (now) became like an owl in the wilderness of unreality.

Like Adam, he was left far away from Paradise, driving an ox on the earth for the purpose of sowing.

He was shedding tears and crying, "O Hindú mighty (in craft)[1], thou hast made the lion[2] a captive of the cow's tail[3].

O wicked fleshly soul with thy chill breath, thou hast acted disloyally to the King who answers every call for help.

In thy greed for a grain of wheat thou hast chosen (to enter) the trap, and every grain of its wheat has become a scorpion to (sting) thee.

4790    The vain fancy of egoism came into thy head: (now) behold a shackle weighing fifty *mann* on thy foot!"

In this fashion was he mourning for his soul, saying, "Why did I become the antagonist of my sovereign?"

(Then) he came to himself and asked pardon of God, and with his repentance he combined something else.

The pain that arises from dread of losing one's faith—take pity (on him who is thus afflicted), for that is the irremediable pain.

May no human being have a perfect (new and spotless)

---

[1] *I.e.* the carnal soul.    [2] *I.e.* the spirit.    [3] *I.e.* the body.

raiment! As soon as he is delivered from enduring (poverty)
he at once seeks the seat of honour.

May no human being possess a fist and nails! (for) then he 4795
never thinks of devotion and righteousness.

'Tis best for a man to be killed (mortified) in tribulation: the
carnal soul is an ingrate and one that has gone astray.

*How God addressed Azrael, saying, "Of all these creatures whose
souls thou hast seized, whom didst thou pity most?" and the
answer given by Azrael to the Lord.*

God was saying to Azrael, "O marshal, whom of all the
miserable ones didst thou pity (most)?"

He replied, "My heart burns with grief for them all, but I
am afraid to neglect the (Divine) command,

So that I should say, 'Would that God might sacrifice me in
exchange for the (generous) youth!'"

God asked, "For whom didst thou feel the greatest pity? On 4800
account of whom was thy heart most filled with flame and
grilled?"

"One day," said he, "by (Thy) command I wrecked a ship
on the fierce waves, so that it went to pieces.

Then Thou bad'st me take the souls of them all, except one
woman and one child belonging to that company.

The twain were left on a plank, and the plank was being
driven on by the waves.

Then Thou saidst, 'Take the mother's soul and leave the
child alone in obedience to the command *Be!*'

When I parted the child from its mother, Thou thyself 4805
knowest how bitter 'twas to me.

Often have I seen sighs (heaved) in great mournings, (but) the
bitter grief of that child has never gone from my recollection."

God said, "Of My grace I bade the waves cast that child[1]
into a forest—

A forest abounding in lilies and sweet basils and roses, full of
trees laden with fruit good to eat,

And fountains of sweet limpid water. I fostered the child
with a hundred endearments.

Myriads of melodious singing-birds poured forth a hundred 4810
songs in that garden.

I made for him a couch of wild-rose leaves; I made him
secure from the shock of afflictions.

I told the sun not to scorch him; I told the wind to blow on
him gently;

I told the clouds not to rain upon him; I told the lightning
not to dart at him.

---

[1] The child was Nimrod. See v. 4843 *infra*.

I said, 'O December, do not cut off the mild weather[1] from this orchard; O November, do not let thy fist fall[2] on this garden.'"

### *The miracles of Shaybán Rá'í, may God sanctify his venerable spirit!*

4815    Just as Shaybán Rá'í (the shepherd), because of the froward wolf, used to draw a line round his flock at the hour of the Friday prayers,

In order that no sheep should go beyond that line, and that no wolf or mischievous robber should come inside.

'Twas on the model of Húd's circle of refuge[3], in which his followers were safe from the *ṣarṣar* wind[4].

(Húd said to them), "Stay quietly within this line for eight days and view the terrible mutilation (which is being inflicted) outside."

It (the wind) lifted (the unbelievers) into the air and flung them on the stones, so that flesh and bone were torn asunder.

4820    One party it hurled against each other in the air, so that their bones crumbled like poppy-seed.

There is no room in the *Mathnawí* to describe fully that chastisement whereat Heaven trembled.

If, O icy wind, thou art doing this by (thine own) nature, (then) try to invade[5] the line and circle drawn by Húd!

O natural philosopher, perceive that this kingdom (of God) is above Nature, or else come and (if thou canst) wipe out this (narrative) from the Holy Book!

Prohibit those who recite the *Qur'án* (professionally) and impose a ban (upon them), or punish the teacher and put terror into him!

4825    Thou art helpless and unable to understand the cause of this helplessness: thy helplessness is a reflexion (foretaste) of the Day of Retribution.

O perverse man, thou hast many a helpless plight before thee: (when) the hour comes, lo, the hide-aways will emerge!

Happy is he whose (spiritual) food is this helplessness and bewilderment and who in both worlds is sleeping in the shadow (protection) of the Beloved.

He (such an one) is conscious of being helpless both in the stable (of the present life) and in the last (future) state: he is dead (to self), he has adopted "the old women's religion[6]."

(He is) like Zalíkhá, (who), when Joseph beamed upon her, found the way from decrepitude to youth.

4830    Life depends on dying (to self) and on suffering tribulation: the Water of Life is in the (Land of) Darkness.

---

[1] Literally, "the equable temperature."
[2] Literally, "do not rub thy fist."
[3] See translation of Book I, *v.* 854 foll.
[4] Literally, "the *ṣarṣar* wind was safety (no danger) to his followers."
[5] Literally, "prowl round."          [6] *I.e.* unquestioning faith.

*Resuming the Story of the most High God's bringing up Nimrod in his childhood without the intervention of mother and nurse.*

"In short, that garden, like the (spiritual) orchard of gnostics, was secure from the simoom and the ṣarṣar wind.

A leopardess (there) had newly given birth to cubs: I bade her give milk to him (Nimrod), and she obeyed.

So she gave him milk and tended him till he grew up and became strong and valiant.

When he was weaned, I told the peris (Jinn) to teach him how to discourse and deal justice.

I gave him nourishment from that garden: how should (the description of) My artfulness be contained in words? 4835

I bestowed on Job a father's love in order that he might entertain the worms hospitably and do them no harm.

I bestowed on the worms love for him like that of children for their father. Look, here is (a token of My) Power, here is (a token of My) Hand!

I have taught mothers to care (for their children): how (infinite) must be the kindness that I have kindled!

(Unto him) I showed a hundred favours and (knit) a hundred ties (of obligation), that he might experience My kindness directly,

And not be distracted by any secondary cause, to the end that every call for help should be made by him to Me, 4840

Or at least that he should have no excuse (for turning elsewhere) and no occasion to complain of any evil companion.

He enjoyed this tender care (cemented) by a hundred ties, for I fostered him (Myself) without an intermediary.

His thanks, O honoured servant, were this, that he became Nimrod and the burner of Khalíl (Abraham)"—

Just as this prince, in return for the favours of the King, showed arrogance and sought to aggrandise himself,

Saying, "Why should I become the follower of another when I possess empire and new (splendid) fortune?" 4845

(Hence) the King's favours, of which the tale has been told above, were veiled from his heart (in oblivion) by his outrageous insolence—

"Even so did Nimrod ignorantly and blindly trample underfoot those favours (of Mine).

Now he has become an infidel and is waylaying (the faithful): he is acting with arrogance and pretending to Divinity.

By means of three vultures he has gone (flown) towards august Heaven in order to battle with Me,

And has killed a hundred thousand innocent children (in the hope) that he may find Abraham; 4850

For the astrologers declared that, according to the forecast for the year, there would be born an adversary to combat him,

(And said), 'Hark, take precautions to repel that enemy'; (so) in his craziness he would fain kill every child that was born.

(But), to confound him, the inspired child was saved; the blood of (all) the others remained (as a burden of guilt) upon his neck.

Oh, 'tis wonderful! Did he obtain that empire from his father so that (in consequence) he was befooled by the darkness[1] of noble lineage?

4855    (Nay); if father and mother were an obstacle (cause of delusion) to others, he derived the jewels in his pocket from Me."

Assuredly thy wicked carnal soul is a rapacious wolf: why art thou laying the blame on every comrade (neighbour)?

In its misguidedness the foul disbelieving unconscionable carnal soul is (like) a cap for (concealing the diseased condition of) a hundred baldpates.

For this reason, O poor slave (of God), I am always saying, "Do not remove the collar from the neck of the cur."

(Even) if this cur has become a teacher, it is a cur still: be thou one whose carnal soul is abased, for it is evil-natured.

4860    Thou wilt perform thy bounden duty if thou go round about (one like) Suhayl (Canopus, and absorb his light)[2] as Ṭá'if hide (absorbs the rays),

In order that Suhayl may redeem thee from the vices of the skin (corporeality), and that thou mayst fit the foot of the Beloved like a boot.

The entire *Qur'án* is a description of the viciousness of carnal souls: look into the Holy Book! Where is thine eye?

('Tis) an account of the carnal soul of people like 'Ád, which (whenever it) found weapons took the utmost pains[3] to combat the prophets.

From generation to generation, the wickedness of the undisciplined carnal soul was the cause of the world being suddenly set on fire (by Divine wrath).

*Returning to the Story of the prince who was smitten by a (mortal) blow from the heart of the King and departed from this world before he was fully endowed with the other (spiritual) excellences.*

4865    Abridge the tale: after a year (had passed) the indignation of that jealous one (the King of China) brought him (the prince) to the grave.

When the King emerged from the state of self-effacement (*mahw*) into consciousness, (he found that) his martial eye had wrought that bloodshed.

---

[1] *I.e.* false and unenlightened notions.
[2] *I.e.* "if thou consort with an illustrious saint and become purified by his spiritual influence."
[3] Literally, "was splitting hairs."

When the peerless (King) looked at his quiver he perceived that one arrow was missing from his quiver.

He said (to himself), "Where is that arrow?" and requested God (to inform him). He (God) replied, "In his (the prince's) throat, for 'tis by thy arrow (that he has been slain)."

The King, whose heart was like an ocean, pardoned him; but, alas, the arrow had struck a vital spot.

He was slain, and the King wept in mourning for him, (for) 4870 he (the King) is all: he is both the slayer and the next of kin;

For if he be not both, then he is not all; (but) he is both the slayer of people and a mourner (for them).

(Meanwhile) the pale-cheeked martyr was thanking (God) that it (the arrow) had smitten his body and had not smitten that which is real.

The visible body is doomed to go at last, (but) that which is real (the pure spirit) shall live rejoicing for ever.

If that punishment was inflicted, yet it fell only on the skin: the lover went unscathed to the Beloved.

Although he laid hold of the Emperor's saddle-strap[1], (yet) in 4875 the end he was (only) admitted (to union with his Beloved) by the eye whose glances kill[2].

And the third (brother) was the laziest of the three: he won (the prize) completely—the form (appearance) as well as the reality.


*The injunctions given by a certain person that after he died his property should be inherited by whichever of his three sons was the laziest.*

Long ago a certain person, in giving injunctions on his death-bed, had spoken (as follows)—

(For) he had three sons like three moving cypresses: to them he had devoted his (vital) soul and his (rational) spirit.

He said, "Whichever of these three is the laziest, let him take all the goods and gold in my possession."

He told the cadi and enjoined him strictly: after that, he 4880 drained the wine-cup of death.

The sons said to the cadi, "O noble sir, we three orphans will not depart from his decision.

We accept and obey: (the right of) control belongs to him: what he has commanded must be executed by us.

We are like Ishmael: we will not recoil from our Abraham though he is offering us in sacrifice."

---

[1] *I.e.* devoted himself to the Emperor's service.
[2] Literally, "the eye of perfection," *i.e.* the jealous eye of the Beloved which blasts the lover's self-conceit.

The cadi said, "Let each one (of you), using his intelligence, give some account of his laziness,

4885 That I may perceive the laziness of each and know beyond any doubt (how stands) the case of every one (of you)."

The gnostics are the laziest folk in the two worlds, because they get their harvest without ploughing.

They have made laziness their prop (and rely upon it) since God is working for them.

The vulgar do not see God's working and (therefore) never rest from toil at morn or eve.

"Come," (said the cadi), "define[1] (your) laziness, so that from the disclosure of the secret I may learn its (essential) definition (and nature)."

4890 'Tis unquestionable that every tongue is a curtain over the heart: when the curtain is moved, the mysteries (hidden behind it) reach us.

A little curtain like a slice of roast-meat conceals the forms of a hundred suns.

Even if the oral explanation is false, yet the scent (the impression produced by the speaker) makes one acquainted with his veracity or falsehood.

The zephyr that comes from a garden is distinct from the simoom (pestilential wind) of the ash-heap.

The scents of truth and fool-catching (plausible) falsehood are apparent in the breath, like musk and garlic.

4895 If you cannot distinguish a (sincere) friend from a double-hearted[2] person, complain of your own rotten sense of smell.

The voices of poltroons and brave courageous men are as distinct as the characteristics of the fox and the lion.

Or, (again), the tongue is just like the lid of a cooking-pot: when it is moved you know what sort of food is inside;

(But) one whose sense (of smell) is keen can tell by the vapour (issuing from the closed pot) whether it is a pot of sweetmeat or sour *sikbáj* (stew flavoured with vinegar).

When a man taps a new pot with his hand at the time when he is buying it, he detects the cracked one (by its sound).

4900 He (one of the three brothers) said (to the cadi), "I know a man at once by his mouth (speech); and if he do not speak, I know him within three days."

The second said, "I know him if he speak, and if he do not speak, I engage him in conversation."

He (the cadi) said, "(But) if he has (already) heard of this device (of yours), he will close his lips and take refuge in silence."

---

[1] Literally, "declare (in words) the (essential) definition of."
[2] Literally, "having ten hearts."

*Parable.*

The case is like that of the mother who said to her child, "If a ghost come to you in the night,

Or if in a graveyard and frightful place you behold a black bogle full of rage,

Keep a stout heart and rush at it, and immediately it will turn 4905 its face away from you."

"(But)," said the child, "suppose the devilish bogle's mother has said this (same thing) to it;

(If) I rush at it, by its mother's orders it will fall on my neck: what shall I do then?

You are teaching me to stand firm, (but) the ugly bogle has a mother too."

The instructor of (the race of) devils and of mankind is the One (God): through Him the enemy prevails (even) if he is in small force.

On whichever side that Gracious One may be, go and for 4910 God's sake, for God's sake, be thou also on that side!

He (the cadi) said, "Suppose the worthy man is not induced to speak by your device and has (already) perceived the trick,

Tell me truly, how can you know his hidden nature?" He replied, "I sit before him in silence

And make patience a ladder to climb upwards[1]: patience is the key to success.

And if in his presence there should gush from my heart a speech beyond this (realm of) joy and sorrow,

I know that he has sent it to me from the depths of a soul 4915 (illumined) like Canopus (rising) in Yemen.

The speech in my heart comes from that auspicious quarter[2], for there is a window between heart and heart."

[1] Literally, "towards the ascending stages."
[2] Literally, "right wing (of an army)."